Saunders Handbook of

VETERINARY DRUGS

SECOND EDITION

MARK G. PAPICH, DVM, MS
Professor of Clinical Pharmacology
College of Veterinary Medicine
North Carolina State University
Raleigh, North Carolina

11830 Westline Industrial Drive
St. Louis, Missouri 63146

Saunders Handbook of Veterinary Drugs ISBN-13: 978-1-4160-5914-1
ISBN-10: 1-4160-5914-8

ISBN-13: 978-1-4160-5914-1
ISBN-10: 1-4160-5914-8

Publishing Director: Linda L. Duncan
Acquisitions Editor: Anthony Winkel
Developmental Editor: Maureen Slaten
Publishing Services Manager: Melissa Lastarria
Project Manager: Kelly E.M. Steinmann
Design Direction: Bill Drone

Printed in the United States of America

Last digit is the print number: 9 8 7 6 5 4 3 2

This is dedicated to the students and veterinarians who provided suggestions and input, and to my wife, Marcy, for her support and encouragement in the preparation of this second edition.

Mark G. Papich

DISCLAIMER

Doses listed are species-specific, unless otherwise listed. The safety and efficacy for other animal species not listed is not assured.

Many of the doses listed are extra-label or are human drugs used in an off-label or extra-label manner. Federal regulations allow use of extra-label veterinary drugs and human drugs in non–food-producing animals when there is a valid veterinarian-client-patient relationship. However, there are restrictions for using these drugs in food-producing animals under the The Animal Medicinal Drug Use Clarification Act of 1994 (AMDUCA). These drugs are prohibited from use in food-producing animals unless certain requirements are met, which include extended withdrawal times for meat and milk. These requirements can be found at: http://www.fda.gov/cvm/amducatoc.htm.

Doses listed are based on best available evidence at the time of the drug handbook preparation; however, the author cannot assure efficacy of drugs used according to recommendations in this book. Other patient factors, or actions of the drug not known at the time of the book preparation, may affect efficacy. Adverse effects may be possible from drugs listed in this handbook, of which the author was not aware at the time of the handbook's preparation.

Veterinarians using this handbook are encouraged to check current literature, product label, federal Freedom of Information (FOI), and the manufacturer's disclosure for information regarding efficacy and any known adverse effects or contraindications not identified at the time of preparation of this handbook.

Mark G. Papich

Preface

The second edition of this handbook was developed with input and helpful suggestions from veterinarians and students who were familiar with the first edition. The drugs listed represent the most important medications used in companion animals and livestock. In the second edition, an effort was made to include the most recently approved drugs for animals, as well as human medications for which veterinary uses have been identified. Approximately 130 drugs are now included that were not available for inclusion in the first edition. In addition, veterinarians had asked for new sections on regulatory requirements, as well as drug stability and storage, which include compounding information. To make it easier to locate important information for each medication, the sections are broken up into separate categories for drug interactions, precautions, pharmacology, and clinical use. Veterinarians and students also asked for tables and quick-reference information in an appendix. Therefore, I have included new appendix tables not available in the first edition that include helpful information such as weight–body-surface conversions, antibiotic of choice, drug interactions, regulatory information, phone numbers and internet sites for drug information, and a section on drug dose calculations.

Overall, the handbook is designed for the busy practitioner and student who need to use their time efficiently and locate accurate and reliable drug information quickly for each of the major veterinary species. The format is consistent from drug to drug and quickly will become familiar with each use of the handbook to allow readers to rapidly locate concise information about each drug.

In preparing this handbook, my priorities were accuracy and reliability. As in the first edition, the indications for use and drug dosing information were developed from a review of the literature or derived from reviews presented by clinical experts. In some cases, dosages were derived from clinical studies; in other cases, they represent a consensus of clinical experience. Manufacturers' recommendations are considered in the dosing recommendations, but other suggestions (off-label indications and uses) also may be listed where the use and dosage have gone beyond those listed on the product's label. Where dosage recommendations have varied among sources, I have applied my clinical judgment and over 20 years of experience in veterinary clinical pharmacology to derive a scientifically valid dose. In some cases, it may have been necessary to derive a dose based on extrapolations from human medicine, but this was limited to drugs for which the therapeutic index of the drug is high. To derive withdrawal times for food animals, the highest priority has been given to the withdrawal time approved by the U.S. Food and Drug Administration (FDA). When there was not an FDA-approved withdrawal time, suggestions made by the Food Animal Residue Avoidance Databank (FARAD) (www.farad.com) were used. If neither of these was available, I listed a conservative estimate for a suggested withdrawal time based on the drug's pharmacokinetics and likelihood that it may cause harmful residues.

Each drug is listed primarily by its official name (USAN) that is recognized by the United States Pharmacopeia (USP), www.usp.org. Following each drug name is the brand or trade name and other synonyms by which the drug also may be known. Not all of the generic names are necessarily listed. Drugs are listed alphabetically according to their official name. There are tables presented in the front section of the book that cross-reference each drug's USAN to other names by which the drug is known. There is also a cross-reference table that lists drugs according to their functional classification and drug use. It may not cover all of the uses for a drug but does represent the most common use or uses.

As clinical experience increases and our knowledge of the pharmacology of various drugs expands, new information may become available for drugs listed in this book. I welcome feedback relating to adverse effects observed, clinical experience, and omissions or errors identified; I can be reached at mark_papich@ncsu.edu. Adverse drug events also should be reported to the drug sponsor directly or the FDA using this web site: http://www.fda.gov/cvm/adetoc.htm.

Thanks to my editor Tony Winkel, Kelly Steinmann, and Tom Pohlman and their editorial, book production, and multimedia teams at Elsevier for all their hard work and dedication that made this edition possible. The careful editing provided by Graphic World Publishing Services is also very much appreciated. I hope that this edition will be helpful to busy veterinarians who work to provide therapy to animals.

Mark G. Papich
Raleigh, North Carolina

Contents

Listing of Drugs According to Functional and Therapeutic Classification

Drug Classification	Drug Name
Acidifying agent	Ammonium chloride Racemethionine
Adrenal suppressant	Trilostane
Adrenergic agonist	Ephedrine hydrochloride Epinephrine Phenylpropanolamine hydrochloride Pseudoephedrine hydrochloride
Adrenolytic agent	Mitotane
Alkalinizing agent	Potassium citrate Sodium bicarbonate
Alpha-2 antagonist	Atipamezole hydrochloride Yohimbine
Analgesic	Acetaminophen Tramadol
Analgesic, nonsteroidal antiinflammatory drug	Aspirin Carprofen Deracoxib Etodolac Firocoxib Flunixin meglumine Ibuprofen Indomethacin Ketoprofen Ketorolac tromethamine Meclofenamate sodium; Meclofenamic acid Meloxicam Naproxen Phenylbutazone Piroxicam Tepoxalin
Analgesic, opioid	Acetaminophen + codeine Buprenorphine hydrochloride Butorphanol tartrate Fentanyl citrate Fentanyl transdermal Hydromorphone Loperamide hydrochloride Meperidine Methadone hydrochloride Morphine sulfate Oxymorphone hydrochloride Pentazocine Sufentanil citrate
Analgesic, opioid, antitussive	Codeine
Anesthetic	Ketamine hydrochloride Propofol Tiletamine + zolazepam
Anesthetic, alpha-2 agonist	Detomidine hydrochloride Medetomidine hydrochloride Romifidine hydrochloride Xylazine hydrochloride
Anesthetic, barbiturate	Methohexital sodium Pentobarbital sodium Thiopental sodium

Continued

Listing of Drugs According to Functional and Therapeutic Classification—cont'd

Drug Classification	Drug Name
Anesthetic, inhalant	Enflurane Halothane Isoflurane Methoxyflurane Sevoflurane
Antacid	Aluminum hydroxide, and aluminum carbonate
Antiarrhythmic	Amiodarone Carvedilol Disopyramide Mexiletine Procainamide hydrochloride Quinidine Quinidine gluconate Quinidine polygalacturonate Quinidine sulfate Tocanide hydrochloride
Antiarrhythmic, calcium channel blocker	Diltiazem hydrochloride Verapamil hydrochloride
Antiarthritic agent	Chondroitin sulfate Glucosamine + chondroitin sulfate Polysulfated glycosaminoglycan
Antibacterial	Chloramphenicol Clofazimine Dapsone Florfenicol Linezolid Methenamine Nitrofurantoin Pyrimethamine Rifampin
Antibacterial, aminoglycoside	Amikacin Gentamicin sulfate Kanamycin sulfate Neomycin Tobramycin sulfate
Antibacterial, antidiarrheal	Sulfasalazine
Antibacterial, antiparasitic	Metronidazole Metronidazole benzoate Metronidazole hydrochloride Ronidazole
Antibacterial, beta-lactam	Amoxicillin Amoxicillin + clavulanate potassium Ampicillin Ampicillin + sulbactam Carbenicillin Cefaclor Cefadroxil Cefazolin sodium Cefdinir Cefepime Cefixime Cefotaxime sodium Cefotetan disodium Cefoxitin sodium

Listing of Drugs According to Functional and Therapeutic Classification—cont'd

Drug Classification	Drug Name
Antibacterial, Beta-lactam—cont'd	Cefpodoxime proxetil
	Ceftazidime
	Ceftiofur crystalline free acid
	Ceftiofur hydrochloride
	Ceftiofur sodium
	Cephalexin
	Cephalothin sodium
	Cephapirin sodium
	Cephradine
	Cloxacillin sodium
	Dicloxacillin sodium
	Ertapenem
	Imipenem + cilastatin
	Meropenem
	Oxacillin sodium
	Penicillin G
	Piperacillin sodium
	Ticarcillin + clavulanate potassium
	Ticarcillin disodium
Antibacterial, fluroroquinolone	Enrofloxacin
	Ciprofloxacin hydrochloride
	Danofloxacin mesylate
	Difloxacin hydrochloride
	Marbofloxacin
	Moxifloxacin
	Norfloxacin
	Orbifloxacin
Antibacterial, glycopeptide	Vancomycin
Antibacterial, lincosamide	Clindamycin hydrochloride
	Clindamycin palmitate
	Clindamycin phosphate
	Lincomycin hydrochloride
	Lincomycin hydrochloride monohydrate
Antibacterial, macrolide	Azithromycin
	Clarithromycin
	Erythromycin
	Tilmicosin phosphate.
	Tulathromycin
	Tylosin
Antibacterial, potentiated sulfonamide	Ormetoprim + sulfadimethoxine
	Trimethoprim + sulfadiazine
	Trimethoprim + sulfamethoxazole
Antibacterial, sulfonamide	Sulfachlorpyridazine
	Sulfadiazine
	Sulfadimethoxine
	Sulfamethazine
	Sulfamethoxazole
	Sulfaquinoxaline
Antibacterial, tetracycline	Chlortetracycline
	Doxycycline
	Minocycline hydrochloride
	Oxytetracycline
	Tetracycline
	Tetracycline hydrochloride

Continued

Listing of Drugs According to Functional and Therapeutic Classification—cont'd	
Drug Classification	**Drug Name**
Antibiotic, aminocyclitol	Spectinomycin Spectinomycin dihydrochloride pentahydrate Spectinomycin sulfate tetrahydrate
Anticancer agent	Asparaginase (L-asparaginase) Bleomycin sulfate Busulfan Carboplatin Chlorambucil Cisplatin Cyclophosphamide Cytarabine Dacarbazine Doxorubicin hydrochloride Fluorouracil Hydroxyurea Lomustine Melphalan Mercaptopurine Methotrexate Mitoxantrone hydrochloride Plicamycin Streptozocin Thioguanine Thiotepa Vinblastine sulfate Vincristine sulfate
Anticholinergic	Aminopentamide Atropine sulfate. Glycopyrrolate Hyoscyamine Oxybutynin chloride
Anticholinesterase agent	Neostigmine Physostigmine Pyridostigmine bromide
Anticoagulant	Dalteparin Dipyridamole Enoxaparin Heparin sodium Warfarin sodium
Anticonvulsant	Bromide Clonazepam Clorazepate dipotassium Felbamate Levetiracetam Lorazepam Midazolam hydrochloride Oxazepam Phenobarbital Phenobarbital sodium Phenytoin Phenytoin sodium Primidone Valproate sodium Valproic acid Zonisamide

Listing of Drugs According to Functional and Therapeutic Classification—cont'd	
Drug Classification	**Drug Name**
Anticonvulsant, analgesic	Gabapentin
Anticonvulsant, tranquilizer	Diazepam
Antidiabetic agent	Glyburide
Antidiarrheal	Bismuth subsalicylate
	Diphenoxylate
	Kaolin + pectin
	Mesalamine
	Olsalazine sodium
	Paregoric
	Propantheline bromide
Antidote	Charcoal, activated
	Deferoxamine mesylate
	Dimercaprol
	Edetate calcium disodium
	Flumazenil
	Fomepizole
	Leucovorin calcium
	Methylene blue 0.1%
	Penicillamine
	Pralidoxime chloride
	Succimer
	Trientine hydrochloride
Antiemetic	Aprepitant
	Dolasetron mesylate
	Dronabinol
	Granisetron hydrochloride
	Meclizine
	Ondansetron hydrochloride
	Trimethobenzamide
Antiemetic, antidiarrheal	Prochlorperazine edisylate
	Prochlorperazine maleate (each with isopropamide iodide)
Antiemetic, phenothiazine	Chlorpromazine
	Prochlorperazine edisylate
	Prochlorperazine maleate
	Trifluoperazine hydrochloride
	Triflupromazine hydrochloride
	Trimeprazine tartrate
Antiemetic, phenothiazine, antihistamine	Promethazine hydrochloride
	Propiopromazine hydrochloride
Antiemetic, prokinetic agent	Metoclopramide hydrochloride
Antiestrogen	Tamoxifen citrate
Antifungal	Amphotericin B
	Enilconazole
	Fluconazole
	Flucytosine
	Griseofulvin
	Itraconazole
	Ketoconazole
	Terbinafine hydrochloride
	Voriconazole
Antifungal, expectorant	Potassium iodide

Continued

Listing of Drugs According to Functional and Therapeutic Classification—cont'd

Drug Classification	Drug Name
Antihistamine	Astemizole
	Cetirizine hydrochloride
	Chlorpheniramine maleate
	Clemastine fumarate
	Cyproheptadine hydrochloride
	Dimenhydrinate
	Diphenhydramine hydrochloride
	Hydroxyzine
	Tripelennamine citrate
Antihypercalcemic agent	Alendronate
	Etidronate disodium
Antihypercalcemic agent, antidote	Pamidronate disodium
Antihyperglycemic agent	Gemfibrozil
	Glipizide
	Metformin
Anti-inflammatory	Allopurinol
	Colchicine
	Dimethyl sulfoxide (DMSO)
	Niacinamide
	Pentoxifylline
Anti-inflammatory, corticosteroid	Betamethasone
	Budesonide
	Desoxycorticosterone pivalate
	Dexamethasone
	Dexamethasone sodium phosphate
	Flumethasone
	Hydrocortisone
	Isoflupredone acetate
	Methylprednisolone
	Prednisolone
	Prednisolone acetate
	Prednisolone sodium succinate
	Prednisone
	Triamcinolone acetonide
	Triamcinolone diacetate
	Triamcinolone hexacetonide
Antimyasthenic	Edrophonium chloride
Antiparasitic	Albendazole
	Amitraz
	Amprolium
	Bunamidine hydrochloride
	Dichlorvos
	Diethylcarbamazine citrate
	Dithiazanine Iodide
	Doramectin
	Epsiprantel
	Febantel
	Fenbendazole
	Furazolidone
	Ivermectin
	Ivermectin + praziquantel
	Levamisole hydrochloride
	Lufenuron
	Lufenuron + milbemycin oxime
	Mebendazole

Listing of Drugs According to Functional and Therapeutic Classification—cont'd

Drug Classification	Drug Name
Antiparasitic—cont'd	Melarsomine Milbemycin oxime Moxidectin Nitenpyram Oxfendazole Oxibendazole Paromomycin sulfate Piperazine Praziquantel Pyrantel pamoate Pyrantel tartrate Quinacrine hydrochloride Selamectin Thenium closylate Thiabendazole Thiacetarsamide sodium
Antiplatelet agent	Clopidogrel
Antiprotozoal	Diclazuril Imidocarb hydrochloride Metronidazole Metronidazole benzoate Metroniadzole HCl Nitazoxanide Ponazuril Pyrimethamine + sulfadiazine Ronidazole Tinidazole Toltrazuril
Antispasmodic	N-butylscopolammonium bromide (Butylscopolamine bromide)
Antithyroid agent	Carbimazole Ipodate Methimazole Propylthiouracil
Antitussive, analgesic	Dextromethorphan Hydrocodone bitartrate
Antiulcer agent	Misoprostol Sucralfate
Antiulcer agent, H_2-blocker	Cimetidine hydrochloride Famotidine Nizatidine Ranitidine hydrochloride
Antiulcer agent, proton-pump inhibitor	Omeprazole Pantoprazole
Antiviral	Acyclovir Lysine (L-Lysine) Zidovudine
Antiviral analgesic	Amantadine
Behavior-modifying drug	Buspirone hydrochloride
Behavior-modifying drug, SSRI	Fluoxetine hydrochloride Paroxetine

Continued

Listing of Drugs According to Functional and Therapeutic Classification—cont'd

Drug Classification	Drug Name
Behavior-modifying drug, Tricyclic	Amitriptyline hydrochloride Clomipramine hydrochloride Doxepin Imipramine hydrochloride
Beta-agonist	Isoproterenol hydrochloride
Beta-blocker	Atenolol Esmolol hydrochloride Metoprolol tartrate Propranolol hydrochloride Sotalol hydrochloride
Bronchodilator	Aminophylline Oxtriphylline Theophylline
Bronchodilator, beta-agonist	Albuterol sulfate Clenbuterol Metaproterenol sulfate Terbutaline sulfate
Calcium supplement	Calcitriol Calcium carbonate Calcium chloride Calcium citrate Calcium gluconate and calcium borogluconate Calcium lactate
Cardiac inotropic agent	Digitoxin Digoxin Dobutamine hydrochloride Pimobendan
Cardiac inotropic agent, beta-agonist	Dopamine hydrochloride
Cholinergic	Bethanechol chloride
Corticosteroid, hormone	Fludrocortisone acetate
Dermatologic agent	Isotretinoin
Diuretic	Acetazolamide Chlorothiazide Dichlorphenamide Furosemide Hydrochlorothiazide Mannitol Methazolamide Spironolactone Triamterene
Diuretic, laxative	Glycerin
Dopamine agonist	Bromocriptine mesylate Levodopa Pergolide Pergolide mesylate Selegiline hydrochloride
Emetic	Apomorphine hydrochloride Ipecac
Expectorant; muscle relaxant	Guaifenesin

Drug Classification	Drug Name
Fluid replacement	Dextran
	Dextrose solution
	Hetastarch
	Lactated Ringer's solution
	Pentastarch
	Ringer's solution
	Sodium chloride 0.9%
	Sodium chloride 7.2%
Hepatic protectant	S-adenosylmethionine (SAMe)
	Silymarin
Hormone	Colony-stimulating factors
	Corticotropin
	Cosyntropin
	Danazol
	Desmopressin acetate
	Diethylstilbestrol
	Epoetin alpha (erythropoietin)
	Estradiol cypionate
	Gonadorelin hydrochloride, gonadorelin diacetate tetrahydrate
	Gonadotropin, chorionic
	Growth hormone
	Insulin
	Levothyroxine sodium
	Liothyronine sodium
	Medroxyprogesterone acetate
	Megestrol acetate
	Mibolerone
	Testosterone
	Urofollitropin
	Vasopressin
Hormone, anabolic agent	Boldenone undecylenate
	Methyltestosterone
	Nandrolone decanoate
	Oxymetholone
	Stanozolol
Hormone antagonist	Finasteride
Hormone, labor induction	Oxytocin
Hormone, thyroid	Thyroid-releasing hormone
	Thyrotropin
Immunostimulant	Interferon
	Lithium carbonate
Immunosuppressive agent	Auranofin
	Aurothioglucose
	Azathioprine
	Cyclosporine
	Gold sodium thiomalate
	Mycophenolate
	Tacrolimus
Iodine supplement	Sodium iodide (20%)
Iron supplement	Hemoglobin glutamer

Table title: Listing of Drugs According to Functional and Therapeutic Classification—cont'd

Continued

Listing of Drugs According to Functional and Therapeutic Classification—cont'd

Drug Classification	Drug Name
Laxative	Bisacodyl Cascara sagrada Castor oil Docusate Lactulose Magnesium citrate Magnesium hydroxide Mineral oil Polyethylene glycol electrolyte solution Psyllium Senna Ursodeoxycholic acid Ursodiol
Laxative, antiarrhythmic	Magnesium sulfate
Local anesthetic	Bupivacaine hydrochloride Mepivacaine
Local anesthetic, antiarrhythmic	Lidocaine hydrochloride
Mineral supplement	Ferrous sulfate Iron dextran
Mucolytic, antidote	Acetylcysteine
Muscle relaxant	Atracurium besylate Dantrolene sodium Methocarbamol Pancuronium bromide
Nutritional supplement	MCT oil Taurine Zinc
Opioid antagonist	Naloxone hydrochloride Naltrexone
Pancreatic enzyme	Pancrelipase
Phosphate supplement, urine acidifier	Potassium phosphate
Potassium supplement	Potassium chloride Potassium gluconate
Prokinetic agent	Cisapride Domperidone Metronidazole
Prostaglandin	Dinoprost tromethamine Prostaglandin F-2 alpha
Respiratory stimulant	Doxapram hydrochloride
Tranquilizer, benzodiazepine	Alprazolam
Tranquilizer, phenothiazine	Acepromazine maleate
Vasodilator	Hydralazine hydrochloride Irbesartan Isosorbide dinitrate Isosorbide mononitrate Isoxsuprine Nitroglycerin Nitroprusside (sodium nitroprusside) Phenoxybenzamine hydrochloride Phentolamine mesylate Prazosin

Listing of Drugs According to Functional and Therapeutic Classification—cont'd

Drug Classification	Drug Name
Vasodilator, ACE-inhibitor	Benazepril hydrochloride Captopril Enalapril maleate Lisinopril Ramipril Trandolapril
Vasodilator, calcium channel blocker	Amlodipine besylate Losartan Nifedipine
Vasopressor	Methoxamine Phenylephrine hydrochloride
Vitamin	Ascorbic acid Cyanocobalamin Dihydrotachysterol Ergocalciferol Phytonadione Riboflavin Thiamine hydrochloride Vitamin A Vitamin E Vitamin K

List of Trade and Brand Names Cross-Referenced to Drug Names

Trade Names and Other Names	Drug Name as Listed in Handbook
2-PAM	Pralidoxime chloride
4-Methylpyrazole	Fomepizole
5-Fluorouracil	Fluorouracil
A180	Danofloxacin mesylate
Abbocillin	Penicillin G
ABCD	Amphotericin B
ABELCET	Amphotericin B
Accutane	Isotretinoin
ACE	Acepromazine maleate
Aceproject	Acepromazine maleate
Aceprotabs	Acepromazine maleate
Acetadote	Acetylcysteine
Acetylpromazine	Acepromazine maleate
Acetylsalicylic acid	Aspirin
Achromycin V	Tetracycline
ActaChar	Charcoal activated
ACTH	Cosyntropin
Acthar	Corticotropin
Actigall	Ursodeoxycholic acid
Actigall	Ursodiol
Adalat	Nifedipine
adenosylmethionine (SAMe)	S-adenosylmethionine (SAMe)
Adequan Canine	Polysulfated glycosaminoglycan
Adequan IA	Polysulfated glycosaminoglycan
Adequan IM	Polysulfated glycosaminoglycan
Adrenaline	Epinephrine
Adriamycin	Doxorubicin hydrochloride
Adrucil	Fluorouracil
Adspec	Clenbuterol
Advil	Ibuprofen
Aarane	Isoflurane
Aarane	Sevoflurane
Aggrenex	Dipyridamole
Albon	Sulfadimethoxine
Aldactone	Spironolactone
Aleve	Naproxen
Alinia	Nitazoxanide
Alkeran	Melphalan
Allopur	Allopurinol
Alpha-tocopherol	Vitamin E
Alupent	Metaproterenol sulfate
AmBisome	Amphotericin B
Amiglyde-V	Amikacin
Amikin	Amikacin
Aminophylline	Theophylline
Aminosalicylic acid	Mesalamine
Ammonium chloride	Ammonium chloride
Amoxicillin trihydrate	Amoxicillin
Amoxi-Drops	Amoxicillin
Amoxi-Inject	Amoxicillin
Amoxil	Amoxicillin
Amoxi-Tabs	Amoxicillin
Amp-Equine	Ampicillin

List of Trade and Brand Names Cross-Referenced to Drug Names—cont'd

Trade Names and Other Names	Drug Name as Listed in Handbook
Amphogel	Aluminum hydroxide
Amphotec	Amphotericin B
Amprol	Amprolium
Amtech iron dextran	Iron dextran
AmVet	Calcium borogluconate
AmVet	Calcium gluconate
Anadrol	Oxymetholone
Anafen	Ketoprofen
Anafranil	Clomipramine hydrochloride
Anaplasmosis block	Chlortetracycline
Ancef	Cefazolin sodium
Ancobon	Flucytosine
Andro-Cyp	Testosterone
Android	Methyltestosterone
Andronate	Testosterone
Anipryl	Selegiline hydrochloride
Anthelcide EQ	Oxibendazole
Antilirium	Physostigmine
Antirobe	Clindamycin palmitate
Antisedan	Atipamezole hydrochloride
Antivert	Meclizine
Antizole	Fomepizole
Antizol-Vet	Fomepizole
Anzemet	Dolasetron mesylate
APL	Gonadotropin chorionic
Apomorphine	Apomorphine hydrochloride
Apresoline	Hydralazine hydrochloride
Aquacillin	Penicillin G
AquaMEPHYTON	Phytonadione
AquaMEPHYTON	Vitamin K
Aquasol E	Vitamin E
Aquasol-A	Vitamin A
Ara-C	Cytarabine
Aredia	Pamidronate disodium
Aristocort	Triamcinolone
Arm & Hammer pure baking soda	Sodium bicarbonate
Arquel	Meclofenamic acid
ASA	Aspirin
Asacol	Mesalamine
Ascriptin	Aspirin
Atabrine	Quinacrine hydrochloride
Atarax	Hydroxyzine
Atgard	Dichlorvos
Ativan	Lorazepam
Atopica	Cyclosporine
Atravet	Acepromazine maleate
Atropine	Atropine sulfate
Augmentin	Amoxicillin + clavulanate potassium
Aureomycin soluble calf tablets	Chlortetracycline
Aureomycin soluble powder	Chlortetracycline
Aureomycin tablets	Chlortetracycline
Avapro	Irbesartan
Avelox	Moxifloxacin
Axid	Nizatidine

Continued

List of Trade and Brand Names Cross-Referenced to Drug Names—cont'd

Trade Names and Other Names	Drug Name as Listed in Handbook
Azium	Dexamethasone
Azulfidine	Sulfasalazine
Bactrim	Trimethoprim + sulfamethoxazole
Bactrovet	Sulfadimethoxine
Baking soda	Sodium bicarbonate
BAL in oil	Dimercaprol
Banamine	Flunixin meglumine
Basalgel	Aluminum carbonate
Baycox	Toltrazuril
Baytril	Enrofloxacin
Benadryl	Diphenhydramine hydrochloride
Benylin	Dextromethorphan
Benza-Pen	Penicillin G
Benzelmin	Oxfendazole
Betamethasone acetate	Betamethasone
Betamethasone benzoate	Betamethasone
Betapace	Sotalol hydrochloride
Bewon	Thiamine hydrochloride
Biaxin	Clarithromycin
Biomox	Amoxicillin
Biomycin	Oxytetracycline
Biomycin 200	Oxytetracycline
Biosol	Neomycin
Blenoxane	Bleomycin sulfate
Bonine	Meclizine
Brethine	Terbutaline sulfate
Brevibloc	Esmolol hydrochloride
Brevital	Methohexital sodium
Bricanyl	Terbutaline sulfate
British anti-lewisite	Dimercaprol
Bufferin	Aspirin
Buprenex	Buprenorphine hydrochloride
Buscopan	Butylscopolamine bromide
BuSpar	Buspirone hydrochloride
Butazolidin	Phenylbutazone
Bute	Phenylbutazone
Butylscopolamine bromide	*N*-butylscopolammonium bromide
Calan	Verapamil hydrochloride
Calciferol	Ergocalciferol
Calcijex	Calcitriol
Calci-mix	Calcium carbonate
Calcium	Calcium chloride
Calcium	Calcium lactate
Calcium disodium ethylenediaminetetra-acetate	Edetate calcium disodium
Calcium disodium versenate	Edetate calcium disodium
Calcium ipodate	Ipodate
Calf scour bolus	Chlortetracycline
Cal-Nate	Calcium borogluconate
Cal-Nate	Calcium gluconate
Canopar	Thenium closylate
Caparsolate	Thiacetarsamide sodium
Capoten	Captopril
Capstar	Nitenpyram
Carafate	Sucralfate

List of Trade and Brand Names Cross-Referenced to Drug Names—cont'd

Trade Names and Other Names	Drug Name as Listed in Handbook
Carbocaine-V	Mepivacaine
Cardioquin	Quinidine
Cardizem	Diltiazem hydrochloride
Cardoxin	Digoxin
Caricide	Diethylcarbamazine citrate
Carmilax	Magnesium hydroxide
Castor	Castor oil
CCNU	Lomustine
Ceclor	Cefaclor
CeeNU	Lomustine
Cefa-Drops	Cefadroxil
Cefadyl	Cephapirin sodium
Cefa-Tabs	Cefadroxil
Cefotan	Cefotetan disodium
Celestone	Betamethasone
CellCept	Mycophenolate
Centrine	Aminopentamide
Ceptaz	Ceftazidime
Cestex	Epsiprantel
Charcodote	Charcoal activated
Chemet	Succimer
Cheque-drops	Mibolerone
Chloramphenicol palmitate	Chloramphenicol
Chloramphenicol sodium succinate	Chloramphenicol
Chloromycetin	Chloramphenicol
Chloromycetin	Chloramphenicol
Chlor-Trimeton	Chlorpheniramine maleate
Choledyl-SA	Oxtrlphylllne
Chondroitin sulfate	Glucosamine + chondroitin sulfate
Chronulac	Lactulose
Cin-Quin	Quinidine
Cipro	Ciprofloxacin hydrochloride
Citracal	Calcium citrate
Citrocarbonate	Sodium bicarbonate
Citroma	Magnesium citrate
Citro-Mag	Magnesium citrate
Citro Nesia	Magnesium citrate
Claforan	Cefotaxime sodium
Clavamox	Amoxicillin + clavulanate potassium
Cleocin	Clindamycin palmitate
ClinaFarm-EC	Enilconazole
Clincox	Diclazuril
Clindamycin	Clindamycin hydrochloride
Clindamycin	Clindamycin phosphate
Clindrops	Clindamycin palmitate
Clinsol	Clindamycin palmitate
Clintabs	Clindamycin palmitate
Clomicalm	Clomipramine hydrochloride
Cloxapen	Cloxacillin sodium
Codeine phosphate	Codeine
Codeine sulfate	Codeine
Colace	Docusate
Co-Lav	Polyethylene glycol electrolyte solution
ColBENEMID	Colchicine

Continued

List of Trade and Brand Names Cross-Referenced to Drug Names—cont'd

Trade Names and Other Names	Drug Name as Listed in Handbook
Colyte	Polyethylene glycol electrolyte solution
Compazine	Prochlorperazine edisylate
Contac	Clemastine fumarate
Cordarone	Amiodarone
Coreg	Carvedilol
Corid	Amprolium
Corrective mixture	Paregoric
Cortef	Hydrocortisone
Cortrosyn	Cosyntropin
Cosequin	Glucosamine + chondroitin sulfate
Cosequin	Chondroitin sulfate
Cotazym	Pancrelipase
Coumadin	Warfarin sodium
Cozaar	Losartan potassium
Creon	Pancrelipase
Crysticillin	Penicillin G
Crystodigin	Digitoxin
CSA	Cyclosporine
CTX	Cyclophosphamide
Cuprimine	Penicillamine
Cyclosporin A	Cyclosporine
Cycrin	Medroxyprogesterone acetate
Cydectin	Moxidectin
Cystorelin	Gonadorelin diacetate tetrahydrate
Cytomel	Liothyronine sodium
Cytosar	Cytarabine
Cytosine arabinoside	Cytarabine
Cytotec	Misoprostol
Cytoxan	Cyclophosphamide
D5W	Dextrose solution
Danocrine	Danazol
Dantrium	Dantrolene sodium
Daranide	Dichlorphenamide
Daraprim	Pyrimethamine
Darbazine	Prochlorperazine edisylate
Darbazine	Prochlorperazine maleate
DDAVP	Desmopressin acetate
DDVP	Dichlorvos
Decadron	Dexamethasone
Decadron	Dexamethasone
Deca-Durabolin	Nandrolone decanoate
Dectomax	Doramectin
Delta-Cortef	Prednisolone
Deltasone	Prednisone
Demerol	Meperidine
Denosyl	S-adenosylmethionine (SAMe)
Depakene	Valproate sodium
Depakote	Valproate sodium
Depen	Penicillamine
Depo-Provera	Medroxyprogesterone acetate
Depo-Estradiol	Estradiol cypionate
Depo-Medrol	Methylprednisolone acetate
Depo-Testosterone	Testosterone
Deprenyl	Selegiline hydrochloride

List of Trade and Brand Names Cross-Referenced to Drug Names—cont'd

Trade Names and Other Names	Drug Name as Listed in Handbook
Deramaxx	Deracoxib
DES	Diethylstilbestrol
Desferal	Deferoxamine mesylate
Dexaject	Dexamethasone
Dexaject SP	Dexamethasone
Dexasone	Dexamethasone
Dexasone	Dexamethasone
Dexatrim	Phenylpropanolamine hydrochloride
Dexavet	Dexamethasone
Dex-A-Vet	Dexamethasone
Dextran 70	Dextran
DHT	Dihydrotachysterol
Diabeta	Glyburide
Diaminodiphenylsulfone	Dapsone
Diamox	Acetazolamide
Dibenzyline	Phenoxybenzamine hydrochloride
Dichlorvos	Dichlorvos
Dicural	Difloxacin hydrochloride
Didronel	Etidronate disodium
Diflucan	Fluconazole
Dilacor	Diltiazem hydrochloride
Dilantin	Phenytoin
Dilaudid	Hydromorphone
Dinoprost	Dinoprost tromethamine
Dinoprost	Prostaglandin F_2 alpha
Dipentum	Olsalazine sodium
Diprivan	Propofol
Di-Trim	Trimethoprim + sulfadiazine
Ditropan	Oxybutynin chloride
Diuril	Chlorothiazide
Divalproex	Valproate sodium
Dizan	Dithiazanine iodide
DMSO	Dimethyl sulfoxide (DMSO)
Dobutrex	Dobutamine hydrochloride
DOCA pivalate	Desoxycorticosterone pivalate
DOCP	Desoxycorticosterone pivalate
Docusate calcium	Docusate
Docusate sodium	Docusate
Dolophine	Methadone hydrochloride
Domitor	Medetomidine hydrochloride
Domoso	Dimethyl sulfoxide (DMSO)
Dopram	Doxapram hydrochloride
Dormosedan	Detomidine hydrochloride
Doxan	Docusate
Doxidan	Docusate
Doxy Caps	Doxycycline
Dramamine	Dimenhydrinate
Draxxin	Tulathromycin
Drisdol	Ergocalciferol
Droncit	Praziquantel
Drontal	Praziquantel
Droxia	Hydroxyurea
DSS	Docusate
DTIC	Dacarbazine

Continued

List of Trade and Brand Names Cross-Referenced to Drug Names—cont'd

Trade Names and Other Names	Drug Name as Listed in Handbook
Dulcolax	Bisacodyl
Duracillin	Penicillin G
Duragesic	Fentanyl transdermal
Duramycin	Tetracycline
Duraquin	Quinidine
Duricef	Cefadroxil
Dynapen	Dicloxacillin sodium
Dyrenium	Triamterene
ECP	Estradiol cypionate
EDTA	Edetate calcium disodium
Elavil	Amitriptyline hydrochloride
Eldepryl	Selegiline hydrochloride
Elspar	Asparaginase
Emend	Aprepitant
Enacard	Enalapril maleate
Enisyl-F	Lysine (L-Lysine)
Enterocort	Budesonide
Ephedrine	Ephedrine hydrochloride
Epival	Valproate sodium
EPO	Epoetin alpha (erythropoietin)
Epogen	Epoetin alpha (erythropoietin)
Epsom salts	Magnesium sulfate
Equidone	Domperidone
Equigard	Dichlorvos
Equimax	Ivermectin + praziquantel
Equimectrin	Ivermectin
Equipoise	Boldenone undecylenate
Equisyn-T4 (equine powder)	Levothyroxine sodium
Equizole	Thiabendazole
Eqvalan liquid	Ivermectin
Ergamisol	Levamisole hydrochloride
Erythro-100	Erythromycin
Erythropoietin	Epoetin alpha (erythropoietin)
Eskacillin	Penicillin G
Ethrane	Enflurane
EtoGesic	Etodolac
Excede	Ceftiofur crystalline free acid
Excenel	Ceftiofur hydrochloride
Factrel	Gonadorelin diacetate tetrahydrate
Felbatol	Felbamate
Feldene	Piroxicam
Fenesin	Guaifenesin
Fermycin	Chlortetracycline
Ferospace	Ferrous sulfate
Ferrodex	Iron dextran
Fertagyl	Gonadorelin diacetate tetrahydrate
Fertelin	Gonadorelin diacetate tetrahydrate
Fertinex	Urofollitropin
Filaribits	Diethylcarbamazine citrate
FK506	Tacrolimus
Flagyl	Metronidazole
Flavor Tabs	Lufenuron + milbemycin oxime
Florinef	Fludrocortisone acetate
Flovent	Fluticasone propionate

List of Trade and Brand Names Cross-Referenced to Drug Names—cont'd

Trade Names and Other Names	Drug Name as Listed in Handbook
Flucort	Flumethasone
Fluopromazine	Triflupromazine hydrochloride
Fluothane	Halothane
Folex	Methotrexate
Fortaz	Ceftazidime
Fortekor	Benazepril hydrochloride
Fosamax	Alendronate
Fragmin	Dalteparin
FSH	Urofollitropin
Fulvicin P/G	Griseofulvin
Fulvicin U/F	Griseofulvin
Fungizone	Amphotericin B
Furadantin	Nitrofurantoin
Furalan	Nitrofurantoin
Furatoin	Nitrofurantoin
Furoxone	Furazolidone
Gabapetin	Gabapentin
Gallimycin-100	Erythromycin
Gallimycin-200	Erythromycin
Gantanol	Sulfamethoxazole
GastroGard	Omeprazole
Gengraf	Cyclosporine
Gentocin	Gentamicin sulfate
Gentran-70	Dextran
Geocillin	Carbenicillin indanyl sodium
Geocolate	Guaifenesin
Geopen	Carbenicillin
Glibenclamide	Glyburide
Glucophage	Metformin
Glucotrol	Glipizide
Glycerol	Glycerin
Glycoflex	Chondroitin sulfate
Glycoflex	Glucosamine + chondroitin sulfate
Glycotuss	Guaifenesin
Glyceryl guaiacolate	Guaifenesin
Glynase	Glyburide
Glytuss	Guaifenesin
GnRh	Gonadorelin diacetate tetrahydrate
Golytely	Polyethylene glycol electrolyte solution
Gonadorelin	Gonadorelin hydrochloride
Gravol	Dimenhydrinate
Grifulvin	Griseofulvin
Grisactin	Griseofulvin
GrisPEG	Griseofulvin
Guailaxin	Guaifenesin
Guaiphenesin	Guaifenesin
Gyrocaps	Theophylline
Heartguard	Ivermectin
HemaJect	Iron dextran
Hepalean	Heparin sodium
HES	Hetastarch
Hespan	Hetastarch
Hetastarch	Hetastarch
Hiprex	Methenamine

Continued

List of Trade and Brand Names Cross-Referenced to Drug Names—cont'd

Trade Names and Other Names	Drug Name as Listed in Handbook
Hismanal	Astemizole
HSS	Sodium chloride 7.2%
Humabid LA	Guaifenesin
Humatin	Paromomycin sulfate
Humatrope	Growth hormone
Humulin (human insulin)	Insulin
Hycodan	Hydrocodone bitartrate
Hydrea	Hydroxyurea
HydroDiuril	Hydrochlorothiazide
Hydrostat	Hydromorphone
Hypertonic saline	Sodium chloride 7.2%
Hytakerol	Dihydrotachysterol
Hytuss	Guaifenesin
Imaverol	Enilconazole
Imizol	Imidocarb hydrochloride
Immiticide	Melarsomine
Imodium	Loperamide hydrochloride
Imuran	Azathioprine
Inderal	Propranolol hydrochloride
Indocin	Indomethacin
Interceptor	Milbemycin oxime
Intropin	Dopamine hydrochloride
Invanz	Ertapenem
Iodopen	Sodium iodide (20%)
Isoprenaline hydrochloride	Isoproterenol hydrochloride
Isoptin	Verapamil hydrochloride
Isorbid	Isosorbide dinitrate
Isordil	Isosorbide dinitrate
Isuprel	Isoproterenol hydrochloride
Itrafungol	Itraconazole
Ivercare	Ivermectin
Ivercide	Ivermectin
IverEase	Ivermectin
Ivermax	Ivermectin
Ivomec	Ivermectin
Kalcinate	Calcium borogluconate
Kalcinate	Calcium gluconate
Kantrim	Kanamycin sulfate
Kaon	Potassium gluconate
KaoPectate	Kaolin + pectin
Keflex	Cephalexin
Keflin	Cephalothin sodium
Kefzol	Cefazolin sodium
Keppra	Levetiracetam
Ketalar	Ketamine hydrochloride
Ketavet	Ketamine hydrochloride
Ketofen	Ketoprofen
Klonopin	Clonazepam
K-Phos	Potassium phosphate
Kytril	Granisetron hydrochloride
Lamisil	Terbinafine hydrochloride
Lamprene	Clofazimine
Lanoxin	Digoxin
Lanvis	Thioguanine

List of Trade and Brand Names Cross-Referenced to Drug Names—cont'd

Trade Names and Other Names	Drug Name as Listed in Handbook
Largactil	Chlorpromazine
Larodopa	Levodopa
Lasix	Furosemide
L-Asparaginase	Asparaginase
L-deprenyl	Selegiline hydrochloride
L-dopa	Levodopa
Lente insulin	Insulin
Leukeran	Chlorambucil
Leukine	Colony-stimulating factors
Levasole	Levamisole hydrochloride
Levo-Powder	Levothyroxine sodium
Levsin	Hyoscyamine
LHRH	Gonadorelin diacetate tetrahydrate
Lincocin	Lincomycin hydrochloride monohydrate
Lincomix	Lincomycin hydrochloride monohydrate
Lincomycin	Lincomycin hydrochloride
Lincomycin	Lincomycin hydrochloride monohydrate
Liquaemin	Heparin sodium
Liquamycin-LA 200	Oxytetracycline
Liqui-cal	Calcium carbonate
Liqui-Char	Charcoal activated
Lithotabs	Lithium carbonate
LMWH	Dalteparin
LMWH	Enoxaparin
Lodine	Etodolac
Lomotil	Diphenoxylate
Lopid	Gemfibrozil
Lopressor	Metoprolol tartrate
Lopurin	Allopurinol
Losec	Omeprazole
Lotensin	Benazepril hydrochloride
Lovenox	Enoxaparin
LRS	Lactated ringer's solution
Luminal	Phenobarbital
Lutalyse	Dinoprost tromethamine
Lutalyse	Prostaglandin F_2 alpha
Lysodren	Mitotane
Maalox	Calcium carbonate
Macrodantin	Nitrofurantoin
Magnalax	Magnesium hydroxide
Malogen	Testosterone propionate ester
Mandelamine	Methenamine mandelate
Marbocyl	Marbofloxacin
Marcaine	Bupivacaine hydrochloride
Marin	Silymarin
Marinol	Dronabinol
Marquis	Ponazuril
Mavik	Trandolapril
Maxipime	Cefepime
Maxolon	Metoclopramide hydrochloride
Meclofen	Meclofenamic acid
Meclofenamate sodium	Meclofenamic acid
Meclofenamic acid	Meclofenamate sodium

Continued

List of Trade and Brand Names Cross-Referenced to Drug Names—cont'd

Trade Names and Other Names	Drug Name as Listed in Handbook
Meclozine	Meclizine
Medium chain triglycerides	MCT oil
Medrol	Methylprednisolone
Mefoxin	Cefoxitin sodium
Megace	Megestrol acetate
Mephyton	Phytonadione
Mephyton	Vitamin K
Merrem	Meropenem
Mesalazine	Mesalamine
Mesasal	Mesalamine
Mestinon	Pyridostigmine bromide
Metacam	Meloxicam
Metamucil	Psyllium
Metaprel	Metaproterenol sulfate
Methadose	Methadone hydrochloride
Methenamine hippurate	Methenamine
Methio-Form	Racemethionine
Methylpyrazole	Fomepizole
Meticorten	Prednisone
Metofane	Methoxyflurane
Metrodin	Urofollitropin
Metronidazole benzoate	Metronidazole
Metronidazole hydrochloride	Metronidazole
Mexate	Methotrexate
Mexitil	Mexiletine
Micotil	Tilmicosin phosphate
Micronase	Glyburide
Milk of Magnesia	Magnesium hydroxide
Milk Thistle	Silymarin
Mineral oil	Mineral oil
Minipress	Prazosin
Minocin	Minocycline hydrochloride
Mitaban	Amitraz
Mithracin	Plicamycin
Mithramycin	Plicamycin
Mobic	Meloxicam
Modrenal	Trilostane
Monodox	Doxycycline
Monoket	Isosorbide mononitrate
Motilium	Domperidone
Motrin	Ibuprofen
MS Contin	Morphine sulfate
MTX	Methotrexate
Mucinex	Guaifenesin
Mucomyst	Acetylcysteine
Mylepsin	Primidone
Myleran	Busulfan
Myochrysine	Gold sodium thiomalate
Mysoline	Primidone
Naprosyn	Naproxen
Narcan	Naloxone hydrochloride
Nature's Remedy	Cascara sagrada
Navigator	Nitazoxanide
Naxcel	Ceftiofur sodium

List of Trade and Brand Names Cross-Referenced to Drug Names—cont'd

Trade Names and Other Names	Drug Name as Listed in Handbook
Naxen	Naproxen
N-butylscopolammonium bromide	Butylscopolamine bromide
Nebcin	Tobramycin sulfate
Nemacide	Diethylcarbamazine citrate
Nembutal	Pentobarbital sodium
Nemex	Pyrantel
Neomercazole	Carbimazole
Neoral	Cyclosporine
Neosar	Cyclophosphamide
Neostigmine bromide	Neostigmine
Neostigmine methylsulfate	Neostigmine
Neo-synephrine	Phenylephrine hydrochloride
Neptazane	Methazolamide
Neupogen	Colony-stimulating factors
Neurontin	Gabapentin
Neurosyn	Primidone
Neutra-Phos-K	Potassium phosphate
New Methylene Blue	Methylene Blue
Nicotinamide	Niacinamide
Niravam	Alprazolam
Nitro-bid	Nitroglycerin
Nitrol	Nitroglycerin
Nitropress	Nitroprusside (sodium nitroprusside)
Nitrostat	Nitroglycerin
Nizoral	Ketoconazole
Nolvadex	Tamoxifen citrate
Normal saline	Sodium chloride 0.9%
Noroxin	Norfloxacin
Norpace	Disopyramide
Norvasc	Amlodipine besylate
Novantrone	Mitoxantrone hydrochloride
NPH insulin	Insulin
Nufluor	Florfenicol
Numorphan	Oxymorphone hydrochloride
Nuprin	Ibuprofen
Nutropin	Growth hormone
Omega	Interferon
Omnicef	Cefdinir
Omnipen	Ampicillin
Omnipen-N	Ampicillin
Omnizole	Thiabendazole
Oncovin	Vincristine sulfate
op-DDD	Mitotane
Optimmune	Cyclosporine
Oramorph SR	Morphine sulfate
Orbax	Orbifloxacin
Orbenin	Cloxacillin sodium
Orciprenaline sulphate	Metaproterenol sulfate
Oragrafin	Ipodate
Orudis-KT	Ketoprofen
Osmitrol	Mannitol
Ovaban	Megestrol acetate
OvaCyst	Gonadorelin diacetate tetrahydrate
Oxpentifylline	Pentoxifylline

Continued

List of Trade and Brand Names Cross-Referenced to Drug Names—cont'd

Trade Names and Other Names	Drug Name as Listed in Handbook
Oxy 1000	Oxytetracycline
Oxy 500	Oxytetracycline
Oxybiotic	Oxytetracycline
Oxyglobin	Hemoglobin glutamer
Oxy-Tet	Oxytetracycline
PAM	Pralidoxime chloride
Panacur	Fenbendazole
Pancoate	Pancrelipase
Pancrease	Pancrelipase
Pancrezyme	Pancrelipase
Panectyl	Trimeprazine tartrate
Panmycin	Tetracycline
Paraplatin	Carboplatin
Parencillin	Penicillin G
Parlodel	Bromocriptine mesylate
Pavulon	Pancuronium bromide
Paxil	Paroxetine
PBZ	Phenylbutazone
PBZ	Phenylbutazone
Pedameth	Racemethionine
PEG	Polyethylene glycol electrolyte solution
Pelamine	Tripelennamine citrate
Pentahydrate	Spectinomycin
Pentasa	Mesalamine
Pentaspan	Pentastarch
Pentothal	Thiopental sodium
Pen-Vee	Penicillin V
Pepcid	Famotidine
Pepto Bismol	Bismuth subsalicylate
Percorten-V	Desoxycorticosterone pivalate
Pergolide mesylate	Pergolide
Periactin	Cyproheptadine hydrochloride
Permax	Pergolide
Persantine	Dipyridamole
Pfizerpen	Penicillin G
PGF_2 alpha	Prostaglandin F_2 alpha
PG F_2alpha	Dinoprost tromethamine
Phenergan	Promethazine hydrochloride
Phenetron	Chlorpheniramine maleate
Phenobarbital sodium	Phenobarbital
Phenobarbitone	Phenobarbital
Phenytoin sodium	Phenytoin
Phylloquinone	Phytonadione
Phylloquinone	Vitamin K
Phytomenadione	Phytonadione
Phytomenadione	Vitamin K
Pipa-Tabs	Piperazine
Pipracil	Piperacillin sodium
Pitocin	Oxytocin
Pitressin	Vasopressin
Platinol	Cisplatin
Plavix	Clopidogrel
Polycillin	Ampicillin
Polycillin-N	Ampicillin

List of Trade and Brand Names Cross-Referenced to Drug Names—cont'd

Trade Names and Other Names	Drug Name as Listed in Handbook
PolyFlex (ampicillin trihydrate)	Ampicillin
Polymox	Amoxicillin
Potassium	Potassium chloride
Potassium bromide	Bromide
PPA	Phenylpropanolamine hydrochloride
Predef 2X	Isoflupredone acetate
Prednisolone acetate	Prednisolone
PrednisTab	Prednisolone
Pregnyl	Gonadotropin chorionic
Prepulsid	Cisapride
Previcox	Firocoxib
Priex	Pyrantel
Prilosec	Omeprazole
Primaxin	Imipenem + cilastatin
Primor	Ormetoprim + sulfadimethoxine
Principen	Ampicillin
Prinivil	Lisinopril
Privermectin	Ivermectin
Pro-Banthine	Propantheline bromide
Procardia	Nifedipine
Prochlorperazine maleate	Prochlorperazine edisylate
Profasi	Gonadotropin chorionic
Program	Lufenuron
ProHeart	Moxidectin
Proin-ppa	Phenylpropanolamine hydrochloride
ProMACE	Acepromazine maleate
Pronestyl	Procainamide hydrochloride
Propagest	Phenylpropanolamine hydrochloride
Propalin	Phenylpropanolamine hydrochloride
Propoflo	Propofol
Propulsid	Cisapride
Propyl-Thyracil	Propylthiouracil
Proscar	Finasteride
Prospec	Clenbuterol
Prostaglandin F_2alpha	Dinoprost tromethamine
ProstaMate	Dinoprost tromethamine
Pro-staphlin	Oxacillin sodium
Prostigmin	Neostigmine
Prostin F_2 alpha	Dinoprost tromethamine
Protamine zinc insulin	Insulin
Protonix	Pantoprazole
Protopam chloride	Pralidoxime chloride
Protopic	Tacrolimus
Protropin	Growth hormone
Proventil	Albuterol sulfate
Provera	Medroxyprogesterone acetate
Prozac	Fluoxetine hydrochloride
PTU	Propylthiouracil
Pulmotil tilmicosin premix	Tilmicosin phosphate
Purinethol	Mercaptopurine
Pyopen	Carbenicillin
Pyran	Pyrantel
Pyrantel pamoate	Pyrantel
Pyrantel tartrate	Pyrantel

Continued

List of Trade and Brand Names Cross-Referenced to Drug Names—cont'd

Trade Names and Other Names	Drug Name as Listed in Handbook
Pyr-A-Pam	Pyrantel
PZI	Insulin
PZI Vet	Insulin
Quadrinal	Potassium iodide
Quest	Moxidectin
Quinidine gluconate	Quinidine
Quinidine polygalacturonate	Quinidine
Quinidine sulfate	Quinidine
Quinaglute	Quinidine
Quinora	Quinidine
Rapinovet	Propofol
ReBalance	Pyrimethamine + sulfadiazine
Regitine	Phentolamine mesylate
Reglan	Metoclopramide hydrochloride
Regonol	Pyridostigmine bromide
Retinol	Vitamin A
Retrovir	Zidovudine
Revolution	Selamectin
Rheumatrex	Methotrexate
r-HuEPO	Epoetin alpha (erythropoietin)
Rhythmodan	Disopyramide
Ridaura	Auranofin
Rifadin	Rifampin
Rifampicin	Rifampin
Rimadyl	Carprofen
Ringers	Ringer's solution
Rintal	Febantel
Ripercol	Levamisole hydrochloride
Robamox-V	Amoxicillin
Robaxin-V	Methocarbamol
Robinul-V	Glycopyrrolate
Robitussin	Dextromethorphan
Rocaltrol	Calcitriol
Rogitine	Phentolamine mesylate
Romazicon	Flumazenil
Rompun	Xylazine hydrochloride
SafeGuard	Fenbendazole
SafeHeart	Milbemycin oxime
Salazopyrin	Sulfasalazine
Salbutamol	Albuterol sulfate
Saline solution	Sodium chloride 0.9%
SAMe	S-adenosylmethionine (SAMe)
Sandimmune	Cyclosporine
Scolaban	Bunamidine hydrochloride
Sedivet	Romifidine hydrochloride
Senokot	Senna
Sentinel	Milbemycin oxime
Sentinel tablets	Lufenuron + milbemycin oxime
Septra	Trimethoprim + sulfamethoxazole
Serax	Oxazepam
Silybin	Silymarin
Simplicef	Cefpodoxime proxetil
Sinequan	Doxepin
Slo-bid	Theophylline

List of Trade and Brand Names Cross-Referenced to Drug Names—cont'd

Trade Names and Other Names	Drug Name as Listed in Handbook
Soda Mint	Sodium bicarbonate
Sodium bromide	Bromide
Sodium ascorbate	Ascorbic acid
Solganal	Aurothioglucose
Soloxine	Levothyroxine sodium
Solu-Cortef	Hydrocortisone sodium succinate
Solu-Delta-Cortef	Prednisolone sodium succinate
Solu-Medrol	Methylprednisolone sodium succinate
Somatrem	Growth hormone
Somatropin	Growth hormone
Sorbitrate	Isosorbide mononitrate
Spectam	Clenbuterol
Spectinomycin dihydrochloride	Spectinomycin
Spectinomycin sulfate tetrahydrate	Spectinomycin
Spectogard	Clenbuterol
Sporanox	Itraconazole
Stelazine	Trifluoperazine hydrochloride
Stiglyn	Neostigmine
Streptozotocin	Streptozocin
Strongid	Pyrantel
Sublimaze	Fentanyl citrate
Sudafed	Pseudoephedrine hydrochloride
Sufenta	Sufentanil citrate
Sulcrate	Sucralfate
Sulfa-Nox	Sulfaquinoxaline
Sulmet	Sulfamethazine
Suprax	Cefixime
Surfak	Docusate
Symmetrel	Amantadine
Synanthic	Oxfendazole
Synthroid	Levothyroxine sodium
Syntocinon	Oxytocin
Syprine	Trientine hydrochloride
Syrup of Ipecac	Ipecac
T4	Levothyroxine sodium
Tagamet	Cimetidine hydrochloride
Talwin-V	Pentazocine
Tapazole	Methimazole
Task	Dichlorvos
Tavist	Clemastine fumarate
Tazicef	Ceftazidime
Tazidime	Ceftazidime
TBZ	Thiabendazole
Tegopen	Cloxacillin sodium
Telezol	Tiletamine + zolazepam
Telmin	Mebendazole
Telmintic	Mebendazole
Temaril	Trimeprazine tartrate
Temaril-P (with prednisolone)	Trimeprazine tartrate
Tenormin	Atenolol
Tensilon	Edrophonium chloride
Terramycin	Oxytetracycline
Terramycin scours tablets	Oxytetracycline
Terramycin soluble powder	Oxytetracycline

Continued

List of Trade and Brand Names Cross-Referenced to Drug Names—cont'd

Trade Names and Other Names	Drug Name as Listed in Handbook
Testex	Testosterone propionate ester
Testosterone cypionate ester	Testosterone
Tetracosactide	Cosyntropin
Tetracosactrin	Cosyntropin
Tetracycline hydrochloride	Tetracycline
Theo-Dur	Theophylline
Theophylline	Aminophylline
Theophylline sustained-release	Theophylline
Thibenzole	Thiabendazole
Thioplex	Thiotepa
Thorazine	Chlorpromazine
Thyrogen	Thyrotropin
Thyroid powder	Levothyroxine sodium
Thyro-L	Levothyroxine sodium
ThyroMed	Levothyroxine sodium
Thyro-Tabs	Levothyroxine sodium
Thytropar	Thyrotropin
Ticar	Ticarcillin disodium
Ticillin	Ticarcillin + clavulanate potassium
Tigan	Trimethobenzamide
Timentin	Ticarcillin + clavulanate potassium
Tindamax	Tinidazole
Titralac	Calcium carbonate
Tocopherol	Vitamin E
Tofranil	Imipramine hydrochloride
Tonocard	Tocainide hydrochloride
Toradol	Ketorolac tromethamine
Torbugesic	Butorphanol tartrate
Torbutrol	Butorphanol tartrate
Torpex equine inhaler	Albuterol sulfate
Totacillin	Ampicillin
Totacillin-N	Ampicillin
Toxiban	Charcoal activated
Tracurium	Atracurium besylate
Tramisol	Levamisole hydrochloride
Tranvet	Propiopromazine hydrochloride
Tranxene	Clorazepate dipotassium
Trental	Pentoxifylline
Trexan	Naltrexone
Trexonil	Naloxone hydrochloride
TRH	Thyroid releasing hormone
Triamcinolone acetonide	Triamcinolone
Triamcinolone diacetate	Triamcinolone
Triamcinolone hexacetonide	Triamcinolone
Triamtabs	Triamcinolone
Tribrissen	Trimethoprim + sulfadiazine
Tribrissen	Sulfadiazine
Trimox	Amoxicillin
TSH	Thyrotropin
Tucoprim	Trimethoprim + sulfadiazine
Tumil-K	Potassium gluconate
Tums	Calcium carbonate
Tylan	Tylosin
Tylenol	Acetaminophen

List of Trade and Brand Names Cross-Referenced to Drug Names—cont'd

Trade Names and Other Names	Drug Name as Listed in Handbook
Tylenol with codeine	Acetaminophen + codeine
Tylocine	Tylosin
Tylosin tartrate	Tylosin
UlcerGard	Omeprazole
Ultralente insulin	Insulin
Ultram	Tramadol
Ultramectin	Ivermectin
Ultrase	Pancrelipase
Unasyn	Ampicillin + sulbactam
Uniprim	Trimethoprim + sulfadiazine
Uracid	Racemethionine
Urecholine	Bethanechol chloride
Urex	Methenamine
UriCon	Phenylpropanolamine hydrochloride
Urocit-K	Potassium citrate
Uroeze	Racemethionine
Ursodeoxycholic acid	Ursodiol
Valbazen	Albendazole
Valium	Diazepam
Valproate sodium	Valproic acid
Vancocin	Vancomycin
Vancoled	Vancomycin
Vantin	Cefpodoxime proxetil
Vasodilan	Isoxsuprine
Vasotec	Enalapril maleate
Vasotop	Ramipril
Vasoxyl	Methoxamine
Veda-K1	Vitamin K
Velban	Vinblastine sulfate
Velosef	Cephradine
Ventipulmin	Clenbuterol
Ventolin	Albuterol sulfate
Vercom	Febantel
Verdisol	Dichlorvos
Vermox	Mebendazole
Versed	Midazolam hydrochloride
Vesprin	Triflupromazine hydrochloride
Veta-K1	Phytonadione
Veta-K1	Vitamin K
Vetalar	Ketamine hydrochloride
Vetalog	Triamcinolone
Vetalog	Triamcinolone
Vetergesic	Buprenorphine hydrochloride
Vetisulid	Sulfachlorpyridazine
Vetmedin	Pimobendan
Vetoryl	Trilostane
Vetsulin (porcine insulin zinc)	Insulin
Vfend	Voriconazole
Vibramycin	Doxycycline
Vincasar	Vincristine sulfate
Viokase	Pancrelipase
Virbagen	Interferon
Vitamin AD	Vitamin A
Vitamin B_1	Thiamine hydrochloride

Continued

List of Trade and Brand Names Cross-Referenced to Drug Names—cont'd

Trade Names and Other Names	Drug Name as Listed in Handbook
Vitamin B_2	Riboflavin
Vitamin B_3	Niacinamide
Vitamin B_{12}	Cyanocobalamin
Vitamin C	Ascorbic acid
Vitamin K_1	Phytonadione
Vitamin K_1	Vitamin K
Wellcovorin	Leucovorin calcium
Winstrol-V	Stanozolol
Wycillin	Penicillin G
Wymox	Amoxicillin
Xanax	Alprazolam
Xylocaine	Lidocaine hydrochloride
Yobine	Yohimbine
Zanosar	Streptozocin
Zantac	Ranitidine hydrochloride
Zeniquin	Marbofloxacin
Zestril	Lisinopril
Zimecterin	Ivermectin
Zinc acetate	Zinc
Zinc sulfate	Zinc
Zinecarp	Carprofen
Zithromax	Azithromycin
Zofran	Ondansetron hydrochloride
Zolazepam	Tiletamine + zolazepam
Zoletil	Tiletamine + zolazepam
Zonegran	Zonisamide
Zovirax	Acyclovir
Zosyn	Piperacillin sodium
Zubrin	Tepoxalin
Zyloprim	Allopurinol
Zyrtec	Cetirizine hydrochloride
Zyvox	Linezolid

Acepromazine Maleate

ayss-proe′meh-zeen mal′ee-ate

Trade and Other Names: ACE, Aceproject, Aceprotabs, Atravet, and Promace; it sometimes is called acetylpromazine.

Functional Classification: Tranquilizer, phenothiazine tranquilizer

Pharmacology and Mechanism of Action

Phenothiazine tranquilizer. Acepromazine inhibits central dopaminergic receptors to cause sedation and tranquilization. Acepromazine also has antimuscarinic action and blocks norepinephrine at adrenergic receptors (e.g., alpha-receptors).

Indications and Clinical Uses

Acepromazine is used as a sedative, a tranquilizer, a preanesthetic, and an anesthetic adjunct. In small animals, acepromazine can produce antiemetic effects.

Precautionary Information

Adverse Reactions and Side Effects

Sedation and ataxia are common side effects. Extrapyramidal effects (involuntary muscle movements), twitching, dystonia, or Parkinson-like effects are rare, but are possible with the administration of phenothiazines to animals. Some animals may have excessive vagal tone from phenothiazines. This may be especially prominent in brachycephalic breeds. Administration of atropine may be used to treat the signs of high vagal tone. Because of alpha-adrenergic antagonism, hypotension is possible in animals. In horses, persistent penile prolapse has been reported from use. This effect is unpredictable and apparently not related to dose.

Contraindications and Precautions

Use cautiously in animals that are prone to seizures. However, seizures have not been a common clinical problem and were not reported to be a clinical problem in a retrospective study of seizure patients.

Do not use in animals that have problems with dystonia or that have had extrapyramidal effects from use of phenothiazines.

Phenothiazines can cause hypotension (via alpha-receptor blockade), therefore use cautiously with other hypotensive drugs or in conditions that may exacerbate hypotension.

Drug Interactions

Acepromazine may potentiate other drugs that cause vasodilation. Acepromazine may increase the risk of seizures if administered with other drugs that lower seizure threshold. Acepromazine has been used to sedate dogs for glucose tolerance testing (0.1 mg/kg), without adversely affecting the results.

Instructions for Use

Acepromazine can be administered PO, IV, or IM. When used with general anesthetics, lower doses of general anesthetics can be used, especially when administering barbiturates and inhalant anesthetics. Clinical signs from acepromazine administration are most prominent during the first 3-4 hours after administration, but may persist for 7 hours.

Patient Monitoring and Laboratory Tests

Monitor blood pressure in animals susceptible to hypotension.

Formulations
Acepromazine is available in 5, 10, and 25 mg tablets and in a 10 mg/mL injection. Acepromazine oral granules and powder are available in Canada.

Stability and Storage
Store in tightly sealed container, protected from light, and at room temperature. Stability of compounded formulations has not been investigated.

Small Animal Dosage
Dogs
- 0.025-0.1 mg/kg IM, IV, or SQ in a single dose. Do not exceed 3 mg total in dogs.
- Sedation: 0.5-2.2 mg/kg q6-8h PO.

Cats
- 0.025-0.1 mg/kg IM, IV, or SQ in a single dose.
- Sedation: 1.1-2.2 mg/kg q6-8h PO.

Large Animal Dosage
Cattle
- 0.13-0.26 mg/kg PO, 0.03-0.1 mg/kg IM, or 0.01-0.02 mg/kg IV.

Pigs
- Adult: 60 mg q12h IM.

Regulatory Information
Withdrawal times: None established in U.S.
Canada: 7 days for meat; 48 hours for milk.
Extralabel use: establish a withdrawal time of at least 7 days for meat and 48 hours for milk.
RCI Classification: 3

Acetaminophen
ah-seet-ah-mee′noe-fen

Trade and Other Names: Tylenol and generic brands

Functional Classification: Analgesic

Pharmacology and Mechanism of Action
Analgesic drug. Exact mechanism of action is not known, however acetaminophen probably inhibits centrally mediated pain transmission. Acetaminophen is not a prostaglandin synthesis inhibitor.

Indications and Clinical Uses
Acetaminophen is used as an analgesic and used for pain control in dogs. **Do not use in cats**. It is considered relatively weak as an analgesic. Often used in combination with an opiate (e.g., codeine).

Precautionary Information
Adverse Reactions and Side Effects
Acetaminophen is well tolerated in dogs at doses listed; however, high doses have caused liver toxicity. It causes severe toxicosis in cats because of their inability to excrete metabolites. Clinical signs of toxicity include methemoglobinemia, acute hepatic toxicosis, swelling of paws, and Heinz body anemia.

Contraindications and Precautions

Do not administer to cats. In people, toxic episodes are more likely when administered with drugs that alter the activity of hepatic drug enzymes. Such a reaction also is possible in animals.

Drug Interactions

In people, other drugs (especially alcohol) will increase risk of hepatotoxicosis. It is not known if other drugs increase this risk in animals.

Instructions for Use

Many OTC formulations are available. Acetaminophen with codeine may have greater analgesic efficacy in some animals. See other entries for formulations that contain codeine.

Patient Monitoring and Laboratory Tests

Monitor liver enzyme levels periodically to look for evidence of hepatotoxicity.

Formulations

Acetaminophen is available in 120, 160, 325, and 500 mg tablets.

Stability and Storage

Acetaminophen is stable in aqueous solutions. Maximum stability is at pH of 5-7.

Small Animal Dosage

Dogs

- 15 mg/kg q8h PO.

Cats

Contraindicated.

Large Animal Dosage

Calves

50 mg/kg PO, followed by 30 mg/kg PO, q6h.
No other doses have been reported for large animals.

Regulatory Information

No regulatory information is available. For extralabel use withdrawal interval estimates, contact FARAD at 1-888-USFARAD (1-888-873-2723) or send e-mail to FARAD@ncsu.edu.
RCI Classification: 4

Acetaminophen + Codeine

ah-seet-ah-mee′noe-fen + koe′deen

Trade and Other Names: Tylenol with codeine and many generic brands

Functional Classification: Analgesic, Opioid

Pharmacology and Mechanism of Action

Analgesic agent. Exact mechanism of action for acetaminophen is not known, however, a centrally mediated mechanism is likely. It is not a prostaglandin synthesis inhibitor. The opiate codeine is added to enhance analgesia.

Indications and Clinical Uses

Acetaminophen + Codeine is used for analgesia in dogs (e.g., postoperative use). Codeine or codeine with acetaminophen is indicated for treatment of moderate pain.

It also has been used as an antitussive. Despite the widespread use of codeine in humans, the efficacy in animals for its antitussive use or analgesic use has not been established.

Oral absorption in dogs is low. Because codeine is converted to morphine (10% of dose) for its activity and the duration of morphine is short in dogs, the clinical effectiveness of codeine in dogs may be questionable.

Precautionary Information

Adverse Reactions and Side Effects

Acetaminophen + Codeine is well tolerated in dogs at doses listed; however, high doses have caused liver toxicity. **Do not administer to cats.**

Contraindications and Precautions

Codeine is Schedule II controlled substance. Do not administer to cats because of acetaminophen component.

Drug Interactions

In people, other drugs (especially alcohol) will increase risk of hepatotoxicity. It is not known if other drugs increase this risk in animals.

Instructions for Use

There are many generic preparations available. Consider that other ingredients may be present in tablets (e.g., ibuprofen or caffeine).

Patient Monitoring and Laboratory Tests

Monitor liver enzyme levels periodically to look for evidence of hepatotoxicity caused by acetaminophen.

Formulations

Acetaminophen + Codeine is available in oral solution and tablets. A variety of formulations are available, for example, 300 mg acetaminophen plus 15, 30, or 60 mg codeine.

Stability and Storage

Acetaminophen is stable in aqueous solutions. Maximum stability is at pH of 5-7.

Small Animal Dosage

Dogs

- Follow dosing recommendations for codeine. Administer dose to deliver doses of codeine equivalent to 0.5-1.0 mg/kg q4-6h PO.

Large Animal Dosage

No dose has been reported for large animals.

Regulatory Information

Acetaminophen + Codeine is a Schedule III drug controlled by DEA. Do not administer to animals intended for food.

Acetazolamide

ah-seet-ah-zole'a-mide

Trade and Other Names: Diamox

Functional Classification: Diuretic

Pharmacology and Mechanism of Action

Carbonic anhydrase inhibitor. Acetazolamide, like other carbonic anhydrase inhibitors, produces a diuresis through inhibition of the uptake of bicarbonate in proximal renal tubules via enzyme inhibition. This action results in loss of bicarbonate in the urine and a diuresis. The action of carbonic anhydrase inhibitors results in urine loss of bicarbonate, alkaline urine, and water loss.

Indications and Clinical Uses

Acetazolamide is rarely used as a diuretic any longer. There are more potent and effective diuretic drugs available such as the loop diuretics (furosemide).

Acetazolamide, like other carbonic anhydrase inhibitors are used primarily to lower intraocular pressure in animals with glaucoma. Methazolamide is used more often than acetazolamide for this purpose, and other treatment regiments are used more often than carbonic anhydrase inhibitors.

Acetazolamide, like other carbonic anhydrase inhibitors, is sometimes used to produce more alkaline urine for management of some urinary calculi.

Precautionary Information

Adverse Reactions and Side Effects

Acetazolamide can potentially produce hypokalemia in some patients.

Contraindications and Precautions

Do not use in patients with acidemia. Use cautiously in any animal sensitive to sulfonamides.

Drug Interactions

Acetazolamide will produce alkaline urine, which may affect clearance of some drugs. Alkaline urine may potentiate the effects of some antibacterial drugs (e.g., macrolides and quinolones).

Instructions for Use

Acetazolamide, in combination with other agents, is usually used to decrease intraocular pressure in the treatment of glaucoma. Acetazolamide has been used to produce alkaline urine to prevent formation of some urinary calculi. However, unless there is supplementation with bicarbonate, the urine alkalinization will not be sustained with repeated administration.

Patient Monitoring and Laboratory Tests

Monitor patient's ocular pressure when used to treat glaucoma.

Formulations

Acetazolamide is available in 125 and 250 mg tablets.

Stability and Storage

Stable if stored in tight containers. Compounded solutions are stable at least 60 days.

Small Animal Dosage

Dogs

- Glaucoma: 5-10 mg/kg q8-12h PO.
- Other diuretic uses: 4-8 mg/kg q8-12h PO.

Large Animal Dosage

No dose has been reported for large animals.

Regulatory Information

No regulatory information is available. For extralabel use withdrawal interval estimates, contact FARAD at 1-888-USFARAD (1-888-873-2723) or send e-mail to FARAD@ncsu.edu.
RCI Classification: 4

Acetylcysteine

ah-see-til-sis′tay-een

Trade and Other Names: Mucomyst and Acetadote

Functional Classification: Mucolytic, Antidote

Pharmacology and Mechanism of Action

Acetylcysteine decreases viscosity of secretions and is used as mucolytic agent in eyes and in bronchial nebulizing solutions. Acetylcysteine is a sulfhydryl compound and acts to increase synthesis of glutathione in the liver. Glutathione subsequently acts as an antioxidant and facilitates conjugation to toxic metabolites, particularly the toxic metabolites of acetaminophen.

Indications and Clinical Uses

As a donator of sulfhydryl group, it is used as antidote for intoxications (e.g., acetaminophen toxicosis in cats). When treating poisoning, it is important that acetylcysteine be administered as soon as possible for optimum effectiveness.

Precautionary Information

Adverse Reactions and Side Effects

None reported in animals. Allergic reactions have been reported in people, which resemble anaphylactic reactions when it is given IV.

Contraindications and Precautions

Acetylcysteine may cause sensitization with prolonged topical administration. It may react with certain materials in nebulizing equipment.

Drug Interactions

Acetylcysteine acts to donate sulfhydryl groups and may facilitate drug conjugation.

Instructions for Use

Available as agent for decreasing viscosity of respiratory secretions, but most common use is as a treatment for intoxications. In cats, acetylcysteine is used to treat acetaminophen toxicosis. When treating an intoxication, consult a poison control center for specific guidelines.

Patient Monitoring and Laboratory Tests

When used to treat acetaminophen toxicity, monitor CBC and liver enzyme concentrations.

Formulations

Acetylcysteine is available in a 20% solution.

Stability and Storage

Acetylcysteine is unstable in air and easily oxidizes. It should be protected from light. Discard open vials after 96 hours.

Small Animal Dosage

Dogs and Cats

- Antidote: 140 mg/kg (loading dose) then 70 mg/kg q4h IV or PO for 5 doses.
- Eye solution: 2% solution topically q2h. The oral solution has been previously administered IV.

Large Animal Dosage

No dose has been reported for large animals.

Regulatory Information

No regulatory information is available. However, because it is short-acting and is used primarily for treatment of intoxications, no withdrawal time is suggested. For further information contact FARAD at 1-888-USFARAD (1-888-873-2723) or send e-mail to FARAD@ncsu.edu.

Acyclovir

ay-sye'kloe-veer

Trade and Other Names: Zovirax and generic brands

Functional Classification: Antiviral

Pharmacology and Mechanism of Action

Antiviral drug. Acyclovir is a synthetic purine analogue (acyclic nucleoside analogue). It has antiviral activity against herpes virus. The action is related to the affinity for the enzyme thymidine kinase (TK). However, resistance among some virus forms is possible because of changes in TK or in the DNA polymerase. It is used for treatment of various forms of herpes virus infection in humans. It has also been used for treatment of viral infections in animals. However, feline herpes virus 1 (FHV1) is resistant to acyclovir, and studies are lacking on the susceptibility of other herpes viruses. The half-life is 9.6 hours for horses, 2.3 hours for dogs, and 2.6 hours for cats. By comparison, the half-life in humans is 2.5 hours. Unfortunately it is not absorbed orally in horses, and there is little data to confirm oral absorption in other species. In humans, oral absorption is only 10%. Other forms (e.g., pro-drugs) are better absorbed in people, but these have been too expensive to use in animals.

Indications and Clinical Uses

Acyclovir is an antiviral drug. The use in veterinary medicine is limited because the activity against some viruses (e.g., FHV1) is either poor or unknown. In cats, acyclovir had poor absorption and produced toxicity. Acyclovir is able to inhibit replication of equine herpes virus (EHV1) in vitro. However, acyclovir oral absorption in horses was poor and inconsistent.

Precautionary Information

Adverse Reactions and Side Effects

The most serious adverse effect in humans is acute renal insufficiency. This may be prevented by slow intravenous infusion and proper hydration. Phlebitis can occur with intravenous administration. No adverse effects were identified in limited studies performed in horses.

Contraindications and Precautions

Do not use in animals with compromised renal function.

Drug Interactions

Do not mix with biological solutions (e.g., blood products). Do not mix with fluids that contain bacteriostatic preservatives. Do not use with other nephrotoxic drugs.

Instructions for Use

To prepare injectable formulation, dilute each vial with 10 or 20 mL of water to make 50 mg/mL. Do **not** use bacteriostatic water that contains benzyl alcohol or parabens. Further dilute solution to at least 100 mL to a concentration of 7 mg/mL or less.

Patient Monitoring and Laboratory Tests

Monitor BUN and creatinine during use.

Formulations

Acyclovir is available in 400 and 800 mg tablets, 200 mg capsules, 1 g and 500 mg vials for injection (50 mg/mL), and 40 mg/mL oral suspension.

Stability and Storage

After reconstitution of solution, at 50 mg/mL, it is stable for 12 hours at room temperature. More dilute solutions are stable for 24 hours. If refrigerated, a precipitate will form, which should be redissolved at room temperature before use. Store tablets and capsules in tightly sealed container, protected from light, and at room temperature.

Small Animal Dosage

Dogs and Cats

- Systemic doses have not been determined. Doses have been extrapolated from human use: 3 mg/kg PO 5 times daily for 10 days, up to 10 mg/kg PO 5 times daily for 10 days. Alternatively 10-20 mg/kg IV q8h (slow infusion for 1 hour).

Large Animal Dosage

Horses

- 10 mg/kg q12h IV. Even after 20 mg/kg, oral acyclovir is not absorbed in horses well enough for systemic treatment.

Regulatory Information

Because of mutagenicity, it should not be administered to animals intended for food.

Albendazole

al-ben′dah-zole

Trade and Other Names: Valbazen

Functional Classification: Antiparasitic

Pharmacology and Mechanism of Action

Benzimidazole antiparasitic drug. Albendazole inhibits glucose uptake in parasites.

Indications and Clinical Uses

Albendazole is used to treat a variety of intestinal helminth parasites. It has been used for treating parasitic infections of the respiratory tract, including *Capillaria aerophilia, Paragonimus kellicotti, Aelurostrongylus abstrusus, Filaroides* spp., and

Oslerus osleri. It is also effective for treatment of Giardia in small animals. However, because albendazole has been associated with bone marrow suppression in dogs and cats, other drugs have been used for Giardia.

Precautionary Information

Adverse Reactions and Side Effects

High doses have been associated with bone marrow toxicity (*J Am Vet Med Assoc*, 213: 44-46, 1998) in dogs and cats, and it should be used cautiously in small animals. In other species, at approved doses, there is a wide margin of safety. Adverse effects can include anorexia, lethargy, and bone marrow toxicity.

Contraindications and Precautions

Adverse effects are more likely when administered for longer than 5 days. Avoid high doses.

Drug Interactions

No drug interactions are reported in animals.

Instructions for Use

Used primarily as antihelmintic but also has demonstrated efficacy for giardiasis.

Patient Monitoring and Laboratory Tests

Monitor CBC in animals experiencing signs suspicious of adverse effects.

Formulations

Albendazole is available in a 113.6 mg/mL suspension and 300 mg/mL paste.

Stability and Storage

Store in tightly sealed container, protected from light, and at room temperature. Stability of compounded formulations has not been investigated.

Small Animal Dosage

- Anthelmintic dose: 25-50 mg/kg q12h PO for 3 days.
- Respiratory parasites: 50 mg/kg q24h PO for 10-14 days.
- Giardia: 25 mg/kg q12h PO for 2 days.

Large Animal Dosage

Cattle

- Antiparasitic: 10 mg/kg oral paste or 10 mg/kg (suspension) PO.

Horses

- *Dictyocaulus arnfieldi:* 25 mg/kg q12h for 5 days.
- *Strongylus vulgaris:* 50 mg/kg q12h for 2 days.

Sheep

- 7.5 mg/kg oral suspension.

Regulatory Information

Cattle withdrawal time: 27 days meat. Do not use in lactating dairy cattle. Do not use during first 45 days of pregnancy.

Albuterol Sulfate

al-byoo′ter-ole sul′fate

Trade and Other Names: Proventil, Ventolin, and Torpex equine inhaler. Also known as Salbutamol outside the US.

Functional Classification: Bronchodilator, Beta-agonist

Pharmacology and Mechanism of Action

$Beta_2$-adrenergic agonist. Albuterol stimulates $beta_2$-receptors to relax bronchial smooth muscle. It may also inhibit release of inflammatory mediators, especially from mast cells.

Indications and Clinical Uses

Albuterol is indicated in a variety of airway diseases for bronchodilation. Except for equine use, doses are primarily derived from extrapolation of human dose. Efficacy studies for small animal use are not reported. Onset of action is 15-30 minutes, and duration of action may be as long as 8 hours.

Albuterol is used as an inhaler (Torpex) in horses for treatment of airway disease. It provides immediate relief of bronchospasm and bronchoconstriction in horses.

Precautionary Information

Adverse Reactions and Side Effects

Excessive beta-adrenergic stimulation at high doses results in tachycardia and muscle tremors. Arrhythmias are possible with high doses. All $beta_2$-agonists will inhibit uterine contractions at the end of gestation in pregnant animals.

Contraindications and Precautions

Avoid use in pregnant animals. IM or SQ injections can be painful.

Drug Interactions

All beta-agonists will interact with other drugs that act on beta-adrenergic receptor.

Instructions for Use

Administration to horses requires adaptor to facilitate metered dose inhaler.
For injection, dilute solution to 0.01 mg/mL (10 mcg/mL) before injection and further dilute to 50/50 with saline or 5% dextrose before injection.

Patient Monitoring and Laboratory Tests

Monitor heart rate and rhythm in animals with cardiovascular disease.

Formulations

Albuterol is available in 2, 4, and 5 mg tablets and 2 mg/5 mL syrup. Solutions for injection are 0.83 mg/mL and 5 mg/mL.

Stability and Storage

Store in well-closed containers and protected from light. Aqueous solutions are stable if kept at an acidic pH (2.2-5).

Small Animal Dosage

Dogs and Cats

- 20-50 mcg/kg q6-8h, up to a maximum of 100 mcg/kg q6h.

Large Animal Dosage

Horses

- 120 mcg albuterol per actuation. Six actuations per dose 4 times daily.
- 48 hours or longer for urine clearance prior to testing.

Regulatory Information

Do not administer to animals intended for food.
RCI Classification: 3

Alendronate

ah-len′droe-nate

Trade and Other Names: Fosamax

Functional Classification: Antihypercalcemic

Pharmacology and Mechanism of Action

Bisphosphonate drug. Drugs in this class include pamidronate, risedronate, and etidronate. This is a group of drugs characterized by a germinal bisphosphonate bond. They slow the formation and dissolution of hydroxyapatite crystals. Their clinical use is in their ability to inhibit bone resorption. These drugs decrease bone turnover by inhibiting osteoclast activity, retarding bone resorption, and decreasing the rate of osteoporosis. Alendronate is 100-1000 times more potent than older drugs such as etidronate. Unfortunately, alendronate is poorly absorbed orally (3%-7%), and use of oral formulations in animals may not be effective. In dogs, half-life in plasma is short (1-2 hours), but bone shows prolonged update and half-life of 300 days.

Indications and Clinical Uses

Alendronate, like other bisphosphonate drugs, is used in people to treat osteoporosis and treatment of hypercalcemia of malignancy.

In animals, alendronate is used to decrease calcium in conditions that cause hypercalcemia, such as cancer and vitamin D toxicosis. It may be helpful for managing neoplastic complications associated with pathologic bone resorption. It also may provide pain relief in patients with pathologic bone disease. Most experimental work performed in dogs has been performed with pamidronate rather than alendronate.

Precautionary Information

Adverse Reactions and Side Effects

No serious adverse effects identified, however use in animals has been uncommon. In people, esophageal injury and erosion are important problems. When administering to animals, ensure that the entire medication is swallowed and followed with water.

Contraindications and Precautions

Do not administer with foods or medications containing calcium. Food will decrease absorption.

Drug Interactions

Do not mix with a solution containing calcium (e.g., Lactated Ringer's solution). Do not give with foods containing calcium.

Instructions for Use

When administering oral medication, ensure that no drug is trapped in esophagus. Food will significantly reduce oral absorption. Wait at least 30 minutes before feeding.

Patient Monitoring and Laboratory Tests

Monitor serum calcium and phosphorus.

Formulations

Alendronate is available in 5, 10, 35, 40, and 70 mg tablets.

Stability and Storage

Store in tightly sealed container, protected from light, and at room temperature.

Small Animal Dosage

Dogs

- 0.5-1 mg/kg q24h PO.

Large Animal Dosage

No dose has been reported for large animals.

Regulatory Information

Withdrawal times are not established for animals that produce food. For extralabel use withdrawal interval estimates, contact FARAD at 1-888-USFARAD (1-888-873-2723) or send e-mail to FARAD@ncsu.edu.

Allopurinol

al-oh-pyoo′rih-nole

Trade and Other Names: Lopurin, Zyloprim, and Allopur (Europe)

Functional Classification: Antiinflammatory

Pharmacology and Mechanism of Action

Purine analogue. Allopurinol decreases the production of uric acid by inhibiting enzymes responsible for uric acid synthesis.

Indications and Clinical Uses

Allopurinol is indicated to decrease formation of uric acid uroliths in at-risk animals. Allopurinol also is used to treat clinical signs associated with leishmaniasis. When used for leishmaniasis it is administered with pentavalent antimonial compounds such as meglumine antimonite (Glutamine) or sodium stibogluconate (Pentosan). In parasites, allopurinol is metabolized to products that disrupt RNA synthesis and interfere with protein synthesis. Allopurinol does not eliminate Leishmania or cure the disease, but it may improve cutaneous lesions and induce remission.

Precautionary Information

Adverse Reactions and Side Effects

Allopurinol may cause skin reactions (hypersensitivity). In dogs that were treated for leishmaniasis for several months, no adverse effects were reported.

Contraindications and Precautions

No contraindications reported for animals.

Drug Interactions

Allopurinol may inhibit drug metabolism of certain drugs. Do not use with azathioprine because it interferes with xanthine oxidase, an important enzyme for metabolizing azathioprine, and will enhance toxicity.

Instructions for Use

In people, allopurinol is used primarily for treating gout.

In animals, it is used to decrease formation of uric acid uroliths and for treating signs associated with leishmaniasis. No single drug or combination is completely effective for treating leishmaniasis, but allopurinol will improve skin lesions. Allopurinol is often administered with other drugs for leishmaniasis. For example, it has been administered with either amphotericin B or pentavalent antimony compounds.

Patient Monitoring and Laboratory Tests

Dose adjustments for treating leishmaniasis are based on monitoring clinical signs. Allopurinol will not cure the underlying disease, but it will decrease some clinical signs.

Formulations

Allopurinol is available in 100 and 300 mg tablets.

Stability and Storage

Store in well-closed containers at room temperature. Stable for at least 60 days in compounded formulations. Maximum stability in solutions at pH of 3-3.4.

Small Animal Dosage

Dogs

- Urate urolith prevention: 10 mg/kg q8h PO, then reduce to 10 mg/kg q24h PO.
- Leishmaniasis: 10 mg/kg q12h PO for at least 4 months. For leishmaniasis, some clinicians have used 15 mg/kg q12h, and then if there is a response, administer 7-10 mg/kg q12-24h PO.

Large Animal Dosage

Horses

- 5 mg/kg PO.

Regulatory Information

No regulatory information is available. For extralabel use withdrawal interval estimates, contact FARAD at 1-888-USFARAD (1-888-873-2723) or send e-mail to FARAD@ncsu.edu.

Alprazolam

al-pray′zoe-lam

Trade and Other Names: Xanax and Niravam

Functional Classification: Tranquilizer, CNS depressant

Pharmacology and Mechanism of Action

Benzodiazepine. Central-acting CNS depressant. Mechanism of action appears to be via potentiation of GABA-receptor mediated effects in CNS. A drug that has similar effects is diazepam.

Indications and Clinical Uses

Alprazolam is used to treat behavior problems in dogs and cats, particularly those associated with anxiety. Alprazolam has been used in dogs for the short-term treatment of thunderstorm phobia. For thunderstorm phobia, it may be more effective if combined with long-term clomipramine treatment.

Precautionary Information

Adverse Reactions and Side Effects

Sedation is the most common side effect. Alprazolam may cause paradoxical excitement in dogs. It also causes polyphagia. In cats, idiopathic fatal hepatic necrosis has been reported from diazepam, but this has not been reported from alprazolam, probably because of differences in metabolism. Alprazolam is not as extensively metabolized as diazepam. Chronic administration in any species may lead to dependence and a withdrawal syndrome if discontinued.

Contraindications and Precautions

No serious contraindications. In rare individuals, benzodiazepines have caused paradoxical excitement.

Drug Interactions

Other drugs may decrease hepatic metabolism (e.g., ketoconazole, chloramphenicol, and itraconazole).

Instructions for Use

Use in animals has been primarily derived from empirical use. There are no well-controlled clinical studies or efficacy trials to document clinical effectiveness.

When treating thunderstorm phobia, it is helpful in some dogs to administer 0.02 mg/kg of clomipramine 1 hour before a storm, in addition to alprazolam.

The Niravam tablets are rapidly dissolving and may be easier to administer to animals that are difficult to medicate. Tablets easily dissolve on the tongue without requiring water and can be cut for accurate dosing.

Patient Monitoring and Laboratory Tests

Monitor hepatic enzymes in animals with chronic use.

Formulations

Alprazolam is available in 0.25, 0.5, 1, and 2 mg tablets and 1 and 2 mg scored tablets.

Rapidly dissolving tablets (Niravam) are available in 0.25, 0.5, 1, and 2 mg that can be cut for accurate dosing.

Stability and Storage

Store in tightly sealed container, protected from light, and at room temperature. Stable in some compounded formulations for 60 days.

Small Animal Dosage

Dogs

- 0.025-0.1 mg/kg q8h PO.

Cats

- 0.125 mg q12h PO (1/2 of 0.25 mg tablet) or 0.0125-0.025 mg/kg q12h PO.

Large Animal Dosage

No dose has been reported for large animals.

Regulatory Information

No regulatory information is available. For extralabel use withdrawal interval estimates, contact FARAD at 1-888-USFARAD (1-888-873-2723) or send e-mail to FARAD@ncsu.edu.
RCI Classification: 2

Aluminum Hydroxide and Aluminum Carbonate

ah-loo′mih-num hye-droks′ide, ah-loo′mih-num kar′boe-nate

Trade and Other Names: Aluminum hydroxide gel (Amphogel) and Aluminum carbonate gel (Basalgel)

Functional Classification: Antacid

Pharmacology and Mechanism of Action

Aluminum is an antacid and phosphate binder in intestine. It is used in both the aluminum hydroxide and aluminum carbonate formulations.

Indications and Clinical Uses

A common use of aluminum hydroxide is for its antacid properties to treat or manage gastrointestinal ulcers. Also, it is used as a phosphate binder. It is indicated in animals with hyperphosphatemia associated with chronic renal failure, often in combination with phosphorus restricted diets. Because of the decreased availability of products containing aluminum, other drugs are used to decrease hyperphosphatemia in patients, such as calcium carbonate and calcium citrate.

Precautionary Information

Adverse Reactions and Side Effects

They are generally safe. However, there has been some concern expressed that these drugs may increase the systemic levels of aluminum, which may lead to some forms of aluminum toxicoses. The evidence for this as a clinical problem in veterinary medicine is lacking.

Contraindications and Precautions

Aluminum decreases oral absorption of some drugs (e.g., fluoroquinolones). If fluoroquinolone antimicrobials are used concurrently, separation of oral doses should be considered.

Drug Interactions

Aluminum will bind and chelate some drugs and prevent the gastrointestinal absorption. Drugs bound to aluminum include tetracyclines and quinolone antibiotics.

Instructions for Use

Antacid doses are designed to neutralize stomach acid, but duration of acid suppression is short. Although aluminum hydroxide is often used to prevent hyperphosphatemia, this drug may not be available in some pharmacies. A substitute for this indication is calcium citrate or calcium carbonate.

Patient Monitoring and Laboratory Tests

Phosphate plasma levels should be monitored to determine success of therapy.

Formulations

Aluminum hydroxide gel is available in 64 mg/mL oral suspension and 600 mg tablet. Aluminum carbonate gel is available in capsules (equivalent to 500 mg aluminum hydroxide). Note: Products containing aluminum may no longer be available from many sources.

Stability and Storage

Store in tightly sealed container, protected from light, and at room temperature.

Small Animal Dosage

Dogs

- Aluminum hydroxide gel: 10-30 mg/kg q8h PO (with meals).
- Aluminum carbonate gel: 10-30 mg/kg q8h PO (with meals).

Cats

- Aluminum hydroxide gel: 10-30 mg/kg q8h PO (with meals).
- Aluminum carbonate gel: 10-30 mg/kg q8h PO (with meals).

Large Animal Dosage

Horses

- Antacid: 60 mg/kg q8h PO.

Regulatory Information

No regulatory information is available. For extralabel use withdrawal interval estimates, contact FARAD at 1-888-USFARAD (1-888-873-2723) or send e-mail to FARAD@ncsu.edu.

Amantadine

ah-man'tah-deen

Trade and Other Names: Symmetrel and generic brands

Functional Classification: Antiviral

Pharmacology and Mechanism of Action

Amantadine is an antiviral drug. The action against viruses is not entirely known. For treating other conditions in people (Parkinson's disease) its effects are attributed to an increase in dopamine in the CNS. However it also is an N-methyl-D-aspartate (NMDA) receptor antagonist. As an NMDA antagonist, it will decrease tolerance to other analgesic drugs (e.g., opiates), but probably does not possess many analgesic properties when used alone. Pharmacokinetics have not been investigated for veterinary uses, but they are completely absorbed in people and cross the blood-brain barrier.

Indications and Clinical Uses

Amantadine is an antiviral drug used to treat influenza infections in people. It also is used in people to treat Parkinson's disease and extrapyramidal reactions, especially those that are drug induced. It also has been used to manage muscular weakness in humans with multiple sclerosis. However, its use in veterinary medicine has primarily been for treating pain in dogs and cats. It is used for treating pain when other drugs have been ineffective or when it is desirable to use in combination with multiple drugs ("multimodal therapy").

Precautionary Information

Adverse Reactions and Side Effects

Toxicity has not been seen in dogs and cats until doses are exceeded by at least two times. Dizziness, confusion, and other CNS disturbances have been reported in people.

Contraindications and Precautions

Amantadine is embryotoxic and teratogenic at high doses in laboratory animals. Use with caution in pregnancy.

Drug Interactions

Do not use with other drugs that increase dopamine concentrations (e.g., selegiline). If used with other CNS stimulants, it may enhance the effects.

Instructions for Use

Use in animals is primarily for the analgesic effect. In people, antiviral dose is 1.5-3 mg/kg once or twice a day.

Patient Monitoring and Laboratory Tests

No specific monitoring is necessary.

Formulations

Amantadine is available in 100 mg capsules, 100 mg tablets, and 10 mg/mL syrup.

Stability and Storage

Store in tightly sealed container, protected from light, and at room temperature. Stability of compounded formulations has not been evaluated.

Small Animal Dosage

Dogs and Cats

3 mg/kg q24h PO for 21 days after surgery.

Large Animal Dosage

No dose has been reported for large animals.

Regulatory Information

No regulatory information is available. For extralabel use withdrawal interval estimates, contact FARAD at 1-888-USFARAD (1-888-873-2723) or send e-mail to FARAD@nesu.edu

Amikacin

am-ih-kay'sin

Trade and Other Names: Amiglyde-V (veterinary preparation), Amikin (human preparation), and generic brands

Functional Classification: Antibacterial

Pharmacology and Mechanism of Action

Aminoglycoside antibiotic. Action is to inhibit bacteria protein synthesis via binding to 30S ribosome. Amikacin is bactericidal with a broad spectrum of activity except against streptococci and anaerobic bacteria. Amikacin may be more active than gentamicin against many gram-negative bacteria, especially enteric species. Amikacin is not absorbed from oral administration.

Indications and Clinical Uses

Amikacin is indicated in bacterial infections, especially for treatment of serious infections caused by gram-negative bacteria. When resistance to gentamicin is anticipated, amikacin is often used in its place. In horses, amikacin also is used for local administration as an intrauterine lavage to treat metritis and other infections of the genital tract caused by gram-negative bacteria. In horses, amikacin also is used for regional limb perfusion.

Precautionary Information

Adverse Reactions and Side Effects

Nephrotoxicity is the most dose-limiting toxicity. Ensure that patients have adequate fluid and electrolyte balance during therapy. Ototoxicity and vestibulotoxicity also are possible.

Contraindications and Precautions

Do not use in animals with renal insufficiency or renal failure. Do not use in dehydrated animals.

Drug Interactions

Do not mix in vial or syringe with other antibiotics. Amikacin is incompatible with other drugs and compounds when mixed in same vial or syringe. This effect is particularly important when mixing with other antibiotics. When used with anesthetic agents, neuromuscular blockade is possible.

Instructions for Use

Once daily doses are designed to maximize peak-to-minimum inhibitory concentration (MIC) ratio. Consider therapeutic drug monitoring to decrease risk of renal toxicosis. Activity against some bacteria (e.g., *Pseudomonas*) enhanced when combined with a beta-lactam antibiotic. Nephrotoxicity is increased with persistently high trough concentrations.

Patient Monitoring and Laboratory Tests

Susceptibility testing: CLSI (NCCLS) MIC break point is less than or equal to 16 mcg/mL. Monitor BUN, serum creatinine, and urine for evidence of renal toxicity. Plasma or serum drug concentrations can be monitored to measure for problems with systemic clearance. When monitoring trough levels in patient doses daily, the trough levels should fall below the limit of detection. Alternatively measure half-life from samples taken at 1 hour and 2 to 4 hours post-dosing. Clearance should be above 1.0 mL/kg/min and half-life should be <2 hours.

Formulations

Amikacin is available in 50 or 250 mg/mL injection.

Stability and Storage

Store in tightly sealed container, protected from light, and at room temperature. Amikacin will be unstable if mixed with other drugs.

Small Animal Dosage

Dogs

- 15-30 mg/kg q24h IV, IM, or SQ.

Cats

- 10-14 mg/kg q24h IV, IM, or SQ.

Large Animal Dosage

Horses

- Adult: 4.4-6.6 mg/kg q12h IM or IV or 10 mg/kg q24h IV or IM.
- Foal: 20-25 mg/kg q24h IV or IM or 6.6 mg/kg q8h IV or IM.
- Intrauterine use: Administer 2 grams (8 mL) diluted in 200 mL sterile saline solution in uterus once per day for 3 days.
- Regional limb perfusion: doses have ranged from 125 mg to 500 mg per limb, diluted in 60 mL saline.

Cattle

- Adult: 10 mg/kg q24h IM, IV, or SQ.
- Calf (<2 weeks of age): 20 mg/kg q24h IV or IM.

Regulatory Information

Withdrawal times have not been established for extralabel use in animals used for food. Long duration of drug in tissues (renal) is expected after administration. Amikacin, like other aminoglycoside antibiotics, should not be administered to animals that produce food because of a risk of residue problems.

Aminopentamide

ah-mee-noe-pent'ah-mide

Trade and Other Names: Centrine

Functional Classification: Anticholinergic

Pharmacology and Mechanism of Action

Antidiarrheal drug. Anticholinergic (blocks acetylcholine at parasympathetic synapse).

Indications and Clinical Uses

Aminopentamide has been used to decrease GI motility and decrease GI secretions in animals. It also has been used to treat diarrhea, but long-term use for this purpose is not recommended.

Precautionary Information

Adverse Reactions and Side Effects

Use cautiously in animals with GI stasis or when anticholinergic drugs are contraindicated (e.g., glaucoma). Aminopentamide will cause significant ileus in animals and should not be administered for conditions in which intestinal stasis may worsen the underlying condition.

Contraindications and Precautions

Aminopentamide is contraindicated in patients with glaucoma.

Drug Interactions

Like other anticholinergic drugs, it will inhibit the action of drugs that act through cholinergic mechanisms (e.g., metoclopramide).

Instructions for Use

Dosing guidelines based on manufacturer's recommendation.

Patient Monitoring and Laboratory Tests

Monitor for problems caused by intestinal stasis because of anticholinergic effect.

Formulations

Aminopentamide is available in 0.2 mg tablets and 0.5 mg/mL injection.

Stability and Storage

Store in tightly sealed container, protected from light, and at room temperature. Stability of compounded formulations has not been evaluated.

Small Animal Dosage

Dogs

- 0.01-0.03 mg/kg q8-12h IM, SQ, or PO.

Cats

- 0.1 mg/cat q8-12h IM, SQ, or PO.

Large Animal Dosage

No dose has been reported for large animals.

Regulatory Information

No regulatory information is available. For extralabel use withdrawal interval estimates, contact FARAD at 1-888-USFARAD (1-888-873-2723) or send e-mail to FARAD@ncsu.edu.

Aminophylline

am-in-off'ih-lin

Trade and Other Names: Generic brands

Functional Classification: Bronchodilator

Pharmacology and Mechanism of Action

Bronchodilator. Aminophylline is a salt of theophylline, formulated to enhance oral absorption without gastric side effects. It is converted to theophylline after ingestion. Mechanism of action is same as theophylline. Theophylline's action is to inhibit phosphodiesterase (PDE) and increase cyclic AMP. Other antiinflammatory mechanisms also may play a role in its clinical effects.

Indications and Clinical Uses

Aminophylline is indicated for control of reversible airway constriction, to prevent bronchoconstriction, and as an adjunct with other respiratory disease treatment. The uses are similar to the indications for theophylline, because it is a salt form of theophylline. It is used for inflammatory airway disease in cats (feline asthma), dogs, and horses. In dogs, the uses include collapsing trachea, bronchitis, and other airway diseases. It has not been effective for respiratory diseases in cattle.

Precautionary Information

Adverse Reactions and Side Effects

Aminophylline causes excitement and possible cardiac side effects with high concentrations. Cardiac adverse effects include tachycardia and arrhythmias. GI side effects include nausea, vomiting, and diarrhea. CNS adverse effects include excitement, tremors, and seizures.

Contraindications and Precautions

Use cautiously in animals with cardiac arrhythmias. Use cautiously in animals prone to seizures. Horses may become excited from IV administration. However, side effects appear more common in people than small animals.

Drug Interactions

Use cautiously with other phosphodiesterase inhibitors such as sildenafil (Viagra) and pimobendan. Many drugs will inhibit the metabolism of theophylline and potentially increase concentrations (e.g., cimetidine, erythromycin, fluoroquinolones, and propranolol). Some drugs will decrease concentrations by increasing metabolism (e.g., phenobarbital and rifampin).

Instructions for Use

Therapeutic drug monitoring is recommended for chronic therapy. When dosing with salts or other formulations of theophylline, adjust dose for the amount of the parent drug.

Patient Monitoring and Laboratory Tests

Plasma concentrations of theophylline should be monitored in patients receiving therapy with aminophylline. Maintain plasma concentrations between 10 and 20 mcg/mL.

Formulations

Aminophylline is available in 100 and 200 mg tablets and 25 mg/mL injection. A dose of 25 mg/mL of anhydrous aminophylline is equivalent to 19.7 mg of anhydrous theophylline per mL.

Stability and Storage

Store in tightly sealed container, protected from light, and at room temperature. Compounded oral formulations have been stable for 60 days.

Small Animal Dosage

Dogs

- 10 mg/kg q8h PO, IM, or IV.

Cats

- 6.6 mg/kg q12h PO.

Large Animal Dosage

Horses

- Treatment of recurrent airway obstructions: 12 mg/kg initial dose, followed by 5 mg/kg q12h PO. Although aminophylline has been administered IV to horses, this administration has caused transient excitement and restlessness. Give intravenous administration slowly.

Cattle

- 10 mg/kg q8h IV or 23 mg/kg PO.

Regulatory Information

Cattle: No established withdrawal times.

No regulatory information is available. For extralabel use withdrawal interval estimates, contact FARAD at 1-888-USFARAD (1-888-873-2723) or send e-mail to FARAD@nesu.edu

RCI Classification: 3

Amiodarone

ah-mee-oe′dah-rone

Trade and Other Names: Cordarone

Functional Classification: Antiarrhythmic

Pharmacology and Mechanism of Action

Antiarrhythmic drug, Class-III. Antiarrhythmic effects are primarily caused by blocking the outward potassium channel in cardiac tissues. Amiodarone prolongs the action potential and the refractory period in all cardiac tissues. It also may have some alpha-adrenergic receptor, beta-adrenergic receptor, and calcium-channel blocking properties. Half-life is several days in duration, and in some animals the half-life may be as long as 100 days with chronic therapy. In horses the terminal half-life was 38-84 hours.

Indications and Clinical Uses

Amiodarone is used to treat refractory ventricular arrhythmias. It is reserved for treating life-threatening arrhythmias that have been refractory to other treatments. Use as last resort for recurrent hemodynamically unstable ventricular tachycardia.

In horses, IV amidarone has been used to treat atrial fibrillation.

Precautionary Information

Adverse Reactions and Side Effects

Most common effect in dogs is decreased appetite. Prolonged Q-T interval is a concern. Other adverse effects include bradycardia, CHF, hypotension, AV block, thyroid dysfunction (decreased T3 and T4), pulmonary fibrosis, and hepatotoxicity. Hepatopathy has been reported in dogs. In one study, doses up to 12.5 mg/kg IV produced no acute cardiovascular reactions, however, with acute intravenous administration, severe cardiac reactions are possible.

No adverse clinical signs were observed in horses after single administration IV, but for treating atrial fibrillation, mild signs of shifting weight and hind limb weakness were reported.

Contraindications and Precautions

Severe reactions including hepatopathy and cardiac arrhythmias have been seen in dogs. Use only when arrhythmia has been refractory to other treatments or when dogs are at risk for sudden death.

Drug Interactions

Use amiodarone with beta-blockers, calcium-channel blockers, and digoxin cautiously, because it may slow conduction. Do not mix intravenous solution with mixtures containing bicarbonate.

Instructions for Use

Typically, loading doses are administered, followed by maintenance dose. Oral dosing in dogs has used 10-15 mg/kg q12h for 1 week, then 5-7.5 mg/kg q12h for 2 weeks, followed by maintenance dose of 7.5 mg/kg q24h. If intravenous therapy is used, doses should be given slowly; initial infusion rate should not exceed 30 mg per minute.

Patient Monitoring and Laboratory Tests

Amiodarone can be toxic in dogs. It is highly recommended to monitor CBC for anemia and neutropenia and monitor hepatic indices with biochemical profile during treatment. Monitor ECG during treatment as prolonged Q-T interval may occur. Monitor thyroid function during treatment. Therapeutic range in plasma is 1-2.5 mcg/mL.

Formulations
Amiodarone is available in 200 mg tablets and 50 mg/mL injection.

Stability and Storage
Store in tightly sealed container, protected from light, and at room temperature.

Small Animal Dosage
Dogs
- 10-15 mg/kg q12h PO for 1 week, then 5-7.5 mg/kg q12h for 2 weeks, followed by maintenance dose of 7.5 mg/kg q24h.
- Boxer or Doberman: 400 mg q12h for 1 week, followed by 200 mg q12h.
- Refractory situations: 25 mg/kg q12h PO for 4 days, followed by 25 mg/kg q24h PO.

Cats

No dose has been reported for cats.

Large Animal Dosage
Horses

Treatment of atrial fibrillation: 5 mg/kg/hr for 1 hour, followed by 0.83 mg/kg/hr for 23 hours IV. Oral absorption was low and inconsistent and has not been recommended.

Regulatory Information
No regulatory information is available. For extralabel use withdrawal interval estimates, contact FARAD at 1-888-USFARAD (1-888-873-2723) or send e-mail to FARAD@ncsu.edu.

Amitraz
am'ih-traz

Trade and Other Names: Mitaban

Functional Classification: Antiparasitic

Pharmacology and Mechanism of Action
Antiparasitic drug for ectoparasites. Amitraz inhibits monoamine oxidase (MAO) in mites. Mammals are resistant to this inhibition. However, administration of amitraz can interact with other MAO inhibitors (MAOIs).

Indications and Clinical Uses
Amitraz is indicated for the topical treatment of mites, including Demodex. It is applied topically as a dip. It should not be administered systemically. The approved dose is effective in many animals; however, in more resistant cases of Demodex, higher doses have been applied. As the dose increases, the risk of adverse effects also increases.

Precautionary Information
Adverse Reactions and Side Effects

Amitraz causes sedation in dogs caused by the agonist activity on alpha$_2$-adrenergic receptors, which may be reversed by yohimbine or atipamezole. When high doses are used, other side effects reported include pruritus, polyuria/polyclipsia, bradycardia, hypothermia, hyperglycemia, and (rarely) seizures.

Contraindications and Precautions

Adverse effects are more common when high doses are administered.

Drug Interactions

Do not administer with MAOIs, such as selegiline (Deprenyl, Anipryl). Do not administer with other alpha$_2$-agonists.

Instructions for Use

Manufacturer's dose should be used initially. But, for refractory cases, this dose has been exceeded to produce increased efficacy.

Patient Monitoring and Laboratory Tests

Monitor by performing periodic skin scrapings and examining for presence of mites.

Formulations

Amitraz is available in 10.6 mL concentrated dip (19.9%).

Stability and Storage

Store in tightly sealed container, protected from light, and at room temperature. Stability of compounded formulations has not been evaluated.

Small Animal Dosage

Dogs

- 10.6 mL/7.5 L water (0.025% solution). Apply 3-6 topical treatments every 14 days. For refractory cases, this dose has been exceeded to improve efficacy. Doses that have been used include: 0.025%, 0.05%, and 0.1% concentration applied once or twice per week. For refractory cases, a dose of 0.125% has been used by applying to only one half of the dog's body one day, then to the other half of the body the following day. This alternating schedule has been repeated every day for 4 weeks and up to 5 months to achieve cures, but should be considered only in extreme cases.

Large Animal Dosage

No dose has been reported for large animals.

Regulatory Information

No regulatory information is available. For extralabel use withdrawal interval estimates, contact FARAD at 1-888-USFARAD (1-888-873-2723) or send e-mail to FARAD@ncsu.edu.

RCI Classification: 3

Amitriptyline Hydrochloride

am-ih-trip'tih-leen hye-droe-klor'ide

Trade and Other Names: Elavil and generic brands

Functional Classification: Behavior modification, Tricyclic antidepressant (TCA)

Pharmacology and Mechanism of Action

TCA drug. Amitriptyline, like other TCAs, acts via inhibition of uptake of serotonin and other transmitters at presynaptic nerve terminals. The action in cats for treating cystitis is unknown, but may be either through reducing anxiety or via anticholinergic effects.

Indications and Clinical Uses

Like other TCAs, amitriptyline is used in animals to treat variety of behavioral disorders (e.g., anxiety). However, there are few studies documenting efficacy in animals.

For treatment of some disorders, such as obsessive compulsive disorder (1 mg/kg q12h up to 2 mg/kg), it was not as effective in animals as clomipramine. For treatment of aggressive behavior in dogs (2 mg/kg q12h) there was no difference between amitriptyline and placebo.

Amitriptyline has been used in cats for chronic idiopathic cystitis. However, when used for short-term treatment of idiopathic cystitis (10 mg per cat, q24h) it was not effective. In another study, at 5 mg/cat per day for 7 days (0.55-1.2 mg/kg), there was no difference on recovery from hematuria and pollakiuria between amitryptiline and placebo, leading to a conclusion that short-term treatment is not helpful.

Precautionary Information

Adverse Reactions and Side Effects

Amitriptyline has a bitter taste and is difficult to administer orally. Multiple side effects are associated with TCAs, such as antimuscarinic effects (dry mouth and rapid heart rate) and antihistamine effects (sedation). High doses can produce life-threatening cardiotoxicity. In cats, reduced grooming, weight gain, and sedation are possible.

Contraindications and Precautions

Use cautiously in patients with heart disease.

Drug Interactions

Do not use with other behavior modification drugs, such as serotonin reuptake inhibitors. Do not use with monoamine oxidase inhibitors (MAOIs).

Instructions for Use

Doses are primarily based on empiricism. There are no controlled efficacy trials available for animals. There is evidence for success treating idiopathic cystitis in cats. (*J Am Vet Med Assoc,* 213: 1282-1286, 1998). Amitriptyline was not effective for treatment of aggressive behavior in dogs, compared to behavior modification alone (*J Am Anim Hosp Assoc,* 37: 325-330, 2001). Amitriptyline applied transdermally is not systemically absorbed in cats.

Patient Monitoring and Laboratory Tests

Monitor patient's cardiovascular status during therapy, such as heart rate and rhythm. Like other TCAs, amitriptyline may decrease total T4 and free-T4 concentrations in dogs.

Formulations

Amitriptyline is available in 10, 25, 50, 75, 100, and 150 mg tablets and 10 mg/mL injection.

Stability and Storage

Store in tightly sealed container, protected from light, and at room temperature. Stability of compounded formulations has not been evaluated.

Small Animal Dosage

Dogs

- 1-2 mg/kg q12-24h PO.

Cats

- 2-4 mg per cat/day PO (0.5-1.0 mg/kg PO per day). The dose for cats may be divided into 12 hour intervals.
- Idiopathic cystitis: 2 mg/kg/day (or a range of 2.5-7.5 mg/cat/day).

Large Animal Dosage

No dose has been reported for large animals.

Regulatory Information

No regulatory information is available. For extralabel use withdrawal interval estimates, contact FARAD at 1-888-USFARAD (1-888-873-2723) or send e-mail to FARAD@ncsu.edu.

RCI Classification: 2

Amlodipine Besylate

am-loe'dih-peen bess'ih-late

Trade and Other Names: Norvasc

Functional Classification: Calcium-channel blocker

Pharmacology and Mechanism of Action

Calcium-channel blocking drug. Amlodipine is a calcium-channel blocker of the dihydropyridine class. It decreases calcium influx in cardiac and vascular smooth muscle. Its greatest effect is as a vasodilator. Hypertension in cats has been defined as systolic blood pressure >190 mm Hg and diastolic pressure >120 mm Hg.

Indications and Clinical Uses

In cats and dogs it is used to treat systemic hypertension (high blood pressure). Amlodipine is considered the drug of choice by many clinicians for treating hypertension in cats. By comparison, angiotensin-converting enzyme (ACE) inhibitors are less effective in cats. Amlodipine may improve survival in cats with hypertensive kidney disease.

Precautionary Information

Adverse Reactions and Side Effects

Adverse effects can include hypotension and bradycardia.

Contraindications and Precautions

Use cautiously in animals with poor cardiac reserve and prone to hypotension. Do not use in dehydrated animals.

Drug Interactions

Use cautiously with other vasodilators. Drug interactions are possible from concurrent use with phenylpropanolamine, theophylline, and beta-agonists.

Instructions for Use

In cats, efficacy has been established at 0.625 mg/cat once daily. If cats are large size (>4.5 kg) or refractory, increase dose to 1.25 mg/cat q24h PO *(J Vet Intern Med*, 12: 157-162, 1998).

Patient Monitoring and Laboratory Tests

Monitor patient's blood pressure if possible. For example, cats with high pressures of systolic 160-190 mm Hg and diastolic 100-120 mm Hg should be considered at risk of clinical effects from hypertension, and cats with pressures above these values are at risk.

Formulations
Amlodipine is available in 2.5, 5, and 10 mg tablets. (Tablets are difficult to split for small animals.)

Stability and Storage
Amlodipine is an unstable drug and potency and stability are not assured if the original formulation is disrupted or compounded. Store in tightly sealed container and protect from light.

Small Animal Dosage
Dogs
- 2.5 mg/dog or 0.1 mg/kg q24h PO.

Cats
- 0.625 mg/cat initially q24h PO and increase if needed to 1.25 mg/cat. Average recommended dose for most cats is 0.18 mg/kg; once daily for hypertension.

Large Animal Dosage
No dose has been reported for large animals.

Regulatory Information
No regulatory information is available. For extralabel use withdrawal interval estimates, contact FARAD at 1-888-USFARAD (1-888-873-2723) or send e-mail to FARAD@ncsu.edu.

RCI Classification: 4

Ammonium Chloride
ah-moe'nee-um klor'ide

Trade and Other Names: Generic brands

Functional Classification: Acidifier

Pharmacology and Mechanism of Action
Urine acidifier. After oral administration, ammonium chloride induces acidic urine.

Indications and Clinical Uses
Compounds containing ammonium are administered to patients to acidify the urine, primarily to manage cystic calculi or chronic UTIs.

Precautionary Information
Adverse Reactions and Side Effects

Ammonium chloride has a bitter taste when added to food. It may cause acidemia in some patients if administered at high doses.

Contraindications and Precautions

Do not use in patients with systemic acidemia. Use cautiously in patients with renal disease. It may be unpalatable when added to some animals' food.

Drug Interactions

No drug interactions are reported in animals.

Instructions for Use

Doses are designed to maximize urine acidifying effect.

Patient Monitoring and Laboratory Tests

Monitor patient's acid/base status.

Formulations

Ammonium is available as crystals.

Stability and Storage

Store in tightly sealed container, protected from light, and at room temperature. Stability of compounded formulations has not been evaluated.

Small Animal Dosage

Dogs

- 100 mg/kg q12h PO.

Cats

- 800 mg/cat (approximately 1/3 to 1/4 tsp) mixed with food daily.

Large Animal Dosage

Horses

- Acidifier: 100-250 mg/kg q24h PO.

Regulatory Information

No regulatory information is available. It is not expected to pose a residue risk and no withdrawal is recommended for food animals.

Amoxicillin

ah-moks-ih-sill'in

Trade and Other Names: Amoxicillin: Amoxi-Tabs, Amoxi-Drops, Amoxi-Inject, Robamox-V, Biomox, and other brands. Amoxil, Trimox, Wymox, Polymox (human preparation), and Amoxicillin trihydrate

Functional Classification: Antibacterial

Pharmacology and Mechanism of Action

Beta-lactam antibiotic. Amoxicillin inhibits bacterial cell wall synthesis. Amoxicillin generally has broad spectrum activity that includes both gram-negative and gram-positive activity; however resistance is common, especially among enteric gram-negative bacilli and staphylococci. Amoxicillin oral absorption in small animals is higher than ampicillin (two times higher in some animals). Amoxicillin oral absorption in adult horses is <10% and is not recommended.

Indications and Clinical Uses

Amoxicillin is used for a variety of infections in all species, including urinary tract infection, soft tissue infections, and pneumonia. It is generally more effective for infections caused by gram-positive bacteria. Because of a short half-life, frequent administration is needed for treating gram-negative infections. In addition, break point for susceptibility is higher for gram-negative versus gram-positive organisms. Oral absorption in horses is <10%, and it is not suitable for treatment of adult horses. However, oral absorption in foals is 36%-43%. Oral absorption in small animals is 50%-60%

Precautionary Information

Adverse Reactions and Side Effects

Amoxicillin is usually well tolerated. Allergic reactions are possible. Diarrhea and vomiting are common with oral doses. Oral administration to horses or cattle can cause diarrhea and/or enteritis.

Contraindications and Precautions

Use cautiously in animals allergic to penicillin-like drugs.

Drug Interactions

Do not mix with other drugs in compounded formulations.

Instructions for Use

Dose recommendations vary depending on the susceptibility of bacteria and location of infection. Generally, more frequent or higher doses needed for gram-negative infections.

Patient Monitoring and Laboratory Tests

Susceptibility testing: CLSI (NCCLS) break point for sensitive organisms is less than or equal to 8 mcg/mL for gram-negative bacilli and enterococci and less than or equal to 0.25 mcg/mL for staphylococci and streptococci. For canine urinary tract pathogens, use a break point of less than or equal to 8 mcg/mL. For cattle pathogens use a break point of less than or equal to 0.25 mcg/mL. For equine respiratory pathogens (streptococci) use a break point of less than or equal to 0.25 mcg/mL.

Formulations

Amoxicillin is available in 50, 100, 150, 200, and 400 mg tablets and 250 and 500 mg capsules (human preparations).

Amoxicillin trihydrate is available in 50, 100, 200, and 400 mg tablets, 50 mg/mL amoxicillin trihydrate oral suspension, and 250 mg/mL amoxicillin trihydrate for injection.

Stability and Storage

Store in tightly sealed container at room temperature. Oral liquid suspensions are stable for 14 days. Other formulations should be protected from moisture. Optimum stability is at pH 5.8-6.5. Above this pH, hydrolysis occurs.

Small Animal Dosage

Dogs and Cats

- 6.6-20 mg/kg q8-12h PO.

Large Animal Dosage

Calves

- Nonruminating: 10-22 mg/kg q8-12h PO.

Cattle and horses

- 6.6-22 mg/kg q8-12h PO (suspension). Note: Oral doses in large animals are not well absorbed (except in foals), and amoxicillin is generally not administered via this route.

Regulatory Information

Withdrawal time: (Cattle only) 25 days meat, 96 hours milk. Amoxicillin intramammary infusion: withdrawal time 12 days meat, 60 hours milk.

Amoxicillin + Clavulanate Potassium

ah-mox-ih-sill'in + klav-yoo-lan'ate poe-tah'see-um

Trade and Other Names: Clavamox (veterinary preparation) and Augmentin (human preparation)

Functional Classification: Antibacterial

Pharmacology and Mechanism of Action

Beta-lactam antibiotic + beta-lactamase inhibitor (clavulanate potassium). Amoxicillin activity and spectrum is as described for amoxicillin. Clavulanate has no antibacterial effects alone, but it is a strong inhibitor of the beta-lactamase enzyme that causes resistance among gram-positive and gram-negative bacteria. By adding clavulanate to amoxicillin, the spectrum is extended.

Indications and Clinical Uses

Amoxicillin + clavulanate is a broad-spectrum antibacterial drug used for skin infections, UTIs, wound infections, and respiratory infections. It is indicated for treatment of bacterial infections (gram-positive and gram-negative) that may otherwise be resistant to amoxicillin owing to bacterial beta-lactamase production.

Precautionary Information

Adverse Reactions and Side Effects

It is usually well tolerated. Allergic reactions are possible. Diarrhea is common with oral doses and has also caused vomiting in some animals.

Contraindications and Precautions

Use cautiously in animals allergic to penicillin-like drugs.

Drug Interactions

No drug interactions are reported in animals.

Instructions for Use

Dose recommendations vary depending on the susceptibility of bacteria and location of infection. Generally, more frequent or higher doses needed for gram-negative infections. It has been the experience of many veterinarians that an oral dose of double the manufacturer's recommendation should be used for treating skin infections (i.e., 25 mg/kg q12h). Oral human dose forms are sometimes substituted for veterinary drugs. Note that veterinary dose formulations contain amoxicillin and clavulanate in a 4:1 ratio. Human dose forms (Augmentin) contain these drugs in ratios of 2:1 to as high as 7:1.

Patient Monitoring and Laboratory Tests

Susceptibility testing: CLSI (NCCLS) break point for sensitive organisms is less than or equal to 4/2 mcg/mL for staphylococci and less than or equal to 16/8 mcg/mL for other organisms. (The "/" distinguishes the amoxicillin from the clavulanate concentrations.)

Formulations

Amoxicillin + clavulanate is available in veterinary dose form: 62.5, 125, 250, and 375 mg tablets and 62.5 mg/mL suspension in a ratio of amoxicillin/clavulanate of 4:1. Amoxicillin + clavulanate is available in human dose form: 250/125, 500/125, and 875/125 mg tablets. Amoxicillin + clavulanate is available in 125/31.25,

200/28.5, 250/62.5, 400/57 mg chewable tablets and oral suspension 125/31.25, 200/28.5, 250/62.5, and 400/57 mg per 5 mL.

Stability and Storage

Store in tightly sealed container, protected from light, and below 24°C. Avoid exposure to humidity or moisture. Reconstituted oral products are stable for 10 days.

Small Animal Dosage

Dogs

- 12.5-25 mg/kg q12h PO. (Dose is based on combined ingredients: amoxicillin and clavulanate.)

Cats

- 62.5 mg/cat q12h PO. Consider administering these doses every 8 hours for gram-negative infections.

Large Animal Dosage

Amoxicillin + clavulanate is only available in an oral formulation. Because these components are not absorbed orally in large animal species, this drug is not recommended.

Regulatory Information

No regulatory information is available. However, it is anticipated that withdrawal times will be similar as for amoxicillin.

Amphotericin B

am-foe-tare′ih-sin

Trade and Other Names: Fungizone (traditional formulation), and liposomal forms of Amphotec, ABCD, ABELCET, and AmBisome

Functional Classification: Antifungal

Pharmacology and Mechanism of Action

Antifungal drug. Amphotericin B is a fungicidal for systemic fungi that damages fungal membranes. There is a conventional formulation of amphotericin B that has been used most often in veterinary medicine. However, new formulations of amphotericin B have been used in people. Although they have not gained widespread use in veterinary medicine because of their high cost, they have distinct advantages; the most important over the traditional formulations is that they are less toxic. These new formulations are lipid-based complexes or cholesteryl complexes of amphotericin B that allow higher doses to be administered with less nephrotoxicity. Amphotericin B lipid complex (ABELCET) is a suspension of amphotericin B complexed with two phospholipids at a concentration of 100 mg/20 mL. This formulation was shown to be safe and effective for treating blastomycosis in dogs at a cumulative dose of 8-12 mg/kg, by administering 1 mg/kg every other day. Amphotericin B cholesteryl sulfate complex (Amphotec, ABCD) is a colloidal dispersion of amphotericin B. It has been effective in studies in which it was administered at doses higher than the traditional amphotericin B formulation. The liposomal complex of amphotericin B (AmBisome) is a unilaminar liposomal formulation. When reconstituted, it produces small vesicles of encapsulated amphotericin B. This formulation has been used safely and effectively in some dogs for blastomycosis.

Indications and Clinical Uses

Amphotericin B is indicated in patients with a variety of systemic mycoses. It is used to treat blastomycosis, coccidioidomycosis, and histoplasmosis. It also has been used to treat leishmaniasis in dogs. It may be administered for treatment of aspergillosis, but this is not a common use in veterinary medicine.

Precautionary Information

Adverse Reactions and Side Effects

Amphotericin B produces a dose-related nephrotoxicity. Also produces fever, phlebitis, and tremors. Renal toxicity is dose-dependent and cumulative. It is more likely when cumulative doses approach, or exceed, 6 mg/kg.

Contraindications and Precautions

Do not use in patients who have renal disease or where renal clearance is not known. Do not use in dehydrated animals or animals with electrolyte imbalances.

Drug Interactions

When preparing intravenous solution, do not mix Amphotericin B with electrolyte solutions; instead use 5% dextrose in water.

Instructions for Use

Administer IV via slow infusion diluted in 5% dextrose in water and monitor renal function closely. Administer sodium chloride fluid loading IV to patients before therapy to decrease risk of renal toxicosis. One study administered amphotericin B subcutaneously *(Aust Vet J,* 73: 124, 1996). Dilute Abelcet in 5% dextrose to 1 mg/mL has been infused over 1-2 hours. Amphotericin B has been mixed as a solution of amphotericin B (one vial of 50 mg) with 40 mL of sterile water and 10 mL of Intralipid 10% (soybean oil). Doses of this mixture of 1-2 mg/kg have been used for treating systemic leishmaniasis. For other indications, this mixture has been administered at a dose of 1-2.5 mg/kg two times per week for 8-10 treatments. This liposomal complex of amphotericin B was used in a study for treatment of canine *Leishmania infantum* at a dose of 3-3.3 mg/kg. Although there was rapid clinical improvement, dogs remained positive for leishmaniasis.

Patient Monitoring and Laboratory Tests

Monitor renal function closely during treatment. After treatment many animals will have an elevated creatinine and blood urea nitrogen. Persistent azotemia may be a cause for discontinuation of treatment and replacement with another antifungal.

Formulations

Amphotericin B is available in 50 mg injectable vial.

Stability and Storage

Stable if stored in original vial. Amphotericin B for intravenous infusion will react with light and should be protected from light during infusions. Store reconstituted solutions in refrigeration. However, unrefrigerated solutions may be stable for up to 1 week. Optimum pH is 6-7.

Small Animal Dosage

Dogs

Conventional formulation: 0.5 mg/kg q48 h IV (slow infusion), to a cumulative dose of 4-8 mg/kg. The liposomal formulations are administered at a dose of 3 mg/kg/day at a rate of over 60-120 minutes for up to 9-12 treatments. This dose may be administered three times per week, rather than every day. A goal for the total cumulative dose for liposomal formulations is 24-27 mg/kg.

Cats

- Cats have received similar regimens as those used for dogs. However, many clinicians will start with lower doses in cats. For liposomal formulations in cats, use 1 mg/kg IV three times per week for up to 12 treatments.

Large Animal Dosage

Horses

- 0.3 mg/kg IV on day 1, followed by 3 consecutive days and repeat after 24-48 hour drug-free interval. Expense has prevented common usage in horses.

Regulatory Information

No regulatory information is available. For extralabel use withdrawal interval estimates, contact FARAD at 1-888-USFARAD (1-888-873-2723) or send e-mail to FARAD@ncsu.edu.

Ampicillin

am-pih-sill'in

Trade and Other Names: Omnipen, Principen, Totacillin, and Polycillin (human preparations), Omnipen-N, Polycillin-N, and Totacillin-N (injectable preparations), and Amp-Equine and Ampicillin trihydrate (Polyflex) (veterinary preparations)

Functional Classification: Antibacterial

Pharmacology and Mechanism of Action

Beta-lactam antibiotic. Ampicillin inhibits bacterial cell wall synthesis. Ampicillin generally has a broad spectrum of activity that includes both gram-positive and gram-negative bacteria. However, resistance is common, especially among enteric gram-negative bacilli and staphylococci.

Indications and Clinical Uses

Ampicillin is indicated in patients with bacterial infections, such as wound infections, UTIs, and pneumonia. It is generally more effective in gram-positive infections.

Elimination half-life is approximately 1 hour in dogs and cats; therefore frequent administration is needed for treating gram-negative infections. In addition, break point for susceptibility is higher for gram-negative versus gram-positive organisms. Half-life in horses is 0.6-1.5 hours after intravenous administration, but longer after intramuscular injection. Oral absorption is less than 50% in dogs and cats, and less than 4% in horses.

Precautionary Information

Adverse Reactions and Side Effects

Adverse effects of penicillin drug are most commonly caused by drug allergy. This can range from acute anaphylaxis when administered IV to other signs of allergic reaction when other routes are used. Diarrhea is possible, when administered orally, especially with high doses.

Contraindications and Precautions

Use cautiously in animals allergic to penicillin-like drugs. Ampicillin contains 3 mEq of sodium per gram.

Drug Interactions
Do not mix in vials with other drugs.

Instructions for Use

Dose requirements vary depending on susceptibility of bacteria. It is absorbed approximately 50% less compared to amoxicillin when administered orally. When selecting doses, more frequent or higher doses are needed for gram-negative infections. Note that higher concentrations (and higher doses) are required for gram-negative bacilli and enterococci. Doses as high as 300 mg/kg/day (in divided doses) have been used to treat enterococci.

Patient Monitoring and Laboratory Tests

Susceptibility testing: CLSI (NCCLS) break point for sensitive organisms is less than or equal to 8 mcg/mL for gram-negative bacilli and enterococci and less than or equal to 0.25 mcg/mL for staphylococci and streptococci. For canine urinary tract pathogens use a break point of less than or equal to 8 mcg/mL. For cattle pathogens use a break point of less than or equal to 0.25 mcg/mL. For equine respiratory pathogens (streptococci) use a break point of less than or equal to 0.25 mcg/mL.

Formulations

Ampicillin is available in 250 and 500 mg capsules and 125, 250, and 500 mg vials of ampicillin sodium. Amp-Equine is available in 1 and 3 g vials for injection. (However, this formulation has been discontinued by some suppliers.) Ampicillin trihydrate (Polyflex) is available in 10 and 25 g vials for injection.

Stability and Storage

Store in tightly sealed container at room temperature. After reconstitution of ampicillin sodium, 90% potency is retained for 2-8 hours at room temperature or up to 72 hours refrigerated. Oral suspensions are stable for 14 days if refrigerated. Ampicillin trihydrate for injection is stable for 12 months refrigerated and 3 months at room temperature. Other formulations should be protected from moisture. Optimum stability is at pH 5.8. Above this pH, hydrolysis occurs.

Small Animal Dosage

Ampicillin Sodium

Dogs and Cats

- 10-20 mg/kg q6-8h IV, IM, or SQ or 20-40 mg/kg q8h PO. Doses as high as 100 mg/kg have been used for some resistant infections such as those caused by enterococci.

Ampicillin Trihydrate

Dogs

- 10-50 mg/kg q12-24h IM or SQ.

Cats

- 10-20 mg/kg q12-24h IM or SQ.

Large Animal Dosage

Ampicillin Sodium

Horses

- 6.6 mg/kg up to 10-20 mg/kg q6-8h IM or IV.
- Refractory infections: up to 25-40 mg/kg q6-8h.

Cattle and Calves

Ampicillin Trihydrate

- 4.4 to 11 mg/kg q24h IM.

Regulatory Information

Cattle withdrawal time: 6 days meat; 48 hours milk (at 6 mg/kg).
Pig withdrawal time: In Canada, 6 days.

Ampicillin + Sulbactam

am-pih-sill'in + sul-bak'tam

Trade and Other Names: Unasyn

Functional Classification: Antibacterial

Pharmacology and Mechanism of Action

Ampicillin plus a beta-lactamase inhibitor (sulbactam). Sulbactam has similar activity as clavulanate (ingredient in amoxicillin-clavulanate), but it is not as active as clavulanate against some gram-negative enzymes (e.g., TEM). Because of the addition of sulbactam, it has broader spectrum of activity than ampicillin alone.

Indications and Clinical Uses

This combination is indicated for general bacterial infections. It has been used for acute infections such as pneumonia, sepsis, and prophylaxis in neutropenic patients. Because of the addition of sulbactam, it has a broader spectrum than ampicillin alone. Therefore, it is used for treating infections for which ampicillin resistance may be expected. It is given by injection in situations where ampicillin-clavulanate (e.g., Clavamox and Augmentin) may be used as an alternative.

Precautionary Information

Adverse Reactions and Side Effects

Adverse effects of penicillin drug are most commonly caused by drug allergy. This can range from acute anaphylaxis when administered to other signs of allergic reaction when other routes are used.

Contraindications and Precautions

Use cautiously in animals allergic to penicillin-like drugs.

Drug Interactions

Do not mix in vials with other drugs.

Instructions for Use

Dosage recommendations vary depending on the susceptibility of bacteria and location of infection. Generally, more frequent or higher doses are needed for gram-negative infections.

Patient Monitoring and Laboratory Tests

Susceptibility testing: CLSI (NCCLS) break point for sensitive organisms is less than or equal to 8/4 mcg/mL for staphylococci and gram-negative bacilli. (The "/" distinguishes the ampicillin from the sulbactam concentrations.)

Formulations

Ampicillin + sulbactam is available in a 2:1 combination for injection and 1.5 and 3 g vials.

Stability and Storage

Store in tightly sealed container at room temperature. Optimum stability is at pH 5.8. Above this pH, hydrolysis occurs. Stability after reconstitution is same as listed for ampicillin sodium.

Small Animal Dosage

Cats and Dogs

- Doses are similar to dose used for ampicillin (when dosed according to ampicillin component) 10-20 mg/kg q8h IV or IM.

Large Animal Dosage

Horses and Ruminants

Doses used should be same as for ampicillin component.

6.6 mg/kg up to to 10-20 mg/kg q6-8hr, IM or IV.

Regulatory Information

Withdrawal time exists for ampicillin, but not sulbactam. Because sulbactam has a similar half-life and presents little risk for toxicity, the withdrawal times listed for ampicillin are suggested.

Cattle withdrawal time: 6 days meat; 48 hours milk (at 6 mg/kg).

Pig withdrawal time: In Canada, 6 days.

Amprolium

am-proe'lee-um

Trade and Other Names: Amprol and Corid

Functional Classification: Antiparasitic

Pharmacology and Mechanism of Action

Antiprotozoal drug. This drug is a vitamin B_1 or thiamine structural analogue. Amprolium antagonizes thiamine in parasites and is used for treatment of coccidiosis.

Indications and Clinical Uses

Amprolium is used to control and treat coccidiosis in calves, sheep, goats, puppies, and birds. It is administered orally, often mixed with food.

Precautionary Information

Adverse Reactions and Side Effects

Toxicity is observed only at high doses. CNS signs are caused by thiamine deficiency, which may be reversed by adding thiamine to the diet.

Contraindications and Precautions

Do not administer to debilitated animals.

Drug Interactions

No drug interactions are reported in animals.

Instructions for Use

Usually administered as feed additive to livestock. For dogs, 30 mL of 9.6% amprolium has been added to 3.8 liters of drinking water for control of coccidiosis.

Patient Monitoring and Laboratory Tests

No specific monitoring is necessary.

Formulations

Amprolium is available in 9.6% (9.6 grams/100 mL) oral solution and a soluble powder in a 22.6 g packet.

Stability and Storage

Store in tightly sealed container, protected from light, and at room temperature. Stability of compounded formulations has not been evaluated.

Small Animal Dosage

Dogs and Cats

- Treatment of coccidiosis: Add 1.25 grams of 20% amprolium powder to daily feed or 30 mL of 9.6% amprolium solution to 3.8 L of drinking water for 7 days.

Large Animal Dosage

Calves

- Prevention of coccidiosis: 5 mg/kg q24h for 21 days.
- Treatment of coccidiosis: 10 mg/kg q24h for 5 days PO.

Regulatory Information

Withdrawal time for cattle (meat): 24 hours before slaughter.

A withdrawal period has not been established for this product in preruminating calves. Do not use in calves to be processed for veal.

Apomorphine Hydrochloride

ah-poe-mor′feen hye-droe-klor′-ide

Trade and Other Names: Generic brands

Functional Classification: Emetic

Pharmacology and Mechanism of Action

Emetic drug. Apomorphine is a potent lipophilic dopamine agonist. It easily crosses the blood-brain barrier after administration. It promptly causes vomiting in dogs.

Indications and Clinical Uses

Apomorphine is indicated for inducing emesis in animals that have ingested toxic agents. After subcutaneous administration, the onset of effect is 10 minutes or shorter. It is promptly effective for inducing vomiting in dogs but less so in cats. Xylazine often is a more reliable emetic in cats.

Precautionary Information

Adverse Reactions and Side Effects

Apomorphine produces emesis before serious adverse effects can occur.

Contraindications and Precautions

Use cautiously in cats that may be sensitive to opiates.

Drug Interactions

No drug interactions are reported in animals. However, some drugs will diminish the emetic action of apomorphine (e.g., acepromazine, atropine, and other antiemetics).

Instructions for Use

Consult local poison center or pharmacist for availability. Apomorphine should be available in most emergency practices for prompt treatment of poisoning.

Patient Monitoring and Laboratory Tests

No specific monitoring is necessary. If used to induce vomiting from a toxicant, monitor for signs of toxicity, because vomiting is able to eliminate less than half of the ingested toxicant.

Formulations

Apomorphine is available in 6 mg tablets as well as other forms made by compounding pharmacists. It is also available as 10 mg/mL in 3 mL preloaded syringes.

Stability and Storage

Solutions decompose when exposed to air and light. A green color indicates decomposition. Store in tightly sealed container at room temperature.

Small Animal Dosage

Dogs and Cats

- 0.02-0.04 mg/kg IV or IM.
- 0.1 mg/kg SQ.
- Dissolve 6 mg tablet in 1-2 mL of saline and instill directly in conjunctiva of eye. After animal vomits, the conjunctiva may be rinsed of residual drug with an eye wash solution.

Large Animal Dosage

No dose has been reported for large animals.

Regulatory Information

Do not administer to animals intended for food.
RCI Classification: 1

Aprepitant

ap-reh'pih-tant

Trade and Other Names: Emend

Functional Classification: Antiemetic

Pharmacology and Mechanism of Action

Aprepitant is an antiemetic. Aprepitant is the first substance P/neurokinin 1 (NK1) receptor antagonist. It is used primarily with drugs known to be highly emetic, such as cisplatin. This drug is effective because chemotherapy drugs release substance P, which is highly emetic. It also blocks stimulation that induces vomiting from other stimuli, but use in small animals has been somewhat limited because of the high expense. In dogs, aprepitant is extensively metabolized after administration.

Indications and Clinical Uses

Aprepitant is an effective anti-emetic for people, particularly when used to treat vomiting associated with cancer chemotherapy. It may be used with corticosteroids (dexamethasone) and serotonin (5HT3) antagonists. However, despite its broad effects to decrease vomiting in people, there are no reports of effective use in dogs or cats.

Precautionary Information

Adverse Reactions and Side Effects

There are no reported adverse effects in animals.

Contraindications and Precautions

No contraindications reported for animals.

Drug Interactions

Drug interactions are possible, because aprepitant is both an inducer and inhibitor of Cytochrome P450 enzymes. Potent inhibitors of Cytochrome P450 (see Appendix) can potentially affect aprepitant clearance.

Instructions for Use

Use in patients refractory to other antiemetic drugs. It may be combined with other antiemetics.

Patient Monitoring and Laboratory Tests

No specific monitoring is necessary.

Formulations

Aprepitant is available in 80 and 125 mg capsules.

Stability and Storage

Store in tightly sealed container, protected from light, and at room temperature. The Granules must remain intact for oral absorption.

Small Animal Dosage

Dogs and Cats

- 1 mg/kg q24h PO. Increase to 2 mg/kg q24h PO in refractory patients.

Large Animal Dosage

No dose has been reported for large animals.

Regulatory Information

No regulatory information is available. For extralabel use withdrawal interval estimates, contact FARAD at 1-888-USFARAD (1-888-873-2723) or send e-mail to FARAD@ncsu.edu.

Ascorbic Acid

ah-skor′bik ass′id

Trade and Other Names: Vitamin C and sodium ascorbate. There are many brand names available.

Functional Classification: Vitamin

Pharmacology and Mechanism of Action

Ascorbic acid is vitamin C. It is an important co-factor in a variety of metabolic functions.

Indications and Clinical Uses

Ascorbic acid is used to treat vitamin C deficiency and occasionally used as urine acidifier. There is insufficient data to show that ascorbic acid is effective for preventing cancer, treating infectious diseases, or preventing cardiovascular disease.

Precautionary Information

Adverse Reactions and Side Effects

Adverse effects have not been reported in animals. High doses may increase the risk of oxalate urolith formation.

Contraindications and Precautions

No contraindications reported for animals.

Drug Interactions

No drug interactions are reported in animals.

Instructions for Use

Not necessary to supplement in animals with well-balanced diets. However, high doses have been used as adjunctive treatment for some diseases. Evidence shows that at doses of 15 and 50 mg/kg in dogs, the increase in absorption was nonlinear. Therefore, higher doses may not produce proportionately higher blood levels as lower doses. Comparison of crystalline ascorbic acid and the vitamin C product, Ester-C, produced similar levels of vitamin C in the plasma.

Patient Monitoring and Laboratory Tests

No specific monitoring is necessary.

Formulations

Ascorbic acid is available in tablets of various sizes and injection. Typically the injection form is 250 mg sodium ascorbate/mL. The formulation of Ester-C appears to be absorbed similarly to the crystalline form of vitamin C.

Stability and Storage

Light sensitive. It will oxidize, darken, and decompose when exposed to air and light. The injectable solution in a vial may build up pressure with storage, which may be decreased by storing in refrigerator. Otherwise, store at room temperature protected from light.

Small Animal Dosage

Dogs and Cats

- Dietary supplementation: 100-500 mg/animal/day PO.
- Urinary acidification: 100 mg/animal q8h PO. Injectable dose ranges from 1-10 mL (250 mg per mL), depending on size of animal, IM or IV.

Guinea Pigs

- 16 mg/kg twice weekly IM.

Large Animal Dosage

Large Animals

- Vitamin C supplementation: 1-10 mL IM or IV. Repeat daily as needed.
- 1-2 grams q24h PO.

Regulatory Information

Withdrawal time: 0 days for all animals intended for food.

Asparaginase (L-Asparaginase)

ah-spar'a-jin-aze

Trade and Other Names: Elspar and Asparaginase

Functional Classification: Anticancer agent

Pharmacology and Mechanism of Action

Anticancer agent. Asparaginase is an enzyme that converts asparagine to aspartic acid and ammonia. This action depletes cancer cells of asparagine. Normal cells are capable of synthesizing their own asparagine, but certain malignant cells, especially malignant lymphocytes, are not. Therefore, asparagine is an essential amino acid for cancer cell survival, especially lymphocytes. Because cancer cells in patients treated with L-asparaginase are depleted of asparagine, this treatment interferes with DNA, RNA, and protein synthesis in cancer cells. It is specific for the G1 phase of the cell cycle. In dogs it has a long half-life of 1-2 days.

Indications and Clinical Uses

Asparaginase has been used in some lymphoma protocols and has been effective for melanoma and mast cell tumors. It has been administered IV, IM, or SQ, but results of one study favored intramuscular administration over subcutaneous administration. In cats, it has been used in combination protocols at a dose of 400 units per kg SQ on Day One of protocols combined with doxorubicin.

Precautionary Information

Adverse Reactions and Side Effects

The most common adverse effect is hypersensitivity (allergic) reactions. A patient can develop hypersensitivity to asparaginase with repeated administrations. Hepatotoxic reactions, pancreatitis, and hyperglycemia also have been reported.

Contraindications and Precautions

Do not use in animals with known sensitivity (allergic reaction).

Drug Interactions

No drug interactions are reported in animals. It has been used with other anticancer drugs.

Instructions for Use

Asparaginase is usually used in combination with other drugs in cancer chemotherapy protocols (e.g., doxorubicin). Studies have shown that intramuscular dosing is more effective than subcutaneous dosing in dogs with lymphoma (*J Am Vet Med Assoc*, 214: 353-356, 1999). Asparaginase has minimal effect on the bone marrow; therefore it can be used in combination with other myelosuppressive drugs in a protocol. Tumor cells can develop resistance by developing a capacity to synthesize asparagine.

Patient Monitoring and Laboratory Tests

Monitoring CBC during chemotherapy is recommended.

Formulations

Asparaginase is available in 10,000 units per vial for injection. (Distribution of this drug to veterinarians by the manufacturer has been temporarily discontinued or may be limited.)

Stability and Storage

Stable if stored in manufacturer's original vial.

Small Animal Dosage

Dogs

- 400 units/kg IM weekly
- 10,000 units/m^2 weekly for 3 weeks.

Cats

- 400 units/kg weekly SQ.

Large Animal Dosage

No dose has been reported for large animals.

Regulatory Information

Withdrawal times are not established for animals that produce food. This drug should not be used in animals that produce food, because it is an anticancer agent.

Aspirin

as'pir-in

Trade and Other Names: ASA, acetylsalicylic acid, Bufferin, Ascriptin, and many generic brands

Functional Classification: Nonsteroidal antiinflammatory

Pharmacology and Mechanism of Action

Nonsteroidal antiinflammatory drug (NSAID). Antiinflammatory action is caused by inhibition of prostaglandins. Aspirin binds irreversibly to the cyclo-oxygenase (COX) enzyme in tissues to inhibit synthesis of prostaglandins. At low doses it may be more specific for COX-1 than COX-2. Antiinflammatory effects are attributed to inhibition of COX, but other antiinflammatory mechanisms—attributed to salicylates—may also contribute to the antiinflammatory action, such as inhibition of NF kappa-B. Pharmacokinetics are variable in animals, ranging from 1 hour in horses, 6 hours in pigs, 8.5 hours in dogs to 38 hours in cats.

Indications and Clinical Uses

Aspirin is used as an analgesic, antiinflammatory, and antiplatelet drug. At low doses, aspirin is a more specific COX-1 selective inhibitor and antiplatelet drug than other NSAIDs. Therefore, low doses have been used in animals specifically to prevent thromboemboli formation. Although aspirin has been available for many years, it is not registered by FDA for use in any species. There are no published controlled studies to document efficacy. Use of aspirin in animals is primarily based on empiricism, rather than published data.

Precautionary Information

Adverse Reactions and Side Effects

Narrow therapeutic index. High doses frequently cause vomiting. Other GI effects can include ulceration and bleeding. Inhibits platelets and increases risk of bleeding.

Contraindications and Precautions

Cats are susceptible to salicylate intoxication because of slow clearance. Use cautiously in patients with coagulopathies because of platelet inhibition (e.g., von Willebrand's disease). Do not administer to animals prone to GI ulcers.

Drug Interactions

Do not administer with other ulcerogenic drugs such as corticosteroids. Do not administer with other drugs that may cause coagulopathy and increase risk of bleeding problems.

Instructions for Use

Analgesic and antiinflammatory doses have primarily been derived from empiricism. Antiplatelet doses are lower because of prolonged effect of aspirin on platelets. Aspirin is only available in oral form. Because it is a weak acid, it is ordinarily absorbed best in the acidic environment of the upper GI tract; however considerable absorption takes place in the intestine as well. In dogs, enteric-coated aspirin reduces gastric irritation, but absorption from this form is erratic and often incomplete. Buffering does not affect absorption but may protect the stomach from injury when high doses are administered. Buffering has less of a beneficial effect when low doses are administered and is not expected to protect the stomach from the more serious effects of GI ulceration, bleeding, and perforations.

Patient Monitoring and Laboratory Tests

Monitor patients for signs of gastric upset, gastroduodenal ulcers, and bleeding. Effective plasma concentrations: 20-50 mcg/mL for pain and fever and 150-200 mcg/mL for inflammation. Aspirin decreased thyroid concentrations in dogs after 2-4 weeks of dosing.

Formulations

Aspirin is available in 81 mg (Children's aspirin) and 325 mg tablets.

For large animals, aspirin is available in 240 grain bolus (14,400 mg) and 3.9, 15.6, and 31.2 g tablets.

Stability and Storage

Store in tightly sealed container at room temperature. After exposure to moisture, it will decompose to acetic acid and salicylic acid. If stored at pH 7 at 25°C, it has a half-life of 52 hours.

Small Animal Dosage

Mild analgesia.

Dogs

- 10 mg/kg q12h PO.

Cats

- 10 mg/kg q48h PO.

Antiinflammatory

Dogs

- 20-25 mg/kg q12h PO.

Cats

- 10-20 mg/kg q48h PO.

Antiplatelet

Dogs

- 5-10 mg/kg q24-48h PO.

Cats

- 80 mg/cat q48h PO.

Large Animal Dosage

Ruminants

- 100 mg/kg q12h PO. Doses as high as 333 mg/kg have been administered to cattle.

Swine

- 10 mg/kg q6-8h PO.

Horses

- 25-50 mg/kg q12h PO (up to 100 mg/kg PO).

Regulatory Information

Extralabel use: Although considered extralabel in animals intended for food, consider a withdrawal time of at least 1 day for meat and 24 hours for milk.

RCI Classification: 4

Astemizole

ast-em′eh-zole

Trade and Other Names: Hismanal

Functional Classification: Antihistamine

Pharmacology and Mechanism of Action

Discontinued July 1999. Antihistamine (H_1-blocking) drug. This is one of the second-generation antihistamines, which usually do not have the side effect of sedation as compared to other antihistamines. It is primarily used for allergic disease; in people used as adjunct for asthma.

Indications and Clinical Uses

This drug has been discontinued from human medicine. There have been no indications identified for veterinary use.

Precautionary Information

Adverse Reactions and Side Effects

Adverse effects have not been reported in small animals, but cardiotoxicity is a potential problem with high doses.

Contraindications and Precautions

Do not administer to animals with risk of cardiac problems.

Drug Interactions

Do not administer with other drugs known to cause inhibition of drug metabolizing enzymes (cytochrome P-450 enzymes; see Appendix) and do not administer with drugs that may inhibit p-glycoprotein.

Instructions for Use

Astemizole is available as tablets and oral suspension. Doses are primarily derived from extrapolation from human dose. Efficacy trials and dose titration have not been performed, but initial studies failed to demonstrate efficacy for pruritus in dogs.

Patient Monitoring and Laboratory Tests

No specific monitoring is necessary.

Formulations

Astemizole is available in 10 mg tablets. Discontinued in 1999 but may still be available through compounding pharmacies.

Stability and Storage

Store in tightly sealed container, protected from light, and at room temperature. Stability of compounded formulations has not been evaluated.

Small Animal Dosage

Dogs

- 0.2 mg/kg q24h PO, up to 1.0 mg/kg q12h PO.

Large Animal Dosage

No dose has been reported for large animals.

Regulatory Information

Do not administer to animals intended for food.

Atenolol

(ah-ten'oe-lole)

Trade and Other Names: Tenormin

Functional Classification: Beta-antagonist

Pharmacology and Mechanism of Action

Beta-adrenergic blocker. Relatively selective for beta$_1$-receptor. Atenolol is a water-soluble beta-blocker and relies on the kidney for clearance. (By comparison, drugs such as propranolol and metoprolol are more lipophilic and rely on liver for clearance.) In dogs, oral absorption is 90%.

Indications and Clinical Uses

Atenolol is used primarily as an antiarrhythmic or for other cardiovascular conditions in which it is needed to slow sinus rate. In cats, this drug is commonly used to treat heart disease from cardiomyopathy or hyperthyroidism.

Precautionary Information

Adverse Reactions and Side Effects

Bradycardia and heart block are possible. Atenolol may produce bronchospasm in sensitive patients.

Contraindications and Precautions

Use cautiously in animals with airway disease, myocardial failure, and cardiac conduction disturbances. Use cautiously in animals with low cardiac reserve.

Drug Interactions

Use cautiously with other drugs that may decrease cardiac contraction or heart rate.

Instructions for Use

Dosing precautions are similar to other beta-blocking drugs. Atenolol is reported to be less affected by changes in hepatic metabolism than other beta-blockers. Dose in animals based on published reports. *(Am J Vet Res*, 57: 1050-1053, 1996). In cats, amlodipine (calcium-channel blocker) is sometimes used with atenolol to control hypertension.

Patient Monitoring and Laboratory Tests

Monitor patient's heart rate and rhythm.

Formulations

Atenolol is available in 25, 50, and 100 mg tablets, 25 mg/mL oral suspension, and 0.5 mg/mL ampules for injection. (Tablets can be split for small animals.)

Stability and Storage

Store in tightly sealed container at room temperature. Oral suspensions are stable for 14 days. Atenolol is water soluble. Compounded oral formulations have been stable for 60 days.

Small Animal Dosage

Dogs

- 6.25-12.5 mg/dog q12h (or 0.25-1.0 mg/kg q12-24h) PO. Doses in dogs have been increased to 3 mg/kg q12-24h PO for some conditions.

Cats

- 6.25-12.5 mg/cat q12h (approx. 3 mg/kg) PO.
- Although an injectable form is available, its use has not been reported in small animals. A dose of 0.1 mg/kg IV, slowly, over 5 minutes is suggested.

Large Animal Dosage

No dose has been reported for large animals.

Regulatory Information

No regulatory information is available. For extralabel use withdrawal interval estimates, contact FARAD at 1-888-USFARAD (1-888-873-2723) or send e-mail to FARAD@ncsu.edu.

RCI Classification: 3

Atipamezole Hydrochloride

ah-tih-pam'eh-zole hye-droe-klor'ide

Trade and Other Names: Antisedan

Functional Classification: Anesthetic

Pharmacology and Mechanism of Action

Alpha$_2$-antagonist. It binds to alpha$_2$-receptors to antagonize other drugs that act as agonists, such as medetomidine and xylazine. Other alpha$_2$-antagonists include yohimbine.

Indications and Clinical Uses

Atipamezole is used to reverse $alpha_2$-agonists such as medetomidine (Domitor) and xylazine. Arousal from sedation should occur within 5-10 minutes of injection.

Precautionary Information

Adverse Reactions and Side Effects

Atipamezole can cause some initial excitement in some animals shortly after reversal. There may be a transient decrease in blood pressure after injection.

Contraindications and Precautions

No contraindications reported for animals.

Drug Interactions

Atipamezole is an $alpha_2$-antagonist. As such, it will antagonize other drugs that bind to the alpha-receptor and prevent their action. Such drugs that may be antagonized include xylazine, medetomidine, detomidine, and some $alpha_1$-agonists.

Instructions for Use

When used to reverse medetomidine, inject same volume as volume of medetomidine that was administered.

Patient Monitoring and Laboratory Tests

Monitor cardiovascular status when using $alpha_2$-agonists. Providing oxygen during recovery may help recovery from $alpha_2$-agonists.

Formulations

Atipamezole is available in a 5 mg/mL injection.

Stability and Storage

Store in tightly sealed container, protected from light, and at room temperature. Stability of compounded formulations has not been evaluated.

Small Animal Dosage

- Inject same volume as used for medetomidine. The range of doses is 0.32 mg/kg for small animals (8.5 pounds), 0.23 mg/kg for medium-sized animals (24 pounds), and up to 0.14 mg/kg for large-sized animals (100 pounds).

Large Animal Dosage

- 30-60 mcg/kg (0.03-0.06 mg/kg) IV. However, in horses, doses of 60-80 mcg/kg IV were more effective than smaller doses.

Regulatory Information

Do not administer to animals intended for food.

Atracurium Besylate

ah-trah-kyoor′ee-um bess′ih-late

Trade and Other Names: Tracurium

Functional Classification: Muscle relaxant

Pharmacology and Mechanism of Action

Neuromuscular blocking agent (nondepolarizing). Atracurium competes with acetylcholine at neuromuscular end plate. Used primarily during anesthesia or other conditions in which it is necessary to inhibit muscle contractions. It has a shorter duration of action than pancuronium.

Indications and Clinical Uses

Atracurium is a paralytic agent used to paralyze skeletal muscle during surgery and mechanical ventilation.

Precautionary Information

Adverse Reactions and Side Effects

Atracurium produces respiratory depression and paralysis. Neuromuscular-blocking drugs have no effect on analgesia.

Contraindications and Precautions

Do not use in patients unless it is possible to provide ventilation support. The action of neuromuscular-blocking agents may be antagonized by acetylcholinesterase inhibitors.

Drug Interactions

No drug interactions are reported in animals.

Instructions for Use

Administer only in situations in which careful control of respiration is possible. Doses may need to be individualized for optimum effect. Do not mix with alkalinizing solutions or Lactated Ringer's solution.

Patient Monitoring and Laboratory Tests

Monitoring of respiratory and cardiovascular indices is critical during use. If possible monitor oxygenation of patient during use.

Formulations

Atracurium is available in 10 mg/mL injection.

Stability and Storage

Store in tightly sealed container, protected from light, and at room temperature. Stability of compounded formulations has not been evaluated.

Small Animal Dosage

Dogs and Cats

- 0.2 mg/kg IV initially, then 0.15 mg/kg q30min.
- Constant Rate Infusion (CRI): 0.3-0.5 mg/kg IV loading dose, followed by 4-9 mcg/kg/min.

Large Animal Dosage

Horses

- 0.05-0.07 mg/kg IV.

Regulatory Information

Do not administer to animals intended for food.

A

Atropine Sulfate

ah'troe-peen sul'fate

Trade and Other Names: Generic brands

Functional Classification: Anticholinergic

Pharmacology and Mechanism of Action

Anticholinergic agent (blocks acetylcholine effect at muscarinic receptors), parasympatholytic.

As an antimuscarinic agent, it blocks cholinergic stimulation and causes decrease in GI motility and secretions, decrease in respiratory secretions, increased heart rate (anti-vagal effect), and mydriasis.

Indications and Clinical Uses

Atropine is used primarily as adjunct to anesthesia or other procedures to increase heart rate and decrease respiratory and GI secretions. Atropine is also used as antidote for organophosphate intoxication.

Precautionary Information

Adverse Reactions and Side Effects

Side effects include xerostomia, ileus, constipation, tachycardia, and urine retention.

Contraindications and Precautions

Do not use in patients with glaucoma, intestinal ileus, gastroparesis, or tachycardia. Use high doses (e.g., 0.04 mg/kg) cautiously, because it will increase oxygen demand.

Drug Interactions

Do not mix with alkaline solutions. Atropine will antagonize the effects of any cholinergic drugs administered (e.g., metoclopramide).

Instructions for Use

Atropine is used ordinarily as adjunct with anesthesia or other procedures. Do not mix with alkaline solutions. Compared to lower doses, in dogs 0.06 mg/kg was more effective than 0.02 mg/kg *(Am J Vet Res,* 60: 1000-1003, 1999). Atropine may be used during cardiac resuscitation, however high doses may cause sustained tachycardia and increased myocardial oxygen demand. During cardiac resuscitation, doses of 0.04 mg/kg IV may be used, but for treating sinus bradycardia, consider lower doses of 0.01 mg/kg.

Patient Monitoring and Laboratory Tests

Monitor patient's heart rate and rhythm.

Formulations

Atropine is available in 400, 500, and 540 mcg/mL injection and 15 mg/mL injection.

Stability and Storage

Store in tightly sealed container at room temperature.

Small Animal Dosage

Dogs

- 0.02-0.04 mg/kg q6-8h IV, IM, or SQ (complete dose range has been from 0.01 mg/kg to 0.06 mg/kg, depending on the indication).
- Sinus bradycardia: 0.005-0.01 mg/kg, but for use during CPR use up to 0.04 mg/kg.

Cats

- 0.02-0.04 mg/kg q6-8h IV, IM, or SQ.

Dogs

- For organophosphate and carbamate toxicosis: 0.2-0.5 mg/kg as needed, IV, IM, or SQ.

Cats

- For organophosphate and carbamate toxicosis: 0.2-0.5 mg/kg as needed.

Large Animal Dosage

Note that in large animals, atropine has a potent effect on inhibiting GI motility.

Horses

- Antidote to organophosphates or cholinesterase inhibitors: 0.02-0.04 mg/kg IM or SQ, and repeat as needed.
- Recurrent Airway Obstruction (RAO, formerly called COPD): 0.022 mg/kg, once, IV.

Pigs

- Antidote to organophosphates or cholinesterase inhibitors: 0.1 mg/kg IV followed by 0.4 mg/kg IM.
- Anesthesia adjunct: 0.02 mg/kg IV or 0.04 mg/kg IM.

Ruminants

- Antidote to organophosphates or cholinesterase inhibitors: 0.1 mg/kg IV, followed by 0.4 mg/kg IM and repeat as needed.
- Anesthesia adjunct to prevent salivation: 0.02 mg/kg IV or 0.04 mg/kg IM.

Regulatory Information

Withdrawal time: None established in U.S. The manufacturer of large animal products lists 0 days milk and meat; however, it is listed as 14 days for meat and 3 days for milk in the U.K.

RCI Classification: 3

Auranofin

or-an′oe-fin

Trade and Other Names: Ridaura

Functional Classification: Immunosuppressive

Pharmacology and Mechanism of Action

Used for gold therapy (chrysotherapy). Mechanism of action is unknown but may relate to immunosuppressive effect on lymphocytes.

Indications and Clinical Uses

Auranofin (gold therapy) is used primarily for immune-mediated diseases. It has been used with some success to control immune-mediated skin diseases, such as pemphigus and immune-mediated arthritis. It has been suggested that this product (oral) is not as effective as injectable products such as aurothioglucose.

Precautionary Information

Adverse Reactions and Side Effects

Adverse effects include dermatitis, nephrotoxicity, and blood dyscrasias.

Contraindications and Precautions

Do not use in animals with suppressed bone marrow, or animals already receiving bone-marrow suppressing agents.

Drug Interactions

No drug interactions are reported in animals.

Instructions for Use

Use of this drug has not been evaluated in veterinary medicine. No controlled clinical trials are available to determine efficacy in animals.

Patient Monitoring and Laboratory Tests

Monitor patient's CBC periodically, because gold salts have caused blood dyscrasias.

Formulations

Auranofin is available in 3 mg capsules.

Stability and Storage

Store in tightly sealed container, protected from light, and at room temperature. Stability of compounded formulations has not been evaluated.

Small Animal Dosage

Dogs and Cats

- 0.1-0.2 mg/kg q12h PO.

Large Animal Dosage

No dose has been reported for large animals.

Regulatory Information

Do not administer to animals intended for food.

Aurothioglucose

or-oh-thye-oe-gloo'kose

Trade and Other Names: Solganal

Functional Classification: Immunosuppressive

Pharmacology and Mechanism of Action

Used for gold therapy (chrysotherapy). Mechanism of action is unknown but may relate to immunosuppressive effect on lymphocytes.

Indications and Clinical Uses

Aurothioglucose (gold therapy) is used primarily for immune-mediated diseases. It has been used with some success to control immune-mediated skin diseases, such as pemphigus and immune-mediated arthritis. However, because of a lack of controlled trials to demonstrate efficacy and adverse effects that have been observed, the use in veterinary medicine has been uncommon.

Precautionary Information

Adverse Reactions and Side Effects

Adverse effects include dermatitis, nephrotoxicity, and blood dyscrasias.

Contraindications and Precautions

Do not use in animals with suppressed bone marrow, or animals already receiving bone-marrow suppressing agents.

Drug Interactions

No drug interactions are reported in animals.

Instructions for Use

Use of this drug has not been evaluated in veterinary medicine. No controlled clinical trials are available to determine efficacy in animals. This drug is often used in combination with other immunosuppressive drugs such as corticosteroids.

Patient Monitoring and Laboratory Tests

Monitor patient's CBC periodically, because gold salts have caused blood dyscrasias.

Formulations

Aurothioglucose is available in 50 mg/mL injection.

Stability and Storage

Store in tightly sealed container, protected from light, and at room temperature. Stability of compounded formulations has not been evaluated.

Small Animal Dosage

Dogs

- Dogs <10 kg: 1 mg IM first week, 2 mg IM second week, 1 mg/kg/week maintenance. Dogs >10 kg: 5 mg IM first week, 10 mg IM second week, 1 mg/kg/week maintenance.

Cats

- 0.5-1 mg/cat every 7 days IM.

Large Animal Dosage

Horses

- 1 mg/kg per week IM.

Regulatory Information

Do not administer to animals intended for food.

Azathioprine

ay-za-thye′oe-preen

Trade and Other Names: Imuran

Functional Classification: Immunosuppressive

Pharmacology and Mechanism of Action

Thiopurine immunosuppressive drug. Acts to inhibit T-cell lymphocyte function. This drug is metabolized to 6-mercaptopurine (6-MP), which may account for immunosuppressive effects, because 6-MP interferes with purine metabolism in lymphocytes. Other cells can use salvage pathways for purine synthesis but not lymphocytes.

Indications and Clinical Uses

Azathioprine is used to treat various immune-mediated diseases in animals, including immune-mediated hemolytic anemia, pemphigus, and inflammatory bowel disease. It is often administered with prednisone or prednisolone. Onset of action may be delayed for 4-6 weeks in some patients.

Precautionary Information

Adverse Reactions and Side Effects

Bone marrow suppression is the most serious concern. Additional adverse effects in dogs include diarrhea, increased risk of secondary infections, and vomiting. There has been some association with development of pancreatitis when administered with corticosteroids. Sensitivity to the adverse effects may be because of a deficiency of metabolizing enzymes, thiopurine methyltransferase (TPMT) in certain individuals. In people, about 10% are deficient. Some dogs and many cats are also deficient. However in dogs, toxicity has not yet been correlated with status of TPMT levels. Cats are particularly susceptible to toxicity and are reported to have low levels of TPMT. Individuals who have higher sensitivity to the suppressing effects of bone marrow should have dose reduced.

Hepatotoxicosis after administration of azathioprine also has been reported. One of the metabolites produced may be hepatotoxic.

Contraindications and Precautions

Exercise extreme caution and careful monitoring when administering to cats.

Drug Interactions

Administer with caution with other drugs that may suppress the bone marrow (e.g., cyclophosphamide and anticancer drugs). There is some evidence that concurrent use with corticosteroids may increase risk of pancreatitis. Do not administer with allopurinol because antagonism of xanthine oxidase may interfere with metabolism.

Instructions for Use

Azathioprine is usually used in combination with other immunosuppressive drugs (e.g., corticosteroids) to treat immune-mediated disease. Some evidence suggests that it is contraindicated in cats because of bone marrow effects. Doses of 2.2 mg/kg to cats have produced toxicity, but most experts recommend starting cats with doses of 0.3 mg/kg/day.

Patient Monitoring and Laboratory Tests

Monitor patient's CBC periodically because some animals are sensitive to the effects of azathioprine and its metabolite 6-MP. After 2 weeks of treatment, a CBC is essential. Because of risk of hepatotoxicity, monitor hepatic enzymes and bilirubin regularly.

Formulations

Azathioprine is available in 50 mg tablets and 10 mg/mL for injection.

Stability and Storage

Store in tightly sealed container at room temperature. Compounded oral suspensions are stable for 60 days.

Small Animal Dosage

Dogs

- 2 mg/kg q24h PO initially then 0.5-1 mg/kg q48h. In dogs, doses as high as 1.5 mg/kg q48h PO have been used with prednisolone.

Cats (use cautiously)

- 1 mg/kg q48h PO has been used. However, in cats one should start with 0.3 mg/kg q24h PO and adjust dose after careful monitoring.

Large Animal Dosage

No dose has been reported for large animals.

Regulatory Information

Do not administer to animals intended for food.

Azithromycin

ay-zith-roe-my'sin

Trade and Other Names: Zithromax

Functional Classification: Antibacterial

Pharmacology and Mechanism of Action

Azalide antibiotic. Similar mechanism of action as macrolides (e.g., erythromycin), which is to inhibit bacteria protein synthesis via inhibition of ribosome. Spectrum of activity is primarily gram-positive cocci, including streptococci and staphylococci. It also has good activity against Mycoplasma, Chlamydia, and some intracellular pathogens. The activity against Toxoplasma has been questionable. Pharmacokinetic data shows extremely long plasma, tissue, and leukocyte half-lives in dogs, cats, and horses. Plasma half-life is 18 hours in horses, 35 hours in cats, and 30 hours in dogs. Volume of distribution also is large with values exceeding 10 L/kg.

Indications and Clinical Uses

Azithromycin is indicated for treatment of bacterial infections. Antimicrobial spectrum is primarily gram-positive. Azithromycin is not recommended for serious gram-negative infections. It may be used to treat infections caused by mycoplasma and other atypical organisms. Azithromycin has been used to treat intracellular organisms because of its ability to concentrate in leukocytes. One of the uses has been to treat infections caused by *Rhodococcus equi* in foals. However, in one comparative study, clarithromycin plus rifampin had better clinical success in foals than azithromycin plus rifampin. Azithromycin has been used in cats to treat upper respiratory infections. There are no controlled clinical trials to document success for this use, however, this treatment has been common among veterinarians. Azithromycin administered to cats with infections caused by *Chlamydophilia felis* (formerly *Chlamydia psittaci*), at 10-15 mg/kg once daily for 3 days and thereafter two times per week, was not effective for eliminating the organism, although clinical signs improved. When azithromycin was administered to dogs with pyoderma at a dose of either 10 mg/kg on day 1, followed by 5 mg/kg on days 2 through 5, or alternatively, 5 mg/kg given 2 days per week for 3 weeks, the response was equal statistically to cephalexin at 22 mg/kg twice daily. In dairy calves, azithromycin administration significantly suppressed shedding of *Cryptosporidium parvum* and improved clinical signs.

Precautionary Information

Adverse Reactions and Side Effects

Adverse effects to azithromycin have not been reported in publications. However, vomiting is likely with high doses. Diarrhea may occur in some patients. Diarrhea has been reported in horses that were administered recommended doses.

Contraindications and Precautions

Use cautiously in animals with history of vomiting. Administration to adult horses has been associated with diarrhea. Use with caution in adult horses.

Drug Interactions

Drug interactions have not been reported in animals. This class of drugs has the potential to inhibit some cytochrome P450 enzymes that are involved in drug metabolism, but azithromycin is less likely than erythromycin or clarithromycin to interfere with Cytochrome P450 enzymes.

Instructions for Use

Azithromycin may be better tolerated than erythromycin. Primary difference from other antibiotics is the high intracellular concentrations achieved. Azithromycin has been commonly used for upper respiratory tract infections in cats. Although, there are uncontrolled studies that demonstrate efficacy, well-controlled studies have not been performed.

Patient Monitoring and Laboratory Tests

Susceptibility testing: CLSI (NCCLS) break point for sensitive organisms is less than or equal to 2 mcg/mL.

Formulations

Azithromycin is available in 250 mg capsules, 250 and 600 mg tablets, 100 and 200 mg/5 mL oral suspension, and 500 mg vials for injection. 1 g packets are available for mixing with water.

Stability and Storage

Stable if maintained in manufacturer's original formulation. Stability has not been reported for compounded formulations.

Small Animal Dosage

Dogs

- 10 mg/kg once every 5 days or 3.3 mg/kg, once daily for 3 days, PO.

Cats

- 5-10 mg/kg, once daily for 7 days, PO, followed by administration q48h.

Large Animal Dosage

Horses

- For *R. equi:* 10 mg/kg q24h, PO, initially, then q48h after a response is seen.

Calves

- For cryptosporidiosis: 33 mg/kg once daily for 7 days, PO.

Regulatory Information

Withdrawal times have not been established for animals producing food.

Benazepril Hydrochloride

ben-ay'zeh-pril hye-droe-klor'ide

Trade and Other Names: Lotensin (human preparation) and Fortekor (veterinary preparation)

Functional Classification: Vasodilator, Angiotensin-converting enzyme (ACE) inhibitor

Pharmacology and Mechanism of Action

ACE inhibitor. Inhibits conversion of angiotensin I to angiotensin II. Angiotensin II is a potent vasoconstrictor and will also stimulate sympathetic stimulation, stimulate renal hypertension, and stimulate synthesis of aldosterone. The ability of aldosterone to cause sodium and water retention contribute to congestion. Benazepril, like other ACE inhibitors, will cause vasodilation and decrease aldosterone-induced congestion; but ACE inhibitors also contribute to vasodilation by increasing concentrations of some vasodilating kinins and prostaglandins. Unlike enalapril, it has a dual mode of elimination through the kidneys and liver. Duration of ACE-inhibiting action is 16-23 hours, despite a short plasma half-life, because of high affinity binding to ACE.

Indications and Clinical Uses

Benazepril, like other ACE inhibitors, is used to treat hypertension and CHF. It is primarily used in dogs, but may benefit some cats in heart failure or with systemic hypertension. Some cats with hypertension may not respond, and ACE inhibitors are not considered a primary treatment for hypertension in cats. In cats, benazepril may be effective in slowing the progression of renal failure. In studies in which it has been used in cats with renal insufficiency, it was associated with a small reduction in systemic hypertension and an increase in glomerular filtration rate (GFR). In clinical cases, it had limited antihypertensive effects in cats with naturally occurring renal disease.

Precautionary Information

Adverse Reactions and Side Effects

Benazepril may cause azotemia in some patients; carefully monitor patients receiving high doses of diuretics.

Contraindications and Precautions

Discontinue ACE inhibitors in pregnant animals. ACE inhibitors cross the placenta and have caused fetal malformations and death of the fetus.

Drug Interactions

Use cautiously with other hypotensive drugs and diuretics. Nonsteroidal antiinflammatory drugs (NSAIDs) may decrease vasodilating effects.

Instructions for Use

Dose is based on approved use in dogs in Europe and Canada. Monitor renal function and electrolytes 3-7 days after initiating therapy and periodically thereafter. In studies in cats there was no benefit to doses higher than 0.5-1.0 mg/kg/day.

Patient Monitoring and Laboratory Tests

Monitor patients carefully to avoid hypotension. With all ACE inhibitors, monitor electrolytes and renal function 3-7 days after initiating therapy and periodically thereafter.

Formulations
Benazepril is available in 5, 10, 20, and 40 mg tablets.

Stability and Storage
Store in tightly sealed container, protected from light, and at room temperature. Stability of compounded formulations has not been evaluated.

Small Animal Dosage
Dogs
- 0.25 to 0.5 mg/kg q24h PO.

Cats
- Systemic hypertension and renal disease: 0.5-1.0 mg/kg/day PO. Alternative dose for cats is 2.5 mg per cat per day, for cats up to 5 kg body weight, PO.

Large Animal Dosage
No dose has been reported for large animals.

Regulatory Information
Do not administer to animals intended for food.
RCI Classification: 3

Betamethasone
bay-tah-meth'ah-sone

Trade and Other Names: Celestone, betamethasone acetate, and betamethasone benzoate

Functional Classification: Corticosteroid

Pharmacology and Mechanism of Action
Potent, long-acting corticosteroid. Antiinflammatory and immunosuppressive effects are approximately thirty times more than cortisol. Antiinflammatory effects are complex but primarily via inhibition of inflammatory cells and suppression of expression of inflammatory mediators.

Indications and Clinical Uses
Betamethasone is used for treatment of inflammatory and immune-mediated disease. It is used for similar indications as prednisolone and dexamethasone.

Precautionary Information
Adverse Reactions and Side Effects
Side effects from corticosteroids are many and include polyphagia, polydipsia/polyuria, and hypothalamic-pituitary-adrenal (HPA) axis suppression. Adverse effects include GI ulceration, hepatopathy, diabetes, hyperlipidemia, decreased thyroid hormone, decreased protein synthesis, delayed wound healing, and immunosuppression. Secondary infections can occur as a result of immunosuppression and include demodex, toxoplasmosis, fungal infections, and UTIs. In horses, additional adverse effects include risk of laminitis.

Contraindications and Precautions
Use cautiously in patients prone to ulcers or infection, or in animals in which wound healing is necessary. Use cautiously in diabetic animals, animals with renal failure, or pregnant animals.

Drug Interactions
No drug interactions are reported in animals.

Instructions for Use
Betamethasone is used for similar indications as dexamethasone because of similar potency and duration of effect. Topical forms of betamethasone also are available.

Patient Monitoring and Laboratory Tests
Monitor CBC and plasma cortisol.

Formulations
Betamethasone is available in 600 mcg (0.6 mg) tablets and 3 mg/mL sodium phosphate injection.

Stability and Storage
Store in tightly sealed container, protected from light, and at room temperature. Stability of compounded formulations has not been evaluated.

Small Animal Dosage
Dogs and Cats
- Antiinflammatory effects: 0.1-0.2 mg/kg q12-24h PO.
- Immunosuppressive effects: 0.2-0.5 mg/kg q12-24h PO.

Large Animal Dosage
- 0.05-0.1 mg/kg q24h IM or PO.

Regulatory Information
No withdrawal times are established for animals intended for food (extralabel use).
RCI Classification: 4

Bethanechol Chloride
beh-than′eh-kole klor′ide

Trade and Other Names: Urecholine

Functional Classification: Cholinergic

Pharmacology and Mechanism of Action
Muscarinic, cholinergic agonist. Parasympathomimetic. Bethanechol stimulates gastric and intestinal motility. It also stimulates contraction of urinary bladder via muscarinic receptor activation.

Indications and Clinical Uses
Bethanechol is used in small animals to increase contraction of urinary bladder. In large animals it may increase gastrointestinal motility, but the efficacy for treating GI stasis problems is questionable.

Precautionary Information
Adverse Reactions and Side Effects
High doses of cholinergic agonists will increase motility of GI tract and cause abdominal discomfort and diarrhea. Bethanechol can cause circulatory depression in sensitive animals and may cause abdominal discomfort.

Contraindications and Precautions
Do **not** use in patients with suspected GI or urinary obstruction.

Drug Interactions
Anticholinergic drugs (atropine, scopolamine, etc) will antagonize effects of bethanechol.

Instructions for Use

Administer injection SQ only. Doses are derived from extrapolation of human doses or via empiricism. There are no well-controlled efficacy studies available for veterinary species.

Bethanechol is no longer available from commercial sources, but some veterinary compounding pharmacists may be able to supply veterinarians.

Patient Monitoring and Laboratory Tests

Monitor GI function.

Formulations

Bethanechol is available in 5, 10, 25, and 50 mg tablets and 5 mg/mL injection. (Commercial preparations are no longer available but are available through some compounding pharmacies.)

Stability and Storage

Store in tightly sealed container at room temperature. Compounded oral suspensions prepared from tablets are not stable.

Small Animal Dosage

Dogs
- 5-15 mg/dog q8h PO.

Cats
- 1.25-5 mg/cat q8h PO.

Large Animal Dosage

Horses
- 0.025 mg/kg IV.

Cattle
- 0.7 mg/kg IV.

Regulatory Information

No withdrawal times are established for animals intended for food (extralabel use). However, FARAD (1-888-873-2723, FARAD@ncsu.edu) recommends a 21 day withdrawal time for slaughter.
RCI Classification: 4

Bisacodyl

biss-ah-koe'dil

Trade and Other Names: Dulcolax

Functional Classification: Laxative

Pharmacology and Mechanism of Action

Laxative/cathartic. Bisacodyl acts via local stimulation of GI motility, most likely by irritation of bowel.

Indications and Clinical Uses

Bisacodyl is used as laxative or for procedures in which bowel evacuation is necessary. It may be used with polyethylene glycol electrolyte solution (e.g., GoLYTELY) to cleanse bowel prior to endoscopy or surgical procedures.

Precautionary Information

Adverse Reactions and Side Effects
Abdominal discomfort. Fluid and electrolyte loss. Avoid chronic use.

Contraindications and Precautions
Avoid use in patients with renal disease. Avoid overuse.

Drug Interactions
No drug interactions are reported in animals.

Instructions for Use
Bisacodyl is available as an OTC tablet. Doses are derived from extrapolation of human doses or via empiricism. There are no well-controlled efficacy studies available for veterinary species. Onset of action is approximately 1 hour after administration.

Patient Monitoring and Laboratory Tests
Monitor electrolytes in animals if used chronically.

Formulations
Bisacodyl is available in 5 mg tablets.

Stability and Storage
Store in tightly sealed container, protected from light, and at room temperature. Stability of compounded formulations has not been evaluated.

Small Animal Dosage

Dogs and Cats
- 5 mg/animal q8-24h PO.

Large Animal Dosage
No dose has been reported for large animals.

Regulatory Information
Do not administer to animals intended for food.

Bismuth Subsalicylate
biz'muth sub-sal-iss'ih-late

Trade and Other Names: Pepto-Bismol

Functional Classification: Antidiarrheal

Pharmacology and Mechanism of Action
Antidiarrheal agent and GI protectant. Precise mechanism of action is unknown, but antiprostaglandin action of salicylate component may be beneficial for enteritis. The bismuth component is efficacious for treating infections caused by spirochete bacteria (Helicobacter gastritis). Bismuth subsalicylate in Pepto-Bismol contains five sources of salicylate, which are absorbed systemically after oral administration.

Indications and Clinical Uses
Bismuth subsalicylate is used for symptomatic treatment of diarrhea in small and large animals. Efficacy has not been established for animals. However, in people it

has been shown effective for treating or preventing diarrhea caused by enterotoxigenic *Escherichia coli* (ETEC).

Precautionary Information

Adverse Reactions and Side Effects

Adverse effects are uncommon. Owners should be warned that bismuth will discolor stools black.

Contraindications and Precautions

Salicylate component is absorbed systemically and overuse should be avoided in animals that cannot tolerate salicylates (such as cats and animals allergic to aspirin).

Drug Interactions

No drug interactions are reported in animals. However, it may possibly exacerbate effects of other nonsteroidal antiinflammatory drugs (NSAIDs) administered to animals. The bismuth component may prevent oral absorption of some drugs.

Instructions for Use

Bismuth subsalicylate is available as an OTC product. Doses are derived from extrapolation of human doses or via empiricism. There are no well-controlled efficacy studies available for veterinary species.

Patient Monitoring and Laboratory Tests

No specific monitoring is necessary.

Formulations

Bismuth subsalicylate is available in oral suspension in 262 mg/15 mL or 525 mg/mL in extra strength formulation and 262 mg tablets. Two tablespoons (30 mL) contain 270 mg salicylate.

Stability and Storage

Store in tightly sealed container, protected from light, and at room temperature. Stability of compounded formulations has not been evaluated.

Small Animal Dosage

Dogs and Cats

- 1-3 ml/kg/day (in divided doses) PO.

Large Animal Dosage

Calves

- 30 mL q30min for 8 doses PO.

Horses

- 1-2 mL/kg q6-8h PO.

Regulatory Information

No withdrawal times are established for animals intended for food (extralabel use). Because salicylate component may be systemically absorbed, withdrawal times should be considered for the salicylate component (similar to aspirin).

Bleomycin Sulfate

blee-oh-mye′sin sul′fate

Trade and Other Names: Blenoxane

Functional Classification: Anticancer agent

Pharmacology and Mechanism of Action

Anticancer antibiotic agent. Exact mechanism of action is unknown, but it may bind to DNA and prevent synthesis.

Indications and Clinical Uses

Bleomycin is used for treatment of various sarcomas and carcinomas.

Precautionary Information

Adverse Reactions and Side Effects

Bleomycin causes local reaction at site of injection, pulmonary toxicity, fever, and chills in people. Side effects are not well documented in veterinary species.

Contraindications and Precautions

Do not use in animals with suppressed bone marrow.

Drug Interactions

No drug interactions are reported in animals.

Instructions for Use

Injectable solution usually used in combination with other anticancer agents. Consult anticancer protocols for details regarding use.

Patient Monitoring and Laboratory Tests

Monitor CBC during treatment.

Formulations

Bleomycin is available in 15 unit vials for injection.

Stability and Storage

Store in tightly sealed container, protected from light, and at room temperature. Refrigerate vials after opening. Stability of compounded formulations has not been evaluated.

Small Animal Dosage

Dogs

- 10 units/m^2 IV or SQ for 3 days, then 10 units/m^2 weekly. (Maximum cumulative dose 200 units/m^2.)

Large Animal Dosage

No dose has been reported for large animals.

Regulatory Information

Withdrawal times are not established for animals that produce food. Because it is an anticancer agent, do not administer to food-producing animals.

Boldenone Undecylenate

bole′de-none un-de-sil-en′ate

Trade and Other Names: Equipoise

Functional Classification: Hormone, anabolic agent

Pharmacology and Mechanism of Action

Anabolic steroid. Boldenone is a steroid ester designed to maximize anabolic effects, while minimizing androgenic action (see also methyltestosterone). Anabolic agents have been used for reversing catabolic conditions, increasing weight gain, increasing muscling in animals, and stimulating erythropoiesis. Other similar drugs used in horses include stanozolol. There are no documented differences in efficacy among the anabolic steroids.

Indications and Clinical Uses

Boldenone is an anabolic agent. It is used, primarily in horses, to improve nitrogen balance, reduce overexertion associated with exercise, and improve training. It may also improve appetite and improve weight gain when used with a well-balanced diet. Boldenone is a long-lasting agent and effects may persist for 6 weeks after an intramuscular injection.

Precautionary Information

Adverse Reactions and Side Effects

Adverse effects from anabolic steroids can be attributed to the pharmacologic action of these steroids. Increased masculine effects are common. Increased aggressiveness may be observed. Increased incidence of some tumors has been reported in people and 17alpha-methylated oral anabolic steroids (oxymetholone, stanozolol, and oxandrolone) are associated with hepatic toxicity.

Contraindications and Precautions

This drug is abused by humans to enhance athletic performance. Do not administer to animals intended for food. Do not administer to pregnant animals.

Drug Interactions

There are no significant drug interactions known, however, use cautiously with other drugs that may affect liver function.

Instructions for Use

For many indications, use in animals is based on experience in people or anecdotal experience in animals.

Patient Monitoring and Laboratory Tests

Monitor liver enzymes for signs of hepatic injury (cholestatic) during treatment.

Formulations

Boldenone is available in 25 and 50 mg/mL injection in sesame oil.

Stability and Storage

Store in tightly sealed container, protected from light, and at room temperature. Do not freeze. Do not mix with aqueous solutions.

Small Animal Dosage

Doses have not been reported for small animals.

Large Animal Dosage

Horses

- 1.1 mg/kg IM. Injection may be repeated every 3 weeks.

Regulatory Information

Do not administer to animals intended for food.
Schedule III controlled drug
RCI Classification: 4

Bromide

broe′mide

Trade and Other Names: Potassium bromide and Sodium bromide

Functional Classification: Anticonvulsant

Pharmacology and Mechanism of Action

Anticonvulsant. Exact mechanism of action is uncertain. Anticonvulsant action is to stabilize neuronal cell membranes. By changing the chloride conductance in neuronal membranes, it may stabilize epileptic foci in the brain. In dogs oral absorption is 46%. It is not metabolized, and most is eliminated by the kidneys. The half-life is long: 11 days in cats and has ranged from 25 days to 46 days in dogs. Bromide is available in two forms: sodium bromide (78% bromide) and potassium bromide (67% bromide).

Indications and Clinical Uses

Bromide ordinarily is used in patients with seizure disorders that have been refractory to phenobarbital. Usually, patients are treated with both phenobarbital and bromide. However, some patients have been treated with bromide as a single therapy for epilepsy. If bromide is added to phenobarbital therapy, it allows for a reduction in phenobarbital dose (reduce by 25% every 6 weeks). Bromide has not been as effective for treating cats with seizure disorders as in dogs. Cats have more adverse effects and are less well controlled.

Precautionary Information

Adverse Reactions and Side Effects

Adverse effects are related to high levels of bromide. Signs of toxicosis are CNS depression, weakness, and ataxia. Hind limb stiffness and abnormal gait also may be a sign of bromide toxicosis.

Nausea and pancreatitis have been reported in dogs. Some dogs show paradoxical excitement with bromide treatment. In cats, bronchitis, resembling allergic airway disease, has been observed. In cats this may be characterized by coughing.

Contraindications and Precautions

Consider using sodium bromide, rather than potassium bromide, in patients with hypoadrenocorticism or any patients in which potassium regulation is a problem. Likewise, consider the sodium content of administration in animals with CHF or hypertension. Monitor plasma concentrations and adjust dose as necessary whenever changing diets as increasing chloride in the diet will shorten the half-life and vice versa. If diet is high in chloride (Hill's h/d, s/d, I/d, and others), higher starting doses may be necessary. Diets high in chloride will cause shorter half-life and need for higher dose. Administration of bromide will interfere with some blood chemistry analysis (e.g., false elevation of chloride).

Drug Interactions

Diets high in chloride will cause shorter half-life and need for higher dose. Administration of bromide will interfere with some blood chemistry analysis (e.g., false elevation of chloride).

Instructions for Use

Bromide usually is administered in combination with phenobarbital. Sodium bromide can be substituted for potassium bromide. When considering doses for sodium bromide, slight dose adjustments should be considered. Potassium bromide is 67% bromide and sodium bromide is 78% bromide. The dose of sodium bromide should be approximately 15% less (e.g., 30 mg/kg of potassium bromide is equivalent to 25 mg/kg of sodium bromide).

Patient Monitoring and Laboratory Tests

Monitor serum bromide concentrations to adjust dose. Effective plasma concentrations should be 1-2 mg/mL (100-200 mg/dL), but if used alone (without phenobarbital) higher concentrations of 2-2.5 mg/mL (200-250 mg/dL) (and as high as 4 mg/mL) may be needed. Most veterinary laboratories can perform a test for bromide in plasma or serum.

Formulations

Bromide is usually prepared as oral solution. Although there are no commercial forms approved by the FDA, compounding pharmacists can prepare a solution. The intravenous solution should be prepared by a pharmacist in sterile water and filtered to remove impurities.

Stability and Storage

Store in tightly sealed container protected from light. Stability of compounded formulations of sodium bromide and potassium bromide has been evaluated. Compounded formulations in aqueous solutions are stable for at least 60 days. Refrigerate to prevent bacterial growth. Do not mix with salt-containing flavorants or solutions.

Small Animal Dosage

Cats

- 30 mg/kg q24h PO.

Dogs

- 30-40 mg/kg q24h PO. If administered without phenobarbital, higher doses of up to 40-50 mg/kg may be needed. If animals are on diets high in chloride, higher doses may be needed. Adjust doses by monitoring plasma concentrations.
- Oral loading dose: 600 mg/kg divided over 3-5 days, PO. Alternatively, 60 mg/kg/day have been administered for 15 days to achieve a plasma concentration of 100 mg/dL, and 200 mg/dL by 60 days.
- IV loading dose for sodium bromide: 800 to 1200 mg/kg infused over 8 hours (it is critical to use sodium bromide instead of potassium bromide for this use).

Large Animal Dosage

No dose has been reported for large animals.

Regulatory Information

Do not administer to animals intended for food.

Bromocriptine Mesylate

broe-moe-krip′teen mess′ih-late

Trade and Other Names: Parlodel

Functional Classification: Dopamine agonist

Pharmacology and Mechanism of Action

Dopaminergic agonist. Antiprolactin agent. Bromocriptine is a lactation inhibitor. It reduces serum prolactin concentration by inhibition of release from anterior pituitary gland. The action binds to dopamine (D_2) receptors in the CNS. The binding of D_2 receptors restores hormonal function in the pituitary. Through the action on the dopamine pituitary receptors, bromocriptine may decrease corticotropin (ACTH) release and has been used in animals (especially horses) for treating pituitary-dependent hyperadrenocorticism (PDH). It also stimulates postsynaptic dopamine receptors and has been used to treat dopamine-deficient neurodegenerative diseases.

Indications and Clinical Uses

In people, bromocriptine is used for its antiparkinson effect and to inhibit lactation associated with excess prolactin. It also has been used to treat acromegaly. Bromocriptine has been used to treat disorders in animals associated with dopamine deficiency. In dogs, bromocriptine has been used to terminate pregnancy when used in combination with a prostaglandin (dinoprost or cloprostenol). In this combination, it was 100% effective for terminating pregnancy in dogs. In horses, bromocriptine may decrease ACTH release and has been used in treating equine pituitary pars intermedia dysfunction (Cushing's syndrome), but pergolide is usually a preferred treatment.

Precautionary Information

Adverse Reactions and Side Effects

Pyometra may occur in dogs after it has been used to induce abortion. Bromocriptine may cause mammary gland enlargement. When terminating pregnancy, bromocriptine is used in combination with prostaglandin F_2alpha. Adverse effects (vomiting, nausea, and retching) may occur as a result of the prostaglandin. Bromocriptine will inhibit lactation.

Contraindications and Precautions

Except when used for termination of pregnancy, do not use in pregnant animals. Do not use in nursing animals.

Drug Interactions

No drug interactions have been reported in animals. However, it will exacerbate the effects of selegiline. Do not administer with monoamine oxidase inhibitors (MAOIs).

Instructions for Use

Use of bromocriptine is limited to treatment of some endocrine disorders. Studies of efficacy are limited. Bromocriptine has been used to terminate pregnancy in dogs, in combination with prostaglandin F_2alpha. Use for termination of pregnancy: administer 15 mcg/kg q12h PO on day 1, 20 mcg/kg 12h PO on days 2 and 3, and 30 mcg/kg q12h PO thereafter for an average of 4-5 days. Ten days may be needed in some dogs. A prostaglandin (cloprostenol sodium) was used at a dose of 1 mcg/kg q48h SQ during this regimen.

Patient Monitoring and Laboratory Tests

Monitor pregnant animals carefully, especially if bromocriptine has been used to terminate pregnancy.

Formulations

Bromocriptine is available in 5 mg capsules and 2.5 mg tablets.

Stability and Storage

Store in tightly sealed container, protected from light, and at room temperature. Stability of compounded formulations has not been evaluated.

Small Animal Dosage

Dogs

- Termination of pregnancy: 15 mcg/kg q12h PO on day 1, 20 mcg/kg 12h PO on days 2 and 3, and 30 mcg/mkg q12h PO thereafter for an average of 4-5 days. For treatment success, it should be administered in combination with prostaglandin F_2alpha.
- Other conditions: 0.02-0.04 mg/kg q12h PO.

Cats

- 0.02-0.04 mg/kg q12h PO.

Large Animal Dosage

No dose has been reported for large animals.

Regulatory Information

Do not administer to animals intended for food.

Budesonide

byoo-dess'oh-nide

Trade and Other Names: Enterocort

Functional Classification: Antiinflammatory, corticosteroid

Pharmacology and Mechanism of Action

Budesonide is a locally acting corticosteroid. It has been used in people, but there has been only limited use in small animals. Budesonide granules are contained in an ethylcellulose matrix that is coated with methacrylic acid polymer. This coating does not release the drug until the pH is >5.5. Therefore, the drug is not usually released until it reaches the distal GI tract. If any is absorbed, 80%-90% is inactivated by metabolism first pass effects. Therefore, systemic glucocorticoid effects are minimized. In humans it has been as effective as other drugs for treatment of Crohn's disease. Budesonide is 1000 times more active than prednisolone as a corticosteroid.

Indications and Clinical Uses

In animals it has been used to treat inflammatory bowel disease. The most common use has been for treating colitis. There is only limited experience with budesonide in dogs and cats, but some animals have benefited from its administration.

Precautionary Information

Adverse Reactions and Side Effects

There is some systemic absorption as evidenced by decreased response to ACTH after 30-day treatment to dogs at 3 mg/m^2, but other side effects were not observed.

Contraindications and Precautions

No known contraindications. However, some of the drug may be absorbed systemically, therefore use with caution in animals that should not receive corticosteroids.

Drug Interactions

Do not administer with drugs that increase stomach pH (antacids, antisecretory drugs). Because budesonide is metabolized by Cytochrome P450 enzymes, other drugs that inhibit these enzymes (see Appendix) may inhibit metabolism.

Instructions for Use

Use in animals has been limited to anecdotal experience. The capsules should not be crushed or compounded for animals.

Patient Monitoring and Laboratory Tests

Monitor corticosteroid effects and, preferably, ACTH-stimulation test to determine degree of adrenal suppression with chronic use.

Formulations

Budesonide is available in 3 mg capsules.

Stability and Storage

Store in tightly sealed container, protected from light, and at room temperature. Do not crush capsules.

Small Animal Dosage

Dogs and Cats

- 0.125 mg/kg q6-8h PO. Dose interval may be increased to every 12 hours when condition improves.

Large Animal Dosage

No dose has been reported for large animals.

Regulatory Information

No regulatory information is available. Because of minimal systemic absorption expected, no withdrawal time is suggested.
RCI Classification: 4

Bunamidine Hydrochloride

byoo-nam'ih-deen hye-droe-klor'ide

Trade and Other Names: Scolaban

Functional Classification: Antiparasitic

Pharmacology and Mechanism of Action

Bunamidine hydrochloride damages integrity of protective integument on cestode parasites. Effective against various species of tapeworms in animals.

Indications and Clinical Uses

Bunamidine is used as an anticestodal agent to treat tapeworm infections in dogs and cats.

Precautionary Information

Adverse Reactions and Side Effects

Vomiting and diarrhea have occurred after use.

Contraindications and Precautions
Avoid use in young animals.

Drug Interactions
No drug interactions are reported in animals.

Instructions for Use
Do not break tablets. Administer tablets on empty stomach. Do not feed for 3 hours after administration.

Patient Monitoring and Laboratory Tests
Monitor fecal samples for evidence of parasites.

Formulations
Bunamidine is available in 400 mg tablets.

Stability and Storage
Store in tightly sealed container, protected from light, and at room temperature. Stability of compounded formulations has not been evaluated.

Small Animal Dosage
Dogs and Cats
- 20-50 mg/kg once PO.

Large Animal Dosage
No dose has been reported for large animals.

Regulatory Information
No regulatory information is available. For extralabel use withdrawal interval estimates, contact FARAD at 1-888-USFARAD (1-888-873-2723) or send e-mail to FARAD@ncsu.edu.

Bupivacaine Hydrochloride
byoo-piv′ah-kane hye-droe-klor′ide

Trade and Other Names: Marcaine and generic brands

Functional Classification: Local anesthetic

Pharmacology and Mechanism of Action
Local anesthetic. Bupivacaine inhibits nerve conduction via sodium channel blockade. It is longer acting and more potent than lidocaine or other local anesthetics.

Indications and Clinical Uses
Bupivacaine is used for local anesthesia and epidural analgesia/anesthesia. It is administered by local infiltration or by epidural injection.

Precautionary Information
Adverse Reactions and Side Effects
Adverse effects rare with local infiltration. High doses absorbed systemically can cause nervous system signs (tremors and convulsions). After epidural administration, respiratory paralysis is possible with high doses.

Contraindications and Precautions

When using for epidural anesthesia, respiratory support should be available. Some formulations contain epinephrine (1:200,000).

Drug Interactions

No drug interactions are reported in animals.

Instructions for Use

Used for local infiltration or infusion into epidural space. One may mix 0.1 mEq sodium bicarbonate per 10 mL solution to increase pH, decrease pain from injection, and speed of onset of action. Use immediately after mixing with bicarbonate because of risk of precipitation. Increasing the pH will accelerate the onset of anesthetic action.

Patient Monitoring and Laboratory Tests

No specific monitoring is necessary.

Formulations

Bupivacaine is available in 2.5 and 5 mg/mL solution injection.

Stability and Storage

Store in tightly sealed container at room temperature. Avoid mixing with strongly acidic or alkalinic solutions. If solutions change to a yellow, pink color, or darker color, they should not be used. If pH is adjusted by mixing with alkalinizing solutions (e.g., bicarbonate) the drug is stable if used soon after mixing.

Small Animal Dosage

Dogs and Cats

- 1 mL of 0.5% solution per 10 cm for an epidural.

Large Animal Dosage

- Local infiltration for surgery has been used.

Regulatory Information

No withdrawal times are established for animals intended for food (extralabel use). When used for local infiltration, clearance from animal is expected to be rapid. For extralabel use withdrawal interval estimates, contact FARAD at 1-888-USFARAD (1-888-873-2723) or send e-mail to FARAD@ncsu.edu.

RCI Classification: 2

Buprenorphine Hydrochloride

byoo-preh-nor′feen hye-droe-klor′ide

Trade and Other Names: Buprenex (Vetergesic in the UK)

Functional Classification: Analgesic, Opioid

Pharmacology and Mechanism of Action

Opioid analgesic. Buprenorphine is a partial mu-receptor agonist and kappa-receptor antagonist. It is twenty-five to fifty times more potent than morphine. Buprenorphine may cause less respiratory depression than other opiates.

Indications and Clinical Uses

Buprenorphine is an opiate analgesic that is used for pain control in dogs and cats. It has lower efficacy (lower ceiling) than pure mu-receptor agonists such as morphine.

Buprenorphine has been shown to be effective in animal studies for treating postoperative pain. In cats it has been administered for transmucosal absorption (buccal administration). In animals, it may have longer action than other opioids because of higher affinity for the mu-receptor. Duration of effect may be 3-8 hours, although this has not been established in well-controlled studies.

Precautionary Information

Adverse Reactions and Side Effects

Adverse effects are similar to other opiate agonists, except there may be less respiratory depression. Dependency from chronic use of buprenorphine may be less than with pure agonists.

Contraindications and Precautions

Patients receiving buprenorphine may require higher doses of naloxone for reversal.

Drug Interactions

As a partial agonist, it may reverse or antagonize some of the mu-receptor effects of other opiates, such as morphine or fentanyl.

Instructions for Use

Buprenorphine is used for analgesia, often in combination with other analgesics or in conjunction with general anesthesia. It is longer acting than morphine and only partially reversed by naloxone.

Patient Monitoring and Laboratory Tests

Monitor patient's heart rate and respiration. Although bradycardia rarely needs to be treated when it is caused by an opioid, if necessary atropine can be administered. If serious respiratory depression occurs, the opioid can be reversed with naloxone. Patients receiving buprenorphine may require higher doses of naloxone for reversal.

Formulations

Buprenorphine is available in 0.3 mg/mL solution.

Stability and Storage

Store in tightly sealed container, protected from light, and at room temperature. Use sodium chloride for infusions. Stability of compounded formulations has not been evaluated. Schedule II drug, store in locked compartment.

Small Animal Dosage

Dogs

- 0.006-0.02 mg/kg q4-8h IV, IM or SQ.

Cats

- 0.005-0.01 mg/kg q4-8h IV or IM.
- Buccal administration: 0.01-0.02 mg/kg q12h. (Equivalent to 0.066 mL per kg.) This may be applied to the cat's gingival or oral mucosa (i.e., sublingual).

Large Animal Dosage

Horses

- 0.005-0.01 mg/kg (short acting in horses)

Regulatory Information

The drug is controlled by the DEA. Do not administer to animals intended for food.
Schedule III controlled drug
RCI Classification: 2

Buspirone Hydrochloride

byoo-speer'own hye-droe-klor'ide

Trade and Other Names: BuSpar

Functional Classification: Behavior modification

Pharmacology and Mechanism of Action

Antianxiety agent of the azapirone class. Buspirone acts to block release of serotonin by binding to presynaptic receptors.

Indications and Clinical Uses

In veterinary medicine, buspirone has been primarily used for treatment of urine spraying (urine marking) in cats. In cats there are published studies demonstrating efficacy. However, some cats relapse after treatment is discontinued. In dogs, it has occasionally been used to treat behavior problems, such as anxiety disorders.

Precautionary Information

Adverse Reactions and Side Effects

Few side effects in cats compared to other drugs. Some cats show increased aggression; some cats show increased affection to owners.

Contraindications and Precautions

Do not use in animals with sensitivity to serotonin agonists.

Drug Interactions

Do not use with other serotonin antagonists, selective serotonin reuptake inhibitors (SSRIs), or monoamine oxidase inhibitors (MAOIs; e.g., selegiline).

Instructions for Use

Some efficacy trials suggest effectiveness for treating urine spraying in cats. There may be a lower relapse rate compared to other drugs.

Patient Monitoring and Laboratory Tests

No specific monitoring is necessary.

Formulations

Buspirone is available in 5 and 10 mg tablets.

Stability and Storage

Store in tightly sealed container, protected from light, and at room temperature. Stability of compounded formulations has not been evaluated.

Small Animal Dosage

Cats

- 2.5-5 mg/cat q12h PO, which may be increased to 5-7.5 mg per cat twice daily for some cats, (0.5-1 mg/kg q12h PO).

Dogs

- 2.5-10 mg/dog q24h or q12h PO.
- 1.0 mg/kg q12h PO.

Large Animal Dosage

Horses

- 100-250 mg/horse q24h PO.

Regulatory Information

Do not administer to animals intended for food.
RCI Classification: 2

Busulfan

byoo-sul′fan

Trade and Other Names: Myleran

Functional Classification: Anticancer agent

Pharmacology and Mechanism of Action

Anticancer agent. Busulfan is a bifunctional alkylating agent and acts to disrupt DNA of tumor cells.

Indications and Clinical Uses

Busulfan is used primarily for lymphoreticular neoplasia.

Precautionary Information

Adverse Reactions and Side Effects

Leukopenia is most severe side effect.

Contraindications and Precautions

Do not use in animals with suppressed bone marrow.

Drug Interactions

No drug interactions are reported in animals.

Instructions for Use

Busulfan is usually used in combination with other anticancer agents. Consult specific protocol for details.

Patient Monitoring and Laboratory Tests

Monitor CBC in animals during treatment.

Formulations

Busulfan is available in 2 mg tablets.

Stability and Storage

Store in tightly sealed container, protected from light, and at room temperature. Stability of compounded formulations has not been evaluated.

Small Animal Dosage

Dogs and Cats

- 3-4 mg/m^2 q24h PO.

Large Animal Dosage

No dose has been reported for large animals.

Regulatory Information

Withdrawal times are not established for animals that produce food. This drug should not be used in food animals because it is an anticancer agent.

Butorphanol Tartrate

byoo-tor'fah-nole tar'trate

Trade and Other Names: Torbutrol and Torbugesic

Functional Classification: Analgesic, Opioid

Pharmacology and Mechanism of Action

Opioid analgesic. Opiate that acts as kappa receptor agonist and weak mu-receptor antagonist (some authorities classify the antagonist effect as a "partial agonist" effect). As a kappa-agonist, butorphanol produces sedation and analgesia in animals. It is considered a mild analgesic compared to pure mu-receptor opiates. It is often used in combination with other anesthetics.

Indications and Clinical Uses

Butorphanol is used for perioperative analgesia, chronic pain, and as an antitussive agent. Butorphanol is considered a weak analgesic compared to drugs that are pure mu-receptor agonists. In dogs, at doses of 0.4 mg/kg, butorphanol produces analgesia for a duration of 1.0 hour or less. In cats, butorphanol at 0.4 mg/kg may have a duration of effect for as long as 3 hours. In horses it is used IV, IM, and as constant rate infusion (CRI). CRI has been shown effective in controlled studies.

Precautionary Information

Adverse Reactions and Side Effects

Adverse effects are similar to other opioid analgesic drugs. Sedation is common at analgesic doses. Respiratory depression can occur with high doses. Although bradycardia rarely needs to be treated when it is caused by an opioid, if necessary atropine can be administered. If serious respiratory depression occurs, the opioid can be reversed with naloxone. Dysphoric effects have been observed with agonist/antagonist drugs; this effect has been observed in cats. Decreased intestinal peristalsis and constipation may occur in some animals. Decrease in intestinal motility may be a particular concern in some horses.

Contraindications and Precautions

Schedule IV controlled substance. Compatible with many other analgesics and used in combination treatment for analgesia.

Drug Interactions

Since butorphanol is an agonist/antagonist, it may antagonize some effects of drugs that are pure agonists (e.g., fentanyl, morphine, and oxymorphone). However, the clinical significance of this antagonism has been debated among experts. Do not mix with sodium barbiturates.

Instructions for Use

Butorphanol is often used in combination with anesthetic agents or in conjunction with other analgesic drugs. For most indications, a dose of 0.4 mg/kg is considered optimum, and there is no reason to increase the dose above 0.8 mg/kg as this is considered the ceiling dose. Above 0.8 mg/kg there is no benefit. Butorphanol has a short duration of effect of less than 2 hours and usually only 1 hour.

Patient Monitoring and Laboratory Tests

Monitor patient's heart rate and respiration.

Formulations

Butorphanol is available in 1, 5, and 10 mg tablets and 0.5 and 1.0 mg/mL injection.

Stability and Storage

Store in tightly sealed container, protected from light, and at room temperature. Stability of compounded formulations has not been evaluated.

Small Animal Dosage

Dogs

- Antitussive: 0.055 mg/kg q6-12h SQ or 0.5-1.0 mg/kg q6-12h PO.
- Preanesthetic: 0.2-0.4 mg/kg (with acepromazine) IV, IM, or SQ.
- Analgesic: 0.2-0.4 mg/kg q2-4h IV, IM, or SQ or 1-4 mg/kg q6h PO.
- CRI: Loading dose of 0.2-0.4 mg/kg IV, followed by 0.1-0.2 mg/kg/hr.

Cats

- Analgesic: 0.2-0.8 mg/kg q2-6h IV or SQ or 1.5 mg/kg q4-8h PO.
- Constant rate infusions for dogs and cats: loading dose of 0.2-0.4 mg/kg IV, followed by 0.1-0.2 mg/kg/hr.

Large Animal Dosage

Horses

- Pain: 0.2-0.4 mg/kg q3-4h IV. In some instances, lower doses of 0.02-0.1 mg/kg IV or 0.04-0.2 mg/kg IM have been used. Lower doses of 0.1 mg/kg IV have been used to minimize the decrease in intestinal motility.
- Sedation: 0.01-0.06 mg/kg IV.
- CRI: 13-24 mcg/kg/hr IV, with lower dose shown to produce analgesia in horses.

Ruminants

- 0.05-0.2 mg/kg IV.

Cattle

- In combination with xylazine: 0.01-0.02 mg/kg IV.

Regulatory Information

Drug controlled by DEA, Schedule IV.
Do not administer to animals intended for food.
RCI Classification: 2

Calcitriol

kal-sih-trye'ole

Trade and Other Names: Rocaltrol and Calcijex

Functional Classification: Calcium supplement

Pharmacology and Mechanism of Action

Vitamin D analogue. Action of calcitriol is to increase calcium absorption in intestine.

Indications and Clinical Uses

Calcitriol is used to treat calcium deficiency and diseases such as hypocalcemia associated with hypoparathyroidism. Most often it is used to lower calcium in cats that have had parathyroid glands removed. Calcitriol has been used to reduce parathyroid hormone (PTH) concentrations in dogs with chronic renal disease. Calcitriol should not be used as a vitamin D supplement.

Precautionary Information

Adverse Reactions and Side Effects

Overdose can result in hypercalcemia.

Contraindications and Precautions

Do not use in patients that are at risk of hypercalcemia.

Drug Interactions

Calcitriol may cause hypercalcemia if used with thiazide diuretics.

Instructions for Use

Doses should be adjusted in each patient according to response and monitoring calcium plasma concentration. When used for treating dogs with chronic kidney disease, the dose was 2.5 ng/kg/day, but ranged from 0.75 to 5 ng/kg/day based on adjustments from measuring calcium concentrations.

Patient Monitoring and Laboratory Tests

Monitor plasma ionized calcium concentration. Adjust doses as necessary to maintain normal calcium concentration. Monitor PTH concentrations if possible.

Formulations

Calcitriol is available as injection (Calcijex) in a 1 and 2 mcg/mL and in 0.25 and 0.5 mcg capsules (Rocaltrol).

Stability and Storage

Store in tightly sealed container, protected from light, and at room temperature. Stability of compounded formulations has not been evaluated.

Small Animal Dosage

Dogs

- 0.25-0.5 mcg/dog/day PO or approximately 12-25 ng/kg/day PO (0.012-0.025 mcg/kg/day).
- Chronic kidney disease: 2.5-3.5 ng/kg/day have been used and adjusted as needed on the basis of calcium monitoring.

Cats

- Hypocalcemia: 0.25 mcg/cat q48h PO or 0.01-0.04 mcg/kg/day PO (10-40 ng/kg/day).

Large Animal Dosage

No dose has been reported for large animals.

Regulatory Information

No regulatory information is available. For extralabel use withdrawal interval estimates, contact FARAD at 1-888-USFARAD (1-888-873-2723) or send e-mail to FARAD@ncsu.edu.

Calcium Carbonate

Trade and Other Names: Titralac, Calci-mix, Liqui-cal, Maalox, Tums, and generic brands

Functional Classification: Calcium supplement

Pharmacology and Mechanism of Action

Calcium supplement. Calcium is essential for the functional integrity of several body systems. Calcium carbonate is equivalent to 400 mg of calcium ion per gram. Calcium carbonate neutralizes stomach acid for treating and preventing stomach ulcers.

Indications and Clinical Uses

Calcium carbonate is used as oral calcium supplement for hypocalcemia. Used as antacid to treat gastric hyperacidity and GI ulcers. Also used as intestinal phosphate binder for hyperphosphatemia associated with renal failure.

Precautionary Information

Adverse Reactions and Side Effects

Few side effects. High calcium concentrations are possible. With any calcium supplements, constipation and intestinal bloating can occur.

Contraindications and Precautions

Do not administer to animals predisposed to forming calcium-containing renal or cystic calculi. When calcium carbonate or calcium citrate are used as a phosphate binder to prevent hyperphosphatemia, caution is advised to avoid hypercalcemia in patients with renal failure.

Drug Interactions

Oral administration of calcium supplements may interfere with absorption of other drugs such as fluoroquinolones (e.g., enrofloxacin, orbifloxacin, marbofloxacin), bisphosphonates, zinc, iron, and tetracyclines.

Instructions for Use

Calcium carbonate is equivalent to 400 mg of calcium ion per gram. Doses are primarily derived from extrapolation of human doses. When used as calcium supplement, doses should be adjusted according to serum calcium concentrations. Some tablets also contain vitamin D. Doses are based on calcium carbonate, not the ion concentration (e.g., a 650 mg tablet contains 260 mg calcium ion).

Patient Monitoring and Laboratory Tests

Monitor serum calcium levels, particularly if patients have renal failure.

Formulations

Calcium carbonate is available in tablets or oral suspension, most of which are OTC. One gram of calcium carbonate is equivalent to 400 mg of calcium ion. Calci-mix and Liqui-cal are available in 1.25 and 1.5 mg capsules. OTC tablets are available in 650 and 667 mg and 1, 1.25, and 1.5 g. Oral suspension (Titralac) is 1 g per 5 mL or 1.25 g per 5 mL.

Stability and Storage

Store in tightly sealed container, protected from light, and at room temperature. Stability of compounded formulations has not been evaluated. Do not mix with other compounds that may chelate with calcium.

Small Animal Dosage

Dogs and Cats

- Calcium supplementation: 70-185 mg/kg/day given with food PO.
- Phosphate binder: 60-100 mg/kg/day in divided doses usually given with food PO.

Large Animal Dosage

No dose has been reported for large animals. Usually other calcium salts are used for supplementation in cattle.

Regulatory Information

No withdrawal times are available. Because this is a normal dietary supplement, with little risk from residues, no withdrawal time is suggested for animals intended for food.

Calcium Chloride

Trade and Other Names: Generic brands

Functional Classification: Calcium supplement

Pharmacology and Mechanism of Action

Calcium supplement. Calcium is essential for the functional integrity of several body systems. Injection is 27.2 mg of calcium ion [1.36 mEq] per mL. Calcium chloride increases ionized calcium in blood greater than other calcium salts.

Indications and Clinical Uses

Calcium chloride is used in acute situations to supplement as electrolyte replacement or as a cardiotonic. It is administered to cows for hypocalcemia (milk fever).

Precautionary Information

Adverse Reactions and Side Effects

Overdose with calcium is possible. Do not administer intravenous solution SQ or IM, because it may cause tissue necrosis.

Contraindications and Precautions

Do not administer rapidly. Rapid intravenous administration to cows can cause cardiac arrhythmias and even death.

Drug Interactions

Calcium chloride will precipitate with sodium bicarbonate. Do not mix with compounds known to chelate with calcium.

Instructions for Use

Injection is 27.2 mg of calcium ion [1.36 mEq] per mL. Usually used in emergency situations. Intracardiac administrations have been performed but avoid injections into the myocardium.

Patient Monitoring and Laboratory Tests

Monitor serum calcium concentration. Monitor heart rhythm during administration.

Formulations

Calcium chloride is available in a 10% (100 mg/mL) solution. This supplies 1.36 mEq calcium ion per mL. Preparations for cattle usually contain 8.5-11.5 g calcium per 500 mL. Many formulations also contain magnesium.

Stability and Storage

Store in tightly sealed container, protected from light, and at room temperature. Stability of compounded formulations has not been evaluated. Do not mix with other compounds that may chelate with calcium.

Small Animal Dosage

Dogs and Cats

- 0.1-0.3 mL/kg IV (slowly).

Large Animal Dosage

Cows

- 2 g/100 kg body weight, IV at a rate of 1 g/min.

Horses

- 1-2 grams per adult horse IV slowly.

Regulatory Information

No withdrawal times are available. Because this is a normal supplement, with little risk from residues, no withdrawal time is suggested for animals intended for food.

Calcium Citrate

Trade and Other Names: Citracal (OTC)

Functional Classification: Calcium supplement

Pharmacology and Mechanism of Action

Calcium supplement. Calcium is essential for the functional integrity of several body systems. Administered orally to supply calcium to the diet.

Indications and Clinical Uses

Calcium citrate is used in treatment of hypocalcemia, such as with hypoparathyroidism. Also used as intestinal phosphate binder for hyperphosphatemia associated with renal failure.

Precautionary Information

Adverse Reactions and Side Effects

Hypercalcemia possible with over supplementation. With any calcium supplements, constipation and intestinal bloating can occur.

Contraindications and Precautions

When calcium carbonate or calcium citrate are used as a phosphate binder to prevent hyperphosphatemia, caution is advised to avoid hypercalcemia in patients with renal failure.

Drug Interactions

Oral administration of calcium supplements may interfere with absorption of other drugs such as fluoroquinolones (e.g., enrofloxacin, orbifloxacin, marbofloxacin), bisphosphonates, zinc, iron, and tetracyclines.

Instructions for Use

Doses should be adjusted according to serum calcium concentration.

Patient Monitoring and Laboratory Tests

Monitor serum calcium levels, particularly if patients have renal failure.

Formulations

Calcium citrate is available in 950 mg tablets (contains 200 mg calcium ion).

Stability and Storage

Store in tightly sealed container, protected from light, and at room temperature. Stability of compounded formulations has not been evaluated. Do not mix with other compounds that may chelate with calcium.

Small Animal Dosage

Cats

- 10-30 mg/kg q8h (with meals) PO.

Dogs

- 20 mg/kg/day (with meals) PO.

Dogs and Cats

- Phosphate binder (prevent hyperphosphatemia): 10-20 mg/kg per day in divided doses, with meals PO.

Large Animal Dosage

No dose has been reported for large animals.

Regulatory Information

No withdrawal times are available. Because this is a normal dietary supplement, with little risk from residues, no withdrawal time is suggested for animals intended for food.

Calcium Gluconate and Calcium Borogluconate

Trade and Other Names: Kalcinate, Calcium borogluconate, AmVet, Cal-Nate, and generic brands

Functional Classification: Calcium supplement

Pharmacology and Mechanism of Action

Calcium supplement. Calcium is essential for the functional integrity of several body systems. It is administered orally to supply calcium to the diet, or injected for acute conditions.

Indications and Clinical Uses

Calcium gluconate and calcium borogluconate are used in treatment of hypocalcemia, such as with hypoparathyroidism. Used in electrolyte deficiency. Calcium supplements are administered to cattle for treatment of hypocalcemia (milk fever).

Precautionary Information

Adverse Reactions and Side Effects

Hypercalcemia possible with over supplementation. Calcium supplements may cause constipation. Subcutaneous or intramuscular injections of calcium salts may cause tissue injury at the site of injection.

Contraindications and Precautions

Avoid rapid intravenous administration. Avoid use in patients that are prone to calcium-containing renal or cystic calculi. Avoid administration of intravenous solution IM or SQ, because it will cause tissue necrosis.

Drug Interactions

Do not mix with any bicarbonates (sodium bicarbonate) phosphates, sulfates, and tartrates, because it may precipitate. Specific drugs that can precipitate with calcium gluconate include oxytetracycline, promethazine, sulfamethazine, tetracycline, cephalothin, and amphotericin B. Calcium supplements may interfere with the oral absorption of iron, tetracyclines, and fluoroquinolones.

Instructions for Use

The 500 mg tablets contain 45 mg of calcium ion. The 10% injection contains 97 mg [9.3 mg of calcium ion (0.47 mEq)] per mL.

Patient Monitoring and Laboratory Tests

Monitor serum calcium concentration. Monitor heart rate during intravenous administration.

Formulations

Calcium gluconate is available as 10% (100 mg/mL) injection. Calcium gluconate 10% contains 9.3 mg of calcium ion per mL, or 0.465 mEq per mL. Calcium gluconate is available in tablets in sizes of 325, 500, 650, 975, and 1 gram. Each gram contains 90 mg of calcium ion. Chewable tablets are available in 650 and 1 gram tablets for people.

Calcium borogluconate is available as 230 mg/mL (AmVet Calcium Gluconate 23% and Cal Nate).

Stability and Storage

Store in tightly sealed container, protected from light, and at room temperature. Solutions should be clear. If crystals are present, warm vial up to 30-40° C (86-104° F) to dissolve crystals. Stability of compounded formulations has not been evaluated. Do not mix with other compounds that may chelate with calcium.

Small Animal Dosage

Dogs and Cats

- 75-500 mg IV, slowly.

Large Animal Dosage

Calcium Borogluconate

Cattle and Horses

- 5-12 g IV, slowly.

Pigs and Sheep

- 0.5-1.5 g IV, slowly.

Dairy Cows

- 2 g/100 kg body weight at a rate of 1 g/min.

Horses

- 50-70 mg/kg, diluted in 5% dextrose and infused slowly, IV.

Regulatory Information

No withdrawal times are available. Because this is a normal dietary supplement, with little risk from residues, no withdrawal time is suggested for animals intended for food.

Calcium Lactate

Trade and Other Names: Generic brands

Functional Classification: Calcium supplement

Pharmacology and Mechanism of Action

Calcium supplement. Calcium is essential for the functional integrity of several body systems.

Indications and Clinical Uses

Calcium lactate is used in treatment of hypocalcemia, such as with hypoparathyroidism, and in electrolyte deficiency.

Precautionary Information

Adverse Reactions and Side Effects

Hypercalcemia possible with over supplementation.

Contraindications and Precautions

Avoid use in patients that are prone to calcium-containing renal or cystic calculi.

Drug Interactions

Calcium supplements may interfere with the oral absorption of iron, tetracyclines, and fluoroquinolones.

Instructions for Use

Calcium lactate contains 130 mg of calcium ion per gram.

Patient Monitoring and Laboratory Tests

Monitor serum calcium concentrations.

Formulations

Calcium lactate is available in 325 mg (42.25 mg of calcium ion) and 650 mg (84.5 mg of calcium ion) OTC tablets.

Stability and Storage

Store in tightly sealed container, protected from light, and at room temperature. Stability of compounded formulations has not been evaluated. Do not mix with other compounds that may chelate with calcium.

Small Animal Dosage

Dogs

- 0.5-2.0 g/day (in divided doses) PO.

Cats

- 0.2-0.5 g/day (in divided doses) PO.

Large Animal Dosage

No dose has been reported for large animals.

Regulatory Information

No withdrawal times are available. Because this is a normal dietary supplement, with little risk from residues, no withdrawal time is suggested for animals intended for food.

Captopril

kap'toe-pril

Trade and Other Names: Capoten

Functional Classification: Vasodilator, Angiotensin-converting enzyme (ACE) inhibitor

Pharmacology and Mechanism of Action

ACE inhibitor. Captopril inhibits conversion of angiotensin I to angiotensin II, leading to vasodilation. Angiotensin II is a potent vasoconstrictor, and also will stimulate sympathetic stimulation, renal hypertension, and synthesis of aldosterone. The ability of aldosterone to cause sodium and water retention contribute to congestion. Captopril, like other ACE inhibitors, will cause vasodilation and decrease aldosterone-induced congestion; but ACE inhibitors also contribute to vasodilation by increasing concentrations of some vasodilating kinins and prostaglandins. Unlike enalapril, it has has not been studied for clinical use in dogs and cats.

Indications and Clinical Uses

Captopril, like other ACE inhibitors, is used to treat hypertension and CHF. It is primarily used in dogs, but may benefit some cats with heart failure or with systemic hypertension. ACE inhibitors are not considered a primary treatment for hypertension in cats.

However, because of low potency and short duration of action, captopril is not used as much as other ACE inhibitors, which include enalapril, benazepril, and lisinopril.

Precautionary Information

Adverse Reactions and Side Effects

Hypotension is possible with excessive doses. Captopril may cause azotemia in some patients, especially when administered with potent diuretics (e.g., furosemide). GI side effects, predominantly anorexia, are common in dogs.

Contraindications and Precautions

Discontinue ACE inhibitors in pregnant animals; they cross the placenta and have caused fetal malformations and death of the fetus.

Drug Interactions

Use cautiously with diuretics and potassium supplements. Nonsteroidal antiinflammatory drugs (NSAIDs) may diminish antihypertensive effect.

Instructions for Use

Use of captopril has been replaced by enalapril and benazepril in small animal practice.

Patient Monitoring and Laboratory Tests

Monitor patients carefully to avoid hypotension. With all ACE inhibitors, monitor electrolytes and renal function 3-7 days after initiating therapy and periodically thereafter.

Formulations

Captopril is available in 12.5, 25, 50, and 100 mg tablets.

Stability and Storage

Store in tightly sealed container at room temperature. More stable at acidic pH. Oral compounded solutions are stable for 30 days refrigerated. However, tap water should not be used; purified water is necessary to ensure stability.

Small Animal Dosage

Dogs

- 0.5-2 mg/kg q8-12h PO.

Cats

- 3.12-6.25 mg/cat q8h PO.

Large Animal Dosage

No dose has been reported for large animals.

Regulatory Information

Do not administer to animals intended for food.

RCI Classification: 3

Carbenicillin

kar-ben-ih-sill'in

Trade and Other Names: Geopen and Pyopen Carbenicillin indanyl sodium (Geocillin)

Functional Classification: Antibacterial

Pharmacology and Mechanism of Action

Beta-lactam antibiotic. Carbenicillin has an action similar to ampicillin, which inhibits bacterial cell wall synthesis. Carbenicillin has a broad spectrum of activity that includes both gram-positive and gram-negative bacteria. However, resistance is possible, especially among beta-lactamase positive strains. The difference between carbenicillin and ampicillin is that it is active against *Pseudomonas aeruginosa* and other gram-negative bacteria that are resistant to other beta-lactam drugs. Half-life is short, and clearance is rapid in animals, therefore requires frequent administration.

Indications and Clinical Uses

Carbenicillin is used to treat gram-negative infections in animals, including infections caused by *Pseudomonas aeruginosa*. Indanyl sodium carbenicillin (Geocillin) is poorly absorbed orally and should not be used for systemic infections. It may produce high enough urine concentrations for treating some infections of lower urinary tract.

C

Precautionary Information

Adverse Reactions and Side Effects

Carbenicillin like other penicillin drugs may cause allergy. Carbenicillin may cause bleeding problems in some animals by interfering with platelets.

Contraindications and Precautions

Use cautiously in patients sensitive to penicillins (e.g., allergy).

Drug Interactions

No drug interactions are reported in animals. Do not mix in vial with other drugs, because inactivation may result.

Instructions for Use

Carbenicillin injection often is administered with an aminoglycoside. Do not mix with aminoglycosides prior to administration or inactivation will result. Carbenicillin indanyl sodium is the oral formulation of carbenicillin but attains concentrations that are only sufficient for treating UTIs. Do not use for systemic infections.

Patient Monitoring and Laboratory Tests

Culture and sensitivity testing recommended to guide therapy. CLSI (NCCLS) break points are less than or equal to 128 mcg/mL when testing for *Pseudomonas* susceptible organisms and less than or equal to 16 mcg/mL for other gram-negative organisms.

Formulations

Carbenicillin is available in 1, 2, 5, 10, and 30 g vials for injection. Carbenicillin indanyl sodium is available in 500 mg tablets.

Stability and Storage

Store in tightly sealed container, protected from light, and at room temperature. Stable at pH of 6.5, but rate of degradation is greater at higher or lower pH.

Small Animal Dosage

Dogs and Cats

- Carbenicillin: 40-50 mg/kg and up to 100 mg/kg q6-8h IV, IM, or SQ.
- Carbenicillin indanyl sodium: 10 mg/kg q8h PO.

Large Animal Dosage

No dose has been reported for large animals.

Regulatory Information

No regulatory information is available. For extralabel use withdrawal interval estimates, contact FARAD at 1-888-USFARAD (1-888-873-2723) or send e-mail to FARAD@ncsu.edu.

Carbimazole

kar-bih'mah-zole

Trade and Other Names: Neomercazole

Functional Classification: Antithyroid drug

Pharmacology and Mechanism of Action

Antithyroid drug similar to methimazole, but it may have fewer side effects, such as less frequent GI problems compared to methimazole.

Indications and Clinical Uses

Carbimazole has been used to decrease thyroid function in cats and to treat hyperthyroidism. Experience in the U.S. is limited because of lack of availability.

Precautionary Information

Adverse Reactions and Side Effects

In cats, lupus-like reactions are possible, such as vasculitis and bone marrow changes. In people, it has caused agranulocytosis and leukopenia.

Contraindications and Precautions

Do not use in cats with bone marrow suppression or thrombocytopenia.

Drug Interactions

No drug interactions are reported in animals.

Instructions for Use

Carbimazole is used in Europe; clinical experience in U.S. is limited.

Patient Monitoring and Laboratory Tests

Monitor thyroid concentrations to adjust dose. Monitor CBC to look for bone marrow suppression.

Formulations

Registration is not available in the United States. This drug has been obtained in Europe.

Stability and Storage

Store in tightly sealed container, protected from light, and at room temperature. Stability of compounded formulations has not been evaluated.

Small Animal Dosage

Cats

- 5 mg/cat q8h (induction), followed by 5 mg/cat q12h PO.

Large Animal Dosage

No dose has been reported for large animals.

Regulatory Information

Do not administer to animals intended for food.

Carboplatin

kar-boe-plat′in

Trade and Other Names: Paraplatin

Functional Classification: Anticancer agent

Pharmacology and Mechanism of Action

Anticancer agent. Carboplatin is a second-generation platinum compound and is related to cisplatin. Action is similar to cisplatin. It is believed to be similar to bifunctional alkylating agents and interrupts replication of DNA in tumor cells. Major route of elimination is via the kidneys.

Indications and Clinical Uses

Carboplatin has been used for squamous cell carcinoma and other carcinomas, melanoma, osteosarcomas, and other sarcomas. When used in dogs, myelosuppression has been the most dose-limiting factor.

Precautionary Information

Adverse Reactions and Side Effects

Adverse effects are dose related. Dose-limiting toxicosis is myelosuppression. Carboplatin may cause anemia, leukopenia, or thrombocytopenia. In dogs, nadir of myelosuppression occurs at 14 days, but recovery occurs by 21-28 days. In cats, the nadir is 21 days and recovery occurs by 28 days. Carboplatin may induce renal toxicity. Compared to cisplatin, carboplatin is less emetogenic and less nephrotoxic. In dogs, the other most common adverse effects relate to GI system toxicity (gastroenteritis, vomiting, anorexia, and diarrhea).

Contraindications and Precautions

In one study, small dogs were more prone to adverse effects than larger dogs.

Drug Interactions

Do not use with other nephrotoxic drugs.

Instructions for Use

Available for reconstitution for injection. It is stable for 1 month when reconstituted with 5% dextrose. It may be frozen at –4° C to prolong the stability of a reconstituted vial. Do not use with administration sets containing aluminum because of incompatibility. Usually administered in specific anticancer protocols. In dogs, it has been dosed on a milligram per square meter dose, but in these protocols smaller dogs have a higher incidence of adverse effects than larger dogs. However, smaller dogs also were more likely to respond.

Patient Monitoring and Laboratory Tests

Monitoring of CBC and platelets is recommended during treatment.

Formulations

Carboplatin is available in 50 and 150 mg vial for injection.

Stability and Storage

Store in tightly sealed container, protected from light, and at room temperature. Stable for 1 month if reconstituted with 5% dextrose solution. It is stable if frozen at –4° C.

Small Animal Dosage

Dogs

- 300 mg/m^2 q21d IV. Is is also administered at 300 mg/m^2 for dogs <15 kg and 350 mg/m^2 for dogs >15 kg.

Cats

- 200-250 mg/m^2 every 4 weeks for 4 treatments IV.

Large Animal Dosage

No dose has been reported for large animals.

Regulatory Information

Withdrawal times are not established for animals that produce food. This drug should not be used in animals intended for food, because it is an anticancer agent.

Carprofen

car-proe'fen

Trade and Other Names: Rimadyl and Zinecarp (Europe)

Functional Classification: NSAID

Pharmacology and Mechanism of Action

Carprofen is a nonsteroidal antiinflammatory drug (NSAID). Like other drugs in this class, carprofen has analgesic and antiinflammatory effects by inhibiting the synthesis of prostaglandins. The enzyme inhibited by NSAID is the cyclo-oxygenase enzyme (COX). The COX enzyme exists in two isoforms, called COX-1 and COX-2. COX-1 is primarily responsible for synthesis of prostaglandins important for maintaining a healthy GI tract, renal function, platelet function, and other normal functions. COX-2 is induced and responsible for synthesizing prostaglandins that are important mediators of pain, inflammation, and fever. (There may be crossover of COX-1 and COX-2 effects in some situations.) Carprofen is relatively COX-1 sparing compared to older NSAIDs, but it is not known if the specificity for COX-1 or COX-2 determines efficacy or safety. In horses, carprofen is not as COX-2 selective as it is in dogs. As an analgesic agent the mechanism of action may involve other mechanisms other than inhibition of prostaglandin synthesis.

Indications and Clinical Uses

Carprofen is used primarily for treatment of musculoskeletal pain and acute pain related to surgery or trauma. It is used primarily for treatment of dogs. Long-term safe use in cats has not been established. However, it is registered in Europe for one-time administration in cats at 4 mg/kg injection. Although use in large animals is uncommon, in cattle, carprofen has been shown to reduce inflammation associated with *Escherichia coli mastitis.* Cows were administered 0.7 mg/kg IV. Inhibition of COX enzymes in horses does not appear to show same specificity as in dogs.

Precautionary Information

Adverse Reactions and Side Effects

Safety of carprofen in dogs was established prior to marketing. However, the most common adverse effect in dogs has been in the GI tract (vomiting, anorexia, and diarrhea). GI ulcers, perforation, and bleeding are uncommon in dogs. In rare cases, carprofen has caused idiosyncratic acute hepatic toxicity in dogs. Signs of toxicity appear 2-3 weeks after exposure. There were no adverse effects on kidneys when carprofen was evaluated in anesthetized dogs. Carprofen has produced toxicity in cats if administered at same dose rates as for dogs.

Contraindications and Precautions

Do not use in cats at doses intended for dogs. Do not administer to animals prone to GI ulcers. Do not administer with ulcerogenic drugs such as corticosteroids. If a patient has had previous adverse effects from NSAIDs, carprofen should be used cautiously.

Drug Interactions
Use NSAIDs cautiously with other drugs known to cause GI injury (e.g., corticosteroids). The efficacy of angiotensin-converting enzyme (ACE) inhibitors and diuretics (e.g., furosemide) may be diminished when administered concurrently with NSAIDs.

Instructions for Use

Doses are based on clinical investigations in dogs with arthritis. Dogs may receive carprofen either once daily or twice daily with similar effectiveness. The only approved dose for cats is 4 mg/kg as a one-time injection for surgical pain. However, for long-term use, pharmacokinetic extrapolations suggest a long-term dose of 0.5 mg/kg q24h PO. Long-term safety at this dose has not been established.

Patient Monitoring and Laboratory Tests

After administration has begun, one should monitor hepatic enzymes for evidence of drug-induced hepatic toxicity approximately 7-14 days after treatment has started. If liver enzymes are elevated, discontinue the medication and contact the drug manufacturer.

Formulations

Carprofen is available in 25, 75, and 100 mg caplets; 25, 75 and 100 mg chewable tablets; and injectable solution: 50 mg/mL.
(Zinecarp injection has been available in Europe.)

Stability and Storage

Store in tightly sealed container, protected from light, and at room temperature. Stability of compounded formulations has not been evaluated.

Small Animal Dosage

Dogs

- 2.2 mg/kg, q12h PO or 4.4 mg/kg q24h PO.
- 2.2 mg/kg q12h SQ or 4.4 mg/kg q24h SQ.

Cats

- 4 mg/kg given once by injection or 0.5 mg/kg q24h PO for long-term use.

Large Animal Dosage

Carprofen is not approved in large animals; safety and efficacy studies have not been published.

Horses

- 0.7 mg/kg q24h IV.

Cattle

- 0.7 mg/kg q24h IV.

Regulatory Information

Extralabel use in animals intended for food. Caution is advised when considering carprofen for cattle, because it has a longer half-life in cows compared to other animals (30-40 hours).
RCI Classification: 4

Carvedilol

kar-ved′ih-lole

Trade and Other Names: Coreg

Functional Classification: Antiarrhythmic

Pharmacology and Mechanism of Action

Antiarrhythmic. Nonselective beta-receptor blocker. Carvedilol blocks both $beta_1$-receptors and $beta_2$-receptors in heart and other tissues. Carvedilol is unique because it also has alpha-receptor blocking properties that will produce vasodilation. It also is reported to have antioxidant properties.

In dogs the half-life is short (1.5 hrs) and oral absorption is low and variable because of high first pass effects. Average oral absorption in one study was 19%, but highly variable, but in another study was only 1.6% (range 0.4% to 54%), making the oral use of carvedilol in dogs unpredictable.

Indications and Clinical Uses

Carvedilol is used to treat arrhythmias in animals. It is used to treat systemic hypertension and to block beta-cardiac receptors in animals with rapid heart rates. Efficacy has been based on anecdotal accounts, extrapolation from humans, and limited studies in healthy dogs. In healthy dogs, 0.2 mg/kg PO decreased heart rate and 0.4 mg/kg PO decreased heart rate *and* lowered blood pressure. At 0.4 mg/kg, the effects in healthy dogs persisted for 36 hours. Because oral absorption is inconsistent in dogs (discussed in pharmacology section), the response may be variable. Elimination is rapid after oral administration to dogs, but clinical pharmacodynamic effects may persist for up to 12 hours.

Precautionary Information

Adverse Reactions and Side Effects

Bradycardia can occur resulting from beta-receptor blockade. Carvedilol increases risk of myocardial depression and decreased cardiac output. Adverse effects from nonselective beta-receptor blockade are possible in other tissues.

Contraindications and Precautions

Use carefully in patients with limited cardiac reserve. Do not administer to dehydrated or hypotensive animals. Use carefully in patients with respiratory disease as the $beta_2$-blocking properties can worsen bronchoconstriction.

Drug Interactions

Use with other beta-blockers will increase its effect. Do not administer with other drugs that may cause hypotension.

Instructions for Use

Doses in dogs established through clinical experience and limited trials. In a dose titration study in dogs, the effective dose was 0.2-0.4 mg/kg q24h, PO.

Patient Monitoring and Laboratory Tests

Monitor patient's heart rate and rhythm carefully during treatment. During initial phase of dosing, monitor patients for worsening of heart failure.

Formulations

Carvedilol is available in 3.125, 6.25, 12.5, and 25 mg tablets.

Stability and Storage

Store in tightly sealed container, protected from light, and at room temperature. Carvedilol is not soluble in water. Stability of compounded formulations has not been evaluated.

Small Animal Dosage

Dogs

- Initial recommendations published were 0.2 mg/kg q24h PO, followed by gradually titrating dose up to q12h, followed by increases up to a maximum of 0.4 mg/kg q12h. More recent evidence suggests a dose of 1.5 mg/kg q12h PO.

Cats

Dose not established.

Large Animal Dosage

No dose has been reported for large animals.

Regulatory Information

No regulatory information is available. For extralabel use withdrawal interval estimates, contact FARAD at 1-888-USFARAD (1-888-873-2723) or send e-mail to FARAD@ncsu.edu.

RCI Classification: 3

Cascara Sagrada

kass-kar'ah sah-grah'dah

Trade and Other Names: Nature's Remedy and generic brands

Functional Classification: Laxative

Pharmacology and Mechanism of Action

Stimulant cathartic. Action is believed to be by local stimulation of bowel motility.

Indications and Clinical Uses

Laxative used to treat constipation or evacuate bowel for procedures.

Precautionary Information

Adverse Reactions and Side Effects

Overuse can cause electrolyte losses.

Contraindications and Precautions

Do not use in cases where there may be intestinal obstruction.

Drug Interactions

No drug interactions are reported in animals.

Instructions for Use

Available in various OTC products.

Patient Monitoring and Laboratory Tests

Monitor electrolytes with chronic therapy.

Formulations

Cascara sagrada is available in 100 and 325 mg tablets.

Stability and Storage

Store in tightly sealed container, protected from light, and at room temperature. Stability of compounded formulations has not been evaluated.

Small Animal Dosage

Dogs
- 1-5 mg/kg/day PO.

Cats
- 1-2 mg/cat/day PO.

Large Animal Dosage

No dose has been reported for large animals.

Regulatory Information

Do not administer to animals intended for food.

Castor Oil

kas'tar oil

Trade and Other Names: Generic brands

Functional Classification: Laxative

Pharmacology and Mechanism of Action

Stimulant cathartic. Action is believed to be by local stimulation of bowel motility.

Indications and Clinical Uses

Castor oil is used as laxative to treat constipation or evacuate bowel for procedures.

Precautionary Information

Adverse Reactions and Side Effects

Overuse can cause electrolyte losses. Castor oil has been known to stimulate premature labor in pregnancy.

Contraindications and Precautions

Do not use in pregnant animals. It may induce labor.

Drug Interactions

No drug interactions are reported in animals.

Instructions for Use

Use in animals is strictly empirical. It is available as an OTC product. Pet owners should be discouraged from repeated administration to pets.

Patient Monitoring and Laboratory Tests

No specific monitoring is necessary.

Formulations

Castor oil is available in an oral liquid (100%).

Stability and Storage

Store in tightly sealed container, protected from light, and at room temperature. Stability of compounded formulations has not been evaluated.

Small Animal Dosage

Dogs
- 8-30 mL/day PO.

Cats
- 4-10 mL/day PO.

Large Animal Dosage

No dose has been reported for large animals.

Regulatory Information

No regulatory information is available.

Cefaclor

sef'ah-klor

Trade and Other Names: Ceclor

Functional Classification: Antibacterial

Pharmacology and Mechanism of Action

Cephalosporin antibiotic. Action is similar to other beta-lactam antibiotics, which inhibits synthesis of bacterial cell wall leading to cell death. Cephalosporins are divided into first-, second-, third-, and fourth-generation drugs depending on spectrum of activity. Cefaclor, like other second-generation cephalosporins, is more active against gram-negative bacteria and has been used to treat infections caused by bacteria resistant to first-generation drugs.

Indications and Clinical Uses

Cefaclor is not used commonly in veterinary medicine. However, it may be indicated for treatment of infections caused by bacteria that are resistant to first-generation cephalosporins. Although it has been used as oral therapy, efficacy availability is not available for dogs or cats.

Precautionary Information

Adverse Reactions and Side Effects

All cephalosporins are generally safe, however, sensitivity can occur in individuals (allergy). Rare bleeding disorders have been known to occur with some cephalosporins.

Contraindications and Precautions

Do not use in animals with allergic sensitivity to other beta-lactams, especially other cephalosporins. However, the incidence of cross sensitivity between penicillins and cephalosporins is small (<10% in people). Some cephalosporins should not be used in animals with bleeding problems or that are receiving warfarin anticoagulants. These cephalosporins are those that have an N-methylthiotetrazole (NMTT) side chain and include cefotetan, cefamandole, and cefoperazone.

Drug Interactions

No drug interactions are reported in animals. However, do not mix with other drugs in a compounded formulation, because inactivation may result.

Instructions for Use

Used primarily when resistance has been demonstrated to first-generation cephalosporins.

Patient Monitoring and Laboratory Tests

Susceptibility testing: CLSI (NCCLS) break point for sensitive organisms is less than or equal to 8 mcg/mL for all organisms.

Formulations

Cefaclor is available in 250 and 500 mg capsules and 25 mg/mL oral suspension.

Stability and Storage

Store in tightly sealed container, protected from light, and at room temperature. Stability of compounded formulations has not been evaluated.

Small Animal Dosage

Dogs

- 15-20 mg/kg q8h PO.

Cats

- 15-20 mg/kg q8h PO.

Large Animal Dosage

No dose has been reported for large animals.

Regulatory Information

Withdrawal times are not established for animals that produce food. However, because of relatively short plasma half-life, residues should not be a risk. For extralabel use withdrawal interval estimates, contact FARAD at 1-888-USFARAD (1-888-873-2723) or send e-mail to FARAD@ncsu.edu.

Cefadroxil

sef-ah-drox'il

Trade and Other Names: Cefa-Tabs and Cefa-Drops (veterinary preparation) and Duricef and generic (human preparation)

Functional Classification: Antibacterial

Pharmacology and Mechanism of Action

Cephalosporin antibiotic. Action is similar to other beta-lactam antibiotics, which inhibits synthesis of bacterial cell wall leading to cell death. Cephalosporins are divided into first-, second-, third-, and fourth-generation drugs depending on spectrum of activity. Cefadroxil is a first-generation cephalosporin. Like other first-generation cephalosporins, it is active against *Streptococcus* and *Staphylococcus* species and some gram-negative bacilli, such as *Pasteurella, Escherichia coli,* and *Klebsiella pneumoniae.* However, resistance is common among gram-negative bacteria. It is not active against *Pseudomonas aeruginosa.* Methicillin-resistant *Staphylococcus aureus* (MRSA) and *Staphylococcus* resistant to oxacillin will be resistant to first-generation cephalosporins.

Indications and Clinical Uses

Like other first-generation cephalosporins, it is indicated for treating common infections in animals, including UTIs, soft tissue infections, pyoderma and other dermal infections, and pneumonia. Efficacy against infections caused by anaerobic bacteria is unpredictable.

Precautionary Information

Adverse Reactions and Side Effects

All cephalosporins are generally safe, however sensitivity can occur in individuals (allergy). Rare bleeding disorders have been known to occur with some cephalosporins. Cefadroxil has been known to cause vomiting after oral administration in dogs. Some estimates show that this can occur in as many as 10% of treated dogs.

Contraindications and Precautions

Do not use in animals with allergic sensitivity to other beta-lactams, especially other cephalosporins. However, the incidence of cross sensitivity between penicillins and cephalosporins is small (<10% in people). Some cephalosporins should not be used in animals with bleeding problems or that are receiving warfarin anticoagulants. These cephalosporins are those that have an N-methylthiotetrazole (NMTT) side chain and include cefotetan, cefamandole, and cefoperazone.

Drug Interactions

No drug interactions are reported in animals. However, do not mix with other drugs in a compounded formulation, because inactivation may result.

Instructions for Use

Spectrum of cefadroxil is similar to other first-generation cephalosporins. For susceptibility test, use cephalothin as test drug.

Patient Monitoring and Laboratory Tests

Susceptibility testing: CLSI (NCCLS) break point for sensitive organisms is less than or equal to 8 mcg/mL for all organisms. Cephalothin is used as a marker to test for sensitivity to cephalexin, cefadroxil, and cephradine.

Formulations

Cefadroxil is available in 50 mg/mL oral suspension and 50, 100, 200, 1000 mg tablets for veterinary use. However, availability of veterinary-labeled tablets has been inconsistent. It is also available in 500 mg capsules and 25, 50, and 100 mg/mL suspension for human use.

Stability and Storage

Store in tightly sealed container, protected from light, and at room temperature. Stability of compounded formulations has not been evaluated. Avoid moisture to prevent hydrolysis.

Suspension is stable for 14 days refrigerated and 10 days at room temperature. Stability of compounded formulations has not been evaluated.

Small Animal Dosage

Dogs

- 22 mg/kg q12h PO, up to 30 mg/kg q12h PO.

Cats

- 22 mg/kg q24h PO.

Large Animal Dosage

Foals

- 30 mg/kg q12h PO. Note: Oral absorption is adequate only in foals and not in adults or ruminants.

Regulatory Information

Withdrawal times are not established for animals that produce food. However, because of relatively short plasma half-life, residues should not be a risk. For extralabel use withdrawal interval estimates, contact FARAD at 1-888-USFARAD (1-888-873-2723) or send e-mail to FARAD@ncsu.edu.

Cefazolin Sodium

sef-ah'zoe-lin so'dee-um

Trade and Other Names: Ancef, Kefzol, and generic brands

Functional Classification: Antibacterial

Pharmacology and Mechanism of Action

Cephalosporin antibiotic. Action is similar to other beta-lactam antibiotics, which inhibits synthesis of bacterial cell wall leading to cell death. Cephalosporins are divided into first-, second-, third-, and fourth-generation drugs depending on spectrum of activity. Cefazolin is a first-generation cephalosporin. Like other first-generation cephalosporins, it is active against *Streptococcus* and *Staphylococcus* species and some gram-negative bacilli, such as *Pasteurella, Escherichia coli,* and *Klebsiella pneumoniae.* The difference between cefazolin and other first generation cephalosporins is that it is slightly more active against gram-negative *Enterobacteriaceae,* and its spectrum resembles some second-generation drugs. Nevertheless, resistance is common among gram-negative bacteria. It is not active against *Pseudomonas aeruginosa.* Methicillin-resistant *Staphylococcus aureus* and *Staphylococcus* resistant to oxacillin will be resistant to first-generation cephalosporins.

Indications and Clinical Uses

Like other first-generation cephalosporins, it is indicated for treating common infections in animals, including UTIs, soft tissue infections, pyoderma and other dermal infections, and pneumonia. Efficacy against infections caused by anaerobic bacteria is unpredictable. Cefazolin, because it is injectable, is the most common drug to be administered prophylactically, prior to surgery.

Precautionary Information

Adverse Reactions and Side Effects

All cephalosporins are generally safe; however sensitivity can occur in individuals (allergy). Rare bleeding disorders have been known to occur with some cephalosporins, however, bleeding problems have not been observed from cefazolin. Some cephalosporins have caused seizures, but this is a rare problem.

Contraindications and Precautions

Do not use in animals with allergic sensitivity to other beta-lactams, especially other cephalosporins. However, the incidence of cross sensitivity between penicillins and cephalosporins is small (<10% in people). Some cephalosporins should not be used in animals with bleeding problems or that are receiving warfarin anticoagulants. These cephalosporins are those that have an N-methylthiotetrazole (NMTT) side chain and include cefotetan, cefamandole, and cefoperazone.

Drug Interactions

No drug interactions are reported in animals. However, do not mix in a vial or syringe with other drugs, because inactivation may result.

Instructions for Use

Cefazolin is a commonly used first-generation cephalosporin as injectable drug for prophylaxis for surgery as well as acute therapy for serious infections. Use cephalothin to test susceptibility.

Patient Monitoring and Laboratory Tests

Susceptibility testing: CLSI (NCCLS) break point for sensitive organisms is less than or equal to 8 mcg/mL for all organisms.

Formulations

Cefazolin is available in 50 and 100 mg/50 mL for injection.

Stability and Storage

Store in tightly sealed container, protected from light, and at room temperature. If slight yellow discoloration occurs, the solution is still stable. After reconstitution, it is stable for 24 hours at room temperature and 14 days refrigerated. Stable if frozen for 3 months.

Small Animal Dosage

Dogs and Cats

- 20-35 mg/kg q8h IV or IM.
- Constant rate infusion (CRI): 1.3 mg/kg loading dose, followed by 1.2 mg/kg/hr.
- Perisurgical use: 22 mg/kg IV every 2 hours during surgery.

Large Animal Dosage

Horses

- 25 mg/kg q6-8h IM or IV.

Regulatory Information

Withdrawal times are not established for animals that produce food. However, because of relatively short plasma half-life, residues should not be a risk. For extralabel use withdrawal interval estimates, contact FARAD at 1-888-USFARAD (1-888-873-2723) or send e-mail to FARAD@ncsu.edu.

Cefdinir

sef'dih-neer

Trade and Other Names: Omnicef

Functional Classification: Antibacterial

Pharmacology and Mechanism of Action

Cephalosporin antibiotic. Action is similar to other beta-lactam antibiotics, which inhibits synthesis of bacterial cell wall leading to cell death. Cephalosporins are divided into first-, second-, third-, and fourth-generation drugs depending on spectrum of activity. It is an oral third-generation cephalosporin and is active against staphylococci and many gram-negative bacilli.

Indications and Clinical Uses

Cefdinir is an oral third-generation cephalosporin used in people. However, its use in animals has not been reported. It has potential efficacy for infections of the skin, soft tissues, and urinary tract, however, in most instances cefpodoxime proxetil may be substituted instead.

Precautionary Information

Adverse Reactions and Side Effects

All cephalosporins are generally safe, however, sensitivity can occur in individuals (allergy). Rare bleeding disorders have been known to occur with some cephalosporins.

Contraindications and Precautions

Do not use in animals with allergic sensitivity to other beta-lactams, especially other cephalosporins. However, the incidence of cross sensitivity between penicillins and cephalosporins is small (<10% in people). Some cephalosporins should not be used in animals with bleeding problems or that are receiving warfarin anticoagulants. These cephalosporins are those that have an N-methylthiotetrazole (NMTT) side chain and include cefotetan, cefamandole, and cefoperazone.

Drug Interactions

No drug interactions are reported in animals. However, do not mix with other drugs in a compounded formulation, because inactivation may result.

Instructions for Use

Use in veterinary medicine has not been reported. Use and doses are extrapolated from human preparations.

Patient Monitoring and Laboratory Tests

Susceptibility testing: CLSI (NCCLS) break point for sensitive organisms is less than or equal to 2 mcg/mL for all organisms.

Formulations

Cefdinir is available in 300 mg capsules and 25 mg/mL oral suspension.

Stability and Storage

Store in tightly sealed container, protected from light, and at room temperature. Stability of compounded formulations has not been evaluated.

Small Animal Dosage

Dogs and Cats

Dose not established. Human dose is 7 mg/kg q12h PO.

Large Animal Dosage

No dose has been reported for large animals.

Regulatory Information

Withdrawal times are not established for animals that produce food. However, because of relatively short plasma half-life, residues should not be a risk. For extralabel use withdrawal interval estimates, contact FARAD at 1-888-USFARAD (1-888-873-2723) or send e-mail to FARAD@ncsu.edu.

Cefepime

sef'ah-peem

Trade and Other Names: Maxipime

Functional Classification: Antibacterial

Pharmacology and Mechanism of Action

Antibacterial drug of the cephalosporin class. Action against bacterial cell walls is similar to other cephalosporins. Cefepime is one of the fourth-generation cephalosporins. It has an enhanced, extended spectrum that is beyond that of the older cephalosporins. Its activity includes gram-positive cocci and gram-negative bacilli. It has been active against organisms resistant to other beta-lactams such as *Escherichia coli* and *Klebsiella*. It is active against most *Pseudomonas aeruginosa*. It is not active against methicillin-resistant staphylococci, *Bacteroides fragilis*, or penicillin-resistant enterococci.

Indications and Clinical Uses

Cefepime is a fourth-generation cephalosporin. Although it has a broader spectrum than other cephalosporins, the use has been limited in veterinary medicine. Experimental studies have been conducted in foals, adult horses, and dogs to establish doses, but reports of efficacy are not available.

Precautionary Information

Adverse Reactions and Side Effects

Cefepime is generally safe. However, consider the same side effects as for other cephalosporins, which include the possibility of bleeding disorders, allergy, vomiting, and diarrhea.

Contraindications and Precautions

Do not administer to patients with sensitivity or allergy to cephalosporins. Reduce dose to less frequent intervals (e.g., every 12 hours or every 24 hours) in patients with renal failure.

Drug Interactions

No drug interactions are reported in animals. However, do not mix in a vial or syringe with other drugs, because inactivation may result.

Instructions for Use

Reconstitute with sterile water, sodium chloride, and 5% dextrose. It may be reconstituted with 1% lidocaine if pain from injection is a problem. Reconstituted solutions are stable for 24 hours at room temperature and 7 days in the refrigerator. Do not mix with other injectable antibiotics. Injection vials also contain L-arginine.

Patient Monitoring and Laboratory Tests

Susceptibility testing: CLSI (NCCLS) break point for sensitive organisms is less than or equal to 8 mcg/mL for all organisms.

Formulations

Cefepime is available in 500 mg, 1 g, and 2 g vials for injection

Stability and Storage

Store in tightly sealed container, protected from light, and at room temperature. Observe manufacturer's recommendations for stability after vial is reconstituted.

Small Animal Dosage

Dogs

- 40 mg/kg q6h IM or IV.
- Contstant rate infusion (CRI): 1.4 mg/kg loading dose, followed by 1.1 mg/kg/hr.

Large Animal Dosage

Foals

• 11 mg/kg q8h IV.

Regulatory Information

Withdrawal times are not established for animals that produce food. However, because of relatively short plasma half-life, residues should not be a risk. For extralabel use withdrawal interval estimates, contact FARAD at 1-888-USFARAD (1-888-873-2723) or send e-mail to FARAD@ncsu.edu.

Cefixime

sef-iks′eem

Trade and Other Names: Suprax

Functional Classification: Antibacterial

Pharmacology and Mechanism of Action

Cephalosporin antibiotic. Action is similar to other beta-lactam antibiotics, which inhibits synthesis of bacterial cell wall leading to cell death. Cephalosporins are divided into first-, second-, third-, and fourth-generation drugs depending on spectrum of activity. Consult package insert or specific reference for spectrum of activity of individual cephalosporin. Cefixime is a third-generation cephalosporin.

Indications and Clinical Uses

Cefixime is one of the few oral third-generation cephalosporins. It has been administered orally in dogs and cats to treat infections of the skin, soft tissues, and urinary tract. It is not as active as cefpodoxime against *Staphylococcus.* In most instances cefpodoxime proxetil may be substituted instead.

Precautionary Information

Adverse Reactions and Side Effects

All cephalosporins are generally safe, however sensitivity can occur in individuals (allergy). Rare bleeding disorders have been known to occur with some cephalosporins.

Contraindications and Precautions

Do not use in animals with allergic sensitivity to other beta-lactams, especially other cephalosporins. However, the incidence of cross sensitivity between penicillins and cephalosporins is small (<10% in people). Some cephalosporins should not be used in animals with bleeding problems or that are receiving warfarin anticoagulants. These cephalosporins are those that have an N-methylthiotetrazole (NMTT) side chain and include cefotetan, cefamandole, and cefoperazone.

Drug Interactions

No drug interactions are reported in animals. However, do not mix with other drugs in a compounded formulation, because inactivation may result.

Instructions for Use

Although not approved for veterinary use, pharmacokinetic studies in dogs have provided recommended doses. Note that break point for sensitivity is lower than for other cephalosporins, indicating that organisms tested as sensitive to other cephalosporins, may not be sensitive to cefixime.

Patient Monitoring and Laboratory Tests

Susceptibility testing: CLSI (NCCLS) break point for sensitive organisms is less than or equal to 1 mcg/mL for all organisms.

Formulations

Cefixime is available in 20 mg/mL oral suspension and 200 and 400 mg tablets. (Availability of commercial forms of cefixime has been inconsistent.)

Stability and Storage

Store in tightly sealed container, protected from light, and at room temperature. Stability of compounded formulations has not been evaluated.

Small Animal Dosage

Dogs and Cats

- 10 mg/kg q12h PO.
- Cystitis: 5 mg/kg q12-24h PO.

Large Animal Dosage

No dose has been reported for large animals.

Regulatory Information

Withdrawal times are not established for animals that produce food. However, because of relatively short plasma half-life, residues should not be a risk. For extralabel use withdrawal interval estimates, contact FARAD at 1-888-USFARAD (1-888-873-2723) or send e-mail to FARAD@ncsu.edu.

Cefotaxime Sodium

sef-oh-taks′eem so′dee-um

Trade and Other Names: Claforan

Functional Classification: Antibacterial

Pharmacology and Mechanism of Action

Cephalosporin antibiotic. Action is similar to other beta-lactam antibiotics, which inhibits synthesis of bacterial cell wall leading to cell death. Cephalosporins are divided into first-, second-, third-, and fourth-generation drugs depending on spectrum of activity. Cefotaxime is a third-generation cephalosporin. Like other third-generation cephalosporins, it has enhanced activity against gram-negative bacilli, especially *Enterobacteriaceae*, which may be resistant to first- and second-generation cephalosporins, ampicillin derivatives, and other drugs. It is active against *Escherichia coli, Klebsiella pneumoniae, Enterobacteriaceae, Pasteurella* species, and *Salmonella* species, among others. It is generally not active against *Pseudomonas aeruginosa*. It is active against streptococci, but *Staphylococcus* species are less sensitive. All methicillin-resistant strains of staphylococci will be resistant. Activity against anaerobic bacteria is unpredictable.

Indications and Clinical Uses

Cefotaxime is used when resistance is encountered to other antibiotics or when infection is in CNS. Because it is injectable, expensive, and must be administered frequently, it is not used for routine infections in veterinary medicine when other drugs will be active.

Precautionary Information

Adverse Reactions and Side Effects

All cephalosporins are generally safe, however, sensitivity can occur in individuals (allergy). Rare bleeding disorders have been known to occur with some cephalosporins.

Contraindications and Precautions

Do not use in animals with allergic sensitivity to other beta-lactams, especially other cephalosporins. However, the incidence of cross sensitivity between penicillins and cephalosporins is small (<10% in people). Some cephalosporins should not be used in animals with bleeding problems or that are receiving warfarin anticoagulants. These cephalosporins are those that have an N-methylthiotetrazole (NMTT) side chain and include cefotetan, cefamandole, and cefoperazone.

Drug Interactions

No drug interactions are reported in animals. However, do not mix in a vial or syringe with other drugs, because inactivation may result.

Instructions for Use

Third-generation cephalosporin is used when resistance encountered to first- and second-generation cephalosporins.

Patient Monitoring and Laboratory Tests

Susceptibility testing: CLSI (NCCLS) break point for sensitive organisms is less than or equal to 8 mcg/mL for all organisms.

Formulations

Cefotaxime is available in 500 mg and 1, 2, and 10 g vials for injection.

Stability and Storage

Store in tightly sealed container, protected from light, and at room temperature. Maximum stability is at pH of 5-7. Do not mix with alkalilne solutions. Yellow or amber color does not indicate instability. After reconstitution, cefotaxime is stable for 12 hours at room temperature; 5 days when stored in plastic syringes or a vial if kept in refrigerator. It is stable for 13 weeks if frozen. IV solutions in 1000 mL are stable for 24 hrs at room temperature or 5 days in refrigerator. Do not re-freeze.

Small Animal Dosage

Dogs

- 50 mg/kg q12h IV, IM, or SQ.
- Contstant rate infusion (CRI): 3.2 mg/kg loading dose, followed by 5 mg/kg/hr.

Cats

- 20-80 mg/kg q6h IV or IM.

Large Animal Dosage

Foals

- 40 mg/kg q6h IV.

Regulatory Information

Withdrawal times are not established for animals that produce food. However, because of relatively short plasma half-life, residues should not be a risk. For extralabel use withdrawal interval estimates, contact FARAD at 1-888-USFARAD (1-888-873-2723) or send e-mail to FARAD@ncsu.edu.

Cefotetan Disodium

sef′oh-tee-tan dye-soe′dee-um

Trade and Other Names: Cefotan

Functional Classification: Antibacterial

Pharmacology and Mechanism of Action

Cephalosporin antibiotic. Action is similar to other beta-lactam antibiotics, which inhibits synthesis of bacterial cell wall leading to cell death. Cephalosporins are divided into first-, second-, third-, and fourth-generation drugs depending on spectrum of activity. Cefotetan is second-generation cephalosporin. Cefotetan is in the cephamycin group of cephalosporins, which have greater stability against the beta-lactamases of anaerobic bacteria such as those of the *Bacteroides* group. It is slightly more active (lower minimum inhibitory concentration [MIC] values) compared to cefoxitin against many bacteria.

Indications and Clinical Uses

Cefotetan, a second-generation cephalosporin of the cephamycin group has greater activity against anaerobic bacteria and gram-negative bacilli than other cephalosporins. Therefore, it has been used to treat infections in dogs and cats in which enteric gram-negative bacilli or anaerobes are suspected, including abdominal infections, soft tissue wounds, and prior to surgery.

Precautionary Information

Adverse Reactions and Side Effects

All cephalosporins are generally safe, however, sensitivity can occur in individuals (allergy). Rare bleeding disorders have been known to occur with some cephalosporins.

Contraindications and Precautions

Do not use in animals with allergic sensitivity to other beta-lactams, especially other cephalosporins. However, the incidence of cross sensitivity between penicillins and cephalosporins is small (<10% in people). Some cephalosporins should not be used in animals with bleeding problems or that are receiving warfarin anticoagulants. These cephalosporins are those that have an N-methylthiotetrazole (NMTT) side chain and include cefotetan, cefamandole, and cefoperazone.

Drug Interactions

No drug interactions are reported in animals. However, do not mix in a vial or syringe with other drugs, because inactivation may result.

Instructions for Use

Second-generation cephalosporin similar to cefoxitin but may have longer half-life in dogs.

Patient Monitoring and Laboratory Tests

Susceptibility testing: CLSI (NCCLS) break point for sensitive organisms is less than or equal to 16 mcg/mL for all organisms.

Formulations

Cefotetan is available in 1, 2, and 10 g vials for injection.

Stability and Storage

Store in tightly sealed container, protected from light, and at room temperature. Observe manufacturer's recommendations for stability after vial is reconstituted.

Small Animal Dosage

Dogs and Cats

- 30 mg/kg q8h IV or SQ.

Large Animal Dosage

No dose has been reported for large animals.

Regulatory Information

Withdrawal times are not established for animals that produce food. However, because of relatively short plasma half-life, residues should not be a risk. For extralabel use withdrawal interval estimates, contact FARAD at 1-888-USFARAD (1-888-873-2723) or send e-mail to FARAD@ncsu.edu.

Cefoxitin Sodium

se-fox'ih-tin soe'dee-um

Trade and Other Names: Mefoxin

Functional Classification: Antibacterial

Pharmacology and Mechanism of Action

Cephalosporin antibiotic. Action is similar to other beta-lactam antibiotics, which inhibits synthesis of bacterial cell wall leading to cell death. Cephalosporins are divided into first-, second-, third-, and fourth-generation drugs depending on spectrum of activity. Consult package insert or specific reference for spectrum of activity of individual cephalosporin. Cefoxitin is a second-generation cephalosporin. Cefoxitin is in the cephamycin group of cephalosporins, which have greater stability against the beta-lactamases of anaerobic bacteria such as those of the Bacteroides group.

Indications and Clinical Uses

Cefoxitin, a second-generation cephalosporin of the cephamycin group has greater activity against anaerobic bacteria and gram-negative bacilli than other cephalosporins. Therefore, it has been used to treat infections in dogs and cats in which enteric gram-negative bacilli or anaerobes are suspected, including abdominal infections, soft tissue wounds, and prior to surgery.

Precautionary Information

Adverse Reactions and Side Effects

All cephalosporins are generally safe, however, sensitivity can occur in individuals (allergy). Rare bleeding disorders have been known to occur with some cephalosporins.

Contraindications and Precautions

Do not use in animals with allergic sensitivity to other beta-lactams, especially other cephalosporins. However, the incidence of cross sensitivity between penicillins and cephalosporins is small (<10% in people). Some cephalosporins should not be used in animals with bleeding problems or that are receiving warfarin anticoagulants. These cephalosporins are those that have an N-methylthiotetrazole (NMTT) side chain and include cefotetan, cefamandole, and cefoperazone.

Drug Interactions

No drug interactions are reported in animals. However, do not mix in a vial or syringe with other drugs, because inactivation may result.

Instructions for Use

Second-generation cephalosporin is often used when activity against anaerobic bacteria is desired.

Patient Monitoring and Laboratory Tests

Susceptibility testing: CLSI (NCCLS) break point for sensitive organisms is less than or equal to 8 mcg/mL for all organisms.

Formulations

Cefoxitin is available in 1, 2, and 10 g vials for injection.

Stability and Storage

Store in tightly sealed container, protected from light, and at room temperature. Observe manufacturer's recommendations for stability after vial is reconstituted.

Small Animal Dosage

Dogs and Cats

- 30 mg/kg q6-8h IV.

Large Animal Dosage

Calves and Horses

- 20 mg/kg q4-6h IV or IM.

Regulatory Information

Withdrawal times are not established for animals that produce food. However, because of relatively short plasma half-life, residues should not be a risk. For extralabel use withdrawal interval estimates, contact FARAD at 1-888-USFARAD (1-888-873-2723) or send e-mail to FARAD@ncsu.edu.

Cefpodoxime Proxetil

sef-poe-doks'eem prahx'ih-til

Trade and Other Names: Simplicef (veterinary preparation) and Vantin (human preparation)

Functional Classification: Antibacterial

Pharmacology and Mechanism of Action

Cephalosporin antibiotic. Action is similar to other beta-lactam antibiotics, which inhibits synthesis of bacterial cell wall leading to cell death. Cephalosporins are divided into first-, second-, third-, and fourth-generation drugs depending on spectrum of activity. Cefpodoxime is a third-generation cephalosporin, which indicates greater activity against gram-negative bacilli compared to first-generation cephalosporins. It is one of the three currently available third-generation oral cephalosporins. It is combined with proxetil to produce an ester to improve oral absorption. Therefore, as the ester, it is actually a pro-drug that needs to be converted to the active cefpodoxime. Oral absorption in dogs is approximately 63%. Half-life is 7.2 hours in horses and 5.6 hours in dogs.

Indications and Clinical Uses

Cefpodoxime is indicated for treatment of skin and other soft-tissue infections in dogs caused by susceptible organisms. Cefpodoxime has greater activity against gram-negative bacilli than first-generation cephalosporins, therefore may be effective for some gram-negative infections. Although not currently registered for treatment of UTIs, approximately 50% of administered dose is excreted in urine and expected to be active for treating UTIs caused by common pathogens. Although not registered for cats, or tested in cats, no adverse effects have been reported from occasional use.

Precautionary Information

Adverse Reactions and Side Effects

All cephalosporins are generally safe, however, sensitivity can occur in individuals (allergy). Rare bleeding disorders have been known to occur with some cephalosporins.

Contraindications and Precautions

This drug is best taken with food to improve oral absorption. Do not use in animals with allergic sensitivity to other beta-lactams, especially other cephalosporins. However, the incidence of cross sensitivity between penicillins and cephalosporins is small (<10% in people). Some cephalosporins should not be used in animals with bleeding problems or that are receiving warfarin anticoagulants. These cephalosporins are those that have an N-methylthiotetrazole (NMTT) side chain and include cefotetan, cefamandole, and cefoperazone.

Drug Interactions

There are no important drug interactions, except that oral absorption in people of cefpodoxime is inhibited by H_2 blockers (e.g., cimetidine and ranitidine) and antacids, which can decrease oral absorption by 30%. Cephalosporins may be administered with other antibiotics to increase the spectrum of activity and produce a synergistic effect. However, do not mix with other drugs in a compounded formulation, because inactivation may result.

Instructions for Use

Registration in dogs includes skin and UTI, although based on spectrum and tissue distribution, it has been used for other infections. There has also been occasional use in cats on an extra-label basis. Note that break point for sensitivity is lower than for other cephalosporins, indicating that organisms tested as sensitive to other cephalosporins may not be sensitive to cefpodoxime.

Patient Monitoring and Laboratory Tests

Susceptibility testing: CLSI (NCCLS) break point for sensitive organisms is less than or equal to 2 mcg/mL for all organisms. Strains of *Escherichia coli* and *Klebsiella* that have extended spectrum beta lactamase (ESBL) may be clinically resistant.

C

Formulations

Cefpodoxime proxetil is available in 100 and 200 mg tablets and 10 and 20 mg/mL oral suspension (human preparation).

Stability and Storage

Store in tightly sealed container, protected from light, and at room temperature. Stability of compounded tablets has not been evaluated. Avoid exposure to moisture.

Small Animal Dosage

Dogs

- Skin infections: 5-10 mg/kg q24h PO.
- Treatment of other serious infections: 10 mg/kg q12h.

Cats

A dose has not been established by the manufacturer for cefpodoxime proxetil. Some veterinarians have extrapolated from the canine dose.

Large Animal Dosage

Horses

- 10 mg/kg oral q6-12h. The 12-hour interval is appropriate for *Klebsiella*, *Pasteurella*, and streptococci. More frequent intervals may be needed for more resistant organisms.

Regulatory Information

Withdrawal times are not established for animals that produce food. However, because of relatively short plasma half-life, residues should not be a risk. For extralabel use withdrawal interval estimates, contact FARAD at 1-888-USFARAD (1-888-873-2723) or send e-mail to FARAD@ncsu.edu.

Ceftazidime

sef-tah'zih-deem

Trade and Other Names: Fortaz, Ceptaz, Tazicef, and Tazidime

Functional Classification: Antibacterial

Pharmacology and Mechanism of Action

Cephalosporin antibiotic. Action is similar to other beta-lactam antibiotics, which inhibits synthesis of bacterial cell wall leading to cell death. Cephalosporins are divided into first-, second-, third-, and fourth-generation drugs depending on spectrum of activity. Ceftazidime is a third-generation cephalosporin. In addition to activity against many gram-negative bacilli, ceftazidime has more activity than other cephalosporins against *Pseudomonas aeruginosa*.

Indications and Clinical Uses

Ceftazidime is a third-generation cephalosporin with activity against many gram-negative bacteria resistant to other drugs. Its activity against *P. aeruginosa* distinguishes it from other cephalosporins. Therefore, it has been used to treat infections in dogs and cats in which enteric gram-negative bacilli or *P. aeruginosa* are suspected, including abdominal infections, skin infections, soft tissue wounds, and prior to surgery.

Precautionary Information

Adverse Reactions and Side Effects

All cephalosporins are generally safe, however, sensitivity can occur in individuals (allergy). Rare bleeding disorders have been known to occur with some cephalosporins.

Contraindications and Precautions

Do not use in animals with allergic sensitivity to other beta-lactams, especially other cephalosporins. However, the incidence of cross sensitivity between penicillins and cephalosporins is small (<10% in people). Some cephalosporins should not be used in animals with bleeding problems or that are receiving warfarin anticoagulants. These cephalosporins are those that have a N-methylthiotetrazole (NMTT) side chain and include cefotetan, cefamandole, and cefoperazone.

Drug Interactions

Do not mix in a vial or syringe with other drugs, because inactivation may result. In particular, there may be mutual inactivation if mixed with aminoglycosides. If mixed with vancomycin, precipitation may occur.

Instructions for Use

Ceftazidime may be reconstituted with 1% lidocaine for intramuscular injection to reduce pain. Ceftazidime contains l-arginine. To make up vial of vials containing sodium carbonate, carbon dioxide will form upon reconstitution. Venting may be necessary to release gas. Doses listed for dogs and cats are sufficient for treating infections caused by *P. aeruginosa*.

Patient Monitoring and Laboratory Tests

Susceptibility testing: CLSI (NCCLS) break point for sensitive organisms is less than or equal to 8 mcg/mL for all organisms. Resistance to ceftazidime has been used to test for extended spectrum beta lactamase (ESBL) producing strains of *Escherichia coli* or *Klebsiella*.

Formulations

Ceftazidime is available in 0.5, 1, 2, and 6 g vials reconstituted to 280 mg/mL.

Stability and Storage

Store in tightly sealed container, protected from light, and at room temperature. Slight discoloration to yellow or amber may occur without losing potency. Do not mix in vial with other drugs, but may be mixed with intravenous fluid solutions. After reconstitution, solutions are stable for at least 18 hours at room temperature, or 7 days if refrigerated. Solutions may be frozen at –20° C to retain potency for 3 months. Once thawed, it should not be refrozen. Thawed solutions are stable for 8 hours at room temperature and for 4 hours if refrigerated.

Small Animal Dosage

Dogs and Cats

- 30 mg/kg q6h IV or IM.
- Dogs: 30 mg/kg q4-6h SQ.
- Constant IV infusion: Give loading dose of 1.2 mg/kg, followed by 1.56 mg/kg/hr delivered in IV fluids.

Large Animal Dosage

Horses

- 20 mg/kg q8h IV or IM.

Regulatory Information

Withdrawal times are not established for animals that produce food. However, because of relatively short plasma half-life, residues should not be a risk. For extralabel use withdrawal interval estimates, contact FARAD at 1-888-USFARAD (1-888-873-2723) or send e-mail to FARAD@ncsu.edu.

Ceftiofur Crystalline Free Acid

sef'tee-oh-fer

Trade and Other Names: Excede

Functional Classification: Antibacterial

Pharmacology and Mechanism of Action

Cephalosporin antibiotic. Ceftiofur hydrochloride and ceftiofur sodium have similar action and spectrum. Action is similar to other beta-lactam antibiotics, which inhibits synthesis of bacterial cell wall leading to cell death. Cephalosporins are divided into first-, second-, third-, and fourth-generation drugs depending on spectrum of activity. Ceftiofur most closely resembles the activity of a third generation cephalosporin. It has good activity against most gram-negative bacilli, especially *Enterobacteriaceae.* It has potent activity against bovine and swine respiratory pathogens such as *Mannheimia, Actinobaclllus pleuropneumoniae, Pasteurella multocida, Salmonella choleraesuis, Haemophilus,* and *Streptococcus.* Ceftiofur has activity against some gram-positive cocci, such as streptococci, but activity against *Staphylococcus* is not as high as other cephalosporins. Ceftiofur is metabolized after administration to metabolites such as desfuroylceftiofur, which is active against bacteria.

Indications and Clinical Uses

Ceftioifur crystalline free acid is indicated for treatment of swine respiratory disease (SRD) caused by *A. pleuropneumoniae, P. multocida, S. choleraesuis, Haemophilus parasuis,* and *Streptococcus suis.* In cattle, it is used for treatment of bovine respiratory disease (BRD) caused by *Mannheimia haemolytica, P. multocida, and Histophilus somni* (formerly *Haemophilus somnus*). It also can be administered to control respiratory disease in cattle at high risk of developing BRD associated with *M. haemolytica, P. multocida,* and *H. somnus.* Ceftiofur hydrochloride and ceftiofur crystalline free acid have also been administered extra-label intramammary to dairy cattle. However, there are specific products designed for intramammary use (Spectramast).

Precautionary Information

Adverse Reactions and Side Effects

All cephalosporins are generally safe, however, sensitivity can occur in individuals (allergy). Rare bleeding disorders have been known to occur with some cephalosporins. For ceftiofur, doses that have exceeded the approved label recommendations have caused bone marrow suppression in dogs. Thrombocytopenia and anemia occurred at doses of 6.6 mg/kg and 11 mg/kg when administered to dogs. High doses have caused diarrhea in horses.

Contraindications and Precautions

Do not administer to animals prone to sensitivity to beta-lactams. Do not administer to animals at high doses. Ceftiofur crystalline free acid should not be used interchangeably with ceftiofur sodium or ceftiofur hydrochloride without consulting label information for difference in dosing and withdrawal times.

Drug Interactions

No drug interactions are reported in animals. However, do not mix in a vial or syringe with other drugs, because inactivation may result.

Instructions for Use

Dosing information is available for pigs and cattle; it is not available for other animals. Ceftiofur sodium has been used in horses and dogs but there is no information available on the use of ceftiofur crystalline free acid in these species.

Patient Monitoring and Laboratory Tests

Monitor CBC if high doses are administered for long periods. Sensitivity testing: CLSI (NCCLS) guidelines for susceptible bacteria indicate that susceptible bacteria have minimum inhibitory concentration (MIC) values less than or equal to 2 mcg/mL. (Note that for other cephalosporins, the MIC values for susceptibility are usually less than or equal to 8.0 mcg/mL.)

Formulations

Ceftiofur crystalline freed acid is available in an injectable suspension for cattle at 200 mg/mL ceftiofur equivalents (CE).

Ceftiofur crystalline freed acid is available in an injectable suspension for pigs at 100 mg/mL CE.

Stability and Storage

Store at room temperature. Shake well before administration. Protect from freezing.

Small Animal Dosage

Dogs and Cats

Dose not established for this product. See ceftiofur sodium for small animal dosage.

Large Animal Dosage

Cattle

- 6.6 mg/kg, with a single SQ injection in the middle third of the posterior aspect of the ear.

Pigs

- 5.0 mg/kg IM injection in the postauricular region of the neck.

Regulatory Information

Pig withdrawal times: 14 days.

Cattle withdrawal time (slaughter): 13 days. A withdrawal period has not been established in preruminating calves. Do not use in calves to be processed for veal. Milk withdrawal: Zero days.

Ceftiofur Hydrochloride

sef'tee-oh-fer hye-droe-klor'ide

Trade and Other Names: Excenel

Functional Classification: Antibacterial

Pharmacology and Mechanism of Action

Cephalosporin antibiotic. Ceftiofur hydrochloride and ceftiofur sodium have similar action and spectrum. Action is similar to other beta-lactam antibiotics, which inhibits synthesis of bacterial cell wall leading to cell death. Cephalosporins are divided into first-, second-, third-, and fourth-generation drugs depending on spectrum of activity. Ceftiofur most closely resembles the activity of a third generation cephalosporin. Ceftiofur has good activity against most gram-negative bacilli, especially *Enterobacteriaceae.* It has potent activity against bovine respiratory pathogens such as *Pasteurella multocida, Mannheimia haemolytica*, and *Histophilus somni* (formerly *Haemophilus somnus*). Ceftiofur has activity against some gram-positive cocci, such as streptococci, but activity against *Staphylococcus* is not as high as other cephalosporins. Ceftiofur is metabolized after administration to metabolites such as desfuroylceftiofur, which is active against bacteria. Ceftiofur hydrochloride has been administered intramammary to dairy cattle.

Indications and Clinical Uses

Ceftiofur hydrochloride is used in cattle and pigs for treatment and control of infections caused by susceptible pathogens. It is registered for treatment of respiratory disease in cattle caused by *Mannheimia, P. multocida,* and *H. somni* (formerly *H. somnus*). It is used for interdigital necrobacillosis (foot rot) in cattle caused by *Fusobacterium necrophorum* or *Bacteroides melaninogenicus.* Ceftiofur hydrochloride has been shown to be effective for treatment of acute postpartum metritis in dairy cows when administered at 2.2 mg/kg. Ceftiofur hydrochloride is used for treatment of swine respiratory disease (SRD) caused by *Actinobacillus, P. multocida, Salmonella choleraesuis,* and *Streptococcus suis.* Ceftiofur hydrochloride and ceftiofur crystalline free acid have also been administered via the intramammary route to dairy cattle. For intramammary use, a specific formulation is recommended (Spectramast DC).

Precautionary Information

Adverse Reactions and Side Effects

All cephalosporins are generally safe, however sensitivity can occur in individuals (allergy). Rare bleeding disorders have been known to occur with some cephalosporins. For ceftiofur, doses that have exceeded the approved label recommendations have caused bone marrow suppression in dogs. Thrombocytopenia and anemia occurred at doses of 6.6 mg/kg and 11 mg/kg when administered to dogs. High doses have caused diarrhea in horses.

Contraindications and Precautions

Do not administer to animals prone to sensitivity to beta-lactams. Do not administer to animals at high doses. Ceftiofur hydrochloride is a sterile suspension and should not be used interchangeably with ceftiofur sodium which is a solution.

Drug Interactions

No drug interactions are reported in animals. However, do not mix in a vial or syringe with other drugs, because inactivation may result.

Instructions for Use

Although dosing information is not available for other species, it has been used safely in pigs and cattle. Dose in cattle may be extended beyond 3 days if necessary. Alternatively doses have been administered to cattle for bovine respiratory disease (BRD) at 2.2 mg/kg at 48 hour intervals. Ceftiofur sodium has been used in horses and dogs but there is no information available on the use of ceftiofur hydrochloride in these species.

Patient Monitoring and Laboratory Tests

Monitor CBC if high doses are administered for long periods. Susceptibility testing: CLSI (NCCLS) guidelines for susceptible bacteria indicate that susceptible bacteria have minimum inhibitory concentration (MIC) values less than or equal to 2 mcg/mL. (Note that for other cephalosporins, the MIC values for susceptibility are usually less than or equal to 8.0 mcg/mL.)

Formulations

Ceftiofur hydrochloride is available in 50 mg/mL sterile suspension.

Stability and Storage

Store at room temperature. Shake well before administration. Protect from freezing.

Small Animal Dosage

Dogs and Cats

Dose not established for this product. See ceftiofur sodium for small animal dose.

Large Animal Dosage

Cattle

- 1.1-2.2 mg/kg q24h for 3 days IM or SQ.

Dairy Cows

- Treatment of postpartum metritis: 2.2 mg/kg once daily for 5 days SQ or IM.

Pigs

- 3-5 mg/kg q24h for 3 days IM.

Regulatory Information

Cattle withdrawal time: 0 days for milk; 3 days for meat.
Pig withdrawal time: 4 days.

Ceftiofur Sodium

sef′tee-oh-fer soe′dee-um

Trade and Other Names: Naxcel

Functional Classification: Antibacterial

Pharmacology and Mechanism of Action

Cephalosporin antibiotic. Ceftiofur hydrochloride and ceftiofur sodium have similar action and spectrum. Action is similar to other beta-lactam antibiotics, which inhibits synthesis of bacterial cell wall leading to cell death. Cephalosporins are divided into first-, second-, third-, and fourth-generation drugs depending on spectrum of activity. Ceftiofur most closely resembles the activity of a third generation cephalosporin. Ceftiofur has good activity against most gram-negative bacilli, especially *Enterobacteriaceae*. It has potent activity against bovine and swine respiratory pathogens such as *Mannheimia*, *Actinobacillus pleuropneumoniae*, *Pasteurella multocida*, *Salmonella choleraesuis*, *Haemophilus*, and *Streptococcus*. Ceftiofur has activity against some gram-positive cocci, such as streptococci, but activity against *Staphylococcus* is not as high as other cephalosporins. Ceftiofur is metabolized after administration to metabolites such as desfuroylceftiofur, which is active against bacteria.

Indications and Clinical Uses

Ceftiofur sodium is used in cattle and pigs for treatment and control of infections caused by susceptible pathogens. It is registered for treatment of respiratory disease and interdigital necrobacillosis (foot rot) in lactating cows in many countries. Ceftiofur has been used for treatment of *Salmonella* in calves. At 5 mg/kg q24h IM, it decreased diarrhea and temperature but did not eradicate organism. Ceftiofur sodium has been administered intramammary for treatment of coliform mastitis, but this is an extralabel use. Ceftiofur sodium is used in horses for treatment of streptococcal respiratory infections (registered treatment) as well as extralabel use for treating other infections such as those caused by gram-negative bacilli, including *Escherichia coli*, *Klebsiella pneumoniae*, and *Salmonella*. Higher doses should be used for nonstreptococcal bacteria in horses. Ceftiofur sodium is registered for a daily subcutaneous injection for treatment of UTIs in dogs.

Precautionary Information

Adverse Reactions and Side Effects

All cephalosporins are generally safe, however sensitivity can occur in individuals (allergy). Rare bleeding disorders have been known to occur with some cephalosporins. For ceftiofur, doses that have exceeded the approved label recommendations have caused bone marrow suppression in dogs. Thrombocytopenia and anemia occurred at doses of 6.6 mg/kg and 11 mg/kg when administered to dogs. High doses have caused diarrhea in horses.

Contraindications and Precautions

Do not administer to animals prone to sensitivity to beta-lactams. Do not administer to animals at high doses.

Drug Interactions

No drug interactions are reported in animals. However, do not mix in a vial or syringe with other drugs, because inactivation may result.

Instructions for Use

Although dosing information is not available for other species, it has been used safely in dogs, sheep, pigs, horses, and cattle and is expected to be safe for other animals. To produce active systemic concentrations for infections other than UTIs, the higher dose of 4.4 mg/kg is recommended.

Patient Monitoring and Laboratory Tests

Monitor CBC if high doses are administered for long periods. Susceptibility testing: CLSI (NCCLS) guidelines for susceptible bacteria indicate that susceptible bacteria have minimum inhibitory concentration (MIC) values less than or equal to 2 mcg/mL. (Note that for other cephalosporins, the MIC values for susceptibility are usually less than or equal to 8.0 mcg/mL.)

Formulations

Ceftiofur sodium is available in 50 mg/mL vials for injection.

Stability and Storage

Store in tightly sealed container, protected from light, and at room temperature. After reconstitution, solutions are potent for 7 days if refrigerated and 12 hours at room temperature. If frozen, solutions are stable for 8 weeks. Do not refreeze. Slight discoloration may occur without losing potency.

Small Animal Dosage

Dogs

- UTI: 2.2 to 4.4 mg/kg q24h SQ.

Cats

- Dose not established but has been extrapolated from canine dose.

Large Animal Dosage

Horses

- 2.2-4.4 mg/kg q24h IM or 2.2 mg/kg q12h IM for as long as 10 days. Up to 11 mg/kg/day IM has been given to horses. Treatment of some gram-negative infections may require doses at the higher range.

Cattle

- Bovine respiratory disease (BRD): 1.1-2.2 mg/kg (0.5-1.0 mg/pound) q24h for 3 days IM. Additional doses may be given on days 4 and 5 if necessary.

Pigs

- Respiratory infections: 3-5 mg/kg (1.36-2.27 mg/pound) q24h for 3 days IM.

Sheep and Goats

- 1.1-2.2 mg/kg (0.5-1.0 mg/pound) q24h for 3 days IM. Additional doses may be given on days 4 and 5 if necessary.

Regulatory Information

Cattle and goat withdrawal time: 0 days for milk and 4 days for meat.
Pig withdrawal time: 4 days.

Cephalexin

sef-ah-lex'in

Trade and Other Names: Keflex and generic brands

Functional Classification: Antibacterial

Pharmacology and Mechanism of Action

Cephalosporin antibiotic. Action is similar to other beta-lactam antibiotics, which inhibits synthesis of bacterial cell wall leading to cell death. Cephalosporins are divided into first-, second-, third-, and fourth-generation drugs depending on spectrum of activity. Cephalexin is a first-generation cephalosporin. Like other first-generation cephalosporins, it is active against *Streptococcus* and *Staphylococcus* species and some gram-negative bacilli, such as *Pasteurella, Escherichia coli,* and *Klebsiella pneumoniae*. However, resistance is common among gram-negative bacteria. It is not active against *Pseudomonas aeruginosa. Staphylococcus* spp. resistant to methicillin and oxacillin will be resistant to first-generation cephalosporins.

Indications and Clinical Uses

Like other first-generation cephalosporins, it is indicated for treating common infections in animals, including UTIs, soft tissue infections, pyoderma and other dermal infections, and pneumonia. Although not approved in U.S. for animals, at this time it is registered in other countries, and there are published efficacy studies documenting its effectiveness. Efficacy against infections caused by anaerobic bacteria is unpredictable. In horses, half-life is short at only 1.6 hours and oral absorption is only 5%.

Precautionary Information

Adverse Reactions and Side Effects

All cephalosporins are generally safe, however sensitivity can occur in individuals (allergy). Rare bleeding disorders have been known to occur with some cephalosporins.

Contraindications and Precautions

Do not use in animals with allergic sensitivity to other beta-lactams, especially other cephalosporins. However, the incidence of cross sensitivity between penicillins and cephalosporins is small (<10% in people). Some cephalosporins should not be used in animals with bleeding problems or that are receiving warfarin anticoagulants. These cephalosporins are those that have a N-methylthiotetrazole (NMTT) side chain and include cefotetan, cefamandole, and cefoperazone.

Drug Interactions

No drug interactions are reported in animals. However, do not mix with other drugs in a compounded formulation, because inactivation may result.

Instructions for Use

Although not approved for veterinary use, trials in dogs show efficacy for treating pyoderma. For cephalexin, use cephalothin to test susceptibility.

Patient Monitoring and Laboratory Tests

Susceptibility testing: CLSI (NCCLS) break point for sensitive organisms is less than or equal to 8 mcg/mL for all organisms. Cephalothin is used as a marker to test for sensitivity to cephalexin, cefadroxil, and cephradine. Cephalexin may cause a false-positive test for urine glucose. The test may be positive with test strips that use either the copper reduction test or an enzymatic reaction.

Formulations

Cephalexin is available in 250 and 500 mg capsules, 250 and 500 mg tablets, 100 mg/mL oral suspension, and 125 and 250 mg/5 mL oral suspension.

Stability and Storage

Store in tightly sealed container, protected from light, and at room temperature. Suspensions should be stored in refrigerator and discarded after 14 days. Cephalexin is compatible with enteral products if used immediately after mixing.

Small Animal Dosage

Dogs

- 10-30 mg/kg q6-12h PO.
- Pyoderma: 22-35 mg/kg q12h PO.

Cats

- 15-20 mg/kg q12h PO.

Large Animal Dosage

Horses

- 30 mg/kg q8h PO for susceptible gram-positive bacteria (minimum inhibitory concentration less than or equal to 0.5 mcg/mL).

Regulatory Information

Withdrawal times are not established for animals that produce animals. However, because of relatively short plasma half-life and poor oral absorption, residues should not be a risk. For extralabel use withdrawal interval estimates, contact FARAD at 1-888-USFARAD (1-888-873-2723) or send e-mail to FARAD@ncsu.edu.

Cephalothin Sodium

sef-ahl'oe-thin soe'dee-um

Trade and Other Names: Keflin

Functional Classification: Antibacterial

Pharmacology and Mechanism of Action

First-generation cephalosporin antibiotic. Action is similar to other beta-lactam antibiotics, which inhibits synthesis of bacterial cell wall leading to cell death. Cephalosporins are divided into first-, second-, third-, and fourth-generation drugs depending on spectrum of activity. Cephalothin is a first-generation cephalosporin. Like other first-generation cephalosporins, it is active against *Streptococcus* and *Staphylococcus* species and some gram-negative bacilli, such as *Pasteurella, Escherichia coli,* and *Klebsiella pneumoniae.* However, resistance is common among gram-negative bacteria. It is not active against *Pseudomonas aeruginosa. Staphylococcus* spp. resistant to methicillin and oxacillin will be resistant to first-generation cephalosporins.

Indications and Clinical Uses

Although not often available commercially, like other first-generation cephalosporins, it is indicated for treating common infections in animals, including UTIs, soft tissue infections, pyoderma and other dermal infections, and pneumonia. Efficacy against infections caused by anaerobic bacteria is unpredictable.

Precautionary Information

Adverse Reactions and Side Effects

All cephalosporins are generally safe, however sensitivity can occur in individuals (allergy). Rare bleeding disorders have been known to occur with some cephalosporins.

Contraindications and Precautions

Do not use in animals with allergic sensitivity to other beta-lactams, especially other cephalosporins. However, the incidence of cross sensitivity between penicillins and cephalosporins is small (<10% in people). Some cephalosporins should not be used in animals with bleeding problems or that are receiving warfarin anticoagulants. These cephalosporins are those that have a N-methylthiotetrazole (NMTT) side chain and include cefotetan, cefamandole, and cefoperazone.

Drug Interactions

No drug interactions are reported in animals. However, do not mix in a vial or syringe with other drugs, because inactivation may result.

Instructions for Use

Used as test drug for susceptibility tests of other first-generation cephalosporins.

Patient Monitoring and Laboratory Tests

Susceptibility testing: CLSI (NCCLS) break point for sensitive organisms is less than or equal to 8 mcg/mL for all organisms. Cephalothin is used as a marker to test for sensitivity to cephalexin, cefadroxil, and cephradine.

Formulations

Cephalothin sodium is available in 1 and 2 g vials for injection (availability is limited).

Stability and Storage

Store in tightly sealed container, protected from light, and at room temperature. Manufacturer's recommendation for stability after vial is reconstituted is 96 hours if refrigerated. Stable if frozen for 6 weeks.

Small Animal Dosage

Dogs and Cats

- 10-30 mg/kg q4-8h IV or IM.

Large Animal Dosage

No dose has been reported for large animals.

Regulatory Information

Withdrawal times are not established for animals that produce food. However, because of relatively short plasma half-life, residues should not be a risk. For extralabel use withdrawal interval estimates, contact FARAD at 1-888-USFARAD (1-888-873-2723) or send e-mail to FARAD@ncsu.edu.

Cephapirin Sodium

sef-ah-peer'in so'dee-um

Trade and Other Names: Cefadyl

Functional Classification: Antibacterial

Pharmacology and Mechanism of Action

Cephalosporin antibiotic. Action is similar to other beta-lactam antibiotics, which inhibits synthesis of bacterial cell wall leading to cell death. Cephapirin is a first-generation cephalosporin. Like other first-generation cephalosporins, it is active against *Streptococcus* and *Staphylococcus* species and some gram-negative bacilli, such as *Pasteurella, Escherichia coli,* and *Klebsiella pneumoniae.* However, resistance is common among gram-negative bacteria. It is not active against *Pseudomonas aeruginosa. Staphylococcus* spp. resistant to methicillin and oxacillin will be resistant to first-generation cephalosporins.

Indications and Clinical Uses

Like other first-generation cephalosporins, it is indicated for treating common infections in animals, including UTIs, soft tissue infections, pyoderma and other dermal infections, and pneumonia. Efficacy against infections caused by anaerobic bacteria is unpredictable. Cephapirin is used as an intramammary treatment for mastitis in dairy cattle.

Precautionary Information

Adverse Reactions and Side Effects

All cephalosporins are generally safe, however, sensitivity can occur in individuals (allergy). Rare bleeding disorders have been known to occur with some cephalosporins.

Contraindications and Precautions

Do not use in animals with allergic sensitivity to other beta-lactams, especially other cephalosporins. However, the incidence of cross sensitivity between penicillins and cephalosporins is small (<10% in people). Some cephalosporins should not be used in animals with bleeding problems or that are receiving warfarin anticoagulants. These cephalosporins are those that have an N-methylthiotetrazole (NMTT) side chain and include cefotetan, cefamandole, and cefoperazone.

Drug Interactions

No drug interactions are reported in animals. However, do not mix in a vial or syringe with other drugs, because inactivation may result.

Instructions for Use

Cephapirin is increasingly unavailable in commercial forms.

Patient Monitoring and Laboratory Tests

Susceptibility testing: CLSI (NCCLS) break point for sensitive organisms is less than or equal to 8 mcg/mL for all organisms. Cephalothin is used as a marker to test for sensitivity to cephalexin, cephapirin, cefadroxil, and cephradine.

Formulations

Cephapirin sodium is available in 500 mg, 1, 2, and 4 g vials for injection. (No longer commercially available in the U.S.)

Stability and Storage

Store in tightly sealed container, protected from light, and at room temperature. Observe manufacturer's recommendations for stability after vial is reconstituted.

Small Animal Dosage

Dogs and Cats

- 10-30 mg/kg q4-8h IV or IM.

Large Animal Dosage

Horses

- 20-30 mg/kg q4-6h IM or IV.

Regulatory Information

Intramammary cephapirin withdrawal time: 4 days meat; 96 hours milk.

For other formulations, withdrawal times are not established for animals that produce food. However, because of relatively short plasma half-life, residues should not be a risk. Contact FARAD at 1-888-USFARAD (1-888-873-2723) or send e-mail to FARAD@ncsu.edu. for a more accurate estimate of a withdrawal time.

Cephradine

sef′ra-deen

Trade and Other Names: Velosef

Functional Classification: Antibacterial

Pharmacology and Mechanism of Action

Cephalosporin antibiotic. Action is similar to other beta-lactam antibiotics, which inhibits synthesis of bacterial cell wall leading to cell death. Cephalosporins are divided into first-, second-, third-, and fourth-generation drugs depending on spectrum of activity. Cephradine is a first-generation cephalosporin. Like other first-generation cephalosporins, it is active against *Streptococcus* and *Staphylococcus* species and some gram-negative bacilli, such as *Pasteurella, Escherichia coli,* and *Klebsiella pneumoniae.* However, resistance is common among gram-negative bacteria. It is not active against *Pseudomonas aeruginosa. Staphylococcus* spp. resistant to methicillin and oxacillin will be resistant to first-generation cephalosporins.

Indications and Clinical Uses

Although not often available in commercial formulations, like other first-generation cephalosporins, it is indicated for treating common infections in animals, including UTIs, soft tissue infections, pyoderma and other dermal infections, and pneumonia. Efficacy against infections caused by anaerobic bacteria is unpredictable.

Precautionary Information

Adverse Reactions and Side Effects

All cephalosporins are generally safe, however, sensitivity can occur in individuals (allergy). Rare bleeding disorders have been known to occur with some cephalosporins.

Contraindications and Precautions

Do not use in animals with allergic sensitivity to other beta-lactams, especially other cephalosporins. However, the incidence of cross sensitivity between penicillins and cephalosporins is small (<10% in people). Some cephalosporins should not be used in animals with bleeding problems or that are receiving warfarin anticoagulants. These cephalosporins are those that have an N-methylthiotetrazole (NMTT) side chain and include cefotetan, cefamandole, and cefoperazone.

Drug Interactions

No drug interactions are reported in animals. However, do not mix with other drugs in a compounded formulation, because inactivation may result.

Instructions for Use

Cephradine may not be commercially available in some areas. Therapeutically, cephradine is equivalent to cephalexin and cefadroxil.

Patient Monitoring and Laboratory Tests

Susceptibility testing: CLSI (NCCLS) break point for sensitive organisms is less than or equal to 8 mcg/mL for all organisms. Cephalothin is used as a marker to test for sensitivity to cephalexin, cefadroxil, and cephradine.

Formulations

Cephalothin is available in 250 and 500 mg capsules and 250 and 500 mg, and 1 and 2 g vials for injection.

Stability and Storage

Store in tightly sealed container, protected from light, and at room temperature. Observe manufacturer's recommendations for stability after vial is reconstituted.

Small Animal Dosage

Dogs and Cats

- 10-25 mg/kg q6-8h PO.

Large Animal Dosage

No dose has been reported for large animals.

Regulatory Information

Withdrawal times are not established for animals that produce food. However, because of relatively short plasma half-life, residues should not be a risk. For extralabel use withdrawal interval estimates, contact FARAD at 1-888-USFARAD (1-888-873-2723) or send e-mail to FARAD@ncsu.edu.

Cetirizine Hydrochloride

seh-teer′ih-zeen hye-droe-klor′ide

Trade and Other Names: Zyrtec

Functional Classification: Antihistamine

Pharmacology and Mechanism of Action

Antihistamine (H_1-blocker). Cetirizine is the active metabolite of hydroxyzine. Similar to other antihistamines, it acts by blocking the histamine type-1 (H_1) receptor and suppresses inflammatory reactions caused by histamine. The H_1 blockers have been used to control pruritus and skin inflammation, rhinorrhea, and airway inflammation. Cetirizine is considered a second-generation antihistamine to distinguish it from other, older antihistamines. The most important difference between cetirizine and older drugs is that it does not cross the blood-brain barrier as readily and produces less sedation. In cats, studies have shown cetirizine to be well absorbed after oral administration.

Indications and Clinical Uses

Cetirizine is used to treat and prevent allergic reactions in people. It is preferred over older drugs because it has fewer side effects. In dogs and cats it has been considered for pruritus therapy, allergic airway disease, rhinitis, and other allergic conditions. In cats, 1 mg/kg (5 mg/cat) has produced plasma concentrations considered effective. However, there are no published clinical trials to document efficacy for these diseases.

Precautionary Information

Adverse Reactions and Side Effects

Sedation is not as likely as with other antihistamines. However, with higher doses sedation is still possible. Antimuscarinic effects (atropine-like effects) also are possible, but cetirizine may produce less antimuscarinic effects than other antihistamines.

Contraindications and Precautions

Because antimuscarinic effects (atropine-like effects) are possible, do not use in conditions for which anticholinergic drugs may be contraindicated, such as glaucoma, ileus, or cardiac arrhythmias.

Drug Interactions

Do not use with other antimuscarinic drugs.

Instructions for Use

Use of cetirizine has been mostly empirical. There are no clinical studies to document efficacy.

Patient Monitoring and Laboratory Tests

No specific monitoring is necessary.

Formulations

Cetirizine hydrochloride is available in 1 mg/mL oral syrup and 5 and 10 mg tablets.

Stability and Storage

Store in tightly sealed container, protected from light, and at room temperature. Stability of compounded formulations has not been evaluated.

Small Animal Dosage

Dogs and Cats

- 1 mg/kg daily, PO.

Large Animal Dosage

No dose has been reported for large animals.

Regulatory Information

No regulatory information is available. For extralabel use withdrawal interval estimates, contact FARAD at 1-888-USFARAD (1-888-873-2723) or send e-mail to FARAD@ncsu.edu.

RCI Classification: 4

Charcoal, Activated

Trade and Other Names: ActaChar, Charcodote, Liqui-Char, Toxiban, and generic brands

Functional Classification: Antidote

Pharmacology and Mechanism of Action

Adsorbent. It will bind to other drugs and prevent their absorption from the intestine. It may reduce the absorption of a poison by as much as 75%.

Indications and Clinical Uses

Used primarily to adsorb drugs and toxins in intestine to prevent their absorption. Ordinarily, a single dose is administered, but multiple doses will increase clearance of drugs that may undergo enterohepatic circulation.

Precautionary Information

Adverse Reactions and Side Effects

Not absorbed systemically. Safe for oral administration.

Contraindications and Precautions

Used primarily as treatment for intoxication.

Drug Interactions

Charcoal will adsorb most other drugs administered orally to prevent their absorption.

Instructions for Use

Charcoal is available in variety of forms and usually used as treatment of poisoning. Many commercial preparations contain sorbitol, which acts as flavoring agent, and promotes intestinal catharsis.

Patient Monitoring and Laboratory Tests

When used as treatment for intoxication, careful monitoring of effects of toxin is necessary because charcoal will not adsorb all of the toxicant.

Formulations

Charcoal is available in oral suspension and granules. Strengths of formulations vary from 15 g/72 mL to 50/240 mL.

Stability and Storage

Store in tightly sealed container at room temperature. Do not mix with other compounds as it will adsorb other chemicals.

Small Animal Dosage

Dogs and Cats

- 1-4 gm/kg PO (granules) or 6-12 mL/kg (suspension). Administer a single dose shortly after poisoning.

Large Animal Dosage

Large animal use is not reported, but may be considered for treatment of a poisoning. Consider a dose of 1 gram/kg PO (granules) or 6-10 mL/kg (suspension) PO.

Regulatory Information

No residue concerns. Withdrawal time: 0 days.

Chlorambucil

klor-am′byoo-sil

Trade and Other Names: Leukeran

Functional Classification: Anticancer agent

Pharmacology and Mechanism of Action

Cytotoxic agent. Acts in similar manner as cyclophosphamide as alkylating agent.

Indications and Clinical Uses

Used for treatment of various tumors and immunosuppressive therapy. It is often used as an alternative to azathioprine. Chlorambucil has been used in cats more often than other species for treatment of immune disorders. There are reports of successful treatment of eosinophilic granuloma complex (EGC) in cats.

Precautionary Information

Adverse Reactions and Side Effects

Myelosuppression is possible. Cystitis does not occur with chlorambucil as with cyclophosphamide. Diarrhea and anorexia may occur in some patients.

Contraindications and Precautions
Cytotoxic, potentially immunosuppressive agent. Do not use in animals with suppressed bone marrow.

Drug Interactions
Chlorambucil will potentiate other immunosuppressive drugs.

Instructions for Use

Consult anticancer drug protocol for specific regimens. Chlorambucil often is combined with prednisolone for treatment of immune-mediated disorders.

Patient Monitoring and Laboratory Tests

Monitor CBC in animals during treatment.

Formulations

Chlorambucil is available in a 2 mg tablet.

Stability and Storage

Store in tightly sealed container, protected from light, and at room temperature. It is not stable if mixed with water. Chlorambucil can decompose rapidly in compounded formulations.

Small Animal Dosage

Dogs

- 2-6 mg/m^2 q24h initially, then q48h PO. (Equivalent dose is 0.1-0.2 mg/kg.)

Cats

- 0.1-0.2 mg/kg q24h initially, then q48h PO.

Large Animal Dosage

No dose has been reported for large animals.

Regulatory Information

Withdrawal times are not established for animals that produce food. This drug should not be used in animals intended for food because it is an anticancer agent.

Chloramphenicol

klor-am fen'ih-kole

Trade and Other Names: Chloramphenicol palmitate, Chloromycetin, Chloramphenicol sodium succinate, and generic brands

Functional Classification: Antibacterial

Pharmacology and Mechanism of Action

Antibacterial drug. Mechanism of action is inhibition of protein synthesis via binding to ribosome. Broad spectrum of activity that include gram-positive cocci, gram-negative bacilli (including *Enterobacteriaceae*), and *Rickettsia*. Chloramphenicol sodium succinate is an injectable solution converted to chloramphenicol by hepatic metabolism.

Indications and Clinical Uses

Antibacterial agent used to treat infections caused by a broad spectrum of organisms, including gram-positive cocci, gram-negative bacilli (including *Enterobacteriaceae*), anaerobic bacteria, and *Rickettsia*. Florfenicol acts via similar mechanism and has been substituted in some animals. (See florfenicol.) Chloramphenicol is known for its ability to penetrate lipid membranes and has been used to penetrate tissues with barriers, such as the blood-brain barrier. However, efficacy for treating infections of the CNS has been poor.

Precautionary Information

Adverse Reactions and Side Effects

Bone marrow suppression is possible with high doses or prolonged treatment. This effect is possible in any species with prolonged use, but cats appear particularly susceptible. Bone marrow changes have been observed after 14 days of treatment in cats.

Contraindications and Precautions

Avoid use in pregnant or neonatal animals. Avoid long-term use in cats.
Warn animal owners that human exposure to chloramphenicol may pose a risk. Exposure to small doses has caused aplastic anemia in people.

Drug Interactions

Chloramphenicol is a potent microsomal enzyme (Cytochrome P450) inhibitor. By inhibiting P450 enzymes it will increase the concentrations of other drugs (e.g., barbiturates) and increase their risk of toxicity. Use cautiously with any other drug that requires metabolism for its clearance.

Instructions for Use

Chloramphenicol use based on susceptibility data. Chloramphenicol palmitate requires active enzymes and should not be administered to fasted (or anorectic) animal.

Patient Monitoring and Laboratory Tests

Susceptibility testing: CLSI (NCCLS) break point for sensitive organisms is less than or equal to 4 mcg/mL for streptococci and less than or equal to 8 mcg/mL for other organisms.

Formulations

Chloramphenicol palmitate is available in a 30 mg/mL oral suspension.
Chloramphenicol is available in 250 mg capsules and 100, 250, and 500 mg tablets.
Chloramphenicol sodium succinate is available in 100 mg/mL injection. Some forms of chloramphenicol are no longer available in the U.S.

Stability and Storage

Store in tightly sealed container, protected from light, and at room temperature. Chloramphenicol palmitate is insoluble in water. Chloramphenicol is stable at pH of 2-7. Chloramphenicol sodium succinate is stable for 30 days at room temperature and 6 months if frozen.

Small Animal Dosage

Chloramphenicol and Chloramphenicol palmitate

Dogs

- 40-50 mg/kg q8h PO.

Cats

- 12.5-20 mg/kg q12h PO.

Chloramphenicol sodium succinate

Dogs

- 40-50 mg/kg q6-8h IV or IM.

Cats

- 12.5-20 mg/cat q12h IV or IM.

Large Animal Dosage

Horses

- 35-50 mg/kg q6-8h PO.

Regulatory Information

It is illegal to administer chloramphenicol to animals that produce food; therefore, there are no withdrawal times established.

Chlorothiazide

klor-oh-thye'ah-zide

Trade and Other Names: Diuril

Functional Classification: Diuretic

Pharmacology and Mechanism of Action

Thiazide diuretic. Chlorothiazide inhibits sodium reabsorption in distal renal tubules to produce a more dilute urine.

Indications and Clinical Uses

Chlorothiazide is used as diuretic and antihypertensive. Because it decreases renal excretion of calcium, it also has been used to prevent uroliths containing calcium.

Precautionary Information

Adverse Reactions and Side Effects

Chlorothiazide may cause electrolyte imbalance such as hypokalemia.

Contraindications and Precautions

Do not use in patients with hypercalcemia.

Drug Interactions

Avoid administering calcium and vitamin D supplements.

Instructions for Use

Not as effective as high-ceiling diuretics (e.g., furosemide) for producing a diuresis.

Patient Monitoring and Laboratory Tests

Electrolytes should be monitored during chronic therapy.

Formulations

Chlorothiazide is available in 250 and 500 mg tablets, 50 mg/mL oral suspension, and injection vials of 500 mg (with mannitol).

Stability and Storage

Store in tightly sealed container, protected from light, and at room temperature. Reconstituted solutions are stable for 24 hours.

Small Animal Dosage

Dogs and Cats

- 20-40 mg/kg q12h PO.

Large Animal Dosage

No dose has been reported for large animals.

Regulatory Information

Withdrawal times are not established for animals that produce food. For extralabel use withdrawal interval estimates, contact FARAD at 1-888-USFARAD (1-888-873-2723) or send e-mail to FARAD@ncsu.edu.
RCI Classification: 4

Chlorpheniramine Maleate

klor-fen-eer'ah-meen mal'ee-ate

Trade and Other Names: Chlortrimeton and Phenetron

Functional Classification: Antihistamine

Pharmacology and Mechanism of Action

Antihistamine (H_1-blocker). Similar to other antihistamines, it acts by blocking the H_1 receptor and suppresses inflammatory reactions caused by histamine. The H_1-blockers have been used to control pruritus and skin inflammation in dogs and cats. Commonly used antihistamines include clemastine, chlorpheniramine, diphenhydramine, and hydroxyzine.

Indications and Clinical Uses

Chlorpheniramine is used to prevent allergic reactions and for pruritus therapy in dogs and cats. However, success rates for treatment of pruritus have not been high. In addition to the antihistamine effect for treating allergies, these drugs block the effect of histamine in the vomiting center, vestibular center, and other centers that control vomiting in animals.

Precautionary Information

Adverse Reactions and Side Effects

Sedation is most common side effect. Sedation is the result of inhibition of histamine N-methyltransferase. Sedation may also be attributed to block of other CNS receptors such as those for serotonin, acetylcholine, and alpha-receptors. Antimuscarinic effects (atropine-like effects) also are common, such as dry mouth and decreased GI secretions.

Contraindications and Precautions

Antimuscarinic effects (atropine-like effects) are common. Do not use in conditions for which anticholinergic drugs may be contraindicated, such as glaucoma, ileus, or cardiac arrhythmias.

Drug Interactions

No drug interactions are reported in animals.

Instructions for Use

Chlorpheniramine is included as an ingredient in many OTC cough, cold, and allergy medications.

Patient Monitoring and Laboratory Tests

No specific monitoring is necessary.

Formulations

Chlorpheniramine maleate is available in 4 and 8 mg tablets, 2 mg chewable tablets, 2 mg/5 mL syrup, 10 mg/mL vials for injection.

Stability and Storage

Store in tightly sealed container, protected from light, and at room temperature. Protect from freezing. Stability of compounded formulations has not been evaluated.

Small Animal Dosage

Dogs

- 4-8 mg/dog q12h PO (up to a maximum of 0.5 mg/kg q12h).

Cats

- 2 mg/cat q12h PO.

Large Animal Dosage

No dose has been reported for large animals.

Regulatory Information

Withdrawal times are not established for animals that produce food. For extralabel use withdrawal interval estimates, contact FARAD at 1-888-USFARAD (1-888-873-2723) or send e-mail to FARAD@ncsu.edu.

RCI Classification: 4

Chlorpromazine

klor-proe′mah-zeen

Trade and Other Names: Thorazine and Largactil

Functional Classification: Antiemetic, Phenothiazine

Pharmacology and Mechanism of Action

Phenothiazine tranquilizer/antiemetic. Inhibits action of dopamine as neurotransmitter. The action is similar to acepromazine.

Indications and Clinical Uses

Chlorpromazine is most often used as a centrally acting antiemetic. It is also used for sedation and preanesthetic purposes, although acepromazine has been much more commonly used.

Precautionary Information

Adverse Reactions and Side Effects

Causes sedation. May lower seizure threshold and causes alpha-adrenergic blockade. It produces extrapyramidal side effects in some individuals. In horses it has produced undesirable side effects, including violent reactions.

Contraindications and Precautions

Use caution in animals with seizure disorders. Avoid use in horses.

Drug Interactions

It will potentiate effects from other sedatives.

Instructions for Use

Chlorpromazine is used for vomiting caused by toxins, drugs, or GI disease. Higher doses than listed in dose section have been used with cancer chemotherapy (2 mg/kg q3h SQ). It may produce anticholinergic effects in some animals.

Patient Monitoring and Laboratory Tests

No specific monitoring is necessary.

Formulations

Chlorpromazine is available in a 25 mg/mL injection solution.

Stability and Storage

Store in tightly sealed container, protected from light, and at room temperature. Slight discoloration does not affect stability. Some sorption (loss) occurs if stored in polyvinyl chloride (soft plastic) containers.

Small Animal Dosage

All doses listed are a one-time injection.

Dogs

- 0.5 mg/kg q6-8h IM or SQ.

Cats

- 0.2-0.4 mg/kg q6-8h, up to 0.5 mg/kg q8h IM or SQ.

Large Animal Dosage

All doses listed are a one-time injection.

Horses

Avoid use.

Cattle

- 0.22 mg/kg IV or 1.1 mg/kg IM.

Sheep and Goats

- 0.55 mg/kg IV or 2.2 mg/kg IM.

Pigs

- 0.5 mg/kg IM.

Regulatory Information

Withdrawal times are not established for animals that produce food. For extralabel use withdrawal interval estimates, contact FARAD at 1-888-USFARAD (1-888-873-2723) or send e-mail to FARAD@ncsu.edu.
RCI Classification: 2

Chlortetracycline

klor-tet′rah-sye-kleen

Trade and Other Names: Anaplasmosis block, Aureomycin soluble powder, Aureomycin tablets, Aureomycin soluble calf tablets, Calf Scour Bolus, Fermycin, and generic brands

Functional Classification: Antibacterial

Pharmacology and Mechanism of Action

Tetracycline antibacterial drug. Inhibits bacterial protein synthesis by interfering with peptide elongation by ribosome. Chlortetracycline is a bacteriostatic agent with a broad spectrum of activity, which includes gram-positive bacteria and mycoplasma.

Indications and Clinical Uses

Broad spectrum activity. It is used for routine infections and intracellular pathogens. However, chlortetracycline is poorly absorbed orally and other tetracyclines are preferred for systemic treatment of infections. The most common use for chlortetracycline is as a feed additive to control respiratory and enteric infections in livestock.

Precautionary Information

Adverse Reactions and Side Effects

Chlortetracycline may bind to bone and developing teeth in young animals. High doses have caused renal injury.

Contraindications and Precautions

Avoid use in young animals.

Drug Interactions

Chlortetracycline, like other tetracyclines, will bind to other cations orally administered that will prevent its absorption. Oral absorption will be decreased if it is administered products with calcium, zinc, aluminum, magnesium, or iron.

Instructions for Use

Chlortetracycline is not administered for systemic use in small animals. Doxycycline has replaced most other tetracyclines for treatment in small animals. Most chlortetracycline used is in powdered form and added to feed of livestock.

Patient Monitoring and Laboratory Tests

Susceptibility testing: CLSI (NCCLS) break point for sensitive organisms is less than or equal to 2 mcg/mL for streptococci and less than or equal to 4 for other organisms. Tetracycline is used as a marker to test susceptibility for other drugs in this class such as doxycycline, minocycline, and oxytetracycline.

Formulations

Chlortetracycline is available as a powdered feed additive in 25 g/lb or 64 g/lb. It is also available as an anaplasmosis block in 2.5 g/lb and in 25 and 500 mg tablets. (A range of concentrations exists for premix.)

Stability and Storage

Store in tightly sealed container, protected from light, and at room temperature. Do not mix with ions that may chelate tetracyclines (calcium, magnesium, iron, aluminum, etc.).

Small Animal Dosage

Dogs and Cats

- 25 mg/kg q6-8h PO.

Large Animal Dosage

Cattle

- Prophylaxis for anaplasmosis: 0.36-0.7 mg/kg/day. (Approximately one block per 10 animals.)
- Tablets: 11 mg/kg q12h for 3-5 days PO.
- Powdered feed additive: 22 mg/kg/day added to water. Actual dose will be affected by feed and water consumption for each animal.

Pigs

- Powdered feed additive: 22 mg/kg/day added to water. Actual dose will be affected by feed and water consumption for each animal.

Regulatory Information

Cattle withdrawal time for meat: Withdrawal times vary from product to product from 1, 2, 5, or 10 days. Most products list a withdrawal time of 1 day for cattle. Pig withdrawal time for meat: 1-5 days.

Note that for chlortetracycline, withdrawal times may vary considerably from one product to another. One should consult specific product packaging to determine exact withdrawal time.

Chondroitin Sulfate

kon-droy'ten sul'fate

Trade and Other Names: Cosequin and Glycoflex

Functional Classification: Nutritional supplement

Pharmacology and Mechanism of Action

Nutritional supplement for patients with osteoarthritis. According to the manufacturer, and supported by some experimental evidence, chondroitin sulfate provides precursors to stimulate synthesis of articular cartilage and inhibits degradation and improves healing of articular cartilage.

Pharmacokinetic studies have produced conflicting results depending on formulation, species studied, and assay technique. There may be limited oral absorption of the intact molecule.

It is usually administered in combination with glucosamine. See Glucosamine section for further details.

Indications and Clinical Uses

Chondroitin sulfate is used primarily for treatment of degenerative joint disease and is usually found in formulations in combination with glucosamine. See glucosamine for additional details.

Precautionary Information

Adverse Reactions and Side Effects

Adverse effects have not been reported, although hypersensitivity is possible. Chondroitin is most often administered with glucosamine. See glucosamine for potential adverse effects.

Contraindications and Precautions

No contraindications have been reported.

Drug Interactions

No drug interactions are reported in animals.

Instructions for Use

Doses are based primarily on empiricism and manufacturer's recommendations. No published trials of efficacy or dose titrations are available to determine optimal dose. Doses listed are general recommendations and products available may vary.

Patient Monitoring and Laboratory Tests

No specific monitoring is necessary.

Formulations

Because several chondroitin sulfate formulations are available, veterinarians are encouraged to carefully examine product label to ensure proper strength. One product (Cosequin) is available in regular strength (RS) and double strength (DS) capsules. RS capsules contain 250 mg glucosamine, 200 mg chondroitin sulfate and mixed glycosaminoglycans, 5 mg manganese, and 33 mg manganese ascorbate. The DS tablets contain double of each of these amounts.

Stability and Storage

Store in tightly sealed container, protected from light, and at room temperature. Stability of compounded formulations has not been evaluated.

Small Animal Dosage

Use the Cosequin RS and DS strength as a general guide.

Dogs

- 1-2 RS capsules per day.
- 2-4 capsules of DS for large dogs.

Cats

- 1 RS capsule daily.

Large Animal Dosage

Horses: 12 mg/kg glucosamine + 3.8 mg/kg chondroitin sulfate twice daily PO, × 4 weeks, then 4 mg/kg glucosamine + 1.3 mg/kg chondroitin sulfate thereafter.

It is common to initiate treatment in horses with a higher dose of 22 mg/kg glucosamine + 8.8 mg/kg chondroitin sulfate, daily, PO.

Regulatory Information

Withdrawal times are not established for animals that produce food. For extralabel use withdrawal interval estimates, contact FARAD at 1-888-USFARAD (1-888-873-2723) or send e-mail to FARAD@ncsu.edu.

Cimetidine Hydrochloride

sye-met′ih-deen hye-droe-klor′ide

Trade and Other Names: Tagamet (OTC and prescription)

Functional Classification: Antiulcer agent

Pharmacology and Mechanism of Action

Histamine$_2$ antagonist (H_2-blocker). Blocks histamine stimulation of gastric parietal cell to decrease gastric acid secretion. Increases stomach pH.

Indications and Clinical Uses

Cimetidine is used to treat gastric ulcers and gastritis. Although it is often used for animals with vomiting, there is no efficacy data to indicate that it is effective. There is no efficacy data to support its use for preventing nonsteroidal antiinflammatory drug (NSAID) induced bleeding and ulcers. In horses, cimetidine has been used to prevent or treat GI ulcers. However, the efficacy for these indications has not been proven. For example, studies in horses showed that at 18 g/kg q8h PO, it did not cause healing of ulcers. The poor efficacy may be because of short duration of effect (2-6 hours). In calves, cimetidine will increase abomasal pH.

Precautionary Information

Adverse Reactions and Side Effects

Adverse effects usually seen only with decreased renal clearance. In people, CNS signs may occur with high doses.

Contraindications and Precautions

Use cautiously with drugs that rely on hepatic metabolism for clearance.

Drug Interactions

Cimetidine is a well-known cytochrome P450 enzyme inhibitor. It may increase concentrations of other drugs used concurrently (e.g., theophylline) because of inhibition of hepatic enzymes. Cimetidine will increase the pH of the stomach, which can inhibit oral absorption of some drugs (e.g., itraconazole and ketoconazole). Cimetidine will inhibit the oral absorption of iron supplements.

Instructions for Use

Efficacy for treating ulcers in animals has not been established. Frequent dosing may be necessary for suppression of stomach acid. Doses are derived from gastric secretory studies in experimental animals.

Patient Monitoring and Laboratory Tests

No specific monitoring is necessary.

Formulations

Cimetidine is available in 100, 150, 200, 300, 400, and 800 mg tablets, an oral solution 60 mg/mL, and a 150 mg/mL injection.

Stability and Storage

Store in tightly sealed container, protected from light, and at room temperature. Do not store injection formulation in refrigerator. Solutions are stable for at least 14 days. Stable if mixed with various enteral products.

Small Animal Dosage

Dogs and Cats

- 10 mg/kg q6-8h IV, IM, or PO.
- Renal failure: 2.5-5 mg/kg q12h IV or PO.

Large Animal Dosage

Horses

- 3 mg/kg diluted in fluid solution and infused IV over 2 minutes, q8h.
- 40-60 mg/kg/day PO. However, oral doses in horses produce inconsistent results.

Calves

- Abomasal ulcers in milk-fed calves: 100 mg/kg q8h PO.

Regulatory Information

Withdrawal times are not established for animals that produce food. For extralabel use withdrawal interval estimates, contact FARAD at 1-888-USFARAD (1-888-873-2723) or send e-mail to FARAD@ncsu.edu.

RCI Classification: 5

Ciprofloxacin Hydrochloride

sip-roe-floks'ah-sin hye-droe-klor'ide

Trade and Other Names: Cipro and generic brands

Functional Classification: Antibacterial

Pharmacology and Mechanism of Action

Fluoroquinolone antibacterial. Acts to inhibit DNA gyrase and cell DNA and RNA synthesis. Bactericidal. Broad antimicrobial activity. Ciprofloxacin is active against gram-negative bacilli, including *Enterobacteriaceae.* Ciprofloxacin is more active against *Pseudomonas aeruginosa* than other fluoroquinolones. Oral absorption of ciprofloxacin has been reported in only a few limited studies. Estimates derived from independent studies in dogs indicate that oral absorption has ranged from 74% to 97% and perhaps as low as only 42%. Oral absorption in horses is <10% and should not be used orally. In cats oral absorption is low 22%-33% and would not be effective for gram-positive bacteria even at 10 mg/kg; but at 10 mg/kg q12h, it was able to reach therapeutic targets against susceptible gram-negative bacteria. Other fluoroquinolones registered for animals have near complete bioavailability.

Indications and Clinical Uses

Ciprofloxacin, although a human drug, has been used in small animals for treatment of a wide variety of infections, including skin infections, pneumonia, and soft tissue infections. Ciprofloxacin is not registered for animals. However, it can be used legally by veterinarians, as long as it is not administered to animals that produce food or are intended for food. The use would be considered extralabel and subject to other extralabel restrictions. The potentially low ciprofloxacin oral availability for dogs and cats suggests that doses should be higher than the doses currently used for drugs such as enrofloxacin, marbofloxacin, or orbifloxacin.

Precautionary Information

Adverse Reactions and Side Effects

High concentrations may cause CNS toxicity, especially in animals with renal failure. Causes occasional vomiting. Intravenous solution should be given slowly (over 30 minutes). At high doses, it may cause some nausea, vomiting, and diarrhea. Blindness in cats has not been reported for ciprofloxacin. All of the fluoroquinolones may cause arthropathy in young animals. Dogs are most sensitive in the age group of 4 weeks to 28 weeks of age. Large, rapidly growing dogs are the most susceptible.

Contraindications and Precautions

Avoid use in young animals because of risk of cartilage injury. Use cautiously in animals that may be prone to seizures, such as epileptics.

Drug Interactions

Fluoroquinolones may increase concentrations of theophylline if used concurrently. Coadministration with divalent and trivalent cations, such as products containing aluminum (e.g., sucralfate), iron, and calcium, may decrease absorption. Do not mix in solutions or in vials with aluminum, calcium, iron, or zinc, because chelation may occur.

Instructions for Use

Doses are based on plasma concentrations needed to achieve sufficient plasma concentration above minimum inhibitory concentration (MIC). Efficacy studies have not been performed in dogs or cats. Ciprofloxacin is not absorbed orally as well as enrofloxacin. Injectable ciprofloxacin is available in a human preparation, usually 10 mg/mL (in sterile water) or 2 mg/mL (premixed with 5% dextrose). Dilute the concentrated form to 1-2 mg/mL prior to intravenous use with an intravenous solution and infuse the final solution over 60 minutes. Do not infuse concurrently with other medications (e.g., in a piggy-back), because inactivation may occur.

Patient Monitoring and Laboratory Tests

Susceptibility testing: CLSI (NCCLS) break point for sensitive organisms is less than or equal to 1.0 mcg/mL. Most sensitive gram-negative bacteria of the

Enterobacteriaceae have MIC values <0.1 mcg/mL. If ciprofloxacin is used to treat *Pseudomonas,* it may be several times more active than other fluoroquinolones. Otherwise, one should assume that if the organism is susceptible to ciprofloxacin, it is likely susceptible to others.

Formulations Available

Ciprofloxacin is available in 250, 500, and 750 mg tablets and 2 mg/mL injection.

Stability and Storage

Store in tightly sealed container, protected from light, and at room temperature. Aqueous solutions of 0.5 to 2 mg/mL retain potency up to 14 days when stored. Do not mix with products that contain ions (e.g., iron, aluminum, magnesium, and calcium).

Small Animal Dosage

Dogs

- 10-20 mg/kg q24h PO.
- 5-10 mg/kg q24h IV.

Cats

- 20 mg/kg q24h, PO.
- 10 mg/kg q24h IV.

Large Animal Dosage

- No dosing data available. Ciprofloxacin has poor oral absorption in horses (<10%).

Regulatory Information

There are no withdrawal times established because this drug should not be administered to animals that produce food.

Cisapride

siss'ah-pride

Trade and Other Names: Propulsid (Prepulsid in Canada)

Functional Classification: Prokinetic agent

Pharmacology and Mechanism of Action

Prokinetic agent. Its mechanism is believed to be as an agonist for the 5-hydroxytryptamine (5-HT_4) receptor on myenteric neurons (5-HT_4 ordinarily stimulates cholinergic transmission in the myenteric neurons). It also acts as an *antagonist* for the 5-HT_3 receptor. Via this mechanism, or independently, cisapride may enhance release of acetylcholine at the myenteric plexus. Cisapride increases the motility of the stomach, small intestine, and colon. It accelerates the transit of contents in the bowel and intestines.

Indications and Clinical Uses

Cisapride is used to stimulate motility for treating gastric reflux, gastroparesis, ileus, and constipation. The most common uses in animals have been to prevent stomach regurgitation, decrease postoperative ileus, and to treat constipation and megacolon in cats. However, cisapride was removed from the human market and is no longer commercially available. Compounding pharmacies have made cisapride available to veterinarians in compounded forms. However, these formulations are not licensed and are unregulated.

Precautionary Information

Adverse Reactions and Side Effects

Adverse cardiac effects have been reported in people and are the cause for discontinuation in human medicine. These cardiac effects have not been reported in animals.

Contraindications and Precautions

Contraindicated in patients with GI obstruction.

Drug Interactions

Anticholinergic drugs, such as atropine, will diminish the action. Cisapride should not be used with drugs that inhibit metabolism (Cytochrome P450 inhibitors) or drugs that inhibit p glycoprotein. Toxicity may result. See Appendix.

Instructions for Use

Not currently available commercially. Cisapride was discontinued by manufacturer in July 2000. However, some veterinary pharmacies can fill some orders or prepare compounded formulations for animals. Consult local compounding pharmacist about availability. Doses are based on extrapolation from human doses, experimental studies, and anecdotal evidence. Efficacy studies have not been performed in dogs or cats.

Patient Monitoring and Laboratory Tests

In humans, cardiac effects have been reported (arrhythmias). Monitor ECG in susceptible patients.

Formulations

Cisapride is available in 10 mg tablet (no longer commercially available from manufacturer).

Stability and Storage

Store in tightly sealed container, protected from light, and at room temperature. Some compounded formulations have been stable for 60 days if the pH is kept neutral.

Small Animal Dosage

Dogs

- 0.1-0.5 mg/kg q8-12h PO, (up to 0.5-1.0 mg/kg).

Cats

- 2.5-5 mg/cat q8-12h PO, (up to 1 mg/kg q8h).

Large Animal Dosage

Horses

- 0.1 mg/kg IV. (This formulation is not commercially available, but an intravenous form has been made by combining 40 mg with 1.0 mL of tartaric acid and diluted to obtain a total volume of 10 mL.)

Regulatory Information

Withdrawal times are not established for animals that produce food. This drug should not be used in animals intended for food, because it poses a risk to humans.

Cisplatin

sis-plah'tin

Trade and Other Names: Platinol

Functional Classification: Anticancer agent

Pharmacology and Mechanism of Action

Anticancer agent. Platinum compound that has action believed to be similar to bifunctional alkylating agents and interrupts replication of DNA in tumor cells. Carboplatin is a second-generation platinum compound used in patients who may not tolerate cisplatin.

Indications and Clinical Uses

Cisplatin is used for treating various solid tumors, including bronchiogenic carcinoma, osteosarcoma, transitional cell carcinoma, and mast cell tumors. It has been shown to be effective for increasing the survival of dogs that have undergone amputations for osteosarcoma.

Precautionary Information

Adverse Reactions and Side Effects

Nephrotoxicity is the most limiting factor to cisplatin therapy. In cats, it causes a dose-related, species-specific, primary pulmonary toxicosis. Vomiting may occur in dogs with administration. Transient thrombocytopenia may occur in dogs.

Contraindications and Precautions

Do not use in cats.

Drug Interactions

Cisplatin may be used with other cancer chemotherapy agents.

Instructions for Use

To avoid toxicity, fluid loading before administration using sodium chloride should be performed. Antiemetic agents are often administered before therapy to decrease vomiting.

Patient Monitoring and Laboratory Tests

Monitor renal function in treated animals.

Formulations

Cisplatin is available in a 1 mg/mL injection.

Stability and Storage

Store in tightly sealed container, protected from light, and at room temperature.

Small Animal Dosage

Dogs

- 60-70 mg/m^2 q3-4wks IV (administer fluid for diuresis with therapy).

Large Animal Dosage

No dose has been reported for large animals.

Regulatory Information

Withdrawal times are not established for animals that produce food. This drug should not be used in animals intended for food, because it is an anticancer agent.

Clarithromycin

klah-rith'roe-mye'sin

Trade and Other Names: Biaxin and generic brands

Functional Classification: Antibiotic

Pharmacology and Mechanism of Action

Macrolide antibiotic, with bacteriostatic activity. It is a substituted 14-carbon macrolide. Compared to erythromycin it has higher absorption, longer half-life, and increased intracellular uptake. Site of action is similar to other macrolide antibiotics, which is the 50-S ribosomal subunit in susceptible bacteria. Spectrum includes primarily gram-positive bacteria. Resistance is expected for most gram-negative bacteria. In foals, half-life is 4.8 hours, with a maximum concentration of 0.9 mcg/mL.

Indications and Clinical Uses

Most common use in people is for treatment of *Helicobacter* gastritis and respiratory infections. In small animals, clarithromycin has been used for indications such as skin infections and respiratory infections. In foals, clarithromycin has been used for treatment of infections caused by *Rhodococcus equi* (in combination with rifampin) and produced better clinical success than azithromycin.

Precautionary Information

Adverse Reactions and Side Effects

The most common adverse effect from clarithromycin and related drugs is diarrhea. Many animals may develop soft feces or mild diarrhea. In studies in healthy foals, diarrhea was uncommon from oral doses and was self-limiting. However, if diarrhea becomes severe, treatment should be discontinued.

Contraindications and Precautions

Administer with caution to adult horses, ruminants, rodents, and rabbits because diarrhea and enteritis may develop. Use cautiously to pregnant animals.

Drug Interactions

Many macrolide antibiotics are cytochrome P450 enzyme inhibitors and can decrease metabolism of other drugs. However, specific drug interactions of this nature have not been documented in animals.

Instructions for Use

Clarithromycin should be given twice daily to animals because of short half-life and need for long time above the minimum inhibitory concentration (MIC).

Patient Monitoring and Laboratory Tests

In absence of a specific value for clarithromycin, use susceptibility for erythromycin to guide use of clarithromycin. MIC values for *R. equi* were 0.12 mcg/mL.

Formulations

Clarithromycin is available in 250 and 500 mg tablets and 25 and 50 mg/mL oral suspension.

Stability and Storage

Store in tightly sealed container, protected from light, and at room temperature. Stability of compounded formulations has not been evaluated.

Small Animal Dosage

Dogs and Cats

- 7.5 mg/kg q12h PO.

Large Animal Dosage

Foals

- 7.5 mg/kg PO q12h PO (Often combined with rifampin at 10 mg/kg q12h).

Regulatory Information

No regulatory information is available. For extralabel use withdrawal interval estimates, contact FARAD at 1-888-USFARAD (1-888-873-2723) or send e-mail to FARAD@ncsu.edu.

Clemastine Fumarate

klem′ass-teen fyoo′mar-ate

Trade and Other Names: Tavist, Contac 12-hour allergy, and generic brands

Functional Classification: Antihistamine

Pharmacology and Mechanism of Action

Antihistamine (H_1-blocker). Similar to other antihistamines, it acts by blocking the H_1 receptor and suppresses inflammatory reactions caused by histamine. The H_1-blockers have been used to control pruritus and skin inflammation in dogs and cats; however, success rates in dogs have not been high. Commonly used antihistamines include clemastine, chlorpheniramine, diphenhydramine, and hydroxyzine.

Indications and Clinical Uses

Used primarily for treatment of allergy. Some reports have suggested that clemastine is effective for pruritus in dogs. However, the half-life in dogs is rapid (3.8 hours), and it has rapid clearance. After oral administration the oral absorption is only 3% (20%-70% in humans). At a high dose of 0.5 mg/kg PO, it did not suppress intradermal skin reactions. This evidence suggests that oral administration may not be as effective in dogs as previously thought. Oral absorption studies in horses indicated that it is not absorbed when given orally (bioavailability was only 3%).

Precautionary Information

Adverse Reactions and Side Effects

Sedation is most common side effect. Sedation is the result of inhibition of histamine N-methyltransferase. Sedation may also be attributed to block of other CNS receptors such as those for serotonin, acetylcholine, and alpha-receptors. Antimuscarinic effects (atropine-like effects) also are possible, such as dry mouth and decreased GI secretions.

Contraindications and Precautions

No contraindications reported for animals.

Drug Interactions

No drug interactions are reported in animals.

Instructions for Use

Clemastine fumarate is used for short-term treatment of pruritus in dogs. It may be more efficacious when combined with other antiinflammatory drugs. Tavist syrup contains 5.5% alcohol.

Patient Monitoring and Laboratory Tests

No specific monitoring is necessary.

Formulations

Clemastine fumarate is available in 1.34 mg tablets (OTC), 2.64 mg tablets (prescription), and 0.134 mg/mL syrup.

Stability and Storage

Store in tightly sealed container, protected from light, and at room temperature. Stability of compounded formulations has not been evaluated.

Small Animal Dosage

Dogs

- 0.05-0.1 mg/kg q12h PO, up to 0.5-1.5 mg/kg q12h PO.
- Dogs <10 kg in weight: 1/2 of tablet. (Dose based on q12h treatment and 1.34 mg tablet.)
- Dogs 10-25 kg in weight: 1 tablet. (Dose based on q12h treatment and 1.34 mg tablets.)
- Dogs >25 kg: 1.5 tablets. (Dose based on q12h treatment and 1.34 mg tablets.)
- 0.1 mg/kg IV.

Large Animal Dosage

Horses

- 50 mcg/kg (0.05 mg/kg) q8h IV. It is not absorbed orally in horses.

Regulatory Information

Do not administer to animals that produce food.
RCI Classification: 3

Clenbuterol

klen-byoo'ter-ole

Trade and Other Names: Ventipulmin

Functional Classification: Bronchodilator, Beta-agonist

Pharmacology and Mechanism of Action

$Beta_2$-adrenergic agonist. Bronchodilator. Stimulates $beta_2$-receptors to relax bronchial smooth muscle. It also may inhibit release of inflammatory mediators, especially from mast cells. Compared to terbutaline, it has lower efficacy because of lower intrinsic activity, and it is only a partial agonist. Clenbuterol differs from other beta-agonists because it resists O-sulfate ester conjugation, which produces longer half-life. It also has better oral absorption (83%) than other beta-agonists in horses. In horses, the plasma half-life is 13 hours, but in urine it can be detected for 12 days.

Indications and Clinical Uses

Clenbuterol is indicated for treatment of animals with reversible bronchoconstriction such as horses with recurrent airway obstruction (RAO), formerly called chronic obstructive pulmonary disease (COPD), now known as recurrent airway obstruction (RAO).

Studies have demonstrated effects in horses, but there are no reports of use in other species. It should not be used in animals intended for food.

Precautionary Information

Adverse Reactions and Side Effects

Clenbuterol may produce excessive beta-adrenergic stimulation at high doses (tachycardia and tremors). Arrhythmias occur at high doses.

Contraindications and Precautions

Do not administer to animals intended for food.

Drug Interactions

Because clenbuterol is a beta-agonist, other adrenergic drugs will potentiate the action. In addition, beta-blocking drugs will decrease action. Use with caution with any other drug that may stimulate the heart.

Instructions for Use

Oral administration for horses. Clenbuterol has not been used in small animals. It is prohibited for use in animals intended for food.

Patient Monitoring and Laboratory Tests

Monitor heart rate in animals during treatment. Clenbuterol can be detected in urine for 12 days. Effective plasma concentrations are 500 pg/mL.

Formulations

Clenbuterol is available in 100 and 33 mL bottles of 72.5 mcg/mL syrup.

Stability and Storage

Store in tightly sealed container, protected from light, and at room temperature. Stability of compounded formulations has not been evaluated.

Small Animal Dosage

Dogs and Cats

No dose has been reported for small animals.

Large Animal Dosage

Horses

- Recurrent Airway Obstruction (RAO, formerly called COPD): 0.8 mcg/kg (0.008 mg/kg) twice daily PO. If initial dose is not effective, increase dose to two, three, and four times the initial dose, up to 3.2 mcg/kg. Duration of effect is approximately 6-8 hours.

Regulatory Information

There are no withdrawal times established because clenbuterol should not be administered to animals that produce food. In horses, clenbuterol can be detected in urine for 12 days.

RCI Classification: 3

Clindamycin Hydrochloride

klin-dah-mye′sin hye-droe-klor′ide

Trade and Other Names: Antirobe, Clindrops, Clintabs, Clinsol, and generic (veterinary preparations) and Cleocin (human preparations)

Functional Classification: Antibacterial

Pharmacology and Mechanism of Action

Antibacterial drug of the lincosamide class (similar in action to macrolides). It inhibits bacterial protein synthesis via inhibition of bacterial ribosome. Clindamycin is bacteriostatic with a spectrum of activity primarily against gram-positive bacteria and anaerobes. Clindamycin, like the macrolide antibiotics, can concentrate in leukocytes and many tissues. Action of clindamycin is primarily against gram-positive organisms such as *Staphylococcus, Streptococcus,* and gram-positive rods such as *Corynebacterium*. Clindamycin also is active against mycoplasma and anaerobic organisms, although not all *Bacteroides species* are susceptible. Activity against *Toxoplasma* is controversial.

Indications and Clinical Uses

Clindamycin is primarily used for gram-positive or anaerobic bacterial infections involving the skin, respiratory tract, or oral cavity. Resistance with *Staphylococcus* may occur. It is effective for some oral infections and anaerobic infections. It also has been used for *Mycoplasma* infections. Although it has been used to treat toxoplasmosis in cats, the evidence for efficacy is lacking.

Precautionary Information

Adverse Reactions and Side Effects

Clindamycin is generally well tolerated in dogs and cats. Oral liquid product may be unpalatable to cats, possibly because of the high alcohol content (8.6%). High doses have caused vomiting and diarrhea in cats. Lincomycin and clindamycin may alter bacterial population in intestine and cause diarrhea.

Contraindications and Precautions

Do not administer to rodents or rabbits, because it may cause diarrhea. Do not administer orally to horses or ruminants, because diarrhea, enteritis, and perhaps death can result. The oral liquid (Antirobe) contains 8.6% ethyl alcohol which may be unpalatable to cats.

Drug Interactions

There are no drug interactions identified in small animals.

Instructions for Use

Most doses are based on manufacturer's drug approval data and efficacy trials. Although every 12 hour frequency is recommended most often for dogs, there are studies that demonstrate efficacy when administered at 11 mg/kg every 24 hours for treatment of pyoderma. An injectable formulation is also available (Cleocin) which is clindamycin phosphate. This may be injected either IV or IM. If administering clindamycin IV, it should be diluted and administered by slow infusion. It contains benzyl alcohol, and this vehicle has produced toxic reactions in young infants (and perhaps small animals). Efficacy of clindamycin for treating toxoplasmosis is controversial. Some studies have shown that clindamycin improved clinical signs, but it did not resolve the infection. Another study showed that clindamycin inhibited killing of *Toxoplasma* organisms by leukocytes.

Patient Monitoring and Laboratory Tests

Susceptibility testing: CLSI (NCCLS) break point for sensitive organisms is less than or equal to 0.25 mcg/mL for streptococci and less than or equal to 0.5 mcg/mL for other organisms.

Formulations

Clindamycin is available in oral liquid (Aquadrops) 25 mg/mL, 25, 75, 150, and 300 mg capsules, 25, 75, and 150 mg tablets and 150 mg/mL injection (Cleocin).

Stability and Storage

Store in tightly sealed container, protected from light, and at room temperature. Protect from freezing. Reconstituted solutions are stable for 2 weeks. Stability of compounded formulations is at least 60 days.

Small Animal Dosage

Dogs

- Staphylococcal infections: 11 mg/kg q12h PO or 22 mg/kg q24h PO.
- Refractory infections: doses up to 33 mg/kg q12h PO. (Label dose for dogs is 5.5-33 mg/kg q12h PO.)
- Anaerobic infections and periodontal infections: 11-33 mg/kg q12h PO.
- 10 mg/kg q12h IV or IM. For IV use, it should be diluted and administered by slow infusion.

Cats

- 5.5 mg/kg q12h or 11 mg/kg q24h PO.
- Refractory infections: doses up to 33 mg/kg q24h PO. (Label dose for cats is 11-33 mg/kg q24h, PO.)
- Anaerobic infections and periodontal infections: 11-33 mg/kg q24h PO.
- Toxoplasmosis: 12.5 mg/kg, up to 25 mg/kg q12h for 4 weeks PO.
- 10 mg/kg q12h IV or IM. For IV use, it should be diluted and administered by slow infusion.

Large Animal Dosage

Do not administer clindamycin orally to large animals.

Regulatory Information

No regulatory information is available. For extralabel use withdrawal interval estimates, contact FARAD at 1-888-USFARAD (1-888-873-2723) or send e-mail to FARAD@ncsu.edu.

Clofazimine

kloe-fah'zih-meen

Trade and Other Names: Lam-prene

Functional Classification: Antibacterial

Pharmacology and Mechanism of Action

Antimicrobial agent used to treat feline leprosy. It produces a slow bactericidal effect on *Mycobacterium leprae*.

Indications and Clinical Uses

Clofazimine has had limited use in veterinary medicine. Its use is limited to treating infections caused by Mycobacterium, such as feline leprosy.

C

Precautionary Information

Adverse Reactions and Side Effects

Adverse effects have not been reported in cats. In people, the most serious adverse effects are gastrointestinal.

Contraindications and Precautions

No contraindications reported for animals.

Drug Interactions

No drug interactions are reported in animals.

Instructions for Use

Doses based on empiricism or extrapolation of human studies.

Patient Monitoring and Laboratory Tests

No specific monitoring is necessary.

Formulations

Clofazimine is available in 50 and 100 mg capsules.

Stability and Storage

Store in tightly sealed container, protected from light, and at room temperature. Stability of compounded formulations has not been evaluated.

Small Animal Dosage

Cats

- 1 mg/kg up to a maximum of 4 mg/kg/day PO.

Large Animal Dosage

No dose has been reported for large animals.

Regulatory Information

No regulatory information is available. For extralabel use withdrawal interval estimates, contact FARAD at 1-888-USFARAD (1-888-873-2723) or send e-mail to FARAD@ncsu.edu.

Clomipramine Hydrochloride

kloe-mip′rah-meen hye-droe-klor′ide

Trade and Other Names: Clomicalm (veterinary preparation) and Anafranil (human preparation)

Functional Classification: Behavior modification

Pharmacology and Mechanism of Action

Tricyclic antidepressant drug (TCA). Used in people to treat anxiety and depression. Action is via inhibition of uptake of serotonin at presynaptic nerve terminals. Beneficial effects may be caused primarily by blocking reuptake of serotonin. Clomipramine has more serotonin-reuptake blocking effects than other TCA drugs. Side effects are caused from antimuscarinic effects caused by active metabolite, desmethylclomipramine. However, animals produce less of this metabolite than people.

Indications and Clinical Uses

Like other TCAs, clomipramine is used in animals to treat variety of behavioral disorders, including obsessive-compulsive disorders (OCDs) and separation anxiety. In dogs, it has been superior to amitriptyline for treating OCD. In dogs, it may not decrease aggression when used for dominance-related aggression. In cats, with long-term treatment it has been effective for decreasing urine spraying (*J Am Vet Med Assoc*, 226: 378-382, 2005). It was equally effective as fluoxetine for urine spraying in cats, but treated animals returned to urine marking abruptly after drug was discontinued.

Precautionary Information

Adverse Reactions and Side Effects

Reported adverse effects include sedation and reduced appetite. Other side effects associated with TCAs are antimuscarinic effects (dry mouth, rapid heart rate, and urine retention), and antihistamine effects (sedation). In cats, sedation and weight gain have been observed. For clomipramine, antimuscarinic effects may be caused by an active metabolite. Clomipramine can decrease total T4 and free-T4 concentrations in dogs, but it may still be within normal reference ranges. Overdoses can produce life-threatening cardiotoxicity. In trials performed in cats, no significant adverse effects were observed.

Contraindications and Precautions

Use cautiously in patients with heart disease.

Drug Interactions

Do not use with other behavior-modifying drugs such as serotonin reuptake inhibitors. Do not use with monoamine oxidase inhibitors (MAOIs), such as selegiline or amitraz.

Instructions for Use

When adjusting doses, one may initiate therapy with low dose and increase gradually. There may be a 2-4 week delay after initiation of therapy before beneficial effects are seen. (*J Am Vet Med Assoc*, 213: 1760-1766, 1998). After achieving a favorable response, the dose can be gradually lowered in some animals. In cats, doses of 1.25 to 2.5 mg per cat have been administered once daily for psychogenic alopecia. In cats, up to 5 mg per cat, once a day has been used for urine spraying.

Patient Monitoring and Laboratory Tests

Monitor animal's heart rate and rhythm periodically during treatment. Like other TCAs, clomipramine may decrease total T4 and free-T4 concentrations in dogs.

Formulations

Clomipramine is available in 20, 40, and 80 mg tablets (veterinary preparation) and 25, 50, and 75 mg capsules (human preparation).

Stability and Storage

Store at room temperature. Protect from moisture. It has been compounded in a tuna-flavored liquid for cats, without a decrease in efficacy.

Small Animal Dosage

Dogs

- 1-3 mg/kg/day q12h PO. Start at lower dose and gradually increase. Increases in dose should be made approximately every 14 days until desired effect is observed.

Cats

- 1-5 mg per cat q12-24h PO (0.5 mg/kg per day).

Large Animal Dosage

No dose has been reported for large animals.

Regulatory Information

No regulatory information is available. For extralabel use withdrawal interval estimates, contact FARAD at 1-888-USFARAD (1-888-873-2723) or send e-mail to FARAD@ncsu.edu.

RCI Classification: 2

Clonazepam

kloe-nah'zih-pam

Trade and Other Names: Klonopin and generic brands

Functional Classification: Anticonvulsant

Pharmacology and Mechanism of Action

Benzodiazepine. Action is to enhance inhibitory effects of GABA in CNS. Used for anticonvulsant action, sedation, and treatment of some behavioral disorders.

Indications and Clinical Uses

Clonazepam has been used as an anticonvulsant in dogs and cats. As a benzodiazepine, it also is used to treat behavior problems in dogs and cats, particularly those associated with anxiety. Tolerance may develop to the anticonvulsant effects with long-term use.

Precautionary Information

Adverse Reactions and Side Effects

Side effects include sedation and polyphagia. Some animals may experience paradoxical excitement.

Contraindications and Precautions

No contraindications reported for animals.

Drug Interactions

No drug interactions are reported in animals. However, it will potentiate effects from other sedatives and CNS depressants.

Instructions for Use

Doses are based primarily on reports from human medicine, empiricism, or experimental studies. No clinical efficacy studies have been performed in dogs or cats. Doses as low as 0.1-0.2 mg/kg have been used in animals sensitive to the higher doses listed in the dosage section.

Patient Monitoring and Laboratory Tests

Samples of plasma or serum may be analyzed for concentrations of benzodiazepines. However, there are no readily available tests for monitoring in many veterinary laboratories. Laboratories that analyze human samples may have nonspecific for benzodiazepines.

Formulations

Clonazepam is available in 0.5, 1, and 2 mg tablets.

Stability and Storage

Store in tightly sealed container, protected from light, and at room temperature. Clonazepam, like other benzodiazepines, will exhibit adsorption to plastic, especially soft plastic (polyvinyl chloride). Compounded oral products are stable for 60 days.

Small Animal Dosage

Dogs

- 0.5 mg/kg q8-12h PO.

Cats

- 0.1-0.2 mg/kg q12-24h PO.

Large Animal Dosage

No dose has been reported for large animals.

Regulatory Information

Do not administer to animals intended for food.
Schedule IV controlled drug.
RCI Classification: 2

Clopidogrel

kloe-pid'oh-grel

Trade and Other Names: Plavix

Functional Classification: Antiplatelet drug

Pharmacology and Mechanism of Action

Clopidogrel is a platelet inhibitor. It is a thienopyridine and inhibits adenosine diphosphate (ADP) receptor-mediated platelet activity. Because this mechanism is different from the aspirin inhibiting effect on platelets, clopidogrel has been used concurrently with aspirin. Clopidogrel is metabolized to an active metabolite that exerts its antiplatelet effect. In cats, clopidogrel produced antiplatelet effects that persisted for 3 days after discontinuation of the drug. Clopidogrel administration also decreased serotonin release from platelets in cats, which may be important because serotonin release may contribute to clinical signs of thromboemboli in cats.

Indications and Clinical Uses

Clopidogrel is used to inhibit platelets in patients that are prone to forming blood clots. In patients with high risk for thrombi and emboli, clopidogrel will inhibit mechanisms that are not effected by aspirin alone. A similar drug is ticlopidine (Ticlid) and is not used in cats because it produces adverse reactions. In cats, clopidogrel has been recommended to prevent cardiogenic arterial thromboembolism associated with cats with heart disease.

Precautionary Information

Adverse Reactions and Side Effects

Bleeding in susceptible patients. No adverse effects have been identified in cats, but in people pruritus and skin rash have been reported.

Contraindications and Precautions

Do not use in patients that have a high risk of bleeding.

Drug Interactions

Use cautiously with other drugs that may inhibit blood clotting.

Instructions for Use

Administer with, or without, aspirin in patients prone to thrombi and emboli. The dose of 19 mg is approximately 1/4 of a human tablet. It is likely that smaller doses are effective, but they have not been evaluated because it is impractical to divide the human 75 mg tablet into fractions smaller than 1/4.

Patient Monitoring and Laboratory Tests

Monitor for bleeding.

Formulations

Clopidogrel is available in 75 mg tablets.

Stability and Storage

Store in tightly sealed container, protected from light, and at room temperature. Stability of compounded formulations has not been evaluated.

Small Animal Dosage

Cats

- 19 mg per cat (1/4 tablet) q24h PO.

(Smaller doses may be effective, but have not been evaluated in cats.)

Large Animal Dosage

No dose has been reported for large animals.

Regulatory Information

Do not administer to animals that produce food.

Clorazepate Dipotassium

klor-az'eh-pate dye-poe-tah'see-um

Trade and Other Names: Tranxene

Functional Classification: Anticonvulsant

Pharmacology and Mechanism of Action

Benzodiazepine. Clorazepate is one of the active metabolites of diazepam. After oral absorption it is quickly converted to the active drug, referred to as nordiazepam or desmethyldiazepam. Action is to enhance inhibitory effects of GABA in CNS.

Indications and Clinical Uses

Clorazepate is used for antiseizure action, sedation, and treatment of some behavioral disorders. It has been used in dogs and cats when other drugs are not effective. It has been used in refractory epileptics, but tolerance may develop to the anticonvulsant effects with long-term use.

Precautionary Information

Adverse Reactions and Side Effects

Side effects include sedation and polyphagia. Some animals may experience paradoxical excitement. Chronic administration may lead to dependence and a withdrawal syndrome if discontinued.

Contraindications and Precautions

No serious contraindications. In rare individuals, benzodiazepines have caused paradoxical excitement. It may cause fetal abnormalities early in pregnancy, but this has not been reported with veterinary use.

Drug Interactions

No drug interactions are reported in animals. However, it will potentiate effects from other sedatives and CNS depressants.

Instructions for Use

Doses are based primarily on reports from human medicine, empiricism, or experimental studies. No clinical efficacy studies have been performed in dogs or cats. Clorazepate tablets degrade quickly in presence of light, heat, or moisture.

Patient Monitoring and Laboratory Tests

Samples of plasma or serum may be analyzed for concentrations of benzodiazepines. Plasma concentrations in the range of 100-250 ng/mL have been cited as the therapeutic range for people. Other references have cited this range as 150 to 300 ng/mL. However, there are no readily available tests for monitoring in many veterinary laboratories. Laboratories that analyze human samples may have nonspecific tests for benzodiazepines. With these assays, there may be cross-reactivity among benzodiazepine metabolites.

Formulations Available

Clorazepate is available in 3.75, 7.5, 11.25, 15, and 22.5 mg tablets.

Stability and Storage

Keep in original packaging or store in tightly sealed container, protected from light, and at room temperature. Stability of compounded formulations has not been evaluated.

Small Animal Dosage

Dogs

- 2 mg/kg q12h PO.

Cats

- 0.2-0.4 mg/kg q12-24h, up to 0.5-2.2 mg/kg PO.

Large Animal Dosage

No dose has been reported for large animals.

Regulatory Information

Do not administer to animals intended for food.
RCI Classification: 2

Cloxacillin Sodium

kloks-ah-sill'in soe'dee-um

Trade and Other Names: Cloxapen, Orbenin, and Tegopen

Functional Classification: Antibacterial

Pharmacology and Mechanism of Action

Beta-lactam antibiotic. Inhibits bacterial cell wall synthesis by binding to penicillin-binding proteins. Spectrum is limited to gram-positive bacteria, especially staphylococci.

Indications and Clinical Uses

The spectrum of cloxacillin includes gram-positive bacilli, including beta-lactamase producing strains of *Staphylococcus.* Therefore, it has been used to treat staphylococcal infections in animals, including pyoderma. Because of the availability of other beta-lactam drugs for treating gram-positive infections such as *Staphylococcus*, cloxacillin is used infrequently in small animals.

Precautionary Information

Adverse Reactions and Side Effects

Adverse effects of penicillin-drugs are most commonly caused by drug allergy. This can range from acute anaphylaxis when administered to other signs of allergic reaction when other routes are used. When administered orally (especially with high doses), diarrhea is possible.

Contraindications and Precautions

Use cautiously in animals allergic to penicillin-like drugs.

Drug Interactions

No drug interactions are reported in animals. However, do not mix with other drugs, because inactivation may result.

Instructions for Use

Doses based on empiricism or extrapolation from human studies. No clinical efficacy studies available for dogs or cats. Oral absorption is poor; administer if possible on empty stomach.

Patient Monitoring and Laboratory Tests

Culture and sensitivity testing: Use oxacillin as a guide for sensitivity testing.

Formulations

Cloxacillin is available in 250 and 500 mg capsules and 25 mg/mL oral solution.

Stability and Storage

Store in tightly sealed container, protected from light, and at room temperature. Stability of compounded formulations has not been evaluated.

Small Animal Dosage

Dogs and Cats

- 20-40 mg/kg q8h PO.

Large Animal Dosage

No dose has been reported for large animals.

Regulatory Information

Dairy cows (intramammary use) withdrawal time for milk: is 30 days for dry-cow treatment.

Cattle withdrawal time for meat: 10 days for meat and 48 hours for milk for the lactating cow treatment.

Codeine

koe′deen

Trade and Other Names: Generic, codeine phosphate, and codeine sulfate

Functional Classification: Analgesic, Opioid, Antitussive

Pharmacology and Mechanism of Action

Opiate agonist, analgesic. Mechanism is similar to morphine, except with approximately 1/10 potency of morphine. Action is to bind to mu-receptors and kappa-opiate receptors on nerves and inhibit release of neurotransmitters involved with transmission of pain stimuli (such as Substance P). Also may inhibit release of some inflammatory mediators. Central sedative and euphoric effects are related to mu-receptor effects in brain.

Indications and Clinical Uses

Codeine, or codeine with acetaminophen, is indicated for treatment of moderate pain. It also has been used as an antitussive. Despite the widespread use of codeine in humans, the efficacy in animals for its antitussive or analgesic use has not been established. Oral absorption in dogs is low. Because codeine is converted to morphine (10% of dose) for its activity, and duration of morphine is short in dogs, the clinical effectiveness of codeine in dogs may be questionable.

Precautionary Information

Adverse Reactions and Side Effects

Like all opiates, side effects from codeine are predictable and unavoidable. Side effects include sedation, constipation, and bradycardia. Respiratory depression occurs with high doses.

Contraindications and Precautions

Schedule II controlled substance. Tolerance and dependence occurs with chronic administration. Cats are more sensitive to excitement than other species.

Drug Interactions

No drug interactions are reported in animals. However, it will potentiate effects from other sedatives and CNS depressants.

Instructions for Use

Available as codeine phosphate and codeine sulfate oral tablets. Doses listed for analgesia are considered initial doses; individual patients may need higher doses depending on degree of tolerance or pain threshold.

Patient Monitoring and Laboratory Tests

Monitor patient's heart rate and respiration. Although bradycardia rarely needs to be treated when it is caused by an opioid, if necessary atropine can be administered. If serious respiratory depression occurs, the opioid can be reversed with naloxone.

Formulations

Codeine is available in 15, 30, and 60 mg tablets, 5 mg/mL syrup, and 3 mg/mL oral solution.

Stability and Storage

Store in tightly sealed container, protected from light, and at room temperature. Stability of compounded formulations has not been evaluated.

Small Animal Dosage

Dogs

- Analgesia: 0.5-1 mg/kg q4-6h PO.
- Antitussive: 0.1-0.3 mg/kg q4-6h PO.

Cats

- Analgesia: 0.5 mg/kg q6h PO. Increase dose as needed to control pain.
- Antitussive: 0.1 mg/kg q6h PO.

Large Animal Dosage

No dose has been reported for large animals.

Regulatory Information

Drug controlled by DEA. Schedule II; some antitussive forms are Schedule V.
RCI Classification: 1

Colchicine

kol'chih-seen

Trade and Other Names: Generic brands

Functional Classification: Antiinflammatory agent

Pharmacology and Mechanism of Action

Antiinflammatory agent. It inhibits fibrosis and formation of collagen.

Indications and Clinical Uses

In people, colchicine is used to treat gout. In animals it has been used as an antifibrotic agent to decrease fibrosis and development of hepatic failure (possibly by inhibiting formation of collagen). It has been used in animals to control amyloidosis. In Shar-pei dogs, colchicine has been used to treat a fever syndrome, possibly because of its use in people for treating Mediterranean fever.

Precautionary Information

Adverse Reactions and Side Effects

Adverse effects are not well documented in animals. Colchicine may cause dermatitis in people.

Contraindications and Precautions

Do not administer to pregnant animals.

Drug Interactions

There are no drug interactions reported for small animals.

Instructions for Use

Doses based on empiricism. There are no well-controlled efficacy studies in veterinary species.

Patient Monitoring and Laboratory Tests

No specific monitoring is necessary.

Formulations

Colchicine is available in 500 and 600 mcg tablets and 500 mcg/mL ampule injection.

Stability and Storage

Store in tightly sealed container, protected from light, and at room temperature. Stability of compounded formulations has not been evaluated.

Small Animal Dosage

Dogs and Cats

- 0.01-0.03 mg/kg q24h PO.

Large Animal Dosage

No dose has been reported for large animals.

Regulatory Information

No regulatory information is available. For extralabel use withdrawal interval estimates, contact FARAD at 1-888-USFARAD (1-888-873-2723) or send e-mail to FARAD@ncsu.edu.

Colony-Stimulating Factors

Trade and Other Names: Leukine and Neupogen

Functional Classification: Hormone

Pharmacology and Mechanism of Action

Stimulates granulocyte development in bone marrow. Two drugs in this class include filgrastim (rG-CSG) and sargramostim (rGM-CSF).

Indications and Clinical Uses

Colony-stimulating factors are used primarily to regenerate blood cells to recover from cancer chemotherapy or other bone marrow suppressing therapy. Their use is uncommon in animals.

Precautionary Information

Adverse Reactions and Side Effects

Pain at injection site. Edema has been reported in people.

Contraindications and Precautions

There are none identified in small animals.

Drug Interactions

There are no drug interactions reported for small animals.

Instructions for Use

Doses based on limited experimental information.

Patient Monitoring and Laboratory Tests

Monitor CBC to assess treatment. Treatment can be discontinued when neutrophils recover.

Formulations

Colony-stimulating factors are available in 300 mcg/mL (Neupogen) and 500 mcg/mL (Leukine).

Stability and Storage

Store in tightly sealed container protected from light.

Small Animal Dosage

Dogs and Cats

Doses for filgrastim have not been established for animals, but in people the dose is 5 mg/kg IV or SQ once a day after last day of chemotherapy. In people, sargramostim is used at a dose of 250 mg/m^2 per day as IV infusion or SQ.

Large Animal Dosage

No dose has been reported for large animals.

Regulatory Information

Do not administer to animals intended for food.

Corticotropin

kor-tih-koe-troe'pin

Trade and Other Names: Acthar

Functional Classification: Hormone

Pharmacology and Mechanism of Action

Corticotropin (ACTH). Corticotropin is a natural hormone, which results from 39 amino acids formulated into a gel. It stimulates normal synthesis of cortisol and other hormones from adrenal cortex.

Indications and Clinical Uses

ACTH is used for diagnostic purposes to evaluate adrenal gland function. Another closely related synthetic product, cosyntropin, is also used for the same purpose. The availability of Acthar gel has been limited. Compounded formulations may not be equivalent.

Precautionary Information

Adverse Reactions and Side Effects

Adverse effects unlikely when used as single injection for diagnostic purposes.

Contraindications and Precautions

Do not administer IV.

Drug Interactions

There are no drug interactions reported for small animals.

Instructions for Use

Doses are established by measuring normal adrenal response in animals. See also cosyntropin, which is sometimes preferred for clinical use. However, availability and cost of cosyntropin and ACTH are the factors that usually determine which is used in small animals.

Patient Monitoring and Laboratory Tests

Monitor cortisol concentrations. Post-ACTH response should be <20-25 units/dL for normal response.

Formulations

ACTH is available in 80 units/mL gel.

Stability and Storage

Store in tightly sealed container protected from light.

Small Animal Dosage

Dogs

- ACTH response test: Collect pre-ACTH sample and inject 2.2 International Units/kg IM. Collect post-ACTH sample at 2 hours.

Cats

- ACTH response test: Collect pre-ACTH sample and inject 2.2 International Units/kg IM. Collect post-ACTH sample 1.5 and 2 hours.

Large Animal Dosage

No dose has been reported for large animals.

Regulatory Information

No withdrawal times are available. Because clearance is rapid, and there is little risk from residues, no withdrawal time is suggested for food animals.

Cosyntropin

koe-sin-troe′pin

Trade and Other Names: Cortrosyn, Synthetic corticotropin, Tetracosactrin, and Tetracosactide

Functional Classification: Hormone

Pharmacology and Mechanism of Action

Cosyntropin is a synthetic form of corticotropin (ACTH). It is also known in international formularies as Tetracosactrin or Tetracosactide. Cosyntropin is an aqueous solution, whereas ACTH is a gel. Therefore cosyntropin can be administered IV, but ACTH gel cannot. Cosyntropin is also more potent than ACTH. Administration of cosyntropin will stimulate secretion of cortisol from adrenal glands. Administration of cosyntropin also will stimulate secretion of sex hormones of adrenal origin.

Indications and Clinical Uses

Cosyntropin is used for diagnostic purposes to evaluate adrenal gland function. Maximum peak cortisol secretion occurs at 60-90 minutes. It is used for same purpose as corticotropin, but in humans it is preferred over corticotropin because it is less allergenic.

Precautionary Information

Adverse Reactions and Side Effects

Adverse effects unlikely when used as single injection for diagnostic purposes. In people, cosyntropin is preferred over ACTH gel because cosyntropin is less allergenic.

Contraindications and Precautions

Maximum dose for dogs should be 250 mcg.

Drug Interactions

There are no drug interactions reported for small animals.

Instructions for Use

Use for diagnostic purposes only; it is not intended for treatment of hypoadrenocorticism. Cosyntropin is preferred to ACTH gel because it is available in a formulation that is easier to use in dogs and cats. In dogs, cosyntropin has been administered at 5 mcg/kg IV, 250 mcg/dog IM, and 5 mcg/kg IM. All three protocols produce similar results. Compounded formulations of ACTH may produce similar results at 60 min post-injection, but may have lower cortisol concentrations at 90 and 120 minutes compared to proprietary formulation. One may split reconstituted Cortrosyn into aliquots of 50 mcg each (250 mcg vial split into 5 aliquots) or 25 mcg each (250 mcg vial split into 10 aliquots) and frozen in plastic syringes.

Patient Monitoring and Laboratory Tests

Monitor cortisol concentrations. Post-cosyntropin response: 6-17 mcg/dL normal, 17-25 mcg/dL borderline, 25-30 mcg/dL suggestive, and >30 mcg/dL is highly likely for hyperadrenocorticism.

If monitoring sex hormones of adrenal origin, a sample for analysis should be taken at 60 minutes after injection.

Formulations

Cosyntropin is available in 250 mcg per vial.

Stability and Storage

Once prepared, this formulation can be kept in refrigerator for 4 months. Frozen cosyntropin can be stored in aliquots. For example, it can be stored in small syringes and frozen at –20° C for up to 6 months (*J Am Vet Med Assoc*, 212: 1569, 1998). Some compounded formulations are stable, but may give different results from the proprietary preparation.

Small Animal Dosage

Dogs

- Response test: collect pre-cosyntropin sample and inject 5 mcg/kg IV or IM and collect post sample at 30 and 60 minutes or one sample at 60 minutes. Maximum dose for dog should be 250 mcg. The following chart can be used for dosing: under 5 kg: 25 mcg; 5-10 kg: 50 mcg; 10-15 kg: 75 mcg; 15-20 kg: 100 mcg; 20-25 kg: 125 mcg; 25-30 kg: 150 mcg; 30-40 kg: 200 mcg; 40-50 kg: 225 mcg; and over 50 kg: 250 mcg (1 vial).

Cats

- Response test: collect pre-cosyntropin sample and inject 125 mcg (0.125 mg) IV or IM per cat and collect post sample at 60 and 90 min after IV administration or at 30 and 60 minutes after intramuscular administration.

Large Animal Dosage

Horses

- Collect a baseline sample at 8:00 am, inject 100 units IV per horse. Then, collect a second sample at 2 hours after injection.

Regulatory Information

No withdrawal times are available. Because clearance is rapid, and there is little risk from residues, no withdrawal time is suggested for animals intended for food.

Cyanocobalamin

sye-ahn-oh-koe-bahl′ah-min

Trade and Other Names: Vitamin B_{12}

Functional Classification: Vitamin

Pharmacology and Mechanism of Action

Vitamin B_{12} supplement.

Indications and Clinical Uses

Vitamin B_{12} has been used to treat some conditions of anemia. Vitamin B_{12} is used to manage vitamin B deficiencies associated with cobalt deficiency, inadequate intake, or intestinal malabsorption.

Precautionary Information

Adverse Reactions and Side Effects

Adverse effects are rare, except in high overdoses, because water soluble vitamins are easily excreted in the urine.

Contraindications and Precautions

No contraindications reported for animals.

Drug Interactions

There are no drug interactions reported for small animals.

Instructions for Use

Not necessary to supplement in animals with well-balanced diets.

Patient Monitoring and Laboratory Tests

Monitor CBC when used to treat anemia.

Formulations

Cyanocobalamin is available in tablets ranging from 25 to 1000 mcg. Injection formulations range from 1000 to 5000 mcg/mL. Vitamin B complex solutions may contain 10-100 mcg/mL of vitamin B_{12}.

Stability and Storage

Store in tightly sealed container, protected from light, and at room temperature. Stability of compounded formulations has not been evaluated.

Small Animal Dosage

Dogs

- 100-200 mcg/day PO
- 250-500 mcg/day IM or SQ.

Cats

- 50-100 mcg/day PO.
- 250 mcg/day IM or SQ.

Large Animal Dosage

Doses listed are on a per animal basis.

Calves and Foals

- 500 mcg once or twice weekly IM or SQ.

Lambs and Pigs

- 500 mcg once or twice weekly IM or SQ.

Cattle and Horses

- 1000-2000 mcg once or twice weekly IM or SQ.

Regulatory Information

No withdrawal times are available. Because clearance is rapid, and there is little risk from residues, no withdrawal time is suggested for animals intended for food.

Cyclophosphamide

sye-kloe-foss'fah-mide

Trade and Other Names: Cytoxan, Neosar, and CTX

Functional Classification: Anticancer agent

Pharmacology and Mechanism of Action

Cytotoxic and anticancer agent. Cyclophosphamide belongs to the group of nitrogen mustards. They are alkylating agents (bifunctional alkylating agents) that alkylate various macromolecules, but preferentially alkylate the N-7 of the guanine base of DNA. They are cytotoxic to cancer cells and are toxic to the rapidly dividing cells of the bone marrow. Cyclophosphamide must be metabolized to active metabolites for pharmacologic effect, which requires P-450 enzyme activation. The metabolites, hydroxyphosphamide and aldophosphamide, are cytotoxic. Aldophosphamide is converted at the tissue site to phosphoramide mustard and acrolein. Phosphoramide mustard is responsible for the antitumor effect, and acrolein is responsible for the cytotoxic action that causes toxicity (e.g., hemorrhagic cystitis). The half-life of the parent drug in dogs is 4-6.5 hours.

Indications and Clinical Uses

Cyclophosphamide is used primarily as adjunct for cancer chemotherapy and as immunosuppressive therapy. Cyclophosphamide is probably the most potent of the nitrogen mustards. It is used in chemotherapy protocols for a variety of tumors, carcinomas, sarcomas, feline lymphoproliferative diseases, mast cell tumor, mammary carcinoma, and especially lymphoproliferative tumors (lymphoma). Cancer protocols such as Cyclophosphamide, Oncovin, and prednisone (COP) and cyclophosphamide, hydroxydaunomycin, Oncovin, and prednisone (CHOP), incorporate cyclophosphamide as one of the agents. The other major use of cyclophosphamide is for immunosuppression. Although it has been used for various immune-mediated disorders in animals (immune-mediated hemolytic anemia, pemphigus, systemic lupus erythematosus [SLE]), efficacy has not been reported in controlled studies for these diseases. In one trial it was shown that cyclophosphamide (50 mg/m^2) had no benefit over prednisolone alone for treatment of immune-mediated hemolytic anemia (*J Vet Intern Med*, 17: 206-212, 2003).

Precautionary Information

Adverse Reactions and Side Effects

Cyclophosphamide is toxic to the bone marrow in a dose-dependent manner. After a single large bolus dose, the nadir of toxicity occurs in 7-10 days, but the effect is reversible because stem cells are sparred. Recovery usually occurs in 21-28 days. Vomiting and diarrhea may occur in some patients. Sterile, hemorrhagic cystitis is a serious and limiting complication to therapy. It is caused by the toxic effects of metabolites on the bladder epithelium (especially acrolein) that are concentrated and excreted in the urine. Various attempts are used to decrease the injury to the bladder epithelium. Corticosteroids are usually administered with cyclophosphamide to induce polyuria and decrease inflammation of the bladder. The drug mesna (Mesnex, mercaptoethane sulfonate) provides free active thiol groups to bind metabolites of cyclophosphamide in the urine. Furosemide (2.2 mg/kg) administered at same time as the cyclophosphamide dose may decrease risk of sterile hemorrhagic cystitis. Cats are less susceptible to developing cystitis compared to dogs. Cyclophosphamide may cause hair loss when used in some chemotherapeutic protocols. Dogs most susceptible are those with continuously growing hair (e.g., poodles and Old English sheepdogs). Cats do not tend to lose hair from cyclophosphamide treatment.

Contraindications and Precautions

Bone marrow suppressive and immunosuppressive. Use cautiously in animals at risk for infection. Teratogenic and embryotoxic. Do not use in pregnancy.

Drug Interactions

Use cautiously with other drugs that may cause bone marrow suppression. Although this drug is highly metabolized to active metabolites, it is not known what effect other drugs have on enzyme activity.

Instructions for Use

Cyclophosphamide is usually administered with other drugs (other cancer drugs in cancer protocols or corticosteroids when used for immunosuppressive therapy). Consult specific anticancer protocols for specific regimens. For example, the **COAP** protocol (COAP is a combination of cyclophosphamide, vincristine, prednisolone, and cytosine arabinoside) uses 50 mg/m^2 orally, every 48 hours, with vincristine, cytosine arabinoside, and prednisone for 8 weeks, but one **CHOP** protocol uses 100-150 mg/m^2 IV on the first day of the protocol, followed by other drugs such as doxorubicin, vincristine, and prednisone.

Patient Monitoring and Laboratory Tests

Monitor CBC in animals during treatment. Monitor urinalysis in dogs during treatment.

Formulations

Cyclophosphamide is available in 25 mg/mL injection and 25 and 50 mg tablets.

Stability and Storage

Store in tightly sealed container, protected from light, and at room temperature. Do not let temperatures exceed 30° C. Subject to hydrolysis in aqueous solutions. Use reconstituted solutions within 24 hours at room temperature and within 6 days if refrigerated, although some refrigerated solutions have been stable for 60 days.

Small Animal Dosage

Dogs

- Anticancer dose: 50 mg/m^2 (approx. 2.2 mg/kg) q48h or once daily 4 days/week PO. Alternatively, some protocols use 150-300 mg/m^2 IV and repeat in 21 days.
- Immunosuppressive therapy: Dog: 50 mg/m^2 q48h PO or 2.2 mg/kg once daily for 4 days/week.

Cats

- 6.25-12.5 mg/cat once daily 4 days/week.

Large Animal Dosage

No dose has been reported for large animals.

Regulatory Information

Withdrawal times are not established for animals that produce food. This drug should not be used in animals intended for food, because it is an anticancer agent.

Cyclosporine, Cyclosporin A

sye'kloe-spor-een

Trade and Other Names: Atopica (veterinary preparation), Neoral (human preparation), Sandimmune, Optimune (ophthalmic), Gengraf, and generic brands

Functional Classification: Immunosuppressive drug

Pharmacology and Mechanism of Action

Immunosuppressive drug. Cyclosporine binds to a specific cellular receptor on calcineurin and inhibits the T-cell receptor-activated signal transduction pathway. Particularly important are its effects to suppress interleukin-2 (IL-2) and other cytokines and blocks proliferation of activated T-lymphocytes. The action of cyclosporine is more specific for T-cells as compared to B-cells. The half-life of cyclosporine is 8-9 hours (average) in dogs and 8-10 hours (average) in cats. However, there is high variability on both species.

Indications and Clinical Uses

Cyclosporine use for keratoconjunctivitis sicca (KCS) is limited to topical administration. Systemic uses for cyclosporine include immune-mediated hemolytic anemia, atopy in dogs, and perianal fistulas. Other diseases have been treated with cyclosporine, such as sebaceous adenitis, idiopathic sterile nodular panniculitis, immune-mediated hemolytic anemia (IMHA), inflammatory bowel disease (IBD), immune-mediated polyarthritis, and aplastic anemia. It has also been used for treatment of granulomatous meningoencephalitis (3-6 mg/kg q12h). In dogs evidence is established for treatment of atopic dermatitis, for which there is similar efficacy as prednisolone. However, there is minimal effectiveness for immune-mediated pemphigus. In cats, cyclosporine has shown beneficial effects for treatment of eosinophilic granuloma complex, atopic dermatitis, stomatitis, and airway disease (feline asthma). In horses it is effective for localized treatment of anterior uveitis.

Precautionary Information

Adverse Reactions and Side Effects

The most common adverse effect in dogs is GI problems (vomiting, diarrhea, and anorexia). Nephrotoxicity may occur, but this is from high concentrations, which are rare with current dose recommendations. Cyclosporine may induce new hair growth in dogs. Neurotoxicity has been seen in dogs from high doses, which can be seen as tremors. However, this is uncommon from recommended doses. Although renal injury has been reported with older formulations, it has not been reported from use of current formulations of cyclosporine. Cyclosporine can inhibit pancreatic beta-cells, but diabetes has not been reported in pets from clinical use. Gingival hyperplasia and papillomas have been observed in dogs with chronic use. In cats, secondary infections, tumors, and toxoplasmosis have been reported from its use. Unlike other immunosuppressive drugs, it does not cause myelosuppression.

Contraindications and Precautions

If used with other drugs, consult Drug Interactions section for possible interference.

Drug Interactions

Cimetidine, erythromycin, or ketoconazole may increase cyclosporine concentrations when used concurrently. Doses of ketoconazole of 2.5 to 10 mg/kg/day in dogs have been shown to substantially decrease the clearance of cyclosporine and reduce the required dose by one-half or more. Grapefruit juice also inhibits clearance and will reduce the required dose. Food will decrease oral absorption by 15%-22%.

Instructions for Use

Atopica (veterinary) and Neoral (human) are identical formulations, except that sizes of capsules vary. After animals have been treated with initial doses of 5 mg/kg per day and are stable, doses may be adjusted by increasing interval to once every other day, or every third day, rather than lowering daily dose. Individual doses may be adjusted by monitoring of blood concentrations, but monitoring is not necessary for routine use. Atopica and Neoral oral products are absorbed more predictably than Sandimmune. Atopica and Neoral may produce 50% higher blood concentrations in some patients or reduce the variability in absorption that was associated with the Sandimmune formulations. Feeding may reduce oral absorption in dogs, but does not decrease efficacy. Generic formulations are available but have not been evaluated for bioequivalence to Atopica in dogs. Oral solution can be diluted to make it more palatable. To reduce the dose, some veterinarians have administered ketoconazole or other enzyme-inhibiting compounds concurrently. When used to treat animals for organ transplantation, the doses are generally higher, and the blood concentrations maintained at a higher level.

Patient Monitoring and Laboratory Tests

Although routine blood concentration monitoring is not necessary, it may be helpful to identify drug interactions, poor absorption, or poor compliance. When monitoring, collect whole blood in ethylenediaminetetraacetic acid (EDTA; purple-top) tube for submission to laboratory. Suggested trough blood concentration range (whole blood assay) is 300-400 ng/mL, although in some studies, levels as low as 200 ng/mL have been effective. If the assay uses fluorescence polarization immunoassay (FPIA) with a commercially available test system (commonly referred to as the TDx method), the feline measured concentration should be multiplied by 0.5 to arrive at a true value; the canine measured concentration should be multiplied by 0.65 to arrive at a drug value.

Formulations

Cyclosporine is available in 10, 25, 50, and 100 mg capsules (Atopica) and 25 and 100 microemulsion capsules and 100 mg/mL oral solution (Neoral, for microemulsion), 100 mg/mL oral solution and 25, 100 mg capsules (Sandimmune), 0.2% ophthalmic ointment (Optimune) and generic human capsules (Gengraf).

Stability and Storage

Store in tightly sealed container, protected from light, and at room temperature. Do not refrigerate, but store at below 30° C. Compounded ophthalmic products are stable at room temperature for 60 days, but do not refrigerate.

Small Animal Dosage

Dogs

- 3-7 mg/kg/day PO. The typical starting dose is 5 mg/kg/day, PO. After induction period, some dogs with atopic dermatitis have been controlled with doses as low as 5 mg/kg every other day to every third day.

- Perianal fistulas and immune-mediated diseases (e.g., IMHA) higher doses and more frequent administration have been used (every 12 hours).
- For immune suppression associated with organ transplantation: doses should be higher, e.g., 3-7 mg/kg q12h PO.

Cats

- 3-5 mg/kg/day PO. Higher doses of 5-10 mg/kg/day, PO, have been used in many cats every other day.
- For immune suppression associated with organ transplantation, doses should be higher, e.g., 3-5 mg/kg q12h PO.

Large Animal Dosage

Only local administration has been used in horses (ocular). No other dose has been reported for large animals.

Regulatory Information

Withdrawal times are not established for animals that produce food. This drug should not be used in animals intended for food, because it may have mutagenic potential.

Cyproheptadine Hydrochloride

sih'proe-hep'tah-deen hye-droe-klor'ide

Trade and Other Names: Periactin

Functional Classification: Antihistamine

Pharmacology and Mechanism of Action

Phenothiazine with antihistamine and antiserotonin properties. Used as appetite stimulant (probably by altering serotonin activity in appetite center).

Indications and Clinical Uses

Cyproheptadine is used in some cats for treatment of feline asthma if serotonin is considered a component of the airway inflammation. Used in some instances for treating inappropriate urination (urine spraying) in cats. Cyproheptadine has been used to treat equine pituitary pars intermedia dysfunction (Cushing's syndrome) at 0.6-1.2 mg/kg, but results have been controversial. It has been considered as a treatment for animals that have "serotonin syndrome" from antidepressant drugs, although efficacy has not been documented for this use.

Precautionary Information

Adverse Reactions and Side Effects

Stimulates hunger. May cause polyphagia and weight gain. Cyproheptadine also has antihistamine effects, antiserotonin effects, and antimuscarinic effects. In horses, it has been used at high doses without adverse effects.

Contraindications and Precautions

None reported for animals.

Drug Interactions

There are no drug interactions reported for small animals.

Instructions for Use

Clinical studies have not been performed in veterinary medicine. Use is based primarily on empiricism and extrapolation from human results. Syrup contains 5% alcohol.

Patient Monitoring and Laboratory Tests

Monitor weight gain in animals.

Formulations Available

Cyproheptadine is available in 4 mg tablets and 2 mg/5 mL syrup.

Stability and Storage

Store in tightly sealed container, protected from light, and at room temperature. Do not freeze the syrup. Stability of compounded formulations has not been evaluated.

Small Animal Dosage

Dogs and Cats

- Antihistamine: 0.5-1.1 mg/kg q8-12h PO, or 2-4 mg/cat PO q12-24h.
- Appetite stimulant: 2 mg/cat PO.
- Feline asthma: 1-2 mg/cat PO q12h.
- Use for inappropriate urination: 2 mg/cat q12h PO, then reduce dose to 1 mg/cat q12h PO.

Large Animal Dosage

Horses

- 0.5 mg/kg q12h PO.

Regulatory Information

No regulatory information is available. For extralabel use withdrawal interval estimates, contact FARAD at 1-888-USFARAD (1-888-873-2723) or send e-mail to FARAD@ncsu.edu.

RCI Classification: 4

Cytarabine

sye-tare′ah-been

Trade and Other Names: Cytosar, Ara-C, and Cytosine arabinoside

Functional Classification: Anticancer agent

Pharmacology and Mechanism of Action

Anticancer agent. Cytarabine (Cytosar) is a compound isolated from a sea sponge. It has also been referred to as cytosine arabinoside and Ara-C. Cytarabine is metabolized to an active drug that inhibits DNA synthesis. It was once thought that its action was via inhibition of the enzyme DNA polymerase, but the exact mechanism of action may not be known.

Indications and Clinical Uses

Cytarabine has been used for lymphoma and leukemia protocols. The most common use of cytarabine is treatment of lymphoma and myelogenous leukemia. It is usually administered as an intramuscular or subcutaneous injection, because it has a short half-life (< 20 minutes) when administered IV. Another use of cytarabine in dogs is for treatment of granulomatous meningoencephalomyelitis as an alternative to corticosteroids.

Cytarabine has been administered at a dose of 50 mg/m^2 SQ, twice daily for 2 days and repeated every 3 weeks.

Precautionary Information

Adverse Reactions and Side Effects

Cytarabine is bone marrow suppressive and can cause granulocytopenia, especially when delivered via continuous rate infusions. In addition, it may cause nausea and vomiting.

Contraindications and Precautions

Use cautiously in animals administered other bone marrow suppressing drugs.

Drug Interactions

There are no drug interactions reported for small animals.

Instructions for Use

Consult anticancer protocols for precise dosing regimens.

Patient Monitoring and Laboratory Tests

Monitor CBC to assess toxicity.

Formulations

Cytarabine is available in 100 mg vial for injection.

Stability and Storage

Store in tightly sealed container, protected from light, and at room temperature. Stability of compounded formulations has not been evaluated.

Small Animal Dosage

Dogs

- Lymphoma: 100 mg/m^2 once daily or 50 mg/m^2 twice daily for 4 days IV or SQ. Alternatively, 100 mg/m^2 as a 48 hour infusion.
- Granulomatous meningoencephalomyelitis: 50 mg/m^2 twice daily for 2 days and repeated every 3 weeks SQ.

Cats

- 100 mg/m^2 once daily for 2 days.

Large Animal Dosage

No dose has been reported for large animals.

Regulatory Information

Withdrawal times are not established for animals that produce food. This drug should not be used in animals intended for food, because it is an anticancer agent.

Dacarbazine

dah-kar'bah-zeen

Trade and Other Names: DTIC

Functional Classification: Anticancer agent

Pharmacology and Mechanism of Action

Anticancer agent. Dacarbazine (DTIC) is a monofunctional alkylating agent, thus it effectively blocks RNA synthesis. Its action is cell-cycle nonspecific.

Indications and Clinical Uses

DTIC has been primarily used for malignant melanoma and lymphoreticular neoplasms.

Precautionary Information

Adverse Reactions and Side Effects

Most common adverse effects are leukopenia, nausea, vomiting, and diarrhea.

Contraindications and Precautions

Do not use in cats.

Drug Interactions

There are no drug interactions reported for small animals.

Instructions for Use

Consult anticancer protocol for specific regimens.

Patient Monitoring and Laboratory Tests

Monitor CBC during treatment.

Formulations

DTIC is available in 200 mg vial for injection.

Stability and Storage

Store in tightly sealed container, protected from light, and at room temperature. Stability of compounded formulations has not been evaluated.

Small Animal Dosage

Dogs

- 200 mg/m^2 for 5 days q3wks IV or 800-1000 mg/m^2 q3wks IV.

Large Animal Dosage

No dose has been reported for large animals.

Regulatory Information

Withdrawal times are not established for animals that produce food. This drug should not be used in animals intended for food, because it is an anticancer agent.

Dalteparin

dahl'tah-pare-in

Trade and Other Names: Fragmin and LMWH

Functional Classification: Anticoagulant

Pharmacology and Mechanism of Action

Low-molecular weight heparin (LMWH). Fragmented heparin. LMWHs produce their effect by increasing antithrombin III mediated inhibition of synthesis and activity of coagulation factor Xa. LMWHs have several advantages compared to conventional heparin and include more complete and predictable absorption from injection, longer duration, and a more predictable anticoagulant response in animals.

Dalteparin has a half-life that is two to four times longer than heparin. LMWHs are classified on the basis of their Anti-factor Xa/Anti-factor IIa ratio. For dalteparin, the ratio is 2.7:1.

LMWHs currently available include tinzaparin (Innohep), enoxaparin (Lovenox), and dalteparin (Fragmin).

Indications and Clinical Uses

Dalteparin, like other LMWHs, is used to treat and prevent coagulation disorders such as thromboembolism, venous thrombosis, and pulmonary thromboembolism. LMWH, such as dalteparin, has been used with other supportive therapy for pulmonary thromboembolism, thromboembolism in cats, and as a prophylactic in animals at risk for disseminated intravascular coagulopathy (DIC).

Precautionary Information

Adverse Reactions and Side Effects

Although better tolerated than regular heparin, bleeding is a risk. However, LMWHs produce less bleeding problems than administration of conventional heparin. LMWHs are associated with a lower incidence of heparin-induced thrombocytopenia. No effects on platelet aggregation are expected.

Contraindications and Precautions

Do not administer IM; administer SQ only.

Drug Interactions

Do not mix with other injectable drugs. Use cautiously in animals that are already receiving other drugs that can interfere with coagulation, such as aspirin and warfarin. Although a specific interaction has not been identified, use cautiously in animals that may be receiving certain chondroprotective compounds such as glycosaminoglycans for treatment of arthritis.

Instructions for Use

Dosing recommendations are empirical because these compounds have not been used commonly in veterinary medicine. In cats 100 units/kg SQ produced anti-factor Xa activity. LMWHs are expensive compared to heparin. When dosing, do **not** interchange doses on a unit for unit basis with other heparins.

Patient Monitoring and Laboratory Tests

Monitoring patients for bleeding problems is important, but mechanism of action of LMWH is through binding antithrombin III and inhibiting clotting factors Xa and IIa. Because LMWH have a preference for factor Xa, the activity is measured as the factor Xa/factor IIa ratio. Therefore, dalteparin does not significantly affect prothrombin time (PT), thrombin time (TT), or activated partial thromboplastin time (APTT). Monitoring these clotting times could be misleading. Prolonged APTT is a sign of overdosing. Monitor anti-factor Xa activity if available.

Formulations

Dalteparin is available in 2500 units anti-factor Xa (16 mg dalteparin sodium) per 0.2 mL in a single dose syringe; 5000 units anti-factor Xa (32 mg dalteparin sodium) per 0.2 mL in a single dose syringe; and 10,000 units anti-factor Xa (64 mg dalteparin sodium) per mL in a 9.5 mL multiple-dose vial.

Stability and Storage

Use multiple-dose vial within 2 weeks of initial penetration. Store in tightly sealed container protected from light.

Small Animal Dosage

Dogs

- Prophylaxis: 70 units/kg once daily SQ.
- Treatment of thromboembolism: 200 units/kg once daily SQ.

Cats

- 100 units/kg q24h SQ. Increase interval to q12h in high-risk patients and use a lower dose of 50 units/kg SQ in low-risk patients.

(Human dose is 100 units/kg twice daily SQ for treatment of deep vein thrombosis.)

Large Animal Dosage

Horses

- 50 units/kg/day SQ. High-risk patients should receive 100 units/kg/day.

Regulatory Information

Extralabel withdrawal times are not established. However, 24 hour withdrawal times are suggested because this drug has little risk from residues.

Danazol

dan'ah-zole

Trade and Other Names: Danocrine

Functional Classification: Hormone

Pharmacology and Mechanism of Action

Gonadotropin inhibitor. Danazol suppresses luteinizing hormone (LH) and follicle-stimulating hormone (FSH), and estrogen synthesis.

Its mechanism of action for treating immune-mediated diseases is not understood. It may interfere with antibody production or interfere with the binding of complement or antibody to the platelet or red blood cell. It may also reduce receptors on monocytes for antibodies bound to platelets or red blood cells.

Indications and Clinical Uses

Danazol has hormone effects (antiestrogen) that are used for endometriosis in women. Danazol (Danocrine) also has been used for treating refractory patients with immune-mediated thrombocytopenia and immune-mediated hemolytic anemia.

Precautionary Information

Adverse Reactions and Side Effects

Danazol may cause signs similar to other androgenic drugs. Adverse effects have not been reported in animals.

Contraindications and Precautions

It is absolutely contraindicated in pregnancy.

Drug Interactions

It has been used with other drugs in the treatment of immune-mediated diseases without reported interactions.

Instructions for Use

When used to treat autoimmune disease, usually used in conjunction with other drugs (e.g., corticosteroids).

Patient Monitoring and Laboratory Tests

Monitor CBC if used for treatment of immune-mediated diseases.

Formulations

Danazol is available in 50, 100, 200 mg capsules.

Stability and Storage

Store in tightly sealed container, protected from light, and at room temperature. Stability of compounded formulations has not been evaluated.

Small Animal Dosage

Dogs and Cats

- 5-10 mg/kg q12h PO.

Large Animal Dosage

No dose has been reported for large animals.

Regulatory Information

Danazol is an anabolic agent and should not be administered to animals intended for food.

RCI Classification: 4

Danofloxacin Mesylate

dan-oh-floks'ah-sin mess'ih-late

Trade and Other Names: A180

Functional Classification: Antibacterial

Pharmacology and Mechanism of Action

Danofloxacin like other fluoroquinolones has activity against a broad spectrum of bacteria, including gram-negative bacilli, especially *Enterobacteriaceae (Escherichia coli, Klebsiella, Salmonella),* some gram-positive cocci, such as *Staphylococcus.* In particular it has good activity against pathogens in cattle, such as *Pasteurella multocida, Mannheimia haemolytica,* and *Histophilus somni* (formerly *Haemophilus somnus*). In cattle, subcutaneous absorption is high. Half-life is 3-6 hours.

When used to treat bovine respiratory disease (BRD) in cattle (*Am J Vet Res,* 66: 342-349, 2005) danofloxacin produced area under the curve (AUC): minimum inhibitory concentration (MIC) ratios >125.

Indications and Clinical Uses

Danofloxacin is indicated for the treatment of BRD caused by *P. multocida, M. haemolytica,* and *H. somni* (formerly *H. somnus*). As a fluoroquinolone with a broad spectrum of activity, other organisms are susceptible. However, extralabel use in animals intended for food for other diseases is prohibited. There are no published reports of danofloxacin use in other animals.

Precautionary Information

Adverse Reactions and Side Effects

All fluoroquinolones at high concentrations may cause CNS toxicity. In safety studies in cattle, when high doses were administered it caused lameness, articular cartilage lesions, and CNS problems (tremors, nystagmus, etc.). Subcutaneous injections may cause tissue irritation. All of the fluoroquinolones may cause arthropathy in young animals, but this effect has not been examined in other species for danofloxacin. In field trials, danofloxacin was associated with lameness in some calves. Fluoroquinolones have caused blindness in cats, but this has not been reported in any species from danofloxacin.

Contraindications and Precautions

Do not inject more than 15 mL in one site. Do not use extralabel. Do not use in other species for which safety information is not available. Do not use in animals prone to seizures.

Drug Interactions

Fluoroquinolones may increase concentrations of theophylline if used concurrently. Do not mix in solutions or in vials with aluminum, calcium, iron, or zinc, because chelation may occur.

Instructions for Use

Inject SQ in neck of cattle.

Patient Monitoring and Laboratory Tests

No specific monitoring is necessary. CLSI (NCCLS) break points for sensitive organisms is less than or equal to 0.25 mcg/mL for cattle respiratory pathogens. Most organisms have minimum inhibitory concentration (MIC) values ≤0.06 mcg/mL.

Formulations

Danofloxacin is available in an injectable solution of 180 mg/mL (with 2-pyrrolidone and polyvinyl alcohol).

Stability and Storage

Store below 30° C, protected from light, and protected from freezing. A slight yellow or amber color is acceptable.

Small Animal Dosage

Dogs and Cats

No small animal dose has been reported.

Large Animal Dosage

Cattle

- 6 mg/kg (1.5 mL per 100 pounds), once per 48 hours, SQ.

Equine and Swine

No dose has been reported.

Regulatory Information

Do not use in calves intended for veal.

Cattle withdrawal time (for meat): 4 days. Not established for milk because it cannot be used in lactating cattle. It is prohibited to use extralabel.

Dantrolene Sodium

dan'troe-leen soe'dee-um

Trade and Other Names: Dantrium

Functional Classification: Muscle relaxant

Pharmacology and Mechanism of Action

Muscle relaxant. Dantrolene inhibits calcium leakage from sarcoplasmic reticulum. By inhibiting calcium initiation of muscle contraction, it relaxes muscle.

Indications and Clinical Uses

Dantrolene is used as a muscle relaxant. However, in addition to muscle relaxation, it has been used for malignant hyperthermia and it also has been used to relax urethral muscle in cats.

In horses, it has improved clinical signs associated with exertional rhabdomyolysis ("tying up").

Precautionary Information

Adverse Reactions and Side Effects

Muscle relaxants can cause weakness in some animals. Use of dantrolene in people has caused hepatitis in some cases.

Contraindications and Precautions

Do not use in animals with hepatic disease. Use with caution in weak or debilitated animals.

Drug Interactions

Do not mix or reconstitute the intravenous solution with acidic solutions, because they are incompatible.

Instructions for Use

Give oral doses on empty stomach. Doses have been primarily extrapolated from experimental studies or extrapolation of human studies. No clinical trials available in veterinary medicine. To relax urethra in cats, most effective dose is 1 mg/kg IV. When administering dantrolene for treatment of malignant hyperthermia, because of dilute solution in vial, several vials may be needed in large animals.

Patient Monitoring and Laboratory Tests

When used for treatment of malignant hyperthermia, monitor body temperature, and acid-base balance. In people, dantrolene may cause hepatitis and tests of liver injury (e.g., liver enzymes) and/or function are monitored.

Formulations

Dantrolene is available in 100 mg capsules and 20 mg vial for injection, when reconstituted is equal to 0.33 mg/mL injection.

Stability and Storage

When intravenous solution is prepared, it is stable for a short time (6 hours). It may be mixed with solutions such as 5% dextrose and 0.9% sodium chloride. Do not use intravenous solution if cloudiness or precipitation is present in vial. Compounded oral suspensions are stable for 150 days if mixed with acid solutions (e.g., citric acid). Store in tightly sealed container, protected from light, and at room temperature.

Small Animal Dosage

Dogs

- Prevention of malignant hyperthermia: 2-3 mg/kg IV.
- Malignant hyperthermia crisis: doses of 2.5-3 mg/kg IV rapid bolus.
- Muscle relaxation: 1-5 mg/kg q8h PO.
- Urethral relaxation: 1-5 mg/kg q8h PO or 0.5-1.0 mg/kg IV.

Cats

- Muscle relaxation: 0.5-2 mg/kg q12h PO.
- Relaxation of urethra: 1-2 mg/kg q8h PO.

Large Animal Dosage

Horses

- 4 mg/kg PO.

Pigs

- Malignant hyperthermia: 1-3 mg/kg IV once.
- Prophylaxis: 5 mg/kg PO.

Regulatory Information

No regulatory information is available. For extralabel use withdrawal interval estimates, contact FARAD at 1-888-USFARAD (1-888-873-2723) or send e-mail to FARAD@ncsu.edu.

RCI Classification: 4

Dapsone

dap'sone

Trade and Other Names: Generic brands

Functional Classification: Antibacterial

Pharmacology and Mechanism of Action

Antimicrobial drug used for treatment of mycobacterium. It may have some immunosuppressive properties or inhibit function of inflammatory cells.

Indications and Clinical Uses

Although originally used as an antibacterial drug, in veterinary medicine it is used primarily for dermatologic diseases in dogs, especially subcorneal pustular dermatosis and dermatitis herpetiformis. It also has been used for canine pemphigus.

Precautionary Information

Adverse Reactions and Side Effects

Hepatitis and blood dyscrasias may occur. Because it shares similar properties as a sulfonamide, the same reactions seen with sulfonamides can be seen with dapsone and include anemia, neutropenia, thrombocytopenia, hepatotoxicosis, and skin drug eruptions. It is toxic to cats and will cause neurotoxicosis and anemia.

Contraindications and Precautions

Do not administer to cats. Do not administer to animals that are sensitive to sulfonamides.

Drug Interactions

Use caution when administering dapsone with trimethoprim/sulfonamide combinations. Trimethoprim may increase blood concentrations of dapsone, because it inhibits excretion and potentiates dapsone adverse effects.

Instructions for Use

Doses are derived from extrapolation of human doses or empiricism. No well-controlled clinical studies have been performed in veterinary medicine.

Patient Monitoring and Laboratory Tests

Monitor for signs of hepatic reactions. Monitor CBC occasionally because bone marrow toxicity has occurred in some animals.

Formulations

Dapsone is available in 25 and 100 mg tablets.

Stability and Storage

Store in tightly sealed container, protected from light, and at room temperature. Dapsone may discolor without change in potency. Compounded suspension formulations have been stable for 21 days when mixed with citric acid.

Small Animal Dosage

Dogs

- 1.1 mg/kg q8-12h PO.

Cats

Contraindicated.

Large Animal Dosage

No dose has been reported for large animals.

Regulatory Information

No regulatory information is available. For extralabel use withdrawal interval estimates, contact FARAD at 1-888-USFARAD (1-888-873-2723) or send e-mail to FARAD@ncsu.edu.

Deferoxamine Mesylate

deh-fer-oks′ah-meen mess′ih-late

Trade and Other Names: Desferal

Functional Classification: Antidote

Pharmacology and Mechanism of Action

Chelating agent with strong affinity for trivalent cations. Used to treat acute iron toxicosis.

Indications and Clinical Uses

Deferoxamine is indicated in cases of severe poisoning, especially iron toxicosis. Deferoxamine also has been used to chelate aluminum and facilitate removal.

Precautionary Information

Adverse Reactions and Side Effects

Adverse effects have not been reported in animals. Allergic reactions and hearing problems have occurred in people.

Contraindications and Precautions

No contraindications reported for animals.

Drug Interactions

Deferoxamine will chelate with cations; avoid mixing with cations prior to administration.

Instructions for Use

One hundred mg of deferoxamine binds 8.5 mg of ferric iron. Contact local poison control center for guidance on dosing.

Patient Monitoring and Laboratory Tests

Monitor serum iron concentrations to determine severity of intoxication and success of therapy. Successful therapy is indicated by monitoring urine color (orange-rose color change to urine indicates chelated iron is being eliminated).

Formulations

Deferoxamine is available in a 500 mg vial for injection.

Stability and Storage

Deferoxamine is soluble in water. Stable when stored in solution for 14 days. Store in tightly sealed container, protected from light, and at room temperature. Do not refrigerate and do not mix solutions with other medications.

Small Animal Dosage

Dogs and Cats

- 10 mg/kg q2h for 2 doses IV or IM, then 10 mg/kg q8h for 24 hours.

Large Animal Dosage

No dose has been reported for large animals.

Regulatory Information

No regulatory information is available. For extralabel use withdrawal interval estimates, contact FARAD at 1-888-USFARAD (1-888-873-2723) or send e-mail to FARAD@ncsu.edu.

Deracoxib

dare-ah-koks'ib

Trade and Other Names: Deramaxx

Functional Classification: Antiinflammatory

Pharmacology and Mechanism of Action

Deracoxib is a nonsteroidal antiinflammatory drug (NSAID). Like other drugs in this class, deracoxib produces analgesic and antiinflammatory effects by inhibiting the synthesis of prostaglandins. The enzyme inhibited by NSAID is the cyclo-oxygenase enzyme (COX). The COX enzyme exists in two isoforms, called COX-1 and COX-2.

COX-1 is primarily responsible for synthesis of prostaglandins important for maintaining a healthy GI tract, renal function, platelet function, and other normal functions. COX-2 is induced and responsible for synthesizing prostaglandins that are important mediators of pain, inflammation, and fever. (There may be some crossover of COX-1 and COX-2 effects in some situations.) Deracoxib, using in vitro assays, is more COX-1 sparing compared to older NSAIDs and is a selective inhibitor of COX-2. The COX-1/COX-2 ratio is high compared to some other drugs registered for dogs. It also is a selective COX-2 inhibitor in cats. It has not been established if the specificity for COX-1 or COX-2 is related to efficacy or safety.

Deracoxib has a half-life of 3 hours in dogs at 2-3 mg/kg and 19 hours at 20 mg/kg. It is highly protein bound. Oral absorption is 90% in dogs. Feeding delays absorption, but does not diminish overall absorption.

Indications and Clinical Uses

Deracoxib is used to decrease pain, inflammation, and fever. It has been used for the acute and chronic treatment of pain and inflammation in dogs. One of the most common uses is osteoarthritis but also has been used for pain associated with surgery. Use in large animals has not been reported.

Precautionary Information

Adverse Reactions and Side Effects

GI problems are the most often adverse effects associated with NSAIDs and can include vomiting, diarrhea, nausea, ulcers, and erosions of the GI tract. Gastric and duodenal ulcers have been reported from use of deracoxib in dogs. Both acute and long-term safety and efficacy have been established for dogs. In field trials, vomiting was the most often reported adverse effect. In studies performed in dogs, higher doses (five times the dose) caused azotemia in normal dogs. Renal toxicity, especially in dehydrated animals or animals with preexisting renal disease has been shown for some NSAIDs.

Contraindications and Precautions

Dogs and cats with preexisting GI problems or renal problems may be at a greater risk of adverse effects from NSAIDs. Safety in pregnancy is not known, but adverse effects have not been reported. Safety studies are not available for dogs <4 months of age, pregnant animals, or lactating animals.

Drug Interactions

Do not administer with other NSAIDs or with corticosteroids. Corticosteroids have been shown to exacerbate the GI adverse effects. Some NSAIDs may interfere with the action of diuretic drugs and angiotensin-converting enzyme (ACE) inhibitors.

Instructions for Use

Use according to manufacturer's dosing guidelines. Chewable tablets can be administered with or without food. Although long-term studies have not been completed in cats, only single-dose studies have been reported.

Patient Monitoring and Laboratory Tests

Monitor GI signs for evidence of diarrhea, GI bleeding, or ulcers. Because of risk of renal injury, monitor renal parameters (water consumption, BUN, creatinine, and urine specific gravity) periodically during treatment. Deracoxib does not appear to affect thyroid hormone assays in dogs.

Formulations

Deracoxib is available in 25 and 100 mg chewable tablets.

Stability and Storage

Store in tightly sealed container, protected from light, and at room temperature. Stability of compounded formulations has not been evaluated.

Small Animal Dosage

Dogs

- Postoperative pain: 3-4 mg/kg once daily as needed for up to 7 days.
- Chronic use: 1-2 mg/kg once daily PO.

Cats

- Long-term safety in cats has not been determined.

Large Animal Dosage

No dose has been reported for large animals.

Regulatory Information

Do not administer to animals that produce food.
RCI Classification: 4

Desmopressin Acetate

dess-moe-press'in ass'ih-tate

Trade and Other Names: DDAVP

Functional Classification: Hormone

Pharmacology and Mechanism of Action

Synthetic peptide similar to antidiuretic hormone (ADH). It produces similar effects as natural ADH and is used to treat diabetes insipidus (DI) in animals. This action is related to stimulation of water reabsorption in the distal renal tubule. The difference between DDAVP and natural ADH is that DDAVP is longer acting and produces fewer vasoconstriction effects. In addition to the hormone effects, in humans administration of DDAVP results in twofold to fivefold increase in the plasma von Willebrand factor. It may induce a 50% increase in von Willebrand factor in some but not as consistently as when administered to people.

Indications and Clinical Uses

Desmopressin is used as replacement therapy for patients with DI and also has been used for treatment of patients with mild to moderate von Willebrand's disease prior to surgery or other procedure that may cause bleeding. However, the response in von Willebrand deficient dogs is not as consistent or as great as in people.

Precautionary Information

Adverse Reactions and Side Effects

No side effects reported. In people, it rarely has caused thrombotic events.

Contraindications and Precautions

There are no specific contraindications.

Drug Interactions

Administration of urea and fludrocortisone will increase the antidiuretic effects.

Instructions for Use

Desmopressin is used only for central DI. Duration of effect is variable (8-20 hours) but typically has a duration of 8-12 hours. It is ineffective for treatment of nephrogenic diabetes insipidus or polyuria from other causes. Intranasal product has been administered as eye drops in dogs. Onset of effect is within 1 hour. (*J Am Vet Med Assoc,* 205: 170, 1994; *J Am Vet Med Assoc,* 209: 1884, 1996.) Oral tablets are available for humans.

Patient Monitoring and Laboratory Tests

Monitor water intake and urinalysis to assess therapy. Desmopressin may be used as a test for DI in animals. To perform this test, administer 2 mcg/kg SQ or IV or 20 mcg intranasally or in the eye. This should be followed by monitoring of urine concentration and animal's body weight. Increase in urine concentrating ability may indicate a diagnosis of DI.

Formulations

Desmopressin is available in a 4 and 15 mcg/mL injection, acetate nasal solution 100 mcg/mL (0.01%) metered spray, and 0.1 and 0.2 mg tablets.

Stability and Storage

Store in tightly sealed container, protected from light, and at room temperature. Stability of compounded formulations has not been evaluated.

Small Animal Dosage

- DI: 2-4 drops (2 mcg) q12-24h intranasal or in eye. The intranasal form can be injected if necessary at a dose of 0.5-2 mcg/dog q12-24h IV or SQ.
- 0.05-0.1 mg q12h PO or as needed. The oral dose may be increased to 0.1-0.2 mg/kg as needed.
- von Willebrand's disease treatment: 1 mcg/kg (0.01 mL/kg), diluted in 20 mL of saline administered SQ, or over 10 min IV.

Large Animal Dosage

No dose has been reported for large animals.

Regulatory Information

Withdrawal times are not established. However, this drug has rapid clearance, with little risk from residues; therefore, a short withdrawal time is suggested for food animals.

Desoxycorticosterone Pivalate

dess-oks-ih-kor-tik-oh-steer′one piv′ah-late

Trade and Other Names: Percorten-V, DOCP, and DOCA pivalate

Functional Classification: Corticosteroid

Pharmacology and Mechanism of Action

Mineralocorticoid with no glucocorticoid activity. Desoxycorticosterone mimics the effects of aldosterone by retaining sodium. The pivalate formulation produces a long-lasting effect from a single administration.

Indications and Clinical Uses

Desoxycorticosterone is used for adrenocortico-insufficiency (hypoadrenocorticism). Some dogs also may require concurrent glucocorticosteroid therapy when it is used to treat insufficiency.

Precautionary Information

Adverse Reactions and Side Effects

Excessive mineralocorticoid effects are possible with high doses. Signs of iatrogenic hyperadrenocorticism are not expected with this drug.

Contraindications and Precautions

Do not use in pregnant animals. Do not use in patients with CHF or renal disease.

Drug Interactions

Aldosterone antagonists (spironolactone) will blunt the effect.

Instructions for Use

Initial dose based on average response in clinical patients, but individual doses may be based on monitoring electrolytes in patients. The actual interval between doses may range from 14-35 days. (*J Vet Intern Med*, 11: 43-49, 1997.)

Patient Monitoring and Laboratory Tests

Monitor serum sodium and potassium.

Formulations

Desoxycorticosterone is available in 25 mg/mL suspension for injection.

Stability and Storage

Store in tightly sealed container, protected from light, and at room temperature. Stability of compounded formulations has not been evaluated.

Small Animal Dosage

Dogs

- 1.5-2.2 mg/kg q25days IM. Adjust dose by monitoring electrolytes.

Large Animal Dosage

No dose has been reported for large animals.

Regulatory Information

Withdrawal times are not established. However, because of low risk of residues, no withdrawal times are suggested.
RCI Classification: 4

Detomidine Hydrochloride

deh-toe′mih-deen hye-droe-klor′ide

Trade and Other Names: Dormosedan

Functional Classification: $Alpha_2$ Analgesic

Pharmacology and Mechanism of Action

$Alpha_2$ adrenergic agonist. $Alpha_2$ agonists decrease release of neurotransmitters from the neuron. The proposed mechanism whereby they decrease transmission is via binding to presynaptic $alpha_2$ receptors (negative feedback receptors). The result is decreased sympathetic outflow, analgesia, sedation, and anesthesia. Other drugs in this class include xylazine, medetomidine, and clonidine.

Indications and Clinical Uses

Detomidine is used primarily as a sedative, anesthetic adjunct, and analgesia. It is used in horses more often than in other species. Detomidine also has been administered for epidural analgesia. For pain, detomidine appears to be more potent and longer acting than xylazine.

Precautionary Information

Adverse Reactions and Side Effects

At typical doses, sedation, ataxia, swaying, and bradycardia are common. Cardiac depression, AV block, and hypotension possible with high doses. In some horses, hyperresponsiveness to stimuli occurs. Diuresis occurs as a consequence of the hyperglycemia produced by $alpha_2$ agonists such as detomidine. Yohimbine (0.11 mg/kg) can be used to reverse effects of $alpha_2$ agonists such as detomidine.

Contraindications and Precautions

Concurrent use of detomidine with sulfonamides IV can lead to cardiac arrhythmias. Xylazine causes problems in pregnant animals and this should be considered for other $alpha_2$ agonists as well. Use cautiously in animals that are pregnant, because it may induce labor. In addition, it may decrease oxygen delivery to fetus in late gestation.

Drug Interactions

Other drugs that depress the heart may increase risk for arrhythmias.

Instructions for Use

Doses not established for small animals, it is used primarily for horses. Atropine (0.01 to 0.02 mg/kg) has been used to prevent bradycardia but is not necessary for routine use.

Patient Monitoring and Laboratory Tests

Monitor heart rate, and, if possible the ECG during treatment with this class of drugs. If available, blood pressure monitoring may be indicated in some patients.

Formulations

Detomidine is available in a 10 mg/mL injection.

Stability and Storage

Store in tightly sealed container, protected from light, and at room temperature. Stability of compounded formulations has not been evaluated.

Small Animal Dosage

Doses not established for small animals.

Large Animal Dosage

Horses

- Sedation: 20-40 mcg/kg (0.02-0.04 mg/kg) IV or IM. Lower doses are sometimes used in practice. For example, doses of 10 mcg/kg (0.01 mg/kg) will produce slightly less ataxia and sedation. Doses as low as 5 mcg/kg have been used in draft horses.
- Analgesia: 20 mcg/kg (0.02 mg/kg) IV or IM. Duration of analgesia may be longer if a dose of 40 mcg/kg is used.

Cattle

- 2-10 mcg/kg (0.002-0.1 mg/kg) IV or 5-40 mcg/kg (0.005-0.04 mg/kg) IM.

Regulatory Information

Cattle withdrawal times (extralabel): 3 days meat; 72 hours milk.
RCI Classification: 3

Dexamethasone

deks-ah-meth′ah-sone

Trade and Other Names: Azium solution in polyethylene glycol, Dexaject, Dex-A-Vet, Decadron, Dexasone, Voren suspension, and generic brands

Functional Classification: Corticosteroid

Pharmacology and Mechanism of Action

Corticosteroid. Antiinflammatory and immunosuppressive effects are approximately thirty times more potent than cortisol. Antiinflammatory effects are complex but primarily via inhibition of inflammatory cells and suppression of expression of inflammatory mediators. Use is for treatment of inflammatory and immune-mediated disease. This dexamethasone solution differs from dexamethasone sodium phosphate in that the sodium phosphate form is water-soluble and appropriate for intravenous administration. Dexamethasone solution is in a polyethylene glycol vehicle that should not be administered rapidly IV. Dexamethasone-21-isonicotinate is a suspension registered for IM use.

Indications and Clinical Uses

Dexamethasone is used for treatment of inflammatory and immune-mediated disease. The use of dexamethasone at high doses for treatment of shock is controversial. Most recent evidence does not support administration of dexamethasone for this use. Large animal uses include induction of parturition (cattle) and treatment of inflammatory conditions. In cattle, corticosteroids also have been used in the treatment of ketosis. In horses, dexamethasone has been used to treat recurrent airway obstruction (RAO).

Precautionary Information

Adverse Reactions and Side Effects

Side effects from corticosteroids are many, and include polyphagia, polydipsia/polyuria, and hypothalamic-pituitary-adrenal (HPA) axis suppression. Adverse effects include GI ulceration, hepatopathy, diabetes, hyperlipidemia, decreased thyroid hormone, decreased protein synthesis, delayed wound healing, and immunosuppression. Secondary infections can occur as a result of immunosuppression and include demodex, toxoplasmosis, fungal infections, and UTIs. In horses, additional adverse effects include risk of laminitis.

Contraindications and Precautions

Use cautiously in patients prone to ulcers, infection, or in animals in which wound healing is necessary. Use cautiously in diabetic animals, animals with renal failure, or pregnant animals. Intravenous injections should be done slowly because formulations contain polyethylene glycol which can cause reactions from rapid intravenous injection (hemolysis, hypotension, and collapse). Do not administer dexamethasone-21-isonicotinate intravenously (IM use only).

Drug Interactions

Administration of corticosteroids with nonsteroidal antiinflammatory drugs (NSAIDs) will increase the risk of GI injury. pH is 7-8.5. Do not mix with acidifying solutions. Otherwise is compatible with most intravenous fluid solutions.

Instructions for Use

Dosing schedules are based on desired effect. Antiinflammatory effects are seen at doses of 0.1-0.2 mg/kg and immunosuppressive effects at 0.2-0.5 mg/kg. Dexamethasone is used to test for hyperadrenocorticism. Low-dose dexamethasone suppression test: dogs 0.01 mg/kg (or 0.015 mg/kg in some references) IV and cats 0.1 mg/kg IV; collect sample at 0, 4, and 8 hours. For high-dose dexamethasone suppression test: dogs 0.1 mg/kg (or 1.0 mg/kg in some references) and cats: 1.0 mg/kg.

Patient Monitoring and Laboratory Tests

For low-dose and high-dose dexamethasone suppression test, administer either 0.01 or 0.1 mg/kg and collect cortisol sample at 0, 4, and 8 hours after administration. Normal cortisol concentration after suppression test should be <30-40 nmol/L (1.1-1.3 mcg/dL). Dexamethasone suppression test for horses: administer 0.04 mg/kg IM and collect postcortisol sample 24 hours later. Normal suppression in horses is <1 mcg/dL.

Formulations

Dexamethasone is available in a 2 mg/mL solution, which contains 500 mg polyethylene glycol, 0.25, 0.5, 0.75, 1, 1.5, 2, 4, and 6 mg tablets, 0.1 and 1 mg/mL oral solution, and 10 mg per 15 g powder. Dexamethasone-21-isonicotinate suspension is 1 mg/mL.

Stability and Storage

Store in tightly sealed container, protected from light, and at room temperature. Dexamethasone formulated in various oral mixtures to enhance flavoring were stable for 26 weeks at room temperature or refrigerated. Dexamethasone sodium phosphate is freely soluble in water, but dexamethasone solution (in polyethylene glycol) is practically insoluble in water.

Small Animal Dosage

Dogs and Cats

- Antiinflammatory: 0.07-0.15 mg/kg q12-24h IV, IM, or PO.
- Low-dose dexamethasone suppression test: 0.01 mg/kg IV (dog) and 0.1 mg/kg IV (cat).
- High-dose dexamethasone suppression test: 0.1 mg/kg IV (dog) and 1.0 mg/kg IV (cat).
- Dexamethasone-21-isonicotinate: 0.03-0.05 mg/kg IM.

Large Animal Dosage

Cattle and Horses

- 0.04-0.15 mg/kg per day IV or IM. Some product labeling lists a total dose of 5-20 mg/animal, which corresponds to 0.01 to 0.04 mg/kg/day. However, for some conditions, higher doses may be needed.
- Induction of parturition (cattle): 0.05 mg/kg (25 mg/animal) as a single dose during the last week or 2 weeks of pregnancy. A dose of prostaglandin PG-F_2 alpha may be administered concurrently (0.5 mg/animal).
- Dexamethasone-21-isonicotinate: 0.01-0.04 mg/kg IM.

Sheep

- Induction of parturition: 0.15 mg/kg/day IM for 1-5 days during the last week of gestation.

Regulatory Information

Dexamethasone is approved for use in cattle, but withdrawal times are not established. Although withdrawal times are not listed on the label, at least 96 hours should be used for milk, and 4-8 days for meat. Allow at least 3 weeks to eliminate residues from kidney and liver and 6 weeks to deplete drug from intramuscular injection site. RCI Classification: 4

Dexamethasone Sodium Phosphate

Trade and Other Names: Sodium phosphate: Dexaject SP, Dexavet, and Dexasone. Decadron and generic brand tablets

Functional Classification: Corticosteroid

Pharmacology and Mechanism of Action

Corticosteroid. Antiinflammatory and immunosuppressive effects are approximately thirty times more potent than cortisol. Antiinflammatory effects are complex but primarily occur via inhibition of inflammatory cells and suppression of expression of inflammatory mediators. Half-life in plasma for dexamethasone ranges from 3 to 6 hours, but duration of action is 36-48 hours.

Indications and Clinical Uses

Use of dexamethasone is for treatment of inflammatory and immune-mediated disease. The use of dexamethasone at high doses for treatment of shock is controversial. Most recent evidence does not support administration of dexamethasone for this use. Large animal uses include induction of parturition (cattle) and treatment of inflammatory conditions. In cattle, corticosteroids also have been used in the treatment of ketosis.

Precautionary Information

Adverse Reactions and Side Effects

Side effects from corticosteroids are many and include polyphagia, polydipsia/polyuria, and hypothalamic-pituitary-adrenal (HPA) axis suppression. Adverse effects include GI ulceration, hepatopathy, diabetes, hyperlipidemia, decreased thyroid hormone, decreased protein synthesis, delayed wound healing, and immunosuppression. Secondary infections can occur as a result of immunosuppression and include *Demodex,* toxoplasmosis, fungal infections, and UTIs. In horses, additional adverse effects include risk of laminitis.

Contraindications and Precautions

Use cautiously in patients prone to ulcers, infection, or in animals in which wound healing is necessary. Use cautiously, or not at all, in animals receiving nonsteroidal antiinflammatory drugs (NSAIDs), because these drugs administered concurrently will increase the risk of GI ulceration. Use cautiously in diabetic animals, animals with renal failure, or pregnant animals.

Drug Interactions

Administration of corticosteroids with NSAIDs will increase the risk of GI injury.

Instructions for Use

Dosing schedules are based on desired effect. Antiinflammatory effects are seen at doses of 0.1-0.2 mg/kg and immunosuppressive effects at 0.2-0.5 mg/kg. Dexamethasone is used for testing hyperadrenocorticism. Low-dose dexamethasone suppression test (for dogs) 0.01 mg/kg (or 0.015 mg/kg in some references) IV and 0.1 mg/kg IV (for cats). For high-dose dexamethasone suppression test in dogs use 0.1 mg/kg (or 1.0 mg/kg in some references) and in cats use 1.0 mg/kg. For horses, dexamethasone suppression test administer 40 mcg/kg.

Patient Monitoring and Laboratory Tests

Monitor CBC periodically during treatment to assess effects. For monitoring a low-dose dexamethasone suppression test collect samples at 4 and 8 hours after dexamethasone. Normal suppression test should be cortisol <30-40 nmol/L (1.1-1.4 mcg/dL). For dexamethasone suppression in horses, collect samples at 17 and 19 hours. Normal horses should have cortisol <1.0 mcg/dL.

Formulations

Sodium phosphate solution is available as 4 mg/mL, equivalent to 3.0 mg/mL of dexamethasone base.

Stability and Storage

Store in tightly sealed container, protected from light, and at room temperature. Dexamethasone sodium phosphate in other aqueous solutions have been stable for 28 days. Dexamethasone sodium phosphate is freely soluble in water, but dexamethasone solution (in polyethylene glycol) is practically insoluble in water. If dexamethasone sodium phosphate is mixed with 5% dextrose solution or saline, it is stable for 24 hours.

Small Animal Dosage

Dogs and Cats

- Antiinflammatory: 0.07-0.15 mg/kg q12-24h IV or IM.
- Shock, spinal injury (efficacy in question): 2.2-4.4 mg/kg IV.
- Low-dose dexamethasone suppression test: 0.01 mg/kg or 0.015 mg/kg IV (for dogs) and 0.1 mg/kg IV (for cats) and collect sample at 0, 4, and 8 hours.
- High-dose dexamethasone suppression test: 0.1 mg/kg or 1.0 mg/kg IV (for dogs) and 1.0 mg/kg IV (for cats).

Large Animal Dosage

Cattle and Horses

- Treatment of inflammation: 0.04-0.15 mg/kg/day IV or IM.
- Ketosis (cattle): 0.01 to 0.04 mg/kg IV or IM.
- Induction of parturition (cattle): 0.05 mg/kg (25 mg per animal) as a single dose during the last week or 2 weeks of pregnancy. A dose of prostaglandin $PG\text{-}F_2$ alpha may be administered concurrently (0.5 mg/animal).
- Dexamethasone suppression test in horses: 40 mcg/kg and collect samples at 17 and 19 hours.

Sheep

- Induction of parturition: 0.15 mg/kg/day IM for 1-5 days during the last week of gestation.

Regulatory Information

Although withdrawal times are not established, at least 96 hours is required for milk and 4-8 days for meat. However, at least 3 weeks are required to eliminate residues from kidney and liver and 6 weeks for intramuscular injection site.

Dextran

deks'tran

Trade and Other Names: Dextran 70 and Gentran-70

Functional Classification: Fluid replacement

Pharmacology and Mechanism of Action

Synthetic colloid used for volume expansion. Dextrans are glucose polymers and are available as low molecular weight (Dextran 40) and high molecular weight (Dextran 70). Dextran 70 is the most often used. The colloids such as dextrans are large molecular weight molecules that remain in the vessels because of their size. Therefore, they increase colloid osmotic pressure within the vasculature to prevent intravascular fluid loss and inhibit tissue edema. Other colloids used are hetastarch and pentastarch.

Indications and Clinical Uses

Dextran is a high molecular weight compound administered IV to maintain intravascular volume. It is used for acute treatment of hypovolemia and shock. Duration of effect is approximately 24 hours.

Precautionary Information

Adverse Reactions and Side Effects

Only limited use in veterinary medicine, and adverse effects have not been reported. In people, coagulopathies are possible because of decreased platelet function and antithrombotic effects. Acute renal failure has occurred, and anaphylactic shock also has occurred in people.

Contraindications and Precautions

Do not use in animals that are prone to bleeding problems. Dextrans can interfere with cross-matching of blood for transfusion.

Drug Interactions

Compatible with most intravenous fluid solutions, including 0.9% saline solution and 5% dextrose solution.

Instructions for Use

Used primarily in critical care situations. Delivered slowly via constant rate infusion (60-90 minutes). In emergency use, bolus doses of 20 mL/kg can be administered rapidly.

Patient Monitoring and Laboratory Tests

Monitor patient's cardiopulmonary status carefully during administration. Dextrans can interfere with cross-matching of blood.

Formulations

Dextran is available in 250, 500, and 1000 mL solution for injection.

Stability and Storage

Store in tightly sealed container, protected from light, and at room temperature. Stability of compounded formulations has not been evaluated.

Small Animal Dosage

Dogs

- 10-20 mL/kg/day IV to effect, usually administerd over 30-60 minutes.

Cats

- 5-10 mL/kg/day IV, administered over 30-60 minutes.

Large Animal Dosage

Horses and Cattle

- 10 mL/kg/day IV.

Regulatory Information

Withdrawal times are not established. However, this drug presents little risk from residues; therefore, a short withdrawal time is suggested for animals intended for food.

Dextromethorphan

deks-troe-meth-or′fan

Trade and Other Names: Benylin and others

Functional Classification: Antitussive

Pharmacology and Mechanism of Action

Centrally acting antitussive drug. Dextromethorphan shares similar chemical structure as opiates but does not affect opiate receptors and appears to directly affect cough receptor. Dextromethorphan is the d-isomer of levorphan (the l-isomer, levorphan, is an opiate with addictive properties, but the d-isomer does not). Dextromethorphan produces mild analgesia and modulates pain via its ability to act as an n-methyl D-aspartate (NMDA) antagonist, but this is unrelated to the antitussive action.

Indications and Clinical Uses

Dextromethorphan has been used for suppression of nonproductive cough. However, its efficacy for reducing cough has been questioned because of a lack of proof. Dextromethorphan also has been used as an adjunct for treating pain because of NMDA antagonism. Pharmacokinetic studies in dogs indicated that dextromethorphan does not attain effective concentrations after oral administration. Even after intravenous administration, concentrations of the parent drug and active metabolite persisted for only a short time after dosing. Therefore, routine use in dogs is not recommended until more data is available to establish safe and effective doses. Data has not been reported for the pharmacokinetics in cats.

Precautionary Information

Adverse Reactions and Side Effects

Adverse effects not reported in veterinary medicine. High overdose may cause sedation. After administration to dogs, dextromethorphan produced adverse effects seen as vomiting after oral doses and CNS reactions after intravenous administration. Some preparations contain alcohol, which can be unpalatable in small animals, especially cats.

Contraindications and Precautions

There are no contraindications identified for animals. However, pet owners should be cautioned that many OTC preparations contain other drugs that may produce significant side effects. For example, some combinations also contain acetaminophen, which can be toxic to cats. Some preparations also contain a decongestant, such as pseudoephedrine, which can cause excitement and other side effects.

Drug Interactions

There are no direct interactions identified for dogs. However, interactions are possible when used with other drugs that may interfere with cytochrome P-450 metabolism.

Instructions for Use

Many OTC preparations may contain other ingredients (e.g., antihistamines, decongestants, ibuprofen, and acetaminophen). Adverse effects from each of these ingredients, such as toxic reactions caused by acetaminophen, CNS excitement from decongestants, and GI toxicity from ibuprofen, can occur in animals.

Patient Monitoring and Laboratory Tests

No specific monitoring is necessary.

Formulations

Dextromethorphan is available in syrup, capsules, and tablets in many OTC products. There are many preparations available without a prescription in liquid and tablet form. OTC formulations may vary in concentration but typically contain 2, 5, 10, or 15 mg/mL and in 15-20 mg tablets.

Stability and Storage

Store in tightly sealed container, protected from light, and at room temperature. Stability of compounded formulations has not been evaluated.

Small Animal Dosage

Dogs and Cats

- 0.5-2 mg/kg q6-8h PO (however, use is not recommended because efficacy at these doses has not been shown).

Large Animal Dosage

No dosing information available. It has little value for treating large animals.

Regulatory Information

No regulatory information is available. For extralabel use withdrawal interval estimates, contact FARAD at 1-888-USFARAD (1-888-873-2723) or send e-mail to FARAD@ncsu.edu.

RCI Classification: 4

Dextrose Solution

deks'trose

Trade and Other Names: D5W

Functional Classification: Fluid replacement

Pharmacology and Mechanism of Action

Dextrose is a sugar added to fluid solutions. It is isotonic as delivered. Five percent dextrose contains 50 grams of dextrose per liter. The pH of this solution is 3.5-6.5. Alternatively, 50% dextrose solution can be added to intravenous fluids to supplement dextrose. For example, 100 mL of 50% dextrose added to 1000 mL supplies 5% dextrose.

Indications and Clinical Uses

Five percent dextrose is an isotonic fluid solution used for intravenous administration. Dextrose is considered only for short-term use, because it is deficient in electrolytes. After the glucose is metabolized, the water is rapidly distributed out of the vascular space. For emergency treatment of hypoglycemia or to supplement fluids, a 50% dextrose solution (500 mg/mL) is used.

Precautionary Information

Adverse Reactions and Side Effects

High doses produce pulmonary edema.

Contraindications and Precautions

Use cautiously in animals with low electrolyte concentrations. Five percent dextrose solution is not a suitable maintenance solution, because it does not provide electrolytes. It should not be considered as a replacement solution; it supplies only 170 kcal/L.

Drug Interactions

No interactions. Five percent dextrose solution is compatible with fluids and most intravenous drugs.

D

Instructions for Use

Dextrose is a commonly used fluid solution administered via constant rate infusion. However, it is **not** a maintenance solution. Dextrose 50% solution can also be added to fluids to supply dextrose. For example, 50 mL of 50% dextrose is added to 1000 mL fluids to achieve a final 2.5% solution.

Patient Monitoring and Laboratory Tests

Monitor patient's hydration status and evidence of pulmonary edema during infusion. Monitor acid-base status.

Formulations

Fluid solution for intravenous administration is 5% dextrose—contains 5 grams of glucose per 100 mL (50 grams/L)—and 50% dextrose—contains 500 mg/mL (50 grams/100 mL).

Stability and Storage

Store in tightly sealed container at room temperature.

Small Animal Dosage

Dogs and Cats

- 5% dextrose solution: 40-50 mL/kg q24h IV.
- In emergency hypoglycemic crisis: 1 mL 50% dextrose solution IV diluted with saline.

Large Animal Dosage

Calves, Cattle, and Horses

- 5% dextrose solution: 45 mL/kg q24h IV.

Regulatory Information

Withdrawal times are not established. However, this drug presents little risk from residues; therefore, no withdrawal time is suggested for animals intended for food.

Diazepam

dye-ay'zeh-pam

Trade and Other Names: Valium and generic brands

Functional Classification: Anticonvulsant

Pharmacology and Mechanism of Action

Benzodiazepine. Central acting CNS depressant. Mechanism of action appears to be via potentiation of GABA-receptor mediated effects in CNS because it binds to the

GABA binding site. Diazepam metabolized to desmethyldiazepam (nordiazepam) and oxazepam.

In dogs, intravenous half-life of diazepam is short (<1 hour), but active metabolites are produced. In cats, intravenous half-life is approximately 5 hours.

Indications and Clinical Uses

Diazepam is used for sedation, anesthetic adjunct, anticonvulsant, and behavioral disorders. Although it is used as a muscle relaxant, its efficacy for this use is not established. In cats, diazepam has been administered IV for short-term stimulation of appetite. In cats, oral administration has been effective for decreasing urine spraying, but relapses are common when drug is discontinued.

Precautionary Information

Adverse Reactions and Side Effects

Sedation is most common side effect. Diazepam may cause paradoxical excitement in dogs and causes polyphagia. In cats, idiopathic fatal hepatic necrosis has been reported. Chronic administration may lead to dependence and a withdrawal syndrome if discontinued. Administration IM or SQ can be painful and irritating. Intravenous injection can cause phlebitis.

Contraindications and Precautions

Diazepam is highly dependent on liver blood flow for metabolism. Do not administer to patients with impaired liver function. Long-term use in cats should be avoided because of risk of liver toxicity. Its use for ivermectin-induced CNS intoxication is controversial.

Drug Interactions

Diazepam is highly lipophilic and will bind to (adsorb) soft plastic containers, infusion, sets, and fluid bags. Storage of diazepam in such containers is not recommended. Diazepam is not soluble in aqueous solutions. Admixing with aqueous solutions or fluids can result in precipitation.

Instructions for Use

Clearance in dogs is many times faster than in people (half-life in dogs less than 1 hour) requiring frequent administration. For treatment of status epilepticus, diazepam may be administered IV or rectally. Avoid IM administration because of pain from injection and unpredictable absorption.

Patient Monitoring and Laboratory Tests

Plasma concentrations in the range of 100-250 ng/mL have been cited as the therapeutic range for people. Other references have cited this range as 150 to 300 ng/mL. Although plasma or serum may be analyzed for concentrations of benzodiazepines, there are no readily available tests for monitoring in many veterinary laboratories. Laboratories that analyze human samples may have nonspecific tests for benzodiazepines. With these assays, there may be cross-reactivity among diazepam and the metabolites desmethyldiazepam and oxazepam.

Formulations

Diazepam is available in 2, 5, and 10 mg tablets and 5 mg/mL solution for injection.

Stability and Storage

Do not store in soft plastic (PVC) containers or fluid bags. Significant adsorption occurs to soft plastic. However, it is compatible with hard plastic, such as syringes. Do not expose to light. Compounded formulations, especially those prepared for transdermal application, may not be stable. Diazepam is practically insoluble in water, but is soluble in alcohol and propylene glycol. Diazepam undergoes hydrolysis in water. Diazepam prepared as an oral suspension (1 mg/mL) in various vehicles (pH 4.2) was stable for 60 days.

Small Animal Dosage

Dogs and Cats

- Preanesthetic: 0.5 mg/kg IV.
- Status epilepticus: 0.5 mg/kg IV or 1 mg/kg rectal, repeat if necessary.
- Constant rate infusion (CRI): 4-16 mcg/kg/min or 0.2 mg/kg/hr.
- Appetite stimulant (cats): 0.2 mg/kg IV.
- Behavioral treatment (cats): 1-4 mg/cat q12-24h PO.

Large Animal Dosage

Cattle, Sheep, and Goats

- 0.02-0.08 mg/kg IV, up to 0.5 mg/kg slowly IV. Dose according to desired effect. Cows may be recumbent after 0.5 mg/kg. Do not administer IM.

Regulatory Information

No regulatory information is available. For extralabel use withdrawal interval estimates, contact FARAD at 1-888-USFARAD (1-888-873-2723) or send e-mail to FARAD@ncsu.edu.

Schedule IV controlled drug

RCI Classification: 2

Dichlorphenamide

dye-klor-fen'ah-mide

Trade and Other Names: Daranide

Functional Classification: Diuretic

Pharmacology and Mechanism of Action

Carbonic anhydrase inhibitor. Diuretic. Dichlorphenamide, like other carbonic anhydrase inhibitors, produces a diuresis through inhibition of the uptake of bicarbonate in proximal renal tubules via enzyme inhibition. This action results in loss of bicarbonate in the urine and a diuresis. The action of carbonic anhydrase inhibitors results in urine loss of bicarbonate, alkaline urine, and water loss.

Indications and Clinical Uses

Dichlorphenamide is rarely used as a diuretic any longer. There are more potent and effective diuretic drugs available such as the loop diuretics (furosemide). Dichlorphenamide, like other carbonic anhydrase inhibitors, is used primarily to lower intraocular pressure in animals with glaucoma. Methazolamide is used more often than dichlorphenamide or acetazolamide for this purpose, and other treatment regiments are used more often than carbonic anhydrase inhibitors. Dichlorphenamide, like other carbonic anhydrase inhibitors, is sometimes used to produce a more alkaline urine for management of some urinary calculi.

Precautionary Information

Adverse Reactions and Side Effects

Sulfonamide derivative. Some animals sensitive to sulfonamides may be sensitive to dichlorphenamide. Hypokalemia may occur in some patients. Severe metabolic acidosis is rare.

Contraindications and Precautions

Use cautiously in animals sensitive to sulfonamides.

Drug Interactions

Dichlorphenamide will produce alkaline urine, which may affect clearance of some drugs. Alkaline urine may potentiate the effects of some antibacterial drugs (e.g., macrolides and quinolones).

Instructions for Use

Dichlorphenamide is not used as diuretic but is most commonly employed to treat glaucoma. It has been combined with other antiglaucoma agents.

Patient Monitoring and Laboratory Tests

Monitor ocular pressure for glaucoma treatment. Monitor serum potassium and acid-base status during treatment.

Formulations

Dichlorphenamide is available in 50 mg tablets.

Stability and Storage

Store in tightly sealed container, protected from light, and at room temperature. Stability of compounded formulations has not been evaluated.

Small Animal Dosage

Dogs and Cats

- 3-5 mg/kg q8-12h PO.

Large Animal Dosage

No large animal doses are reported.

Regulatory Information

No regulatory information is available. For extralabel use withdrawal interval estimates, contact FARAD at 1-888-USFARAD (1-888-873-2723) or send e-mail to FARAD@ncsu.edu.

RCI Classification: 4

Dichlorvos

dye'klor-vos

Trade and Other Names: Task, Dichlorovos, Atgard, DDVP, Verdisol, and Equigard

Functional Classification: Antiparasitic

Pharmacology and Mechanism of Action

Antiparasitic drug. Kills parasites by anticholinesterase action.

Indications and Clinical Uses

Dichlorvos is used primarily to treat intestinal parasites. Parasites that may be treated include *Toxocara canis* and *Toxascaris leonina* (roundworms), *Ancylostoma caninum Uncinaria stenocephala* (hookworms), and *Trichuris vulpis* (whipworms). Efficacy against *T. vulpis* may be erratic. In horses, it may be used for the removal and control of bots *(Gastrophilus intestinalis, G. nasalis)*, large strongyles *(Strongylus vulgaris,*

S. equinus, S. edentatus), small strongyles [of the genera *Cyathostomum, Cylicocercus, Cylicodontophorus, Triodontophorus, Poteriostomum, pinworms (Oxyuris equi)*, and large roundworm *(Parascaris equorum)*]. In pigs, it is used to treat and control of mature, immature, and/or fourth-stage larvae of the whipworm *(Trichuris suis)*, nodular worm (*Oesophagostomum* sp.), large roundworm *(Ascaris suum)*, and the thick stomach worm *(Ascarops strongylina)*.

Precautionary Information

Adverse Reactions and Side Effects

Overdoses can cause organophosphate intoxication (treat with pralidoxime chloride and atropine). Signs of toxicity include salivation, diarrhea, difficulty breathing, and muscle twitching.

Contraindications and Precautions

Do not use in heartworm positive patients. Do not administer within 2 days of administration of a cholinesterase-inhibiting drug. Use a split dosage schedule in animals which are old, heavily parasitized, anemic, or otherwise debilitated. Do not use in young foals, kittens, or puppies. Its use may exacerbate clinical signs in animals with respiratory disease, such as bronchitis and obstructive pulmonary disease. Do not allow birds access to feed containing this preparation or to fecal excrement from treated animals.

Drug Interactions

Do not use with other anticholinesterase drugs. Do not use with other antifilarial agents, muscle relaxants, CNS depressants, or tranquilizers.

Instructions for Use

Administer on about one third of the regular canned dog food ration or in ground meat. Dogs may be treated with any combination of capsules and/or pellets so that the animal receives a single dose. One half of the single recommended dosage may be given, and the other half may be administered 8 to 24 hours later. For horses, administer in the grain portion of the ration. It may be administered at one half of the single recommended dosage and repeated 8 to 12 hours later for treatment of old, emaciated, or debilitated subjects or those reluctant to consume medicated feed. Split the dose if heavy parasitism may cause concern over mechanical blockage of the intestinal tract.

Patient Monitoring and Laboratory Tests

Monitor for parasites as part of a regular parasite control program.

Formulations

Dichlorvos is available in 10 and 25 mg tablets. Manufacture of equine formulations has been discontinued.

Stability and Storage

Store in tightly sealed container, protected from light, and at room temperature. Stability of compounded formulations has not been evaluated.

Small Animal Dosage

Dogs

- 26.4-33 mg/kg once PO.

Cats

- 11 mg/kg once PO.

Large Animal Dosage

Pigs

- 11.2-21.6 mg/kg once PO. For pregnant sows, mix into a gestation feed to provide 1000 mg/head daily during last 30 days of gestation, mixed at a rate of

334-500 g/ton of feed. For other pigs, mix at 334 per ton of feed and feed as sole ration for 2 consecutive days (rate of 8.4 pounds of feed per head until the medicated feed has been consumed).

Horses

- 31-41 mg/kg once PO.

Regulatory Information

Do not administer to horses intended for food.

For other animals, no regulatory information is available. For extralabel use withdrawal interval estimates, contact FARAD at 1-888-USFARAD (1-888-873-2723) or send e-mail to FARAD@ncsu.edu.

Diclazuril

dih-klaz'yoor-il

Trade and Other Names: Clincox

Functional Classification: Antiprotozoal

Pharmacology and Mechanism of Action

Coccidiostat. Diclazuril is a triazinone antiprotozoal that is effective for treating infections caused by *Isospora* spp., *Toxoplasma gondii, Eimeria* spp., and has been used for treating coccidiosis. It also has been used in horses to treat equine protozoal myeloencephalitis (EPM) caused by *Sarcocystis neurona*. Toltrazuril sulfone (ponazuril) is an active metabolite found in serum and cerebrospinal fluid (CSF) of treated horses. Because of the availability of a commercial formulation of ponazuril *(Marquis)*, it is preferred by many veterinarians for treating infections in horses.

Indications and Clinical Uses

Dosage information for diclazuril has been based on experimental studies, pharmacokinetic data, and limited clinical experience. Diclazuril has been replaced by ponazuril for treating most cases of EPM in horses.

Precautionary Information

Adverse Reactions and Side Effects

No specific adverse effects have been reported.

Contraindications and Precautions

No contraindications have been reported.

Drug Interactions

No drug interactions have been reported.

Instructions for Use

Administer orally to horses.

Patient Monitoring and Laboratory Tests

No specific monitoring is necessary.

Formulations

Diclaruzil is available as a feed additive for poultry in other countries and has been imported into the United States with permission from FDA.

Stability and Storage

Store in tightly sealed container, protected from light, and at room temperature. Stability of compounded formulations has not been evaluated.

Small Animal Dosage

No dosing information has been reported for small animals.

Large Animal Dosage

Horses

- Treatment of EPM: 2.5 mg/kg q12h PO for a minimum of 21 days.

Regulatory Information

Do not administer to horses intended for food. For other animals, no regulatory information is available. For extralabel use withdrawal interval estimates, contact FARAD at 1-888 USFARAD (1-888-873-2723) or send e-mail to FARAD@ncsu.edu.

Dicloxacillin Sodium

dye-kloks-ah-sill′in soe′dee-um

Trade and Other Names: Dynapen

Functional Classification: Antibacterial

Pharmacology and Mechanism of Action

Dicloxacillin is a beta-lactam antibiotic. Like other antibiotics in this class, it inhibits bacterial cell wall synthesis by binding to penicillin-binding proteins and weakening the cell wall. The spectrum is limited to gram-positive bacteria, especially staphylococci.

Indications and Clinical Uses

Dicloxacin has a relatively narrow spectrum of activity. Like cloxacillin and oxacillin, the spectrum of dicloxacillin includes gram-positive bacilli, including beta-lactamase producing strains of *Staphylococcus.* Therefore, it has been used to treat staphylococcal infections in animals, including pyoderma. Because of availability of other drugs for small animals to treat this spectrum of bacteria, dicloxacillin is not used commonly. Because it is an oral drug with limited absorption in large animals, its use is limited to small animal oral administration.

Precautionary Information

Adverse Reactions and Side Effects

Adverse effects of penicillin-drugs are most commonly caused by drug allergy. This can range from acute anaphylaxis when administered to other signs of allergic reaction when other routes are used. When administered orally (especially with high doses), diarrhea is possible.

Contraindications and Precautions

Use cautiously in animals allergic to penicillin-like drugs.

Drug Interactions

There are no specific drug interactions. Dicloxacillin is absorbed better in dogs on an empty stomach.

Instructions for Use

No clinical efficacy studies available for dogs or cats. In dogs, oral absorption is low and may not be suitable for therapy. (*J Vet Pharmacol Ther*, 21:414-417, 1998.) Administer if possible on empty stomach.

Patient Monitoring and Laboratory Tests

Use oxacillin as a guide for sensitivity testing.

Formulations

Dicloxacillin is available in 125, 250, and 500 mg capsules and 12.5 mg/mL oral suspension.

Stability and Storage

Store in tightly sealed container, protected from light, and at room temperature. Do not mix with other drugs. Reconstituted oral suspension is stable for 14 days refrigerated. Compounded formulations, especially aqueous formulations, may not be stable.

Small Animal Dosage

Dogs and Cats

- 11-55 mg/kg q8h PO.

Large Animal Dosage

No dose has been reported for large animals.

Regulatory Information

No regulatory information is available. Because oral absorption is expected to be minimal, when using systemically to food animals, apply similar withdrawal times as for ampicillin.

Alternatively, contact FARAD at 1-888-USFARAD (1-888-873-2723) or send e-mail to FARAD@ncsu.edu.

Diethylcarbamazine Citrate

dye-eth-il-kar-bam′eh-zeen sih′trate

Trade and Other Names: Caricide, Filaribits, and Nemacide

Functional Classification: Antiparasitic

Pharmacology and Mechanism of Action

Heartworm preventative and anthelmintic. Produces neuromuscular blockade in parasite through inhibition of neurotransmitter that causes paralysis of worms.

Indications and Clinical Uses

Caricide tablets and some other brands used for heartworm prevention have been voluntarily withdrawn from the sponsor. Diethylcarbamazine has been used to prevent infection caused by heartworms in dogs. It is administered regularly during heartworm season in endemic areas. It is not effective to treat heartworms once infection is established. Other uses of diethylcarbamazine include control of ascarids infections (*Toxocara canis* and *Toxascaris leonina*) and as an aid in treatment of ascarid infections at higher doses (55 to 110 mg/kg). In cats, diethylcarbamazine has been used to treat ascarid worm infections (55-110 mg/kg).

Precautionary Information

Adverse Reactions and Side Effects

Overdoses cause vomiting. If administered to an animal with positive microfilaria, reactions are possible that include pulmonary reactions. This drug is a piperazine derivative, which is a class of antiparasitic drugs considered generally safe in animals.

Contraindications and Precautions

Dogs with established heartworm infections caused by *Dirofilaria immitis* should **not** receive diethylcarbamazine until they have been treated with an adulticide to kill the adult heartworms, followed by appropriate microfilaricidal treatment. Reactions can occur in animals with positive microfilaria. However, there are no breed sensitivities or other specific contraindications.

Drug Interactions

No specific drug interactions are reported.

Instructions for Use

Specific protocols for heartworm administration may be based on region of country as the time (season) required for heartworm prevention depends on the duration of active mosquitoes during the year. Occasionally some animals vomit immediately after dosing. Administration with food sometimes decreases this reaction.

Patient Monitoring and Laboratory Tests

Monitor heartworm status of patient. It is important to check for microfilaria in animals before prescribing. Manufacturers recommend that animals, which are currently receiving diethylcarbamazine, be checked for microfilaria every 6 months. Reactions can occur in animals with positive microfilaria.

Formulations

Although some brands have been withdrawn by the sponsor, some availability of other diethylcarbamazine tablets may vary with manufacturer and brand name. Not every brand name is available in the sizes listed. Both plain and chewable tablets have been available. Tablet sizes include: 30, 45, 50, 60, 100, 120, 150, 180, 200, 300, and 400 mg. Syrup has been available as 60 mg/mL.

Stability and Storage

Store in tightly sealed container, protected from light, and at room temperature. Stability of compounded formulations has not been evaluated.

Small Animal Dosage

Dogs

- Heartworm prophylaxis: 6.6 mg/kg q24h PO.
- Treatment of ascarids: 55-110 mg/kg PO, as a single treatment (110 mg/kg dose may be divided into twice per day).

Cats

- Ascarid treatment: 55-110 mg/kg PO. When treating Ascarid parasites, consider repeating treatment in 10-20 days to remove immature worms.

Large Animal Dosage

No dose has been reported for large animals.

Regulatory Information

No regulatory information is available.

For extralabel use withdrawal interval estimates, contact FARAD at 1-888-USFARAD (1-888-873-2723) or send e-mail to FARAD@ncsu.edu.

Diethylstilbestrol

dye-eth-il-stil-bess'trole

Trade and Other Names: DES and generic brands

Functional Classification: Hormone

Pharmacology and Mechanism of Action

Diethylstilbestrol, known as DES, is a synthetic estrogen compound. It is used for estrogen replacement in animals. The most common use of DES is treatment of incontinence in dogs. This action is believed to increase sensitivity of alpha-receptors in urinary sphincter to restore continence.

Indications and Clinical Uses

DES is most commonly used to treat estrogen-responsive incontinence in dogs. Phenylpropanolamine (PPA) has been used in dogs when DES therapy is no longer effective. Conjugated estrogens (e.g., Premarin at 20 mcg/kg twice weekly) has been used in some dogs when DES is unavailable. Estriol also has been used in some dogs to treat incontinence. DES also has been used to induce abortion in dogs. Commercial forms of DES are no longer available, but it is available through some compounding pharmacies.

Precautionary Information

Adverse Reactions and Side Effects

Side effects may occur that are caused by excess estrogen. Estrogen therapy may increase risk of pyometra and estrogen-sensitive tumors. Although bone marrow depression (particularly anemia) has been reported from administration of other estrogens in dogs and has been cited as a potential risk, it is rare complication of DES therapy.

Contraindications and Precautions

Although not reported as a significant clinical problem with DES, problems with anemia have occurred with administration of high doses of estrogens to animals.

Drug Interactions

No significant drug interactions have been reported for animals. However, in people, administration of estrogens increases thyroid binding globulin and may decrease active form of thyroid hormone (T4) in patients receiving thyroid supplementation.

Instructions for Use

Doses listed are for treating urinary incontinence and vary depending on response. Titrate dose to individual patient's response. Although used to induce abortion it was not efficacious in one study that administered 75 mcg/kg.

Patient Monitoring and Laboratory Tests

Monitor CBC to detect signs of bone marrow toxicity. Monitor T-4 levels if patients are hypothyroid and receiving supplementation.

Formulations

DES is available in 1 and 5 mg tablets and 50 mg/mL injection. DES is no longer marketed commercially in the U.S., but it is available from compounding pharmacists.

Stability and Storage

Store in tightly sealed container, protected from light, and at room temperature. Stability of compounded formulations has not been reported. However, compounded tablets are available from compounding pharmacies, and there is anecdotal information to indicate that they are effective.

Small Animal Dosage

Dogs

- 0.1-1.0 mg/dog q24h PO. Size of dose is proportional to size of dog. Continue daily dose for 5 days, then reduce frequency of administration to 2 or 3 times per week.

Cats

- 0.05-0.1 mg/cat q24h PO.

Large Animal Dosage

No dose is available for large animals. Use in animals intended for food is prohibited.

Regulatory Information

It is prohibited to administer DES to animals that produce food.

Difloxacin Hydrochloride

dye-floks'ah-sin hye-droe-klor'ide

Trade and Other Names: Dicural

Functional Classification: Antibacterial

Pharmacology and Mechanism of Action

Fluoroquinolone antibacterial drug. Acts via inhibition of DNA gyrase in bacteria to inhibit DNA and RNA synthesis. Bactericidal with broad spectrum of activity. Antibacterial activity includes *Escherichia coli*, *Klebsiella* spp., *Pasteurella* spp., and other gram-negative bacilli. Activity against *Pseudomonas aeruginosa* is less than for other gram-negative bacilli. Activity against gram-positive cocci includes *Staphylococcus*. *Streptococcus* and *Enterococcus* are more resistant.

Indications and Clinical Uses

Difloxacin, like other fluoroquinolones, is used for variety of infections including skin infections, wound infections, and pneumonia. Unlike other fluoroquinolones, difloxacin does not have high renal clearance. Urine concentrations may not be sufficient for some UTIs.

Precautionary Information

Adverse Reactions and Side Effects

High concentrations may cause CNS toxicity, especially in animals with renal failure. Difloxacin may cause some nausea, vomiting, and diarrhea at high doses. All of the fluoroquinolones may cause arthropathy in young animals. Dogs are most sensitive 4 weeks to 28 weeks of age. Large, rapidly growing dogs are the most susceptible. Safety in cats has not been reported. It has not been reported if there is a potential to cause retinal ocular injury in cats.

Contraindications and Precautions

Avoid use in young animals because of risk of cartilage injury. Use cautiously in animals that may be prone to seizures, such as epileptics. Avoid use in cats unless safety has been established.

Drug Interactions

Fluoroquinolones may increase concentrations of theophylline if used concurrently. Coadministration with divalent and trivalent cations, such as products containing aluminum (e.g., sucralfate), iron, or calcium, may decrease absorption. Do not mix in solutions or in vials with aluminum, calcium, iron, or zinc, because chelation may occur.

Instructions for Use

Dose range can be used to adjust dose depending on severity of infection and susceptibility of bacteria. Bacteria with low minimum inhibitory concentration (MIC) values can be treated with a low dose; susceptible bacteria with higher MIC values should be treated with higher dose. Difloxacin is primarily eliminated in feces rather than urine (urine is less than 5% of clearance). Sarafloxacin is an active desmethyl metabolite but produced in low amounts. Oral absorption in horses is 69% and may be effective for bacteria with MIC less than 0.12 mcg/mL.

Patient Monitoring and Laboratory Tests

Susceptibility testing: CLSI (NCCLS) break points for sensitive organisms is less than or equal to 0.5 mcg/mL for canine pathogens. Other fluoroquinolones may be used in some cases to estimate susceptibility to this fluoroquinolone. However, if ciprofloxacin is used to treat *Pseudomonas* it may be several times more active than other fluoroquinolones.

Formulations

Difloxacin is available in 11.4, 45.4, and 136 mg tablets

Stability and Storage

Store in tightly sealed container, protected from light, and at room temperature. Stability of compounded formulations has not been evaluated, but has been mixed with simple syrup (100 mg/mL) for horses.

Small Animal Dosage

Dogs

- 5-10 mg/kg q24h PO.

Cats

No dosing information for cats is available. There is no safety information available.

Large Animal Dosage

Horses: 5 mg/kg PO, q24h.

Regulatory Information

Do not administer to animals intended for food.

Digitoxin

dih-jih-toks'in

Trade and Other Names: Crystodigin

Functional Classification: Cardiac inotropic agent

Pharmacology and Mechanism of Action

Cardiac inotropic agent. Digitoxin increases cardiac contractility and decreases heart rate. The mechanism is via inactivation of cardiac muscle sodium-potassium ATPase and increased intracellular accumulation of calcium, triggering calcium release from sarcoplasmic reticulum. In addition, neuroendocrine effects include sensitization of baroreceptors, which decreases heart rate. Beneficial effects for heart failure may be via these neuroendocrine effects.

Indications and Clinical Uses

Digitoxin is indicated in patients with myocardial failure and to control rate of supraventricular tachycardias. Digitoxin formulation availability for treating patients is limited. Some formulations can no longer be obtained in the U.S. Subsequently, most of the digitoxin use has been replaced by digoxin. Digoxin is an active metabolite of digitoxin and may be used instead of digitoxin.

Precautionary Information

Adverse Reactions and Side Effects

Digitalis glycosides have narrow therapeutic index. Digitoxin may cause variety of arrhythmias in patients (e.g., AV block and ventricular tachycardia). It frequently causes vomiting, anorexia, and diarrhea. Digitoxin has adverse effects potentiated by hypokalemia, reduced by hyperkalemia.

Contraindications and Precautions

Do not administer to animals with AV block or at risk for other serious arrhythmias. Do not administer to animals with potassium electrolyte abnormalities.

Drug Interactions

High potassium will diminish clinical effect; low potassium will enhance effect and toxicity. Quinidine may increase plasma concentrations. Calcium-channel blocking drugs and beta-blockers may potentiate action on AV node conduction.

Instructions for Use

Use of digitoxin has diminished in recent years in favor of digoxin. If available, it may be used with other cardiac drugs.

Patient Monitoring and Laboratory Tests

Monitor serum digoxin concentrations in patients to determine optimum therapy. When monitoring, collect blood samples 2-6 hours after dosing. Therapeutic range is 10-30 ng/mL.

Formulations

Digitoxin is available in 0.05 and 0.1 mg tablets. (No longer available from some distributors).

Stability and Storage

Store in tightly sealed container, protected from light, and at room temperature. Stability of compounded formulations has not been evaluated.

Small Animal Dosage

Dogs and Cats

- 0.02-0.03 mg/kg q8h PO.

Large Animal Dosage

Cattle

- 50-60 mcg/kg q6h IV.

Regulatory Information

Do not administer to cattle intended for food.
RCI Classification: 4

Digoxin

dih-joks'in

Trade and Other Names: Lanoxin and Cardoxin

Functional Classification: Cardiac inotropic agent

Pharmacology and Mechanism of Action

Cardiac inotropic agent. Digoxin increases cardiac contractility and decreases heart rate. The mechanism is via inactivation of cardiac muscle sodium-potassium ATPase and increased intracellular accumulation of calcium, triggering calcium release from sarcoplasmic reticulum. In addition, neuroendocrine effects include sensitization of baroreceptors, which decreases heart rate. Beneficial effects for heart failure may be via these neuroendocrine effects.

Indications and Clinical Uses

Digoxin is used in heart failure for inotropic effect and decrease heart rate. Used in supraventricular arrhythmias to decrease ventricular response to atrial stimulation. Digoxin may be used with other drugs for heart failure such as angiotensin-converting enzyme (ACE) inhibitors (e.g., enalapril), diuretics (furosemide), and vasodilators.

Precautionary Information

Adverse Reactions and Side Effects

Digitalis glycosides have narrow therapeutic index. They may cause variety of arrhythmias in patients (e.g., AV and ventricular tachycardia). Digoxin frequently causes vomiting, anorexia, and diarrhea. Digoxin adverse effects are potentiated by hypokalemia, reduced by hyperkalemia.

Contraindications and Precautions

Some breeds of dogs (Doberman pinscher) and cats are more sensitive to adverse effects.

Drug Interactions

High potassium will diminish clinical effect; low potassium will enhance effect and toxicity. Many drugs may increase digoxin concentrations, including quinidine, aspirin, and chloramphenicol. Administration of phenobarbital chronically may decrease digoxin concentrations by increasing clearance. Calcium-channel blockers and beta-blockers will potentiate action on AV node conduction, increasing risk of AV block.

Instructions for Use

When dosing, calculate dose on lean body weight. Doses should be 10% less for elixir because of increased absorption.

Patient Monitoring and Laboratory Tests

Monitor patients carefully. Monitor serum digoxin concentrations in patients to determine optimum therapy. Therapeutic range is 0.8-2 ng/mL 8-10 hours after a dose.

Some cardiologists recommend concentrations of 1.0 ng/mL and below for treating heart failure. Adverse effects common at concentration above 3.5 ng/mL.
In sensitive patients, this may be as low as 3.0 ng/mL. Patients may be monitored with ECG to detect digoxin-induced arrhythmias.

Formulations

Digoxin is available in 0.0625, 0.125, and 0.25 mg tablets and 0.05, 0.15 mg/mL elixir.

Stability and Storage

Store in tightly sealed container, protected from light, and at room temperature. It is not stable if mixed with low pH solutions (pH <3). Do not compound oral tablets with other medications.

Small Animal Dosage

Dogs

- Dogs <20 kg: 0.005-0.01 mg/kg q12h.
- Dogs >20 kg: 0.22 mg/m^2 q12h PO (subtract 10% for elixir).
- Rapid digitalization: 0.0055-0.011 mg/kg q1h IV to effect.

Cats

- 0.008-0.01 mg/kg q48h PO. (Approximately 1/4 of a 0.125 mg tablet/cat).

Large Animal Dosage

Cattle

- 22 mcg/kg (0.022 mg/kg) IV loading dose, followed by 0.86 mcg/kg/hr IV or multiple doses of 3.4 mcg/kg q4h. Plasma concentrations to monitor are similar as for other animals.

Horses

- 2 mcg/kg (0.002 mg/kg) IV.
- 15 mcg/kg (0.015 mg/kg) q12h PO.

Regulatory Information

Do not administer to animals intended for food.
RCI Classification: 4

Dihydrotachysterol

dye-hye-droe-tak-iss′ter-ole

Trade and Other Names: Hytakerol and DHT

Functional Classification: Vitamin

Pharmacology and Mechanism of Action

Vitamin D analogue. Vitamin D promotes absorption and utilization of calcium.

Indications and Clinical Uses

Dihydrotachysterol is used as treatment of hypocalcemia, especially hypoparathyroidism associated with thyroidectomy. Calcitriol is one of the other drugs used to regulate calcium concentrations in animals. Dihydrotachysterol is used primarily for replacement in cats that have had thyroidectomy for treatment of hyperthyroidism.

Precautionary Information

Adverse Reactions and Side Effects

Overdose may cause hypercalcemia.

Contraindications and Precautions

Avoid use in pregnant animals, because it may cause fetal abnormalities.

Drug Interactions

No specific drug interactions are reported for animals. However, use cautiously with high doses of preparations containing calcium. Use with caution with thiazide diuretics.

Instructions for Use

Doses for individual patients should be adjusted by monitoring serum calcium concentrations.

Patient Monitoring and Laboratory Tests

Monitor serum calcium concentration.

Formulations

Dihydrotachysterol is available in 0.125 mg capsules, 0.5 mg/mL oral liquid (20% alcohol), and 125, 200, and 400 mg tablets.

Stability and Storage

Store in tightly sealed container, protected from light, and at room temperature. Stability of compounded formulations has not been evaluated.

Small Animal Dosage

Dog and Cats

- 0.01 mg/kg/day PO.
- Acute treatment: 0.02 mg/kg initially, then 0.01-0.02 mg/kg q24-48h PO thereafter. The dose should be adjusted on the basis of measuring calcium concentrations. Effective doses can range from 0.1 to 0.3 mg/kg.

Large Animal Dosage

No large animal doses are reported.

Regulatory Information

No regulatory information is available. For extralabel use withdrawal interval estimates, contact FARAD at 1-888-USFARAD (1-888-873-2723) or send e-mail to FARAD@ncsu.edu.

Diltiazem Hydrochloride

dil-tye'ah-zem hye-droe-klor'ide

Trade and Other Names: Cardizem and Dilacor

Functional Classification: Calcium-channel blocker

Pharmacology and Mechanism of Action

Calcium-channel blocking drug. Diltiazem blocks calcium entry into cells via blockade of voltage-dependent slow calcium channel. Via this action, it produces vasodilation, negative chronotropic, and negative inotropic effects. However, the action on cardiac tissue (SA node and AV node) predominates over other effects. Half-life in dogs is approximately 3 hours (range 2.5-4 hrs), and it is shorter in horses (1.5 hrs).

Indications and Clinical Uses

Diltiazem is used primarily for control of supraventricular arrhythmias, systemic hypertension, and hypertrophic cardiomyopathy. It also is used for atrial flutter, AV nodal reentry arrhythmias, and other forms of tachycardia. Diltiazem is more effective on heart tissues (AV node and SA node) than on blood vessels. To produce vasodilation, one of the dihydropyridines (e.g., amlodipine) is preferred. In horses, diltiazem may be effective for atrial fibrillation. However, treated horses had variable results, and some developed hypotension and sinus arrest.

Precautionary Information

Adverse Reactions and Side Effects

Hypotension, myocardial depression, bradycardia, and AV block are the most important adverse effects. If acute hypotension occurs, treat with aggressive fluid therapy and administration of calcium gluconate or calcium chloride. It may cause anorexia in some patients. High doses in cats have caused vomiting. When cats were administered 60 mg of Dilacor XR it produced lethargy, GI disturbances, and weight loss in 36% of cats.

Contraindications and Precautions

Do not inject rapidly when administering IV. Do not administer to hypotensive patients.

Drug Interactions

Calcium-channel blocking drugs have been associated with drug interactions in people by interfering with drug metabolism. These interactions, although possible, have not been documented in veterinary patients. Nevertheless, use with caution when administering other drugs that may be p-glycoprotein (efflux protein produced by MDR gene) substrates. (See Appendix.) Do not mix intravenous solutions with furosemide.

Instructions for Use

Diltiazem is preferred over verapamil in patients with heart failure because of less myocardial depression. See detailed instructions for cats in dosing section.

Patient Monitoring and Laboratory Tests

Monitor heart rate and rhythm during treatment. Monitor blood pressure with acute treatment for atrial fibrillation. If blood concentrations are monitored, to produce a reduction in heart rate 80-290 ng/mL are necessary in people and 60-120 ng/mL in dogs.

Formulations

Diltiazem is available in 30, 60, 90, and 120 mg tablets, 60, 90, 120, 180, 240, and 300 mg extended release capsules, and in a 5 mg/mL solution.

Dilacor XR has three or four tablets in one unit.

Stability and Storage

Store in tightly sealed container, protected from light, and at room temperature. Extended release tablets are difficult to manipulate for pet owners. Compounded transdermal formulations have not been found to be stable. Compounded oral formulations, prepared with various sugars and flavorings, were stable for 50-60 days. Injectable solution may be mixed with intravenous fluids, but should be discarded after 24 hours. Do not freeze.

Small Animal Dosage

Dogs

- 0.5-1.5 mg/kg q8h PO. In some dogs, 5 mg/kg has been used for atrial fibrillation.
- Atrial fibrillation: 0.05-0.25 mg/kg IV administered q5min to effect.
- Injection: 0.25 mg/kg over 2 min IV (repeat if necessary). When treating supraventricular tachycardia, inject 0.25 mg/kg, then wait 20 minutes for response before repeating.

Cats

- 1.75-2.4 mg/kg q8h PO.
- Dilacor XR or Cardizem CD: 10 mg/kg once daily PO. Extended release tablets can be more difficult to use in cats compared to other tablets, but have been used at 30 or 60 mg per cat (See below).
- Injection: 0.25 mg/kg over 2 min IV (repeat if necessary). When treating supraventricular tachycardia, inject 0.25 mg/kg, then wait 20 minutes for response before repeating.

Constant rate infusion (CRI): 0.15-0.25 mg/kg IV over 2 minutes, then 1-8 mcg/kg/min.

Tablets are difficult to break for use in cats. Note that "XR, SR, and CD" all refers to slow-release formulations. Dilacor XR-240 mg contains four 60 mg tablets. XR-180 contains three 60 mg tablets. Slow- and extended-release tablets are not recommended for routine use in cats because they produce inconsistent plasma concentrations that may result in ineffective treatment in some, and adverse effects in others. Based on available information for cats, use either Dilacor XR 30 or Dilacor XR 60. The dose of 30 mg per cat of Dilacor XR (extended release tablets) produced fewer adverse effects than 60 mg per cat. Transdermal administration of diltiazem has not been shown to be effective in cats.

Large Animal Dosage

Horses, for treatment of atrial fibrillation doses of 1-2 mg/kg IV have been studied. However, the authors of that study recommended lower doses produced more effective results.

Regulatory Information

No regulatory information is available. For extrlabel use withdrawal interval estimates, contact FARAD at 1-888-USFARAD (1-888-873-2723) or send e-mail to FARAD@ncsu.edu.

RCI Classification: 4

Dimenhydrinate

dye-men-hye'drih-nate

Trade and Other Names: Dramamine and (Gravol in Canada)

Functional Classification: Antihistamine

Pharmacology and Mechanism of Action

Antihistamine (H_1-blocker). Similar to other antihistamines, it acts by blocking the H_1 receptor and suppresses inflammatory reactions caused by histamine. The H_1-blockers have been used to control pruritus and skin inflammation in dogs and cats; however, success rates in dogs have not been high. Commonly used antihistamines include clemastine, chlorpheniramine, diphenhydramine, and hydroxyzine. Dimenhydrinate is converted to active diphenhydramine. Dimenhydrinate also has central acting antiemetic properties, possibly by acting on the vomiting center or via the chemoreceptor-trigger zone (CRTZ).

Indications and Clinical Uses

Dimenhydrinate is used to prevent allergic reactions and for pruritus therapy in dogs and cats. However, success rates for treatment of pruritus have not been high. In addition to the antihistamine effect for treating allergies, dimenhydrinate, like other antihistamines, act as an antiemetic via the effects on the drugs centers that control vomiting in animals. Antihistamines used as antiemetics are administered for motion sickness, vomiting induced by chemotherapy, and GI disease that stimulates vomiting.

Precautionary Information

Adverse Reactions and Side Effects

Sedation is most common side effect. Sedation is the result of inhibition of histamine N-methyltransferase. Sedation may also be attributed to block of other CNS receptors such as those for serotonin, acetylcholine, and alpha-receptors. Antimuscarinic effects (atropine-like effects) also are common, including dry mouth and decreased GI secretions.

Contraindications and Precautions

Antimuscarinic effects (atropine-like effects) are common. Do not use in conditions for which anticholinergic drugs may be contraindicated, such as glaucoma, ileus, or cardiac arrhythmias.

Drug Interactions

No drug interactions are reported. However, use with other sedatives and tranquilizers may increase sedation.

Instructions for Use

Like other antihistamines, there have been no clinical studies on the use of dimenhydrinate. It is primarily used empirically for treatment of vomiting and to prevent allergic reactions. Diphenhydramine is the active moiety of dimenhydrinate.

Patient Monitoring and Laboratory Tests

No specific monitoring is necessary.

Formulations

Dimenhydrinate is available in 50 mg tablets and 50 mg/mL injection.

Stability and Storage

Store in tightly sealed container, protected from light, and at room temperature. Stability of compounded formulations has not been evaluated.

Small Animal Dosage

Dogs

- 4-8 mg/kg q8h PO, IM, or IV.

Cats

- 12.5 mg/cat q8h IV, IM, or PO.

Large Animal Dosage

No large animal doses have been reported.

Regulatory Information

No regulatory information is available. For extralabel use withdrawal interval estimates, contact FARAD at 1-888-USFARAD (1-888-873-2723) or send e-mail to FARAD@ncsu.edu.

RCI Classification: 3

Dimercaprol

dye-mer-cap′role

Trade and Other Names: British anti-lewisite (BAL) in oil

Functional Classification: Antidote

Pharmacology and Mechanism of Action

Chelating agent. Dimercaprol is also known as BAL. It is a dithiol chelating agent for chelating with heavy metals. It binds to arsenic, lead, and mercury to treat toxicosis.

Indications and Clinical Uses

Used to treat lead, gold, mercury, and arsenic toxicity. There are two formulations, dimercaptopropane-1-sulfonic acid (DMPS) and meso-2,3-dimercaptosuccinic acid. Because these are not readily available, they may be compounded from a bulk source.

Precautionary Information

Adverse Reactions and Side Effects

Adverse effects not reported in veterinary medicine. In people, sterile abscesses occur at injection site. High doses have caused seizures, drowsiness, and vomiting.

Contraindications and Precautions

Dimercaprol is used only to treat intoxications.

Drug Interactions

There are no drug interactions reported.

Instructions for Use

Use as soon as possible after intoxicant exposure. Alkalinization of urine will increase toxin removal. For lead intoxication, dimercaprol may be used with edetate calcium.

Patient Monitoring and Laboratory Tests

Heavy metal concentrations can be measured to assess treatment.

Formulations

Dimercaprol is available in an injection that must be prepared by compounding.

Stability and Storage

Store in tightly sealed container, protected from light, and at room temperature.

Small Animal Dosage

- 4 mg/kg q4h IM.

Large Animal Dosage

- 4 mg/kg q4h IM.

Regulatory Information

Withdrawal time: 5 days for milk and meat (extralabel use).

Dimethyl Sulfoxide (DMSO)

di-meth-il sulf-oks′ide

Trade and Other Names: DMSO and Domoso

Functional Classification: Antiinflammatory

Pharmacology and Mechanism of Action

DMSO is a solvent that is a byproduct of the paper-making process. It is highly hygroscopic (water absorbing). It readily displaces water and will penetrate cell membranes, skin, and mucosa easily. It produces antiinflammatory, antifungal, and antibacterial properties. The clinical antiinflammatory action of DMSO is uncertain. It may produce antiinflammatory or protective effects on cell membranes via its ability to scavenge oxygen-derived free radicals. In horses, at a dose of 1 gm/kg, the half-life is 8.6 hours. Twenty-six percent of the administered dose was excreted in the urine. In dogs, the half-life is 36 hours.

Indications and Clinical Uses

DMSO is administered topically and systemically (IV) for treatment of various inflammatory conditions. It is popular in horses for treatment of laminitis, arthritis, pneumonia, intestinal ischemia, synovitis, and nervous system injuries. Despite popular use, there are no published reports of efficacy for clinical use. Effectiveness at the doses used (approximately 1 g/kg) is controversial.

Precautionary Information

Adverse Reactions and Side Effects

DMSO is irritating to skin and mucosal membranes. It is hygroscopic and also induces release of histamine in skin. Long-term use has produced ocular lens changes in laboratory animals. Concentrated DMSO, when administered IV, will cause significant hemolysis. Intravenous use also has been associated with hemoglobinemia, acute colic, diarrhea, myositis, muscle tremors, and collapse. These reactions are more likely at doses of 2 g/kg or greater. DMSO produces a strong odor when administered.

Contraindications and Precautions

DMSO is not registered for systemic use, although many veterinarians administer it systemically. It may enhance transdermal absorption of toxicants and contaminants on the skin. Do not administer IV at concentrations >10% or at doses >1 g/kg.

Drug Interactions

DMSO is a strong solvent. It will dissolve other compounds. It may act as a penetration enhancer and increase transmembrane penetration of other compounds.

Instructions for Use

Dilute prior to use to 10% for intravenous infusion. Doses vary widely among veterinarians. Dose listed of 1 g/kg is common, but ranges of 0.2 to 4 g/kg have been cited in the literature for horses.

Patient Monitoring and Laboratory Tests

Monitor CBC during use.

Formulations

DMSO is available in a solution.

Stability and Storage

Store in tightly sealed container, protected from light, and at room temperature. Do not mix with other compounds, unless it is done immediately prior to administration.

Small Animal Dosage

Dogs and Cats

- 1 g/kg IV slowly. Do not administer solutions stronger than 10%.

Large Animal Dosage

Horses and Cattle

- 1 g/kg IV slowly. Dilute prior to use. Do not administer concentrations >10%. For most conditions, administration is every 12 hours.

Regulatory Information

Not approved for use in animals intended for food. No withdrawal times are available.

RCI Classification: 5

Dinoprost Tromethamine

dye'noe-prahst troe-meth'ah-meen

Trade and Other Names: Lutalyse, Dinoprost, Prostin F_2 alpha, ProstaMate, Prostaglandin F_2 alpha, and PGF_2 alpha

Functional Classification: Prostaglandin

Pharmacology and Mechanism of Action

Dinoprost is a prostaglandin (PGF_2 alpha) that induces luteolysis. It will also act to contract smooth muscle.

Indications and Clinical Uses

Dinoprost is used for estrous synchronization in cattle and horses by causing luteolysis. In horses and cattle it is used to control timing of estrus in estrus cycling females and in clinically anestrous females that have a corpus luteum. In pigs, dinoprost is used to induce parturition when given within 3 days of farrowing. In dogs, dinoprost has been used to treat open pyometra. In cattle, dinoprost has been used for treatment of chronic endometritis.

In large animals, dinoprost is used to induce abortion in first 100 days of gestation, but use for inducing abortion in small animals has been questioned.

Precautionary Information

Adverse Reactions and Side Effects

Prostaglandin F_2 alpha causes increased smooth muscle tone, resulting in diarrhea, abdominal discomfort, bronchoconstriction, and increase in blood pressure. In small animals, other side effects include vomiting. Induction of abortion may cause retained placenta.

Contraindications and Precautions

Do not administer IV. Dinoprost induces abortion in pregnant animals. Use caution when handling this drug by veterinarians, animal owners, and technical help. It should not be handled by pregnant women. Absorption through the skin is possible. People with respiratory problems also should not handle dinoprost.

Drug Interactions

According to the label, dinoprost should not be used with nonsteroidal antiinflammatory drugs (NSAIDs), because these drugs inhibit synthesis of prostaglandins. However, NSAIDs should not affect concentrations of PGF_2 alpha administered by this product. When using oxytocin concurrently, it should be used cautiously, because there is a risk of uterine rupture.

Instructions for Use

Use in treating pyometra should be monitored carefully. If pyometra is not open, severe consequences may result. When used in cattle, after a single injection, cattle should be bred at the usual time relative to estrus. When administering two injections, cattle can be bred after the second injection either at the usual time relative to detected estrus or at about 80 hours after the second injection. Estrus is expected to occur 1 to 5 days after injection if a corpus luteum was present. Cattle that do not become pregnant will be expected to return to estrus in about 18 to 24 days. When used in cattle to induce abortion, it should be used only during first 100 days of gestation. Cattle that abort will abort within 35 days after injection.

In pigs, administer within 3 days of predicted farrowing for parturition induction. Farrowing should start in approximately 30 hours.

Patient Monitoring and Laboratory Tests

When used for estrus synchronization, monitor for signs of estrus. Animals should be bred at usual time relative to estrus.

Formulations

Dinoprost is available in 5 mg/mL solution for intramuscular injection.

Stability and Storage

Store in tightly sealed container, protected from light, and at room temperature. Stability of compounded formulations has not been evaluated.

Small Animal Dosage

Dogs

- Pyometra: 0.1-0.2 mg/kg, once daily for 5 days SQ.
- Abortion: 0.025-0.05 mg (25-50 mcg)/kg q12h IM.

Cats

- Pyometra: 0.1-0.25 mg/kg, once daily for 5 days SQ.
- Abortion: 0.5-1 mg/kg IM for 2 injections.

Large Animal Dosage

Cattle

- Induction of abortion: 25 mg total dose, administered once IM.
- Estrus synchronization: 25 mg (5 mL) IM once or twice at 10-12 day intervals.
- Pyometra: 25 mg administered once IM.

Horses

- Estrus synchronization: 1 mg/100 pounds (1 mg/45 kg) or 1-2 mL administered once IM. Mares should return to estrus within 2-4 days and ovulate 8-12 days after treatment.

Pigs

- Induction of parturition: 10 mg (2 mL) administered once IM. Parturition occurs within 30 hours.

Regulatory Information

Do not administer to horses intended for food.
To be used in beef cattle and nonlactating dairy cows only.

Diphenhydramine Hydrochloride

dye-fen-hye′drah-meen hye-droe-klor′ide

Trade and Other Names: Benadryl

Functional Classification: Antihistamine

Pharmacology and Mechanism of Action

Antihistamine (H_1-blocker). Diphenhydramine is the active moiety of dimenhydrinate (Dramamine). Similar to other antihistamines, it acts by blocking the H_1 receptor (H1) and suppresses inflammatory reactions caused by histamine. Commonly used antihistamines include clemastine, chlorpheniramine, diphenhydramine, and hydroxyzine.

Indications and Clinical Uses

Diphenhydramine, like other antihistamines, is used to prevent allergic reactions and for pruritus therapy in dogs and cats. However, success rates for treatment of pruritus have not been high. In addition to the antihistamine effect for treating allergies, these drugs block the effect of histamine in the vomiting center, vestibular center, and other centers that control vomiting in animals.

Precautionary Information

Adverse Reactions and Side Effects

Sedation is most common side effect. Sedation is the result of inhibition of histamine N-methyltransferase. Sedation may also be attributed to block of other CNS receptors such as those for serotonin, acetylcholine, and alpha-receptors. Antimuscarinic effects (atropine-like effects) also are common, including dry mouth and decreased GI secretions. Excitement has been observed in cats and in other animals at high doses.

Contraindications and Precautions

Antimuscarinic effects (atropine-like effects) are common. Do not use in conditions for which anticholinergic drugs may be contraindicated, such as glaucoma, ileus, or cardiac arrhythmias.

Drug Interactions

There are no specific drug interactions. However, because of anticholinergic (atropine-like) effects, it may counteract drugs that are administered for a parasympathomimetic action (e.g., drugs used to stimulate intestinal motility).

Instructions for Use

Antihistamine used primarily for allergic disease in animals. These drugs also can be used to treat or prevent vomiting in animals. Clinical studies documenting efficacy have been limited. Most use is empirical with doses extrapolated from human use.

Patient Monitoring and Laboratory Tests

No specific monitoring is necessary.

Formulations

Diphenhydramine is available OTC in a 2.5 mg/mL elixir, 25 and 50 mg capsules and tablets, and 50 mg/mL injection.

Stability and Storage

Store in tightly sealed container, protected from light, and at room temperature. Stability of compounded formulations has not been evaluated. Protect from freezing.

Small Animal Dosage

Dogs

- 25-50 mg/dog q8h IV, IM, or PO.
- 2.2 mg/kg q8-12h PO.

Cats

- 2-4 mg/kg q6-8h PO.
- 1 mg/kg q8h IV or IM.

Large Animal Dosage

- 0.5-1 mg/kg as a single dose, as needed, IM.

Regulatory Information

No regulatory information is available. For extralabel use withdrawal interval estimates, contact FARAD at 1-888-USFARAD (1-888-873-2723) or send e-mail to FARAD@ncsu.edu.

Diphenoxylate

dye-fen-oks'ih-late

Trade and Other Names: Lomotil

Functional Classification: Antidiarrheal

Pharmacology and Mechanism of Action

Opiate agonist. Binds to mu-opiate receptors in intestine and stimulates smooth muscle segmentation in intestine, decreases peristalsis, and enhances fluid and electrolyte absorption.

Indications and Clinical Uses

Diphenoxylate is used for acute treatment of nonspecific diarrhea. It has primarily a local effect. Loperamide (Imodium) has a similar action and has become more popular for this indication.

Precautionary Information

Adverse Reactions and Side Effects

Adverse effects have not been reported in veterinary medicine. Diphenoxylate is poorly absorbed systemically and produces few systemic side effects. Excessive use can cause constipation.

Contraindications and Precautions

Do not use in patients with diarrhea caused by infectious causes. Opiates should not be used for chronic treatment of diarrhea.

Drug Interactions

There are no specific drug interactions reported. However, use cautiously with other opiates and other drugs that may cause constipation (e.g., antimuscarinic drugs).

Instructions for Use

Doses are based primarily on empiricism or extrapolation of human dose. Clinical studies have not been performed in animals. Diphenoxylate contains atropine, but dose is not high enough for significant systemic effects.

Patient Monitoring and Laboratory Tests

No specific monitoring is necessary.

Formulations

Diphenoxylate is available in 2.5 mg tablets.

Stability and Storage

Store in tightly sealed container, protected from light, and at room temperature. Stability of compounded formulations has not been evaluated.

Small Animal Dosage

Dogs

- 0.1-0.2 mg/kg q8-12h PO.

Cats

- 0.05-0.1 mg/kg q12h PO.

Large Animal Dosage

No use in large animals is reported.

Regulatory Information

No regulatory information is available. For extralabel use withdrawal interval estimates, contact FARAD at 1-888-USFARAD (1-888-873-2723) or send e-mail to FARAD@ncsu.edu.

Schedule V controlled drug

RCI Classification: 4

Dipyridamole

dye-peer-id'ah-mole

Trade and Other Names: Persantine and Aggrenex

Functional Classification: Anticoagulant

Pharmacology and Mechanism of Action

Platelet inhibitor. Mechanism of action is attributed to increased levels of cyclic AMP in platelet, which decreases platelet activation.

Indications and Clinical Uses

Use of dipyridamole has been infrequent in animals. It may be indicated in clinical conditions in which platelet inhibition is desired. Indicated primarily to prevent thromboembolism.

Precautionary Information

Adverse Reactions and Side Effects

Adverse effects have not been reported in animals. However, bleeding problems are expected in animals prone to coagulopathies or receiving other anticoagulants.

Contraindications and Precautions

Do not use in animals with bleeding problems.

Drug Interactions

Aspirin may potentiate effects.

Instructions for Use

Dipyridamole is used primarily in people to prevent thromboembolism. Use in animals has not been reported. When used in people, it is combined with other antithrombotic agents (e.g., warfarin).

Patient Monitoring and Laboratory Tests

It may be necessary to monitor bleeding times in some animals.

Formulations

Dipyridamole is available in 25, 50, and 75 mg tablets and 5 mg/mL injection. It is also available combined with aspirin as 200 mg dipyridamole plus 25 mg aspirin.

Stability and Storage

Store in tightly sealed container, protected from light, and at room temperature. Compounded oral formulations have been stable for 60 days.

Small Animal Dosage

Dogs and Cats

- 4-10 mg/kg q24h PO.

Large Animal Dosage

No use in large animals is reported.

Regulatory Information

No regulatory information is available. For extralabel use withdrawal interval estimates, contact FARAD at 1-888-USFARAD (1-888-873-2723) or send e-mail to FARAD@ncsu.edu.
RCI Classification: 3

Disopyramide

dye-soe-peer'ah-mide

Trade and Other Names: Norpace (Rhythmodan in Canada)

Functional Classification: Antiarrhythmic agent

Pharmacology and Mechanism of Action

Antiarrhythmic agent of Class I. Disopyramide blocks inward sodium channel and depresses myocardial electrophysiologic conduction rate.

Indications and Clinical Uses

Disopyramide is used for control of ventricular arrhythmias. Its use in veterinary medicine is not as common as for other drugs. Studies of efficacy in animals have not been reported.

Precautionary Information

Adverse Reactions and Side Effects

Adverse effects have not been reported in animals. High doses may cause cardiac arrhythmias.

Contraindications and Precautions

At high doses, it may induce arrhythmias in some patients.

Drug Interactions

No drug interactions are reported for animals. Use cautiously with other drugs that may affect the cardiac rhythm.

Instructions for Use

Disopyramide is not commonly used in veterinary medicine because of its short half-life in dogs. Other antiarrhythmic drugs are preferred.

Patient Monitoring and Laboratory Tests

Monitor ECG in treated animals. This drug can be pro-arrhythmogenic.

Formulations

Disopyramide is available in 100 and 150 mg capsules and 10 mg/mL injection (Canada only).

Stability and Storage

Store in tightly sealed container, protected from light, and at room temperature. Compounded oral formulations have been stable for 30 days.

Small Animal Dosage

Dogs

- 6-15 mg/kg q8h PO.

Cats

No dose established

Large Animal Dosage

No use in large animals is reported.

Regulatory Information

No regulatory information is available. For extralabel use withdrawal interval estimates, contact FARAD at 1-888-USFARAD (1-888-873-2723) or send e-mail to FARAD@ncsu.edu.

RCI Classification: 4

Dithiazanine Iodide

dye-thye-az′ah-neen eye′oe-dide

Trade and Other Names: Dizan

Functional Classification: Antiparasitic

Pharmacology and Mechanism of Action

Microfilaricidal drug for dogs. It is also active against hookworms, roundworms, and whipworms.

Indications and Clinical Uses

Dithiazanine is used to eliminate heartworm microfilaria in dogs. It also has been used to treat some intestinal parasites.

Precautionary Information

Adverse Reactions and Side Effects

Adverse effects are rare. Vomiting is reported in some dogs. Dithiazanine causes discoloration of feces.

Contraindications and Precautions

Do not use in animals with reduced renal function. Do not administer to heartworm-positive dogs until 6 weeks after adulticide therapy has been given.

Drug Interactions

There are no specific drug interactions reported.

Instructions for Use

Administer with food. If powder is used, mix with food as top dressing. Before other drugs were available, this was the only microfilaricidal agent for dogs. However, with improved availability of other drugs, it is not commonly used anymore.

Patient Monitoring and Laboratory Tests

Monitor heartworm status after a course of therapy by checking for microfilaria.

Formulations

Dithiazanine is available in 10, 50, 100, and 200 mg tablets. However, it is rarely available in commercial tablets any longer. It is also available in a 200 mg per tablespoon powder.

Stability and Storage

Store in tightly sealed container, protected from light, and at room temperature. Stability of compounded formulations has not been evaluated.

Small Animal Dosage

Dogs

- Heartworm: 6.6-11 mg/kg q24h for 7-10 days PO.
- Roundworms: 22 mg/kg once daily for 3-5 days PO.
- Hookworms: 22 mg/kg once daily for 7 days PO.
- Whipworms: 22 mg/kg once daily for 10-12 days PO.

Cats

No dose has been reported.

Large Animal Dosage

No use in large animals has been reported.

Regulatory Information

No regulatory information is available. For extralabel use withdrawal interval estimates, contact FARAD at 1-888-USFARAD (1-888-873-2723) or send e-mail to FARAD@ncsu.edu.

Dobutamine Hydrochloride

doe-byoo'tah-meen hye-droe-klor'ide

Trade and Other Names: Dobutrex

Functional Classification: Cardiac inotropic agent

Pharmacology and Mechanism of Action

Adrenergic agonist. The action of dobutamine is primarily to stimulate myocardial contractility via its action on $beta_1$ receptors. Some action on alpha receptors may contribute to its action and effects on heart rate. At appropriate infusion rates, dobutamine can improve contractility, without increasing heart rates. Dobutamine has a short half-life in animals (2-3 minutes). Therefore, it must be given via constant intravenous infusion and has a short onset of activity.

Indications and Clinical Uses

Dobutamine is used primarily for the acute treatment of heart failure. It produces an inotropic effect without increasing heart rates. Short treatment regimens (e.g., 48 hours) can have a residual positive effect in some animals.

Precautionary Information

Adverse Reactions and Side Effects

Dobutamine may cause tachycardia and ventricular arrhythmias at high doses or in sensitive individuals. If tachycardia or arrhythmias are detected, stop infusion rate and resume at a lower rate.

Contraindications and Precautions

Do not use in animals with ventricular arrhythmias.

Drug Interactions

Do not mix with alkaline solutions, such as those containing bicarbonate. Do not infuse in intravenous line with heparin, cephalosporins, or penicillins. Otherwise, it is compatible with most fluid solutions. Do not administer to animals receiving monoamine oxidase inhibitors (MAOIs; e.g., selegiline).

Instructions for Use

Dobutamine has a rapid elimination half-life (minutes), and therefore must be administered via carefully monitored constant rate infusion (CRI). Dose rates (infusion rate) can be adjusted by monitoring patient response.

Patient Monitoring and Laboratory Tests

Monitor heart rate and ECG during treatment. Cardiac arrhythmias are possible during infusions, especially at high doses.

Formulations

Dobutamine is available in 250 mg/20 mL (12.5 mg/mL) vial for injection.

Stability and Storage

Usually dilute in 5% dextrose solution (e.g., 250 mg in 1 L 5% dextrose). Slight pink tinge to solution can occur without loss of potency; however do not use if color turns brown.

Small Animal Dosage

Dogs

- 5-20 mcg/kg/min IV infusion. Generally start with low dose and titrate upwards.

Cats

- 2 mcg/kg/min IV infusion.

Large Animal Dosage

Horses

- 5-10 mcg/kg/min (0.005-0.01 mg/kg/min) IV infusion. Observe for increases in heart rate and ventricular arrhythmias. Adjust dose if necessary.

Regulatory Information

No regulatory information is available. Because of a short half-life, no risk of residue is anticipated in food animals.

RCI Classification: 3

Docusate

dok'yoo-sate

Trade and Other Names: Docusate calcium: Surfak and Doxidan, Docusate sodium: DSS, Colace, and Doxan, and generic brands

Functional Classification: Laxative

Pharmacology and Mechanism of Action

Docusate sodium and docusate calcium are stool softeners. They act as surfactants to help increase water penetration into feces. They act to decrease surface tension to allow more water to accumulate in the stool.

Indications and Clinical Uses

Docusate is indicated for medical conditions in which softened feces are desirable, such as after intestinal or anal surgery, to help pass hardened feces, and when administering drugs that slow intestinal transit (e.g., opiates). Docusate is indicated for treatment of constipation.

Precautionary Information

Adverse Reactions and Side Effects

No adverse effects reported in animals. In people, high doses have caused abdominal discomfort.

Contraindications and Precautions

Some formulations of docusate calcium and docusate sodium products have contained the stimulant cathartic phenolphthalein, which should be used cautiously in cats. Examine label of products to ensure absence of phenolphthalein.

Drug Interactions

No specific drug interactions are reported for animals.

Instructions for Use

Doses are based on extrapolations from humans or empiricism. No clinical studies reported for animals.

Patient Monitoring and Laboratory Tests

No specific monitoring is necessary.

Formulations

Docusate calcium is available as 60 mg tablets and 240 mg capsules.
Docusate sodium is available as 50 and 100 mg capsules and 10 mg/mL liquid.

Stability and Storage

Store in tightly sealed container, protected from light, and at room temperature. Stability of compounded formulations has not been evaluated.

Small Animal Dosage

Dogs

- Docusate calcium: 50-100 mg/dog q12-24h PO.
- Docusate sodium: 50-200 mg/dog q8-12h PO.

Cats

- Docusate calcium: 50 mg/cat q12-24h PO.
- Docusate sodium: 50 mg/cat q12-24h PO.

Large Animal Dosage

- Docusate sodium: 10 mg/kg/day PO.

Regulatory Information

No regulatory information is available for animals intended for food. Because docusate has primarily a local acting effect in the intestine, there is a minimal risk of residues in animals intended for food.

Dolasetron Mesylate

doe-lah'seh-tron mess'ih-late

Trade and Other Names: Anzemet

Functional Classification: Antiemetic

Pharmacology and Mechanism of Action

Antiemetic drug from the class of drugs called serotonin antagonists. These drugs act by inhibiting serotonin (5-HT, type 3) receptors. During chemotherapy, there may be 5-HT released from injury to the GI tract, which stimulates vomiting centrally that is blocked by this class of drugs. Serotonin antagonists used for antiemetic therapy include granisetron, ondansetron, dolasetron, and tropisetron.

Indications and Clinical Uses

Like other serotonin antagonists, dolasetron is used primarily for its antiemetic effects during chemotherapy, for which they generally have been superior to other drugs in efficacy. These drugs also may be used to control vomiting from surgery (postoperative nausea and vomiting).

Precautionary Information

Adverse Reactions and Side Effects

Dolasetron adverse effects have not been reported in animals. These drugs have little affinity for other 5-HT receptors. Some effects may be indistinguishable from concurrent cancer drugs.

Contraindications and Precautions

There are no important contraindications identified in animals.

Drug Interactions

No drug interactions are reported. However, dolasetron is subject to effects from cytochrome P450 inducers and inhibitors. (See Appendix.)

Instructions for Use

Dolasetron has been used infrequently in veterinary medicine because of its expense. Doses are derived from anecdotal experience or extrapolation from human studies. These drugs are more effective if used to prevent vomiting, (administered prior to a chemotherapeutic agent) rather than treat ongoing vomiting. This class of drugs may be combined with corticosteroids (e.g., dexamethasone) to enhance the antiemetic action.

Patient Monitoring and Laboratory Tests

Monitor GI signs in vomiting patient.

Formulations

Dolasetron is available in 50 and 100 mg tablets and 20 mg/mL injection.

Stability and Storage

Store in tightly sealed container, protected from light, and at room temperature. It may be added to fluid solutions, but do not mix with other intravenous drugs. Do not use injection after 24 hours when added to fluids. Oral formulations have been added to fruit juice up to 2 hours at room temperature without loss of stability.

Small Animal Dosage

Dogs and Cats

- Prevention of nausea and vomiting: 0.6 mg/kg once daily IV or PO.
- Treating vomiting and nausea: 1.0 mg/kg once daily IV or PO.

Large Animal Dosage

No dose has been reported.

Regulatory Information

Use in animals intended for food is negligible. No regulatory information is available.

Domperidone

dahm-pare′ih-done

Trade and Other Names: Motilium and Equidone

Functional Classification: Prokinetic agent

Pharmacology and Mechanism of Action

Domperidone is a motility modifier with actions similar to metoclopramide, although chemically unrelated. A difference between metoclopramide and domperidone is that the latter does not cross the blood-brain barrier. Therefore, adverse CNS effects are not as much of a problem. Domperidone stimulates motility of upper GI tract, probably through dopaminergic effects or by increasing acetylcholine effects. The action of domperidone is to inhibit dopamine receptors and enhance action of acetylcholine in GI tract.

Indications and Clinical Uses

Domperidone has been used to treat gastroparesis and treatment of vomiting. In horses, domperidone has been used to treat fescue toxicosis and periparturient agalactia. Fescue toxicosis is caused by a fungus that produces a toxin, which causes reproductive problems in horses. The action of domperidone to increase lactation is through the stimulation of prolactin.

Precautionary Information

Adverse Reactions and Side Effects

Adverse effects that are seen with metoclopramide are not as common with domperidone because it does not cross the blood-brain barrier as readily as metoclopramide. It causes a transient increase in aldosterone and prolactin secretion.

Contraindications and Precautions

Do not use in patients with GI obstruction.

Drug Interactions

Acidity is needed for oral administration. Do not administer with stomach antacids such as omeprazole, cimetidine, or antacids.

Instructions for Use

Domperidone has questionable efficacy as a prokinetic agent (for treatment of ileus) in animals. A formulation has been available as an investigational drug for use in horses in the U.S. for treatment of agalactia and fescue toxicosis.

Patient Monitoring and Laboratory Tests

No specific monitoring is required, but clinical monitoring of GI motility is important.

Formulations

Domperidone is not available in U.S. at this time for small animal use. In Canada, it is available as 10 mg tablets. Formulation used in horses is oral gel at 11% (110 mg/mL).

Stability and Storage

Store in tightly sealed container, protected from light, and at room temperature. Stability of compounded formulations has not been evaluated.

Small Animal Dosage

Doses for small animals have not been established; but 2-5 mg per dog or cat q8-12h PO has been used.

Large Animal Dosage

Horses

- Use in horses for fescue toxicity and agalactia.
- Equidone oral gel (11%): 10 days prior to foaling at 1.1 mg/kg daily PO, starting 10 days before the scheduled foaling date. (This dose is equivalent to 5 mL per 500 kg, or 5 mL per adult horse daily PO of the 11% oral gel.) Continue until foaling. If there is not adequate milk production after foaling, continue for 5 additional days.

Regulatory Information

No regulatory information is available. For extralabel use withdrawal interval estimates, contact FARAD at 1-888-USFARAD (1-888-873-2723) or send e-mail to FARAD@ncsu.edu.

Dopamine Hydrochloride

doe'pah-meen hye-droe-klor'ide

Trade and Other Names: Intropin

Functional Classification: Cardiac inotropic agent

Pharmacology and Mechanism of Action

Adrenergic and dopamine agonist. At low doses it stimulates the dopamine (D_1)receptors; at moderate doses it stimulates the adrenergic receptors, and at high doses it acts as an alpha$_1$-receptor agonist (producing vasoconstriction).

Indications and Clinical Uses

Dopamine is used therapeutically to stimulate myocardium via action on cardiac beta$_1$-receptors. At lower doses, stimulation of dopamine receptors (D_1) causes renal arterial vasodilation and natriuresis. Vascular D_1 receptors are located on smooth muscle of arterial beds, particularly in renal and splanchnic tissues. Although dopamine can increase renal blood perfusion and induce natriuresis, clinical evidence for beneficial effect is lacking when using dopamine for treating acute renal failure.

Precautionary Information

Adverse Reactions and Side Effects

Dopamine may cause tachycardia and ventricular arrhythmias at high doses or in sensitive individuals.

Contraindications and Precautions

Dopamine is unstable in alkaline fluids.

Drug Interactions

Do not mix with alkaline solutions. Otherwise, it is compatible with most fluid solutions.

Instructions for Use

Dopamine has a rapid elimination half-life (minutes), and therefore must be administered via carefully monitored constant rate infusion (CRI). Because the actions of dopamine are dose dependent, the rate administered is adjusted to reach the desired clinical effect. Dopamine has been administered at doses of 2-10 mcg/kg/min for the acute management of heart failure and cardiogenic shock. When preparing intravenous solutions, one may admix 200-400 mg of dopamine with 250-500 mL of fluid. Dopamine is unstable in alkaline fluid solutions, such as those containing bicarbonate.

Low dose (vasodilation, D_1 receptor): 0.5-2 mcg/kg/min; medium dose (cardiac stimulating, beta$_1$-receptor): 2-10 mcg/kg/min; and high dose (vasoconstriction, alpha-receptors): >10 mcg/kg/min.

Patient Monitoring and Laboratory Tests

Monitor heart rate and rhythm while administering dopamine.

Formulations

Dopamine is available in 40, 80, and 160 mg/mL for IV injection.

Stability and Storage

Store in tightly sealed container, protected from light, and at room temperature. It may be added to fluids such as 5% dextrose, saline, and lactated Ringer's solution. It is stable for 24 hours after dilution. Do not use if solution turns a brown or purple color.

Small Animal Dosage

Dogs and Cats

- 2-10 mcg/kg/min IV infusion. Dose rate is dependent on desired effects.

Large Animal Dosage

Horses and Cattle

- 1-5 mcg/kg/min IV infusion.

Regulatory Information

No regulatory information is available. Because of a short half-life, no risk of residue is anticipated in food animals.

RCI Classification: 2

Doramectin

dore-ah-mek'tin

Trade and Other Names: Dectomax

Functional Classification: Antiparasitic

Pharmacology and Mechanism of Action

Antiparasitic drug. Avermectins (ivermectin-like drugs) and milbemycins (milbemycin, doramectin, and moxidectin) are macrocyclic lactones and share similarities, including mechanism of action. Neurotoxic to parasites by potentiating effects of inhibitory neurotransmitter, GABA. Therefore, these drugs paralyze and kill susceptible parasites. Ordinarily, mammals are resistant because sufficient concentrations for toxicity are not achieved in the CNS. Doramectin acts in similar manner and mirrors that of ivermectin and other drugs in this class. Doramectin is unique because it is formulated in an oil-based vehicle that delays absorption when injected. Therefore, it produces longer and more sustained plasma concentrations. It is effective against nematodes and arthropods, but has no effect on flukes or tapeworms.

Indications and Clinical Uses

Doramectin is used for treatment or prevention of GI parasite (nematode) infections in livestock, lice infestation, lungworm infection, and treatment of scabies. There are reports of a single injection (200-300 mcg/kg) used in cats for treatment of notoedric mange (infections from the mite *Notoedres cati*).

Precautionary Information

Adverse Reactions and Side Effects

Toxicity may occur at high doses and in breeds in which ivermectin-like drugs cross the blood-brain barrier. Sensitive breeds include collies, Australian shepherds, Shetland sheepdogs, and old English sheepdogs. Toxicity is neurotoxic, and signs include depression, ataxia, impaired vision, coma, and death. Sensitivity to ivermectin-like drugs may be because of mutation in blood-brain barrier (p-glycoprotein deficiency). Treatment of hypodermal larvae in cattle may elicit reactions in tissues from dead larvae. These drugs are safe for pregnant animals. No adverse effects were seen in cats treated with doses as high as 345 mcg/kg.

Contraindications and Precautions

Doramectin is only approved in cattle. Certain breeds of dogs (Shetland sheepdogs and Collie-type breeds) are more sensitive to adverse effects than other breeds.

Drug Interactions

Use cautiously with drugs that may inhibit p-glycoprotein at blood-brain barrier (see Appendix).

Instructions for Use

Doses vary depending on use. In cattle, for treatment of hypodermal larvae, treatment should begin at the end of fly season. Administration to cattle should use a 16- or 18-gauge needle for subcutaneous administration. For intramuscular injection, use a 1.5-inch needle and inject in neck muscle. When administering topical form, remove mud and manure from hide. If it rains within 2 hours of administration, decreased efficacy may occur.

Patient Monitoring and Laboratory Tests

Monitor for microfilaremia prior to administration in small animals.

Formulations

Doramectin is available in a 1% (10 mg/mL) injection and 5 mg/mL (0.5%) topical transdermal solution.

Stability and Storage

Store in tightly sealed container, protected from light, and at room temperature. Stability of compounded formulations has not been evaluated.

Small Animal Dosage

Dogs

- Demodex treatment: 600 mcg/kg/wk for 5-23 weeks SQ.

Cats

- Mite infection: 200-270 mcg/kg once SQ.
- 0.1 mL of 1% solution given once SQ.

Large Animal Dosage

Cattle

- 200 mcg/kg (0.2 mg/kg) or 1 mL per 50 kg (110 pounds), single injection, IM or SQ.
- Transdermal solution: Give 500 mcg (0.5 mg) per kg or 1 mL per 10 kg (4.5 pounds) as a single dose along the animal's back, along the midline.

Pigs

- 300 mcg/kg (0.3 mg/kg) or 1 mL per 34 kg (75 pounds), single injection, IM.

Regulatory Information

Cattle withdrawal time (meat): 35 days.
Pig withdrawal time (meat): 24 days.
Do not administer to lactating dairy cattle.
Do not administer to female dairy cattle older than 20 months of age.
Cattle transdermal solution withdrawal time (meat): 45 days. Do not administer to lactating dairy cattle; do not administer within 2 months of calving.

Doxapram Hydrochloride

doks'ah-pram hye-droe-klor'ide

Trade and Other Names: Dopram

Functional Classification: Respiratory stimulant

Pharmacology and Mechanism of Action

Respiratory stimulant via action on carotid chemoreceptors and subsequent stimulation of respiratory center.

Indications and Clinical Uses

Doxapram is used to treat respiratory depression or to stimulate post-anesthesia respiration, and it may also increase cardiac output. However, efficacy for these indications has not been established and availability of this formulation is questionable.

Precautionary Information

Adverse Reactions and Side Effects

Adverse effects not reported in animals. In people, cardiovascular effects and convulsions have occurred with high doses.

Contraindications and Precautions

Because it contains benzyl alcohol as vehicle, use cautiously in young animals.

Drug Interactions

Do not use with other CNS stimulants.

Instructions for Use

Used for short-term treatment only. No longer available from manufacturer.

Patient Monitoring and Laboratory Tests

Monitor patient's heart and respiratory rate.

Formulations

Doxapram has been available in a 20 mg/mL solution, but has recently become difficult to obtain commercially.

Stability and Storage

Store in tightly sealed container, protected from light, and at room temperature. Stability of compounded formulations has not been evaluated.

Small Animal Dosage

- 5-10 mg/kg IV.
- Neonate: 1-5 mg SQ, sublingual, or via umbilical vein.

Large Animal Dosage

No large animal doses are reported.

Regulatory Information

No regulatory information is available. For extralabel use withdrawal interval estimates, contact FARAD at 1-888-USFARAD (1-888-873-2723) or send e-mail to FARAD@ncsu.edu.
RCI Classification: 2

Doxepin

doks'eh-pin

Trade and Other Names: Sinequan

Functional Classification: Behavior-modifying drug, tricylic

D

Pharmacology and Mechanism of Action

Tricyclic antidepressant (TCA). For treatment of depression, this class of drugs is thought to act by increasing synaptic concentrations of norepinephrine and serotonin (5-HT) in the CNS. Doxepin is only a moderate to weak inhibitor of these neurotransmitters. Doxepin also has antihistamine (H_1) properties.

Indications and Clinical Uses

Doxepin has been used to treat anxiety disorders and dermatologic conditions in dogs and cats. Some use for dermatitis is related to the drug's antihistamine properties. Although it has been used for treating pruritus and dermatitis in small animals, it has not been effective for treating atopic dermatitis in dogs. Doxepin has been used to treat lick granuloma in dogs.

Precautionary Information

Adverse Reactions and Side Effects

Tricyclic antidepressant drugs all have to some degree antimuscarinic effects that may increase heart rate, cause xerostomia, and affect the GI tract. Those with antihistamine properties may cause sedation.

Contraindications and Precautions

As with other TCAs, do not administer with other antidepressant drugs. Do not use in patients with glaucoma. Use cautiously in epileptic patients as it may lower seizure threshold.

Drug Interactions

This drug will increase sedative effects from antihistamines. Do not administer with monoamine oxidase inhibitors (MAOIs).

Instructions for Use

Doxepin has primarily been administered to treat pruritus in dogs. The efficacy for this use has been disappointing.

Patient Monitoring and Laboratory Tests

No specific monitoring is necessary.

Formulations

Doxepin is available in 10, 25, 50, 75, 100, and 150 mg capsules. Generic and Sinequan is available in 10 mg/mL oral solution.

Stability and Storage

Store in tightly sealed container, protected from light, and at room temperature. Oral formulations can be mixed with various flavorings, juices, and foods without loss of stability.

Small Animal Dosage

Dogs

- 1-5 mg/kg q12h PO. Start with low dose and gradually increase.
- Lick granuloma: 0.5-1.0 mg/kg q12h PO. (For comparison, antipruritic dose for people is 10 to 25 mg/person once to three times per day and increased as needed.)

Cats

- 0.5-1 mg/kg q12-24h. Start with low dose initially.

Large Animal Dosage

No large animal doses are reported.

Regulatory Information

No regulatory information is available. For extralabel use withdrawal interval estimates, contact FARAD at 1-888-USFARAD (1-888-873-2723) or send e-mail to FARAD@ncsu.edu.

RCI Classification: 2

Doxorubicin Hydrochloride

doks-oh-roo′bih-sin hye-droe-klor′ide

Trade and Other Names: Adriamycin

Functional Classification: Anticancer agent

Pharmacology and Mechanism of Action

Anticancer agent. Doxorubicin, like other anthracycline antibiotics, damages DNA by inhibition of topoisomerase-II dependent pathways and intercalating between bases of DNA molecule. It subsequently causes cell death by blocking synthesis of RNA and proteins. Other mechanisms that may contribute to its action are binding to cell membranes, alteration of ion transport, and generation of oxygen free radicals, which are toxic to cancer cells. Doxorubicin is administered IV only, usually every 21 days. After intravenous infusion, there are three phases of elimination with the longest phase having a half-life of 26 hours in humans, but 8-10 hours in dogs. Other antitumor antibiotics include mitoxantrone, actinomycin D, and bleomycin.

Indications and Clinical Uses

Doxorubicin is used for treatment of various neoplasia, including lymphoma. Doxorubicin is commonly used in humans for the treatment of breast tumors, various sarcomas, and osteosarcoma. In veterinary medicine it has been used for lymphoma, osteosarcoma, and other carcinomas and sarcomas. It is considered one of the most effective single agents in the treatment of lymphoma.

Precautionary Information

Adverse Reactions and Side Effects

Most common acute effect is anorexia, vomiting, and diarrhea. Some oncologists pre-treat their patients with an antiemetic drug such as metoclopramide, prochlorperazine, or chlorpromazine to minimize side effects. Dose-related toxicity also includes bone marrow suppression, hair loss (in certain breeds), and cardiotoxicity. Bone marrow depression (leukopenia) is common. The nadir is at 7-10 days. The stem cells are usually spared, and recovery occurs within 21 days following each dose. Cardiotoxicity limits the total dose administered. The risk of chronic effects increases as total cumulative doses exceed 200-240 mg/m^2. Most clinicians rarely exceed a total dose of 180 mg/m^2 (not more than 6 doses) to avoid cardiac toxicity. Cardiotoxicity may be caused by doxorubicin forming an intracellular complex with iron that catalyzes formation of oxygen-derived free radical production. These radicals damage myocardial cells. Dexrazoxane (Zinecard) is a potent chelator of iron and has been used to chelate free iron and iron complexed with anthracycline antibiotics, yet it does not interfere with the drug's antitumor effect. Alopecia is common in people, but primarily it is seen only in dogs that have continuously growing hair (e.g., poodles). Cats may lose their whiskers. Hypersensitivity (allergic) reactions have been observed. These reactions are probably not true allergic reactions, but are simply the result of mast cell degranulation that occurs independently of IgG binding. Signs of this reaction are head shaking (ear pruritus) and generalized urticaria and erythema. Many oncologists pre-treat their patients with antihistamines and/or corticosteroids to prevent this reaction.

Contraindications and Precautions

Do not use in animals with cardiomyopathy. Monitor CBC in patients prior to each treatment and adjust dose or alter schedule when neutropenia is severe.

Drug Interactions

No specific drug interactions are reported.

Instructions for Use

Regimen listed may differ for various tumors. Dose must be infused IV (over 20-30 min). Animals may require antiemetic and antihistamine (diphenhydramine) prior to therapy. Most often it is administered on a body surface area rate (mg/m^2); however, dose according to body weight (mg/kg) may be safer for small dogs.

Patient Monitoring and Laboratory Tests

Monitor ECG during therapy. ECGs should be performed periodically in dogs to look for evidence of myocardial toxicity. CBC should be monitored regularly and prior to each treatment because of risk of myelotoxicity.

Formulations

Doxorubicin is available in a 2 mg/mL injection.

Stability and Storage

Store in tightly sealed container, protected from light, and at room temperature.

Small Animal Dosage

Dogs

- 30 mg/m^2 q21days IV.
- Dogs >20 kg: 30 mg/m^2.
- Dogs <20 kg: 1 mg/kg.

Cats

- 20 mg/m^2 (approximately 1.25 mg/kg) q3wks IV.

Large Animal Dosage

No large animal doses are reported.

Regulatory Information

Withdrawal times are not established for animals that produce food. This drug should not be used in animals intended for food, because it is an anticancer agent.

Doxycycline

doks-ih-sye'kleen

Trade and Other Names: Vibramycin, Monodox, Doxy Caps, and generic brands

Functional Classification: Antibacterial

Pharmacology and Mechanism of Action

Tetracycline antibiotic. Mechanism of action of tetracyclines is to bind to the 30S ribosomal subunit and inhibit protein synthesis. The action of tetracyclines is usually bacteriostatic. Broad spectrum of activity including bacteria, some protozoa, *Rickettsia*, and *Ehrlichia*.

Indications and Clinical Uses

Doxycycline is usually the drug of choice for treating tick-borne diseases in animals, and efficacy has been demonstrated in research studies. It is used for treating infections caused by bacteria, some protozoa, *Rickettsia*, and *Ehrlichia*. Doxycycline administered to cats with infections caused by *Chlamydophilia felis* (formerly *Chlamydia psittaci*) at 10-15 mg/kg once daily PO has been effective for eliminating the organism, and improvement of clinical signs.

Precautionary Information

Adverse Reactions and Side Effects

In general, tetracyclines may cause renal tubular necrosis at high doses and can affect bone and teeth formation in young animals. However, doxycycline has not been reported to cause these problems in animals. Doxycycline administered orally to cats has caused esophageal irritation, tissue injury, and esophageal stricture. This may be caused by solid-dose formulations becoming entrapped in the esophagus. Passage into the stomach by giving the cat water or food after administration is advised to prevent this effect. Doxycycline given IV to horses has been fatal; however, it has been administered safely to horses PO. In two studies there were no adverse effects reported. In another study, one of the horses in a pharmacokinetic trial developed signs of enteritis and colic.

Contraindications and Precautions

Do not administer to young animals because it can affect bone and teeth formation. However, it has been better tolerated in children than other tetracyclines. If solid-dose forms are administered to cats, lubricate the tablet/capsule, or follow with food or water to ensure passage into stomach. Do not administer rapidly IV. Do not administer solution IM or SQ. Do **not** administer IV to horses under any circumstances; acute death has been reported from this use.

Drug Interactions

Tetracyclines bind to compounds containing calcium, which decreases oral absorption. However, this is less of a problem with doxycycline than other tetracyclines. Doxycycline has been mixed with milk prior to oral administration to children without decreasing efficacy.

Instructions for Use

Many pharmacokinetic and experimental studies have been conducted in small animals, but no clinical studies. Doxycycline is ordinarily considered the drug of choice for *Rickettsia* and *Ehrlichia* infections in dogs. Doxycycline is more effective than enrofloxacin for *Ehrlichia*. Doxycycline intravenous infusion is stable for only 12 hours at room temperature and 72 hours if refrigerated.

Patient Monitoring and Laboratory Tests

Susceptibility testing: CLSI (NCCLS) Break points for sensitive organisms is less than or equal to 2 mcg/mL for streptococci and less than or equal to 4 for other organisms. Tetracycline is used as a marker to test susceptibility for other drugs in this class, such as doxycycline, minocycline, and oxytetracycline.

D

Formulations

Doxycycline is available in 10 mg/mL oral suspension, 100 mg tablets, and 50 and 100 mg capsules (doxycycline hyclate), and 100 mg injection vial.

Stability and Storage

Store in tightly sealed container, protected from light, and at room temperature. Avoid mixing with cations such as iron, calcium, aluminum, and zinc. However, doxycycline tablets have been mixed with milk and immediately administered to children without loss of potency. Doxycycline hyclate for injection will retain potency for 12 hours at room temperature, or 72 hours refrigerated after reconstitution at concentrations up to 1 mg/mL. IV solutions are stable in LRS or 5% dextrose for 6 hours at room temperature. Protect IV solutions from light. If frozen after reconstitution with sterile water, solutions of 10 mg/mL are potent for 8 weeks.

Small Animal Dosage

Dogs and Cats

- 3-5 mg/kg q12h PO or IV, 10 mg/kg q24h PO.
- *Rickettsia* (dogs): 5 mg/kg q12h.
- *Ehrlichia* (dogs): 5 mg/kg q12h for 14 days.

Large Animal Dosage

- Use has been limited primarily to treating *Ehrlichiosis* in horses. Dose: 10-20 mg/kg q12h PO.

Regulatory Information

No regulatory information is available. For extralabel use withdrawal interval estimates, contact FARAD at 1-888-USFARAD (1-888-873-2723) or send e-mail to FARAD@ncsu.edu.

Dronabinol

droe-nab'ih-nole

Trade and Other Names: Marinol

Functional Classification: Antiemetic

Pharmacology and Mechanism of Action

Antiemetic from the cannabinoid class. The site of action is unknown, but there is some evidence that the active ingredient may affect opiate receptors, or they may affect other receptors in the vomiting center. For dronabinol, the oral absorption is good, but bioavailability is low because of high first-pass effects. The volume of distribution is high.

Indications and Clinical Uses

Cannabinoids have been used in people who have not responded to any other antiemetic drugs (e.g., patients who are receiving anticancer drugs). They have also gained recent popularity to increase the appetite in patients with terminal disease, cancer, and AIDS. Their use has not been reported in veterinary patients, but they have been used by some veterinarians to increase the appetite in cats.

Precautionary Information

Adverse Reactions and Side Effects

Cannabinoids are relatively well tolerated in people, but side effects include drowsiness, dizziness, ataxia, and disorientation. Withdrawal signs may occur after abrupt discontinuation after repeated doses.

Contraindications and Precautions

No known contraindications.

Drug Interactions

No drug interactions reported for animals.

Instructions for Use

Dronabinol is a form of synthetic marijuana (THC) and is available as an antiemetic prescription drug. Most clinical use in animals has been anecdotal. It has been administered to decrease vomiting and improve appetite associated with chemotherapy.

Patient Monitoring and Laboratory Tests

No specific monitoring is necessary.

Formulations

Dronabinol is available in 2.5, 5, and 10 mg capsules.

Stability and Storage

Store in tightly sealed container, protected from light, and at room temperature.

Small Animal Dosage

Dogs and Cats

- 5 mg/m^2 PO, up to 15 mg/m^2 for antiemetic administration prior to chemotherapy.
- Appetite stimulation: start at 2.5 mg before meals.

Large Animal Dosage

No dose has been reported for large animals.

Regulatory Information

Do not administer to animals intended for food.

Edetate Calcium Disodium

ed'eh-tate kal'see-um dye-soe-dee-um

Trade and Other Names: Calcium disodium versenate and calcium disodium ethylenediaminetetra-acetate (EDTA)

Functional Classification: Antidote

E

Pharmacology and Mechanism of Action

Chelating agent. Readily chelates with lead, zinc, cadmium, copper, iron, and manganese.

Indications and Clinical Uses

Edetate calcium disodium is indicated for treatment of acute and chronic lead poisoning. It is sometimes used in combination with dimercaprol.

Precautionary Information

Adverse Reactions and Side Effects

No adverse effects reported in animals. In people, allergic reactions (release of histamine) have occured after intravenous administration.

Contraindications and Precautions

Do not use edetate disodium to substitute for edetate calcium disodium, because it will chelate calcium in the patient.

Drug Interactions

No specific drug interactions are reported. However, it has the potential to chelate other drugs if mixed together.

Instructions for Use

Edetate calcium disodium may be used with dimercaprol. Equally effective when administered IV or IM, but intramuscular injection may be painful. Ensure adequate urine flow before the first dose is administered.

Patient Monitoring and Laboratory Tests

Monitor lead concentrations to assess treatment.

Formulations

Edetate calcium disodium is available in a 20 mg/mL injection.

Stability and Storage

Store in tightly sealed container, protected from light, and at room temperature. Stability of compounded formulations has not been evaluated.

Small Animal Dosage

- 25 mg/kg q6h for 2-5 days SQ, IM, or IV.

Large Animal Dosage

- 25 mg/kg q6h for 2-5 days SQ, IM, or IV.

Regulatory Information

Withdrawal time: 2 days for meat; 2 days for milk (extralabel).

Edrophonium Chloride

ed-roe-foe′nee-um klor′ide

Trade and Other Names: Tensilon and generic brands

Functional Classification: Antimyasthenic, anticholinesterase

Pharmacology and Mechanism of Action

Cholinesterase inhibitor. Edrophonium causes cholinergic effects by inhibiting metabolism of acetylcholine. Its effects do not last long and is used for short-term use only.

Indications and Clinical Uses

Because edrophonium is short acting, it ordinarily is only used for diagnostic purposes (e.g., myasthenia gravis). It also has been used to reverse neuromuscular blockade of nondepolarizing agents (pancuronium).

Precautionary Information

Adverse Reactions and Side Effects

Edrophonium is short acting and side effects are minimal. Excessive muscarinic/cholinergic effects may occur with high doses; these may be counteracted with atropine.

Contraindications and Precautions

Edrophonium will potentiate effects of other cholinergic drugs.

Drug Interactions

Use cautiously with other cholinergic drugs.

Instructions for Use

Edrophonium is used only for determination of diagnosis of myasthenia gravis.

Patient Monitoring and Laboratory Tests

No specific monitoring is necessary.

Formulations

Edrophonium is available in a 10 mg/mL injection.

Stability and Storage

Store in tightly sealed container, protected from light, and at room temperature. Stability of compounded formulations has not been evaluated.

Small Animal Dosage

Dogs

- 0.11-0.22 mg/kg IV.

Cats

- 2.5 mg/cat IV.

Large Animal Dose

No large animal doses have been reported.

Regulatory Information

No regulatory information is available. Because of a short half-life, no risk of residue is anticipated in food animals.

RCI Classification: 3

Enalapril Maleate

eh-nal'ah-prill mal'ee-ate

Trade and Other Names: Enacard (veterinary preparation) and Vasotec (human preparation)

Functional Classification: Vasodilator, angiotensin-converting enzyme (ACE) inhibitor

Pharmacology and Mechanism of Action

ACE inhibitor. Like other ACE inhibitors, it inhibits conversion of angiotensin I to angiotensin II. Angiotensin II is a potent vasoconstrictor and will also stimulate sympathetic stimulation, renal hypertension, and synthesis of aldosterone. The ability of aldosterone to cause sodium and water retention contributes to congestion.

Enalapril, like other ACE inhibitors will cause vasodilation and decrease aldosterone-induced congestion, but ACE inhibitors also contribute to vasodilation by increasing concentrations of some vasodilating kinins and prostaglandins.

Indications and Clinical Uses

Enalapril, like other ACE inhibitors, is used to treat hypertension and CHF. It is primarily used in dogs, but it may benefit some cats in heart failure or with systemic hypertension. Unfortunately, approximately 50% of cats with hypertension do not respond to enalapril, and ACE inhibitors are not considered a primary treatment for hypertension in cats.

Enalapril also is used to treat some forms of renal disease in animals. When glomerular filtration pressures are high, enalapril can benefit patients with renal disease.

Precautionary Information

Adverse Reactions and Side Effects

Enalapril may cause azotemia in some patients; carefully monitor patients receiving high doses of diuretics.

Contraindications and Precautions

Discontinue ACE inhibitors in pregnant animals; they cross the placenta and have caused fetal malformations and death of the fetus.

Drug Interactions

Use cautiously with other hypotensive drugs and diuretics. Nonsteroidal antiinflammatory drugs (NSAIDs) may decrease vasodilating effects.

Instructions for Use

Doses are based on clinical trials conducted in dogs by manufacturer. For dogs, start with once daily administration and increase to q12h if needed. Other drugs used for treatment of heart failure may be used concurrently. In horses, the metabolite enalaprilat at 0.5 mg/kg IV completely inhibited ACE activity (*Am J Vet Res,* 62:1008-1013, 2001). However at this dose, enalaprilat did not change blood pressure or other hemodynamic variables in response to exercise.

Patient Monitoring and Laboratory Tests

Monitor patients carefully to avoid hypotension. With all ACE inhibitors, monitor electrolytes and renal function 3-7 days after initiating therapy and periodically thereafter.

Formulations

Enalapril is available as Vasotec (human preparation) in 2.5, 5, 10, and 20 mg tablets, and as Enacard (veterinary preparation) in 1, 2.5, 5, 10, and 20 mg tablets.

Stability and Storage

Store in tightly sealed container, protected from light, and at room temperature. Enalapril, compounded in a variety of oral suspensions and flavorings, was stable for 60 days. Above pH of 5, degradation occurs more quickly.

Small Animal Dosage

Dogs

- 0.5 mg/kg q12-24h PO. In some animals it may be necessary to increase dose to 1.0 mg/kg.

Cats

- 0.25-0.5 mg/kg q12-24h PO.
- 1.0-1.25 mg/cat/day PO.

Large Animal Dosage

- There are no clinical studies available. However, in horses, the metabolite enalaprilat at 0.5 mg/kg IV completely inhibited ACE activity (*Am J Vet Res,* 62: 1008-1013, 2001). However, at this dose, enalaprilat did not change blood pressure or other hemodynamic variables in response to exercise. Oral absorption is poor in horses.

Regulatory Information

No regulatory information is available. For extralabel use withdrawal interval estimates, contact FARAD at 1-888-USFARAD (1-888-873-2723) or send e-mail to FARAD@ncsu.edu.

RCI Classification: 3

Enflurane

en-floor′ane

Trade and Other Names: Ethrane

Functional Classification: Inhalant anesthetic

Pharmacology and Mechanism of Action

Inhalant anesthetic. Like other inhalant anesthetics, the mechanism of action is uncertain. Enflurane produces a generalized, reversible, depression of the CNS. The inhalant anesthetics vary in their solubility in blood, their potency, and the rate of induction and recovery. Those with low blood/gas partition coefficients are associated with the most rapid rates of induction and recovery. Enflurane has a vapor pressure of 175 mm Hg (at 20° C), a blood/gas partition coefficient of 1.8, and a fat/blood coefficient of 36.

Indications and Clinical Uses

Enflurane, like other inhalant anesthetics, is used for general anesthesia in animals. It has a minimum alveolar concentration (MAC) value of 2.37%, 2.06%, and 2.12% in cats, dogs, and horses, respectively.

Precautionary Information

Adverse Reactions and Side Effects

Like other inhalant anesthetics, enflurane produces vasodilation and increased blood flow to cerebral blood vessels. This may increase intracranial pressure. Like other inhalant anesthetics, it produces a dose-dependent myocardial depression, with accompanying decrease in cardiac output. It also depresses respiratory rate and alveolar ventilation. Like other inhalant anesthetics it increases the risk of ventricular arrhythmias, especially in response to catecholamines.

Contraindications and Precautions

No specific contraindications are reported for animals.

Drug Interactions

No drug interactions are reported for animals.

Instructions for Use

Titrate dose for each individual with anesthetic monitoring.

Patient Monitoring and Laboratory Tests

Monitor anesthesia parameters. During anesthesia, monitor heart rate and rhythm and respiratory rate.

Formulations

Enflurane is available as solution for inhalation.

Stability and Storage

Store in tightly sealed container, protected from light, and at room temperature.

Small Animal Dosage

Induction: 2%-3% Maintenance: 1.5%-3%

Large Animal Dosage

- MAC value: 1.66%.

Regulatory Information

No withdrawal times are established for food animals. Clearance is rapid and short withdrawal times are suggested. For extralabel use withdrawal interval estimates, contact FARAD at 1-888-USFARAD (1-888-873-2723) or send e-mail to FARAD@ncsu.edu.

Enilconazole

en-il-kah′nah-zole

Trade and Other Names: Imaverol and ClinaFarm-EC

Functional Classification: Antifungal

Pharmacology and Mechanism of Action

Azole antifungal agent for topical use only. Like other azoles, enilconazole inhibits membrane synthesis (ergosterol) in fungus and weakens cell wall. It is highly active against dermatophytes.

Indications and Clinical Uses

Enilconazole is used only topically. It is used as a topical agent to apply on the skin for treatment of dermatophytes and as a spray, it is used to treat environment. It may be applied to animal bedding, stall, and cages. In addition to dermatologic use, enilconazole has been instilled into the nasal sinus of dogs for treatment of nasal aspergillosis.

Precautionary Information

Adverse Reactions and Side Effects

Adverse effects have not been reported. However, it is reported that if used on cats, they should be prevented from licking fur after application until the drug has dried.

Contraindications and Precautions

No specific contraindications are reported.

Drug Interactions

No specific interactions are reported. However, like other azoles, systemic treatment may result in cytochrome P450 enzyme inhibition.

Instructions for Use

It is used only topically. Imaverol is available only in Canada as 10% emulsion. In the U.S., Clinafarm EC is available for use in poultry units as 13.8% solution. Dilute solution to at least 50:1 and apply topically every 3-4 days for 2-3 weeks. Enilconazole also has been instilled as 1:1 dilution into nasal sinus for nasal aspergillosis. Enilconazole also has been used—in a diluted form—as a spray to kill fungi on bedding, equine tack, and cages.

Patient Monitoring and Laboratory Tests

No specific monitoring is necessary.

Formulations Available

Enilconazole is available as 10% or 13.8% emulsion.

Stability and Storage

Store in tightly sealed container, protected from light, and at room temperature. Stability of compounded formulations has not been evaluated. When the emulsion is mixed, it should be used immediately and not stored.

Small Animal Dosage

- Nasal aspergillosis: 10 mg/kg q12h instilled into nasal sinus for 14 days (10% solution diluted 50/50 with water).
- Dermatophytes: dilute 10% solution to 0.2% and wash lesion with solution four times at 3-4 day intervals. Solution may be sponged directly on animal. Allow solution to air dry.

Large Animal Dosage

Horses

- Dilute 10% solution to 0.2% and wash lesions with solution four times at 3-4 day intervals.

Regulatory Information

No regulatory information is available. For extralabel use withdrawal interval estimates, contact FARAD at 1-888-USFARAD (1-888-873-2723) or send e-mail to FARAD@ncsu.edu.

Enoxaparin

en-oks'ah-pare-in

Trade and Other Names: Lovenox and low-molecular weight heparin (LMWH)

Functional Classification: Anticoagulant

Pharmacology and Mechanism of Action

LMWHs are also known as fragmented heparin. LMWHs produce their effect by increasing antithrombin III mediated inhibition of synthesis and activity of factor Xa. LMWHs have several advantages compared to heparin that includes more complete and predictable absorption from injection, longer duration, and a more predictable anticoagulant response in animals. LMWHs are classified on the basis of their Anti-factor Xa/Anti-factor IIa ratio. Enoxaparin has a ratio of 3.8:1. By comparison, unfractionated heparin has a ratio of 1:1. LMWHs currently available include tinzaparin (Innohep), enoxaparin (Lovenox), and dalteparin (Fragmin).

Indications and Clinical Uses

Enoxaparin, like other LMWHs, is used to treat and prevent coagulation disorders such as thromboembolism, venous thrombosis, and pulmonary thromboembolism. There are no controlled clinical trials in animals in which LMWHs have been used. However, they have been administered, with other supportive therapy, for pulmonary thromboembolism, thromboembolism in cats, and as a prophylactic in animals at risk for disseminated intravascular coagulopathy (DIC).

Precautionary Information

Adverse Reactions and Side Effects

Although better tolerated than regular heparin, bleeding is a risk. However, LMWHs produce less bleeding problems than administration of heparin. LMWHs are associated with a lower incidence of heparin-induced thrombocytopenia. No effects on platelet aggregation are expected.

Contraindications and Precautions

Use cautiously in animals prone to bleeding problems.

Drug Interactions

Do not mix with intravenous fluids. Do not mix with other drugs. Use cautiously with other anticoagulants or nonsteroidal antiinflammatory drugs (NSAIDs), especially aspirin.

Instructions for Use

Dosing recommendations are empirical, because these compounds have not been used commonly in veterinary medicine. LMWHs are expensive compared to heparin. When dosing, do **not** interchange doses on a unit for unit basis with other heparins.

Patient Monitoring and Laboratory Tests

Patients should be observed for bleeding problems. The mechanism of action of LMWHs is via binding antithrombin III and inhibiting clotting factors Xa and IIa, but they have preference for factor Xa. This activity is measured as the factor Xa/factor IIa ratio. Therefore, enoxaparin does not significantly affect prothrombin time (PT), thrombin time (TT), or activated partial thromboplastin time (APTT) clotting times and monitoring these times could be misleading. Prolonged APTT is a sign of overdosing. Monitor anti-factor Xa activity if available.

Formulations

Enoxaparin is available in 30 mg in 0.3 mL, 40 mg in 0.4 mL, 60 mg in 0.6 mL, 80 mg in 0.8 mL, and 100 mg in 1 mL injection.

Stability and Storage

Store in tightly sealed container, protected from light, and at room temperature. Stability of compounded formulations has not been evaluated.

Small Animal Dosage

Dogs

- 1 mg/kg q12h SQ.

Cats

- Prophylaxis: 0.5 mg/kg q24h SQ.
- Thrombosis: 1 mg/kg q12h SQ.

Large Animal Dosage

Horses

- Prophylaxis: 0.5 mg/kg q24h SQ and 1 mg/kg q24h SQ for high-risk patients.

Regulatory Information

Withdrawal times are not established; 24 hour withdrawal times are suggested, because this drug has little risk from residues.

Enrofloxacin

en-roe-floks'ah-sin

Trade and Other Names: Baytril

Functional Classification: Antibacterial

Pharmacology and Mechanism of Action

Fluoroquinolone antibacterial drug. Enrofloxacin acts via inhibition of DNA gyrase in bacteria to inhibit DNA and RNA synthesis. Enrofloxacin is a bactericidal with a broad spectrum of activity. In most animal species, enrofloxacin is metabolized to ciprofloxacin. Ciprofloxacin is an active desmethyl metabolite of enrofloxacin and may contribute in an additive fashion to the antibacterial effects. At the peak concentration, ciprofloxacin may account for approximately 10% and 20% of the total concentration in cats and dogs, respectively. Susceptible bacteria include *Staphylococcus, Escherichia coli, Proteus, Klebsiella,* and *Pasteurella*. *Pseudomonas aeruginosa* is moderately sensitive but requires higher concentrations. Enrofloxacin has poor activity against *Streptococcus* and anaerobic bacteria.

Indications and Clinical Uses

Enrofloxacin, like other fluoroquinolones, is used to treat susceptible bacteria in a variety of species. Treatment has included infections of skin and soft tissue, UTIs in dogs and cats, soft tissue infections in horses, and bovine respiratory disease (BRD) in cattle.

Enrofloxacin has been shown effective for treating *Rickettsia* infections in dogs. However, it is not effective for treating *Ehrlichia* (see doxycycline). Enrofloxacin is also used in most exotic animal species because of its safety and activity against a wide variety of pathogens.

Precautionary Information

Adverse Reactions and Side Effects

High concentrations may cause CNS toxicity, especially in animals with renal failure. It may cause occasional vomiting and at high doses, may cause some nausea and diarrhea. All of the fluoroquinolones may cause arthropathy in young animals. Dogs are most sensitive at 4 weeks to 28 weeks of age. Large, rapidly growing dogs are the most susceptible.

Cats are relatively resistant to cartilage injury, but foals are susceptible. Blindness in cats has been reported that is caused by retinal degeneration. Affected cats have had permanent blindness. This may be a dose-related effect. Cats administered doses of 20 mg/kg developed retinal degeneration but did not at 5 mg/kg. Therefore, dose restrictions in cats have been employed. Administration of concentrated solution (100 mg/mL) given orally to horses has caused oral mucosal lesions. When injected, this solution (pH 10.5) may be irritating to some tissues.

Contraindications and Precautions

Avoid use in young dogs because of risk of cartilage injury. Do not administer to young foals; injury to articular cartilage has been reported. Use cautiously in animals that may be prone to seizures, such as epileptics. Do not administer to cats at doses >5 mg/kg/day.

Drug Interactions

Fluoroquinolones may increase concentrations of theophylline if used concurrently. Coadministration with divalent and trivalent cations, such as products containing aluminum (e.g., sucralfate), iron, and calcium may decrease absorption.
Do not mix in solutions or in vials with aluminum, calcium, iron, or zinc, because chelation may occur.

Instructions for Use

Low dose of 5 mg/kg/day is used for sensitive organisms with minimum inhibitory concentration (MIC) values of 0.12 mcg/mL or less or urinary tract infection.
A dose of 5-10 mg/kg/day is used for organisms with MIC of 0.12-0.5 mcg/mL (e.g., gram-positive bacteria). A dose of 10-20 mg/kg/day is used for organisms with MIC of 0.5-1.0 mcg/mL (e.g., Pseudomonas *aeruginosa*). The solution is not approved for intravenous use, but it has been administered via this route safely if given slowly. Enrofloxacin was not absorbed in cats after transdermal application in a pluronic gel vehicle. Concentrated enrofloxacin solution (cattle formulation at 100 mg/mL) is basic (pH 10.5), therefore it can be irritating to some animals when injected IM. Also, this formulation may precipitate out of solution if pH is decreased by other solutions.

Patient Monitoring and Laboratory Tests

Susceptibility testing: CLSI (NCCLS). For small animals, break points for sensitive organisms is less than or equal to 0.5 mcg/mL. MIC values greater than or equal to 4 are considered resistant. If MIC values are 1 or 2 mcg/mL, higher doses may be justified. For cattle, break points for sensitive organisms is less than or equal to 0.25 mcg/mL. Other fluoroquinolones may be used in some cases to estimate susceptibility to this fluoroquinolone but a test using a specific drug is recommended. Ciprofloxacin break point for susceptibility is less than or equal to 1.0 mcg/mL. However, if ciprofloxacin is used to treat *Pseudomonas* it may be several times more active than other fluoroquinolones.

Enrofloxacin may cause a false-positive result on urine glucose tests when using tablet (e.g., Clintest) copper reduction test.

Formulations

Enrofloxacin is available in 22.7 and 68 mg tablets; Taste Tabs are 22.7, 68, and 136 mg. It is also available in a 22.7 mg/mL injection and 100 mg/mL preparation for cattle (Baytril-100).

Stability and Storage

Store in tightly sealed container, protected from light, and at room temperature. Stability of compounded formulations has been evaluated and found to be stable with many mixtures. However, do not mix with solutions that contain ions that may chelate with enrofloxacin (iron, magnesium, aluminum, and calcium). The 100 mg/mL solution is alkaline and contains benzyl alcohol and l-arginine as a base. If pH of this solution is lowered, it may precipitate.

Small Animal Dosage

Dogs

- 5-20 mg/kg/day IM, PO, or IV.

Cats

- 5 mg/kg/day PO or IM. (Avoid intravenous use in cats.)

Exotic Animals

- Usually 5 mg/kg/day or in reptiles, every other day.

Birds

- 15 mg/kg q12h IM or PO.

Large Animal Dosage

Horses

- 5 mg/kg q24h IV.
- 7.5-10 mg/kg q24h PO.
- 5 mg/kg of 100 mg/mL solution (Baytril-100) IM.

Cattle

- BRD: 2.5-5 mg/kg/day SQ or 7.5-12.5 mg/kg once SQ.

Regulatory Information

Cattle withdrawal time: 28 days for meat. Not to be used in lactating dairy cattle or calves intended to be used as veal.

Extralabel use of fluoroquinolones in animals that produce food is illegal.

Ephedrine Hydrochloride

eh-fed′rin hye-droe-klor′ide

Trade and Other Names: Generic brands

Functional Classification: Adrenergic agonist

Pharmacology and Mechanism of Action

Adrenergic agonist. Decongestant. Ephedrine acts as an agonist on alpha-adrenergic receptors and beta$_1$-adrenergic receptors but has less effect on beta$_2$ receptors.

Indications and Clinical Uses

Ephedrine is used as a vasopressor, for example when it is administered during anesthesia. It also has been used as a CNS stimulant. Oral formulations have been used to treat urinary incontinence because of action on bladder sphincter muscle. However, most oral dose forms are no longer available.

Precautionary Information

Adverse Reactions and Side Effects

Adverse effects are related to excessive adrenergic activity (e.g., peripheral vasoconstriction and tachycardia).

Contraindications and Precautions

Use in animals with cardiovascular disease is not recommended.

Drug Interactions

No specific drug interactions are reported. However, ephedrine will potentiate any other adrenergic agonist.

Instructions for Use

Most current use is from injection primarily in acute situations to increase blood pressure. Oral use for urinary incontinence in dogs has diminished because of lack of available formulations.

Patient Monitoring and Laboratory Tests

Monitor heart rate and rhythm in patients.

Formulations

Ephedrine is available in 25 and 50 mg/mL injection.

Stability and Storage

Store in tightly sealed container, protected from light, and at room temperature.

Small Animal Dosage

Dogs

- Urinary incontinence: 4 mg/kg or 12.5-50 mg/dog q8-12h PO.
- Vasopressor: 0.75 mg/kg IM or SQ, repeat as needed.

Cats

- Urinary incontinence: 2-4 mg/kg q12h, PO.
- Vasopressor: 0.75 mg/kg IM or SQ, repeat as needed.

Large Animal Dosage

No large animal doses are reported.

Regulatory Information

Withdrawal time: No withdrawal times are established. Ephedrine is metabolized after administration, and a short withdrawal is recommended.
RCI Classification: 2

Epinephrine

eh-pih-nef'rin

Trade and Other Names: Adrenaline and generic brands

Functional Classification: Adrenergic agonist

Pharmacology and Mechanism of Action

Adrenergic agonist. Epinephrine nonselectively stimulates alpha-adrenergic and beta-adrenergic receptors. Epinephrine is a potent adrenergic agonist with a prompt onset and a short duration of action.

Indications and Clinical Uses

Epinephrine is used primarily for emergency situations to treat cardiopulmonary arrest and anaphylactic shock. It is administered IV, IM, or endotracheal for acute use. Epinephrine has been used in horses to test for diagnosis of anhidrosis, but terbutaline sulfate challenge is used more frequently for this test.

Precautionary Information

Adverse Reactions and Side Effects

Overdose will cause excessive vasoconstriction and hypertension. High doses can cause ventricular arrhythmias. When high doses are used for cardiopulmonary arrest, an electrical defibrillator should be available.

Contraindications and Precautions

Avoid repeated administration in patients.

Drug Interactions

Epinephrine will interact with other drugs that are used to either potentiate or antagonize alpha-adrenergic or beta-adrenergic receptors. It is incompatible with alkaline solutions (e.g., bicarbonate), chlorine, bromine, and salts of metals or oxidizing solutions. Do not mix with bicarbonates, nitrates, citrates, and other salts.

Instructions for Use

Doses are based on experimental studies, primarily in dogs. Clinical studies are not available. Intravenous doses are ordinarily used, but endotracheal administration is acceptable when intravenous access is not available. Intraosseous route also has been used, and doses are equivalent to intravenous doses. When endotracheal route is used, the dose is higher and duration of effect may be longer than intravenous administration. When administering doses endotracheally, one can dilute the dose in a volume of 2-10 mL of saline. There appears to be no advantage to intracardiac injection compared to intravenous administration. Solutions are available in 1:1000 and 1:10,000 (either 1 mg/mL or 0.1 mg/mL). Generally, only the 1:10,000 solution is given IV. 1:1000 solutions are intended for SQ and IM use.

Patient Monitoring and Laboratory Tests

Monitor heart rate and rhythm during treatment.

Formulations

Epinephrine is available in 1 mg/mL (1:1,000) injection solution and 0.1 mg/mL (1:10,000) injection solution. The 1:10,000 is most often used IV, and the 1:1000 solution used IM or SQ. Ampules for people are designed to deliver 1 mg/person (approximately 14 mcg/kg).

Stability and Storage

It is compatible with plastic in syringes. When solution becomes oxidized, it turns brown. Do not use if this color change is observed. It is most stable at pH of 3-4. If pH of solution is >5.5, it becomes unstable.

Small Animal Dosage

- Cardiac arrest: 10-20 mcg/kg IV. 100-200 mcg/kg (0.1-0.2 mg/kg) endotracheal (may be diluted in saline before administration).
- Anaphylactic shock: 2.5-5 mcg/kg IV or 50 mcg/kg endotracheal (may be diluted in saline).

- Vasopressor therapy: 100-200 mcg/kg (0.1-0.2) mg/kg IV (high dose) or 10-20 mcg/kg (0.01-0.02 mg/kg) IV (low dose). Administer low dose first, and if no response use high dose.

Large Animal Dosage

- 1 mg/mL (1:1000) solution.
- Anaphylactic shock (cattle, pigs, horses, and sheep): 20 mcg/kg (0.02 mg/kg) IM or 1 mL per 45 kg (1 mL per 100 pounds). 5-10 mcg/kg (0.005-0.01 mg/kg) IV or 0.25 to 0.5 mL per 45 kg (100 pounds).

Regulatory Information

No withdrawal times are established. Epinephrine is rapidly metabolized after administration, and 0 days is recommended for withdrawal.
RCI Classification: 2

Epoetin Alpha (Erythropoietin)

ee-poe'eh-tin

Trade and Other Names: Epogen, epoetin alfa, "EPO," (r-HuEPO), and Erythropoietin

Functional Classification: Hormone

Pharmacology and Mechanism of Action

Human recombinant erythropoietin. Hematopoietic growth factor that stimulates erythropoiesis.

Indications and Clinical Uses

Epoetin alpha is used to treat nonregenerative anemia (*Compendium of Continuing Education*, 14:25-34, 1992; *J Am Vet Med Assoc*, 212:521-528, 1998). It has been used to treat myelosuppression caused by disease or chemotherapy. It also has been used to treat chronic anemia associated with renal failure.

Precautionary Information

Adverse Reactions and Side Effects

Because this product is a human-recombinant product, it may induce local and systemic allergic reactions in animals. Injection site pain and headache have occurred in people. Seizures also have occurred. Delayed anemia may occur because of cross-reacting antibodies against animal erythropoietin (reversible when drug is withdrawn). Anti-epoetin antibodies may increase with long-term use.

Contraindications and Precautions

Stop therapy with epoetin when joint pain, fever, anorexia, or cutaneous reactions are observed.

Drug Interactions

No interactions are reported.

Instructions for Use

The use of epoetin alpha has been limited primarily to dogs and cats. The only form currently available is a human recombinant product. It is used in animals when hematocrit falls below 25%. In cats, 100 units/kg SQ three times a week is administered until a target hematocrit of 30%-40% is attained. Thereafter, twice weekly injections are used. Maintenance dose is usually in a range of 75-100 units/kg SQ once or twice a week.

Patient Monitoring and Laboratory Tests

Monitor hematocrit. Dose should be adjusted to maintain hematocrit in a range of 30%-34%.

Formulations Available

Epoetin alpha is available in 2000 units/mL injection.

Stability and Storage

Store in tightly sealed container, protected from light, and at room temperature. Stability of compounded formulations has not been evaluated.

Small Animal Dosage

Dogs

- 35 or 50 units/kg three times a week, up to 400 units/kg/wk SQ (adjust dose to maintain hematocrit of 30%-34%).

Cats

- Start with 100 units/kg three times weekly; lower to twice weekly and to once weekly when target hematocrit of 30%-40% is attained. In most cats, maintenance dose is 75-100 units/kg SQ twice weekly.

Large Animal Dosage

No large animal doses are reported.

Regulatory Information

No withdrawal times are established for food animals. Erythropoietin in any form is prohibited to be on the premises of racing horses.
RCI Classification: 2

Epsiprantel

ep-sih-pran'til

Trade and Other Names: Cestex

Functional Classification: Antiparasitic

Pharmacology and Mechanism of Action

Anticestodal agent similar to praziquantel. The action of epsiprantel on parasites related to neuromuscular toxicity and paralysis via altered permeability to calcium. Susceptible parasites include: canine cestodes *Dipylidium caninum* and *Taenia pisiformis* and feline cestodes *D. caninum* and *T. taeniaeformis.*

Indications and Clinical Uses

Like praziquantel, epsiprantel is used primarily to treat infections caused by tapeworms.

Precautionary Information

Adverse Reactions and Side Effects

Vomiting occurs at high doses. Anorexia and transient diarrhea have been reported. Epsiprantel is safe in pregnant animals.

Contraindications and Precautions

Do not use in animals younger than 7 weeks. All doses are single-dose.

Drug Interactions

No drug interactions are reported.

Instructions for Use

Administer as directed to treat tapeworm infections.

Patient Monitoring and Laboratory Tests

No specific monitoring is necessary.

Formulations

Epsiprantel is available in 12.5, 25, 50, or 100 mg coated tablets.

Stability and Storage

Store in tightly sealed container, protected from light, and at room temperature. Stability of compounded formulations has not been evaluated.

Small Animal Dosage

Dogs
- 5.5 mg/kg PO.

Cats
- 2.75 mg/kg PO.

Large Animal Dosage

No large animal doses are reported.

Regulatory Information

No regulatory information is available. For extralabel use withdrawal interval estimates, contact FARAD at 1-888-USFARAD (1-888-873-2723) or send e-mail to FARAD@ncsu.edu.

Ergocalciferol

er-go-kal-sif′eh-role

Trade and Other Names: Calciferol and Drisdol

Functional Classification: Vitamin

Pharmacology and Mechanism of Action

Vitamin D analogue. Vitamin D promotes absorption and utilization of calcium.

Indications and Clinical Uses

Ergocalciferol is used for vitamin D deficiency and as treatment of hypocalcemia associated with hypoparathyroidism.

Precautionary Information

Adverse Reactions and Side Effects

Overdose may cause hypercalcemia.

Contraindications and Precautions

Avoid use in pregnant animals, because it may cause fetal abnormalities. Use cautiously with high doses of preparations containing calcium.

Drug Interactions
No drug interactions are reported.

Instructions for Use

Ergocalciferol should not be used for renal secondary hypoparathyroidism because of inability to convert to active compound. Doses for individual patients should be adjusted by monitoring serum calcium concentrations.

Patient Monitoring and Laboratory Tests

Monitor serum calcium concentration

Formulations

Ergocalciferol is available in 400 unit tablets (OTC), 50,000 unit tablets (1.25 mg), and 500,000 unit/mL (12.5 mg/mL) injection.

Stability and Storage

Store in tightly sealed container, protected from light, and at room temperature. Stability of compounded formulations has not been evaluated.

Small Animal Dosage

- 500-2000 units/kg/day PO.

Large Animal Dosage

No large animal doses are reported.

Regulatory Information

No regulatory information is available. For extralabel use withdrawal interval estimates, contact FARAD at 1-888-USFARAD (1-888-873-2723) or send e-mail to FARAD@ncsu.edu.

Ertapenem

er-tah-pen'em

Trade and Other Names: Invanz

Functional Classification: Antibacterial

Pharmacology and Mechanism of Action

Ertapenem is a beta-lactam antibiotic of the carbapenem (penem) class with a broad spectrum of activity. Its action on cell walls is similar to other beta-lactams, which is to bind penicillin-binding proteins (PBP) that weaken or interfere with cell wall formation. The carbapenems bind to a specific PBP (PBP-1) that results in more rapid lysis compared to other beta-lactams. This results in greater bactericidal activity and a longer postantibiotic effect. Carbapenems have a broad spectrum of activity and are among the most active of all antibiotics. Spectrum includes gram-negative bacilli, including *Enterobacteriaceae*. Ertapenem is not as active against *Pseudomonas aeruginosa* as other carbapenems are. It is also active against most gram-positive bacteria, except methicillin-resistant strains of *Staphylococcus* and *Enterococcus.*

Indications and Clinical Use

Ertapenem is indicated primarily for resistant infections caused by bacteria resistant to other drugs. It may be valuable for treating resistant infections caused by

Escherichia coli and *Klebsiella pneumoniae.* The use of ertapenem has not been as common as for meropenem or imipenem. High protein binding and long half-life in people have allowed less frequent administration compared to other carbapenems. However, the pharmacokinetics have not been reported for dogs and cats.

Precautionary Information

Adverse Reactions and Side Effects

Carbapenems pose similar risks as other beta-lactam antibiotics, but adverse effects are rare. There is a risk of CNS toxicity (seizures and tremors) with high doses.

Contraindications and Precautions

Some slight yellowish discoloration may occur after reconstitution. Slight discoloration will not affect potency. However, a darker amber or brown discoloration may indicate oxidation and loss of potency.

Drug Interactions

Do not mix in vial or syringe with other antibiotics.

Instructions for Use

Doses in animals have been based on extrapolation from human studies rather than efficacy trials.

Patient Monitoring and Laboratory Tests

Susceptibility testing: CLSI (NCCLS) break points for sensitive organisms is less than or equal to 4 mcg/mL for all organisms. Sensitivity to imipenem can be used as a marker for ertapenem.

Formulations

Ertapenem is available in a 1 g vial for injection.

Stability and Storage

Store in tightly sealed container, protected from light, and at room temperature.

Small Animal Dosage

Dogs and Cats

- 15 mg/kg q12h IV or SQ.

Large Animal Dosage

No large animal doses have been reported.

Regulatory Information

Withdrawal times are not established for animals that produce food. For extralabel use withdrawal interval estimates, contact FARAD at 1-888-USFARAD (1-888-873-2723) or send e-mail to FARAD@ncsu.edu.

Erythromycin

eh-rith-roe-mye'sin

Trade and Other Names: Gallimycin-100, Gallimycin-200, Erythro-100, and generic brands

Functional Classification: Antibacterial

Pharmacology and Mechanism of Action

Macrolide antibiotic. Like other macrolides, it inhibits bacteria by binding to 50S ribosome and inhibiting protein synthesis. The spectrum of activity of erythromycin is limited primarily to gram-positive aerobic bacteria; it has little or no effect on gram-negative bacteria. Spectrum of activity also includes mycoplasma. In cattle, it is also active against respiratory pathogens such as *Pasteurella multocida, Mannheimia haemolytica,* and *Histophilus somni* (formerly *Haemophilus somnus*).

Indications and Clinical Uses

Erythromycin is used in a variety of species to treat infections caused by susceptible bacteria. Infections treated include respiratory infections (pneumonia), soft tissues infections caused by gram-positive bacteria, and skin and respiratory infections. In foals it is used to treat *Rhodococcus equi* pneumonia, often in combination with rifampin. In some species, including horses, it has been used at low doses to stimulate intestinal motility. Erythromycin has been used to stimulate motility in animals, but this action may be minimal in clinical patients. In horses the dose of erythromycin to stimulate GI motility is lower than the antibacterial dose (1 mg/kg), but the clinical efficacy for this use has not been shown. In experimental calves, 8.8 mg/kg IM significantly increased rumen motility.

The use of erythromycin has diminished because of decreased availability of some dose forms (erythromycin estolate), adverse effects in small animals (vomiting), and diarrhea in horses. Other macrolides (e.g., azithromycin and clarithromycin in small animals and horses, and tilmicosin and tulathromycin in cattle) are used more often instead of erythromycin.

Precautionary Information

Adverse Reactions and Side Effects

Diarrhea in large animals is the most common adverse effect. This is believed to be caused by a disruption of the normal bacterial intestinal flora. This is caused usually from oral administration. Nursing mares have developed diarrhea through exposure to treated foals. Hyperthermia (febrile syndrome) in association with erythromycin treatment has been observed in foals.
In small animals the most common side effect is vomiting (probably caused by cholinergic-like effect or motilin-induced motility). However, in small animals, it also may cause diarrhea. In rodents and rabbits, the diarrhea caused by erythromycin can be serious and even fatal.

Contraindications and Precautions

Do not administer orally to rodents or rabbits. Do not administer erythromycin solutions intended for intramuscular administration by intravenous injection. Only the gluceptate and lactobionate salts should be used intravenously (gluceptate rarely available).

Drug Interactions

Erythromycin, like other macrolides, is known to inhibit the Cytochrome P450 enzymes and may decrease the metabolism of other coadministered drugs. See Appendix.

Instructions for Use

There are several forms of erythromycin, including the ethylsuccinate and estolate esters and stearate salt for oral administration. However, the estolate form is only available as a suspension. There is no convincing data to suggest that one form is absorbed better than another, and dosage is included for all. Only erythromycin gluceptate and lactate are to be administered IV (gluceptate rarely available). Motilin-like effect to stimulate GI motility occurs at low dose and has been studied primarily in experimental horses.

Patient Monitoring and Laboratory Tests

Susceptibility testing: CLSI (NCCLS) break points for sensitive organisms is less than or equal to 0.25 mcg/mL for streptococci and less than or equal to 0.5 for other organisms.

Formulations

Erythromycin is available in several forms that contain either 250 or 500 mg erythromycin base. Oral formulations include 25 and 50 mg/mL erythromycin estolate suspension, 40 mg/mL erythromycin ethylsuccinate suspension, 400 mg ethylsuccinate tablets, and 250 and 500 mg erythromycin stearate tablets. Intravenous formulations include erythromycin lactobionate, but erythromycin gluceptate is rarely available. Erythromycin phosphate, a feed additive available as a powder, has been administered in horses and shown to produce adequate absorption. Erythromycin phosphate is 260 mg per gram, which is equivalent to 231 mg erythromycin base per gram. This is available as an OTC feed additive for poultry.

Stability and Storage

Store in tightly sealed container, protected from light, and at room temperature. Protect from freezing. Erythromycin base is most stable at pH 7-7.5. In acidic solution it may decompose. Ethylsuccinate formulations are stable for 14 days.

Small Animal Dosage

Dogs and Cats

- 10-20 mg/kg q8-12h PO.
- Prokinetic effects: 0.5-1.0 mg/kg q8-12h PO.

Large Animal Dosage

Horses

- *Rhodococcus equi:* erythromycin phosphate or erythromycin estolate 37.5 mg/kg q12h PO or 25 mg/kg q8h PO. Note that in horses, erythromycin base (plain tablets) are poorly absorbed and other forms should be used. (See Instructions for Dosing regarding dosage forms.)
- Erythromycin lactiobionate injection: 5 mg/kg q4-6h IV. To stimulate GI motility: 1 mg/kg.

Cattle

- Abscesses, pododermatitis: 2.2-8.8 mg/kg q24h IM.
- Pneumonia: 2.2-8.8 mg/kg q24h IM or 15 mg/kg q12h IM.

Regulatory Information

Cattle withdrawal times: 6 days meat (at 8.8 mg/kg). Do not use in female dairy cattle older than 20 months of age. Do not slaughter treated animals within 6 days of last treatment. To avoid excess trim, do not slaughter within 21 days of last injection.

In Canada, withdrawal time for meat is 14 days and 72 hours for milk.

Esmolol Hydrochloride

ez'moe-lole hye-droe-klor'ide

Trade and Other Names: Brevibloc

Functional Classification: Beta-blocker, antiarrhythmic

Pharmacology and Mechanism of Action

Beta-blocker. Selective for $beta_1$ receptor. The difference between esmolol and other beta-blockers is the short duration of action is attributed to metabolism by red blood cell esterases; it has a half-life of only 9-10 minutes.

Indications and Clinical Uses

Esmolol is indicated for short-term control of systemic hypertension and tachyarrhythmias. It has been used for emergency therapy or short-term treatment. Long-term treatment is not possible because of short half-life.

Precautionary Information

Adverse Reactions and Side Effects

Adverse effects related to $beta_1$-blocking effects on heart include myocardial depression, lowered cardiac output, and bradycardia.

Contraindications and Precautions

When administering to patient with dilated cardiomyopathy, consider risk of negative cardiac effects. Use cautiously in patients with bronchospasm. Esmolol is contraindicated in patients with bradycardia or AV block.

Drug Interactions

Use cautiously with digoxin, morphine, or warfarin.

Instructions for Use

Esmolol is indicated for short-term intravenous therapy only. Doses are based primarily on empiricism or extrapolation of human dose. No clinical studies have been reported in animals.

Patient Monitoring and Laboratory Tests

Monitor heart rate and rhythm during treatment.

Formulations

Esmolol is available in 10 mg/mL injection.

Stability and Storage

Store in tightly sealed container, protected from light, and at room temperature. Stability of compounded formulations has not been evaluated.

Small Animal Dosage

Dogs and Cats

- 0.5 mg/kg (500 mcg/kg) IV, which may be given as 0.05-0.1 mg/kg slowly every 5 min.
- 0.5 to 1 mg/kg slowly over a 30-second period followed by 50-200 mcg/kg/min infusion.

Large Animal Dosage

No large animal doses have been reported.

Regulatory Information
Withdrawal times are not reported. However, because of short duration of action and rapid metabolism, a short withdrawal period is suggested.
RCI Classification: 3

Estradiol Cypionate
ess-trah-dye'ole sip'ee-oh-nate

Trade and Other Names: ECP, Depo-Estradiol, and generic brands

Functional Classification: Hormone

Pharmacology and Mechanism of Action
Estradiol is used for estrogen replacement in animals. It also has been used to induce abortion in animals.

Indications and Clinical Uses
Estradiol is a semisynthetic estrogen compound. Its effects will mimic that of estrogen in animals. The most common use in small animals has been to terminate pregnancy.

Estradiol benzoate also has been used to terminate pregnancy (5-10 mg/kg divided into two or three subcutaneous injections). This formulation had high efficacy (95%), but it had serious adverse effects and is not recommended. Estradiol cypionate is longer-acting and more potent.

Precautionary Information

Adverse Reactions and Side Effects
Estradiol has a high risk of causing endometrial hyperplasia and pyometra. There is a dose-dependent risk of bone marrow toxicity in animals, particularly dogs. Estradiol cypionate injections have produced leukopenia, thrombocytopenia, and fatal aplastic anemia. Because stem cells can be affected, the bone marrow toxicity may not be reversible.

Contraindications and Precautions
Estradiol is contraindicated in pregnancy, unless used to terminate pregnancy. Do **not** administer to ferrets.

Drug Interactions
No drug interactions are reported for animals. It should not be used with other drugs that may suppress the bone marrow. In people, it has been recommended that these estrogen compounds not be used with other drugs that may cause hepatotoxicity. Estradiol may increase cyclosporine concentrations.

Instructions for Use
To terminate pregnancy, 22 mcg/kg is administered once IM during days 3-5 of estrus or within 3 days of mating. However in one study, a dose of 44 mcg/kg was more efficacious than a dose of 22 mcg/kg when given during estrus or diestrus.

Patient Monitoring and Laboratory Tests
Monitor CBC for evidence of bone marrow suppression.

Formulations
Estradiol is available in a 2 mg/mL injection.

Stability and Storage

Store in tightly sealed container, protected from light, and at room temperature. Stability of compounded formulations has not been evaluated.

Small Animal Dosage

Dogs

- 22-44 mcg/kg IM (total dose not to exceed 1.0 mg).

Cats

- 250 mcg/cat IM, between 40 hrs and 5 days of mating.

Large Animal Dosage

No large animal doses have been reported.

Regulatory Information

Do not use in food-producing animals.

Etidronate Disodium

eh-tih-droe′nate dye-soe′dee-um

Trade and Other Names: Didronel

Functional Classification: Antihypercalcemic agent

Pharmacology and Mechanism of Action

Bisphosphonate drug. These drugs are a group of drugs characterized by a germinal bisphosphonate bond. They slow the formation and dissolution of hydroxyapatite crystals. Their clinical use resides in their ability to inhibit bone resorption. These drugs decrease bone turnover by inhibiting osteoclast activity and retard bone resorption and decrease rate of osteoporosis.

Indications and Clinical Uses

The bisphosphonate group of drugs, which includes etidronate, is used primarily in people to treat osteoporosis and hypercalcemia of malignancy. In animals they are used to decrease calcium in conditions that cause hypercalcemia, such as cancer and vitamin D toxicosis. Studies in people have shown that bisphosphonates may have action in cancer-induced bone disease that is more significant than the effect on osteolysis and bone resorption and also may decrease the tumor burden. Drugs in this class include pamidronate, etidronate, and pyrophosphate. In dogs, more experimental work has been performed with pamidronate than other drugs in this group. Some bisphosphonates have been used to treat navicular disease in horses, but this work is only preliminary and used injectable formulations.

Precautionary Information

Adverse Reactions and Side Effects

Adverse effects not reported for animals. In people, GI problems are common. Esophageal lesions have occurred because of reaction from contact with mucosa. If used in animals, ensure that tablets are completely swallowed.

Contraindications and Precautions

No contraindications have been identified in animals.

Drug Interactions

No drug interactions have been reported in animals. If mixed with other solutions or drugs, avoid mixtures containing calcium.

Instructions for Use

At high doses, etidronate may inhibit mineralization of bone. In people, alendronate has replaced etidronate because of side effects.

Patient Monitoring and Laboratory Tests

Monitor serum calcium and phosphorus. Monitor urea nitrogen, creatinine, and urine specific gravity in treated animals, as well as food intake.

Formulations

Etidronate is available in 200 and 400 mg tablets and 50 mg/mL injection.

Stability and Storage

Store in tightly sealed container, protected from light, and at room temperature. Stability of compounded formulations has not been evaluated.

Small Animal Dosage

Dogs

- 5 mg/kg/day PO.

Cats

- 10 mg/kg/day PO.

Large Animal Dosage

No large animal doses have been reported.

Regulatory Information

Withdrawal times are not established; 24 hour withdrawal times are suggested, because this drug has little risk from residues.

Etodolac

ee-toe'doe-lak

Trade and Other Names: EtoGesic (veterinary preparation) and Lodine (human preparation)

Functional Classification: Nonsteroidal antiinflammatory drug (NSAID)

Pharmacology and Mechanism of Action

Like other NSAIDs, etodolac has analgesic and antiinflammatory effects by inhibiting the synthesis of prostaglandins. The enzyme inhibited by NSAID is the cyclo-oxygenase enzyme (COX). The COX enzyme exists in two isoforms, called COX-1 and COX-2. COX-1 is primarily responsible for synthesis of prostaglandins important for maintaining a healthy GI tract, renal function, platelet function, and other normal functions. COX-2 is induced and responsible for synthesizing prostaglandins that are important mediators of pain, inflammation, and fever. (There may be some crossover of COX-1 and COX-2 effects in some situations.) In dogs, etodolac has a half-life of 7.6 to 14 hours, depending on the study and feeding conditions. In dogs it shows either little preference of COX-2 or COX-1 (nonselective) or slight COX-2 selectivity in vitro. It is not known if selectivity for COX-2 affects efficacy or risk of adverse effects. In horses, etodolac is relatively COX-2 selective and is more potent than in dogs. The half-life in horses is only 3 hours but a duration of effect of approximately 24 hours has been observed in horses with lameness.

Indications and Clinical Uses

Etodolac is indicated for treatment of osteoarthritis in dogs. It also is used as an analgesic and may be used for other painful conditions. Like other NSAIDs, etodolac is expected to reduce fever. Uses in cats have not been established. Etodolac has been used in some horses to relieve pain associated with abdominal surgery and to treat lameness (e.g., caused by navicular disease). Dose regimens are different for horses compared with other animals.

Precautionary Information

Adverse Reactions and Side Effects

NSAIDs may cause GI ulceration. Other adverse effects caused by NSAIDs include decreased platelet function and renal injury. In clinical trials with etodolac at recommended doses, some dogs showed weight loss, loose stools, or diarrhea. At high doses (above label dose), etodolac caused GI ulceration in dogs. Etodolac has been associated with keratoconjunctivitis sicca (KCS) in dogs. In horses at high doses, GI toxicity has been observed.

Contraindications and Precautions

Do not administer to animals prone to GI ulcers. Do not administer with other ulcerogenic drugs, such as corticosteroids. Do not administer to dogs that may be prone to developing KCS. Do not administer to animal with compromised renal function.

Drug Interactions

Use NSAIDs cautiously with other drugs known to cause GI injury (e.g., corticosteroids). The efficacy of angiotensin-converting enzyme (ACE) inhibitors and diuretics (furosemide) may be diminished when administered concurrently with NSAIDs. Etodolac may cross-react with sulfonamides in sensitive animals.

Instructions for Use

Administer as directed and avoid concurrent use of other medications that may increase GI toxicity. Most of the use in dogs has been associated with treatment of osteoarthritis. In horses, it has been shown experimentally to improve lameness associated with navicular disease. When used in horses for this purpose, it was given at 23 mg/kg orally once or twice daily for 3 days. Treated horses improved with either regimen and showed no signs of adverse effects. Experimental horses treated with 20 or 23 mg/kg did not demonstrate adverse effects, but long-term safety has not been reported.

Patient Monitoring and Laboratory Tests

Monitor for signs of GI ulcers and bleeding. Monitor tear production periodically in dogs treated with etodolac and observe for ocular signs of KCS. Monitor liver enzymes in dogs treated with NSAIDs periodically for signs of liver toxicosis. Monitor urea nitrogen and creatinine in treated animals for signs of renal injury. Etodolac has had varying effects on T4, free-T4, and TSH concentrations in dogs. One study showed no effect, and another study showed a decrease in T4 and free-T4 in treated dogs after 2 weeks.

Formulations

Etodolac is available in 150 and 300 mg tablets.

Stability and Storage

Store in tightly sealed container, protected from light, and at room temperature. Etodolac is insoluble in water but is soluble in alcohol or propylene glycol.

Small Animal Dosage

Dogs
• 10-15 mg/kg once daily PO.

Cats
• Dose not established.

Large Animal Dosage

Horses
• 23 mg/kg q24h PO. Long-term safety with this regimen has not been established (see Instructions for Dosing).

Regulatory Information

No withdrawal times have been established. For extralabel use withdrawal interval estimates, contact FARAD at 1-888-USFARAD (1-888-873-2723) or send e-mail to FARAD@ncsu.edu.
RCI Classification: 4

Famotidine

fah-moe'tih-deen

Trade and Other Names: Pepcid

Functional Classification: Antiulcer agent

Pharmacology and Mechanism of Action

Histamine$_2$ antagonist (H_2-blocker). Famotidine blocks histamine stimulation from gastric parietal cell to decrease gastric acid secretion.

Indications and Clinical Uses

Famotidine, like other H_2-receptor blockers, is used to treat ulcers and gastritis in a variety of animals. They have also been used to prevent ulcers caused from nonsteroidal antiinflammatory drugs (NSAIDs), but the efficacy for this use has not been demonstrated.

Precautionary Information

Adverse Reactions and Side Effects

Adverse effects usually seen only with decreased renal clearance. In people, CNS signs may occur with high doses. Give intravenous injections slowly to cats (over 5 minutes), because rapid intravenous injections have caused hemolysis.

Contraindications and Precautions

Intravenous solutions contain benzyl alcohol. IV injections to small animals, especially cats, should be done slowly.

Drug Interactions

Famotidine and other H_2-receptor blockers block secretion of stomach acid. Therefore, they will interfere with oral absorption of drugs dependent on acidity, such as ketoconazole, itraconazole, and iron supplements. Unlike cimetidine, famotidine is not known to inhibit microsomal P450 enzymes.

Instructions for Use

Clinical studies for famotidine have not been performed, therefore optimal dose for ulcer prevention and healing are not known. For intravenous use, dilute with IV solutions (e.g., 0.9% saline) to a total volume of 5-10 mL.

Patient Monitoring and Laboratory Tests

No specific monitoring is necessary.

Formulations

Famotidine is available in 10 mg tablets and 10 mg/mL injection.

Stability and Storage

Store in tightly sealed container, protected from light, and at room temperature. Famotidine is soluble in water. Compounded formulations in cherry syrup have been stable for 14 days. Diluted intravenous solutions in saline are stable for 48 hours at room temperature.

Small Animal Dosage

Dogs

- 0.1-0.2 mg/kg q12h PO, IV, SQ, or IM. Doses as high as 0.5 mg/kg have been administered, but there is no evidence that higher doses improves efficacy.

Cats

- 0.2 mg/kg q24h, up to 0.25 mg/kg q12h IM, SQ, PO, or IV (slowly).

Large Animal Dosage

Horses

- 1-2 mg/kg q6-8h PO.

Regulatory Information

No restrictions on use in animals not intended for food.
RCI Classification: 5

Febantel

feh-ban′tel

Trade and Other Names: Rintal and Vercom. Drontal Plus also contains two other drugs.

Functional Classification: Antiparasitic

Pharmacology and Mechanism of Action

Febantel is an antiparasitic that interferes with carbohydrate metabolism in parasitic worms. It suppresses mitochondrial reactions via inhibition of fumarate reductase and interferes with glucose transport. It is metabolized to a benzimidazole compound that binds to structural protein tubulin and prevents polymerization to microtubules, which results in incomplete digestion and absorption of nutrients by parasite.

A formulation of febantel, pyrantel, and praziquantel (Drontal Plus) has been used in cats for treatment of Giardia, roundworms, hookworms, and whipworms.

Indications and Clinical Uses

Febantel is indicated in the control and treatment of larvae and adult stages of intestinal nematodes. In horses, it is used for removal of large strongyles *(Strongylus vulgaris, S. edentatus, S. equinus)*, ascarids (*Parascaris equorum*, sexually mature and immature), pinworms *(Oxyuris equi*, adult and fourth-stage larvae), and the various small strongyles.

In dogs and cats it is used for treatment of hookworms *(Ancylostoma caninum* and *Uncinaria stenocephala)*, ascarids (*Toxocara canis* and *Toxascaris leonina*), and whipworms *(Trichuris vulpis)*. In dogs, it is used in combination with praziquantel for treatment of hookworms (*A. caninum* and *U. stenocephala*), whipworms (*T. vulpis*), ascarids (*T. canis* and *T. leonina*), and tapeworms (*Dipylidium caninum* and *Taenia pisiformis*).

In cats it is used in combination with praziquantel for removal of hookworms *(A. tubaeforme)*, ascarids *(Toxocara cati)*, and tapeworms (*D. caninum* and *Taenia taeniaeformis*).

Precautionary Information

Adverse Reactions and Side Effects

Vomiting and diarrhea may occur after dosing.

Contraindications and Precautions

Do not use in pregnant animals. Do not use in animals with liver or kidney dysfunction.

Drug Interactions

No drug interactions reported.

Instructions for Use

For horses, the paste may be administered on the base of the tongue or added to a portion of the normal grain ration. For most effective results, retreat in 6-8 weeks. Febantel suspension may be used in combination with trichlorfon oral liquid when combining 1 part febantel suspension with 5 parts trichlorfon liquid.

Patient Monitoring and Laboratory Tests

No specific monitoring is necessary.

Formulations

Febantel is available in an equine paste: 45.5% febantel (455 mg/mL), suspension: 9.3% (2.75 grams per ounce) febantel, and 27.2 and 163.3 mg tablets.

Febantel is also available in combinations; each gram of paste contains 34 mg of febantel and 3.4 mg of praziquantel.

Febantel, pyrantel, and praziquantel are available for small animals.

Stability and Storage

Store in tightly sealed container, protected from light, and at room temperature.

Small Animal Dosage

Dogs

- 10 mg/kg febantel alone or in combination with 1 mg/kg praziquantel PO, with food once daily for 3 days.
- Puppies: 15 mg/kg febantel alone or in combination with 1.5 mg/kg praziquantel PO, with food once daily for 3 days.

Cats

- 10 mg/kg febantel alone or in combination with 1 mg/kg praziquantel PO, in the food once daily for 3 days.
- Kittens: 15 mg/kg febantel alone or in combination with 1.5 mg/kg praziquantel.

Large Animal Dosage

Cattle

- 7.5 mL/100 kg body weight PO.

Sheep and Goats

- 1.0 mL/20 kg body weight or 5 mL/25 kg PO.

Horses

- 6 mg/kg PO.

Regulatory Information

Not for use in horses intended for food. No other regulatory restrictions are listed.

Felbamate

fel'bah-mate

Trade and Other Names: Felbatol

Functional Classification: Anticonvulsant

Pharmacology and Mechanism of Action

Anticonvulsant. Mechanism may be via antagonism at the N-methyl-D-aspartate (NMDA) receptor and block effects of excitatory amino acids. The half-life in dogs is 5-6 hours, which may require frequent administration.

Indications and Clinical Uses

Felbamate is used in dogs when they are refractory to other anticonvulsants. It has been used in conjunction with other anticonvulsants.

Precautionary information

Adverse Reactions and Side Effects

Not documented with use in dogs. In people the most severe reactions have been hepatotoxicity and aplastic anemia.

Contraindications and Precautions

It may increase phenobarbital concentrations.

Drug Interactions

Possible interactions exist with drugs that either alter or are substrates for hepatic cytochrome P450 enzymes. See Appendix. It may increase phenobarbital concentrations if used concurrently.

Instructions for Use

Dosing has been empirical in dogs. There are no controlled studies to document efficacy, but it is usually administered when animals have been refractory to other drugs, such as phenobarbital or bromide.

Patient Monitoring and Laboratory Tests

Monitoring of plasma concentrations is helpful to assess therapy. Assays may be available in some commercial laboratories. Ideal plasma concentrations have not been established for animals. However, concentrations in humans of 24 to 137 mcg/mL in plasma have been effective (mean of 78 mcg/mL).

Formulations

Felbamate is available in120 mg/mL oral liquid and 400 and 600 mg tablets.

Stability and Storage

Store in tightly sealed container, protected from light, and at room temperature. Stability of compounded formulations has not been evaluated.

Small Animal Dosage

Dogs

- Start with 15-20 mg/kg q8h PO. Maximum dose is approximately 70 mg/kg q8h PO.
- Small dogs: 200 mg/dog q8h PO, and increase to a maximum dose of 600 mg/dog q8h.
- Large dogs: 400 mg/dog q8h. Increase dose gradually by 200 mg (15 mg/kg); increments until seizure control. Maximum dose for large dogs is 1200 mg/dog q8h.

Large Animal Dosage

No large animal doses have been reported.

Regulatory Information

No withdrawal times have been established. For extralabel use withdrawal interval estimates, contact FARAD at 1-888-USFARAD (1-888-873-2723) or send e-mail to FARAD@ncsu.edu.

RCI Classification: 3

F

Fenbendazole

fen-ben′dah-zole

Trade and Other Names: Panacur and SafeGuard

Functional Classification: Antiparasitic

Pharmacology and Mechanism of Action

Benzimidazole antiparasitic drug. Like other benzimidazoles, fenbendazole produces a degeneration of the parasite microtubule and irreversibly blocks glucose uptake in parasites. Inhibition of glucose uptake causes depletion of energy stores in parasite, eventually resulting in death. However, there is no effect on glucose metabolism in mammals.

Indications and Clinical Uses

Fenbendazole is effective for treatment of numerous helminth intestinal parasites in animals, including *Toxacara, Toxascaris, Ancylostoma*, and *Trichuris.* In dogs it is effective for most intestinal helminth parasites and also against nematodes. Fenbendazole has been effective for treatment of Giardia (*Am J Vet Res,* 59:61-63, 1998), but higher doses are needed and there may be failure rates as high as 50%. It is effective in cats for treatment of lungworms, flukes, and a variety of helminth parasites.

Precautionary Information

Adverse Reactions and Side Effects

Good safety margin, but vomiting and diarrhea have been reported. When evaluated at doses of three and five times the recommended dose at three times the recommended duration, fenbendazole was well tolerated and no adverse effects reported. There have been rare reports of pancytopenia associated with fenbendazole administration.

Contraindications and Precautions

No known contraindications. It may be used in all ages of animals.

Drug Interactions

There are no known drug interactions.

Instructions for Use

Dose recommendations based on clinical studies by manufacturer. Granules may be mixed with food. Paste may be given to horses and cattle. Presence of food does not affect oral absorption. In studies for treatment of *Giardia,* it was safer than other treatments.

Patient Monitoring and Laboratory Tests

Fecal monitoring may be performed to determine the efficacy of treatment for intestinal parasites.

Formulations Available

Fenbendazole is available in 22.2% (222 mg/g) Panacur granules, 10% (92 g/32 oz), and 100 mg/mL oral suspension.

Stability and Storage

Store in tightly sealed container, protected from light, and at room temperature. Stability of compounded formulations has not been evaluated.

Small Animal Dosage

Dogs

- 50 mg/kg/day for 3 days PO.
  Duration may be extended to 5 days for severe parasitic infestations.

Cats

- 50 mg/kg/day for 3 days PO.
  Duration may be extended to 5 days for severe parasitic infestations.

Large Animal Dosage

Horses

- Intestinal parasites, such as strongyles, pinworms, and ascarids: Panacur granules or paste is administered at a dose of 5.1 mg/kg (2.3 mg/pound) PO. Two packets of 1.15 grams each will treat a 450 kg (1000 pound) horse. Retreatment in 6-8 weeks may be necessary. Panacur paste can be administered to horses at a dose of 5 mg/kg PO. Retreatment at 6-8 weeks may be necessary. For treatment of ascarids *(Parascaris equorum)* in horses, a higher dose of 10 mg/kg is recommended.

Sheep and Goats

- 5 mg/kg PO.

Cattle

- 5 mg/kg PO

Regulatory Information

Cattle withdrawal time (meat): 8 days. There is no withdrawal period for milk.
Goat withdrawal time (meat): 6 days.

F

Fentanyl Citrate

fen'tah-nil sih'trate

Trade and Other Names: Sublimaze and generic brands

Functional Classification: Analgesic, Opioid

Pharmacology and Mechanism of Action

Synthetic opiate analgesic. Fentanyl is approximately 80 to 100 times more potent than morphine. Fentanyl is an agonist for the mu-opiate receptors on nerves and inhibits release of neurotransmitters involved with transmission of pain stimuli (such as Substance P). Central sedative and euphoric effects related to mu-receptor effects in brain.

Indications and Clinical Uses

Fentanyl citrate is used as an intravenous bolus or as a constant rate infusion (CRI) in animals for relief of pain, an adjunct for anesthesia, or as a sedative in combination with other CNS sedatives. Fentanyl administered IV in cats (0.01 mg/kg) produced antinociceptive effects for approximately 2 hours. See fentanyl, transdermal for information about transdermal form.

Precautionary Information

Adverse Reactions and Side Effects

Fentanyl has adverse effects similar to morphine. Like all opiates, side effects are predictable and unavoidable. Side effects include sedation, constipation, and bradycardia. Respiratory depression occurs with high doses. As with other opiates, a slight decrease in heart rate is expected. In most cases this decrease does not have to be treated with anticholinergic drugs (e.g., atropine), but it should be monitored. In horses, undesirable and even dangerous, behavior can follow rapid intravenous opioid administration. Horses should receive a pre-anesthetic of acepromazine or an $alpha_2$ agonist.

Contraindications and Precautions

Fentanyl citrate is a Schedule II controlled substance. Tolerance and dependence occurs with chronic administration. Cats are more sensitive to excitement than other species.

Drug Interactions

There are no specific drug interactions, but fentanyl will decrease other anesthetic requirements. Fentanyl will potentiate other opiates and CNS depressants.

Instructions for Use

Doses are based on empiricism and experimental studies. No clinical studies have been reported. In addition to fentanyl injection, transdermal fentanyl is available.

Patient Monitoring and Laboratory Tests

Monitor analgesic response. Monitor patient's heart rate and respiration. Although bradycardia rarely needs to be treated when it is caused by an opioid, atropine can be administered if necessary. If serious respiratory depression occurs, the opioid can be reversed with naloxone.

Formulations Available

Fentanyl citrate is available as a 250 mg/5 mL injection (50 mg/mL).

Stability and Storage

Store in tightly sealed container, protected from light, and at room temperature. It is soluble in water and slightly soluble in alcohol. It is a Schedule II drug, store in locked compartment.

Small Animal Dosage

Dogs and Cats

- Anesthetic uses: 0.02-0.04 mg/kg q2h IV, SQ, or IM or if administered with acepromazine or diazepam, use 0.01 mg/kg IV, IM, or SQ.
- Analgesic agent, 0.005-0.01 mg/kg q2h IV, IM, or SQ.
- CRI: 0.003 mg/kg IV loading dose, followed by 0.005 mg/kg/hr in dogs or 0.002 mg/kg/hr in cats.

Large Animal Dosage

Small Ruminants

- 5-10 mcg/kg (0.005-0.010 mg/kg) IV.

Regulatory Information

Schedule II controlled drug by DEA.
RCI Classification: 1

Fentanyl Transdermal

fen'tah-nil

Trade and Other Names: Duragesic

Functional Classification: Analgesic, Opioid

Pharmacology and Mechanism of Action

Synthetic opiate analgesic. Fentanyl is approximately 80 to 100 times more potent than morphine. Fentanyl is an agonist for the mu-opiate receptors on nerves and inhibits release of neurotransmitters involved with transmission of pain stimuli (such as Substance P). Central sedative and euphoric effects related to mu-receptor effects in brain. The fentanyl transdermal system delivers fentanyl through the skin at a constant rate to produce systemic effects. Transdermal absorption and effective plasma concentrations have been demonstrated for cats, dogs, horses, and goats. Absorption is determined by the surface area for absorption.

Patches are available that deliver 25, 50, 75, and 100 mcg/hr. Absorption can be variable in animals [e.g., rate of release of fentanyl has varied from 27% to 98% (mean 71%) of the theoretical value]. Cats absorbed the fentanyl at an average rate of approximately one third that of the theoretical delivery rate, but one patch will maintain consistent concentrations of fentanyl in the plasma for at least 118 hours. Fentanyl transdermal patches (two or three 100 mcg/hr patches) have been applied to the skin of horses to relieve pain. In horses, the duration is less than in dogs or cats and may have to be reapplied every 48 hours.

Indications and Clinical Uses

Fentanyl transdermal has same properties as fentanyl citrate administered IV, except in this formulation, it is administered transdermal to produce pain relief and as an adjunct to other drugs in perioperative patients and in patients with chronic pain. In dogs, fentanyl transdermal patches (50 mcg/hr) are appropriate for most average-size dogs. Transdermal fentanyl has been shown effective to relieve postoperative pain in dogs. Transdermal fentanyl has been well tolerated in cats. Fentanyl patches (25 mcg/hr) were effective and safe to relieve pain from onychectomy surgery in cats. Cats that have received fentanyl patches have had improvement in temperament, attitude, and appetite. Transdermal fentanyl has been used alone or combined with nonsteroidal antiinflammatory drugs (NSAIDs) for treating severe pain in horses and may provide pain relief that is superior to NSAIDs alone.

Precautionary Information

Adverse Reactions and Side Effects

Severe adverse effects have not been reported. The patch may cause slight skin irritation at the site of application. If patch delivery of fentanyl is high, some signs of opiate overdose may occur (e.g., excitement in cats or sedation in dogs), however these reactions are rare. Adverse effects have not been reported from the use in horses. If adverse effects are observed in animals (e.g., respiratory depression, excess sedation, or excitement in cats), remove patch and if necessary, administer naloxone.

Contraindications and Precautions

Transdermal fentanyl is a Schedule II controlled substance. Use cautiously in animals of small body weight (e.g., small toy dogs and young or debilitated cats).

Drug Interactions

There are no specific drug interactions, but transdermal fentanyl will decrease other anesthetic requirements. Transdermal fentanyl will potentiate other opiates and CNS depressants.

Instructions for Use

Transdermal fentanyl incorporates fentanyl into adhesive patches applied to skin of dogs and cats. Studies have determined that patches release sustained levels of fentanyl for 72-108 hours in dogs and cats. One 100 mcg/hr patch is equivalent to

10 mg/kg of morphine every 4 hours IM. Patches are available in sizes of 25, 50, 75 and 100 mcg/hr. Patch size is related to release rate of fentanyl. Studies have determined that 25 mcg/hr patches are appropriate for cats; 50 mcg/hr patches are appropriate for dogs weighing 10-20 kg. In horses, two or three 100 mcg/hr patches achieved rapid plasma concentrations within effective ranges in adults, but highly variable. If rate of delivery is too high for cats and adverse reactions are suspected, covering half the adhesive surface area will reduce rate of delivery. Duration of effect in horses is less than in dogs or cats, at only 48 hours. Follow manufacturer's recommendations carefully when applying patches.

Patient Monitoring and Laboratory Tests

Monitor patient's heart rate and respiration. Although bradycardia rarely needs to be treated when it is caused by an opioid, atropine can be administered if necessary. If serious respiratory depression occurs, the opioid can be reversed with naloxone. Monitor for signs of excitement in cats.

Formulations Available

Transdermal fentanyl is available in 25, 50, 75, and 100 mcg/hr patches.

Stability and Storage

Store in tightly sealed container, protected from light, and at room temperature. Do not open fentanyl patch membrane.

Small Animal Dosage

Dogs

- 10-20 kg: 50 mcg/hr patch q72h.

Cats

- 25 mcg patch q118h.

Large Animal Dosage

Horses

- Adults: Two or three transdermal patches of 100 mcg/hr each (10 mg fentanyl, equivalent to 35-110 mcg/kg delivered transdermally.
- Foals: One transdermal patch of 100 mcg/hr.

Sheep and Goats

- 100 mcg/hr patch. (Absorption has been inconsistent.)

Regulatory Information

Schedule II controlled drug by DEA.

Fentanyl should not be administered to animals that produce food. Withdrawal times are not established.

Ferrous Sulfate

fare'us sul'fate

Trade and Other Names: Ferospace and generic brands (OTC)

Functional Classification: Mineral supplement, Iron supplement

Pharmacology and Mechanism of Action

Iron supplement. Replaces iron in animals that are deficient or with iron-deficiency anemia.

Indications and Clinical Uses

Iron supplements are indicated in patients with diseases caused by iron deficiency.

Precautionary Information

Adverse Reactions and Side Effects

High doses cause stomach ulceration. Feces become dark with oral administration.

Contraindications and Precautions

Do not use in animals prone to gastric ulcers. High doses or accidental ingestion may cause sever ulcers and perforation and should be treated as an emergency.

Drug Interactions

Iron supplements will interfere with oral absorption of other drugs such as fluoroquinolones, tetracyclines, and other drugs that may chelate with iron. Cimetidine and other antacids will decrease oral absorption, because an acid environment favors absorption.

Instructions for Use

Recommendations based on dose needed to increase hematocrit. In some animals, injectable Iron Dextran is used instead of oral therapy.

Patient Monitoring and Laboratory Tests

Monitor hematocrit, serum iron levels, and total iron binding capacity.

Formulations

OTC oral formulations are available; 250 mg ferrous sulfate contains 50 mg elemental iron. Injectable forms are usually Iron Dextran. (Iron Dextran is listed in a separate monograph.)

Stability and Storage

Store in tightly sealed container, protected from light, and at room temperature. Do not mix with other drugs as chelation may occur. Ferrous sulfate is soluble in water.

Small Animal Dosage

Dogs

- 100-300 mg/dog q24h PO.

Cats

- 50-100 mg/cat q24h PO.

Large Animal Dosage

No large animal doses have been reported.

Regulatory Information

Extralabel withdrawal times are not established. However, 24 hour withdrawal times are suggested because this drug has little risk from residues.

Finasteride

fin-ass′ter-ide

Trade and Other Names: Proscar

Functional Classification: Hormone antagonist

Pharmacology and Mechanism of Action

Finasteride is a synthetic steroid type-II 5 alpha reductase inhibitor. It inhibits conversion of testosterone to dihydrotestosterone (DHT).

Indications and Clinical Uses

Because DHT stimulates prostate growth, finasteride has been used for benign prostatic hypertrophy. In dogs with benign prostatic hypertrophy (BPH), finasteride has been shown to reduce prostatic size without adversely affecting testosterone production or semen quality *(J Am Vet Med Assoc,* 218:1275-1280, 2001).

Precautionary Information

Adverse Reactions and Side Effects

No adverse effects reported in dogs.

Contraindications and Precautions

Finasteride is contraindicated in pregnant animals.

Drug Interactions

No drug interactions are reported for animals.

Instructions for Use

Doses based on studies in dogs *(J Am Vet Med Assoc,* 59:762-764, 1998; *J Am Vet Med Assoc,* 218:1275-1280, 2001). Information for other animals has not been reported. One study in dogs found significant effects at 0.1 mg/kg q24h. Another study used a dose range of 0.1 to 0.5 mg/kg q24h and reported reduction in prostate size.

Patient Monitoring and Laboratory Tests

No specific monitoring is necessary.

Formulations

Finasteride is available in 5 mg tablets.

Stability and Storage

Store in tightly sealed container, protected from light, and at room temperature. Stability of compounded formulations has not been evaluated.

Small Animal Dosage

- 0.1 mg/kg q24h PO.
- Dogs 10-50 kg: 5 mg tablet q24h PO.

Large Animal Dosage

No large animal doses have been reported.

Regulatory Information

No withdrawal times are established. Do not use in animals intended for food.

Firocoxib

feer-oh-koks'ib

Trade and Other Names: Previcox and Equioxx

Functional Classification: Antiinflammatory

Pharmacology and Mechanism of Action

Firocoxib is a nonsteroidal antiinflammatory drug (NSAID). Like other drugs in this class, firocoxib produces analgesic and antiinflammatory effects by inhibiting the synthesis of prostaglandins. The enzyme inhibited by NSAID is the cyclo-oxygenase enzyme (COX). The COX enzyme exists in two isoforms, called COX-1 and COX-2. COX-1 is primarily responsible for synthesis of prostaglandins important for maintaining a healthy GI tract, renal function, platelet function, and other normal functions. COX-2 is induced and responsible for synthesizing prostaglandins that are important mediators of pain, inflammation, and fever. (There may be some crossover of COX-1 and COX-2 effects in some situations.) Firocoxib, using in vitro assays, is more COX-1 sparing compared to older NSAIDs and is a selective inhibitor of COX-2. The COX-1/COX-2 ratio is greater than for other drugs registered for dogs. It also is a selective COX-2 inhibitor in cats. It has not been established if the specificity for COX-1 or COX-2 is related to efficacy or safety. Firocoxib has a half-life of 7.8 hours in dogs, 9-12 hours in cats, and 30-40 hours in horses. It is highly protein bound (96%-98%). Oral absorption is 38% in dogs and 54%-70% in cats. Feeding delays absorption but does not diminish overall absorption. In horses, oral absorption is 79%, with oral paste at a dose of 0.1 mg per kg.

Indications and Clinical Uses

Firocoxib is used to decrease pain, inflammation, and fever. It has been used for the acute and chronic treatment of pain and inflammation in dogs. One of the most common uses is osteoarthritis but also has been used for pain associated with surgery. In horses it is used for osteoarthritis. In cats, firocoxib has been demonstrated to be effective for attenuating febrile responses. Use in cats is limited to short-term use or long-term use at low doses. Acute response to treating fever in cats also has been demonstrated. Large animal use has been limited.

Precautionary Information

Adverse Reactions and Side Effects

GI problems are the most common adverse effects associated with NSAIDs and can include vomiting, diarrhea, nausea, ulcers, and erosions of the GI tract. Both acute and long-term safety and efficacy have been established for dogs. In field trials, vomiting was the most often reported adverse effect. In studies performed in dogs, higher doses, (5 times dose) caused GI problems. Behavior changes have occurred in dogs and horses, but they are rare. In studies of young juvenile dogs, administration of firocoxib was associated with periportal fatty hepatic changes in some animals. Renal toxicity, especially in dehydrated animals or animals with preexisting renal disease, has been observed for some NSAIDs.

In horses, gastrointestinal problems (diarrhea, loose stool) have been reported in field trials, but they are rare at approved doses. At doses exceeding labeled dose or duration in horses, ulcers, azotemia, renal injury, erosions of skin and oral mucosa, and prolonged bleeding times have been observed.

Contraindications and Precautions

Dogs and cats with preexisting GI problems or renal problems may be at a greater risk of adverse effects from NSAIDs. There is no information on the safety of firocoxib in the treatment of breeding, pregnant, or lactating animals, but adverse effects have not been reported in breeding animals.

In horses, do not exceed recommended duration of treatment. During animal safety studies in horses, toxicity occurred at recommended doses if administration exceeded 30 days.

Drug Interactions

Do not administer with other NSAIDs or with corticosteroids. Corticosteroids have been shown to exacerbate the GI adverse effects. Some NSAIDs may interfere with the action of diuretic drugs and angiotensin-converting enzyme (ACE) inhibitors.

Instructions for Use

Use according to manufacturer's dosing guidelines. Chewable tablets can be administered with or without food. Long-term studies have not been completed in cats, and only single-dose studies have been reported.

Patient Monitoring and Laboratory Tests

Monitor GI signs for evidence of diarrhea, GI bleeding, or ulcers. Because of risk of renal injury, monitor renal parameters (water consumption, BUN, creatinine, and urine specific gravity) periodically during treatment.

Formulations

Firocoxib is available in 57 and 227 mg tablets.
Equine oral paste is available as 8.2 mg per gram of paste (0.82% w/w).

Stability and Storage

Store in tightly sealed container, protected from light, and at room temperature. Stability of compounded formulations has not been evaluated.

Small Animal Dosage

Dogs

- 5 mg/kg once daily PO.

Cats

- 1.5 mg/kg once. Long-term safety in cats has not been determined.

Large Animal Dosage

Horses

- 0.1 mg/kg q24h, PO for up to 14 days.

Regulatory Information

Do not administer to animals that produce food. Do not administer to horses that are used for human consumption.
RCI classification not established, but likely similar to other NSAIDs.

Florfenicol

flore-fen'ih-kole

Trade and Other Names: Nuflor, Aquaflor (fish form)

Functional Classification: Antibacterial

Pharmacology and Mechanism of Action

Florfenicol is a thiamphenicol derivative with same mechanism of action as chloramphenicol (inhibition of protein synthesis). However, it is more active than either chloramphenicol or thiamphenicol. Florfenicol has a broad spectrum of antibacterial activity that includes all organisms sensitive to chloramphenicol, gram-negative bacilli, gram-positive cocci, and other atypical bacteria such as mycoplasma. Florfenicol is highly lipophilic and has been used to treat intracellular pathogens.

Indications and Clinical Uses

Because florfenicol is a derivative of chloramphenicol, it has been used in situations in which chloramphenicol is unavailable or illegal. (Chloramphenicol is illegal to use in food-animals in the United States.) Florfenicol has been shown to be effective for treatment of bovine respiratory disease (BRD) in cattle associated with *Mannheimia haemolytica*, *Pasteurella multocida*, and *Histophilus somni* (formerly *Haemophilus somnus*). It also is used for treatment of bovine interdigital phlegmon (foot rot, acute interdigital necrobacillosis, and infectious pododermatitis) associated with *Fusobacterium necrophorum* and *Bacteroides melaninogenicus*.

In pigs it is used for treatment of swine respiratory disease (SRD) caused by *Actinobacillus pleuropneumoniae*, *Pasteurella multocida*, *Salmonella choleraesuis*, and *Streptococcus suis*.

Administration of florfenicol (40 mg/kg once SQ) at time of arrival to feedlot decreased incidence of BRD. Florfenicol is used to treat pneumonia in pigs.

There is a feed-additive formulation that also has been approved for catfish (10 mg/kg).

Precautionary Information

Adverse Reactions and Side Effects

Use in dogs and cats has been limited, therefore adverse effects have not been reported. Chloramphenicol has been linked to dose-dependent bone marrow depression and similar reactions may be possible with florfenicol. However, there does not appear to be a risk of aplastic anemia as for chloramphenicol. At high doses, florfenicol may cause testicular degeneration. In horses, doses of 20 mg/kg q48h IM changed the bacterial flora and increased risk of diarrhea.

Contraindications and Precautions

Long-term use in animals may cause bone marrow suppression. Administration to horses has caused diarrhea, colitis, and elevations in bilirubin. Administration to horses is not recommended. Do not administer more than 10 mL in a single site.

Drug Interactions

No drug interactions are reported for animals. However, chloramphenicol is well-known to inhibit cytochrome P450 enzymes and decrease metabolism of other drugs (see Appendix). Therefore, it is possible, but not documented, that florfenicol could cause drug interactions.

Instructions for Use

Dose form is only approved for use in cattle, and doses listed have not been thoroughly evaluated in small animals. Doses listed are derived from pharmacokinetic studies. Sustained effect in cattle from intramuscular and subcutaneous administration does not appear to be long lasting in dogs. Injectable formulation for cattle has been administered, if necessary, orally to small animals.

Patient Monitoring and Laboratory Tests

Monitor CBC for evidence of bone marrow depression. Susceptibility testing: laboratories have used chloramphenicol to test for susceptibility to florfenicol. In these cases, CLSI (NCCLS) break points for sensitive organisms is less than or equal to 4 mcg/mL for streptococci and less than or equal to 8 for other organisms.

Formulations

Florfenicol is available in 300 mg/mL injectable solution (cattle), or 23 mg/mL solution to be added to drinking water for pigs.
Medicated feed formulation contains 500 g/kg to be added to fish feed.

Stability and Storage

Store in tightly sealed container, protected from light, and at room temperature. Light yellow or straw color does not affect potency. Stability of compounded formulations has not been evaluated.

Small Animal Dosage

Dogs
- 20 mg/kg q6h IM or PO.

Cats
- 22 mg/kg q8h IM or PO.

Large Animal Dosage

Cattle, BRD
- 20 mg/kg q48h IM (in the neck).
- 40 mg/kg q72h SQ.

Horses

Although florfenicol has been administered, some references cite adverse effects after administration. Until more safety data becomes available, it is suggested to avoid use of florfenicol in horses.

Pigs
- Administer in drinking water at 400 mg per gallon (100 parts per million) for 5 consecutive days.

Regulatory Information

Cattle withdrawal time (meat): 28 days if administered IM, 38 days if administered SQ.
A withdrawal period has not been established in preruminating calves.
Do not use in calves to be processed for veal; not to be used in dairy cattle 20 months of age or older or in veal calves younger than 1 month.
Pig withdrawal time: 16 days of last treatment.

Fluconazole

floo-kahn'ah-zole

Trade and Other Names: Diflucan and generic brands

Functional Classification: Antifungal

Pharmacology and Mechanism of Action

Azole antifungal drug. Fungistatic. Fluconazole inhibits ergosterol synthesis in fungal cell membrane and has activity against dermatophytes, systemic fungi, and yeasts. However, it has weak activity against *Aspergillus.* Compared to other oral azole antifungals, fluconazole is absorbed more predictably and completely, even on an empty stomach.

Indications and Clinical Uses

Fluconazole is efficacious against dermatophytes, yeasts, and variety of systemic fungi. It has been used to treat *Malassezia* dermatitis. In dogs, cats, horses, and exotic animals, it is used to treat systemic fungal infections, yeast infections, and dermatophytes. In cats it has been used to treat *Cryptococcus.* Because it is water soluble, it has been used to treat fungal cystitis.

Precautionary Information

Adverse Reactions and Side Effects

Adverse effects have not been reported from fluconazole administration. Compared to ketoconazole, it has less effect on endocrine function. However, increased liver enzyme concentrations and hepatopathy are possible.

Contraindications and Precautions

Use cautiously in pregnant animals. At high doses in laboratory animals, it has caused fetal abnormalities.

Drug Interactions

Fluconazole is not known to cause inhibition of drug metabolism like other antifungal drugs such as ketoconazole.

Instructions for Use

Doses for fluconazole are primarily based on studies performed in cats for treatment of cryptococcosis. Efficacy for other infections has not been reported. The primary difference between fluconazole and other azoles is that fluconazole attains higher concentrations in the CNS. Oral absorption of fluconazole is more predictable than itraconazole and ketoconazole and less affected by fasting.

Patient Monitoring and Laboratory Tests

Monitor hepatic enzymes periodically in treated animals. Susceptibility testing is possible, but ranges are only established for *Candida*.

Formulations

Fluconazole is available in 50, 100, 150, and 200 mg tablets, 10 and 40 mg/mL oral suspension, and 2 mg/mL intravenous injection.

Stability and Storage

Fluconazole is stable for 14 days after reconstituting oral suspension. Because it is water soluble at a concentration of 8-10 mg/mL, it also may be compounded in formulations for administration to small animals. However, long-term stability, beyond 15 days, of compounded formulations has not been determined.

Small Animal Dosage

Dogs

- 10-12 mg/kg/day PO.
- *Malassezia* treatment: 5 mg/kg q12h PO.

Cats

- 50 mg/cat q12h PO or 50 mg/cat per day PO. In most cases it is administered once daily.

Large Animal Dosage

Horses

- 5 mg/kg q24h PO.

Regulatory Information

No withdrawal times are established for animals intended for food (extralabel use).

Flucytosine

floo-sye′toe-seen

Trade and Other Names: Ancobon

Functional Classification: Antifungal

Pharmacology and Mechanism of Action

Antifungal drug. Action is to penetrate fungal cells and is converted to fluorouracil, which acts as antimetabolite.

Indications and Clinical Uses

Flucytosine is an antifungal drug that is not used in veterinary medicine much, except to treat cryptococcal meningitis. It should be used in combination with other antifungal drugs for treatment of cryptococcosis to improve efficacy and decrease resistance.

Precautionary Information

Adverse Reactions and Side Effects

Anemia and thrombocytopenia are the most common adverse effects.

Contraindications and Precautions

No specific contraindications have been identified for animals.

Drug Interactions

No drug interactions are reported for animals.

Instructions for Use

Flucytosine is used primarily to treat cryptococcosis in animals. Efficacy is based on its ability to attain high concentrations in cerebrospinal fluid (CSF). Flucytosine may be synergistic with amphotericin B.

Patient Monitoring and Laboratory Tests

Monitor CBC during treatment.

Formulations Available

Flucytosine is available in 250 and 500 mg capsules and 75 mg/mL oral suspension.

Stability and Storage

Store in tightly sealed container, protected from light, and at room temperature. Compounded oral suspensions have been stable for 60 days.

Small Animal Dosage

Dogs and Cats

- 25-50 mg/kg q6-8h PO, up to a maximum dose of 100 mg/kg q12h PO.
- Cryptococcal meningitis: 20-40 mg/kg q6h PO.

Large Animal Dosage

No large animal doses have been reported.

Regulatory Information

No withdrawal times are established for animals that are intended for food (extralabel use).

Fludrocortisone Acetate

floo-droe-kor'tih-sone ass'ih-tate

Trade and Other Names: Florinef

Functional Classification: Corticosteroid

Pharmacology and Mechanism of Action

Mineralocorticoid replacement therapy. Fludrocortisone has high potency of mineralocorticoid activity compared to glucocorticoid activity. Fludrocortisone acts to mimic the action of aldosterone in the body, specifically to increase reabsorption of sodium in renal tubules.

Indications and Clinical Uses

Fludrocortisone is used as replacement therapy in animals with adrenocortical insufficiency (Addison's disease). Because of its glucocorticosteroid activity, some animals may not require additional supplementation with glucocorticoids when administering fludrocortisone. Desoxycorticosterone pivalate (DOCP) is used as an alternative in dogs when an intermittent injectable is desired rather than daily oral doses of fludrocortisone.

F

Precautionary Information

Adverse Reactions and Side Effects

Adverse effects are primarily related to glucocorticoid effects with high doses. Polyuria/polydipsia may occur in some animals. Long-term treatment for hypoadrenocorticism may result in glucocorticoid side effects.

Contraindications and Precautions

Although used as a mineralocorticoid, it may produce glucocorticoid side effects. Use cautiously in animals which may be at risk for corticosteroid side effects.

Drug Interactions

No drug interactions are reported for animals.

Instructions for Use

Dose should be adjusted by monitoring patient response (i.e., monitoring electrolyte concentrations). In some patients, it is administered with a glucocorticoid and sodium supplementation. For example, prednisolone/prednisone at a dose of 0.2-0.3 mg/kg/day.

Patient Monitoring and Laboratory Tests

Monitor patient's electrolytes (i.e., sodium and potassium). Dose adjustment should be based on electrolyte monitoring to maintain these within a desired range.

Formulations

Fludrocortisone is available in 100 mcg (0.1 mg) tablets.

Stability and Storage

Store in tightly sealed container, protected from light, and at room temperature. It is insoluble in water. When crushed tablets were prepared in various suspensions, they were stable for 14 days.

Small Animal Dosage

Dogs

- 15-30 mcg/kg/day (0.015-0.03 mg/kg) PO. (*J Vet Intern Med,* 11:43-49, 1997).

Cats

- 0.1-0.2 mg/cat q24h PO.

Large Animal Dosage

No large animal doses have been reported.

Regulatory Information

Extralabel withdrawal times are not established. However, 24 hour withdrawal times are suggested, because this drug has little risk from residues.
RCI Classification: 4

Flumazenil

floo-may'zeh-nil

Trade and Other Names: Romazicon

Functional Classification: Antidote

Pharmacology and Mechanism of Action

Benzodiazepine receptor antagonist. Flumazenil blocks the action of benzodiazepines, such as diazepam, from the action on the GABA receptor.

Indications and Clinical Uses

Flumazenil is used as a reversal agent after benzodiazepine administration in people (not commonly used in veterinary medicine). Because of high first-pass effects, it cannot be administered orally; it must be injected.

Precautionary Information

Adverse Reactions and Side Effects

No adverse effects reported in animals.

Contraindications and Precautions

Flumazenil may precipitate a seizure if used with tricyclic antidepressants (TCAs) or other drugs that can lower seizure threshold.

Drug Interactions

Flumazenil may increase risk of seizures when used with other drugs known to inhibit the inhibitory neurotransmitter GABA.

Instructions for Use

Flumazenil is used primarily to block effects of benzodiazepine drugs. It has been used to reverse overdoses of benzodiazepines (e.g., diazepam). Although it has been used experimentally for treating hepatic encephalopathy, its efficacy for this condition is not established.

Patient Monitoring and Laboratory Tests

No specific monitoring is necessary.

Formulations

Flumazenil is available in a 100 mcg/mL (0.1 mg/mL) injection.

Stability and Storage

Store in tightly sealed container, protected from light, and at room temperature. Stability of compounded formulations has not been evaluated.

Small Animal Dosage

Dogs and Cats

- 0.02 mg/kg IV.
- To reverse benzodiazepines: 0.2 mg (total dose), as needed, IV.

Large Animal Dosage

Horses, Cattle, Swine, and Sheep

- To reverse benzodiazepines: 20 mcg/kg IV (0.02 mg/kg).

Regulatory Information

Do not use in animals intended for food.

Flumethasone

floo-meth'ah-sone

Trade and Other Names: Flucort

Functional Classification: Corticosteroid

Pharmacology and Mechanism of Action

Potent glucocorticoid antiinflammatory drug. Potency is listed by one reference as approximately 15 times that of cortisol and in veterinary references as 30 times that of cortisol and 6 to 7 times the potency of prednisolone. Antiinflammatory effects are complex but primarily via inhibition of inflammatory cells and suppression of expression of inflammatory mediators. Use is for treatment of inflammatory and immune-mediated disease.

Indications and Clinical Uses

Flumethasone, like other corticosteroids, is used to treat a variety of inflammatory and immune-mediated diseases. Dosing section contains range of doses for replacement therapy, antiinflammatory therapy, and immunosuppressive therapy.

Flumethasone is used more often in large animals than small animals. Large-animal uses include treatment of inflammatory conditions, especially musculoskeletal disorders. In horses, flumethasone has been used for treatment of obstruction airway disease (RAO, formerly called chronic obstructive pulmonary disease [COPD]). In cattle, corticosteroids have been used in the treatment of ketosis.

Precautionary Information

Adverse Reactions and Side Effects

Side effects from corticosteroids are many, and include polyphagia, polydipsia/polyuria, and hypothalamic-pituitary-adrenal (HPA) axis suppression. Adverse effects include GI ulceration, hepatopathy, diabetes, hyperlipidemia, decreased thyroid hormone, decreased protein synthesis, and delayed wound healing and immunosuppression. Secondary infections can occur as a result of immunosuppression and include demodicosis, toxoplasmosis, fungal infections, and UTIs. In horses, additional adverse effects include risk of laminitis.

Contraindications and Precautions

Use cautiously in patients prone to ulcers, infection, or in animals in which wound healing is necessary. Use cautiously in diabetic animals, animals with renal failure, or pregnant animals.

Drug Interactions

Administration of corticosteroids with nonsteroidal antiinflammatory drugs (NSAIDs) will increase the risk of GI injury.

Instructions for Use

Doses are based on severity of underlying disease. For example, antiinflammatory conditions require lower doses than immune-mediated conditions. For all conditions, cats often require higher doses than dogs. Note that the approved label dose for cattle and horses is in the range of 1.25 to 5 mg per animal or approximately 0.003-0.006 mg/kg for an adult animal. Considering that the potency of flumethasone may be similar to dexamethasone, many experts feel that the dose should be higher, in the range of 0.04 0.15 mg/kg.

Patient Monitoring and Laboratory Tests

Monitor liver enzymes, blood glucose, and renal function during therapy. Monitor patients for signs of secondary infections. Perform adrenocorticotropic hormone (ACTH) stimulation test to monitor adrenal function.

Formulations

Flumethasone is available in a 0.5 mg/mL injection.

Stability and Storage

Store in tightly sealed container, protected from light, and at room temperature. Stability of compounded formulations has not been evaluated.

Small Animal Dosage

Dogs and Cats

- Antiinflammatory uses: 0.15-0.3 mg/kg q12-24h IV, IM, or SQ.

Large Animal Dosage

Horses

- 1.25-2.5 mg per animal, as a single dose, IM or IV. (Approximately 0.003-0.006 mg/kg.) This is the dose frequently listed on the product label. However, many experts prefer doses of 0.04-0.15 mg/kg, as a single dose IV or IM.

Cattle

- 1.25-5 mg/animal as a single dose IV or IM. This is the dose frequently listed on the product label. However, many experts prefer doses of 0.04-0.15 mg/kg, as a single dose IV or IM.

Regulatory Information

There are no U.S. withdrawal times established.
In Canada, cattle withdrawal time (meat): 4 days.
RCI Classification: 4

Flunixin Meglumine

floo-nix'in meg'loo-meen

Trade and Other Names: Banamine and generic brands

Functional Classification: Nonsteroidal antiinflammatory drug (NSAID)

Pharmacology and Mechanism of Action

Flunixin is an NSAID. Flunixin and other NSAIDs produce analgesic and antiinflammatory effects by inhibiting the synthesis of prostaglandins. The enzyme inhibited by NSAID is the cyclo-oxygenase enzyme (COX). The COX enzyme exists in two isoforms, called COX-1 and COX-2. COX-1 is primarily responsible for synthesis of prostaglandins important for maintaining a healthy GI tract, renal function, platelet function, and other normal functions. COX-2 is induced and responsible for synthesizing prostaglandins that are important mediators of pain, inflammation, and fever. Other antiinflammatory effects may occur (such as effects on leukocytes) but have not been well characterized. In horses, the half-life is 2 hours and oral absorption of paste is 77% and absorption of granules is 85%. However, access to hay will delay peak concentrations and oral absorption from granules and paste mixed with feed may be more erratic.

Indications and Clinical Uses

Flunixin is used primarily for short-term treatment of moderate pain and inflammation. It has been used for abdominal pain in horses, to decrease signs of sepsis in horses, and to decrease clinical signs associated with coliform mastitis in cattle. In horses, as an adjunctive treatment for sepsis, it is used at a low dose of 0.25 mg/kg. It has been used as an adjunctive treatment, with antibiotics, for treatment of bovine respiratory disease (BRD). Flunixin has been used as a single dose for treatment of diarrhea in dairy calves. Flunixin at 2.2 mg/kg IV in cows with endotoxin mastitis did not affect milk production, but it decreased fever and improved rumen motility.

In pigs it is used for pyrexia associated with swine respiratory disease.

In dogs and cats, it has been used occasionally, but treatment is usually confined to one or two treatments because of risk of gastrointestinal toxicity (ulcers and perforation).

Precautionary Information

Adverse Reactions and Side Effects

Most severe adverse effects related to GI system. Flunixin causes gastritis and GI ulceration with high doses or prolonged use. Renal schema has also been documented. Therapy in dogs should be limited to 4 consecutive days. In horses, if given IM it can result in myositis and abscess at injection site.

Contraindications and Precautions

Avoid use in pregnant animals near term. Do not use in calves to be processed for veal. Do not use in bulls intended for breeding as reproductive effects in this class of cattle have not been studied.

Drug Interactions

Ulcerogenic effects are potentiated when administered with corticosteroids. Flunixin, like other NSAIDs, may interfere with the action of diuretics such as furosemide and angiotensin-converting enzyme (ACE) inhibitors. Coadministration with enrofloxacin in dogs increased flunixin plasma concentrations because of reduced clearance.

Instructions for Use

Flunixin is not approved for small animals but has been shown in experimental studies to be an effective prostaglandin synthesis inhibitor. It is approved for use in small animals in Europe.

Patient Monitoring and Laboratory Tests

Monitor for signs of GI bleeding and ulcers during treatment.

Formulations

Flunixin is available in 250 mg packet granules in a 10-gram packet and 10 and 50 mg/mL injection. It is also available as a paste and each 30-gram syringe contains flunixin meglumine equivalent to 1500 milligrams of flunixin.

Stability and Storage

Store in tightly sealed container, protected from light, and at room temperature. Stability of compounded formulations has not been evaluated.

Small Animal Dosage

Dogs and Cats

- 1.1 mg/kg once IV, IM, or SQ.
- 1.1 mg/kg/day 3 day/week PO.
- Ophthalmic: 0.5 mg/kg once IV.

Large Animal Dosage

Horses

- 1.1 mg/kg q24h for up to 5 days IV or IM. Note: In foals, it has been shown that doses as low as 0.25 mg/kg inhibit prostaglandin synthesis during sepsis.
- Banamine paste: 1.1 mg/kg q24h PO.
- Granules: 1.1 mg/kg/day PO (one packet per 500 pounds).

Cattle

- 1.1 to 2.2 mg/kg (slowly) once a day for up to 3 days IV.

Pigs

- 2.2 mg/kg, once IM.

Regulatory Information

Cattle withdrawal time: 4 days meat and 36 hours milk.
Pig withdrawal time: 12 days.
RCI Classification: 4

Fluorouracil

floo-roe-yoo′rah-sil

Trade and Other Names: 5-Fluorouracil, Adrucil

Functional Classification: Anticancer agent

Pharmacology and Mechanism of Action

Anticancer agent. Antimetabolite. Action is via inhibition with nucleic acid synthesis. Fluorouracil is used in anticancer protocols.

Indications and Clinical Uses

Fluorouracil is used in cancer protocols used in dogs. It has been used as a component with other combination cancer regimens.

Precautionary Information

Adverse Reactions and Side Effects

Fluorouracil causes mild leukopenia, thrombocytopenia, and CNS toxicity.

Contraindications and Precautions

Do not use in cats.

Drug Interactions

No drug interactions are reported for animals.

Instructions for Use

Consult anticancer treatment protocol for precise dosage and regimen.

Patient Monitoring and Laboratory Tests

Monitor CBC for evidence of bone marrow toxicity.

Formulations

Fluorouracil is available in 50 mg/mL vial

Stability and Storage

Store in tightly sealed container, protected from light, and at room temperature. Stability of compounded formulations has not been evaluated.

Small Animal Dosage

Dogs

- 150 mg/m^2 once/week IV.

Cats

Do not use.

Large Animal Dosage

No large animal doses have been reported.

Regulatory Information

Withdrawal times are not established for animals that produce food. This drug should not be used in food animals, because it is an anticancer agent.

Fluoxetine Hydrochloride

floo-oks'eh-teen hye-droe-klor'ide

Trade and Other Names: Prozac

Functional Classification: Behavior modification, SSRI

Pharmacology and Mechanism of Action

Antidepressant drug. Fluoxetine, like other drugs in this class, is classified as a selective serotonin reuptake-inhibitor (SSRI). Mechanism of action appears to be via selective inhibition of serotonin reuptake and down regulation of 5-HT$_1$ receptors. SSRI drugs are more selective for inhibiting serotonin reuptake than the tricyclic antidepressant (TCA) drugs. Fluoxetine is metabolized to norfluoxetine, which is an active metabolite. Oral absorption in dogs is 72% with a half-life of 6-10 hours. The metabolite norfluoxetine has a longer half-life of 48-57 hours. In cats, oral absorption is 100% with a half-life of 34-47 hours; with the metabolite norfluoxetine, a half-life of 51-55 hours. Absorption in cats from transdermal administration is only 10%, but 100% from oral administration. Another SSRI used in animals is paroxetine (Paxil).

Indications and Clinical Uses

Fluoxetine, like other SSRI drugs, is used to treat behavioral disorders such as canine compulsive disorders and dominance aggression. In cats, it has been effective for decreasing urine spraying (1 mg/kg/day). In trials comparing fluoxetine with clomipramine for treating urine marking in cats, both drugs were equally effective for long-term use. However, the urine marking returned after discontinuation of the drug.

Precautionary Information

Adverse Reactions and Side Effects

Fluoxetine has fewer adverse effects (especially antihistamine and antimuscarinic effects) compared to other antidepressant drugs. In dogs, at high doses of 10-20 mg/kg it caused tremors, anorexia, aggressive behavior, nystagmus, emesis, and ataxia. Occasionally some of these signs may be seen at lower doses. In cats, nervousness or increased anxiousness have been observed. However, in trials used for treating urine spraying, few adverse effects were reported. Cats have tolerated doses up to 50 mg/kg, but at 5 mg/kg tremors were reported and at 3 mg/kg anorexia and vomiting were observed.

Contraindications and Precautions

Use cautiously in animals prone to aggression, because it may decrease inhibition.

Drug Interactions

Do not use with other behavior-modifying drugs such as other SSRIs or TCAs. Do not use with monoamine oxidase inhibitors (MAOIs). Because it is highly metabolized by the liver, it may be subject to interactions caused by cytochrome P450 inhibitors.

Instructions for Use

Use of fluoxetine in animals is largely experimental. Doses have been derived empirically, and use is based primarily on anecdotal experience. Because of long half-life, accumulation in plasma may take several days to weeks. There may be a delay in the onset of action of 2 weeks.

In some animals, paroxetine (Paxil) is preferred, which is available in tablets and has been used for smaller-size animals. Do not use transdermally; absorption is low.

Patient Monitoring and Laboratory Tests

Use in animals has been relatively safe, and one should only monitor behavior changes.

Formulations

Fluoxetine is available in 10 and 40 mg capsules, 10 mg tablets, and 4 mg/mL oral solution.

Stability and Storage

Store in tightly sealed container, protected from light, and at room temperature. It is soluble in water at 14 mg/mL and in alcohol at 100 mg/mL. Fluoxetine hydrochloride solution has been mixed with various juices, juices, and flavorings and found to be stable for 8 weeks. In one trial it was mixed in tuna-flavored water for cats and retained effectiveness.

Small Animal Dosage

Dogs

- 0.5 mg/kg/day PO, then increase to 1 mg/kg/day PO. (Average dose is 10-20 mg/dog.)

Cats

- 0.5-4 mg/cat q24h PO (0.5-1 mg/kg per day). Start with 1/4 tablet (2.5 mg) per cat.
- Urine marking: 1.0 mg/kg q24h PO and increase to 1.5 mg/kg if there has been inadequate response.

Large Animal Dosage

- Although fluoxetine has been used in horses at a dose of 80 mg per horse once daily, orally for "cribbing behavior," these doses have not been tested for safety or efficacy.

Regulatory Information

Do not administer to animals intended for food.
RCI Classification: 2

Fluticasone Propionate

(floo-tok'ah-sone proe-pee-oe-nayt)

Trade and Other Names: Flovent

Functional Classification: Corticosteroid

Pharmacology and Mechanism of Action

Potent glucocorticoid antiinflammatory drug with potency of 18 times that of desamethasone. In patients with inflammatory airway diseases, glucocorticoids have potent antiinflammatory effects on the bronchial mucosa. Glucocorticoids bind to receptors on cells and inhibit the transcription of genes for the production of mediators (cytokines, chemokines, adhesion molecules) involved in airway inflammation. A decrease in the synthesis of inflammatory mediators such as prostaglandins, leukotrienes, and platelet-activating-factor caused by glucocorticoids also may be important. Glucocorticoids also play a role in enhancing the action of adrenergic agonists on beta-2 receptors in the bronchial smooth muscle, either by modifying the receptor or augmenting muscle relaxation after a receptor has been bound. Corticosteroids also may prevent down-regulation of beta-2 receptors. Topical (inhaled) corticosteroids such as fluticasone or budesonide are used to avoid systemic effects. They typically have high first-pass effects and low systemic exposure if swallowed.

Indications and Clinical Uses

Fluticasone is used as an inhaled (topical) corticosteroid for treatment of airway disease. Most of the use has been established for cats, but it also could be used for dogs, horses, or other animals in which a special adapter can be used to deliver the drug via a metered-dose inhaler. In dogs and cats the most common use is inflammatory airway diseases such as asthma, bronchitis, or bronchospasm. For example, if a cat is given 2 puffs twice a day of a potent inhaled corticosteroid (e.g., budesonide, fluticasone), and allowed 5-7 breaths (10 sec) from a chamber (spacer), it may reduce the need for oral prednisone in cats with feline asthma.

In horses the most common use is for recurrent airway obstruction (RAO), formerly called *chronic obstructive pulmonary disease* (COPD).

Precautionary Information

Adverse Reactions and Side Effects

Although fluticasone systemic absorption is low, some systemic exposure will occur in animals. Side effects can occur but are not expected to be as severe as with systemic corticosteroids. Adrenal suppression is expected to occur in treated animals but may recover once treatment is discontinued.

Contraindications and Precautions

Use cautiously in patients with oral or respiratory tract infections as immunosuppression may occur.

Drug Interactions

Some systemic effects are possible but minimal. Administration of corticosteroids with nonsteroidal antiinflammatory drugs (NSAIDs) will increase the risk of GI injury.

Instructions for Use

The use is based on administration of fluticasone for treatment of airway diseases. It is delivered via a metered-dose inhaler. These inhalers can be used in animals if special adaptations, such as a spacer device which are available for use in pediatrics or for cats and horses, are used.

Patient Monitoring and Laboratory Tests

Monitor liver enzymes, blood glucose, and renal function during therapy. Monitor patients for signs of secondary infections. Perform adrenocorticotropic hormone (ACTH) stimulation test to monitor adrenal function.

Formulations

Metered-dose inhaler at 44, 110, or 220 mcg per puff.

Stability and Storage

Store in original container (metered-dose inhaler). Do not puncture container or attempt to remove drug from pressurized container. Stability of compounded formulations has not been evaluated.

Small Animal Dosage

Dogs and Cats

- Airway diseases: 220 mcg per dose, inhales. A typical dose for fluticasone is 440 mcg (2 puffs from a 220 mcg metered-dose inhaler) per day. After 10 days, decrease the dose to 220 mcg per day. Use a metered-dose inhaler and a spacer to effectively deliver medication.

Horses

- No equine dose is available, however, it can potentially be delivered in the airways for treatment of airway diseases with a metered-dose inhaler.

Regulatory Information

There are no U.S. withdrawal times established.
RCI Classification: not established.

Fomepizole

foh-meh′pih-zole

Trade and Other Names: 4-Methylpyrazole, Antizol-Vet, and Antizole (human preparation)

Functional Classification: Antidote

Pharmacology and Mechanism of Action

Fomepizole is an antidote for ethylene glycol (antifreeze) intoxication. It inhibits dehydrogenase enzyme that converts ethylene glycol to toxic metabolites.

Indications and Clinical Uses

Fomepizole is used for treatment of acute ethylene glycol toxicosis in dogs. In people, it is used for this purpose but also is registered for methanol poisoning. It should be used early for maximum success. Fomepizole was safe and effective in dogs in clinical trials if used within 8 hours of poisoning.

Precautionary Information

Adverse Reactions and Side Effects

No adverse effects have been reported.

Contraindications and Precautions

Treatment should be initiated early for optimum effect.

Drug Interactions

Fomepizole will inhibit the metabolism of other drugs and compounds that share a similar pathway as alcohol. Use cautiously with any other coadministered drugs.

Instructions for Use

The only used documented is for emergency management of ethylene glycol intoxication. Experimental studies have demonstrated effectiveness in dogs, but in cats ethanol is more effective (*J Am Vet Med Assoc,* 209:1880, 1996). Administer 0.9% sodium chloride before administration of fomepizole.

Patient Monitoring and Laboratory Tests

Monitor renal function during treatment. Monitor urine output.

Formulations

Fomepizole is available in a 5% solution in a 1.5 mL vial (Antizol-Vet) and 1 g/mL solution (Antizol), a human preparation.

Stability and Storage

Store in tightly sealed container, protected from light, and at room temperature. Stability of compounded formulations has not been evaluated.

Small Animal Dosage

- 20 mg/kg initially IV, then 15 mg/kg at 12 and 24 hour intervals, then 5 mg at 36 hours.

Large Animal Dosage

No large animal doses have been reported.

Regulatory Information

No withdrawal times are established for animals intended for food. There is little risk of residues in food animals.

Furazolidone

fyoo-rah-zole'ih-done

Trade and Other Names: Furoxone

Functional Classification: Antiparasitic

Pharmacology and Mechanism of Action

Furazolidone is an oral antiprotozoal drug with activity against *Giardia,* and it may have some activity against bacteria in intestine. It is used for only local treatment of intestinal parasites; it is not used for systemic therapy.

Indications and Clinical Uses

Furazolidone has been used to treat protozoal intestinal parasites. However, because efficacy and safety of other oral antiprotozoal drugs are better established, they are used more often.

Precautionary Information

Adverse Reactions and Side Effects

Adverse effects not reported in animals. In people, mild anemia, hypersensitivity, and disturbance of intestinal flora have been reported.

Contraindications and Precautions

No contraindications reported for animals.

Drug Interactions

Do not use with monoamine oxidase inhibitors (MAOIs).

Instructions for Use

Clinical studies have not been reported for animals. Doses and recommendations are based on extrapolation from humans. Other drugs, such as fenbendazole, may be preferred for treating Giardia.

Patient Monitoring and Laboratory Tests

No specific monitoring is necessary.

Formulations

Furazolidone is available in 100 mg tablets.

Stability and Storage

Store in tightly sealed container, protected from light, and at room temperature. Stability of compounded formulations has not been evaluated.

Small Animal Dosage

- 4 mg/kg q12h for 7-10 days PO.

Large Animal Dosage

No large animal doses have been reported.

Regulatory Information

No regulatory information is available. For extra-label use withdrawal interval estimates, contact FARAD at 1-888-USFARAD (1-888-873-2723), or send e-mail to FARAD@ncsu.edu.

Furosemide

fyoo-roe′seh-mide

Trade and Other Names: Lasix and generic brands

Functional Classification: Diuretic

Pharmacology and Mechanism of Action

Furosemide is a loop diuretic, and it inhibits sodium and water transport in ascending loop of Henle, which produces diuresis. Furosemide is one of the most potent and effective diuretics used in veterinary medicine. It also may have vasodilating properties, increasing renal perfusion and decreasing cardiac preload.

Indications and Clinical Uses

Furosemide is indicated in diseases associated with water retention, such as CHF. In horses, the most common use of furosemide is prior to racing. Presumably the effect in race horses is to decrease exercise-induced pulmonary hemorrhage (EIPH). However, the efficacy to reduce EIPH has not been demonstrated in horses. In all animals, duration of effect is short, approximately 2-4 hours.

Precautionary Information

Adverse Reactions and Side Effects

Adverse effects primarily related to diuretic effect (loss of fluid and electrolytes).

Contraindications and Precautions

Administer conservatively in animals receiving angiotensin-converting enzyme (ACE) inhibitors to decrease risk of azotemia.

Drug Interactions

Concurrent use with aminoglycoside antibiotics or amphotericin B may increase risk of nephrotoxicity and ototoxicity. Administration of nonsteroidal antiinflammatory drugs (NSAIDs) with furosemide may diminish the effect. pH of solution is 8-9.8. Furosemide is stable with alkaline drugs, but do not mix with acidifying drug solutions with pH <5.5.

Instructions for Use

Recommendations are based on extensive clinical use of furosemide in animals. Constant rate infusions (CRI) in dogs and horses were shown to be more effective than intermittent bolus.

Patient Monitoring and Laboratory Tests

Monitor electrolyte concentrations (particularly potassium) and hydration status in patients during treatment.

Formulations

Furosemide is available in 12.5, 20, 40, 50 and 80 mg tablets, 20, 40, and 80 mg tablets (human preparation), 10 mg/mL oral solution (syrup), and 50 mg/mL injection. Tablets usually can be easily split.

Stability and Storage

Store in tightly sealed container, protected from light, and at room temperature. Do not mix with acidic solutions. It is compatible in plastic syringes and infusion sets. Furosemide is poorly soluble in water, but may be mixed with 5% dextrose, 0.9% saline, or lactated Ringer's solution at a concentration of 10 mg/mL. These solutions are stable for 8 hours. It is more soluble if the pH is >8, but it readily precipitates when pH is <5.5. Compounded oral formulations in syrups and other flavorings are stable if kept at alkaline pH or in alcohol. However, lower pH will result in instability of formulation. If discoloration occurs, discard formulation.

Small Animal Dosage

Dogs

- 2-6 mg/kg q8-12h (or as needed) IV, IM, SQ, or PO. It may be administered more frequently if needed in critical cases.
- CRI: 0.66 mg/kg bolus dose IV, followed by 0.66 mg/kg/hr for 8 hours.

Cats

- 1-4 mg/kg q8-24h IV, IM, SQ, or PO.

Large Animal Dosage

Horses

- 1 mg/kg q8h or 250 to 500 mg/horse at 6-8 hour intervals IM or IV.
- CRI: 0.12 mg/kg IV followed by 0.12 mg/kg/hr IV.

Cattle

- 500 mg/animal once a day or 250 mg/animal twice a day IM or IV.

Regulatory Information

Cattle withdrawal times: 2 days meat and 48 hours milk.
Horses: Most racing regulations specify that a 250 mg/horse dose may be given by a single intravenous injection no later than 4 hours before racing post time. In most horses this will not produce violations above 100 ng/mL urine threshold at 4 hours.

Gabapentin

gab'ah-pen-tin

Trade and Other Names: Gabapetin, Neurontin, and generic brands

Functional Classification: Anticonvulsant, Analgesic

Pharmacology and Mechanism of Action

Anticonvulsant and analgesic. Gabapentin is an analogue of the inhibitory neurotransmitter GABA. The mechanism of anticonvulsant action and analgesic effects are not clear. It may bind to voltage-sensitive calcium channels in neuronal tissue and inhibit depolarization. Half-life in dogs is only 3-4 hours, which may necessitate frequent administration. Another related drug is pregabalin (Lyrica), which is used in people for neuropathic pain. However, there is no information on pregabalin for treatment in animals.

Gabapentin is eliminated by renal clearance and not as dependent on hepatic metabolism as other anticonvulsants. Therefore, it has been used in animals as a replacement for phenobarbital when liver problems are a concern.

Indications and Clinical Uses

Gabapentin is an anticonvulsant. However, it is also used to treat chronic pain syndromes, including neuropathic pain. It is used for this indication because neuropathic pain often does not respond to nonsteroidal antiinflammatory drugs (NSAIDs) or opiates. Another related drug is pregabalin (Lyrica), which is used in people for neuropathic pain and seizures, but information is lacking on this drug for treatment in animals.

Precautionary Information

Adverse Reactions and Side Effects

Sedation and ataxia are reported adverse effects. In people a withdrawal syndrome from abrupt discontinuation has been described, but it is not reported in animals.

Contraindications and Precautions

Gabapentin oral solutions contains xylitol as a sweetener. Xylitol has been reported to cause hypoglycemia and hepatotoxicity in dogs at doses greater than 0.1 grams/kg.

Drug Interactions

Antacids decrease oral absorption.

Instructions for Use

Gabapentin has been used in some animals as an anticonvulsant when they are refractory to other drugs. It also has been used to treat neuropathic pain syndromes. Most often it is used with other analgesic drugs for treatment of pain. Efficacy for each of these indications is anecdotal; there are no controlled studies published.

Patient Monitoring and Laboratory Tests

No specific monitoring is necessary.

Formulations

Gabapentin is available in 100, 300, and 400 mg capsules, 100, 300, 400, 600, and 800 mg scored tablets, and 50 mg/mL oral solution.

Stability and Storage

Store in tightly sealed container, protected from light, and at room temperature. Stability of compounded formulations has not been evaluated.

Small Animal Dosage

Dogs and Cats

- Anticonvulsant dose: 2.5-10 mg/kg q8-12h PO.
- Neuropathic pain: Start with anticonvulsant dose and increase up to 10-15 mg/kg q8h PO, if necessary.

Large Animal Dosage

No large animal doses have been reported.

Regulatory Information

No regulatory information is available. For extralabel use withdrawal interval estimates, contact FARAD at 1-888-USFARAD (1-888-873-2723) or send e-mail to FARAD@ncsu.edu.

RCI Classification: 4

Gemfibrozil

jem-fih′broe-zil

Trade and Other Names: Lopid

Functional Classification: Antihyperlipidemic agent

Pharmacology and Mechanism of Action

Gemfibrozil is an agent that lowers cholesterol and it reduces plasma triglyceride, very-low-density-lipoprotein (VLDL) and increases high-density lipoproteins (HDL). Mechanism results from inhibition of peripheral lipolysis and reduced hepatic extraction of free fatty acids.

Indications and Clinical Uses

Used for treatment of hyperlipidemia. It has been used in dogs for treatment of some hyperlipidemia syndromes, but the efficacy has not been reported.

Precautionary Information

Adverse Reactions and Side Effects

Adverse effects have not been reported in animals.

Contraindications and Precautions

No reported contraindications in animals.

Drug Interactions

No drug interactions are reported for animals.

Instructions for Use

Used primarily in people to treat hyperlipidemia, but it is used occasionally in dogs. Clinical studies have not been performed in animals.

Patient Monitoring and Laboratory Tests

Monitor cholesterol concentrations.

Formulations
Gemfibrozil is available in 600 mg tablets and 300 mg capsules (Canada only).

Stability and Storage
Store in tightly sealed container, protected from light, and at room temperature. Stability of compounded formulations has not been evaluated.

Small Animal Dosage
Dogs and Cats
- 7.5 mg/kg q12h PO.

Large Animal Dosage
No large animal doses have been reported.

Regulatory Information
No regulatory information is available. For extralabel use withdrawal interval estimates, contact FARAD at 1-888-USFARAD (1-888-873-2723) or send e-mail to FARAD@ncsu.edu.

Gentamicin Sulfate
jen-tah-mye'sin sul'fate

Trade and Other Names: Gentocin

Functional Classification: Antibacterial

Pharmacology and Mechanism of Action
Aminoglycoside antibiotic. Action is to inhibit bacteria protein synthesis via binding to 30S ribosome. Bactericidal. Gentamicin has a broad spectrum of activity that includes most bacterial isolates in animals except streptococci and anaerobic bacteria.

Indications and Clinical Uses
Gentamicin has a rapid, bactericidal action and is indicated for acute serious infections, such as those caused by gram-negative bacilli. Gentamicin has been administered IM, SQ, and IV. It is not absorbed after oral administration, and this use is restricted to labeled use in pigs. Gentamicin, like other aminoglycosides, is synergistic with beta-lactam antibiotics, and its activity is enhanced when administered with penicillins, ampicillin, or cephalosporins. Although gentamicin is generally active against most gram-negative bacilli, amikacin is more consistently active against resistant strains.

Precautionary Information
Adverse Reactions and Side Effects
Nephrotoxicity is the most dose-limiting toxicity. Ensure that patients have adequate fluid and electrolyte balance during therapy. Ototoxicity and vestibulotoxicity also are possible but have not been reported in animals. With high doses, neuromuscular toxicity is possible, although rare.

Contraindications and Precautions
Do not administer to animals with compromised renal function, renal insufficiency, or renal failure. There should be adequate renal clearance for clearance of gentamicin. Use in young animals is accepted, except higher doses may be necessary.

Drug Interactions

When used with anesthetic agents, neuromuscular blockade is possible. Do not mix in vial or syringe with other antibiotics. Ototoxicity and nephrotoxicity potentiated by loop diuretics such as furosemide.

Instructions for Use

Dosing regimens are based on sensitivity of organisms. Some studies have suggested that once daily therapy (combining multiple doses into a single daily dose) is as efficacious as multiple treatments. Activity against some bacteria (e.g., *Pseudomonas*) is enhanced when combined with a beta-lactam antibiotic, such as ceftazidime. Nephrotoxicity is increased with persistently high trough concentrations.

Patient Monitoring and Laboratory Tests

Susceptibility testing: The CLSI (NCCLS) minimum inhibitory concentration (MIC) break point for susceptibility is less than or equal to 2 mcg/mL. Monitor BUN, creatinine, and urine for evidence of renal toxicity. Blood levels can be monitored to measure for problems with systemic clearance. When monitoring trough levels in patient doses once daily, the trough levels should be below the limit of detection. Alternatively measure half-life from samples taken at 1 hour and 2 to 4 hours post-dosing. Clearance should be approximately equal to glomerular filtration rate (GFR) (>1.0 mL/kg/min), and half-life should be less than 2 hours.

Formulations

Gentamicin is available in 50 and 100 mg/mL solution for injection.

Stability and Storage

Store in tightly sealed container, protected from light, and at room temperature. Gentamicin is soluble in water. Do not mix with other drugs, especially in a vial, syringe, or fluid administration set. Inactivation may occur. Avoid long-term storage in plastic containers.

Small Animal Dosage

Dogs

- 2-4 mg/kg q8h or 9-14 mg/kg q24h SQ, IM, or IV.
  Once daily administration is usually the preferred interval.

Cats

- 3 mg/kg q8h or 5-8 mg/kg q24h SQ, IM, or IV.
  Once daily administration is usually the preferred interval.

Large Animal Dosage

Horses

- Adult: 4-6.6 mg/kg q24h IM or IV.
- Foal younger than 2 weeks: 12-14 mg/kg q24h IM or IV.

Pigs

- Colibacillosis, swine dysentery: 1.1-2.2 mg/kg for 3 days in drinking water.

Calves

- Younger than 2 weeks: 12-15 mg/kg q24h IV or IM.
- Adult cattle: 5-6 mg/kg q24h IM or IV.

Regulatory Information

With the exception of licensed products for pigs, aminoglycosides should not be administered to cattle intended for food.

Withdrawal time for pigs: 3 days meat at 1.1 mg/kg PO and 40 days meat at 5 mg/kg IM; 14 days meat at 5 mg/kg PO.
If gentamicin is administered systemically to cattle, an extended withdrawal time is necessary because of persistence of residues in kidney. FARAD recommends 18 months. After systemic administration of 5 mg/kg, milk withdrawal time should be 5 days. If gentamicin is administered intramammary, a milk withdrawal time of at least 10 days should be used.
Contact FARAD for additional information at 1-888-USFARAD (1-888-873-2723) or send e-mail to FARAD@ncsu.edu.

Glipizide

glip-ih'zide

Trade and Other Names: Glucotrol

Functional Classification: Antidiabetic agent, hypoglycemic agent

Pharmacology and Mechanism of Action

Sulfonylurea oral hypoglycemic agent. This drug acts to increase secretion of insulin from beta cells of pancreas, probably by interacting with sulfonylurea receptors on beta cells or by inhibiting adenosine triphosphate (ATP) sensitive potassium channels on the pancreatic beta cells which increases insulin secretion. These drugs also may increase sensitivity of existing insulin receptors. Studies in cats showed that glipizide had a half-life of 17 hours and effective plasma concentration for 50% efficacy (EC_{50}) of 70 mcg/mL.

Indications and Clinical Uses

Glipizide is used as oral treatment in the management of diabetes mellitus, particularly in cats. Response rate in cats is approximately 44%-65% (some reports are 35% or lower). Response rate in dogs is poor. It has been more common to administer the sulfonylurea class of drugs in animals than other oral hypoglycemic drugs, because they have had better efficacy. Glipizide is the most common of this class. Other oral hypoglycemic drugs include acetohexamide, chlorpropamide, glyburide (DiaBeta, Micronase), gliclazide, and tolazamide. Metformin is of the biguanide class of oral drugs for diabetes and has not had efficacy as high as glipizide in cats.

Glipizide transdermal absorption from a pluronic transdermal gel (pluronic organogel [PLO]) vehicle is poor in cats (<20%) and inconsistent. This route is not recommended.

Precautionary Information

Adverse Reactions and Side Effects

It may cause dose-related vomiting, anorexia, increased bilirubin, and elevated liver enzymes in some cats (15%). Vomiting has been common in cats. Glipizide may cause hypoglycemia, but less so than insulin. In people, increased cardiac mortality is possible, but this has not been reported in cats.

Contraindications and Precautions

Many cats do not respond and will require insulin therapy. Do not rely on glipizide in cats that are not stable or if they are dehydrated or debilitated.

Drug Interactions

Many drug interactions have been reported in people. It is not known if these occur in animals. Use cautiously with beta-blockers, antifungal drugs, anticoagulants, fluoroquinolones, sulfonamides, and others.

Instructions for Use

Oral hypoglycemic agents are successful in people only for non–insulin-dependent diabetes. There has been only limited use in animals. Because response to oral hypoglycemic agents in cats is unpredictable, it is recommended to use a trial first of at least 4 weeks. If the cat responds, the drug can be continued, otherwise, insulin may be indicated. Feed cats a high fiber diet when using oral hypoglycemic agents. Transdermal glipizide (5 mg dose) in a PLO gel was evaluated in cats. Although the transdermal formulation produced a modest change in glucose concentrations, systemic absorption was only 20%.

Patient Monitoring and Laboratory Tests

Monitor blood glucose levels to determine if the drug is effective. Monitor liver enzymes. It may increase alanine transaminase (ALT) and alkaline phosphatase.

Formulations

Glipizide is available in 5 and 10 mg tablets.

Stability and Storage

Store glipizide in tightly sealed container, protected from light, and at room temperature. Stability of compounded formulations has not been evaluated.

Small Animal Dosage

Dogs

No effective dose available.

Cats

- 2.5-7.5 mg/cat q12h PO. Usual dose is 2.5 mg/cat initially, then increase to 5 mg/cat, q12h.

Large Animal Dosage

No large animal doses have been reported.

Regulatory Information

No regulatory information is available. For extralabel use withdrawal interval estimates, contact FARAD at 1-888-USFARAD (1-888-873-2723) or send e-mail to FARAD@ncsu.edu.

Glucosamine + Chondroitin Sulfate

gloo-koe′seh-meen + kahn-droy′ten sul′fate

Trade and Other Names: Cosequin, Glycoflex, and generic brands

Functional Classification: Nutritional supplement

Pharmacology and Mechanism of Action

Glucosamine is an amino sugar synthesized from glucose and glutamine. It is a source of glucosamine-6-phosphate and n-acetylglucosamine. It is an intermediate for formation of compounds in the body, including glycosaminoglycans in cartilage. Glucosamine is usually administered as a combination of glucosamine HCl and chondroitin sulfate. According to the manufacturer these compounds stimulate synthesis of synovial fluid, inhibit degradation, and improve healing of articular cartilage. Additional information is available in the section on chondroitin sulfate. Bioavailability studies have produced varying results depending on formulation, assay technique, and species. Horses have lower oral absorption than dogs.

Indications and Clinical Uses

Glucosamine + chondroitin sulfate is used primarily for treatment of degenerative joint disease. It is used as a dietary supplement that modifies disease and is not regulated as a drug.

Precautionary Information

Adverse Reactions and Side Effects

In some animals, soft stools and intestinal gas have been reported. In experimental animals, glucosamine can cause hyperglycemia and insulin suppression. Animals that received glucosamine had a decrease in the metabolic action of insulin. However, the clinical relevance of these findings has not been shown. Otherwise, adverse effects have not been reported, although hypersensitivity is possible.

Contraindications and Precautions

Use with caution in diabetic animals or obese animals that may be prone to developing diabetes. Otherwise, there are no known precautions.

Drug Interactions

No drug interactions are reported. Glucosamine and chondroitin containing products may be used safely with nonsteroidal antiinflammatory drugs (NSAIDs).

Instructions for Use

Doses are based primarily on empiricism and manufacturer's recommendations. There are limited published trials of efficacy or dose titrations are available to determine optimal dose. Doses listed are general recommendations and may vary among products. Glucosamine hydrochloride is more bioavailable than glucosamine sulfate. Products may vary in their stability, purity, and potency. Use products from a reputable supplier.

Patient Monitoring and Laboratory Tests

No routine patient monitoring is necessary. Glucose monitoring may be indicated in animals prone to developing diabetes.

Formulations

Several formulations are available. Veterinarians are encouraged to carefully examine product label to ensure proper strength. One product (Cosequin) is available as Regular ("RS") and double strength ("DS") capsules. Regular strength contains 250 mg glucosamine, 200 mg chondroitin sulfate, and mixed glycosaminoglycans, 5 mg manganese and 33 mg manganese ascorbate. The DS tablets contain double of each of these amounts. Products for horses contain 3.3 grams per scoop, equal to 1800 mg glucosamine and 570 mg chondroitin.

Stability and Storage

Store in tightly sealed container, protected from light, and at room temperature. Products may vary in stability and potency.

Small Animal Dosage

- Glucosamine dose: 22 mg/kg/day PO, and increased to 44 mg/kg/day PO, in patients that do not initially respond. Alternatively, a better response may be anticipated by starting with the higher dose.

Many preparations are administered in combination with chondroitin. For general dosing, use the Cosequin RS and DS strength as a general guide.

Dogs

- 1-2 RS capsules per day.
  (2-4 capsules of DS for large dogs.)

Cats

- 1 RS capsule daily.

Large Animal Dosage

Horses

- 12 mg/kg glucosamine + 3.8 mg/kg chondroitin sulfate twice daily PO for 4 weeks, then 4 mg/kg glucosamine + 1.3 mg/kg chondroitin sulfate thereafter. It is common to initiate treatment in horses with a higher dose of 22 mg/kg glucosamine + 8.8 mg/kg chondroitin sulfate daily PO.

Regulatory Information

No regulatory information is available. Because of low risk of residues, no withdrawal times are suggested.

Glyburide

glye′byoor-ide

Trade and Other Names: Diabeta, Micronase, Glynase, and Glibenclamide (British name)

Functional Classification: Antidiabetic agent, hypoglycemic agent

Pharmacology and Mechanism of Action

Glyburide is a sulfonylurea oral hypoglycemic agent; it is also known as glibenclamide. This drug acts to increase secretion of insulin from pancreas, probably by interacting with sulfonylurea receptors on beta-cells or by interfering with adenosine triphosphate (ATP) sensitive potassium channels on pancreatic beta cells, which increases secretion of insulin. These drugs also may increase sensitivity of existing insulin receptors. It is used as oral treatment in the management of diabetes mellitus, particularly in cats. Response rate is approximately 40%. Sulfonylurea drugs include glipizide (Glucotrol) and glyburide (DiaBeta, Micronase). Metformin is of the biguanide class of oral drugs for diabetes.

Indications and Clinical Uses

Oral hypoglycemic agents are successful in people only for noninsulin dependent diabetes. There has been only limited use in animals. Glyburide is not effective in dogs but has been used in some cats. Similar drugs include acetohexamide, chlorpropamide, glipizide, gliclazide, and tolazamide. There is more experience with glipizide than with other drugs, and it should be used as the first choice.

Precautionary Information

Adverse Reactions and Side Effects

It may cause dose-related vomiting, anorexia, increased bilirubin, and elevated liver enzymes in some cats. Glyburide causes hypoglycemia but less so than insulin. In people, increased cardiac mortality is possible.

Contraindications and Precautions

There are no known contraindications in animals.

Drug Interactions

No drug interactions are reported for animals. Many drug interactions have been reported in people. It is not known if these occur in animals. Use cautiously with beta-blockers, antifungal drugs, anticoagulants, fluoroquinolones, sulfonamides, and others (consult package insert).

Instructions for Use

Because response to oral hypoglycemic agents in cats is unpredictable, it is recommended to use a trial first of at least 4 weeks. If the cat responds, the drug can be continued. Otherwise, insulin may be indicated. Feed cats a high fiber diet when using oral hypoglycemic agents.

Patient Monitoring and Laboratory Tests

Monitor blood glucose levels to determine if the drug is effective. Monitor liver enzymes.

Formulations

Glyburide is available in 1.25, 2.5, and 5 mg tablets (Diabeta and Micronase). Glynase is available in 1.5, 3, and 6 mg micronized tablets.

Stability and Storage

Store in tightly sealed container, protected from light, and at room temperature. Stability of compounded formulations has not been evaluated.

Small Animal Dosage

Dogs

No effective doses have been reported.

Cats

- 0.2 mg/kg daily PO. Alternatively start with 625 mg (½ tablet) per cat once daily.

Large Animal Dosage

No large animal doses have been reported.

Regulatory Information

No regulatory information is available. No withdrawal information is available.

Glycerin

glih'ser-in

Trade and Other Names: Generic

Functional Classification: Diuretic, Laxative

Pharmacology and Mechanism of Action

Glycerin has been administered to lower ocular pressure to treat acute glaucoma. However, intravenous mannitol is used more frequently for this purpose. Glycerin has been used as a laxative; it lubricates the stools and adds water to intestinal contents.

Indications and Clinical Uses

Glycerin is an osmotic agent that draws water into the intestine or renal tubule. Administered systemically, it acts as an osmotic diuretic agent, preventing water reabsorption from the renal tubules. Administered orally, it is not absorbed, but acts as an osmotic laxative, drawing water into the intestine.

Precautionary Information

Adverse Reactions and Side Effects

Glycerin may cause dehydration with frequent use or high doses.

Contraindications and Precautions

Do not administer to dehydrated animals.

Drug Interactions

No drug interactions are reported for animals.

Instructions for Use

Although glycerin may lower ocular pressure, other drugs are used to treat acute glaucoma.

Patient Monitoring and Laboratory Tests

Monitor ocular pressures. Monitor electrolytes in treated animals.

Formulations Available

Glycerin is available in an oral solution or 40 mg/mL emulsion.

Stability and Storage

Store in tightly sealed container, protected from light, and at room temperature. Stability of compounded formulations has not been evaluated.

Small Animal Dosage

- 1-2 mL/kg q8h PO.

Large Animal Dosage

No large animal doses have been reported.

Regulatory Information

No regulatory information is available. Because of low risk of residues, no withdrawal times are suggested.

Glycopyrrolate

glye-koe-peer′oe-late

Trade and Other Names: Robinul-V

Functional Classification: Anticholinergic

Pharmacology and Mechanism of Action

Anticholinergic agent (blocks acetylcholine effect at muscarinic receptor), parasympatholytic.

Glycopyrrolate may have less effect on CNS compared to atropine because of lower penetration to CNS. It may produce a longer duration of action than atropine.

Indications and Clinical Uses

Glycopyrrolate is used to inhibit vagal effects and increase heart rate in animals. It also will decrease respiratory, salivary, and GI secretions. It may be used as an adjunct to anesthesia.

Precautionary Information

Adverse Reactions and Side Effects

Adverse effects attributed to antimuscarinic (anticholinergic) effects. Side effects of therapy include xerostomia, ileus, constipation, tachycardia, and urine retention.

Contraindications and Precautions

Do not use in patients with glaucoma, intestinal ileus, gastroparesis, or tachycardia.

Drug Interactions

No specific drug interactions are reported for animals. However, it is expected that glycopyrrolate, like other anticholinergic drugs, will antagonize drugs that stimulate respiratory and GI secretions and GI motility.

Instructions for Use

Glycopyrrolate is often used in combination with other agents, particularly anesthetic drugs.

Patient Monitoring and Laboratory Tests

Monitor heart rate during treatment.

Formulations

Glycopyrrolate is available as a 0.2 mg/mL injection.

Stability and Storage

Store in tightly sealed container, protected from light, and at room temperature. Stability of compounded formulations has not been evaluated.

Small Animal Dosage

Dogs and Cats

- 0.005-0.01 mg/kg IV, IM, or SQ.

Large Animal Dosage

Cattle and Horses

- Use during anesthesia: 0.005-0.01 mg/kg IM or SQ or 0.0025-0.005 mg/kg IV.

Regulatory Information

No regulatory information is available. For extralabel use withdrawal interval estimates, contact FARAD at 1-888-USFARAD (1-888-873-2723) or send e-mail to FARAD@ncsu.edu.

RCI Classification: 4

Gold Sodium Thiomalate

gold soe′dee-um thye-oh-mah′late

Trade and Other Names: Myochrysine

Functional Classification: Immunosuppressive

Pharmacology and Mechanism of Action

Used for gold therapy (chrysotherapy). Mechanism of action is unknown, but it may relate to immunosuppressive effect on lymphocytes or suppression of sulfhydryl systems.

Indications and Clinical Uses

Gold therapy is used primarily for immune-mediated diseases (such as dermatologic disease) in animals. In people it has been used for rheumatoid arthritis. In animals, there is a lack of controlled clinical trials to document efficacy. Other immunosuppressive drugs are used more commonly.

Precautionary Information

Adverse Reactions and Side Effects

Adverse effects include dermatitis, nephrotoxicity, and blood dyscrasias.

Contraindications and Precautions

Use cautiously in animals with bone marrow suppression or renal disease.

Drug Interactions

Use with penicillamine will increase risk of hematologic adverse effects.

Instructions for Use

Clinical studies have not been performed in animals. Aurothioglucose generally is used more often than gold sodium thiomalate.

Patient Monitoring and Laboratory Tests

CBC should be monitored periodically during treatment.

Formulations Available

Gold sodium thiomalate is available in 10, 25, and 50 mg/mL injection.

Stability and Storage

Store in tightly sealed container, protected from light, and at room temperature. Stability of compounded formulations has not been evaluated.

Small Animal Dosage

Dogs and Cats

- 1-5 mg per animal IM first week, then 2-10 mg IM second week, and then 1 mg/kg once per week IM for maintenance.

Large Animal Dosage

No large animal doses have been reported.

Regulatory Information

No regulatory information is available. For extralabel use withdrawal interval estimates, contact FARAD at 1-888-USFARAD (1-888-873-2723) or send e-mail to FARAD@ncsu.edu.

Gonadorelin Hydrochloride, Gonadorelin Diacetate Tetrahydrate

goe-nad-oh-rell'in hye-droe-klor'ide, goe-nad-oh-rell'in dye-ass'eh-tate tet-ra-hye'drate

Trade and Other Names: Factrel, Fertagyl, Cystorelin, Fertelin, OvaCyst, GnRh, and LHRH

Functional Classification: Hormone

Pharmacology and Mechanism of Action

Gonadorelin stimulates synthesis and release of luteinizing hormone (LH) and to a lesser degree, follicle-stimulating hormone (FSH).

Indications and Clinical Uses

Gonadorelin is used to induce luteinization and ovulation in animals. Gonadotropin has been used to manage various reproductive disorders where stimulation of ovulation is desired. In dairy cattle, it is used to treat ovarian follicular cysts.

Precautionary Information

Adverse Reactions and Side Effects

Adverse effects have not been reported in animals.

Contraindications and Precautions

Do not administer to pregnant animals.

Drug Interactions

No drug interactions in animals are reported.

Instructions for Use

For treatment of dairy cattle, with the diacetate tetrahydrate form, administer 100 mcg per cow as a single intramuscular or intravenous injection for treatment of ovarian cysts. For the hydrochloride formulation, administer 100 mcg IM for the treatment of cystic ovaries (ovarian follicular cysts) in cattle to reduce the time to first estrus.

Patient Monitoring and Laboratory Tests

Monitor treated cattle for ovulation.

Formulations

Gonadorelin is available in 50 mcg gonadorelin diacetate tetrahydrate per mL (equivalent to 43 mcg/mL of gonadorelin) or 50 mcg gonadorelin (as hydrochloride) in aqueous solution.

Stability and Storage

Store in tightly sealed container, protected from light, and at room temperature. Stability of compounded formulations has not been evaluated.

Small Animal Dosage

Dogs

- 50-100 mcg/dog/day q24-48h IM.

Cats

- 25 mcg/cat once IM.

Large Animal Dosage

Cattle

- 100 mcg/cow IM or IV once. (Equivalent to approximately 2 mL per cow for gonadorelin diacetate tetrahydrate.)

Regulatory Information

No withdrawal times are necessary (zero days).

Gonadotropin, Chorionic

go-nad-o-tro′pin, kor-ee-ahn′ik

Trade and Other Names: Profasi, Pregnyl, A.P.L., and generic brands

Functional Classification: Hormone

Pharmacology and Mechanism of Action

Gonadotropin is also referred to as human chorionic gonadotropin (hCG). Action of hCG is identical to that of luteinizing hormone (LH).

Indications and Clinical Uses

Gonadotropin is used to induce luteinization in animals. Gonadotropin has been used to manage various reproductive disorders where stimulation of ovulation is desired.

Precautionary Information

Adverse Reactions and Side Effects

Adverse effects have not been reported in animals.

Contraindications and Precautions

Do not administer to pregnant animals.

Drug Interactions

No specific drug interactions are reported.

Instructions for Use

When used in horses, most ovulate 32-40 hours after treatment.

Patient Monitoring and Laboratory Tests

Monitor treated patients for signs of luteinization and estrus.

Formulations

HCG is available in 5000, 10,000, and 20,000 unit injections.

Stability and Storage

Store in tightly sealed container, protected from light, and at room temperature. Stability of compounded formulations has not been evaluated.

Small Animal Dosage

Dogs

- 22 units/kg q24-48h IM or 44 units once IM.

Cats

- 250 units/cat once IM.

Large Animal Dosage

Horses

- Ovulation induction: 2500 to 5000 units IM or IV.

Regulatory Information

No regulatory information is available for food animals. Because of low risk of residues, no withdrawal times are suggested.

Granisetron Hydrochloride

grah-nih'seh-tron hye-droe-klor'ide

Trade and Other Names: Kytril

Functional Classification: Antiemetic

Pharmacology and Mechanism of Action

Antiemetic drug from the class of drugs called serotonin antagonists. These drugs act by inhibiting serotonin (5-HT, type 3) receptors. During chemotherapy, there may be 5-HT released from injury to the GI tract that stimulates vomiting centrally, which is blocked by this class of drugs. These drugs also have been used to treat vomiting from other forms of gastroenteritis. Serotonin antagonists used for antiemetic therapy include granisetron, ondansetron, dolasetron, azestron, and tropisetron.

Indications and Clinical Uses

Granisetron, like other serotonin antagonists, is used primarily for antiemetic during chemotherapy, for which they generally have been superior to other drugs in efficacy. It may be administered prior to chemotherapy to prevent nausea and vomiting.

Precautionary Information

Adverse Reactions and Side Effects

None reported in dogs or cats. These drugs have little affinity for other serotonin receptors.

Contraindications and Precautions

No contraindications reported in animals.

Drug Interactions

No interactions are reported. It may be used with cancer chemotherapy agents.

Instructions for Use

There have been only limited uses of this class of antiemetic drugs used in veterinary patients. Most doses have been extrapolated from human uses.

Patient Monitoring and Laboratory Tests

No specific monitoring is necessary.

Formulations

Granisetron is available in 1 mg tablets and 1 mg/mL injection.

Stability and Storage

Store in tightly sealed container, protected from light, and at room temperature. Discard opened vial after 30 days. Compounded solutions are stable in various fluids for 24 hours. Oral compounded formulations have been prepared in juices, syrups, and flavorings and were stable for 14 days.

Small Animal Dosage

Dogs and Cats

- 0.01 mg/kg IV; oral doses have been extrapolated from people (1 mg/person PO).

Large Animal Dosage

No large animal doses have been reported.

Regulatory Information

No regulatory information is available for food animals. Because of low risk of residues, no withdrawal times are suggested.

Griseofulvin

grizs-ee-oh-ful'vin

Trade and Other Names: Microsize: Fulvicin U/F, Grisactin, and Grifulvin and Ultramicrosize: Fulvicin P/G, and GrisPEG

Functional Classification: Antifungal

Pharmacology and Mechanism of Action

Antifungal drug. After systemic administration, griseofulvin is deposited in the keratin precursor cells of the skin and hair. It is rapidly taken up into these tissues within 4-8 hours or 48-72 hours (depending on the study) after administration. Once it is incorporated into these cells, mitosis of the fungal cells is inhibited by effects on the mitotic spindle, and eventually fungal cells are killed.

Indications and Clinical Uses

Griseofulvin is one of the drugs of choice when systemic treatment is needed for dermatophyte infections caused by *Microsporum* spp., and *Trichophyton* spp. in dogs and cats. It is sometimes used in combination with topical therapy. Griseofulvin is not effective for the treatment of yeasts or bacteria. At least 4 weeks, and sometimes 3 months or more, are needed for successful therapy. Its use has been replaced by azole antifungal drugs in many cases (itraconazole, fluconazole, etc.). It also has a predilection to accumulate in inflammatory sites of the skin and may be effective for treating some noninfectious, inflammatory dermatoses other than dermatomycosis.

Precautionary Information

Adverse Reactions and Side Effects

Adverse effects in animals include teratogenicity in cats, anemia and leukopenia in cats, anorexia, depression, vomiting, and diarrhea. In cats, feline immunodeficiency virus (FIV) infection may increase the risk of bone marrow toxicosis. Whether the bone marrow problems are caused by high doses or is an idiosyncratic (non-dose related) reaction is not understood. These effects resolve in cats when treatment is stopped, but irreversible idiosyncratic pancytopenia has been reported.

Contraindications and Precautions

Do not administer to pregnant cats. Caution should be used when administering griseofulvin to cats with viral infections (FIV) as this may exacerbate bone marrow effects.

Drug Interactions

Griseofulvin is an enhancer of cytochrome P450 drug enzymes. Therefore, other concurrent drugs may be metabolized and cleared more quickly if given with griseofulvin.

Instructions for Use

A wide range of doses have been reported. Doses listed here represent the current consensus. Oral absorption is favored in the presence of fat. Administration of the drug with a high fat meal can tremendously enhance the extent of absorption.

Administration of a formulation made up of fine particles also will increase absorption. Two formulations are available, microsize and ultramicrosize. Veterinary formulations are generally composed of microsize preparations, and this is reflected in the dosage regimens. If the ultramicrosized preparations are used, the dose may be decreased by half. Shake oral suspension well before using. Dosing recommendations have varied depending on the source. Consider 25 mg/kg q12h initially, and then increase to 50-60 mg/kg q12h for problem cases.

Patient Monitoring and Laboratory Tests

Monitor CBC for evidence of bone marrow toxicity.

Formulations

Griseofulvin is available in 125, 250, and 500 mg microsize tablets, 25 mg/mL oral suspension, 125 mg/mL oral syrup, and 100, 125, 165, 250, and 330 mg ultramicrosized tablets.

Stability and Storage

Store in tightly sealed container, protected from light, and at room temperature. Griseofulvin is insoluble in water but is soluble in alcohol.

Small Animal Dosage

Dogs and Cats

- Microsize: 50 mg/kg per day PO, up to a maximum dose of 110-132 mg/kg/day in divided treatments. Start with 25 mg/kg q12h PO and then increase to 50-60 mg/kg q12h PO for refractory cases.
- Ultramicrosize: 30 mg/kg/day in divided treatments PO.

Large Animal Dosage

Horses

- Dermatophytosis: 5.6 mg/kg q24h of the oral microsize powder. Treatment should be continued for minimum of 10 days.

Regulatory Information

No regulatory information is available for food animals. Because of potential for teratogenic effects, do not administer to food animals.

Growth Hormone

Trade and Other Names: Somatrem, Somatropin, Protropin, Humatrope, and Nutropin

Functional Classification: Hormone

Pharmacology and Mechanism of Action

Growth hormone, also known as human growth hormone (hCG). It is administered to correct growth hormone deficiency in animals. Somatrem is a biosynthetic somatropin.

Indications and Clinical Uses

Growth hormone is used to treat growth hormone deficiencies. The use is rare in veterinary medicine.

Precautionary Information

Adverse Reactions and Side Effects

Growth hormone is diabetogenic in all animals. Excess growth hormone causes acromegaly.

Contraindications and Precautions

No contraindications reported in animals.

Drug Interactions

No drug interactions are reported in animals.

Instructions for Use

There is only limited clinical experience in animals. Dose form must be reconstituted with sterile diluent before use.

Patient Monitoring and Laboratory Tests

Monitor glucose periodically during treatment.

Formulations

Growth hormone is available in 5 and 10 mg/vial (1 mg is equal to 3 units).

Stability and Storage

Prepared solution is stable if refrigerated for 14 days. Otherwise it is stable for only 24 hours.

Small Animal Dosage

- 0.1 units/kg three times a week for 4-6 weeks SQ or IM. (Usual human pediatric dose is 0.18-0.3 mg/kg/week SQ or IM.)

Large Animal Dosage

No large animal doses have been reported.

Regulatory Information

Do not administer to animals that produce food.

Guaifenesin

gwye-fen'eh-sin

Trade and Other Names: Glyderyl guaiacolate, Guaiphenesin, Geocolate, Guailaxin, Glycotuss, Hytuss, Glytuss, Fenesin, Humabid LA, and Mucinex

Functional Classification: Expectorant; Muscle relaxant

Pharmacology and Mechanism of Action

Guaifenesin, which is also known as glyderyl guaiacolate, is a compound that has been an older, traditional therapy for treating cough in people, although the efficacy has been questioned for this effect. For respiratory disease, it is administered orally to produce an expectorant effect. This effect is presumably via stimulation of vagal transmission to produce more viscous bronchial secretions.

As an anesthetic adjunct, it is used as a pre-anesthetic with barbiturates and other drugs. It is a central acting skeletal muscle relaxant and causes sedation and relaxation via depression of nerve transmission. Pharmacokinetic information is limited, but half-life in ponies is 60-84 minutes. Duration of action in horses is approximately 30 minutes.

Indications and Clinical Uses

Guaifenesin is administered IV (particularly in large animals) as an adjunct to anesthesia and orally in animals as an expectorant. Historically, it also has been used as an analgesic and antipyretic. Most often it is used prior to induction of general anesthesia in horses, but it also has been used in other species. Supporting data for an expectorant effect is lacking. It may increase the volume and reduce the viscosity of secretions in the trachea and bronchi. It may also facilitate removal of secretions.

Precautionary Information

Adverse Reactions and Side Effects

Minor leakage outside the vein from an intravenous injection does not cause tissue injury. However, thrombophlebitis from intravenous injection may occur. Hypotension may occur from high doses. Some hemolysis has been observed from intravenous infusion, but this is not significant at concentration less than 15%. A vagal effect (e.g., stimulation of secretions) may occur when the drug is used as an expectorant.

Contraindications and Precautions

Do not administer IV if visible precipitate is observed.
Formulations for people may contain other ingredients such as dextromethorphan or decongestants (e.g., pseudoephedrine). Do not use these combinations in animals sensitive to these drugs, and if possible use only formulations that contain guaifenesin.

Drug Interactions

No significant drug interactions are reported. It has been safely used with acepromazine, xylazine, detomidine, ketamine, thiopental, and pentobarbital.

Instructions for Use

For anesthetic purposes, 5% guaifenesin is prepared from powder (50 grams/L) dissolved in sterile water. It dissolves more readily if the water is warm. Infusion of 110 mg/kg can produce transient recumbency, but usually it is administered with other agents.

Patient Monitoring and Laboratory Tests

Monitoring of animals during anesthesia (heart rate, rhythm, and respiratory rate) is suggested. Hypotension is possible; therefore blood pressure should be monitored.

Formulations

Guaifenesin is available in intravenous solutions and are prepared prior to infusion from powder to a 5% solution. It is also available in 100 and 200 mg tablet, 600 mg extended release tablets, and 20 mg/mL and 40 mg/mL oral solution. Human over-the-counter formulations may contain other ingredients such as dextromethorphan and decongestants.

Stability and Storage

Guaifenesin is soluble in water and in alcohol. It is more soluble in warm water. It will precipitate if the temperature is 22° C or colder. It should be administered orally shortly after preparation because stability is short. However, 10% solutions have been stable for as long as 7 days. For intravenous use it has been mixed with xylazine and ketamine, without apparent loss of stability.

Small Animal Dosage

Dogs

- Expectorant: 3-5 mg/kg q8h PO.
- Anesthetic adjunct: 2.2 mL/kg/hr of a 5% solution intravenously. Administered with $alpha_2$ agonists and ketamine.

Cats

- Expectorant: 3-5 mg/kg q8h PO.

Large Animal Dosage

Horses

- 2.2 mL/kg of a 5% solution (110 mg/kg) infused IV to horses prior to other anesthetic agents, such as ketamine. Guaifenesin solution may be infused rapidly.
- Constant Rate Infusion (CRI): 2.2 mg/kg/hr IV.

Regulatory Information

Withdrawal time (extralabel): 3 days meat and 48 hours milk.

RCI Classification: 4

Halothane

hal'oe-thane

Trade and Other Names: Fluothane

Functional Classification: Inhalant anesthetic

Pharmacology and Mechanism of Action

Inhalant anesthetic. Halothane is a multi-halogenated ethane. It is characterized by rapid induction and recovery, high potency, and few adverse effects. Like other inhalant anesthetics, the mechanism of action is uncertain. They produce generalized, reversible, depression of the CNS. The inhalant anesthetics vary in their solubility in blood, their potency, and the rate of induction and recovery. Those with low blood/gas partition coefficients are associated with the most rapid rates of induction and recovery. Halothane has a vapor pressure of 243 mm Hg (at 20° C), a blood/gas partition coefficient of 2.3, and a fat/blood coefficient of 51. Because of high solubility in fat, its clearance from the body is slower than other agents.

Indications and Clinical Uses

Halothane, like other inhalant anesthetics, is used for general anesthesia in animals. It has a minimum alveolar concentration (MAC) value of 1.04%, 0.87%, and 0.88% in cats, dogs, and horses, respectively. However, it has been replaced by newer inhalant anesthetics (e.g., isoflurane) in many veterinary practices.

Precautionary Information

Adverse Reactions and Side Effects

Like other inhalant anesthetics, halothane produces vasodilation and increased blood flow to cerebral blood vessels. This may increase intracranial pressure. Like other inhalant anesthetics, it produces a dose-dependent myocardial depression, with accompanying decrease in cardiac output. It also depresses respiratory rate and alveolar ventilation. Like other inhalant anesthetics, it increases the risk of ventricular arrhythmias, especially in response to catecholamines. Hepatotoxicity has been reported in people.

Contraindications and Precautions

Administer with caution to patients with cardiovascular problems.

Drug Interactions

No specific drug interactions. Use of other anesthetics in conjunction with halothane will lower the requirement for halothane dose.

Instructions for Use

Use of inhalant anesthetics requires careful monitoring. Dose is determined by depth of anesthesia.

Patient Monitoring and Laboratory Tests

Monitor patient's heart rate and rhythm and respiration during anesthesia.

Formulations

Halothane is available in a 250 mL bottle.

Stability and Storage

Halothane is highly volatile and should be stored in tightly sealed container.

Small Animal Dosage

- Induction: 3%
- Maintenance: 0.5%-1.5%

Large Animal Dosage

- MAC value: 1%

Regulatory Information

No withdrawal times are established for food animals. Clearance is rapid and short withdrawal times are suggested. For extralabel use withdrawal interval estimates, contact FARAD at 1-888-USFARAD (1-888-873-2723) or send e-mail to FARAD@ncsu.edu.

Hemoglobin Glutamer

hee'moe-gloe-bin gloot'am-er

Trade and Other Names: Oxyglobin

Functional Classification: Iron supplement, hemoglobin substitute

Pharmacology and Mechanism of Action

Hemoglobin glutamer (bovine) is used as oxygen-carrying fluid in dogs with varying causes of anemia. Oxyglobin is an ultrapurified polymerized bovine hemoglobin. Osmolality is 300 mOsm/mL. Colloid osmotic pressure is higher than other colloids. Half-life of this drug is 18-43 hours. According to the manufacturer, 95% of a dose is eliminated in 4-9 days.

Indications and Clinical Uses

Hemoglobin glutamer has been used to treat anemia caused by blood loss, hemolysis, or decreased blood cell production. Although licensed for dogs, it also has been used in cats.

Precautionary Information

Adverse Reactions and Side Effects

Transient hemoglobinuria. Adverse pulmonary effects can occur from rapid administration (circulatory overload). Pulmonary hypertension has been observed because of depletion of nitric oxide (NO) and volume overload. Other adverse effects have been skin discoloration, vomiting, diarrhea, and anorexia. Discoloration of skin and mucous membranes can persist for 3-5 days.

Contraindications and Precautions

Hemoglobin glutamer should not be used in dogs with advanced heart disease. Administer with caution to cats, because pulmonary hypertension has been observed in cats.

Drug Interactions

Do not administer with other drugs via the same infusion set. Do not mix with other drugs.

Instructions for Use

Administer using aseptic technique. In 5-7 days, 90% of dose is eliminated.

Patient Monitoring and Laboratory Tests

Patients receiving hemoglobin glutamer should be monitored carefully. Use of Oxyglobin does not require cross-matching. Monitoring packed cell volume (PCV) or hematocrit is not useful for assessing response to Oxyglobin therapy. Oxyglobin will interfere with other monitoring tests, such as blood chemistry analysis. Doses of 30 mL/kg are listed by manufacturer, but many veterinarians use 10-15 mL/kg.

Formulations

Hemoglobin glutamer is available in 13 g/dL polymerized hemoglobin of bovine origin in 125 mL single-dose bags. Availability from manufacturer may be limited.

Stability and Storage

At room temperature, hemoglobin glutamer has a 2-year shelf-life. Do **not** freeze.

Small Animal Dosage

Dogs

- One-time dose of 10-30 mL/kg IV or up to a rate of 10 mL/kg/hr.

Cats

- One-time dose of 3-5 mL/kg IV, slowly.

Large Animal Dosage

No doses reported. Do not use in race horses.

Regulatory Information

No regulatory information is available. Because of low risk of residues, no withdrawal times are suggested. However, hemoglobin glutamer (Oxyglobin) is prohibited to be on the premises of racing horses.
RCI Classification: 2

Heparin Sodium

hep'ah-rin soe'dee-um

Trade and Other Names: Liquaemin and Hepalean (Canada)

Functional Classification: Anticoagulant

Pharmacology and Mechanism of Action

Anticoagulant. Heparin produces its action by increasing antithrombin III mediated inhibition of synthesis and activity of factor Xa. Heparin differs from low-molecular weight heparin (LMWH) by an equal Anti-factor Xa/anti-factor IIa ratio. Heparin has a ratio of 1:1, but the LMWHs have ratios of 2:1 or higher.

Indications and Clinical Uses

Heparin is administered to prevent or treat thrombotic disease in animals.
Use in specific situations is primarily anecdotal. Use for prevention of thrombosis in canine patients with immune-mediated hemolytic anemia has not been effective (300 units/kg q6h).

Precautionary Information

Adverse Reactions and Side Effects

Adverse effects caused by excessive inhibition of coagulation result in bleeding.

Contraindications and Precautions

Do not use in animals unless able to monitor bleeding, because it may be life threatening.

Drug Interactions

Use cautiously in animals that are already receiving other drugs that can interfere with coagulation, such as aspirin and warfarin. Although a specific interaction has not been identified, use cautiously in animals that may be receiving certain chondroprotective compounds, such as glycosaminoglycans for treatment of arthritis.

Instructions for Use

Dose adjustments should be performed by monitoring clotting times. For example, dose is adjusted to maintain activated partial thromboplastin time (APTT) at 1.5 to 2 times normal. For information on other forms of heparin, such as LMWHs, see dalteparin or enoxaparin.

In high-risk patients, doses used include 500 units/kg SQ or IM, followed by reduced doses such as those listed in dosing section q8-12h.

Patient Monitoring and Laboratory Tests

Monitor effect using APTT. Dose is adjusted to maintain APTT at 1.5 to 2 times normal.

Formulations

Heparin sodium is available in 1000 and 10,000 units/mL injection.

Stability and Storage

Store in tightly sealed container, protected from light, and at room temperature.

Small Animal Dosage

Dogs and Cats

- 100-200 units/kg IV loading dose, then 100-300 units/kg q6-8h SQ.
- Low dose prophylaxis (dog and cat): 70 units/kg q8-12h SQ.

Large Animal Dosage

- 125 units/kg SQ or IM q8-12h.

Regulatory Information

No regulatory information is available for food animals. Because of low risk of residues, no withdrawal times are suggested.

Hetastarch

het'ah-starch

Trade and Other Names: HES, Hetastarch, and Hespan

Functional Classification: Fluid replacement

Pharmacology and Mechanism of Action

Hetastarch is a synthetic colloid volume expander that is used to maintain vascular volume in animals with circulatory shock. It is prepared from hydroxyethyl starch and is derived from amylopectin. Because hetastarch is a large molecular weight compound (450 kd), it tends to remain in the vasculature and prevent loss of intravascular volume and prevent tissue edema. There are two hydroxyethyl starch preparations, hetastarch and pentastarch. Other colloids used are dextrans (Dextran 40 and Dextran 70).

Indications and Clinical Uses

Hetastarch is used primarily to treat acute hypovolemia and shock. It is administered IV in acute situations. Hetastarch has a duration of effective volume expansion of 12-48 hours. One of the disadvantages to use of hetastarch is the high cost.

Precautionary Information

Adverse Reactions and Side Effects

Only limited use in veterinary medicine, therefore adverse effects have not been reported. However, it may cause allergic reactions and hyperosmotic renal dysfunction. Coagulopathies are possible, but rare, at usual doses. Nevertheless, do not use in patients with bleeding problems or preexisting coagulopathies.

Contraindications and Precautions

Do not use in animals with bleeding problems (coagulopathies) or active hemorrhage.

Drug Interactions

Hetastarch is available compatible with most fluid solutions.

Instructions for Use

Hetastarch is used in critical care situations, and it is infused via constant rate infusion (CRI). Hetastarch appears to be more effective and produce fewer side effects than Dextran. Infuse slowly.

Patient Monitoring and Laboratory Tests

Monitor patient's hydration status and blood pressure during administration. Monitor heart rate and rhythm and observe patients for evidence of bleeding. Administration of hetastarch may increase patient's amylase for 2-3 days.

Formulations

Hetastarch is available in 6% injectable solution.

Stability and Storage

Hetastarch is stable in original packaging and is compatible with most fluid administration sets.

Small Animal Dosage

Dogs

- CRI: 10-20 mL/kg/day IV (0.4-0.8 mL/kg/hr).

Cats

- CRI: 5-10 mL/kg/day IV (0.2-0.4 mL/kg/hr).

Large Animal Dosage

No large animal doses have been reported.

Regulatory Information

No regulatory information is available for food animals. Because of low risk of residues, no withdrawal times are suggested.

Hydralazine Hydrochloride

hye-drahl'ah-zeen hye-droe-klor'ide

Trade and Other Names: Apresoline

Functional Classification: Vasodilator

Pharmacology and Mechanism of Action

Vasodilator. Antihypertensive. Hydralazine relaxes vascular smooth muscle and reduces blood pressure. In arteriolar vascular beds it relaxes vascular smooth muscle to reduce vascular resistance and improves cardiac output. The mechanism of action is not certain. It may generate nitric oxide or act via other smooth muscle relaxing properties.

Indications and Clinical Uses

Hydralazine is used to dilate arterioles and decrease cardiac afterload. It is primarily used for treatment of CHF, valvular disease of the heart, and other cardiovascular disorders characterized by high peripheral vascular resistance. It may be used with other cardiac drugs. However, its use is not as common as other vasodilator drugs, such as the angiotensin-converting enzyme (ACE) inhibitors.

Precautionary Information

Adverse Reactions and Side Effects

Adverse effects attributed to excess vasodilation and subsequent hypotension which results in tachycardia. Hydralazine may dangerously decrease cardiac output. Allergic reactions (Lupus-like syndrome) have been reported in people and are related to acetylator status but have not been reported in animals.

Contraindications and Precautions

Do not use in hypotensive animals.

Drug Interactions

No specific drug interactions are reported for animals. However, use cautiously with other drugs that may lower blood pressure.

Instructions for Use

Use of hydralazine in heart failure may accompany other drugs, such as digoxin and diuretics. Dosage in animals may be adjusted by monitoring blood pressure.

Patient Monitoring and Laboratory Tests

Monitor patients for hypotension. Monitor blood pressure to adjust dose.

Formulations

Hydralazine is available in 10 mg tablets and 20 mg/mL injection.

Stability and Storage

Store in tightly sealed container, protected from light, and at room temperature. Exposure to light may change color and cause decomposition. Hydralazine is unstable. Mixing with juices, syrups, and flavorings may cause decomposition in as little as 24 hours.

Small Animal Dosage

Dogs

- 0.5 mg/kg (initial dose), titrate to 0.5-2 mg/kg q12h PO.

Cats

- 2.5 mg/cat q12-24h PO.

Large Animal Dosage

Horses

- 1 mg/kg q12h PO or 0.5 mg/kg IV as needed to reduce blood pressure.

Regulatory Information

No regulatory information is available. For extralabel use withdrawal interval estimates, contact FARAD at 1-888-USFARAD (1-888-873-2723) or send e-mail to FARAD@ncsu.edu.
RCI Classification: 3

Hydrochlorothiazide

hye-droe-klor-oh-thye'ah-zide

Trade and Other Names: HydroDiuril and generic

Functional Classification: Diuretic

Pharmacology and Mechanism of Action

Thiazide diuretic. Like other thiazide diuretics, it inhibits sodium reabsorption in distal renal tubules and causes urinary diuresis. Because thiazide diuretics act in the distal tubules (at the point where most water has already been reabsorbed), their diuretic effects are not as great as compared to loop diuretics such as furosemide.

Indications and Clinical Uses

Like other thiazide diuretics, hydrochlorothiazide is used to increase excretion of sodium, potassium, and water. It also has been used as an antihypertensive. Because thiazide diuretics decrease renal excretion of calcium, they also have been used to treat uroliths containing calcium.

Precautionary Information

Adverse Reactions and Side Effects

Hydrochlorothiazide may cause electrolyte imbalance such as hypokalemia.

Contraindications and Precautions

Do not use in patient with high serum calcium. Thiazide diuretics will prevent calcium excretion.

Drug Interactions

Use carefully with other diuretics. It may enhance the effects of other diuretics and antihypertensive agents.

Instructions for Use

Hydrochlorothiazide is not as potent as loop diuretics (e.g., furosemide). Clinical efficacy has not been established in veterinary patients.

Patient Monitoring and Laboratory Tests

Monitor hydration status, electrolytes, and renal function.

Formulations

Hydrochlorothiazide is available in 10 and 100 mg/mL oral solution and 25, 50, and 100 mg tablets.

Stability and Storage

Store in tightly sealed container, protected from light, and at room temperature. Stability of compounded formulations has not been evaluated.

Small Animal Dosage

Dogs and Cats

- 2-4 mg/kg q12h PO.

Large Animal Dosage

No large animal doses have been reported.

Regulatory Information

No regulatory information is available. For extralabel use withdrawal interval estimates, contact FARAD at 1-888-USFARAD (1-888-873-2723) or send e-mail to FARAD@ncsu.edu.

RCI Classification: 4

Hydrocodone Bitartrate

hye-droe-koe′done bye-tar′trate

Trade and Other Names: Hycodan

Functional Classification: Antitussive, Analgesic

Pharmacology and Mechanism of Action

Opioid agonist, analgesic. Like other opioids, hydrocodone is an agonist for mu-opiate and kappa-opiate receptors on nerves and inhibits release of neurotransmitters involved with transmission of pain stimuli (such as Substance P). Central sedative and euphoric effects related to mu-receptor effects in brain. Other opiates used in animals include hydromorphone, codeine, oxymorphone, meperidine, and fentanyl. Hycodan contains homatropine, which is added to decrease abuse by people. Hydrocodone formulations used for antitussive action may also contain guaifenesin or acetaminophen. Hydrocodone may be metabolized to hydromorphone.

Indications and Clinical Uses

Hydrocodone is an opiate agonist. However, its use as a sedative or analgesic in small animals is uncommon. The oral absorption, metabolism, and efficacy have not been studied in animals to document clinical use. However, hydrocodone has been used in animals as an antitussive for symptomatic treatment of airway diseases. There are no preparations marketed for use in the U.S. that do not contain atropine. (Canadian preparations may contain only hydrocodone.) It may also contain other ingredients for treating cough.

Precautionary Information

Adverse Reactions and Side Effects

Like all opiates, side effects from codeine are predictable and unavoidable. Side effects include sedation, constipation, and bradycardia. Respiratory depression occurs with high doses.

Contraindications and Precautions

Opiate may cause sedation. Do not use in patients that may be sensitive to opiate effects or experience dysphoria. Because preparations for oral use contain atropine, do not use in animals in which atropine may be contraindicated.

Drug Interactions

No specific drug interactions are reported for animals.

Instructions for Use

Hydrocodone is combined with atropine in the product Hycodan. Atropine can decrease respiratory secretions but probably does not exert significant clinical effects at doses in this preparation (1.5 mg homatropine per 5 mg tablet).

Patient Monitoring and Laboratory Tests

No specific monitoring is necessary.

Formulations

Hydrocodone is available in 5 mg tablets and 1 mg/mL syrup.

Stability and Storage

Store in tightly sealed container, protected from light, and at room temperature.

Small Animal Dosage

Dogs

- 0.22 mg/kg q4-8 hr PO.

Cats

No dose available.

Large Animal Dosage

No large animal doses have been reported.

Regulatory Information

Hydrocodone is a Schedule III drug controlled by DEA.
No regulatory information is available. For extralabel use withdrawal interval estimates, contact FARAD at 1-888-USFARAD (1-888-873-2723) or send e-mail to FARAD@ncsu.edu.
Schedule II controlled drug
RCI Classification: 1

Hydrocortisone

hye-droe-kor'tih-sone

Trade and Other Names: Hydrocortisone, Cortef and generic brands Hydrocortisone sodium succinate, Solu-Cortef

Functional Classification: Corticosteroid

Pharmacology and Mechanism of Action

Glucocorticoid antiinflammatory drug. Hydrocortisone has weaker antiinflammatory effects and greater mineralocorticoid effects compared with prednisolone or dexamethasone. It is about 1/5 the potency of prednisolone and 1/25 the potency of dexamethasone. Antiinflammatory effects are complex but primarily via inhibition of inflammatory cells and suppression of expression of inflammatory mediators.

Indications and Clinical Uses

Hydrocortisone is used for antiinflammatory effects and for glucocorticoid replacement therapy. Hydrocortisone is not used as commonly as other corticosteroids such as prednisolone or dexamethasone. Hydrocortisone sodium succinate is a rapid acting injectable product that can be used when a prompt response is needed.

Precautionary Information

Adverse Reactions and Side Effects

Side effects from corticosteroids are many and include polyphagia, polydipsia/polyuria, and hypothalamic-pituitary adrenal (HPA) axis suppression. Adverse effects include GI ulceration, hepatopathy, diabetes, hyperlipidemia, decreased thyroid hormone, decreased protein synthesis, delayed wound healing, and immunosuppression. Secondary infections can occur as a result of immunosuppression and include demodicosis, toxoplasmosis, fungal infections, and UTIs. In horses, additional adverse effects include risk of laminitis.

Contraindications and Precautions

Use cautiously in patients prone to ulcers, infection, or in animals in which wound healing is necessary. Use cautiously, in diabetic animals, animals with renal failure, or pregnant animals.

Drug Interactions

Glucocorticoids are often synergistic with other antiinflammatory and immunosuppressive drugs. Administration of corticosteroids with nonsteroidal antiinflammatory drugs (NSAIDs) will increase the risk of GI injury.

Instructions for Use

Dose requirements are related to severity of disease. Typically for replacement therapy (such as in animals with hypoadrenocorticism) doses start at 1 mg/kg/day.

Patient Monitoring and Laboratory Tests

Monitor electrolytes (sodium and potassium) in animals being treated for hypoadrenocorticism. Monitor liver enzymes, blood glucose, and renal function during therapy. Monitor patients for signs of secondary infections. Perform adrenocorticotropic hormone (ACTH) stimulation test to monitor adrenal function.

Formulations

Hydrocortisone is available in 5, 10, and 20 mg tablets and hydrocortisone sodium succinate is available in various size vials for injection.

Stability and Storage

Store in tightly sealed container, protected from light, and at room temperature. Hydrocortisone is slightly soluble in water and is soluble in alcohol. Degradation occurs at high pH above 7-9. Compounded suspensions have been stable for 30 days. Most compounded topical ointments and lotions are stable for 30 days.

Small Animal Dosage

Dogs and Cats

Hydrocortisone

- Replacement therapy: 1-2 mg/kg q12h PO.
- Antiinflammatory: 2.5-5 mg/kg q12h PO.

Hydrocortisone sodium succinate

- Shock: 50-150 mg/kg IV, for 2 doses, 8 hours apart.
- Antiinflammatory: 5 mg/kg q12h IV.

Large Animal Dosage

Horses

- Hydrocortisone sodium succinate: 5 mg/kg q12h IV.

Regulatory Information

No regulatory information is available. For extralabel use withdrawal interval estimates, contact FARAD at 1-888-USFARAD (1-888-873-2723) or send e-mail to FARAD@ncsu.edu.

RCI Classification: 4

Hydromorphone

hye-droe-mor′fone

Trade and Other Names: Dilaudid, Hydrostat, and generic brands

Functional Classification: Analgesic, Opiate

Pharmacology and Mechanism of Action

Opioid agonist, analgesic. Like other opiates, it binds to mu-opiate and kappa-opiate receptors on nerves and inhibits release of neurotransmitters involved with transmission of pain stimuli (such as Substance P). Opiates also may inhibit release of some inflammatory mediators. Central sedative and euphoric effects related to mu-receptor effects in brain. Hydromorphone is 6 or 7 times more potent than morphine. In dogs, the half-life after IV administration was 70-80 minutes. Other opiates used in animals include morphine, codeine, oxymorphone, meperidine, and fentanyl.

Indications and Clinical Uses

Hydromorphone is an opiate agonist, with effects similar to morphine. However, it is more potent than morphine and should be used at lower doses. Because hydromorphone is less expensive than oxymorphone, there is increased use in veterinary medicine. Hydromorphone is approximately half as potent as oxymorphone, and 5-7 times as potent as morphine. Studies in dogs indicate that hydromorphone at equivalent doses, is equal to oxymorphone for producing sedation in dogs (*J Am Vet Med Assoc*, 218:1101-1105, 2001). In cats, duration of effect (0.1 mg/kg) has been 6-7.5 hours. Hydromorphone is used in animals for analgesia, sedation, and as an adjunct for anesthesia. In dogs and cats it is used as a single agent or in combination with other agents.

Precautionary Information

Adverse Reactions and Side Effects

Like all opiates, side effects from hydromorphone are predictable and unavoidable. Side effects from administration include sedation, panting, constipation, urinary retention, and bradycardia.

Respiratory depression occurs with high doses. As with other opiates, a slight decrease in heart rate is expected. In most cases this decrease does not have to be treated with anticholinergic drugs (e.g., atropine) but should be monitored. Tolerance and dependence occurs with chronic administration. In horses, undesirable and even dangerous behavior actions can follow rapid intravenous opioid administration. Horses should receive a pre-anesthetic of acepromazine or an $alpha_2$ agonist.

Contraindications and Precautions

Cats and horses are more sensitive to excitement than other species. Hydromorphone may cause bradycardia and AV block in some patients.

Drug Interactions

No significant interactions. Hydromorphone may be used with other anesthetics. If butorphanol is used, it may diminish the effects of hydromorphone by antagonizing mu-opiate receptors.

Instructions for Use

Hydromorphone may be used interchangeably with morphine, provided that doses are adjusted for potency differences. Oral tablets and solution are available for human use, but use has not been reported for animals.

Patient Monitoring and Laboratory Tests

Monitor patient's heart rate and respiration. Although bradycardia rarely needs to be treated when it is caused by an opioid, if necessary atropine or glycopyrrolate can be administered. If serious respiratory depression occurs, the opioid can be reversed with naloxone.

Formulations

Hydromorphone is available in 1 mg/mL oral solution, 1, 2, 3, 4, 8 mg tablets, and 1, 2, 4, and 10 mg/mL injection.

Stability and Storage

Store in tightly sealed container, protected from light, and at room temperature. Hydromorphone is soluble in water. Compounded solutions in fluids have been stable for 30 days. It is schedule II drug and should be store in locked compartment.

Small Animal Dosage

Dogs

- 0.22 mg/kg IM or SQ. Repeat every 4-6 hours or as needed for pain treatment.
- 0.1-0.2 mg/kg IV, repeated every 2 hours or as necessary. A dose of 0.1 mg/kg may be used with acepromazine.

Cats

- 0.1-0.2 mg/kg IM or 0.05-0.1 mg/kg IV.

In animals, oral doses have not been evaluated and may not be absorbed. Oral doses used in people are generally 0.03 to 0.15 mg/kg q4-6h, as needed for pain.

Large Animal Dosage

No large animal doses have been reported.

Regulatory Information

Hydromorphone is a schedule II drug controlled by DEA.
No regulatory information is available. For extralabel use withdrawal interval estimates, contact FARAD at 1-888-USFARAD (1-888-873-2723) or send e-mail to FARAD@ncsu.edu.
RCI Classification: 1

Hydroxyurea

hye-droks'ih-yoo-ree-ah

Trade and Other Names: Droxia and Hydrea (Canada)

Functional Classification: Anticancer agent

Pharmacology and Mechanism of Action

Antineoplastic agent. Hydroxyurea is a cell-cycle dependent agent, acting primarily at the S-phase of mitosis. Exact mechanism of action is uncertain, but it may interfere with DNA synthesis in cancer cells. The effects on red blood cells (RBCs) occur because of effects on hemoglobin in cells.

Indications and Clinical Uses

In people, hydroxyurea is used for treatment of sickle cell anemia and occasionally other carcinomas. In animals it has been used in combination with other anticancer modalities for treatment of certain tumors. In animals one of the uses has been treatment of polycythemia vera.

Precautionary Information

Adverse Reactions and Side Effects

Because of only limited use in veterinary medicine, no adverse effects have been reported. In people, hydroxyurea causes leukopenia, anemia, and thrombocytopenia.

Contraindications and Precautions

Avoid use in pregnant animals.

Drug Interactions

No specific drug interactions are reported for animals.

Instructions for Use

Hydroxyurea has been used on a limited basis in veterinary medicine. Most of the use is empirical or extrapolated from human medicine.

Patient Monitoring and Laboratory Tests

Monitor CBC in treated animals.

Formulations

Hydroxyurea is available in 200, 300, 400, and 500 mg capsules.

Stability and Storage

Store in tightly sealed container, protected from light, and at room temperature.

Small Animal Dosage

Dogs

- 50 mg/kg PO once daily, 3 days/week.

Cats

- 25 mg/kg PO once daily, 3 days/week.

Large Animal Dosage

No large animal doses have been reported.

Regulatory Information

Withdrawal times are not established for animals that produce food. This drug should not be used in animals intended for food, because it is an anticancer agent.

Hydroxyzine

hye-droks′ih-zeen

Trade and Other Names: Atarax

Functional Classification: Antihistamine

Pharmacology and Mechanism of Action

Antihistamine (H_1 blocker) of the piperazine class. Like other antihistamines, hydroxyzine, it acts by blocking the H_1 receptor and suppresses inflammatory reactions caused by histamine. The H_1 blockers have been used to control pruritus and skin inflammation, rhinorrhea, and airway inflammation. One of the newer drugs—cetirizine—is the active metabolite of hydroxyzine. They are of almost equal potency.

Indications and Clinical Uses

In animals it has been used to treat pruritus. Efficacy in animals for treating pruritus is low. Other uses include allergic airway disease and rhinitis. However, efficacy is not established for these uses.

Precautionary Information

Adverse Reactions and Side Effects

Sedation is most common side effect. Sedation is the result of inhibition of histamine N-methyltransferase. Sedation may also be attributed to block of other CNS receptors such as those for serotonin, acetylcholine, and alpha-receptors. Antimuscarinic effects (atropine-like effects) also are common such as dry mouth and decreased GI secretions.

Contraindications and Precautions

No contraindications reported in animals.

Drug Interactions

No specific drug interactions are reported for animals.

Instructions for Use

Clinical studies have shown hydroxyzine to be somewhat effective for treatment of pruritus in dogs, but efficacy rates are low.

Patient Monitoring and Laboratory Tests
No specific monitoring is necessary.

Formulations
Hydroxyzine is available in 10, 25, and 50 mg tablets and 2 mg/mL oral solution.

Stability and Storage
Store in tightly sealed container, protected from light, and at room temperature. Hydroxyzine is soluble in water. Compounded formulation with syrups was stable for 14 days.

Small Animal Dosage
Dogs
- 1-2 mg/kg q6-8h IM or PO.

Cats
Effective doses have not been established.

Large Animal Dosage
No large animal doses have been reported.

Regulatory Information
No regulatory information is available for food animals. Because of low risk of residues, no withdrawal times are suggested.
RCI Classification: 2

Hyoscyamine
hye-oh-sye′ah-meen

Trade and Other Names: Levsin

Functional Classification: Anticholinergic

Pharmacology and Mechanism of Action
Anticholinergic agent (blocks acetylcholine effect at muscarinic receptor), parasympatholytic.

Indications and Clinical Uses
Hyoscyamine is an anticholinergic drug with actions similar to atropine and related drugs. It will produce an antiemetic effect to decrease vomiting associated with motion sickness, and some GI diseases. It is indicated in animals for conditions in which it is important to block parasympathetic responses. It has been used to decrease GI motility and secretions, decrease salivation, and increase heart rate (to treat bradycardia).

Precautionary Information
Adverse Reactions and Side Effects
Side effects include xerostomia, ileus, constipation, tachycardia, and urine retention.

Contraindications and Precautions
Do not use in patients with glaucoma, intestinal ileus, gastroparesis, or tachycardia.

Drug Interactions
Do not mix with alkaline solutions. Hyoscyamine will antagonize the effects of any cholinergic drugs administered (e.g., metoclopramide).

Instructions for Use

Hyoscyamine is used primarily in dogs for cardiovascular and GI diseases.

Patient Monitoring and Laboratory Tests

Monitor heart rate and intestinal motility during treatment.

Formulations

Hyoscyamine is available in 0.125 mg tablets, 0.375 extended-release tablets, and 0.025 mg/mL solution.

Stability and Storage

Store in tightly sealed container at room temperature.

Small Animal Dosage

Dogs

- 0.003-0.006 mg/kg q8h PO.

Large Animal Dosage

No large animal doses have been reported.

Regulatory Information

Do not use in animals that produce food.

Withdrawal time: None established in U.S. (manufacturer of large animal products lists 0 days milk and meat), but listed as 14 days for meat and 3 days for milk in the U.K.

Ibuprofen

eye-byoo-proe′fen

Trade and Other Names: Motrin, Advil, and Nuprin

Functional Classification: Nonsteroidal antiinflammatory drug (NSAID)

Pharmacology and Mechanism of Action

Like other NSAIDs in this class, ibuprofen produces analgesic and antiinflammatory effects by inhibiting the synthesis of prostaglandins. The enzyme inhibited by NSAIDs is the cyclo-oxygenase enzyme (COX). The COX enzyme exists in two isoforms, called COX-1 and COX-2. COX-1 is primarily responsible for synthesis of prostaglandins important for maintaining a healthy GI tract, renal function, platelet function, and other normal functions. COX-2 is induced and responsible for synthesizing prostaglandins that are important mediators of pain, inflammation, and fever. (There may be some crossover of COX-1 and COX-2 effects in some situations.) Ibuprofen is not selective for either COX-1 or COX-2. Ibuprofen is registered for human use and experience with this drug in veterinary medicine is limited.

Pharmacokinetics have been studied in a variety of animals. In horses, the half-life is approximately 60-90 minutes. Oral absorption is high in horses (80%-90%) regardless of the dose form used, including a compounded paste. Ibuprofen was 90%-100% absorbed when administered orally to dairy goats.

Indications and Clinical Uses

Ibuprofen is not registered for any animals in veterinary medicine. There are drugs in small animals that have been safer for the GI tract and are preferred. Use of ibuprofen in dogs is discouraged because of high risk of GI ulceration. It has been used for musculoskeletal inflammation in horses and ruminants. Administration of 25 mg/kg IV to cows reduced some systemic variables in endotoxin-induced mastitis.

In horses, doses of 10-25 mg/kg have been used, but clinical trials of efficacy have not been reported.

Precautionary Information

Adverse Reactions and Side Effects

Vomiting, severe gastrointestinal ulceration, and hemorrhage have been reported in dogs. Like other NSAIDs, renal injury caused by decrease renal perfusion has occurred with ibuprofen. Ibuprofen may inhibit platelets in animals.

Contraindications and Precautions

Safe doses have not been established for dogs and cats. Do not administer to animals prone to GI ulcers. Do not administer with other ulcerogenic, drugs such as corticosteroids.

Drug Interactions

No specific drug interactions are reported. However, like other NSAIDs ulcerogenic effects are potentiated when administered with corticosteroids. Ibuprofen, like other NSAIDs, may interfere with the action of diuretics, such as furosemide and angiotensin-converting enzymes (ACE) inhibitors.

Instructions for Use

Avoid use in dogs. Safe dose for other species have not been established, although there has been some off-label use in ruminants and horses.

Patient Monitoring and Laboratory Tests

Monitor for signs of GI ulcers. Monitor renal function during therapy.

Formulations

Ibuprofen is available in 200, 400, 600, and 800 mg tablets.

Stability and Storage

Store in tightly sealed container, protected from light, and at room temperature. It has been compounded in alcohol (ethanol), and propylene glycol solutions without loss of stability. It is poorly soluble in water. It has been compounded as an oral paste for horses without compromising the oral absorption.

Small Animal Dosage

Dogs and Cats

Safe dose not established.

Large Animal Dosage

Horses

- 25 mg/kg q8h PO, up to 6 days.

Ruminants

- 14-25 mg/kg/day.

Regulatory Information

No withdrawal times are established for animal intended for food. For extralabel use withdrawal interval estimates, contact FARAD at 1-888-USFARAD (1-888-873-2723) or send e-mail to FARAD@ncsu.edu.

RCI Classification: 4

Imidocarb Hydrochloride

im-id'oh-carb hye-droe-klor'ide

Trade and Other Names: Imizol

Functional Classification: Antiprotozoal

Pharmacology and Mechanism of Action

Imidocarb is an aromatic diamidine. It inhibits nucleic acid metabolism in susceptible organisms. It is used as an antiprotozoal drug, specifically for treating *Babesia* infections.

Indications and Clinical Uses

Imidocarb has been used in animals to treat intracellular tick-borne pathogens. It has been used to treat *Babesia* infections. In addition, it has been used to treat haemobartonellosis in cats caused by the organisms *Mycoplasma haemofelis* and *Mycoplasma haemominutum*. It also has been used to treat *Cytauxzoon felis* infections in cats and ehrlichial infections in dogs and cats.

Precautionary Information

Adverse Reactions and Side Effects

No toxic reactions were observed in trials with experimental cats. Transient pain or discomfort may occur at site of injection.

Contraindications and Precautions

No specific contraindications are reported.

Drug Interactions

No drug interactions reported.

Instructions for Use

Use of imidocarb has been limited in animals. Most protocols are established from small clinical trials or extrapolation from human use.

Patient Monitoring and Laboratory Tests

No specific monitoring is necessary.

Formulations

Imidocarb compounded formulations are available from some pharmacies.

Stability and Storage

Store in tightly sealed container, protected from light, and at room temperature.

Small Animal Dosage

Cats

- 5 mg/kg IM twice, q14d.

Large Animal Dosage

No large animal doses are available.

Regulatory Information

No regulatory information is available. For extralabel use withdrawal interval estimates, contact FARAD at 1-888-USFARAD (1-888-873-2723) or send e-mail to FARAD@ncsu.edu.

Imipenem + Cilastatin

ih-mih-pen′em + sye-lah-stat′in

Trade and Other Names: Primaxin

Functional Classification: Antibacterial

Pharmacology and Mechanism of Action

Imipenem + cilastatin is a beta-lactam antibiotic of the carbapenems class with a broad spectrum of activity. Action on cell wall is similar to other beta-lactams, which is to bind penicillin-binding proteins (PBP) that weaken or interfere with cell wall formation. The carbapenems bind to a specific PBP (PBP-1) that results in more rapid lysis compared to other beta-lactams. This results in greater bactericidal activity and a longer postantibiotic effect. Carbapenems have a broad spectrum of activity and are among the most active of all antibiotics. Spectrum includes gram-negative bacilli, including *Enterobacteriaceae* and *Pseudomonas aeruginosa*. It also is active against most gram-positive bacteria, except methicillin-resistant strains of *Staphylococcus* and *Enterococcus.* Compared to imipenem, meropenem is slightly more active. Cilastatin has no antibacterial activity, but it is a specific inhibitor of renal dipeptidase, dehydropeptidase (DHP-I). Therefore, cilastatin blocks renal tubular metabolism of imipenem and improving urinary recovery of imipenem.

Indications and Clinical Uses

Imipenem is used primarily for infections caused by bacteria resistant to other drugs. Imipenem is especially valuable for treating resistant infections caused by *Pseudomonas aeruginosa, Escherichia coli,* and *Klebsiella pneumoniae.* Although active against gram-positive bacteria, such as staphylococci (but not methicillin-resistant strains), other less expensive drugs should be used for gram-positive infections. Meropenem is a newer drug in the class of carbapenems and has some advantages with respect to activity and convenience of administration.

Precautionary Information

Adverse Reactions and Side Effects

Allergic reactions may occur with beta-lactam antibiotics. With rapid infusion or in patients with renal insufficiency, neurotoxicity may occur. Neurotoxicity in animals has included tremors, nystagmus, and seizures. Nephrotoxicity is possible, but imipenem is combined with cilastatin to decrease renal metabolism. Vomiting and nausea are possible. Intramuscular injections can cause painful reactions.

Contraindications and Precautions

Use cautiously in patients prone to seizures. Seizures may be more likely in patients with renal failure.

Drug Interactions

No known drug interactions. Do not mix with other drugs in vial.

Instructions for Use

Doses and efficacy studies have not been determined in animals. Recommendations are based on extrapolation of studies performed in humans. Reserve the use of this drug for resistant, refractory infections. Observe manufacturer's instructions carefully for proper administration. When vial is initially reconstituted, it should not be given IV. It first must be diluted in a suitable intravenous fluid solution (at least 100 mL). For intravenous administration, add to intravenous fluids. After reconstitution in vial, 250 or 500 mg should be added to not less than 100 mL of fluids and given IV over 30-60 minutes. Intravenous fluid solutions are stable for 48 hours if refrigerated or 8 hours at room temperature. For intramuscular administration, add 2 mL lidocaine (1%). The suspension is stable for only 1 hour. In some hospitals, the intravenous solution has been diluted in fluids and administered SQ without any sign of injection site reactions.

Patient Monitoring and Laboratory Tests

Susceptibility testing: CLSI (NCCLS) break points for sensitive organisms are less than or equal to 4 mcg/mL for all organisms. Most veterinary pathogens have minimum inhibitory concentration (MIC) values less than 1.0 mcg/mL.

Formulations

Imipenem + cilastatin is available in 250 and 500 mg vials for injection. Intramuscular suspension is available in 500 and 750 mg vials.

Stability and Storage

Store in tightly sealed container, protected from light, and at room temperature. After reconstitution it is stable for 4 hours at room temperature and 24 hours refrigerated. Do not freeze intravenous fluid solutions. Slight yellow discoloration is acceptable but discard if color turns brown.

Small Animal Dosage

Dogs and Cats

- 3-10 mg/kg q6-8h IV or IM. Generally, 5 mg/kg q6-8h IV, IM, or SQ.

Large Animal Dosage

Horses

- 10-20 mg/kg q6h by slow IV infusion.

Regulatory Information

Withdrawal times are not established for animals that produce food. For extralabel use withdrawal interval estimates, contact FARAD at 1-888-USFARAD (1-888-873-2723) or send e-mail to FARAD@ncsu.edu.

Imipramine Hydrochloride

im-ip′rah-meen hye-droe-klor′ide

Trade and Other Names: Tofranil and generic brand

Functional Classification: Behavior modification

Pharmacology and Mechanism of Action

Tricyclic antidepressant drug (TCA). Imipramine, like others in this class, is used in people to treat anxiety and depression. Action is via inhibition of uptake of serotonin and norepinephrine at presynaptic nerve terminals. Other TCA drugs used in animals include clomipramine and amitriptyline.

Indications and Clinical Uses

Like other TCAs, imipramine is used in animals to treat variety of behavioral disorders, including obsessive-compulsive disorders, separation anxiety, and inappropriate urination. There have been fewer studies of efficacy with imipramine than with clomipramine or amitriptyline.

Precautionary Information

Adverse Reactions and Side Effects

Multiple side effects are associated with TCAs, such as antimuscarinic effects (dry mouth and rapid heart rate), and antihistamine effects (sedation). Overdoses can produce life-threatening cardiotoxicity.

Contraindications and Precautions

Use cautiously in patients with heart disease.

Drug Interactions

Do not use with other behavior-modifying drugs, such as serotonin reuptake inhibitors. Do not use with monoamine oxidase inhibitors (MAOIs) such as selegiline.

Instructions for Use

Doses are primarily based on empiricism. There are few controlled efficacy trials available for animals to compare with other drugs in this class. There may be a 2-4 week delay after initiation of therapy before beneficial effects are seen.

Patient Monitoring and Laboratory Tests

Monitor heart rate and rhythm in treated animals. Like other TCAs, imipramine may decrease total T4 and free-T4 concentrations in dogs.

Formulations

Imipramine is available in 10, 25, and 50 mg tablets.

Stability and Storage

Store in tightly sealed container, protected from light, and at room temperature. Although imipramine has been compounded for veterinary use, the potency and stability has not been evaluated for compounded products.

Small Animal Dosage

Dogs
- 2-4 mg/kg q12-24h PO.

Cats
- 0.5-1.0 mg/kg q12-24h PO.

Large Animal Dosage

No large animal doses have been reported.

Regulatory Information

Do not administer to animals intended for food.
RCI Classification: 2

Indomethacin

in-doe-meth'ah-sin

Trade and Other Names: Indocin

Functional Classification: Nonsteroidal antiinflammatory drug (NSAID)

Pharmacology and Mechanism of Action

NSAID and analgesic. Like other NSAIDs, indomethacin produces potent analgesic and antiinflammatory effects by inhibiting the synthesis of prostaglandins. The enzyme inhibited by NSAID is the cyclo-oxygenase enzyme (COX). The COX enzyme exists in two isoforms, called COX-1 and COX-2. COX-1 is primarily responsible for synthesis of prostaglandins important for maintaining a healthy GI tract, renal function, platelet function, and other normal functions. COX-2 is induced and responsible for synthesizing prostaglandins that are important mediators of pain, inflammation, and fever. (There may be some crossover of COX-1 and COX-2 effects in some situations.) Indomethacin is considered a prototype for a nonselective drug because it inhibits equally both COX-1 and COX-2. Indomethacin is registered for human use and experience with this drug in veterinary medicine is limited. Indomethacin acts to inhibit COX that synthesizes prostaglandins. Other antiinflammatory effects may occur (such as effects on leukocytes) but have not been well characterized. Used primarily for short-term treatment of moderate pain and inflammation.

Indications and Clinical Uses

Indomethacin, like other NSAIDs, has been used to treat pain and inflammation in people. However, indomethacin has not been used often in clinical veterinary medicine because other safer, registered drugs are available. Indomethacin is used as a prototypical nonselective COX-1 and COX-2 blocker in research. In dogs, the high risk of GI ulceration prohibits its routine use.

Precautionary Information

Adverse Reactions and Side Effects

Indomethacin has produced severe GI ulceration and hemorrhage in dogs. Indomethacin, like other NSAIDs may cause renal injury via inhibition of renal prostaglandins.

Contraindications and Precautions

Do not use in dogs or cats.

Drug Interactions

Like other NSAIDs, there are several drug interactions possible. NSAIDs have the potential to interfere with the action of diuretics such as furosemide and angiotensin-converting enzyme (ACE) inhibitors, such as enalapril. Corticosteroids, when used with NSAIDs, will increase the risk of ulceration.

Instructions for Use

Use cautiously, if at all, because safe doses have not been determined for clinical use in animals.

Patient Monitoring and Laboratory Tests

Monitor for signs of GI toxicity (hemorrhage, ulcers, and perforation).

Formulations

Indomethacin is available in 25 and 50 mg capsules and 5 mg/mL oral suspension.

Stability and Storage

Store in tightly sealed container, protected from light, and at room temperature. Indomethacin is practically insoluble in water but is soluble in ethanol. It decomposes in alkaline conditions and is maximally stable at pH 3.75.

Small Animal Dosage

Dogs and Cats

Safe dose has not been established.

Large Animal Dosage

No large animal doses have been reported.

Regulatory Information

Withdrawal times are not established for animals that produce food. For extralabel use withdrawal interval estimates, contact FARAD at 1-888-USFARAD (1-888-873-2723) or send e-mail to FARAD@ncsu.edu.

RCI Classification: 4

Insulin

in'syoo-lin

Trade and Other Names: Lente insulin, Ultralente insulin, Regular insulin, NPH insulin, Protamine zinc insulin (PZI), Humulin (human insulin; discontinued), Vetsulin is porcine insulin zinc suspension (veterinary), and PZI Vet (veterinary protamine zinc insulin)

Functional Classification: Hormone

Pharmacology and Mechanism of Action

Insulin has multiple effects associated with utilization of glucose. Dog insulin is identical to pork insulin and cat insulin is similar to beef insulin with only one amino acid difference. Most beef-pork insulin combinations for humans have been discontinued. Insulin is available in several preparations:

1. Regular insulin is short acting. Peak is 1-5 hours and duration is 4-10 hours.
2. Neutral Protamine Hagedorn (isophane or also called NPH) is intermediate acting. Peak is 2-10 hours in dogs and 2-8 hours in cats with a duration of action of 4-24 hours in dogs and 4-12 hours in cats.
3. Lente insulin. Peak is 2-10 hours in dogs and 2-8 hours in cats with a duration of action of 4-24 hours in dogs and 4-12 hours in cats.
4. Protamine-zinc insulin (PZI) is long acting. Peak is 4-14 hours in dogs and 5-7 hours in cats, with a duration of 6-28 hours in dogs and cats.
5. Ultralente insulin: peak is 4-16 hours in dogs and 2-14 hours in cats and has a duration of 8-28 hours in dogs and 12-24 hours in cats.
6. Glargine (an insulin analogue) with a slow onset of 4-18 hours and a duration of 24 hours or greater. This analogue is produced by the substitution of glycine for asparagine and addition of two arginine molecules. These changes shift the isoelectric point toward neutral which reduces solubility and causes it to be released slowly from the injection site.
7. Insulin glulisine (Apidra), insulin lispro (Humalog), and insulin aspart (NovoLog) are rapidly-acting insulins used in people. They are used for their rapid onset and short duration of action. In people, they are typically used with a meal and combined with a longer-acting form. These rapid-acting insulin analogues have not been evaluated for animals.

Addition of protamine or zinc to insulin will produce a crystallized insulin in suspension that has a longer absorption rate than dissolved insulin. The lente forms of insulin control their duration by the size of the crystal. For example, semilente is practically amorphous, whereas ultralente has large crystals, and lente is a combination of ultralente and semilente. Availability of some forms of insulin is limited because manufacturers have discontinued the Regular and NPH formulations of pork insulin. Other formulations, such as Humulin U Ultralente and Humulin L Lente also have been discontinued.

Indications and Clinical Uses

Insulin, in the various forms, is used to treat diabetes mellitus in dogs and cats. It is used to replace insulin that is deficient. In some cats (approximately 50%) some oral hypoglycemic drugs have been used to reduce use of insulin. However, diabetic dogs are more insulin dependent. Regular insulin is short acting and more useful for emergencies such as diabetic ketoacidosis or acute nonketotic syndromes.

Intermediate or long acting insulin preparations are used for maintenance. In dogs, the porcine form is preferred because it is identical to canine insulin (e.g., Vetsulin). In cats, once-daily glargine insulin is equivalent to twice-daily lente insulin. It is not recommended for dogs. Insulin is occasionally used to treat severe cases of hyperkalemia.

Precautionary Information

Adverse Reactions and Side Effects

Adverse effects primarily related to overdoses that result in hypoglycemia. Glargine insulin has a low pH (4) and may sting from injection. Other insulins are more neutral.

Contraindications and Precautions

Use cautiously in animals because of the risk of hypoglycemia. Mixing regular insulin and insulins containing zinc in the same syringe will prolong absorption of the regular insulin. Do not mix isophane insulin or phosphate buffered insulin with zinc insulins (lente, ultralente, semilente).

Drug Interactions

Administration of corticosteroids (prednisolone, dexamethasone, etc.) will interfere with action of insulin.

Instructions for Use

Doses should be carefully adjusted in each patient depending on response. When switching dogs from human lente insulin to porcine insulin, use the same dose, but if switching from human ultralente insulin to porcine insulin, reduce dose by 25%.

For cats with ketoacidosis, alternative dosing regimen has used 0.2 units/kg IM initially, then 0.1 units/kg IM every hour until glucose level is less than 300, then 0.25-0.4 units/kg q6h SQ. When protamine zinc insulin is used in cats, twice daily dosing usually is required. However, consider once-daily in cats if blood glucose nadir develops 10 hours or longer after administration of PZI.

Dietary management is essential for optimal glucose control. Feed cats a high protein, low carbohydrate diet. Feed dogs a high fiber, low fat diet.

Pet owners are instructed to use appropriate syringe types for administration (e.g., U-40 vs. U-100).

Patient Monitoring and Laboratory Tests

Monitor blood glucose, glycosylated hemoglobin, and/or fructosamine concentrations. When treating diabetes, it is desirable to maintain glucose concentrations between 100 and 300 mg/dL, with the nadir (lowest point) being 80-150 mg/dL.

Formulations

Insulin is available in 100 units/mL injection (U-100). Porcine insulin for dogs is available as U-40 (Vetsulin). Protamine zinc beef/pork (PZI VET) insulin also may be available as 40 units/mL injection (U-40). In 2005, Eli Lilly discontinued manufacture of four insulin products: Iletin II Pork Insulin (Regular and NPH formulations), Humulin U Ultralente, and Humulin L Lente (Humulin U and Humulin L). Glargine is available only as the U-100 concentration.

Stability and Storage

Proper storage is critical for proper action of insulin: Keep refrigerated. Warm gently and roll vial prior to injection to ensure proper mixing of vial contents. Do **not** freeze vials of insulin. Do **not** allow vials of insulin exposure to heat. Veterinarians should not use formulations of insulin that are compounded in unreliable conditions. Dilution of insulin should only be done by a pharmacist because specific diluents must be used.

Small Animal Dosage

Dogs

- Ketoacidosis for dogs <3 kg: 1 unit/animal initially, then 1 unit/animal q1h; for dogs 3-10 kg: 2 units/animal initially, then 1 unit/animal q1h; and for dogs >10 kg: 0.25 unit/kg initially, then 0.1 unit/kg q1h IM.
- NPH isophane for dogs <15 kg: 1 unit/kg q12-24h SQ (to effect); dogs >25 kg: 0.5 unit/kg q12-24h SQ (to effect).

Cats

- Ketoacidosis: 0.2 unit/kg IM initially, then 0.1 unit/kg IM every hour until glucose level is less than 300 mg/dL and then continue with 0.25-0.4 unit/kg SQ q6h.
- NPH not recommended for cats.
- An initial dose for Ultralente and PZI insulins is 0.5-1.0 unit/kg SQ and then once or twice daily (usually twice is needed). Initially administer a low dose of 0.4 unit/kg (or 1 unit per cat) SQ, twice daily, with subsequent doses adjusted to produce desirable glucose levels, usually no higher than 3 units per cat. Final adjusted dose for most cats is 0.9 (+/– 0.4) unit/kg.

Large Animal Dosage

No large animal doses have been reported.

Regulatory Information

No regulatory information is available for animals intended for food. Because of low risk of residues, no withdrawal times are suggested.

Interferon

in-ter-feer'on

Trade and Other Names: Virbagen omega

Functional Classification: Immunostimulant

Pharmacology and Mechanism of Action

Recombinant omega interferon contained in Virbagen omega is produced by silkworms previously inoculated with interferon-recombinant baculovirus. It allows the production of pure interferon. Omega interferon of feline origin, produced by genetic engineering, is a type 1 interferon closely related to alpha interferon. The exact mechanism of action of interferon omega is not understood, but it may enhance nonspecific defenses in dogs and cats. Interferon does not act directly and specifically on the pathogenic virus but exerts its effect by inhibition of the internal synthesis mechanisms of the infected cells. After injection it has a half-life of 1.4 hours in dogs and 1.7 hours in cats. It is bound to receptors in cells infected by virus.

There are multiple interferons available for human use (e.g., treatment of AIDS related diseases and cancer-associated diseases). These interferons may be alpha-2a, alpha 2b, n-1, and n-3. These types of interferons are not interchangeable.

Indications and Clinical Uses

Interferon is used to stimulate the immune system in patients. It has been used to stimulate immune cells in dogs with parvovirus and in cats with feline retrovirus (Feline Leukemia Virus [FeLV] and Feline Immunodeficiency Virus [FIV]). Human interferon alpha, orally, has improved clinical signs in cats with FIV.

Precautionary Information

Adverse Reactions and Side Effects

It may induce vomiting and nausea. In some animals it may induce hyperthermia 3-6 hours after injection. In cats, it may produce soft feces to mild diarrhea. A slight decrease in white blood cells, platelets and red blood cells, and rise in the concentration of alanine aminotransferase may be observed. These parameters usually return to normal in the week following the last injection. In cats, it may induce transient fatigue during the treatment.

In people, injections of interferon alpha have been associated with influenza-like symptoms. Other effects also have been reported in people such as bone marrow suppression.

Contraindications and Precautions

Do not vaccinate dogs or cats receiving interferon.

Drug Interactions

Do not mix with any other vaccine/immunological product, except the solvent supplied for use with the product.

Instructions for Use

Doses and indications for animals have primarily been based on extrapolation of human recommendations, experimental studies (*J Am Vet Med Assoc*, 199:1477, 1991), or specific studies in cats with viral infections.

Patient Monitoring and Laboratory Tests

Monitor CBC during treatment.

Formulations Available

Interferon is available in 5 and 10 million units/vial. The freeze-dried fraction must be reconstituted with 1 mL of the specific diluent to obtain, depending on the presentation, a solution containing 5 million units or 10 million units of recombinant interferon.

Stability and Storage

Interferon has a shelf life of 2 years. The product should be used immediately after reconstitution and should be stored in original carton. Store and transport at 4° C ± 2° C. Do not freeze.

Small Animal Dosage

Dogs

- 2.5 million units/kg IV once daily for 3 consecutive days.

Cats

- 1.0 million units/kg IV once daily for 5 consecutive days. Three separate 5-day treatments must be performed at day 0, day 14, and day 60.
- 10 units/kg human interferon alpha on an alternate-week schedule, oral.

Large Animal Dosage

No large animal doses have been reported.

Regulatory Information

Do not administer to animals intended for food.

Ipecac

ih'peh-kak

Trade and Other Names: Ipecac and Syrup of ipecac

Functional Classification: Emetic

Pharmacology and Mechanism of Action

Emetic drug. Ipecac contains two alkaloids, cephalin and emetine. These alkaloids stimulate gastric receptors linked to the chemoreceptor trigger zone (CRTZ).

Indications and Clinical Uses

Ipecac is indicated for emergency treatment of poisoning. When used in animals, the administration should be promptly after poisoning. Inducing vomiting with ipecac is not effective beyond 30-60 minutes after poisoning. After successful administration, it is estimated that vomiting removes only 10%-60% of ingested toxicant. Therefore, other systemic antidotes, and/or activated charcoal should be considered.

Precautionary Information

Adverse Reactions and Side Effects

No adverse effects with acute therapy for poisoning. Chronic administration can lead to myocardial toxicity.

Contraindications and Precautions

Do not induce vomiting if patient has ingested caustic chemicals or if there is a risk of aspiration pneumonia.

Drug Interactions

Ipecac is not as effective if drugs that act as antiemetics have been administered. Such drugs include tranquilizers (e.g., acepromazine), anticholinergics (e.g., atropine), antihistamines, and prokinetic agents (e.g., metoclopramide).

Instructions for Use

Ipecac is available as nonprescription drug. Onset of vomiting may require 20-30 minutes.

Patient Monitoring and Laboratory Tests

Poisoned animals should be monitored closely because ipecac may not entirely eliminate ingested toxicant.

Formulations

Ipecac is available in a 30 mL bottle oral solution.

Stability and Storage

Store in tightly sealed container, protected from light, and at room temperature.

Small Animal Dosage

Dogs

- 3-6 mL/dog PO.

Cat

- 2-6 mL/cat PO.

Large Animal Dosage

Not recommended for large animals.

Regulatory Information

No regulatory information is available for animals intended for food. Because of low risk of residues, no withdrawal times are suggested.

Ipodate

ih′poe-date

Trade and Other Names: Orografin and Calcium ipodate

Functional Classification: Antithyroid agent

Pharmacology and Mechanism of Action

Cholecystographic agent. This drug is an iodinated biliary radiocontrast dye. Ipodate inhibits conversion of T4 to T3. It also blocks T3 receptors. It lowers the T-3 level but not the T-4 levels.

Indications and Clinical Uses

Ipodate is used as treatment for hyperthyroidism in cats. The use is not as common as other treatments, but it has been administered as an alternative to methimazole, radiation therapy, or surgery. If iopanoic acid (Telepaque) is used as a substitute, it may be less effective.

Precautionary Information

Adverse Reactions and Side Effects

Ipodate can cause hypothyroidism. No significant adverse effects have been reported in cats, but compounds containing iodide have caused hypersensitivity reactions in people. In humans, chronic high doses of compounds containing iodide can cause sore mouth, swollen tissues, skin reactions, or GI upset.

Contraindications and Precautions

Monitor for lowering of thyroid levels in animals or clinical signs. Relapses have occurred in cats after 10 weeks to 6 months of treatment.

Drug Interactions

No drug interactions have been reported for small animals.

I

Instructions for Use

Use of ipodate has been experimental, and precise doses have not been evaluated. In one study, two-thirds of treated cats responded. More experience is needed to determine if response to treatment is transient.

Patient Monitoring and Laboratory Tests

Monitor serum thyroid. Ipodate lowers the T-3 level but not the T-4 levels.

Formulations

Ipodate is available as either calcium or sodium ipodate. Oragrafin 500 mg capsules have been formulated into 50 mg capsules by pharmacists. (These may have to be specifically formulated for cats.) Availability of Orografin has become a problem for veterinarians. Iopanoic acid (Telepaque) has been used as a substitute.

Stability and Storage

Store in tightly sealed container, protected from light, and at room temperature.

Small Animal Dosage

Cats

- 15 mg/kg q12h PO. Most common dose has been 50 mg/cat twice daily. Dose is equivalent regardless of whether sodium or calcium ipodate is used.

Large Animal Dosage

No large animal doses have been reported.

Regulatory Information

Do not administer to animals intended for food.

Irbesartan

er-beh-sar′tan

Trade and Other Names: Avapro

Functional Classification: Vasodilator

Pharmacology and Mechanism of Action

Vasodilator, angiotensin II receptor blocker. It has been used in people who cannot tolerate angiotension-converting enzyme (ACE) inhibitors. In dogs, it is reported that they do not convert losartan to the active metabolite, and therefore it has little activity in dogs. By contrast irbesartan has been shown to block angiotensin II receptors.

Indications and Clinical Uses

Angiotensin II blockers, such as irbesartan, are used in people as alternatives to ACE inhibitors. However, they are rarely used or indicated in animals. One product (Avalide) contains irbesartan in combination with hydrochlorothiazide.

Precautionary Information

Adverse Reactions and Side Effects

No adverse effects have been reported in animals. Hypotension is a potential problem from overdosing.

Contraindications and Precautions

Do not administer to hypotensive or dehydrated animals. No other contraindications reported for animals.

Drug Interactions

No drug interactions have been reported for small animals. Use cautiously with other vasodilators.

Instructions for Use

In dogs, irbesartan is preferred over losartan, because losartan is not converted to active products in dogs.

Patient Monitoring and Laboratory Tests

Monitor blood pressure and heart rate in treated animals. Monitor electrolytes if it is administered long-term.

Formulations

Irbesartan is available in 75, 150, and 300 mg tablets.

Stability and Storage

Store in tightly sealed container, protected from light, and at room temperature.

Small Animal Dosage

Dogs

- 30-60 mg/kg q12h PO.

Large Animal Dosage

No large animal doses have been reported.

Regulatory Information

Withdrawal times are not established for animals that produce food. For extralabel use withdrawal interval estimates, contact FARAD at 1-888-USFARAD (1-888-873-2723) or send e-mail to FARAD@ncsu.edu.
RCI Classification: 3

Iron Dextran

Trade and Other Names: AmTech Iron Dextran, Ferrodex, and HemaJect

Functional Classification: Mineral supplement

Pharmacology and Mechanism of Action

Iron supplement. Iron dextran is injected in animals (most commonly pigs) for prevention of iron deficiency anemia. Iron dextran injection contains either 100 mg elemental iron per mL or 200 mg per mL. Ferric hydroxide is complexed with a low molecular weight dextran in this formulation.

Indications and Clinical Uses

Use in animals, primarily young pigs, for treatment and prevention of iron deficiency anemia. Injections are usually made IM at 1 to 4 days of age.

Precautionary Information

Adverse Reactions and Side Effects

Injections may produce transient myositis and muscle weakness.

Contraindications and Precautions

No specific contraindications.

Drug Interactions

No drug interactions are reported.

Instructions for Use

Inject in midportion of rear thigh muscle in pigs.

Patient Monitoring and Laboratory Tests

Monitor iron concentrations in treated animals and CBC to monitor effectiveness.

Formulations

Iron Dextran is 100 or 200 elemental iron per mL.

Stability and Storage

Store in tightly sealed container, at room temperature, protected from light. Do not mix with other solutions.

Small Animal Dosage

No dose is reported for small animals.

Large Animal Dosage

Pigs

- 100 mg (1 mL) IM to 2-4 day-old pigs and repeat in 10 days.
- 200 mg (1 mL of higher concentration) IM to pigs at 1-3 days of age.

Regulatory Information

No withdrawal time is necessary.

Isoflupredone Acetate

eye-soe-floo′preh-done ass′ih-tate

Trade and Other Names: Predef 2X

Functional Classification: Corticosteroid

Pharmacology and Mechanism of Action

Corticosteroid. Antiinflammatory and immunosuppressive effects are approximately 17 times more potent than cortisol and 4 times more potent than prednisolone. Antiinflammatory effects are complex, but primarily via inhibition of inflammatory cells and suppression of expression of inflammatory mediators. Use is for treatment of inflammatory and immune-mediated disease.

Indications and Clinical Uses

Isoflupredone acetate is used for treating various musculoskeletal, allergic, and systemic inflammatory diseases. Large animal uses include inflammatory disorders, especially musculoskeletal inflammation, and recurrent airway disease (RAO) (formerly called *chronic obstructive pulmonary disease* [COPD]) in horses. Isoflupredone acetate, like other corticosteroids, has been used to treat ketosis in cattle. In large animals, it also has been used to treat septic shock. However, efficacy for using corticosteroids to treat septic shock is not supported by evidence.

Precautionary Information

Adverse Reactions and Side Effects

Side effects from corticosteroids are many and include polyphagia, polydipsia/polyuria, and hypothalamic-pituitary adrenal (HPA) axis suppression. Adverse effects include GI ulceration, hepatopathy, diabetes, hyperlipidemia, decreased thyroid hormone, decreased protein synthesis, delayed wound healing, and immunosuppression. Secondary infections can occur as a result of immunosuppression and include demodicosis, toxoplasmosis, fungal infections, and UTIs. In horses, additional adverse effects include risk of laminitis.

Contraindications and Precautions

Use with caution in patients prone to infection or GI ulcers. Administration of isoflupredone may induce hepatopathy, diabetes mellitus, or hyperlipidemia. Use cautiously in pregnant animals or in young, rapidly growing animals. Use of corticosteroids may impair healing.

Drug Interactions

Corticosteroids will increase risk of GI ulceration when administered with nonsteroidal antiinflammatory drugs (NSAIDs).

Instructions for Use

When administered to treat primary ketosis in cattle, it is advised to also administer intravenous glucose.

Patient Monitoring and Laboratory Tests
Monitor liver enzymes, blood glucose, and renal function during therapy. Monitor patients for signs of secondary infections. Perform adrenocorticotropic (ACTH) stimulation test to monitor adrenal function.

Formulations
Isoflupredone is available in a 2 mg injection in 10 and 100 mL vials.

Stability and Storage
Store in tightly sealed container, protected from light, and at room temperature.

Small Animal Dosage
- No doses are listed for isoflupredone as it is generally not administered to small animals. However, based on antiinflammatory potency, doses of 0.125-0.25 mg/kg/day IM can be considered.

Large Animal Dosage
Cattle
- 10-20 mg total dose per animal q12-24h IM.
- Ketosis: 10-20 mg as a total single dose per animal q12-24h IM.

Horses
- 5-20 mg total dose per animal q12-24h IM.
- Pulmonary disease: 0.02-0.03 mg/kg q24h.
- Intraarticular: 5-20 mg per joint.

Pigs
- 0.036 mg/kg/day IM.

Regulatory Information
Cattle and pig withdrawal time (meat): 7 days.
No milk withdrawal time is listed for U.S. labeling. In Canada, withdrawal times are listed as 5 days for meat and 72 hours for milk.
For extralabel use withdrawal interval estimates, contact FARAD at 1-888-USFARAD (1-888-873-2723) or send e-mail to FARAD@ncsu.edu.

Isoflurane
eye-soe-floo′rane

Trade and Other Names: Aerrane

Functional Classification: Anesthetic

Pharmacology and Mechanism of Action
Inhalant anesthetic. Like other inhalant anesthetics, the mechanism of action is uncertain. Isoflurane produces a generalized, reversible, depression of the CNS. Inhalant anesthetics vary in their solubility in blood, their potency, and the rate of induction and recovery. Those with low blood/gas partition coefficients are associated with the most rapid rates of induction and recovery. Isoflurane has a vapor pressure of 250 mm Hg (at 20° C), a blood/gas partition coefficient of 1.4, and a fat/blood coefficient of 45.

Indications and Clinical Uses

Isoflurane, like other inhalant anesthetics, is used for general anesthesia in animals. It is associated with rapid induction of anesthesia and rapid recovery rates. It is metabolized to only a small percent (<1%) and has minimal effects on other organs. It has a minimum alveolar concentration (MAC) value of 1.63%, 1.3%, and 1.31% in cats, dogs, and horses, respectively.

Precautionary Information

Adverse Reactions and Side Effects

Adverse effects related to anesthetic effects (e.g., cardiovascular and respiratory depression).

Contraindications and Precautions

Do not administer unless it is possible to control ventilation and monitor heart rate and rhythm.

Drug Interactions

No drug interactions are reported. However, like other inhalant anesthetics, other anesthetic agents act synergistically and will lower dose requirement.

Instructions for Use

Use of inhalant anesthetics requires careful monitoring. Dose is determined by depth of anesthesia.

Patient Monitoring and Laboratory Tests

Monitor respiratory rate, heart rate, and rhythm during administration.

Formulations

Isoflurane is available in a 100 mL bottle.

Stability and Storage

Store in tightly sealed container, protected from light, and at room temperature.

Small Animal Dosage

- Induction: 5%, maintenance: 1.5%-2.5%.

Large Animal Dosage

- MAC value: 1.5%-2%.

Regulatory Information

Withdrawal times are not established for animals that produce food. Clearance is rapid, and short withdrawal times are suggested.

For extralabel use withdrawal interval estimates, contact FARAD at 1-888-USFARAD (1-888-873-2723) or send e-mail to FARAD@ncsu.edu.

Isoproterenol Hydrochloride

eye-soe-proe-teer'eh-nole hye-droe-klor'ide

Trade and Other Names: Isuprel and Isoprenaline hydrochloride

Functional Classification: Beta-agonist

Pharmacology and Mechanism of Action

Adrenergic agonist. Isoproterenol stimulates both $beta_1$ and $beta_2$ adrenergic receptors. Like other beta-agonists, it stimulates activity of adenyl cyclase. In cardiac tissue, isoproterenol is one of the most potent agonists and will increase rate, conduction, and contractility. Beta-agonists will also relax bronchial smooth muscle and arterial smooth muscle.

Indications and Clinical Uses

Isoproterenol is administered when it is necessary for prompt stimulation of the heart (inotropic and chronotropic) or to relieve acute bronchoconstriction. It is short acting and must be administered IV or via inhalation.

Precautionary Information

Adverse Reactions and Side Effects

Isoproterenol causes adverse effects related to excessive adrenergic stimulation, seen primarily as tachycardia and tachyarrhythmias. High doses can cause calcium accumulation in myocardium and tissue injury.

Contraindications and Precautions

Do no use if formulation turns pink or a dark color.

Drug Interactions

Isoproterenol will potentiate other adrenergic agonists. Treatment will potentiate cardiac arrhythmias and should be used cautiously with other arrhythmogenic drugs.

Instructions for Use

Because of a short half-life, isoproterenol must be infused via constant rate infusion (CRI) or repeated if administered IM or SQ. It is recommended for short-term use only because repeated treatment will cause cardiac injury.

Patient Monitoring and Laboratory Tests

Monitor heart rate and rhythm during treatment.

Formulations

Isoproterenol is available in 0.2 mg/mL ampules for injection.

Stability and Storage

Store in tightly sealed container, protected from light, and at room temperature. It is soluble in water with good aqueous stability. It is susceptible to light, and if a dark color is observed, it should be discarded (pink to brownish color). Solutions above pH 6.0 may decompose more rapidly. In 5% dextrose solutions it is stable for 24 hours. It has been added to ultrasonic nebulizers in distilled water for respiratory therapy and was stable in solution for 24 hours. It also is stable if mixed with cromolyn sodium.

Small Animal Dosage

Dogs and Cats

- 10 mcg/kg q6h IM or SQ.
- Dilute 1 mg in 500 mL of 5% dextrose or Lactated Ringer's solution and infuse IV 0.5-1.0 mL/min (1-2 mcg/min) or to effect.
- CRI: administer to effect at 0.01-0.1 mcg/kg/min.

Large Animal Dosage

- 1 mcg/kg q15min IV, until desired response.

Regulatory Information

No regulatory information is available for animals intended for food. Because of low risk of residues, no withdrawal times are suggested.
RCI Classification: 2

Isosorbide Dinitrate, Isosorbide Mononitrate

eye-soe-sor'bide dye-nye'trate, eye-soe-sor'bide mahn-oh-neye'trate

Trade and Other Names: Isosorbide dinitrate: Isordil, Isorbid, and Sorbitrate and Isosorbide mononitrate: Monoket

Functional Classification: Vasodilator

Pharmacology and Mechanism of Action

Nitrate vasodilator. Like other nitrovasodilators, it produces vasodilation via generation of nitric oxide. It relaxes vascular smooth muscle, especially venous. Isosorbide mononitrate is a biologically active form of isosorbide dinitrate. Compared to isosorbide dinitrate, it does not undergo first-pass metabolism and is completely absorbed orally.

Indications and Clinical Uses

Isosorbide dinitrate is used to reduce preload in patients with CHF. In people, it is primarily used to treat angina.

Precautionary Information

Adverse Reactions and Side Effects

Adverse effects are primarily related to overdoses that produce excess vasodilation and hypotension. Tolerance may develop with repeated doses.

Contraindications and Precautions

Do not administer to hypovolemic patients. Use cautiously in animals with low cardiac reserve.

Drug Interactions

No drug interactions are reported.

Instructions for Use

Generally, doses are titrated to individual depending on response. Isosorbide mononitrate is absorbed better than isosorbide dinitrate and may be preferred in clinical situations.

Patient Monitoring and Laboratory Tests

Monitor patient's cardiovascular status during treatment.

Formulations

Isosorbide dinitrate is available in 2.5, 5, 10, 20, 30, and 40 mg tablets and 40 mg capsules.
Isosorbide mononitrate is available in 10 and 20 mg tablets.

Stability and Storage

Store in tightly sealed container, protected from light, and at room temperature.

Small Animal Dosage

Dogs and Cats

- Isosorbide dinitrate: 2.5-5 mg/animal q12h PO or 0.22-1.1 mg/kg q12h PO.
- Isosorbide mononitrate: 5 mg/dog two doses per day 7 hours apart PO.

Large Animal Dosage

No large animal doses have been reported.

Regulatory Information

No regulatory information is available. For extralabel use withdrawal interval estimates, contact FARAD at 1-888-USFARAD (1-888-873-2723) or send e-mail to FARAD@ncsu.edu.

There is a low risk of residue potential.

RCI Classification: 4

Isotretinoin

eye-soe-tret′ih-noe-in

Trade and Other Names: Accutane

Functional Classification: Dermatologic agent

Pharmacology and Mechanism of Action

Isotretinoin is a keratinization stabilizing drug. Isotretinoin reduces sebaceous gland size, inhibits sebaceous gland activity, and decreases sebum secretion.

Indications and Clinical Uses

In people, it is primarily used to treat acne. In animals it has been used to treat sebaceous adenitis.

Precautionary Information

Adverse Reactions and Side Effects

Adverse effects not reported for animals, although experimental studies have demonstrated that it can cause focal calcification (such as in myocardium and vessels).

Contraindications and Precautions

Isotretinoin is absolutely contraindicated in pregnant animals because of fetal abnormalities.

Drug Interactions

No drug interactions are reported.

Instructions for Use

Use in veterinary medicine is confined to limited clinical experience and extrapolation from human reports. High expense of this medication has limited veterinary use.

Patient Monitoring and Laboratory Tests

No monitoring is necessary for animal use.

Formulations

Isotretinoin is available in 10, 20, and 40 mg capsules.

Stability and Storage

Store in tightly sealed container, protected from light, and at room temperature.

Small Animal Dosage

Dogs

- 1-3 mg/kg/day (up to a maximum recommended dose of 3-4 mg/kg/day PO).

Large Animal Dosage

No large animal doses have been reported.

Regulatory Information

Do not use in animals intended for food.

Isoxsuprine

eye-soks′yoo-preen

Trade and Other Names: Vasodilan and generic brands

Functional Classification: Vasodilator

Pharmacology and Mechanism of Action

Vasodilator. The mechanism of action for isoxsuprine has not been identified. It has been suggested to act as a $beta_2$ agonist (for which experimental evidence is not supportive) or by increasing concentrations of nitric oxide. It also may inhibit mechanisms that are calcium dependent. It relaxes vessels in digits of horses.

Indications and Clinical Uses

Isoxsuprine is used in horses for navicular disease and other diseases of the foot, such as laminitis. Note that efficacy has not been established for these indications. There are no reports of its use in other animals.

Precautionary Information

Adverse Reactions and Side Effects

Hypotension is the primary adverse effect. It lowers arterial pressure. In horses, side effects may also include rubbing noses on objects, hyperexcitability, sweating, tachycardia, and restlessness.

Contraindications and Precautions

Do not use in hypotensive or dehydrated animals.

Drug Interactions

No drug interactions are reported.

Instructions for Use

When used in horses, it often is used with other vasodilators and antiinflammatory drugs. It is not known if it acts synergistically with these other medications.

Patient Monitoring and Laboratory Tests

Monitor heart rate in treated animals.

Formulations
Isoxsuprine is available in 10 and 20 mg tablets.

Stability and Storage
Store in tightly sealed container, protected from light, and at room temperature. Although isoxsuprine is compounded for equine use, stability of compounded formulations has not been evaluated.

Small Animal Dosage
No small animal doses are reported.

Large Animal Dosage
Horses

- Navicular disease and laminitis: 0.6 mg/kg q12h PO, for 6 to 14 weeks. In some dosing protocols, if 0.6 mg/kg q12h has not improved horse's condition within 3 weeks, the dose has been doubled.

Regulatory Information
No regulatory information is available. For extralabel use withdrawal interval estimates, contact FARAD at 1-888-USFARAD (1-888-873-2723) or send e-mail to FARAD@ncsu.edu.

Itraconazole
it-rah-kahn'ah-zole

Trade and Other Names: Sporanox and Itrafungol (available in Europe for cats)

Functional Classification: Antifungal

Pharmacology and Mechanism of Action
Azole (triazole) antifungal drug. Itraconazole inhibits ergosterol synthesis in fungal cell membrane. Fungistatic. It is active against dermatophytes and systemic fungi, such as *Blastomyces, Histoplasma,* and *Coccidioides.* It is more potent against these fungi than ketoconazole. Itraconazole can be incorporated into sebum and stratum corneum and can be detected in skin for 3-4 weeks after treatment.

Experience in dogs and cats has shown it to be absorbed orally and doses have been established for treating systemic fungal infections and dermatophytes. In horses, the oral solution is better absorbed than the capsules (65% vs. 12%). The half-life for the solution is 11 hours.

Indications and Clinical Uses
Itraconazole is used to treat dermatophytes and systemic fungi, such as *Blastomyces, Histoplasma,* and *Coccidioides.* It also has been shown effective for treatment of *Malassezia* dermatitis, but doses are lower than for other infections. Although it has been used to treat infections caused by aspergillosis, efficacy has not been as good as with other antifungal drugs such as voriconazole or amphotericin B. Itraconazole is often considered the first choice for dermatophyte infections in cats.

Precautionary Information

Adverse Reactions and Side Effects

Itraconazole is better tolerated than ketoconazole. Ketoconazole inhibits hormone synthesis and can lower concentrations of cortisol, testosterone, and other hormones in animals. However, itraconazole has little effect on these enzymes and will not produce endocrine effects. However, vomiting and hepatotoxicity is possible, especially at high doses. In one study, hepatotoxicity was more likely at high doses. Some 10%-15% of dogs will develop high liver enzyme levels. High doses in cats caused vomiting and anorexia.

Contraindications and Precautions

Use cautiously in any animal with signs of liver disease. Use cautiously in pregnant animals. At high doses in laboratory animals, it has caused fetal abnormalities.

Drug Interactions

Itraconazole is a cytochrome P450 enzyme inhibitor. It may cause drug interactions because of inhibition of P450 enzymes. However, this inhibition is not expected to be as prominent as with ketoconazole.

Instructions for Use

Doses are based on studies in animals in which itraconazole has been used to treat blastomycosis in dogs. Lower doses may be used in cats and dogs for dermatophytes and in dogs for treating *Malassezia* dermatitis. Doses in horses are based on specific pharmacokinetic studies. Other uses or doses are based on empiricism or extrapolation from human literature.

Patient Monitoring and Laboratory Tests

Monitor liver enzyme concentrations.

Formulations Available

Itraconazole is available in 100 mg capsules and 10 mg/mL oral liquid. Itrafungol for cats is 10 mg/mL oral liquid (available in Europe).

Stability and Storage

Itraconazole is practically insoluble in water but is soluble in ethanol. It is unstable and may lose potency if not maintained in manufacturer's original formulation (capsules and solution). Compounded formulations are highly unstable and insoluble. Oral absorption of extemporaneously compounded itraconazole suspensions and capsules has been poor and is not recommended. Oral commercial formulation (in cyclodextran) has a pH of approximately 2.0. Do not freeze.

Small Animal Dosage

Dogs

- 2.5 mg/kg q12h or 5 mg/kg q24h PO.
- Dermatophytes: 3 mg/kg/day for 15 days.
- *Malassezia* dermatitis: 5 mg/kg q24h PO for 2 days, repeated each week for 3 weeks.

Cats

- 5 mg/kg q12h PO.
- Dermatophytes: 1.5-3.0 mg/kg (up to 5 mg/kg) q24h PO for 15 days (although some cats needed an additional 15 day course of therapy).
- 5-10 mg/kg q24h PO for 7 days, then alternating with one week on, one week off.

Large Animal Dosage

Horses

- 5 mg/kg/day (2.5 mg/kg q12h) PO. In horses, the capsules are absorbed poorly and inconsistently. Use the oral solution (Sporanox) for optimum oral absorption.

Regulatory Information

No regulatory information is available. For extralabel use withdrawal interval estimates, contact FARAD at 1-888-USFARAD (1-888-873-2723) or send e-mail to FARAD@ncsu.edu.

Ivermectin

eye-ver-mek'tin

Trade and Other Names: Heartguard, Ivomec, Eqvalan liquid, Equimectrin, IverEase, Zimecterin, Privermectin, Ultramectin, Ivercide, Ivercare, and Ivermax. Acarexx is a topical form for cats.

Functional Classification: Antiparasitic

Pharmacology and Mechanism of Action

Antiparasitic drug. Avermectins (ivermectin-like drugs) and milbemycins (milbemycin and moxidectin) are macrocyclic lactones and share similarities, including mechanism of action. These drugs are neurotoxic to parasites by potentiating glutamate-gated chloride ion channels in parasites. Paralysis and death of the parasite is caused by increased permeability to chloride ions and hyperpolarization of nerve cells. These drugs also potentiate other chloride channels, including ones gated by GABA. Mammals ordinarily are not affected, because they lack glutamate-gated chloride channels, and there is a lower affinity for other mammalian chloride channels. Because these drugs ordinarily do not penetrate the blood-brain barrier, GABA-gated channels in the CNS of mammals are not affected. Ivermectin is active against intestinal parasites, mites, bots, heartworm microfilaria, and developing larvae. Ivermectin has no effect on trematode or cestode parasites.

Indications and Clinical Uses

Ivermectin is used in horses for the treatment and control of large strongyles (adult) (*Strongylus vulgaris, Strongylus edentatus*, and *Triodontophorus* species), small strongyles (adult and fourth stage larvae) (*Cyathostomum* species, *Cylicocyclus* species, *Cylicostephanus* species), pinworms (adult and fourth-stage larvae) *(Oxyuris equi),* large roundworms (adult) *(Parascaris equorum),* hairworms (adult) *(Trichostrongylus axei),* large mouth stomach worms (adult) *(Habronema muscae),* neck threadworms (microfilariae) (*Onchocerca* species), and stomach bots (*Gastrophilus* species). In cattle it is used for treatment and control of GI nematodes (adults and fourth-stage larvae) *(Haemonchus placei, Ostertagia ostertagi)* (including inhibited larvae), *O. lyrata, Trichostrongylus axei, T. colubriformis, Cooperia oncophora, C. punctata, C. pectinata, Oesophagostomum radiatum, Nematodirus helvetianus* (adults only), *N. Spathiger* (adults only), *Bunostomum phlebotomum*; lungworms (adults and fourth-stage larvae) (*Dictyocaulus viviparus)*; grubs (parasitic stages) *(Hypoderma bovis, H. lineatum)*; sucking lice *(Linognathus vituli, Haematopinus eurysternus, Solenopotes capillatus)*; mites (scabies) [*Psoroptes ovis* (syn. *P. communis* var. *bovis*), *Sarcoptes scabiei* var. *bovis*].

In pigs it is used for treatment and control of GI roundworms (adults and fourth-stage larvae) (large roundworm, *Ascaris suum;* red stomach worm, *Hyostrongylus rubidus;* nodular worm, *Oesophagostomum* species; threadworm, *Strongyloides ransomi* (adults only); somatic roundworm larvae (threadworm, *Strongyloides ransomi* [somatic larvae]); lungworms *(Metastrongylus* species [adults only]); lice *(Haematopinus suis);* and mites *(Sarcoptes scabiei* var. *suis.)*.

In small animals (dogs and cats) it is used as a heartworm preventative (low dose) or to treat external parasites (mites) and intestinal parasites at higher doses. Treatment of *Demodex* infections is effective but requires higher doses than for any other indication.

Precautionary Information

Adverse Reactions and Side Effects

Toxicity may occur at high doses and in breeds in which ivermectin crosses the blood-brain barrier. Sensitive breeds include Collies, Australian shepherds, Old English sheepdogs, Longhaired Whippets, and Shetland sheepdogs. Toxicity is neurotoxic and signs include depression, ataxia, difficulty with vision, coma, and death. Sensitivity to ivermectin occurs in certain breeds because of a mutation in the multidrug resistance gene (MDR1) that codes for the membrane pump p-glycoprotein. This mutation that affects the efflux pump in blood-brain barrier. Therefore, ivermectin can accumulate in the brain of susceptible animals. High doses in normal animals may also produce similar toxicosis. Ivermectin at doses of 400 mcg/kg has produced toxicosis in Siamese kittens, and doses as low as 300 mcg/kg have been lethal in kittens. In horses, adverse reactions may include itching because of effects on microfilariae.

Contraindications and Precautions

Do not administer to animals younger than 6 weeks of age. Animals with high numbers of microfilaremia may show adverse reactions to high doses. If dogs are sensitive to ivermectin (see earlier list of breeds), they may be sensitive to other drugs in this class (avermectins). Ivermectin at approved clinical doses for treatment of endoparasites or heartworm prevention has been safe in pregnant animals. At high doses used for treating demodicosis, safety is not known, but there have been no reports of teratogenic effects. In the most sensitive laboratory animal (mouse) the lowest dose that is teratogenic is 400 mcg/kg. Dogs with MDR mutation may also be sensitive to other drugs such as loperamide and anticancer drugs. Ivermectin is excreted in milk.

Drug Interactions

Do not administer with drugs that could potentially increase the penetration of ivermectin across the blood-brain barrier. Such drugs include ketoconazole, itraconazole, cyclosporine, and calcium-channel blockers.

Instructions for Use

Ivermectin is used in a wide range of animals for internal and external parasites. Dosage regimens vary, depending on the species and parasite treated. Heartworm prevention is lowest dose, other parasites require higher doses. Heartguard and a topical form is only form approved for small animals; for other indications, large animal injectable products are often administered PO, IM, or SQ to small animals. Do not administer IV. Injections in pigs should be made in neck only.

Patient Monitoring and Laboratory Tests

Monitor for microfilaremia prior to administration in small animals.

Formulations

Ivermectin is available in 1% (10 mg/mL) and 0.27% (2.7 mg/mL) injectable solution, 10 mg/mL oral solution, 0.8 mg/mL oral sheep drench, 18.7 mg/mL oral paste, 68, 136, and 272 mcg tablets and 55 and 165 mg feline tablets. A water-soluble topical is 0.01% (0.1 mg/mL) available in ampules in foil pouches for treating ear mites in cats.

Stability and Storage

Store in tightly sealed container, protected from light, and at room temperature. Stability of compounded formulations has not been evaluated.

Small Animal Dosage

Dogs

- Heartworm preventative: 6 mcg/kg q30day PO.
- Microfilaricide: 50 mcg/kg PO 2 weeks after adulticide therapy.
- Ectoparasite therapy: 200-400 mcg/kg (0.2-0.4 mg/kg) IM, SQ, or PO.
- Endoparasites: 200-400 mcg/kg (0.2-0.4 mg/kg) weekly SQ or PO.
- Demodicosis therapy: Start with 100 mcg/kg/day (0.1 mg/kg) and increase dose by 100 mcg/kg/day to 600 mcg/kg/day (0.6 mg/kg) for 60-120 days, PO.
- Sarcoptic mange and Cheyletiellosis therapy: 200-400 mcg/kg q7days PO or q14 days SQ for 4-6 weeks.

Cats

- Heartworm preventative: 24 mcg/kg q30 days PO.
- Ectoparasite therapy: 200-400 mcg/kg (0.2-0.4 mg/kg) IM, SQ, or PO.
- Endoparasite therapy: 200-400 mcg/kg (0.2-0.4 mg/kg) weekly SQ or PO.
- Topical: 0.5 mL per ear (0.1 mg/mL) for treating ear mites.

Large Animal Dosage

Horses

- 200 mcg/kg (0.2 mg/kg) IM, oral paste, or oral solution.

Calves

- Slow-release bolus: 5.7-13.8 mg/kg, as a single dose, which has a duration of 135 days.

Cattle and Goats

- Injection solution: 200 mcg (0.2 mg) per kg as a single dose SQ.

Pigs

- 300 mcg (0.3 mg) per kg, SQ as a single dose.

Sheep

- Injection solution: 200 mcg (0.2 mg) per kg as a single dose SQ.
- 200 mcg/kg PO.

Regulatory Information

Pigs withdrawal time (meat): 18 days for SQ in jection.

Cattle and calves withdrawal time (meat): 35 days cattle for SQ injection or 180 days for slow-release bolus. 48 days for topical (pour-on).

Because a withdrawal time in milk has not been established, do not use in female dairy cattle of breeding age.

Sheep withdrawal time (meat): 11 days.

Goats withdrawal time: 11-14 days (meat) and 6-9 hours (milk). When administering SQ to goats use 35 hours for meat and 40 hours for milk.

I

Ivermectin + Praziquantel

eye-ver-mek'tin + pray-zih-kwon'tel

Trade and Other Names: Equimax

Functional Classification: Antiparasitic

Pharmacology and Mechanism of Action

Antiparasitic drug. Ivermectin + Praziquantel are indicated for use in horses for treatment and control of tapeworms, large strongyles (including *Strongylus vulgaris, Strongylus edentatus, S. equines*), and small strongyles, pinworms, ascarids, hairworms, stomach worms, bots, *Habronema spp.*, and other parasites.

Indications and Clinical Uses

Ivermectin has properties as described in the Ivermectin monograph. Praziquantel is added to this formulation to increase the spectrum.

Precautionary Information

Adverse Reactions and Side Effects

Toxicity may occur at high doses. Ivermectin appears to be safe for pregnant animals.

Contraindications and Precautions

Ivermectin can be administered to breeding, pregnant, and lactating animals without adverse effects.

Drug Interactions

Use cautiously with other drugs that may affect penetration across the blood-brain barrier.

Instructions for Use

Use of this drug is similar to individual drugs ivermectin and praziquantel.

Patient Monitoring and Laboratory Tests

Fecal samples should be examined for parasites to monitor effectiveness.

Formulations

Ivermectin + praziquantel is available in a paste composed of 1.87% ivermectin and 14.03% praziquantel.

Stability and Storage

Store in tightly sealed container, protected from light, and at room temperature.

Small Animal Dosage

No dose available for small animals.

Large Animal Dosage

Horses

- 200 mcg/kg Ivermectin and 1 mg/kg Praziquantel PO.

Regulatory Information

No withdrawal times are available for animals intended for food (extralabel use).

Kanamycin Sulfate

kan-ah-mye'sin sul'fate

Trade and Other Names: Kantrim

Functional Classification: Antibacterial

Pharmacology and Mechanism of Action

Aminoglycoside antibiotic. Bactericidal. Like other aminoglycosides, kanamycin acts to inhibit bacteria protein synthesis via binding to 30S ribosome. Kanamycin has a broad spectrum of activity that includes *Staphylococcus spp.*, and gram-negative bacilli. It has weak activity against streptococci and anaerobic bacteria. Kanamycin is not as active against most bacteria as gentamicin or amikacin.

Indications and Clinical Uses

Kanamycin is a broad-spectrum antibiotic used to treat gram-negative infections. It is less active than gentamicin, amikacin, or tobramycin. Therefore, there is little advantage for using kanamycin over the other drugs in this class.

Precautionary Information

Adverse Reactions and Side Effects

Nephrotoxicity is the most dose-limiting toxicity. Ensure that patients have adequate fluid and electrolyte balance during therapy. Ototoxicity and vestibulotoxicity also are possible.

Contraindications and Precautions

Do not use in animals with renal disease. Do not use in dehydrated animals.

Drug Interactions

When used with anesthetic agents, neuromuscular blockade is possible. Do not mix in vial or syringe with other antibiotics. Ototoxicity and nephrotoxicity potentiated by loop diuretics such as furosemide.

Instructions for Use

Kanamycin is not as active as other aminoglycosides. For serious infections consider gentamicin or amikacin.

Patient Monitoring and Laboratory Tests

Susceptibility testing: CLSI (NCCLS) minimum inhibitory concentration (MIC) value break point for susceptibility is less than or equal to 16 mcg/mL. Monitor BUN, creatinine, and urine for evidence of renal toxicity.

Formulations

Kanamycin is available in 200 and 500 mg/mL injection.

Stability and Storage

Store in tightly sealed container, protected from light, and at room temperature. It is soluble in water, but is not stable in compounded formulations. Do not mix with other drugs. Do not freeze.

Small Animal Dosage

Dogs and Cats

- 10 mg/kg q12h IV or IM.
- 20 mg/kg q24h IV or IM.

Large Animal Dosage

Horses

- 10 mg/kg q24h IV.

Regulatory Information

Avoid use in food-producing animals. Extended withdrawal times (as long as 18 months) may be needed for withdrawal time in cattle. For extralabel use withdrawal interval estimates, contact FARAD at 1-888-USFARAD (1-888-873-2723) or send e-mail to FARAD@ncsu.edu.

Kaolin + Pectin

kay'oh-lin + pek'tin

Trade and Other Names: KaoPectate

Functional Classification: Antidiarrheal

Pharmacology and Mechanism of Action

Antidiarrheal compound. Kaolin may act as adsorbent for endotoxins and pectin may protect intestinal mucosa. Commercial forms of kaolin-pectin (Kao Pectate) contain salicylate (8.68 mg/mL). The salicylate component may have antiinflammatory effects to decrease secretory diarrhea caused by bacteria.

Indications and Clinical Uses

Kaolin and pectin combinations are used for the symptomatic treatment of acute diarrhea. Efficacy for treating diarrhea in animals has not been established.

Precautionary Information

Adverse Reactions and Side Effects

Side effects are uncommon.

Contraindications and Precautions

No specific contraindications in animals.

Drug Interactions

No drug interactions are reported. However, the kaolin component may prevent absorption of other drugs. Administer other oral drugs 30 minutes prior to kaolin-pectin to avoid drug interaction.

Instructions for Use

Kaolin-pectin may not change the course of diarrhea but may change the character of the feces.

Patient Monitoring and Laboratory Tests

No specific monitoring is necessary.

Formulations

Kaolin-pectin is available in a 12 oz. oral suspension. Salicylate (8.68 mg/mL) is present in Kao-Pectate.

Kaolin-pectin is available in 1 quart and 1 gallon containers containing 5.8 grams kaolin and 0.139 grams pectin per 30 mL (one ounce).

Stability and Storage

Store in tightly sealed container, protected from light, and at room temperature.

Small Animal Dosage

Dogs and Cats

- 1-2 mL/kg q2-6h PO.

Large Animal Dosage

Horses and Cattle

- 180-300 mL q2-3h PO.

Calves and Foals

- 90-120 mL q2-3h PO.

Regulatory Information

There is little risk of residues in animals that produce food. No withdrawal times are necessary.

Ketamine Hydrochloride

ket'ah-meen hye-droe-klor'ide

Trade and Other Names: Ketalar, Ketavet, and Vetalar

Functional Classification: Anesthetic

K

Pharmacology and Mechanism of Action

Anesthetic agent. Exact mechanism of action is not known, but most evidence suggests that it acts as dissociative agent. Ketamine produces mild analgesia and modulate pain via its ability to act as an n-methyl D-aspartate (NMDA) antagonist. Ketamine is rapidly metabolized in most animals (60 minute half-life in dogs), however metabolite (norketamine) may produce more prolonged NMDA antagonistic effects.

Indications and Clinical Uses

Ketamine is used for short-term anesthetic procedures. Duration of action is generally 30 minutes or less. Ketamine has some analgesic properties via its effects on NMDA receptors and has been administered as an adjunct to other analgesic medications, usually with opiates. Ketamine is often combined in use with other anesthetics and sedatives such as benzodiazepines (diazepam) or $alpha_2$ agonists (medetomidine and xylazine). Such combinations have been synergistic and allowed lower doses of each individual component.

Although ordinarily contraindicated in epileptic patients, it has been used to treat rare cases of refractory status epilepticus through its NMDA receptor effects.

Precautionary Information

Adverse Reactions and Side Effects

Ketamine causes pain with intramuscular injection (pH of solution is 3.5). Tremors, muscle spasticity, and convulsive seizures have been reported. Ketamine will increase heart rate and blood pressure as a result of an increase in sympathetic tone. It will produce an increased cardiac output compared to other anesthetic agents. Salivation, mydriasis, and regurgitation are increased in animals that receive ketamine, which may be reduced by premedication within atropine. Apnea may develop in some animals, and oxygen supplementation should be provided.

Contraindications and Precautions

Do not use in animals with head injury because it may elevate cerebral spinal fluid (CSF) pressure. Use cautiously, if at all, in animals with glaucoma. Do not use in animals prone to seizures.

Drug Interactions

Ketamine hydrochloride is maintained at an acidic pH for stability and solubility. If mixed with alkalinizing solutions instability or precipitation can result.

Instructions for Use

Ketamine is often used in combination with other anesthetics and anesthetic adjuncts, such as xylazine, medetomidine, acepromazine, and diazepam. For use in cats, administration of acepromazine at 0.1 mg/kg and atropine at 0.05 mg/kg is recommended prior to administration of ketamine. Intravenous doses are generally less than intramuscular doses. Animals receiving ketamine will have open eyelids, and artificial tears should be applied to prevent corneal injury.

Patient Monitoring and Laboratory Tests

Monitor heart rate and breathing in patients anesthetized with ketamine.

Formulations

Ketamine is available in 100 mg/mL injection solution.

Stability and Storage

Store in tightly sealed container, protected from light, and at room temperature. Ketamine is soluble in water and ethanol.

Small Animal Dosage

For all animals: Lower doses listed for intravenous use; higher doses listed for intramuscular use.

Dogs

- 5.5-22 mg/kg IV or IM. It is recommended to use adjunctive sedative or tranquilizer treatment.
- Constant Rate Infusion (CRI): Loading dose of 0.3-0.5 mg/kg IV, followed by 0.3-0.6 mg/kg/hr (5-10 mcg/kg/min). This rate may be increased to 1 mg/kg/hr if needed.

Cats

- 2-25 mg/kg IV or IM. It is recommended to use adjunctive sedative or tranquilizer treatment.
- CRI: Loading dose of 0.3-0.5 mg/kg IV, followed by 0.3-0.6 mg/kg/hr (5-10 mcg/kg/min). This rate may be increased to 1 mg/kg/hr if needed.

Large Animal Dosage

Horses, Cattle, Sheep, and Swine

- 2 mg/kg IV.
- 10 mg/kg IM. Often used in combination with other agents, such as xylazine.

Regulatory Information

Extralabel use: establish a withdrawal time of at least 3 days for meat and 48 hours for milk.

Schedule III controlled drug

RCI Classification: 2

Ketoconazole

kee-toe-kah'nah-zole

Trade and Other Names: Nizoral

Functional Classification: Antifungal

Pharmacology and Mechanism of Action

Azole (imidazole) antifungal drug. Ketoconazole has a similar mechanism of action as other azole antifungal agents (itraconazole and fluconazole). It inhibits a P450 enzyme in fungi and inhibits ergosterol synthesis in fungal cell membrane. Fungistatic. It has antifungal activity against dermatophytes and a variety of systemic fungi, such as *Histoplasma, Blastomyces,* and *Coccidioides* and *Malassezia* yeast. Other azole antifungal drugs include voriconazole, itraconazole, and fluconazole.

Indications and Clinical Uses

Ketoconazole is used in dogs, cats, and some exotic animals to treat dermatophytes and systemic fungi, such as *Blastomyces, Histoplasma*, and *Coccidioides.* It also has been shown effective for treatment of *Malassezia* dermatitis. It does not have good activity against *Aspergillus.* Ketoconazole should not be used in horses because oral absorption is poor unless administered with a highly acidic vehicle. In dogs it has been used to reduce doses of cyclosporine.

K

Precautionary Information

Adverse Reactions and Side Effects

Adverse effects in animals include dose-related vomiting, diarrhea, and hepatic injury. Liver enzyme elevations are common. Ketoconazole inhibits hormone synthesis and can lower concentrations of cortisol, testosterone, and other hormones in animals. Ketoconazole has been associated with cataract formation in dogs.

Contraindications and Precautions

Do not administer to pregnant animals. At high doses in laboratory animals, it has caused embryotoxicity and fetal abnormalities. Some of these effects on pregnancy may be because of the inhibition of estrogen synthesis by ketoconazole.

Drug Interactions

Ketoconazole is a potent inhibitor of hepatic cytochrome P450 enzymes and will inhibit metabolism of other drugs (anticonvulsants, cyclosporine, warfarin, and cisapride).

Instructions for Use

Oral absorption depends on acidity in stomach. Do not administer with antisecretory drugs or antacids. Because of endocrine effects, ketoconazole has been used for short-term treatment of hyperadrenocorticism. However, many experts believe that ketoconazole is not an effective long-term treatment for canine Cushing's disease.

Patient Monitoring and Laboratory Tests

Monitor liver enzymes for evidence of toxicity. Ketoconazole will lower serum cortisol levels.

Formulations

Ketoconazole is available in 200 mg tablets and 100 mg/mL oral suspension (Canada).

Stability and Storage

Store in tightly sealed container, protected from light, and at room temperature. Ketoconazole is practically insoluble in water but is soluble in ethanol. When ketoconazole was compounded extemporaneously from tablets with syrups and flavorings, it was stable for 60 days. However, ketoconazole requires acidity for solubility and may not be absorbed from these formulations. If compounded in alkaline conditions, it may precipitate.

Small Animal Dosage

Dogs

- 10-15 mg/kg q8-12h PO.
- *Malassezia canis* infection: 5 mg/kg q24h PO.
- Hyperadrenocorticism: 15 mg/kg q12h PO.

Cats

- 5-10 mg/kg q8-12h PO.

Large Animal Dosage

Horses

Poorly absorbed. Fluconazole, itraconazole, or voriconazole is more completely absorbed.

Regulatory Information

Withdrawal times are not established for animals that produce food. For extralabel use withdrawal interval estimates, contact FARAD at 1-888-USFARAD (1-888-873-2723) or send e-mail to FARAD@ncsu.edu.

Ketoprofen

kee-toe-proe'fen

Trade and Other Names: Orudis-KT (human OTC tablet), Ketofen (veterinary injection), and Anafen (outside the U.S.)

Functional Classification: Nonsteroidal antiinflammatory drug (NSAID)

Pharmacology and Mechanism of Action

Ketoprofen, like other NSAIDs, produce analgesic and antiinflammatory effects by inhibiting the synthesis of prostaglandins. The enzyme inhibited by NSAID is the cyclo-oxygenase enzyme (COX). The COX enzyme exists in two isoforms, called COX-1 and COX-2. COX-1 is primarily responsible for synthesis of prostaglandins important for maintaining a healthy GI tract, renal function, platelet function, and other normal functions. COX-2 is induced and responsible for synthesizing prostaglandins that are important mediators of pain, inflammation, and fever. (There may be some crossover of COX-1 and COX-2 effects in some situations.) Ketoprofen is a nonselective inhibitor of COX-1 and COX-2. There is weak evidence of its ability to inhibit lipoxygenase.

Indications and Clinical Uses

Ketoprofen is an NSAID. Ketoprofen is used for treatment of moderate pain and inflammation. It has a half-life in most animals less than 2 hours, but it has a duration of action for up to 24 hours. Ketoprofen is not registered in U.S. for small animals but has been labeled for dogs and cats in other countries. It has been given by injection for acute treatment and by tablet for long-term use. In the U.S. if it is used in small animals, it is the large animal formulation that is used or the human OTC version. In dogs and cats, it has been shown effective for treating pyrexia. In horses, ketoprofen is used for musculoskeletal inflammation and pain, abdominal pain, and other inflammatory conditions. Ketoprofen also has been used in cattle, goats, sheep, and pigs. In cattle, it has been effective for fever, pain, and inflammation associated with mastitis. It is registered for use in cattle in Canada, but not in the U.S.

Precautionary Information

Adverse Reactions and Side Effects

All NSAIDs share similar adverse effect of GI toxicity. Ketoprofen has been administered for 5 consecutive days in dogs without serious adverse effects. Most common side effect is vomiting. GI ulceration is possible in some animals. In horses, ketoprofen has been less ulcerogenic than phenylbutazone or flunixin meglumine in one study. Bleeding problems can occur if ketoprofen is administered prior or after surgery.

Contraindications and Precautions

Do not administer to animals prone to GI ulcers. Do not administer with other ulcerogenic drugs such as corticosteroids. Do not use extended-release formulations of ketoprofen.

Drug Interactions

Do not administer with other NSAIDs or with corticosteroids. Corticosteroids have been shown to exacerbate the GI adverse effects. Some NSAIDs may interfere with the action of diuretic drugs and angiotensin-converting enzyme (ACE) inhibitors.

Instructions for Use

Although not approved in the U.S., ketoprofen is approved for small animals in other countries. Doses listed are based on approved use in those countries. It is available as OTC drug for humans in the U.S.

Patient Monitoring and Laboratory Tests

Monitor patient for signs of GI intoxication (vomiting and diarrhea). Monitor renal function during chronic treatment.

Formulations

Ketoprofen is available in 12.5 mg tablets (OTC), 25, 50, and 75 mg (human preparation) and 100 mg/mL injection for horses. It is available in 10 mg/mL outside the U.S.

Stability and Storage

Store in tightly sealed container, protected from light, and at room temperature. Ketoprofen is insoluble in water, but it is soluble in ethanol. Stability of oral compounded formulations has not been evaluated.

Small Animal Dosage

Dogs and Cats

- 1 mg/kg q24h PO for up to 5 days. Initial dose can be given via injection at up to 2 mg/kg SQ, IM, or IV.

Large Animal Dosage

Horses

- 2.2-3.3 mg/kg/day IV or IM.

Cattle and Small Ruminants

- 3 mg/kg/day IV or IM for up to 3 days.

Regulatory Information

Extralabel use in U.S.: withdrawal time of at least 7 days for meat and 24 hours for milk.
In Canada a meat withdrawal time of 1 day is established.
RCI Classification: 4

Ketorolac Tromethamine

kee-toe'role-ak troe-meth'eh-meen

Trade and Other Names: Toradol

Functional Classification: Nonsteroidal antiinflammatory drug (NSAID)

Pharmacology and Mechanism of Action

Ketorolac, like other NSAIDs, produce analgesic and antiinflammatory effects by inhibiting the synthesis of prostaglandins. The enzyme inhibited by NSAID is the cyclo-oxygenase enzyme (COX). The COX enzyme exists in two isoforms, called COX-1 and COX-2. COX-1 is primarily responsible for synthesis of prostaglandins important for maintaining a healthy GI tract, renal function, platelet function, and other normal functions. COX-2 is induced and responsible for synthesizing prostaglandins that are important mediators of pain, inflammation, and fever. (There may be some crossover of COX-1 and COX-2 effects in some situations.) Ketorolac is a nonselective inhibitor of COX.

Indications and Clinical Uses

Ketorolac is infrequently used in veterinary medicine. There is only limited data on safety and efficacy for veterinary uses. It has occasionally been used to treat pain and inflammation in dogs.

Precautionary Information

Adverse Reactions and Side Effects

Like other NSAIDs, it may cause GI ulceration and renal ischemia. Ketorolac may cause GI lesions if administered more frequently than every 8 hours.

Contraindications and Precautions

Do not administer more than two doses. Do not administer to animals prone to GI ulcers. Do not administer with other ulcerogenic drugs such as corticosteroids.

Drug Interactions

Do not administer with other NSAIDs or with corticosteroids. Corticosteroids have been shown to exacerbate the GI adverse effects. Some NSAIDs may interfere with the action of diuretic drugs and angiotensin-converting enzyme (ACE) inhibitors.

Instructions for Use

Limited clinical studies in dogs have been conducted. However, it may be effective in some patients for short-term use. Long-term administration is discouraged.

Patient Monitoring and Laboratory Tests

Monitor for signs of GI ulceration.

Formulations

Ketorolac is available in 10 mg tablets, and 15 and 30 mg/mL injection in 10% alcohol.

Stability and Storage

Store in tightly sealed container, protected from light, protected from humidity, and at room temperature. Ketorolac tromethamine is soluble in water and slightly soluble in ethanol. Stability of oral compounded formulations has not been evaluated.

Small Animal Dosage

Dogs

- 0.5 mg/kg q8-12h PO, IM, or IV.

Cats

No safe dose is established.

Large Animal Dosage

No large animal doses are reported.

Regulatory Information

Withdrawal times are not established for animals that produce animals. For extralabel use withdrawal interval estimates, contact FARAD at 1-888-USFARAD (1-888-873-2723) or send e-mail to FARAD@ncsu.edu.

Lactated Ringer's Solution

Trade and Other Names: LRS

Functional Classification: Fluid replacement

Pharmacology and Mechanism of Action

Lactated Ringer's solution is a fluid solution for replacement. Intravenous administration. Lactated Ringer's solution contains a balanced combination of electrolytes and an alkalinizing buffer. This solution contains 28 mEq/L of lactate.

Indications and Clinical Uses

Lactated Ringer's solution is indicated as a replacement or maintenance fluid. It also is used as a vehicle to deliver intravenous medications via constant rate infusion (CRI). It has been administered SQ, intraosseous (in bone medullary cavity), and intraperitoneal (IP) in animals when intravenous access is not possible. It contains lactate, a metabolizable base, but will not correct acidosis as quickly as bicarbonate. Severely acidemic animals may already have high lactate serum levels.

Precautionary Information

Adverse Reactions and Side Effects

No significant adverse effects.

Contraindications and Precautions

Administer intravenous fluids only in patients monitored carefully.

Drug Interactions

Lactated Ringer's solution has a pH of 6-7.5. Do not add medications to this solution if they are unstable at this pH. Lactated Ringer's contains calcium. Do not add drugs to this solution that may bind (chelate) to calcium.

Instructions for Use

Fluid requirements vary depending on animal's needs (replacement versus maintenance). For shock therapy, administer half the calculated dose in first 30 minutes and the remainder CRI. For severe acidemia, consider fluids supplemented with bicarbonate instead of lactate.

Patient Monitoring and Laboratory Tests

Monitor patient's hydration status and electrolyte balance. With high administration rates, monitor patient for signs of pulmonary edema.

Formulations

Lactated Ringer's solution is available in 250, 500, and 1000 mL fluid bags.

Stability and Storage

Store in tightly sealed container. If container has been punctured or transferred to another container, sterility cannot be assured.

Small Animal Dosage

Dogs and Cats

- Moderate dehydration: 15-30 mL/kg/hr IV.
- Severe dehydration: 50 mL/kg/hr IV
- Maintenance: 55-65 mL/kg/day IV, SQ, or IP (2.5 mL/kg/hr).

- During anesthesia: 10-15 mL/kg/hr IV.
- Shock therapy: (for dogs) 90 mL/kg IV and (for cats) 60-70 mL/kg IV.

Large Animal Dosage

Cattle, Horses, and Pigs

- Maintenance: 40-50 mL/kg/day IV.
- Moderate dehydration: 15-30 mL/kg/hr IV.
- Severe dehydration: 50 mL/kg/hr IV.

Calves and Foals

- Moderate dehydration: 45 mL/kg at a rate of 30-40 mL/kg/hr IV.
- Severe dehydration: 80-90 mL/kg at a rate of 30-40 mL/kg/hr IV. In severe cases it may be given as rapidly as 80 mL/kg/hr.

Regulatory Information

There is no risk of harmful residues in animals intended for food. No withdrawal times are necessary.

Lactulose

lak'tyoo-lose

Trade and Other Names: Chronulac and generic brands

Functional Classification: Laxative

L

Pharmacology and Mechanism of Action

Laxative. Lactulose is a disaccharide sugar containing one molecule of fructose and one molecule of galactose. Lactulose produces laxative effect by osmotic effect in colon. It is a nonabsorbed sugar and retains water in the intestine after oral administration via an osmotic effect. Lactulose also will decrease the pH of intestinal lumen.

Indications and Clinical Uses

Lactulose is administered orally for treatment of hyperammonemia (hepatic encephalopathy), because it decreases blood ammonia concentrations via lowering pH of colon, thus ammonia in colon is not as readily absorbed. Lactulose also is administered orally to produce a laxative effect for treatment of constipation

Precautionary Information

Adverse Reactions and Side Effects

Excessive use may cause fluid and electrolyte loss.

Contraindications and Precautions

Use lactulose with caution in animals with diabetes, because it contains lactose and galactose.

Drug Interactions

No drug interactions are reported for animals.

Instructions for Use

In veterinary medicine, clinical studies to establish efficacy are not available. In addition to doses cited, 20-30 mL/kg of 30% solution retention enema has been used in cats.

Patient Monitoring and Laboratory Tests

When used for treating hepatic encephalopathy, monitor the patient's hepatic status.

Formulations

Lactulose is available in 10 g/15 mL liquid solution (3.3 grams per 5 mL).

Stability and Storage

Store in tightly sealed container, protected from light, and at room temperature. It is soluble in water. Darkening of the solution may occur without affecting stability. Avoid freezing.

Small Animal Dosage

Dogs

- Constipation: 1 mL/4.5 kg q8h (to effect) PO.
- Hepatic encephalopathy: 0.5 mL/kg q8h PO.

Cats

- Constipation: 1 mL/4.5 kg q8h (to effect) PO.
- Hepatic encephalopathy: 2.5-5 mL/cat q8h PO.

Large Animal Dosage

Horses and Cattle

- 0.25-0.5 mL/kg/day PO.

Regulatory Information

There is little risk of residues in animals intended for food. No withdrawal times are necessary.

Leucovorin Calcium

loo-koe-vor'in kal'see-um

Trade and Other Names: Wellcovorin and generic brands

Functional Classification: Antidote

Pharmacology and Mechanism of Action

Leucovorin is a reduced form of folic acid that is converted to active folic acid derivatives for purine and thymidine synthesis.

Indications and Clinical Uses

Use of leucovorin is uncommon in animals. It may be used as an antidote for folic acid antagonists. In humans it is primarily used as rescue for overdoses of folic acid antagonists (methotrexate) and treatment of adverse reactions from methotrexate but also may be considered for reactions caused by pyrimethamine.

Precautionary Information

Adverse Reactions and Side Effects

No adverse reactions reported for animals, but allergic reactions have been reported in people.

Contraindications and Precautions

No contraindications reported for animals.

Drug Interactions

Leucovorin will interfere with action of trimethoprim and pyrimethamine.

Instructions for Use

Clinical studies have not been reported in veterinary medicine. Although leucovorin may prevent toxicity from trimethoprim, it will not prevent toxic reactions that may be caused by sulfonamides in animals.

Patient Monitoring and Laboratory Tests

Monitor CBC if this drug is used to treat overdose of folic acid antagonists.

Formulations Available

Leucovorin is available in 5, 10, 15, and 25 mg tablets and 3 and 5 mg/mL injection.

Stability and Storage

Store in tightly sealed container, protected from light, and at room temperature. It is soluble in water but is insoluble in ethanol. Reconstituted solutions have stability for 7 days at room temperature or refrigerated.

Small Animal Dosage

Dogs and Cats

- With methotrexate administration: 3 mg/m^2 IV, IM, or PO.
- As antidote for pyrimethamine toxicosis: 1 mg/kg q24h PO.

Large Animal Dosage

No large animal doses are reported. However, if pyrimethamine toxicosis is suspected in horses, doses listed for small animals may be considered.

Regulatory Information

Withdrawal times are not established for animals that produce food. For extralabel use withdrawal interval estimates, contact FARAD at 1-888-USFARAD (1-888-873-2723) or send e-mail to FARAD@ncsu.edu.

L

Levamisole Hydrochloride

leh-vam′ih-sole hye-droe-klor′ide

Trade and Other Names: Levasole, Ripercol, Tramisol, and Ergamisol

Functional Classification: Antiparasitic

Pharmacology and Mechanism of Action

Levamisole is an antiparasitic drug of the imidazothiazole class. It eliminates a variety of parasites via neuromuscular toxicity. Levamisole has a *immunorestorative* effect in animals, but the mechanism of action on the immune system is unknown. It may activate and stimulate proliferation of T-cells, augment monocyte activation, and stimulate macrophages, including phagocytosis and chemotaxis. It may increase neutrophil mobility. However, it is not cytotoxic.

Indications and Clinical Uses

In cattle and sheep, it is used to treat a variety of nematodes, including stomach worms (*Haemonchus, Trichostrongylus,* and *Ostertagia species*), intestinal worms (*Trichostrongylus, Cooperia, Nematodirus, Bunostomum, Oesophagostomum,* and *Chabertia species*), and lungworms (*Dictyocaulus species*). In pigs it is used to treat nematodes such as large roundworms (*Ascaris suum*), nodular worms (*Oesophagostomum* species), intestinal thread worms (*Strongyloides ransomi*), and lungworms (*Metastrongylus* species). Levamisole has been used for treatment of endoparasites in dogs and as a microfilaricide. In people, levamisole is used as an immunostimulant to aid in treatment of colorectal carcinoma and malignant melanoma. In animals, levamisole also is used as an immunostimulant, but reports of efficacy are lacking.

Precautionary Information

Adverse Reactions and Side Effects

Levamisole may produce cholinergic toxicity. It has produced vomiting in some dogs. The injectable formulation has caused some swelling at the site of injection. In humans, when used as an immunostimulant, it has caused stomatitis, agranulocytosis, and thrombocytopenia.

Contraindications and Precautions

Use cautiously in animals with high heartworm microfilaria burdens. Reactions are possible from heavy kill rate of microfilaria. There are no adverse reactions on fertility and no effects on pregnancy. In rats and rabbits there was no evidence of teratogenicity or embryotoxicity at doses of 180 mg/kg.

Drug Interactions

Do not use with pyrantel because they share the same mechanism of toxicity.

Instructions for Use

In heartworm-positive dogs, it may sterilize female adult heartworms. Levamisole has also been used as an immunostimulant; however, clinical reports of its efficacy are not available. Because of the possibility of contamination at the injection site, use a clean needle between animals and clean the injection site.

Patient Monitoring and Laboratory Tests

Monitor for microfilaria after treatment for heartworm disease.

Formulations

Levamisole is available in 0.184 gram bolus; 2.19 gram bolus; 9, 11.7, and 18.15 grams per packet; 136.5 mg/mL and 182 mg/mL injection (levamisole phosphate); and 50 mg tablet (Ergamisol).

Stability and Storage

Store in tightly sealed container, protected from light, and at room temperature. Stability of compounded formulations has not been evaluated.

Small Animal Dosage

Dogs

- Endoparasites: 5-8 mg/kg once PO (up to 10 mg/kg PO for 2 days).
- Hookworms: 10 mg/kg/day for 2 days.
- Microfilaricide: 10 mg/kg q24h PO for 6-10 days.
- Immunostimulant: 0.5-2 mg/kg 3 times/week PO. (In humans the immunostimulant dose is given q8h for 3 days.)

Cats

- Endoparasites: 4.4 mg/kg once PO.
- Lungworms: 20-40 mg/kg q48h for 5 treatments PO.

Large Animal Dosage

Cattle and Sheep

- 8 mg/kg once PO, or approximately on 2.19 gram bolus per 450-750 pounds (200-340 kg).
- Levamisole injection (for cattle): 8 mg/kg SQ into mid neck area, once, or approximately 2 mL per 100 pounds (45 kg).

Pigs

- 8 mg/kg in drinking water.

Regulatory Information

Cattle withdrawal time (meat): 2 days (PO) and 7 days (SQ injection).
Sheep withdrawal time (meat): 3 days.
Pig withdrawal time (meat): 3 days.

Levetiracetam

lev-eh-teer-ass′eh-tam

Trade and Other Names: Keppra

Functional Classification: Anticonvulsant

Pharmacology and Mechanism of Action

Anticonvulsant. The mechanism of action is not certain, but it does not involve inhibitory neurotransmitters. It inhibits burst firing of neurons without affecting normal neuronal excitement. It does not undergo hepatic metabolism and relies almost completely on renal clearance. It may have advantages for use in patients with hepatic diseases.

Indications and Clinical Uses

Levetiracetam has been used in cats at a dose of 20 mg/kg every 8 hours and found to be effective in some cases. In dogs, levetiracetam has been used refractory to other anticonvulsants. It is used often in combination with other anticonvulsants.

Precautionary Information

Adverse Reactions and Side Effects

Weakness, lethargy, and dizziness have been reported in people. No adverse effects have been reported in animals.

Contraindications and Precautions

No known contraindications.

Drug Interactions

No drug interactions common to other anticonvulsants are anticipated with levetiracetam, because it does not affect the cytochrome P450 enzymes. Interactions with other concurrently used anticonvulsants have not been reported.

Instructions for Use

It is rapidly and completely absorbed, and absorption is not affected by feeding.

Patient Monitoring and Laboratory Tests

Monitor seizure frequency. Currently no clinical monitoring test for serum exists.

Formulations

Levetiracetam is available in 250, 500, and 750 mg tablets.

Stability and Storage

Store in tightly sealed container, protected from light, and at room temperature. Stability of compounded formulations has not been evaluated. It is soluble in water, and it may be acceptable to mix with other foods, syrups, or flavorings immediately prior to oral administration.

Small Animal Dosage

Dogs

- Start with 10 mg/kg q12h PO and increase gradually as necessary, up to as much as 20 mg/kg q8h, PO.

Cats

- 30 mg/kg q12h PO.

Large Animal Dosage

No dose has been reported for large animals.

Regulatory Information

No regulatory information is available. For extralabel use withdrawal interval estimates, contact FARAD at 1-888-USFARAD (1-888-873-2723) or send e-mail to FARAD@ncsu.edu.

Levodopa

lee'voe-doe'pah

Trade and Other Names: Larodopa and L-dopa

Functional Classification: Dopamine agonist

Pharmacology and Mechanism of Action

Dopamine, when administered systemically, does not cross the blood-brain barrier. However, levodopa crosses more easily via a carrier-mediated process and is converted to dopamine after crossing blood-brain barrier. Dopamine is used in neurodegenerative disorders to stimulate CNS dopamine receptors.

Indications and Clinical Uses

In people, levodopa is used for treating Parkinson's disease, and it is used in combination with carbidopa (a peripheral decarboxylase inhibitor) and entacapone (a o-methyltransferase inhibitor) to potentiate therapy. In animals has been used for treating hepatic encephalopathy.

Precautionary Information

Adverse Reactions and Side Effects

Adverse effects in animals have not been reported. In people, dizziness, mental changes, difficult urination, and hypotension are among the reported adverse effects.

Contraindications and Precautions

No specific contraindications for use in animals.

Drug Interactions

Anti-dopamine drugs will interfere with action. Such drugs include metoclopramide, phenothiazines (e.g., acepromazine), and risperidone.

Instructions for Use

Clinical studies have not been reported in veterinary medicine. Titrate dose for each patient.

Patient Monitoring and Laboratory Tests

No specific monitoring is necessary.

Formulations Available

Levodopa is available in 100, 250, and 500 mg tablets or capsules.

Stability and Storage

Store in tightly sealed container, protected from light, and at room temperature. Levodopa is slightly soluble in water but more soluble in acid solutions. It will be rapidly oxidized with exposure to air, which will be indicated by a darkening of the formulation. Injectable solutions have been prepared extemporaneously and found to be stable for 96 hours.

Small Animal Dosage

Dogs and Cats

- Hepatic encephalopathy: 6.8 mg/kg initially, then 1.4 mg/kg q6h.

Large Animal Dosage

No dose has been reported for large animals.

Regulatory Information

No regulatory information is available for animals intended for food. Because of low risk of residues, no withdrawal times are suggested.

Levothyroxine Sodium

lee-voe-thye-roks′een soe′dee-um

Trade and Other Names: T4, Soloxine, Thyro-Tabs, Synthroid, ThyroMed. Leventa and equine powders include Equisyn-T4, Levo-Powder, Thyroid Powder, and Thyro-L

Functional Classification: Hormone

Pharmacology and Mechanism of Action

Thyroid hormone. Levothyroxine is used as replacement therapy for treating patients with hypothyroidism. Levothyroxine is T-4, which is converted in most patients to the active T-3. Requirements and pharmacokinetics vary among animals and doses are adjusted on the basis of thyroid monitoring.

Indications and Clinical Uses

Levothyroxine is used for replacement therapy in animals with thyroid hormone deficiency (hypothyroidism). It has been used in many species, including dogs, cats, and horses. Although it has been suggested for use in treating dogs with von Willebrand's disease, clinical studies failed to show an effect on clotting factors, bleeding times, or von Willebrand's factor (vWf) from levothyroxine treatment (0.04 mg/kg).

Intravenous levothyroxine sodium may be used in dogs for acute treatment of hypothyroid dogs with myxedema coma (4-5 mcg/kg IV).

Precautionary Information

Adverse Reactions and Side Effects

High doses may produce thyrotoxicosis, which is uncommon. Potential adverse effects from IV treatment include arrhythmias or pneumonia.

Contraindications and Precautions

No specific contraindications are reported for small animals. When switching from one brand to another, it is advised to follow-up by testing to ensure that brands are therapeutically equivalent.

Drug Interactions

Patients receiving corticosteroids may have decreased ability to convert T-4 to the active T-3. The following drugs may lower thyroid concentrations when used concurrently: nonsteroidal antiinflammatory drugs (NSAIDs), sulfonamides, and phenobarbital, although results in some dogs may not be clinically significant. Although not reported in animals, in people, administration of estrogens increases thyroid binding globulin and may decrease active form of thyroid hormone (T4) in patients receiving thyroid supplementation. Monitor T4 levels in these patients and increase dose of thyroxine if necessary.

Instructions for Use

Thyroid supplementation should be guided by testing to confirm diagnosis and postmedication monitoring to adjust dose. The brands Soloxine and Synthroid have been equivalent according to studies in dogs. In each case, bioavailability is only 37% (average). When using the liquid formulation (Leventa), use the specially designed syringes for dosing. The starting dose listed in the dosing section for dogs (22 mcg/kg q12) may not be high enough for some dogs and monitoring is recommended to adjust dose appropriately.

Patient Monitoring and Laboratory Tests

Monitor serum T-4 concentrations to guide therapy. Normal thyroxine (T4) baseline levels are 20-55 nmol/L (1.5 to 4.3 mcg/dL). Thyrotropin-releasing hormone (TRH) injection should result in at least 1.5-fold increase in T4. To monitor postpill adequacy of therapy, some feel that the most valuable sample to collect is immediately prior to the next scheduled dose (trough level). Alternatively, some clinicians take a peak concentration by collecting a blood sample 4-6 hours after pill, and the T4 should be between 30 and 60 nmol/L (2.3-4.6 mcg/dL). In horses, postpill peak occurs at 1-2 hours.

Formulations

Levothyroxine is available in 0.1-0.8 mg tablets (in 0.1 mg increments), 0.1-0.8 mg chewable tablets, 1.0 mg/mL oral solution for dogs, and 1 gram per 453.6 of oral powder (1 gram per pound), used for horses.

Stability and Storage

Store in tightly sealed container, protected from light, and at room temperature. Thyroxine is only slightly soluble in water or ethanol. It is more soluble at pH less than 2 or greater than 8. It has been unstable in some compounded formulations. However, it has been added to food products if administered immediately. When it was mixed with ethanol followed by mixing with a syrup, it was stable for 15 days at room temperature and 47 days refrigerated. However, other compounded preparations have been stable for only 15 days (refrigerated) or 11 days (room temperature). Therefore, use of compounded formulations should probably be limited to a storage time of 10-15 days.

The oral solution (Leventa) should be stored refrigerated, but once opened can be stored at room temperature, protected from light, and is stable for 2 months.

Small Animal Dosage

Dogs

- 18-22 mcg/kg (0.018-0.022 mg/kg) q12h PO (adjust dose via monitoring) an alternative dose is 0.5 mg per square meter (0.5 mg/m^2).

- Liquid (1.0 mg/mL): 20 mcg/kg PO, q24h.
- IV therapy for acute treatment: 4-5 mcg/kg IV.

Cats

- 10-20 mcg/kg/day (0.01-0.02 mg/kg) PO (adjust dose via monitoring).

Large Animal Dosage

Horses

- 10-60 mcg/kg (0.01 to 0.06 mg/kg) q24h or 5-30 mcg/kg (0.005-0.03 mg/kg) q12h PO. When using the oral powder for dosing in horses, one level teaspoon contains 12 mg of levothyroxine (T-4), and one tablespoon contains 36 mg of levothyroxine (T-4). This powder may be mixed in with daily ration of grain.

Regulatory Information

No regulatory information is available for animals intended for food. Because of low risk of residues, no withdrawal times are suggested.

Lidocaine Hydrochloride

lye'doe-kane hye-droe-klor'ide

Trade and Other Names: Xylocaine and generic brands

Functional Classification: Local anesthetic, antiarrhythmic

Pharmacology and Mechanism of Action

Local anesthetic. Lidocaine inhibits nerve conduction via sodium channel blockade. Class-1 antiarrhythmic. Decreases Phase 0 depolarization without affecting conduction. After systemic administration lidocaine is metabolized to monoethylglycinexylidide (MEGX), which also has antiarrhythmic properties. Lidocaine also has analgesic properties after systemic administration. During intravenous infusion, it may decrease pain response. In horses it may restore intestinal motility after ileus by inhibiting the sympathetic inhibitory reflexes in the GI tract. Pharmacokinetics in dogs and cats are similar, however, cats have increased sensitivity to the cardiac effects.

Indications and Clinical Uses

Lidocaine is used commonly as a local anesthetic and for acute treatment of ventricular arrhythmias. Lidocaine should be used cautiously for treating supraventricular arrhythmias, because it may increase cardiac conduction. Lidocaine also is used for pain management. It has been administered as a constant rate infusion (CRI) in animals, especially in postsurgical patients. In horses, a CRI may help to restore intestinal motility and is used to treat intestinal ileus.

Precautionary Information

Adverse Reactions and Side Effects

High doses cause CNS effects (tremors, twitches, and seizures) and vomiting. Lidocaine can produce cardiac arrhythmias, but it has greater effect on abnormal cardiac tissue than normal tissue. Intravenous doses of lidocaine in cats have resulted in death. In cats under anesthesia, lidocaine administration has caused decreased cardiac output, cardiovascular depression, and decreased oxygen delivery to tissues. In cats, lidocaine has also produced methemoglobinemia and hemolysis. Intravenous and CRIs doses to horses may cause ataxia, weakness, or tremors, but in most instances have not caused important adverse reactions.

Contraindications and Precautions

Cats are more susceptible to adverse effects, and lower doses should be used for cats. In animals with decreased blood flow to liver (e.g., animals under anesthesia) clearance may be reduced.

Drug Interactions

Lidocaine hydrochloride is maintained as an acidic solution for solubility. Although short-term mixing with alkaline solutions may not interfere with stability, storage in alkalinizing solutions can cause precipitation. If mixed with alkalinizing solutions, it should be administered promptly.

Instructions for Use

When used for local infiltration, many formulations contain epinephrine to prolong activity at injection site. Avoid using formulations that contain epinephrine in patients with cardiac arrhythmias. Note that human formulations may contain epinephrine, but no veterinary formulations contain epinephrine. To increase pH, speed onset of action, and decrease pain from injection, one may add 1 mEq sodium bicarbonate to 10 mL lidocaine (use immediately after mixing).

Patient Monitoring and Laboratory Tests

Monitor for signs of neurotoxicity (e.g., depression, muscle twitching, and seizures). Monitor ECG during treatment for cardiac rate and rhythm in treated animals.

Formulations

Lidocaine is available in 5, 10, 15, and 20 mg/mL injection.

Stability and Storage

Store in tightly sealed container, protected from light, and at room temperature. Topical preparations have been prepared and found to be stable for several weeks.

Small Animal Dosage

Dogs

- Antiarrhythmic: 2-4 mg/kg IV (to a maximum dose of 8 mg/kg over 10 minute period).
- Antiarrhythmic: 25-75 mcg/kg/min IV infusion.
- Antiarrhythmic: 6 mg/kg q1.5h IM.
- Epidural: 4.4 mg/kg of 2% solution.

Cats

- Antiarrhythmic: Start with 0.1 to 0.4 mg/kg initially, and then increase to 0.25-0.75 mg/kg IV slowly if there has been no response.
- Antiarrhythmic: 10-40 mcg/kg/min CRI.
- Epidural: 4.4 mg/kg of 2% solution.

Large Animal Dosage

- Antiarrhythmic: 0.25-0.5 mg/kg q5-15min IV.

Horses

- Post-operative ileus: 1.3 mg/kg IV bolus administered over 15 min, followed by 0.05 mg/kg/min (50 mcg/kg/min) CRI.

Regulatory Information

Extralabel use withdrawal time: 1 day for meat and 24 hours for milk.
Horses: Clearance prior to racing, approximately 2.5 days.
RCI Classification: 2

Lincomycin Hydrochloride, Lincomycin Hydrochloride Monohydrate

lin-koe-mye′sin hye-droe-klor′ide, lin-koe-mye′sin hye-droe-klor′ide mono-hye′drate

Trade and Other Names: Lincocin and Lincomix

Functional Classification: Antibacterial

Pharmacology and Mechanism of Action

Lincosamide antibiotic. Lincomycin is similar in mechanism to clindamycin. Mechanism of action is also similar to macrolides, such as erythromycin, and there may be cross resistance among these drugs. Like the other related drugs, the site of action is the 50S ribosomal subunit. By inhibiting this ribosome, it decreases protein synthesis. In most bacteria it is bacteriostatic. The spectrum includes primarily gram-positive bacteria.

Indications and Clinical Uses

Lincomycin has a gram-positive spectrum and has limited use. In small animals it is used for pyoderma and other soft tissue infections caused by susceptible gram-positive bacteria. It is also active against *Mycoplasma*, *Erysipelothrix*, and *Leptospira* species. In pigs and birds, it is used primarily for treatment of infections caused by *Mycoplasma*. Compared to lincomycin, clindamycin has better activity against anaerobic bacteria.

L

Precautionary Information

Adverse Reactions and Side Effects

Adverse effects are uncommon. Lincomycin has caused vomiting and diarrhea in animals. Severe, and even fatal, enteritis can be caused from oral administration to ruminants.

Contraindications and Precautions

Do **not** administer orally to rodents, horses, ruminants, or rabbits. Oral administration to ruminants and horses can cause severe enteritis.

Drug Interactions

No drug interactions reported for animals.

Instructions for Use

Action of lincomycin and clindamycin are similar enough that clindamycin can be substituted for lincomycin.

Patient Monitoring and Laboratory Tests

Susceptibility testing: CLSI (NCCLS) break points for sensitive organisms are less than or equal to 0.25 mcg/mL for streptococci and less than or equal to 0.5 for other organisms.

Formulations

Lincomycin is available in 100, 200, and 500 mg tablets, 400 mg/g of powder, 16 g/40 g of soluble powder, 10, 20, and 50 g/lb of premix, 50 mg/mL syrup, and 25, 100, and 300 mg/mL solution for injection.

Stability and Storage

Store in tightly sealed container, protected from light, and at room temperature. Stability of compounded formulations has not been evaluated.

Small Animal Dosage

Dogs and Cats

- 15-25 mg/kg q12h PO.
- Pyoderma: 10 mg/kg q12h PO.

Large Animal Dosage

Pigs

- Swine dysentery: 250 mg per gallon of drinking water, which is approximately 8.4 mg/kg/day if given as the only source of drinking water for 5-10 days.
- *Mycoplasma* infections: 11 mg/kg q24h or 11 mg/kg q12h IM injection.

Cattle

- Septic arthritis, mastitis, and abscesses: 5 mg/kg q24h IM for 5-7 days.
- Refractory infections: 10 mg/kg q12h IM.

Sheep

- Septic arthritis: 5 mg/kg q24h for 3-5 days IM.

Regulatory Information

Withdrawal time for pigs: 0, 1, 2, or 6 days, depending on product and route of administration. (For most products, 6 days for oral administration and 2 days for IM administration.) For extra-label use in cattle, FARAD recommends 7 days for meat and 96 hours for milk, at a dose of 5 mg/kg.

Linezolid

lih-neh-zoe'lide

Trade and Other Names: Zyvox

Functional Classification: Antibacterial

Pharmacology and Mechanism of Action

Linezolid is an antibiotic in the oxazolidinone class (synthetic drugs). It is bacteriostatic with a unique mechanism of action. It inhibits protein synthesis by binding to a site on the bacterial 23S ribosomal RNA of the 50S subunit. This prevents formation of the 70S ribosomal unit, and therefore protein synthesis is inhibited. Linezolid has good penetration into cells and extracellular fluid. In dogs the pharmacokinetics are similar to humans. The oral absorption is almost 100%, and the half-life is slightly faster than humans. Linezolid does not undergo hepatic P450 metabolism, and one third of the total clearance relies on the kidneys.

Indications and Clinical Uses

Linezolid is active against streptococci and staphylococci and is indicated for treatment of infections that have become resistant to other drugs, particularly the beta-lactam antibiotics (penicillins, ampicillin derivatives, and cephalosporins). It is not indicated for gram-negative infections. Linezolid is indicated for treatment of methicillin-resistant and oxacillin-resistant strains of *Staphylococcus*. It is often the only oral drug available active against these strains. Linezolid is expensive and not used for routine infections.

Precautionary Information

Adverse Reactions and Side Effects

Adverse effects include diarrhea and nausea. Rarely, anemia and leukopenia have been observed in people.

Contraindications and Precautions

No contraindications reported.

Drug Interactions

No known drug interactions. Linezolid is not expected to affect metabolism of other drugs.

Instructions for Use

Linezolid is reserved for infections that are resistant to other drugs, such as *Enterococcus, Streptococcus,* or *Staphylococcus* infections.

Patient Monitoring and Laboratory Tests

Choice of drug should be selected on the basis of susceptibility monitoring. CLSI (NCCLS) lists the break point for susceptibility as less than or equal to 4.0 mcg/mL for *Staphylococcus* and less than or equal to 2.0 for *Enterococcus.*

Formulations

Linezolid is available in 400 and 600 mg tablets, 20 mg/mL oral suspension, and 2 mg/mL injection.

Stability and Storage

Store in tightly sealed container, protected from light, and at room temperature. Do not mix with other drugs. Oral suspension is stable for 21 days after reconstitution at room temperature.

Small Animal Dosage

Dogs and Cats

- 10 mg/kg q8-12h PO or IV. (Use every 8 hours for serious infections; every 12 hours for less life-threatening infections.)

Large Animal Dosage

No large animal dose is available.

Regulatory Information

Withdrawal times are not established for animals that produce food. For extralabel use withdrawal interval estimates, contact FARAD at 1-888-USFARAD (1-888-873-2723) or send e-mail to FARAD@ncsu.edu.

Liothyronine Sodium

lye-oh-thye′roe-neen soe′dee-um

Trade and Other Names: Cytomel

Functional Classification: Hormone

Pharmacology and Mechanism of Action

Thyroid supplement. Liothyronine is equivalent to T-3. T-3 is more active than T-4, but ordinarily T-4 is converted in animals to the active form of T-3.

Indications and Clinical Uses

Liothyronine is used for similar indications as levothyroxine (T-4), except that in this instance, the active T-3 hormone is administered. In may be indicated in cases in which there is failure to convert T-4 to the active T-3 hormone. In most cases, it is preferred to administer levothyroxine instead of liothyronine.

Precautionary Information

Adverse Reactions and Side Effects

Adverse effects have not been reported.

Contraindications and Precautions

No contraindications reported.

Drug Interactions

No drug interactions reported for animals.

Instructions for Use

Doses of liothyronine should be adjusted on the basis of monitoring T-3 concentrations in patients. It is rarely necessary to administer T3 alone for treatment of hypothyroidism. In most patients drugs that contain T4 should be used (e.g., levothyroxine). Liothyronine has been used as a diagnostic test for cats.

Patient Monitoring and Laboratory Tests

Monitor serum T-3 concentrations. Used for T-3 suppressing test in cats.

Formulations

Liothyronine is available in 60 mcg tablets.

Stability and Storage

Store in tightly sealed container, protected from light, and at room temperature. Stability of compounded formulations has not been evaluated.

Small Animal Dosage

Dogs and Cats

- 4.4 mcg/kg q8h PO.
- T-3 suppression test in cats: Collect pre-sample for T-4 and T-3, administer 25 mcg q8h for 7 doses and then collect post-samples for T-3 and T-4 after last dose.

Large Animal Dosage

No large animal dose is available.

Regulatory Information

Withdrawal times are not established for animals that produce food. For extralabel use withdrawal interval estimates, contact FARAD at 1-888-USFARAD (1-888-873-2723) or send e-mail to FARAD@ncsu.edu.

Lisinopril

lye-sin'oh-pril

Trade and Other Names: Prinivil and Zestril

Functional Classification: Vasodilator, Angiotensin-converting enzyme (ACE) inhibitor

Pharmacology and Mechanism of Action

Like other ACE inhibitors, lisinopril inhibits conversion of angiotensin I to angiotensin II. Angiotensin II is a potent vasoconstrictor and will also stimulate sympathetic stimulation, renal hypertension, and synthesis of aldosterone. The ability of aldosterone to cause sodium and water retention contributes to congestion. Lisinopril, like other ACE inhibitors will cause vasodilation, and decrease aldosterone-induced congestion. But it also contributes to vasodilation by increasing concentrations of some vasodilating kinins and prostaglandins.

Indications and Clinical Uses

Lisinopril, like other ACE inhibitors, is used to treat hypertension and CHF. Enalapril has been used more often in animals. Other uses may include primary hypertension. Lisinopril also may be used to treat some forms of renal disease in animals. When glomerular filtration pressures are high, lisinopril may benefit patients with renal disease.

Precautionary Information

Adverse Reactions and Side Effects

Like other ACE inhibitors, it may cause azotemia in some patients. Carefully monitor patients receiving high doses of diuretics.

Contraindications and Precautions

Discontinue ACE inhibitors in pregnant animals; they cross the placenta and have caused fetal malformations and death of the fetus.

Drug Interactions

Use cautiously with other hypotensive drugs and diuretics. Nonsteroidal antiinflammatory drugs (NSAIDs) may decrease vasodilating effects.

Instructions for Use

Clinical studies using lisinopril in animals have not been reported.

Patient Monitoring and Laboratory Tests

Monitor patients carefully to avoid hypotension. With all ACE inhibitors, monitor electrolytes and renal function 3-7 days after initiating therapy and periodically thereafter.

Formulations

Lisinopril is available in 2.5, 5, 10, 20, and 40 mg tablets.

Stability and Storage

Store in tightly sealed container, protected from light, and at room temperature. Lisinopril has been mixed with syrup for oral administration and found to be stable for 30 days at either room temperature or refrigerated.

Small Animal Dosage

Dogs

- 0.5 mg/kg q24h PO.

Cats

No dose established.

Large Animal Dosage

No large animal dose is available.

Regulatory Information

Withdrawal times are not established for animals that produce food. For extralabel use withdrawal interval estimates, contact FARAD at 1-888-USFARAD (1-888-873-2723) or send e-mail to FARAD@ncsu.edu.

Lithium Carbonate

lih'thee-um kar'boe-nate

Trade and Other Names: Lithotabs

Functional Classification: Immunostimulant

Pharmacology and Mechanism of Action

Lithium stimulates granulopoiesis and elevates neutrophil pool in animals. It also affects the CNS, because it affects the balance of CNS neurotransmitters.

Indications and Clinical Uses

In people lithium is used for treatment of depression. It has also been used experimentally to increase neutrophil counts following cancer therapy.

Precautionary Information

Adverse Reactions and Side Effects

Adverse effects have not been reported in animals. In people, cardiovascular problems, drowsiness and diarrhea are among the adverse effects.

Contraindications and Precautions

Not recommended in cats.

Drug Interactions

No drug interactions are reported.

Instructions for Use

Use in animals is uncommon, and little dosing information is available.

Patient Monitoring and Laboratory Tests

Monitor neutrophil count.

Formulations

Lithium is available in 150, 300, and 600 mg capsules, 300 mg tablets, and 300 mg/5 mL syrup.

Stability and Storage

Store in tightly sealed container, protected from light, and at room temperature. Stability of compounded formulations has not been evaluated.

Small Animal Dosage

Dogs

- 10 mg/kg q12h PO.

Cats

Not recommended.

Large Animal Dosage

No large animal dose is available.

Regulatory Information

Withdrawal times are not established for animals that produce food. For extralabel use withdrawal interval estimates, contact FARAD at 1-888-USFARAD (1-888-873-2723) or send e-mail to FARAD@ncsu.edu.

Lomustine

loe-mus'teen

Trade and Other Names: CeeNu and CCNU

Functional Classification: Anticancer agent

Pharmacology and Mechanism of Action

Anticancer agent. It is one of two nitrosoureas used, lomustine (1-[2-chloroethyl]-3-cyclohexyl-1-chloroethylnitrosourea), known by the abbreviation of CCNU, and carmustine (1,3-bis-2-chloroethyl-1-nitrosourea), known by the abbreviation BCNU. These drugs, in addition to being lipid soluble, are alkylating agents. Both of the nitrosoureas are metabolized spontaneously to alkylating and carbamyolating compounds. The binding occurs preferentially at the O-6 of guanine. Bifunctional interstrand cross-links are responsible for the cytotoxicity of nitrosoureas. Oral absorption and high membrane penetration are attributed to high lipophilicity. Because oral absorption is high, lomustine can be administered effectively as tablets. After absorption, lomustine is metabolized to antitumor metabolites. Both the parent drug and the metabolites are lipid soluble. The CNS penetration of lomustine has been determined from the plasma/cerebrospinal fluid (CSF) ratio, which is 1:3.

Indications and Clinical Uses

Lomustine (CCNU) is used to treat tumors of the CNS and lymphoma in dogs and cats. It has occasionally been used to treat other forms of cancer. Lomustine has been used more often than carmustine.

Precautionary Information

Adverse Reactions and Side Effects

Bone marrow effects are the most serious. In people, lomustine has a delayed nadir of bone marrow toxicity, which is as long as 4-6 weeks with slow recovery. But in dogs the nadir of bone marrow effects are generally seen 6 to 7 days after dosing. Doses in dogs are used to minimize the bone marrow effects. At higher doses—100 mg/m^2—myelosuppression has been reported. Thrombocytopenia also has been reported from lomustine administration as a cumulative effect.

Cats resemble people in that bone marrow nadir of toxicity occurs at 3-4 weeks. Nitrosoureas also can be toxic to the rapidly dividing cells of mucosa. In people, nitrosoureas also have caused pulmonary fibrosis and hepatotoxicity. Hepatotoxicity may be a delayed reaction. The hepatic damage may be irreversible in dogs. In people, carmustine (BCNU) has been associated with a higher rate of hepatic injury than lomustine.

Contraindications and Precautions

Consider risks to bone marrow with use in small animals.

Drug Interactions

Use with caution with any drugs that may cause bone marrow suppression.

Instructions for Use

The nitrosourea drugs are used to treat CNS tumors and other forms of cancer. Protocols used in small animals are quite different from those given to people which are as much as 150-200 mg/m^2. Oral treatment should be given on an empty stomach if possible.

Patient Monitoring and Laboratory Tests

Monitor CBC and liver enzymes in treated patients.

Formulations

Lomustine is available in 10, 40, and 100 mg capsules.

Stability and Storage

Store in tightly sealed container, protected from light, and at room temperature.

Small Animal Dosage

Dogs

- 70-90 mg/m^2 q4wk PO.
- Brain tumors: protocols of 60-80 mg/m^2 q6-8wk PO also have been cited.

Cats

- 50-60 mg/m^2 q3-6wk PO. Alternatively, administer 10 mg/cat q3wk.

Large Animal Dosage

No large animal doses have been reported.

Regulatory Information

Do not administer to animals that produce food.

Loperamide Hydrochloride

loe-pare'ah-mide hye-droe-klor'ide

Trade and Other Names: Imodium and generic brands

Functional Classification: Analgesic, Opioid

Pharmacology and Mechanism of Action

Opiate agonist. Like other opiates, loperamide acts on the mu-opiate receptors of the GI tract. It decreases propulsive intestinal contractions and increases segmentation (an overall constipating effect). It also increases the tone of GI sphincters. In addition to affecting motility, opiates have an antisecretory effect and stimulate absorption of fluid, electrolytes, and glucose. Their effects on secretory diarrhea are probably related to inhibition of calcium influx and decreased calmodulin activity. Action of loperamide is limited to intestine. CNS effects do not occur, because it does not cross the blood-brain barrier.

Indications and Clinical Uses

Loperamide is used for symptomatic treatment of acute nonspecific diarrhea. It has been administered to dogs and cats, and occasionally large animals. Only oral administration is available. Long-term use is discouraged, because it may lead to constipation.

Precautionary Information

Adverse Reactions and Side Effects

Loperamide can cause severe constipation with repeated use. In some dogs that have a mutation in the multi-drug resistance gene (MDR gene), they may lack p-glycoprotein in the blood-brain barrier. In these susceptible animals, loperamide will cross the blood-brain barrier and cause profound sedation. Such cases may be reversed with naloxone. Dogs most susceptible include Collie breeds, Australian shepherds, Old English sheepdogs, Longhaired Whippets, and Shetland sheepdogs.

Contraindications and Precautions

Small dogs and collie-type dogs may be at higher risk or adverse effects.

Drug Interactions

Do not administer with drugs that may act as MDR1 (p-glycoprotein) membrane inhibitors, such as ketoconazole. (Other inhibitors are listed in Appendix.) These inhibitors may increase blood-brain barrier penetration and cause depression.

Instructions for Use

Doses are based primarily on empiricism or extrapolation of human dose. Clinical studies have not been performed in animals.

Patient Monitoring and Laboratory Tests

No specific monitoring is necessary.

Formulations

Loperamide is available in 2 mg tablets, 2 mg capsules and 1 and 0.2 mg/mL oral liquid (OTC).

Stability and Storage

Store in tightly sealed container, protected from light, and at room temperature. Loperamide is slightly soluble in water but only at low pH. Stability of compounded formulations has not been evaluated.

Small Animal Dosage

Dogs

- 0.1 mg/kg q8-12h PO.

Cats

- 0.08-0.16 mg/kg q12h PO.

Large Animal Dosage

No large animal doses have been reported. If administered to horses or ruminants it may induce problems associated with decreased intestinal motility.

Regulatory Information

Withdrawal times are not established for animals that produce food. For extralabel use withdrawal interval estimates, contact FARAD at 1-888-USFARAD (1-888-873-2723) or send e-mail to FARAD@ncsu.edu.

RCI Classification: 4

Lorazepam

lor-ay'zeh-pam

Trade and Other Names: Ativan and generic brands

Functional Classification: Anticonvulsant

Pharmacology and Mechanism of Action

Benzodiazepine. Central acting CNS depressant, with action similar to diazepam. Mechanism of action appears to be via potentiation of GABA-receptor mediated effects in CNS. In animals, lorazepam does not undergo extensive hepatic metabolism, but it is glucuronidated before excretion. In dogs, lorazepam had a half-life of 0.9 hours, with systemic clearance less than half that of diazepam. Oral absorption is 60%. Therefore, the oral formulation may be suitable in dogs for some conditions.

Indications and Clinical Uses

Lorazepam, as a benzodiazepine, may be considered for anxiety disorders in animals, but it has not been used as commonly as other drugs such as diazepam. Lorazepam also is effective for treating seizures, but it is not used as often in animals as other anticonvulsants. In controlled studies, it has been equally as effective as diazepam in dogs.

Precautionary Information

Adverse Reactions and Side Effects

Sedation is most common side effect. Lorazepam causes polyphagia. Some animals may experience paradoxical excitement. Chronic administration may lead to dependence and a withdrawal syndrome if discontinued.

Contraindications and Precautions

Oral administration of another benzodiazepine, diazepam, has caused idiosyncratic liver injury in cats, but this is unlikely for lorazepam.

Drug Interactions

Use cautiously with other drugs that may cause sedation. Do not mix with buprenorphine.

Instructions for Use

Doses based on empiricism. There have been no clinical trials in veterinary medicine, although it is expected to produce effects similar to other benzodiazepines. For intravenous use, dilute 50/50 with 0.9% saline or 5% dextrose prior to use.

Patient Monitoring and Laboratory Tests

No specific monitoring is necessary.

Formulations Available

Lorazepam is available in 0.5, 1, and 2 mg tablets and 2 and 4 mg/mL injection.

Stability and Storage

Store in tightly sealed container, protected from light, and at room temperature. Lorazepam is practically insoluble in water. It is slightly soluble in some infusion solutions (e.g., 0.054 mg/mL in 5% dextrose). Solutions should be discarded if they turn a dark color.

Small Animal Dosage

Dogs

- 0.05 mg/kg q12h PO.
- Seizures: 0.2 mg/kg IV. Repeat every 3-4 hours for seizure control if necessary.

Cats

- 0.05 mg/kg q12-24h PO.

Large Animal Dosage

No large animal doses have been reported.

Regulatory Information

Do not administer to animals intended for food.
Schedule IV controlled drug
RCI Classification: 2

Losartan

loe-zar'tan

Trade and Other Names: Cozaar

Functional Classification: Vasodilator

Pharmacology and Mechanism of Action

Vasodilator, Angioitensin II receptor blocker. It has high affinity and selectivity for the AT1 receptor. It has been used in people who cannot tolerate angiotensin-converting enzyme (ACE) inhibitors. In people it is metabolized to the active carboxylic acid metabolite which is 10-40 times more potent than the parent drug and believed to be responsible for most clinical effects.

Indications and Clinical Uses

In dogs, it is reported that they do not convert losartan to the active metabolite, and therefore it has little activity in dogs. However, a related drug, irbesartan (30 mg/kg q12h) has been shown to block angiotensin II receptors.

Precautionary Information

Adverse Reactions and Side Effects

No adverse reactions reported in animals. In people, hypotension may occur.

Contraindications and Precautions

No specific contraindications for animals. Do not use in pregnant animals.

Drug Interactions

No drug interactions are reported for animals.

Instructions for Use

In dogs, losartan is not converted to the active metabolite. Therefore it has little bioactivity (*J Pharmacol Exp Ther,* 268:1199-1205, 1999). It is suggested instead to consider irbesartan at a dose of 30 mg/kg q12h PO.

Patient Monitoring and Laboratory Tests

Monitor blood pressure in treated animals.

Formulations

Losartan is available in 25 and 50 mg tablets.

Stability and Storage

Store in tightly sealed container, protected from light, and at room temperature. Stability of compounded formulations has not been evaluated.

Small Animal Dosage

Dogs

Not recommended.

Large Animal Dosage

No large animal doses have been reported.

Regulatory Information

Do not administer to animals intended for food.
RCI Classification: 3

Lufenuron

loo-fen'yoo-rahn

Trade and Other Names: Program

Functional Classification: Antiparasitic

Pharmacology and Mechanism of Action

Antiparasitic. Lufenuron is a benzoylurea insecticide. This class of insecticides was previously used on fruits to decrease damage by insects. Lufenuron (Program) has been used for prevention of flea infections in dogs and cats, because it inhibits chitin synthesis. For this use it has been given to dogs at a dose of 10 mg/kg every 30 days and to cats at a dose of 30 mg/kg every 30 days. It may also affect fungal cell membranes, because it inhibits the cell wall of fungi, which contain chitin, as well as other complex polysaccharides. It has been used to treat dermatophytes in small animals because of this effect, but efficacy has been controversial.

Indications and Clinical Uses

Lufenuron is used to control flea infestations by preventing hatching of eggs. It has been used as part of flea control, often with other drugs that kill adult fleas. There are clinical reports of the use of lufenuron for treating dermatophyte infections in cats (*J Am Vet Med Assoc*, 217:1510-1513, 2000). However, other reports have disputed the efficacy and have cited a high incidence of recurrence.

In one study, lufenuron produced effective and rapid treatment of dermatophyte infections in dogs and cats. In cat colonies, where cats may be re-exposed to fungal spores frequently, treat with a minimum dose of 100 mg/kg orally combined with environmental treatment to decrease the spread of fungal spores. House cats and dogs should be treated with 80 mg/kg. Animals that are re-exposed to dermatophytes should be retreated 2 weeks after the first treatment. Cats routinely exposed to dermatophytes may be treated each month. Some dermatologists are skeptical of the efficacy of lufenuron for treatment of dermatophytes. Efficacy has been poor in some follow-up studies. Poor efficacy in some animals has been attributed to inadequate dosing or re-exposure from the environment. In horses it was not absorbed orally and is not effective for treating fungal infections. It does not have any in vitro effect on *Aspergillus fumigatus* or *Coccidioides immitis*. However, there is one report of successful use of lufenuron for treatment of fungal endometritis. In these mares, lufenuron was used as an intrauterine infusion of 540 mg suspended in 60 mL of saline.

Precautionary Information

Adverse Reactions and Side Effects

There is a high margin of safety at doses used for flea control or treatment of dermatophytes. Adverse effects have not been reported. Lufenuron appears to be relatively safe in pregnant and young animals.

Contraindications and Precautions

No contraindications are reported for animals.

Drug Interactions

No drug interactions reported for animals.

Instructions for Use

Lufenuron is a highly lipophilic drug and is absorbed best with a meal. If cats have free access to their food, withhold their food until such time that a meal will be consumed readily before administering the lufenuron oral dose. Lufenuron may control flea development with administration once every 30 days in animals.

Patient Monitoring and Laboratory Tests

No specific monitoring is necessary.

Formulations

Lufenuron is available in 45, 90, 135, 204.9, 409.8 mg tablets and 135 and 270 mg suspension per unit pack.

Stability and Storage

Store in tightly sealed container, protected from light, and at room temperature. Stability of compounded formulations has not been evaluated.

Small Animal Dosage

Dogs

- Flea control: 10 mg/kg q30d PO.
- Dermatophytes: 80 mg/kg.

Cats

- Flea control: 30 mg/kg q30d PO or injection of 10 mg/kg SQ every 6 months.
- Dermatophytes: 80 mg/kg; 100 mg/kg PO is the minimum dose for treating cats in a cattery. These doses should be repeated initially after the first 2 weeks and possibly once per month in animals that may be re-exposed.

Large Animal Dosage

Horses

Not effective.

Regulatory Information

Withdrawal times are not established for animals that produce food. For extralabel use withdrawal interval estimates, contact FARAD at 1-888-USFARAD (1-888-873-2723) or send e-mail to FARAD@ncsu.edu.

Lufenuron + Milbemycin Oxime

loo-fen′yoo-rahn + mil-beh-mye′sin oks′eem

Trade and Other Names: Sentinel tablets and Flavor Tabs

Functional Classification: Antiparasitic

Pharmacology and Mechanism of Action

Combination of two antiparasitic drugs. Refer to sections on lufenuron or milbemycin for details.

Indications and Clinical Uses

Lufenuron + milbemycin is used to protect against fleas, heartworms, roundworms, hookworms, and whipworms.

Precautionary Information

Adverse Reactions and Side Effects

Refer to section on lufenuron or milbemycin for details.

Contraindications and Precautions

No contraindications are reported for animals. Some animals may be sensitive to milbenycin.

Drug Interactions

No drug interactions reported for animals, except those that may pertain to milbemycin.

Instructions for Use

See section on lufenuron or milbemycin for details.

Patient Monitoring and Laboratory Tests

Monitor for heartworm status in dogs before initiating treatment with milbemycin.

Formulations

Milbemycin/Lufenuron ratio is as follows: 2.3/46 mg tablets and 5.75/115, 11.5/230, and 23/460 mg Flavor Tabs.

Stability and Storage

Store in tightly sealed container, protected from light, and at room temperature. Stability of compounded formulations has not been evaluated.

Small Animal Dosage

Dogs

- Administer one tablet every 30 days. Each tablet formulated for size of dog.

Cats

No dose is reported.

Large Animal Dosage

No large animal doses have been reported.

Regulatory Information

Withdrawal times are not established for animals that produce food. For extralabel use withdrawal interval estimates, contact FARAD at 1-888-USFARAD (1-888-873-2723) or send e-mail to FARAD@ncsu.edu.

Lysine (L-Lysine)

lye'seen

Trade and Other Names: Enisyl-F

Functional Classification: Antiviral

Pharmacology and Mechanism of Action

Lysine is an amino-acid based supplement for treating Feline Herpes Virus Type 1 (FHV-1). It acts by antagonism of the growth-promoting effect of arginine which is an essential amino acid of FHV-1.

Indications and Clinical Uses

Lysine-based supplement for treating FHV-1 in cats. It is intended to reduce viral shedding in infected cats. L-Lysine monohydrate can be supplied as a powder and mixed with a small amount of food.

Precautionary Information

Adverse Reactions and Side Effects

No adverse effects reported in cats.

Contraindications and Precautions

No contraindications have been reported.

Drug Interactions

No drug interactions reported for animals.

Instructions for Use

Mix powder with food.

Patient Monitoring and Laboratory Tests

Monitor patient's CBC during treatment.

Formulations

Paste (Enisyl-F) is distributred in syringes in which each mark on the syringe represents 1 mL (250 mg/mL).

Stability and Storage

Store in tightly sealed container, protected from light, and at room temperature.

Small Animal Dosage

Cats

- 400 mg/cat/day PO.
- Paste formulation: 1-2 mL to adult cats and 1 mL to kittens.

Large Animal Dosage

No large animal doses have been reported.

Regulatory Information

No regulatory information is available. Because of low risk of residues, no withdrawal times are suggested.

Magnesium Citrate

Trade and Other Names: Citroma, CitroNesia, and Citro-Mag (Canada)

Functional Classification: Laxative

Pharmacology and Mechanism of Action

Saline cathartic. Acts to draw water into small intestine via osmotic effect. Fluid accumulation produces distension, which promotes bowel evacuation.

Indications and Clinical Uses

Magnesium citrate is administrated orally for constipation and bowel evacuation prior to certain procedures. It is prompt in its cathartic action.

Precautionary Information

Adverse Reactions and Side Effects

Adverse effects have not been reported in animals. However, fluid and electrolyte loss can occur with overuse.

Contraindications and Precautions

Magnesium accumulation may occur in patients with renal impairment. Cathartics containing magnesium decrease oral absorption of ciprofloxacin and other fluoroquinolones.

Drug Interactions

No drug interactions reported for animals. However, it may increase clearance of some drugs administered orally.

Instructions for Use

Magnesium citrate is commonly used to evacuate bowel prior to surgery or diagnostic procedures. Onset of action is rapid.

Patient Monitoring and Laboratory Tests

No specific monitoring is necessary. However, monitor magnesium concentrations in patients if repeated treatments or high doses are administered.

Formulations

Magnesium citrate is available in a 6% oral suspension.

Stability and Storage

Store in tightly sealed container, protected from light, and at room temperature.

Small Animal Dosage

Dogs and Cats

- 2-4 mL/kg/day PO.

Large Animal Dosage

Horses and Cattle

- 2-4 mL/kg once PO.

Regulatory Information

No regulatory information is available. Because of low risk of residues, no withdrawal times are suggested.

Magnesium Hydroxide

Trade and Other Names: Milk of Magnesia, Carmilax, and Magnalax

Functional Classification: Laxative

Pharmacology and Mechanism of Action

Saline cathartic. Magnesium hydroxide acts to draw water into small intestine via osmotic effect. Fluid accumulation produces distension, which promotes bowel evacuation.

Indications and Clinical Uses

Magnesium hydroxide is used for constipation and bowel evacuation prior to certain procedures. It is commonly used to evacuate bowel prior to surgery or diagnostic procedures. Onset of action is rapid. Magnesium hydroxide also is used as oral antacid to neutralize stomach acid. In large animals it is used as an antacid and mild cathartic. In cattle, approximately 1 g/kg as a single dose significantly increases rumen pH and decreases rumen microbial activity.

Precautionary Information

Adverse Reactions and Side Effects

Adverse effects have not been reported in animals. However, fluid and electrolyte loss can occur with overuse.

Contraindications and Precautions

Magnesium accumulation may occur in patients with renal impairment.

Drug Interactions

Cathartics containing magnesium decrease oral absorption of ciprofloxacin and other fluoroquinolones.

Instructions for Use

Administer to patients only if they are properly hydrated.

Patient Monitoring and Laboratory Tests

Monitor electrolytes with chronic use.

Formulations

Magnesium hydroxide is available as oral liquid 400 mg/5 mL (Milk of Magnesia) OTC. Milk of Magnesia is approximately 400 mg per 1 teaspoon. It is also available as 27 g bolus for cattle and sheep and as a powder 310-360 g/lb (approximately 745 g/kg). As a powder, 1.0 pounds of powder is equivalent to 1 gallon of Milk of Magnesia and three 27 g boluses are equal to 1 quart of Milk of Magnesia.

Stability and Storage

Store in tightly sealed container, protected from light, and at room temperature.

Small Animal Dosage

Dogs

- Antacid: 5-10 mL/dog q4-6h PO.
- Cathartic: 15-50 mL/dog q24h PO.

Cats

- Antacid: 5-10 mL/cat q4-6h PO.
- Cathartic: 2-6 mL/cat q24h PO.

Large Animal Dosage

Sheep and Cattle

- 1 g/kg or 1 bolus per 27 kg [60 pounds] PO, once (3-4 boluses for adult cattle).
- If using the powder, mix 1 lb with 1 gallon water and administer 500 mL/45 kg (500 mL per 100 pounds).

Regulatory Information

Withdrawal time for animals intended for food: 12-24 hours (milk) depending on the product.

Magnesium Sulfate

Trade and Other Names: Epsom salts

Functional Classification: Laxative, Antiarrhythmic

Pharmacology and Mechanism of Action

Saline cathartic and antiarrhythmic. Magnesium sulfate when administered orally acts to draw water into small intestine via osmotic effect. Fluid accumulation produces distension, which promotes bowel evacuation. It is used as a replacement for magnesium in deficient patients. When used as an antiarrhythmic it serves as a source of magnesium for treating refractory arrhythmias.

Indications and Clinical Uses

Magnesium sulfate is used for constipation and bowel evacuation prior to certain procedures. Injectable solution of magnesium sulfate is used to treat refractory arrhythmias in critically ill patients. In cattle, magnesium sulfate is used to treat hypomagnesemia, especially in dairy cattle.

Precautionary Information

Adverse Reactions and Side Effects

High doses may cause muscle weakness and respiratory paralysis. With repeated administration, fluid and electrolyte loss can occur with overuse. When treating arrhythmias it has been administered at doses of 0.1-0.2 mEq/kg safely.

Contraindications and Precautions

Magnesium accumulation may occur in patients with renal impairment.

Drug Interactions

Cathartics containing magnesium decrease oral absorption of ciprofloxacin and other fluoroquinolones. Magnesium sulfate is incompatible with alkaline solutions. Some metal ions (e.g., calcium) may form insoluble sulfates.

Instructions for Use

Magnesium sulfate when used as a laxative is administered for its prompt action to evacuate bowel prior to surgery or diagnostic procedures. Onset of action is rapid. For use in cattle (hypomagnesemia) an initial dose can be administered IV, followed by an SQ dose to produce a sustained effect. Monitor animals for hypocalcemia, which can occur simultaneously.

Patient Monitoring and Laboratory Tests
Monitor magnesium and calcium concentrations. Normal magnesium concentrations in animals are 1.32-2.46 mEq/L. Many cattle also have hypocalcemia.

Formulations
Magnesium sulfate is available as solid crystals in generic preparations. Solution for injection is 12.5% mEq/mL. Intravenous and subcutaneous solutions for cattle are usually 1.5-4 g/L.

Stability and Storage
Crystals are stable if stored in dry container. Store injectable solutions at room temperature, in tightly sealed vial, protected from light.

Small Animal Dosage
Dogs
- 8-25 g/dog q24h PO.

Cats
- 2-5 g/cat q24h PO.

Dogs and Cats
- Constant Rate Infusion (CRI) for treating arrhythmias: 0.15-0.3 mEq/kg slowly over 5-15 minutes, followed by 0.75-1.0 mEq/kg/day.
- Use during fluid therapy: supplement fluid solutions with 0.75-1.0 mEq/kg/day.

Large Animal Dosage
Cattle
- 2-3 grams per cow IV over 10 minutes. This may be followed by 200-400 mL per cow of 25% magnesium sulfate, SQ to supply 50-100 grams per cow.

Horses
- 1 g/horse q12-24h PO or 2-4 mg/kg IV.

Regulatory Information
No regulatory information is available. Because of low risk of residues, no withdrawal times are suggested.

Mannitol
man'ih-tole

Trade and Other Names: Osmitrol

Functional Classification: Diuretic

Pharmacology and Mechanism of Action
Hyperosmotic diuretic. Mannitol occurs naturally as a sugar in fruits and vegetables. As an osmotic diuretic, mannitol is filtered by the glomerulus, but it is not reabsorbed by the renal tubule. Therefore it increases osmolality of the urine. Osmotic effect inhibits reabsorption of fluid from the renal tubules, and this produces a strong diuresis. Reabsorption of sodium chloride and solutes also is inhibited. Mannitol, compared to other diuretic drugs, produces a diuretic effect along the entire length of the renal tubule. After intravenous administration, mannitol increases the plasma osmolality which draws fluid from tissues to plasma

which is helpful for treating tissue edema (e.g., cerebral edema). It reduces intracranial pressure. It is also used as an antiglaucoma agent because it lowers intraocular pressure when administered IV.

Indications and Clinical Uses

Mannitol is administered IV for treatment of cerebral edema, acute glaucoma, and conditions associated with tissue edema. Mannitol also has been used to promote urinary excretion of certain toxins and in the management of anuric or oliguric renal failure.

Precautionary Information

Adverse Reactions and Side Effects

Mannitol produces a profound diuresis and can cause significant fluid loss and electrolyte imbalance. Administration rate that is too rapid may expand the extracellular volume excessively.

Contraindications and Precautions

Do not use in dehydrated patients. Use cautiously when intracranial bleeding is suspected, because it may increase bleeding. (This effect is controversial when dealing with intracranial hemorrhage.)

Drug Interactions

Do not administer simultaneously with blood replacement. If blood is administered simultaneously, sodium chloride must be added to each liter of mannitol (20 mEq/L). Mannitol may increase renal clearance of some drugs.

Instructions for Use

Use only in patients in which fluid and electrolyte balance can be monitored.

Patient Monitoring and Laboratory Tests

Monitor hydration and electrolyte balance in treated animals. Monitor intraocular pressure when treating acute glaucoma.

Formulations

Mannitol is available in 5%, 10%, 15%, 20%, and 25% solution for injection.

Stability and Storage

Once solutions are prepared, discard unused portions. If solutions are chilled, crystals may form.

Small Animal Dosage

Dogs and Cats

- Diuretic: 1 g/kg of 5%-25% solution IV to maintain urine flow.
- Glaucoma or CNS edema: 0.25-2 g/kg of 15%-25% solution over 30-60 min IV (repeat in 6 hours if necessary)

Large Animal Dosage

- 0.25-1.0 g/kg (20% solution) IV administered over 1 hour.

Regulatory Information

No regulatory information is available. Because of low risk of residues, no withdrawal times are suggested.

Marbofloxacin

mar-boe-floks'ah-sin

Trade and Other Names: Zeniquin and Marbocyl (European name)

Functional Classification: Antibacterial

Pharmacology and Mechanism of Action

Fluoroquinolone antimicrobial. Marbofloxacin acts via inhibition of DNA gyrase in bacteria to inhibit DNA and RNA synthesis. Marbofloxacin is a bactericidal with a broad spectrum of activity. Sensitive bacteria include *Staphylococcus, Escherichia coli, Proteus, Klebsiella,* and *Pasteurella. Pseudomonas aeruginosa* is moderately sensitive but requires higher concentrations. Marbofloxacin has poor activity against streptococci and anaerobic bacteria.

Indications and Clinical Uses

Marbofloxacin, like other fluoroquinolones, is used to treat susceptible bacteria in a variety of species. Marbofloxacin is registered for use in dogs and cats. Infections treated with marbofloxacin include skin and soft tissue infections, bone infections, UTIs, pneumonia, and infections caused by intracellular organisms. Marbofloxacin also has been used in horses to treat infections caused by susceptible bacteria.

Precautionary Information

Adverse Reactions and Side Effects

High concentrations may cause CNS toxicity. Like other fluoroquinolones, it may cause some nausea, vomiting, and diarrhea at high doses. All of the fluoroquinolones may cause arthropathy in young animals. Dogs are most sensitive at 4 to 28 weeks of age. Large, rapidly growing dogs are the most susceptible. Marbofloxacin at a dose of twice the upper limit caused articular damage in dogs that were 4-5 months old. In cats 8 months old at doses of 17 and 28 mg/kg for 42 days articular cartilage injury was observed. Marbofloxacin has been safe when administered with anesthetic agents in dogs. Blindness in cats has been reported from some quinolones such as enrofloxacin and nalidixic acid. There are no known reports of this reaction with marbofloxacin, and toxicity studies by the manufacturer showed that it did not cause ocular lesions or vision problems in cats. At doses of 17 mg/kg and 28 mg/kg (3 times and 5 times the upper limit of dosing) and it did not produce ocular changes. Marbofloxacin has been administered to horses orally without producing adverse effects in the GI tract.

Contraindications and Precautions

Avoid use in young animals because of risk of cartilage injury. Use cautiously in animals that may be prone to seizures, such as epileptics.

Drug Interactions

Fluoroquinolones may increase concentrations of theophylline if used concurrently. Coadministration with divalent and trivalent cations, such as products containing aluminum (e.g., sucralfate), iron, and calcium may decrease absorption. Do not mix in solutions or in vials with aluminum, calcium, iron, or zinc because chelation may occur.

Instructions for Use

At the registered label dose, marbofloxacin is active against most susceptible bacteria. Within the approved dose range, higher doses are needed for organisms with higher minimum inhibitory concentration (MIC) values. Doses published for European use may be lower than U.S. approved doses. Successful treatment of pyoderma in European studies has been accomplished with doses of 2.0 mg/kg once daily, but in the U.S. the lowest dose is 2.75 mg/kg once daily.

Patient Monitoring and Laboratory Tests

Susceptibility testing: CLSI (NCCLS) break points for sensitive organisms in dogs and cats are less than or equal to 1.0 mcg/mL. If other fluoroquinolones are used to test susceptibility to marbofloxacin, results will be similar. However, marbofloxacin is slightly more active than other veterinary quinolones against *Pseudomonas aeruginosa*, and the human drug ciprofloxacin is more active.

Formulations

Marbofloxacin is available in 25, 50, 100, and 200 mg tablets. Injectable marbofloxacin (Marbocyl) is approved in other countries but not in the U.S.

Stability and Storage

Store in tightly sealed container, protected from light, and at room temperature. Do not compound with ingredients that may chelate with quinolones, such as iron or calcium.

Small Animal Dosage

Dogs

- 2.75-5.5 mg/kg once daily PO.

Cats

- 2.75-5.5 mg/kg once daily PO.

Large Animal Dosage

Horses

- 2 mg/kg once daily IV or PO for treatment of susceptible gram-negative bacteria. (IV formulation not available in the U.S.) An oral dose of 2 mg/kg may not be sufficient for treating other bacteria that cause infections in horses, including gram-positive cocci. However, higher doses have not been tested.

Regulatory Information

Marbofloxacin is prohibited from use in animals intended for food. There are no withdrawal times established, because it should not be administered to animals that produce food.

MCT Oil

Trade and Other Names: Medium chain triglycerides (MCT) oil

Functional Classification: Nutritional supplement

Pharmacology and Mechanism of Action

MCT oil supplements triglycerides in animals.

Indications and Clinical Uses

MCT oil is used to treat lymphangiectasia and as a component of enteral feeding formulas.

Precautionary Information

Adverse Reactions and Side Effects

Adverse effects not reported in veterinary medicine. It may cause diarrhea in some patients.

Contraindications and Precautions

No contraindications reported.

Drug Interactions

No drug interactions reported.

Instructions for Use

Results of clinical trials using MCT oil have not been reported. Many enteral feeding formulas contain MCT oil (many polymeric formulations).

Patient Monitoring and Laboratory Tests

No specific monitoring is necessary.

Formulations

MCT is available as an oral liquid.

Stability and Storage

Store in tightly sealed container, protected from light, at room temperature, and in a cool place. Do not store in plastic container. It may be mixed with fruit juices or food products prior to administration.

Small Animal Dosage

- 1-2 mL/kg daily in food.

Large Animal Dosage

No large animal doses have been reported.

Regulatory Information

No regulatory information is available. Because of low risk of residues, no withdrawal times are suggested.

Mebendazole

meh-ben′dah-zole

Trade and Other Names: Telmintic, Telmin, Vermox (human preparation), and generic brands

Functional Classification: Antiparasitic

Pharmacology and Mechanism of Action

Benzimidazole antiparasitic drug. Like other benzimidazoles, mebendazole produces a degeneration of the parasite microtubule and irreversibly blocks glucose uptake in parasites. Inhibition of glucose uptake causes depletion of energy stores in parasite, eventually resulting in death. However, there is no effect on glucose metabolism in mammals.

Indications and Clinical Uses

Mebendazole is used in horses for treatment of infections caused by large roundworms (*Parascaris equorum*), large strongyles (*Strongylus edentatus, S. equinus,* and *S. vulgaris*), small strongyles, and mature and immature (4th larval stage pinworms [*Oxyuris equi*]). In dogs it has been used for treatment of infections of roundworms (*Toxocara canis*), hookworms (*Ancylostoma caninum* and *Uncinaria stenocephala*), whipworms (*Trichuris vulpis*), and tapeworms (*Taenia pisiformis*).

Precautionary Information

Adverse Reactions and Side Effects

Adverse effects are rare. Mebendazole causes occasional vomiting and diarrhea in dogs. Some reports suggest idiosyncratic hepatic reactions in dogs.

Contraindications and Precautions

No contraindications reported.

Drug Interactions

No drug interactions reported for animals.

Instructions for Use

The powder for horses may be sprinkled directly on the horse's grain or dissolved in 1 L of water and administered via stomach tube. For dogs, it may be added directly to the dog's food.

Patient Monitoring and Laboratory Tests

No specific monitoring is necessary.

Formulations

Mebendazole is available in 40 or 166.7 mg/g powder, 200 mg/g equine paste, 33.3 mg/mL solution, and 100 mg chewable tablets (human preparation).

Some equine formulations contain 83.3 mg mebendazole plus 375 mg trichlorfon in each gram of powder.

Stability and Storage

Store in tightly sealed container, protected from light, and at room temperature. Stability of compounded formulations has not been evaluated.

Small Animal Dosage

Dogs

- 22 mg/kg (mixed with food) q24h for 3 days. May be repeated in 3 weeks.

Large Animal Dosage

Horses

- 8.8 mg/kg PO.

Regulatory Information

Do not administer to horses intended for food.

Withdrawal times are not established for animals that produce food. For extralabel use withdrawal interval estimates, contact FARAD at 1-888-USFARAD (1-888-873-2723) or send e-mail to FARAD@ncsu.edu.

Meclizine

mek'lih-zeen

Trade and Other Names: Antivert, Bonine, Meclozine (British name), and generic brands

Functional Classification: Antiemetic

Pharmacology and Mechanism of Action

Antiemetic. Antihistamine. Like other antihistamines, it blocks effect of histamine on H_1 receptor. However, it also has central anticholinergic actions, which may be responsible for the central acting antiemetic properties.

Indications and Clinical Uses

Meclizine is used to treat vomiting. It may suppress the chemoreceptor trigger zone (CRTZ). It also is used for treatment of motion sickness

Precautionary Information

Adverse Reactions and Side Effects

Adverse effects have not been reported in animals. Anticholinergic (atropine-like) effects may cause side effects.

Contraindications and Precautions

Use cautiously in animals with GI obstruction or glaucoma.

Drug Interactions

No drug interactions reported for animals.

Instructions for Use

Results of clinical studies in animals have not been reported. Use in animals is based on experience in people or anecdotal experiences in animals.

Patient Monitoring and Laboratory Tests

No specific monitoring is necessary.

Formulations

Meclizine is available in 12.5, 25, and 50 mg tablets.

Stability and Storage

Store in tightly sealed container, protected from light, and at room temperature. Stability of compounded formulations has not been evaluated.

Small Animal Dosage

Dogs

- 25 mg per dog q24h PO (for motion sickness, administer 1 hour prior to traveling).

Cats

- 12.5 mg per cat q24h PO.

Large Animal Dosage

No large animal doses have been reported.

Regulatory Information

Withdrawal times are not established for animals that produce food. For extralabel use withdrawal interval estimates, contact FARAD at 1-888-USFARAD (1-888-873-2723) or send e-mail to FARAD@ncsu.edu.

M

Meclofenamate Sodium, Meclofenamic Acid

mek'loe-fen'am-ate soe-dee'um, mek'loe-fen-am'ik ass'id

Trade and Other Names: Arquel and Meclofen

Functional Classification: Nonsteroidal antiinflammatory drug (NSAID)

Pharmacology and Mechanism of Action

Meclofenamate and other NSAIDs have produced analgesic and antiinflammatory effects by inhibiting the synthesis of prostaglandins. The enzyme inhibited by NSAIDs is the cyclo-oxygenase enzyme (COX). The COX enzyme exists in two isoforms, called COX-1 and COX-2. COX-1 is primarily responsible for synthesis of prostaglandins important for maintaining a healthy GI tract, renal function, platelet function, and other normal functions. COX-2 is induced and responsible for synthesizing prostaglandins that are important mediators of pain, inflammation, and fever. Meclofenamic acid is a balanced COX-1/COX-2 inhibitor.

Indications and Clinical Uses

Meclofenamate is also known as meclofenamic acid. It is used in animals for treatment of pain and inflammation. The most common use has been musculoskeletal inflammation. Use in animals has diminished because of decreased availability and increased popularity of other drugs.

Precautionary Information

Adverse Reactions and Side Effects

Adverse effects have not been reported in animals, but adverse effects common to other NSAIDs are possible. These side effects are generally GI in nature (e.g., gastritis, gastric ulcers)

Contraindications and Precautions

Do not administer to animals prone to GI ulcers. Do not administer with other ulcerogenic drugs such as corticosteroids. Manufacturer suggests that duration is limited to 5-7 days.

Drug Interactions

Like other NSAIDs, ulcerogenic effects are potentiated when administered with corticosteroids. Meclofenamic acid, like other NSAIDs, may interfere with the action of diuretics, such as furosemide, and angiotensin-converting enzyme (ACE) inhibitors.

Instructions for Use

Most of the experience with meclofenamate has been with horses. There are no longer commercial formulations marketed for animals. Administer with food.

Patient Monitoring and Laboratory Tests

Monitor for signs of GI ulceration during use.

Formulations

Meclofenamate is available 50 and 100 mg capsules (rarely available commercially any longer), 10 and 20 mg tablets (formulation for dogs), and granules for horses, 5% meclofenamic acid.

Stability and Storage

Store in tightly sealed container, protected from light, and at room temperature. Stability of compounded formulations has not been evaluated.

Small Animal Dosage

Dogs

- 1 mg/kg/day for up to 5 days PO.

Large Animal Dosage

Horses

- 2.2 mg/kg q24h PO.

Regulatory Information

Withdrawal times are not established for animals that produce food. For extralabel use withdrawal interval estimates, contact FARAD at 1-888-USFARAD (1-888-873-2723) or send e-mail to FARAD@ncsu.edu.

RCI Classification: 4

Medetomidine Hydrochloride

meh-deh-toe′mih-deen hye-droe-klor′ide

Trade and Other Names: Domitor

Functional Classification: Analgesic, Alpha$_2$ agonist

Pharmacology and Mechanism of Action

Alpha$_2$ adrenergic agonist. Alpha$_2$ agonists decrease release of neurotransmitters from the neuron. The proposed mechanism whereby they decrease transmission is via binding to presynaptic alpha$_2$ receptors (negative feedback receptors). The result is decreased sympathetic outflow, analgesia, sedation, and anesthesia. Other drugs in this class include xylazine, detomidine, and clonidine. Receptor binding studies indicate that alpha$_2$/alpha$_1$ adrenergic receptor selectivity was 16201 for medetomidine and 160 for xylazine.

Indications and Clinical Uses

Medetomidine, like other alpha$_2$ agonists are used as sedatives, anesthetic adjuncts, and analgesia. It has been used to sedate animals for intradermal skin testing without affecting results. Duration of effect is 0.5-1.5 hours at the low dose and up to 3 hours for the high dose. Compared to xylazine, medetomidine has produced better sedation and analgesia than xylazine in dogs. Many anesthesiologists recommend combinations of medetomidine and ketamine, medetomidine and butorphanol, or medetomidine and hydromorphone, in dogs for sedation and short-term procedures. Medetomidine combined with an opiate (butorphanol or hydromorphone) have produced a longer duration of sedation and more desirable degree of sedation than medetomidine used alone.

Precautionary Information

Adverse Reactions and Side Effects

In small animals, vomiting is the most common acute effect. $Alpha_2$ agonists decrease sympathetic output. Cardiovascular depression may occur. Constant rate infusion (CRI) of 1.5 mcg/kg/hr has caused decreased heart rate and sinus arrhythmia in dogs. Doses as low as 1 mcg/kg IV can reduce cardiac output to less than 40% of resting value. Medetomidine will cause an initial bradycardia and hypertension. If adverse reactions are observed, reverse with atipamezole. Yohimbine also can reverse medetomidine.

Contraindications and Precautions

Use cautiously in animals with heart disease. Use may be contraindicated in older animals with preexisting cardiac disease. Xylazine causes problems in pregnant animals, and this should be considered for other $alpha_2$ agonists as well. Use cautiously in animals that are pregnant, because it may induce labor. In addition, it may decrease oxygen delivery to fetus in late gestation.

Drug Interactions

Do not use with other drugs that may cause cardiac depression. Do not mix in vial or syringe with other anesthetics. Reverse with atipamezole at a dose of 25-300 mcg/kg IM. Use with opioid analgesic drugs will greatly enhance the CNS depression. Consider lowering doses if administered with opioids.

Instructions for Use

Medetomidine and detomidine are more specific for the $alpha_2$ receptor than xylazine. They may be used for sedation, analgesia, and minor surgical procedures. Many veterinarians use doses that are much less than the doses listed on the label. For example, lower doses are sometimes used for short-term sedation and analgesia, particularly when combined with other drugs such as opiates. Reverse with atipamezole at a dose of 25-300 mcg/kg (equal to volume of medetomidine used) IM.

Patient Monitoring and Laboratory Tests

Monitor vital signs during anesthesia. Monitor heart rate, blood pressure, and ECG if possible during anesthesia.

Formulations

Medetomidine is available in 1.0 mg/mL injection.

Stability and Storage

Store in tightly sealed container, protected from light, and at room temperature. Stability of compounded formulations has not been evaluated.

Small Animal Dosage

Dogs

- 750 mcg/m^2 IV or 1000 mcg/m^2 IM. The IV dose is equivalent to 18-71 mcg/kg IV.
- Lower doses are often used for short-term sedation and analgesia of 5-15 mcg/kg (0.005-0.015 mg/kg) IV, IM, or SQ. These doses may be increased up to 60 mcg/kg when severe pain is involved. 20 mcg/kg has been used in combination with butorphanol (0.2 mg/kg), hydromorphone (0.1 mg/kg), or ketamine for short-term procedures.
- CRI: Loading dose of 1 mcg/kg IV, followed by 0.0015 mg/kg/hr (1.5 mcg/kg/hr). CRI may produce adverse cardiovascular effects and should be monitored closely.

Cats

- 750 mcg/m^2 IV or 1000 mcg/m^2 IM. The IV dose is equivalent to 18-71 mcg/kg IV.
- Lower doses are often used for short-term sedation and analgesia of 10-20 mcg/kg (up to 80 mcg/kg for severe pain) IM, IV, or SQ.

Large Animal Dosage

Lambs

- 30 mcg/kg (0.03 mg/kg) IV.

Horses

- 10 mcg/kg IM as a sedative prior to induction for anesthesia. Some horses may need an additional dose of 4 mcg/kg IV. In horses, guaifenesin (5% solution) and ketamine (2.2 mg/kg) have been used in combination.

Regulatory Information

Withdrawal times are not established for animals that produce food. For extralabel use withdrawal interval estimates, contact FARAD at 1-888-USFARAD (1-888-873-2723) or send e-mail to FARAD@ncsu.edu.
RCI Classification: 3

Medroxyprogesterone Acetate

meh-droks'ee-proe-jess'teh-rone ass'ih-tate

Trade and Other Names: Depo-Provera (injection), Provera (tablets), and Cycrin (tablets)

Functional Classification: Hormone

Pharmacology and Mechanism of Action

Progestin hormone. Medroxyprogesterone is a derivative of acetoxyprogesterone. Medroxyprogesterone acetate replaces progesterone in the body and will mimic progesterone's hormone effects. In the Depo-Provera formulation it can produce long-acting effects.

Indications and Clinical Uses

Medroxyprogesterone acetate is used to replace progesterone in animals. Most often it is used as progesterone hormone treatment to control estrous cycle. Also used for management of some behavioral and dermatologic disorders (such as urine spraying in cats and alopecia). However, its use for behavioral therapy in animals is discouraged because of high relapse rates and incidence of hormone-related adverse effects. In horses it has been used to prevent estrous.

Precautionary Information

Adverse Reactions and Side Effects

Adverse effects include polyphagia, polydipsia, adrenal suppression (cats), increased risk of diabetes mellitus, pyometra, diarrhea, and increased risk of neoplasia. In cats a single injection of medroxyprogesterone acetate has produced feline mammary fibroepithelial hyperplasia.

Contraindications and Precautions

Do not use in animals at a high risk for diabetes. In humans it increases the risk of thromboembolic problems. Do not use in pregnant animals.

Drug Interactions

No drug interactions are reported. However, clearance of medroxyprogesterone is increased with drugs known to induce hepatic P450 enzymes (see Appendix).

Instructions for Use

Clinical studies in animals have studied primarily the reproductive use and effects on behavioral use. Medroxyprogesterone acetate may have fewer side effects than megestrol acetate.

Patient Monitoring and Laboratory Tests

It may increase concentrations of serum cholesterol and some liver enzymes.

Formulations

Medroxyprogesterone is available in 150 and 400 mg/mL suspension injection and 2.5, 5, and 10 mg tablets.

Stability and Storage

Store in tightly sealed container, protected from light, and at room temperature. Stability of compounded formulations has not been evaluated.

Small Animal Dosage

Dogs and Cats

- 1.1-2.2 mg/kg every 7 days IM.
- Behavior problems: 10-20 mg/kg SQ.
- Prostatic disease (dogs): 3-5 mg/kg IM or SQ.
- Intervals of administration vary with condition. Intervals may range from once/week, to once/month.

Large Animal Dosage

Horses

- To prevent estrus: 250-500 mg/horse IM.

Regulatory Information

There are no withdrawal times established because this drug should not be administered to animals that produce food.

Megestrol Acetate

meh-jess'trole ass'ih-tate

Trade and Other Names: Ovaban and Megace

Functional Classification: Hormone

Pharmacology and Mechanism of Action

Progestin hormone. Megestrol acetate mimics the effects of progesterone in animals.

Indications and Clinical Uses

Megestrol acetate is used in animals as a progesterone hormone treatment to control estrous cycle. It also has been used for management of some behavioral and dermatologic disorders (such as urine spraying in cats and alopecia). However, its use for behavioral therapy in animals is discouraged because of high relapse rates and incidence of hormone-related adverse effects.

In horses, it has been used to prevent estrus, but at doses of 10-20 mg/day/horse, it failed.

Precautionary Information

Adverse Reactions and Side Effects

Adverse effects include polyphagia, polydipsia, adrenal suppression (cats), increased risk of diabetes, pyometra, diarrhea, and increased risk of neoplasia.

Contraindications and Precautions

Do not use in diabetic animals. Do not use in pregnant animals.

Drug Interactions

No drug interactions are reported. However, clearance of medroxyprogesterone is increased with drugs known to induce hepatic P450 enzymes (see Appendix).

Instructions for Use

Clinical studies in animals have studied primarily the reproductive use and effects on behavioral use. Medroxyprogesterone acetate may have fewer side effects than megestrol acetate.

Patient Monitoring and Laboratory Tests

Because of risk of diabetes mellitus, monitor glucose concentrations during treatment periodically.

M

Formulations

Megestrol acetate is available in 5 mg tablets (veterinary preparation) and 20 and 40 mg tablets (human preparation).

Stability and Storage

Store in tightly sealed container, protected from light, and at room temperature. Stability of compounded formulations has not been evaluated.

Small Animal Dosage

Dogs

- Proestrus: 2 mg/kg q24h PO for 8 days.
- Anestrus: 0.5 mg/kg q24h PO for 30 days.
- Treatment of behavior problems: 2-4 mg/kg q24h for 8 days (reduce dose for maintenance).

Cats

- Dermatologic therapy or urine spraying: 2.5-5 mg/cat q24h PO for 1 week then reduce to 5 mg once or twice/week cat.
- Suppress estrus: 5 mg/cat/day for 3 days, then 2.5-5 mg once/week for 10 weeks.

Large Animal Dosage

Horses

- Suppress estrus: 0.5 mg/kg q24h PO.

Regulatory Information

There are no withdrawal times established because this drug should not be administered to animals that produce food.

Melarsomine

mel-ar'soe-meen

Trade and Other Names: Immiticide

Functional Classification: Antiparasitic

Pharmacology and Mechanism of Action

Organic arsenical compound. Arsenicals alter glucose uptake and metabolism in heartworms.

Indications and Clinical Uses

Melarsomine is used for heartworm adulticide therapy.

Precautionary Information

Adverse Reactions and Side Effects

Melarsomine may cause pulmonary thromboembolism 7-20 days after therapy, anorexia (13% incidence), injection site reaction ([myositis] 32% incidence), or lethargy or depression (15% incidence). It causes elevations of hepatic enzymes. High doses (three times the dose) can cause pulmonary inflammation and death. If high doses are administered, dimercaprol (3 mg/kg IM) may be used as antidote.

Contraindications and Precautions

Use cautiously in animals with high heartworm burden. Specifically, melarsomine is contraindicated in dogs with Class 4 (very severe) heartworm disease.

Drug Interactions

No drug interactions are reported.

Instructions for Use

Dose regimens are based on severity of heartworm disease. Follow product insert carefully for instructions on proper administration. Also consult current reference to determine class of heartworm disease (Class 1-4) before initiating treatment. Class 1 and 2 are least severe. Class 3 is severe and Class 4 is most severe and should not be treated with adulticide before surgery. Avoid human exposure. (Wash hands after handling or wear gloves.)

Patient Monitoring and Laboratory Tests

Monitor heartworm status after treatment. Monitor treated patients carefully for signs of pulmonary thromboembolism.

Formulations

Melarsomine is available in 25 mg/mL injection.

Stability and Storage

After reconstitution, solution retains potency for 24 hours. Do not freeze solutions after they are prepared.

Small Animal Dosage

Dogs

Administer via deep intramuscular injection.

- Class 1-2: 2.5 mg/kg/day for 2 consecutive days.
- Class 3: 2.5 mg/kg once, then in 1 month two additional doses 24 hours apart.

Large Animal Dosage
No large animal doses have been reported.

Regulatory Information
There are no withdrawal times established because this drug should not be administered to animals that produce food.

Meloxicam
mel-oks'ih-kam

Trade and Other Names: Metacam (veterinary preparation), Mobic (human preparation), Metacam suspension (equine preparation, Europe), and Mobicox (human formulation in Canada)

Functional Classification: Antiinflammatory

Pharmacology and Mechanism of Action
Meloxicam is a nonsteroidal antiinflammatory drug (NSAID). Like other drugs in this class, meloxicam has analgesic and antiinflammatory effects by inhibiting the synthesis of prostaglandins. The enzyme inhibited by NSAID is the cyclo-oxygenase enzyme (COX). The COX enzyme exists in two isoforms, called COX-1 and COX-2. COX-1 is primarily responsible for synthesis of prostaglandins important for maintaining a healthy GI tract, renal function, platelet function, and other normal functions. COX-2 is induced and responsible for synthesizing prostaglandins that are important mediators of pain, inflammation, and fever. (There may be some crossover of COX-1 and COX-2 effects in some situations.) Meloxicam is relatively COX-1 sparing compared to older NSAIDs, but it is not known if the specificity for COX-1 or COX-2 is related to efficacy or safety. Meloxicam has a half-life of 23-24 hours in dogs, 15 hours in cats, and 8.5 (range 5-14.5) in horses. Meloxicam is highly protein bound. Oral absorption is almost complete in dogs when administered with food. Absorption is 85%-98% in horses and is not affected significantly by feeding.

Indications and Clinical Uses
Meloxicam is used to decrease pain, inflammation, and fever. It has been used for the acute and chronic treatment of pain and inflammation in dogs and cats. One of the most common uses is osteoarthritis, but it has also been used for pain associated with surgery. Both acute and long-term safety and efficacy have been established for dogs. In studies performed in dogs, higher doses, (up to 0.5 mg/kg) were more effective than lower doses, but also were associated with a higher incidence of GI adverse effects. Use in cats is limited to short-term use or long-term use at low doses. In cats, meloxicam was superior to butorphanol for treating pain associated with onychectomy. Acute response to treating fever in cats also has been demonstrated. In pigs, meloxicam has been used for mastitis-metritis-agalactia syndrome. In horses, meloxicam has been used for treating pain and inflammation associated with surgery. There is an approved registration in horses at a dose of 0.6 mg/kg and published pharmacokinetic and pharmacodynamic studies at this dose.

Precautionary Information

Adverse Reactions and Side Effects

Major adverse effects are GI, including vomiting, diarrhea, and ulceration. Because meloxicam appears to be relatively COX-1 sparing, adverse effects are expected to be less than other NSAIDs that are not as selective, but this has not been demonstrated on controlled clinical trials. Renal toxicity, especially in dehydrated animals or animals with preexisting renal disease has been shown for some NSAIDs. Renal injury has been reported in dogs from doses of 0.3-0.5 mg/kg and higher. GI ulceration has been observed when dogs were administered doses slightly higher than registered doses. In cats at high doses (five times the dose) vomiting and other GI problems were reported. With repeated doses (9 days) of 0.3 mg/kg/day to cats, inflamed GI mucosa and ulceration were observed.

Contraindications and Precautions

Dogs and cats with preexisting GI problems or renal problems may be at a greater risk of adverse effects from NSAIDs. Safety in pregnant animals is not known, but adverse effects have not been reported. The manufacturer does not recommend a second dose of meloxicam injection to cats.

Drug Interactions

Do not administer with other NSAIDs or with corticosteroids. Corticosteroids have been shown to exacerbate the GI adverse effects. Some NSAIDs may interfere with the action of diuretic drugs and angiotensin converting enzyme (ACE) inhibitors.

Instructions for Use

Liquid medication may be added to food for dosing. When using veterinary liquid formulation, the dropper bottle is designed to deliver 0.05 mg per drop or one drop per pound body weight (two drops per kg body weight). Observe manufacturer's instructions when using dosing syringe supplied with product.

Patient Monitoring and Laboratory Tests

Monitor GI signs for evidence of diarrhea, GI bleeding, or ulcers. Because of risk of renal injury, monitor renal parameters (water consumption, BUN, creatinine, and urine specific gravity) periodically during treatment.

Formulations

Meloxicam is available in 1.5 mg/mL (0.05 mg per drop) oral suspension, 5% (5 mg/mL) injection, and 7.5 and 15 mg tablets (human preparation).

In Europe, a 15 mg/mL oral suspension is available for horses.

Stability and Storage

Stability of commercial preparation has been established by manufacturer. However, stability and potency of preparations compounded from human tablets have not been established.

Small Animal Dosage

Dogs

- 0.2 mg/kg initial loading dose PO, SQ, or IV, and then 0.1 mg/kg q24h thereafter PO, SQ, or IV.

Cats

- 0.1 mg/kg q24h PO, with reduction in dose if chronic treatment is pursued. Long-term treatment should be lowered to 0.05 mg/kg q48h, and as low as q72h, PO.
- Single doses of 0.3 mg/kg SQ.

Large Animal Dosage

Pigs

- 0.4 mg/kg IM, which may be repeated in 24 hours.

Horses

- 0.6 mg/kg q24h IV or PO.

Regulatory Information

Registered for use in dogs in U.S. Registered for limited use in Europe in cats and swine.
RCI Classification: 3
Registered for use in horses in Europe. Recommended withdrawal time for racing horses is 3 days for urine testing. No food animal withdrawal times are available.

Melphalan

mel'fah-lan

Trade and Other Names: Alkeran

Functional Classification: Anticancer agent

M

Pharmacology and Mechanism of Action

Anticancer agent. Melphalan is an alkylating agent, similar in action to cyclophosphamide. It alkylates base-pairs in DNA and produces a cytotoxic effect.

Indications and Clinical Uses

Melphalan is not used as an anticancer agent as frequently as other alkylating agents. In animals it is used to treat multiple myeloma and certain carcinomas.

Precautionary Information

Adverse Reactions and Side Effects

Adverse effects related to its action as an anticancer agent. Melphalan causes myelosuppression.

Contraindications and Precautions

Do not use in animals with bone marrow suppression.

Drug Interactions

No drug interactions are reported. It has been used with other anticancer drug protocols.

Instructions for Use

Consult specific anticancer drug protocols for more dosing information.

Patient Monitoring and Laboratory Tests

Monitor CBC for evidence of bone marrow toxicity.

Formulations Available

Melphalan is available in 2 mg tablets and 50 mg vials for injection.

Stability and Storage

Store in tightly sealed container, protected from light, and at room temperature. It is insoluble in water but is soluble in ethanol. After reconstitution, decomposition occurs rapidly and may precipitate. Use within 1 hour of reconstitution. When prepared in a compounded formulation for oral use, it was unstable with rapid decomposition (80% loss in 24 hours).

Small Animal Dosage

Dogs

- 1.5 mg/m^2 (or 0.1-0.2 mg/kg) q24h PO for 7-10 days (repeat every 3 weeks).
- Injectable forms have not been used in animals, but in humans 16 mg/m^2 IV over 15-20 minutes has been used at 2 week intervals for multiple myeloma.

Large Animal Dosage

No large animal doses have been reported.

Regulatory Information

Withdrawal times are not established for animals that produce food. This drug should not be used in animals intended for food, because it is an anticancer agent.

Meperidine Hydrochloride

meh-pare'ih-deen hye-droe-klor'ide

Trade and Other Names: Demerol, Pethidine (European name)

Functional Classification: Analgesic, Opioid

Pharmacology and Mechanism of Action

Meperidine is a synthetic opioid agonist with activity primarily at the mu-opiate receptor. It is called pethidine in Europe. It is similar in action to morphine, except with approximately one seventh of the potency. An intramuscular injection of 75 mg or an oral dose of 300 mg of meperidine has similar potency as 10 mg morphine.

Indications and Clinical Uses

Meperidine has been used for short-term sedative effects, often used with other sedatives and/or anesthetics. For analgesic use, it is short-acting, usually less than 2 hours and often much shorter. Therefore its use for treating pain has not been popular. Meperidine may produce fewer GI motility problems compared to other opioids.

The use of meperidine in human medicine has declined because toxic effects have been observed from accumulation of metabolites.

Precautionary Information

Adverse Reactions and Side Effects

Like all opiates, some side effects are predictable and unavoidable. Side effects include sedation, urine retention, constipation, and bradycardia. Respiratory depression occurs with high doses. Tolerance and dependence occurs with chronic administration. Repeated doses in humans may cause toxicity from accumulation of metabolite. One of the metabolites, normeperidine, accumulates with repeated administration because it has a half-life much longer than meperidine. The accumulation of the metabolite causes excitatory effects. Similar reactions have not been reported from clinical use in animals.

Contraindications and Precautions

Meperidine is a schedule II controlled substance. Cats are more sensitive to excitement than other species, although they have tolerated meperidine relatively well. Avoid repeated doses because accumulation of metabolites may be toxic.

Drug Interactions

Meperidine should not be administered with monoamine oxidase inhibitors (MAOIs), such as selegiline. Meperidine and metabolites may inhibit reuptake of serotonin and cause excess serotonin effect, especially if combined with other drugs that produce similar action, such as selective-serotonin-reuptake inhibitors (e.g., fluoxetine), tricyclic antidepressants (e.g., clomipramine), or other analgesics such as tramadol.

Instructions for Use

Although comparative clinical studies have not been conducted in animals, meperidine may be effective for short duration but has not been used for long-term pain management.

Patient Monitoring and Laboratory Tests

Monitor patient's heart rate and respiration. Although bradycardia rarely needs to be treated when it is caused by an opioid, atropine can be administered if necessary. If serious respiratory depression occurs, the opioid can be reversed with naloxone.

Formulations

Meperidine is available in 50 and 100 mg tablets, 10 mg/mL syrup, and 25, 50, 75, and 100 mg/mL injection.

Stability and Storage

Store in tightly sealed container, protected from light, and at room temperature. It is soluble in water. It may be mixed with 0.9% saline or 5% dextrose for 28 days without loss of potency or stability. It is stable in syrup formulation. Protect from freezing.

Small Animal Dosage

Dogs

- 5-10 mg/kg IV or IM as often as every 2-3 hours (or as needed).

Cats

- 3-5 mg/kg IV or IM every 2-4 hours (or as needed).

Large Animal Dosage

No large animal doses have been reported.

Regulatory Information

Schedule II controlled drug.

Withdrawal times are not established for animals that produce food. For extralabel use withdrawal interval estimates, contact FARAD at 1-888-USFARAD (1-888-873-2723) or send e-mail to FARAD@ncsu.edu.

RCI Classification: 1

Mepivacaine

meh-piv'ah-kane

Trade and Other Names: Carbocaine-V

Functional Classification: Local anesthetic

Pharmacology and Mechanism of Action

Mepivacaine is a local anesthetic of the amide class. It inhibits nerve conduction via sodium channel blockade. Medium potency and duration of action compared to bupivacaine. Compared to lidocaine, it is longer-acting but has equal potency.

Indications and Clinical Uses

Mepivacaine is used as a local anesthetic and for epidural analgesia/anesthesia.

Precautionary Information

Adverse Reactions and Side Effects

Adverse effects are rare with local infiltration. High doses absorbed systemically can cause nervous system signs (tremors and convulsions). After epidural administration, respiratory paralysis is possible with high doses. Mepivacaine may cause less irritation to tissues than lidocaine.

Contraindications and Precautions

No contraindications reported for animals.

Drug Interactions

No drug interactions reported.

Instructions for Use

For epidural use, do not exceed 8 mg/kg total dose. Duration of epidural analgesia is 2.5-3 hours.

Patient Monitoring and Laboratory Tests

No specific monitoring is necessary.

Formulations

Mepivacaine is available in a 2% (20 mg/mL) injection.

Stability and Storage

Store in tightly sealed container, protected from light, and at room temperature. Stability of compounded formulations has not been evaluated.

Small Animal Dosage

Dogs and Cats

Variable dose for local infiltration.

- Epidural: 0.5 mL of 2% solution q30sec until reflexes are absent.

Large Animal Dosage

Horses

Variable doses used for local infiltration, depending on the need.

Regulatory Information

No regulatory information is available. Because of low risk of residues when used for local infiltration, no withdrawal times are suggested.
Horses: Clearance prior to racing is approximately 2 days.
RCI Classification: 2

Mercaptopurine

mer-kap-toe-pyoo′reen

Trade and Other Names: Purinethol

Functional Classification: Anticancer agent

Pharmacology and Mechanism of Action

Anticancer agent. Antimetabolite agent that inhibits synthesis of purines in cancer cells. It is cell-cycle specific and acts at the S-phase of cell division.

Indications and Clinical Uses

Mercaptopurine is used for various forms of cancer, including leukemia and lymphoma. A related drug is azathioprine. Administration of azathioprine is metabolized to 6 mercaptopurine, which is further metabolized to cytotoxic products.

Precautionary Information

Adverse Reactions and Side Effects

Many side effects are possible that are common to anticancer therapy (many of which are unavoidable) including bone marrow suppression and anemia.

Contraindications and Precautions

Do not use in animals with known sensitivity to azathioprine. Do **not** administer to cats.

Drug Interactions

No drug interactions are reported. It has been used with other anticancer drug protocols.

Instructions for Use

Consult specific anticancer protocol for specific regimen.

Patient Monitoring and Laboratory Tests

Monitor CBC for evidence of bone marrow toxicity.

Formulations

Mercaptopurine is available in 50 mg tablets.

Stability and Storage

Store in tightly sealed container, protected from light, and at room temperature. It is prone to oxidation of mixed with alkaline solutions. pH of solutions should be below 8. If mixed with oral vehicles, such as syrups, it was stable for 14 days.

Small Animal Dosage

Dogs
- 50 mg/m^2 q24h PO.

Cats
- Contraindicated.

Large Animal Dosage

No large animal doses have been reported.

Regulatory Information

Withdrawal times are not established for animals that produce food. This drug should not be used in animals intended for food, because it is an anticancer agent.

Meropenem

meer-oh-pen′em

Trade and Other Names: Merrem

Functional Classification: Antibacterial

Pharmacology and Mechanism of Action

Beta-lactam antibiotic of the carbapenems class with broad spectrum of activity. Action on cell wall is similar to other beta-lactams, which is to bind penicillin-binding proteins (PBP) that weaken or interfere with cell wall formation. The carbapenems bind to a specific PBP (PBP-1) that results in more rapid lysis compared to other beta-lactams. This results in greater bactericidal activity and a longer postantiobiotic effect. Carbapenems have a broad spectrum of activity and are among the most active of all antibiotics. Spectrum includes gram-negative bacilli, including *Enterobacteriaceae* and *Pseudomonas aeruginosa*. It also is active against most gram-positive bacteria, except methicillin-resistant strains of *Staphylococcus*. It is not active against *Enterococcus*. Meropenem is the most active of all beta-lactams and active against aerobe and anaerobic gram-positive and gram-negative bacteria.

Indications and Clinical Uses

Meropenem is indicated primarily for resistant infections caused by bacteria resistant to other drugs. It is especially valuable for treating resistant infections caused by *Pseudomonas aeruginosa*, *Escherichia coli*, and *Klebsiella pneumoniae*. Meropenem is slightly more active against some bacteria than imipenem.

Precautionary Information

Adverse Reactions and Side Effects

Carbapenems pose similar risks as other beta-lactam antibiotics, but adverse effects are rare. Meropenem does not cause seizures as frequently as imipenem. Subcutaneous injections may cause slight hair loss at injection site.

Contraindications and Precautions

Some slight yellowish discoloration may occur after reconstitution. Slight discoloration will not affect potency. However, a darker amber or brown discoloration may indicate oxidation and loss of potency.

Drug Interactions

Do not mix in vial or syringe with other antibiotics.

Instructions for Use

Doses in animals have been based on pharmacokinetic studies rather than efficacy trials. Meropenem is more soluble than imipenem and can be injected via bolus rather than administered in fluid solutions. Meropenem has been injected SQ in dogs with no evidence of tissue reaction.

Patient Monitoring and Laboratory Tests

Susceptibility testing: CLSI (NCCLS) break points for sensitive organisms are less than or equal to 4 mcg/mL for all organisms. Sensitivity to imipenem can be used as a marker for meropenem.

Formulations

Meropenem is available in 500 mg in 20 mL vial (25 mg/mL) or 1 gram vial in 30 mL (33 mg/mL) for injection.

Stability and Storage

Stable if stored in manufacturer's original vial. When reconstituted, stability studies have shown that meropenem is stable for up to 25 days if refrigerated. Slight yellow discoloration may occur without loss of potency.

Small Animal Dosage

Dogs and Cats

- 8.5 mg/kg SQ q12h or 24 mg/kg IV q12h.
- UTIs: 8 mg/kg q12h SQ.
- For infections caused by *Pseudomonas aeruginosa* or other similar organisms that may have minimum inhibitory concentration (MIC) values as high as 1.0 mcg/mL: 12 mg/kg q8h SQ or 25 mg/kg q8h IV.

Large Animal Dosage

No large animal doses have been reported. However, doses similar to the range used in small animals are suggested for foals.

Regulatory Information

Withdrawal times are not established for animals that produce food. For extralabel use withdrawal interval estimates, contact FARAD at 1-888-USFARAD (1-888-873-2723) or send e-mail to FARAD@ncsu.edu.

Mesalamine

mez-ahl'ah-meen

Trade and Other Names: Asacol, Mesasal, Pentasa, and Mesalazine

Functional Classification: Antidiarrheal

Pharmacology and Mechanism of Action

Mesalamine is also known as 5-aminosalicylic acid. It is the active component of sulfasalazine, which is commonly administered for treatment of colitis. (See sulfasalazine and olsalazine for additional information.) The action of mesalamine is not precisely known, but it appears to suppress the metabolism of arachidonic acid in the intestine. It inhibits both cyclo-oxygenase and lipoxygenase-mediated mucosal inflammation. Systemic absorption is low; most of the action is believed to be local. There are four formulations of mesalamine used:

1. Asacol. Asacol is a tablet coated with an acrylic-based resin. The resin dissolves at a pH of 7.0 and is designed to release 5-aminosalicylic acid in the colon.

2. Mesasal. Mesasal is a tablet coated with an acrylic-based resin that dissolves at a pH of >6.0. It is designed to release 5-aminosalicylic acid in the terminal ileum and colon. Approximately 35% of the salicylate is absorbed systemically. The dose in people is 1-1.5 g/day.
3. Olsalazine sodium (Dipentum). Olsalazine is a dimer of 2 molecules of 5-aminosalicylic acid linked by an azo bond. It is used in people who cannot tolerate sulfasalazine. Only 2% of the salicylate from this compound is absorbed systemically. The most common adverse effect in people from this preparation has been a watery diarrhea.
4. Pentasa. Pentasa contains microgranules of mesalamine coated with ethyl cellulose, which releases 5-aminosalicylic acid into the small and large intestine gradually regardless of pH.

Indications and Clinical Uses

Mesalamine is used for treatment of inflammatory bowel disease, including colitis in animals. Most often sulfasalazine is used, however in some animals, especially those sensitive to sulfonamides, mesalamine may be indicated.

Precautionary Information

Adverse Reactions and Side Effects

Mesalamine alone has not been associated with side effects in animals.

Contraindications and Precautions

Drug interactions are possible, but they have not been reported in animals, probably because low systemic drug levels are achieved. Mesalamine if absorbed sufficiently can potentially interfere with thiopurine methyltransferase and, therefore, increase the risk of toxicity from azathioprine.

Drug Interactions

No drug interactions are reported in animals. Omeprazole can potentially increase absorption by increasing intestinal pH.

Instructions for Use

Mesalamine usually is used as a substitute for sulfasalazine in animals that cannot tolerate sulfonamides.

Patient Monitoring and Laboratory Tests

No specific monitoring is necessary.

Formulations

Mesalamine is available in 400 mg tablets and 250 mg capsules.

Stability and Storage

Store in tightly sealed container, protected from light, and at room temperature. It is slightly soluble in water and ethanol. It should be protected from air and moisture. Darkening may occur after exposure to air. Do not crush coated tablets.

Small Animal Dosage

Veterinary dose has not been established. The usual human dose is 400-500 mg q6-8h.

Large Animal Dosage

No large animal doses have been reported.

Regulatory Information

No regulatory information is available. Because of low risk of residues, no withdrawal times are suggested.
RCI Classification: 5

Metaproterenol Sulfate

met-ha-proe-teer′eh-nole sul′fate

Trade and Other Names: Alupent, Metaprel, and Orciprenaline sulphate

Functional Classification: Bronchodilator, Beta-agonist

Pharmacology and Mechanism of Action

$Beta_2$ adrenergic agonist. Bronchodilator. Like other $beta_2$ agonists, it stimulates $beta_2$ receptors, activates adenyl cyclase and relaxes bronchial smooth muscle. It also may inhibit release of inflammatory mediators, especially from mast cells.

Indications and Clinical Uses

Metaproterenol is used in animals to relax bronchial smooth muscle to treat bronchitis, obstructive pulmonary disease, and other airway diseases. It is indicated in animals with reversible bronchoconstriction, such as cats with bronchial asthma.

M

Precautionary Information

Adverse Reactions and Side Effects

Metaproterenol causes excessive beta-adrenergic stimulation at high doses (tachycardia and tremors). Arrhythmias occur at high doses or in sensitive individuals. Beta-agonists will inhibit uterine contractions in animals in labor.

Contraindications and Precautions

Use cautiously in animals with cardiac disease.

Drug Interactions

Do not administer with monoamine oxidase inhibitors (MAOIs). Use cautiously with other drugs that may cause cardiac arrhythmias in animals. It may be mixed with cromolyn sodium for nebulization if used within 60-90 minutes. It also has been combined with dexamethasone without loss of stability.

Instructions for Use

Results of clinical studies in animals have not been reported. Use in animals (and doses) is based on experience in people or anecdotal experience in animals. $Beta_2$ agonists also have been used in people to delay labor (inhibit uterine contractions).

Patient Monitoring and Laboratory Tests

Monitor heart rate and rhythm of animals during treatment.

Formulations

Metaproterenol is available in 10 and 20 mg tablets, 5 mg/mL syrup, and inhalers.

Stability and Storage

Store in tightly sealed container, protected from light, and at room temperature. Avoid exposure to air and moisture. Do not freeze. Do not use if formulation turns dark color.

Small Animal Dosage

Dogs and Cats

- 0.325-0.65 mg/kg q4-6h PO.

Large Animal Dosage

No large animal doses have been reported. There is no evidence of oral absorption in large animals.

Regulatory Information

Do not administer to animals that produce food. Other beta-agonists (clenbuterol) are banned for use in food animals.

RCI Classification: 3

Metformin

met-for'min

Trade and Other Names: Glucophage

Functional Classification: Antihyperglycemic

Pharmacology and Mechanism of Action

Metformin is an oral antihyperglycemic agent used to treat diabetes. It is of the biguanide class of oral drugs for diabetes. Metformin does not have a direct effect on pancreatic beta cells, but it lowers blood glucose by reducing hepatic glucose production and improving peripheral utilization of glucose (e.g., in muscle). It thus lowers insulin requirements without any direct effect to increase insulin secretion. It may increase the insulin receptors on tissues. At therapeutic doses, metformin will not cause hypoglycemia. Half-life in cats is 2.75 hours.

Indications and Clinical Uses

In people, metformin is used to treat Type II diabetes. It has been used in people when the sulfonylurea drugs fail. It has been used in cats to treat diabetes. However, in cats treated with 50 mg/cat q12h PO, it showed significant adverse effects and was effective in only one fifth of treated cats. In cats, it has been more common to administer the sulfonylurea class of drugs in animals. Sulfonylurea drugs include glipizide (Glucotrol) and glyburide (DiaBeta, Micronase). Diabetic dogs rarely respond to oral hypoglycemic agents.

Precautionary Information

Adverse Reactions and Side Effects

Metformin has caused lethargy, appetite loss, vomiting, and weight loss in cats. Use has not been common enough to document other effects. However, in people, it has caused lactic acidosis. Metformin also has caused megaloblastic anemia by affecting Vitamin B_{12} absorption. Another drug in people from an unrelated class (thiazolidinediones), troglitazone (Rezulin), was removed from the market in 2001 because of liver toxicity.

Contraindications and Precautions

Metformin is cleared by the kidneys, so doses will need to be adjusted in patients with renal failure.

Drug Interactions

Use cautiously with drugs that may affect glycemic control such as glucocorticoids.

Instructions for Use

Doses published for cats are based on pharmacokinetic studies that demonstrated oral absorption in cats to be 35%-70%. The half-life was 11.5 hrs, which is the basis for the q12h dosage recommendation.

Patient Monitoring and Laboratory Tests

Blood glucose should be monitored carefully. Doses should be adjusted on the basis of glucose monitoring. Some animals may require insulin injections to control hyperglycemia.

Formulations Available

Metformin is available in 500 and 850 mg tablets.

Stability and Storage

Stable if maintained in original formulation.

Small Animal Dosage

Cats

- 25 or 50 mg/cat q12h PO (5-10 mg/kg q12h). (Efficacy is limited.)

Large Animal Dosage

No large animal doses have been reported.

Regulatory Information

Do not administer to animals intended for food.

Methadone Hydrochloride

meth'ah-done hye-droe-klor'ide

Trade and Other Names: Dolophine, Methadose, and generic brands

Functional Classification: Analgesic, Opioid

Pharmacology and Mechanism of Action

Opioid agonist, analgesic. Action of methadone is to bind to mu-opiate and kappa-opiate receptors on nerves and inhibit release of neurotransmitters involved with transmission of pain stimuli (such as Substance P). Methadone also may antagonize NMDA (n-methyl D-aspartate) receptors, which may contribute to side effects, decrease adverse CNS effects, and inhibit tolerance. Other opiates used in animals include morphine, hydromorphone, codeine, oxymorphone, meperidine, and fentanyl.

Indications and Clinical Uses

Methadone is indicated for short-term analgesia, sedation, and as an adjunct to anesthesia. It is compatible with most anesthetics and can be used as part of a multimodal approach to analgesia/anesthesia. Administration of methadone may lower dose requirements for other anesthetics and analgesics used. Oral doses to dogs are not absorbed systemically.

Precautionary Information

Adverse Reactions and Side Effects

Like all opiates, side effects from methadone are predictable and unavoidable. Side effects from methadone administration include sedation, vomiting, constipation, urinary retention, and bradycardia. Panting may occur in dogs as a result of changes in thermoregulation. Effects such as excitement and dysphoria were not observed with intravenous administration of methadone.

Contraindications and Precautions

Methadone is a schedule II controlled substance. Cats may be more sensitive to excitement than other species.

Drug Interactions

No specific drug interactions reported for animals.

Instructions for Use

Oral doses were not absorbed in dogs. Oral doses have not been evaluated in other species.

Patient Monitoring and Laboratory Tests

Monitor patient's heart rate and respiration. Although bradycardia rarely needs to be treated when it is caused by an opioid, atropine can be administered if necessary. If serious respiratory depression occurs, the opioid can be reversed with naloxone.

Formulations

Methadone is available in 1 and 2 mg/mL oral solution, 5, 10, and 40 mg tablets, and 10 mg/mL injectable solution.

Stability and Storage

Store in tightly sealed container, protected from light, and at room temperature. It is soluble in water and ethanol. It may precipitate from a solution if pH is above 6. It has been combined in oral mixtures with juices, syrups, and stable for at least 14 days.

Small Animal Dosage

Dogs

- Analgesia: 0.5-2.2 mg/kg q3-4h SQ or IM.
- Analgesia: 0.1 mg/kg IV.

Cats

- Analgesia: 0.1-0.5 mg/kg q3-4h SQ or IM.
- 0.05-0.1 mg/kg IV.

Large Animal Dosage

Horses

Dose not reported

Regulatory Information

Do not administer to animals intended for food.
Methadone is a Schedule II controlled drug.
RCI Classification: 1

Methazolamide

meth-ah-zole'ah-mide

Trade and Other Names: Neptazane

Functional Classification: Diuretic

Pharmacology and Mechanism of Action

Methazolamide is a carbonic anhydrase inhibitor. Methazolamide, like other carbonic anhydrase inhibitors, produces a diuresis through inhibition of the uptake of bicarbonate in proximal renal tubules via enzyme inhibition. This action results in loss of bicarbonate in the urine and a diuresis. The action of carbonic anhydrase inhibitors results in urine loss of bicarbonate, alkaline urine, and water loss. Methazolamide, like other carbonic anhydrase inhibitors, also decreases formation of cerebrospinal fluid (CSF) by the choroid plexus and decreases the ocular fluid formation by decreasing bicarbonate secretion by the ocular ciliary body. This effect on aqueous humor formation decreases ocular pressure.

Indications and Clinical Uses

Methazolamide is rarely used as a diuretic any longer. There are more potent and effective diuretic drugs available, such as the loop diuretics (furosemide). Methazolamide, like other carbonic anhydrase inhibitors, are used primarily to lower intraocular pressure in animals with glaucoma. Its duration is relatively short in dogs, which may require more frequent administration to maintain low ocular pressure. Methazolamide is used more often than acetazolamide for this purpose because it is more effective and easily available. However, other treatment regimens are commonly used for treatment of glaucoma compared to the carbonic anhydrase inhibitors. Methazolamide, like other carbonic anhydrase inhibitors, are sometimes used to produce more alkaline urine for management of some urinary calculi.

Precautionary Information

Adverse Reactions and Side Effects

Methazolamide can potentially produce hypokalemia in some patients.

Contraindications and Precautions

Do not use in patients with acidemia. Use cautiously in any animal sensitive to sulfonamides. Do not use in patients with hepatic encephalopathy.

Drug Interactions

Use cautiously with other treatments that could cause metabolic acidosis.

Instructions for Use

Methazolamide may be used with other glaucoma agents, such as topical drugs to decrease intraocular pressure.

Patient Monitoring and Laboratory Tests

Monitor ocular pressure in treated patients. Monitor urine pH if it is used to produce alkaline urine.

Formulations Available

Methazolamide is available in 25 and 50 mg tablets.

Stability and Storage

Store in tightly sealed container, protected from light, and at room temperature. Stability of compounded formulations has not been evaluated.

Small Animal Dosage

Dogs and Cats

- 2-3 mg/kg q8-12h PO. There does not seem to be any benefit for increasing the dose to a maximum dose of 4-6 mg/kg, but more frequent administration (every 8 hours) may be beneficial.

Large Animal Dosage

No large animal doses have been reported.

Regulatory Information

Withdrawal times are not established for animals that produce food. For extralabel use withdrawal interval estimates, contact FARAD at 1-888-USFARAD (1-888-873-2723) or send e-mail to FARAD@ncsu.edu.

RCI Classification: 4

Methenamine

meth-en′ah-meen

Trade and Other Names: Methenamine hippurate: Hiprex and Urex; Methenamine mandelate: Mandelamine and generic brands

Functional Classification: Antibacterial

Pharmacology and Mechanism of Action

Methenamine is a urinary antiseptic. Methenamine in the acid environment of the urine is converted to formaldehyde to produce an antibacterial/antifungal effect. A low urine pH of at least 5.5 or below is needed for optimal effect. It is active against a wide range of bacteria. Resistance does not develop. Less effective against *Proteus* species that produce an alkaline urine pH. Because there is no systemic absorption, it is not effective for systemic infections.

Indications and Clinical Uses

Methenamine is used as a urinary antiseptic. There is a lack of well-controlled clinical trials to show its effectiveness. However it has been used in animals to prevent recurrences of lower UTIs. It is probably less effective for treating ongoing infections. It is critical that the urine pH is low for conversion to formaldehyde.

Precautionary Information

Adverse Reactions and Side Effects

Although formaldehyde formation in bladder may be irritating, in people, high doses were required (greater than 8 g/day). In animals, no adverse effects have been reported.

Contraindications and Precautions

High doses may irritate bladder mucosa. Do not administer with sulfonamides, because it may form formaldehyde-sulfonamide complexes.

Drug Interactions

Do not administer with medications that may cause alkaline urine. Because urine acidifers are added with methenamine, acid urine will decrease the activity of fluoroquinolone and aminoglycoside antibiotics.

Instructions for Use

Results of clinical studies in animals have not been reported. Use in animals is based on experience in people or anecdotal experience in animals. Urine must be acidic for methenamine to convert to formaldehyde (monitor pH periodically). pH <5.5 is optimal. Supplement with ascorbic acid or ammonium chloride to lower pH.

Patient Monitoring and Laboratory Tests

No specific monitoring is necessary. Monitor urinalysis or culture of urine to guide therapy of UTI.

Formulations

Methenamine hippurate is available in 1 g tablets and methenamine mandelate is available in 1 g tablets, granules for oral solution, and 50 and 100 mg/mL oral suspension.

Stability and Storage

Store in tightly sealed container, protected from light, and at room temperature. Methenamine is soluble in water and ethanol. In an acidic environment, it is hydrolyzed to form formaldehyde and ammonia by acid. It has been physically incompatible when mixed with some foods and suspensions.

Small Animal Dosage

Dogs

- Methenamine hippurate: 500 mg/dog q12h PO.
- Methenamine mandelate: 10-20 mg/kg q8-12h PO.

Cats

- Methenamine hippurate: 250 mg/cat q12h PO.
- Methenamine mandelate: 10-20 mg/kg q8-12h PO.

Large Animal Dosage

No large animal doses have been reported. It is unlikely to be effective in large animals, because their urine is more alkaline.

Regulatory Information

No regulatory information is available. Because of low risk of residues, no withdrawal times are suggested.

Methimazole

meth-im'ah-zole

Trade and Other Names: Tapazole

Functional Classification: Antithyroid agent

Pharmacology and Mechanism of Action

Antithyroid drug. Action is to serve as substrate for thyroid peroxidase (TPO), to inhibit it and decrease incorporation of iodide into tyrosine molecules. Methimazole inhibits coupling of mono-iodinated and di-iodinated residues to form T4 and T3. Methimazole does not inhibit release of preformed thyroid hormone. It is used for treating hyperthyroidism, primarily in cats. Carbimazole is a similar drug used in Europe that acts via a similar mechanism. Methimazole also may have immunosuppressive effects. Treatment may decrease antithyrotropin-receptor antibodies.

Indications and Clinical Uses

Methimazole is used to treat hyperthyroidism in animals, especially cats. There is good evidence for efficacy when administered to cats at recommended doses. Methimazole is preferred in cats instead of propylthiouracil (PTU), because methimazole has a lower incidence of adverse effects. Evidence supports twice daily dosing in cats to be more effective than once daily. Methimazole has been formulated for use in cats as a transdermal gel for skin absorption (e.g., those combined with pluronic organogel [PLO] gel). These formulations are available through compounding pharmacies. There is published data to indicate that transdermal methimazole is not as rapidly acting, or as effective, as oral dosing, but it can be effective to lower T4 concentrations in many cats.

Precautionary Information

Adverse Reactions and Side Effects

Methimazole is generally well tolerated in dogs. In cats, GI problems are the most common and can include anorexia and vomiting. Most adverse effects caused by methimazole are dose related and can be decreased by lowering the dose. In cats, alopecia and scaling and crusting of the head and face have been observed. In people, it has caused agranulocytosis and leukopenia. In cats, lupus-like reactions are possible, such as vasculitis and bone marrow changes. In cats, abnormal platelet counts and low blood counts can develop after 1-3 months of treatment. Bleeding abnormalities may be related to thrombocytopenia, but tests conducted in cats did not demonstrate prolongation of bleeding times (prothrombin time and activated partial antithromboplastin time). There were fewer adverse GI effects when methimazole was applied as a transdermal gel compared to administration as an oral tablet.

Contraindications and Precautions

Do not administer to animals with thrombocytopenia or bleeding problems. Other drugs such as beta-blockers are safe to administer with methimazole. Warn pet owners that transdermal methimazole can be absorbed through human skin. If an animal has had an adverse reaction to propylthiouracil (PTU), there may also be cross-sensitivity to methimazole. Methimazole has caused fetal abnormalities and should not be used in pregnant animals.

Drug Interactions

There are no drug interactions reported from the use in animals.

Instructions for Use

Use in cats is based on experimental studies in hyperthyroid cats. Methimazole has, for the most part, replaced propylthiouracil (PTU) for use in cats. Adjust maintenance dose by monitoring thyroid (T-4) concentrations in plasma. Because it does not inhibit release of preformed thyroid, it may take 2-4 weeks to achieve maximum effect. When methimazole dosing frequency was been evaluated, dosing with 2.5 mg q12h PO was more effective than 5 mg q24h PO. If prepared as a transdermal gel, it is recommended to use a PLO formulation consisting of 0.15 g methimazole, 100 g lecithin soya, 100 g isopropyl palmitate, 0.66 g of sorbic acid powder, and 20% pluronic F127 gel. Final concentration should be 5 mg/0.1 mL of transdermal gel. Gel can be applied to inner ear. The use of transdermal gel may be less effective than with oral tablets.

Patient Monitoring and Laboratory Tests

Monitor serum T-4 levels. Recheck T4 levels after first month of treatment. Monitor CBC and platelet count in cats every week or 14 days for the first 30 days of treatment.

Formulations

Methimazole is available in 5 and 10 mg tablets.

Stability and Storage

Methimazole is stable if maintained in original formulation. However, if prepared in compounded formulations for cats, potency and stability may be less. Potency is assured for 2 weeks with compounded transdermal gel.

Small Animal Dosage

Cats

- 2.5 mg/cat q12h PO for 7-14 days, then 5-10 mg/cat PO q12h and monitor T-4 concentrations.
- In some cats, once T4 levels have been normalized, dose can be decreased to 10-15 mg/cat once a day.
- Transdermal dose: 2.5 mg/cat transdermally twice daily. Alternate ears with each dose and wear gloves when applying.

Large Animal Dosage

No large animal doses have been reported.

Regulatory Information

Withdrawal times are not established for animals that produce food. This drug should not be used in animals intended for food.

Methocarbamol

meth-oh-kar'bah-mole

Trade and Other Names: Robaxin-V

Functional Classification: Muscle relaxant

Pharmacology and Mechanism of Action

Skeletal muscle relaxant. Methocarbamol depresses polysynaptic reflexes to cause muscle relaxation.

Indications and Clinical Uses

Methocarbamol has been used for treatment of skeletal muscle spasms and increased muscle tone. It has also been used to treat pain that is associated with increased muscle spasms or myositis. Higher doses than listed in the dosing section are recommended if it is used for treating tetanus. However, evidence for efficacy in animals is lacking. For some indications (e.g., muscle spasms) methocarbamol has been replaced by other muscle relaxants such as orphenadrine (Norflex).

Precautionary Information

Adverse Reactions and Side Effects

Methocarbamol may cause depression and sedation of the CNS. Excess salivation, emesis, weakness, and ataxia have been observed from methocarbamol administration. Adverse effects are usually short in duration.

Contraindications and Precautions

Use cautiously with other drugs that depress the CNS.

Drug Interactions

No drug interactions reported for animals.

Instructions for Use

Results of clinical studies in animals have not been reported. Use in animals (and doses) is based on experience in people or anecdotal experience in animals.

Patient Monitoring and Laboratory Tests

No specific monitoring is necessary.

Formulations

Methocarbamol is available in 500 and 750 mg tablets and 100 mg/mL injection.

Stability and Storage

Store in tightly sealed container, protected from light, and at room temperature. Stability of compounded formulations has not been evaluated.

Small Animal Dosage

Dogs and Cats

- 44 mg/kg q8h PO or IV on the first day, and then 22-44 mg/kg q8h PO. Up to 130 mg/kg for severe conditions.

Large Animal Dosage

- 11-22 mg/kg q8h IV or more frequently if needed.

Regulatory Information

Withdrawal times are not established for animals that produce food. For extralabel use withdrawal interval estimates, contact FARAD at 1-888-USFARAD (1-888-873-2723) or send e-mail to FARAD@ncsu.edu.

RCI Classification: 4

Methohexital Sodium

meth-oe-heks′ih-tahl soe′dee-um

Trade and Other Names: Brevital

Functional Classification: Anesthetic, Barbiturate

Pharmacology and Mechanism of Action
Barbiturate anesthetic. Anesthesia is produced by CNS depression without analgesia. Anesthesia is terminated by redistribution in the body. Methohexital is about two to three times more potent than pentothal, but it has a shorter duration.

Indications and Clinical Uses
Methohexital is used as an intravenous anesthetic in animals, given either as a bolus or constant rate infusion (CRI). Frequently other anesthetic adjuncts, such as tranquilizers, are administered prior to methohexital infusion.

Precautionary Information
Adverse Reactions and Side Effects
Adverse effects are related to the anesthetic effects of the drug. Severe adverse effects are caused by respiratory and cardiovascular depression.

Contraindications and Precautions
Overdoses can be caused by rapid or repeated injections. Avoid extravasation outside of vein.

Drug Interactions
No drug interactions reported for animals.

Instructions for Use
Therapeutic index is low. Use only in patients in which it is possible to monitor cardiovascular and respiratory functions. Methohexital is often administered with other anesthetic adjuncts.

M

Patient Monitoring and Laboratory Tests
Monitor heart rate and breathing in patients anesthetized with barbiturates.

Formulations
Methohexital is available in 0.5, 2.5, and 5 g vials for injection.

Stability and Storage
Store in tightly sealed container, protected from light, and at room temperature. Stability of compounded formulations has not been evaluated.

Small Animal Dosage
Dogs and Cats
- 3-6 mg/kg IV (give slowly to effect). Doses as high as 15 mg/kg IV have been administered to dogs over 30 seconds.
- CRI: 0.25 mg/kg/min for 30 minutes, then 0.125 mg/kg/min.

Large Animal Dosage
No large animal doses have been reported.

Regulatory Information
Withdrawal times are not established for animals that produce food. For extralabel use withdrawal interval estimates, contact FARAD at 1-888-USFARAD (1-888-873-2723) or send e-mail to FARAD@ncsu.edu.

Schedule III controlled drug

RCI Classification: 2

Methotrexate

meth-oh-treks′ate

Trade and Other Names: MTX, Mexate, Folex, Rheumatrex, and generic brands

Functional Classification: Anticancer agent

Pharmacology and Mechanism of Action

Anticancer agent. Action is via antimetabolite action. Methotrexate binds and inhibits the dihydrofolate reductase enzyme (DHFR). The DHFR enzyme is a reducing enzyme necessary for purine synthesis. The reduced form of folic acid (tetrahydrofolate-FH4) acts as an important coenzyme for biochemical reactions, particularly DNA, RNA, and protein synthesis. (The structure of methotrexate is similar to folic acid.)

Indications and Clinical Uses

Methotrexate is used for various carcinomas, leukemia, and lymphomas. In people, methotrexate is also commonly used for autoimmune diseases such as rheumatoid arthritis.

Precautionary Information

Adverse Reactions and Side Effects

Its major adverse effects in animals are anorexia, nausea, myelosuppression, and vomiting. Anticancer drugs cause predictable (and sometimes unavoidable) side effects that include bone marrow suppression, leukopenia, and immunosuppression. Hepatotoxicity has been reported in people from methotrexate therapy. In people, higher doses are often used compared to veterinary doses. In people, risk of systemic toxicity is high and rescue therapy with leukovorin (tetrahydrofolic acid) must be used. Leukovorin rescue therapy is used because it is an antagonist of the action of methotrexate on the DHFR enzyme.

Contraindications and Precautions

Do not administer to pregnant animals. It has been used to induce abortion.

Drug Interactions

Concurrent use with nonsteroidal antiinflammatory drugs (NSAIDs) may cause severe methotrexate toxicity. Do not administer with pyrimethamine, trimethoprim, sulfonamides, or other drugs that may affect folic acid synthesis.

Instructions for Use

Use in animals has been based on experimental studies. There is only limited clinical information available. Consult specific anticancer protocols for precise dosage and regimen.

Patient Monitoring and Laboratory Tests

Monitor CBC for evidence of bone marrow toxicity.

Formulations

Methotrexate is available in 2.5 mg tablets and 2.5 and 25 mg/mL injection.

Stability and Storage

Store in tightly sealed container, protected from light, and at room temperature. Stability of compounded formulations has not been evaluated.

Small Animal Dosage

Dogs and Cats

- 2.5-5 mg/m^2 q48h PO (dose depends on specific cancer protocol).
- 0.3-0.5 mg/kg once/week IV.

Cats

- 0.8 mg/kg IV every 2-3 weeks.

Large Animal Dosage

No large animal doses have been reported.

Regulatory Information

Withdrawal times are not established for animals that produce food. This drug should not be used in animals intended for food, because it is an anticancer agent.
RCI Classification: 4

Methoxamine

meh-thahk'seh-meen

Trade and Other Names: Vasoxyl

Functional Classification: Vasopressor

Pharmacology and Mechanism of Action

Alpha$_1$ adrenergic agonist. Methoxamine stimulates alpha$_1$ receptors on vascular smooth muscle to produce vasoconstriction in vascular beds.

Indications and Clinical Uses

Methoxamine is used primarily in critical care patients or during anesthesia to increase peripheral resistance and blood pressure.

Precautionary Information

Adverse Reactions and Side Effects

Adverse effects related to excessive stimulation of alpha$_1$ receptor (prolonged peripheral vasoconstriction). Reflex bradycardia may occur.

Contraindications and Precautions

Use cautiously in animals with heart disease.

Drug Interactions

Do not use with monoamine oxidase inhibitors (MAOIs), such as selegiline.

Instructions for Use

Methoxamine has a rapid onset and short duration of action.

Patient Monitoring and Laboratory Tests

Monitor heart rate and blood pressure in treated patients.

Formulations

Methoxamine is available in 20 mg/mL injection.

Stability and Storage

Store in tightly sealed container, protected from light, and at room temperature. Stability of compounded formulations has not been evaluated.

Small Animal Dosage

Dogs and Cats

- 200-250 mcg/kg (0.2-0.25 mg/kg) IM or 40-80 mcg/kg IV, repeat dose as needed.

Large Animal Dosage

Cattle and Horses

- 100-200 mcg/kg (0.1-0.2 mg/kg) IM once or as needed.

Regulatory Information

No regulatory information is available. Because of low risk of residues, no withdrawal times are suggested.

Methoxyflurane

meh-thahk′seh-floo′rane

Trade and Other Names: Metofane

Functional Classification: Anesthetic, inhalant

Pharmacology and Mechanism of Action

Inhalant anesthetic. Like other inhalent anesthetics, the mechanism of action is uncertain. They produce generalized, reversible, depression of the CNS. The inhalant anesthetics vary in their solubility in blood, their potency, and the rate of induction and recovery. Those with low blood/gas partition coefficients are associated with the most rapid rates of induction and recovery.

Indications and Clinical Uses

Methoxyflurane is not used often as an inhalant anesthetic. In the past 10 years use has declined. Other agents are used more often.

Precautionary Information

Adverse Reactions and Side Effects

Adverse effects related to anesthetic effects (e.g., cardiovascular and respiratory depression). Methoxyflurane has been reported to cause hepatic injury in animals.

Contraindications and Precautions

Use cautiously in animals with cardiac disease.

Drug Interactions

Labeling recommendations in some countries state that flunixin should not be administered to animals receiving methoxyflurane anesthesia.

Instructions for Use

Use of inhalant anesthetics requires careful monitoring. Dose is determined by depth of anesthesia.

Patient Monitoring and Laboratory Tests

Monitor heart rate and breathing in patients undergoing anesthesia with inhalant anesthetics. Monitor hepatic enzymes.

Formulations

Methoxyflurane is available in 4 oz bottle for inhalation.

Stability and Storage

Store in tightly sealed container, protected from light, and at room temperature.

Small Animal Dosage

- Induction: 3%, maintenance: 0.5%-1.5%.

Large Animal Dosage

- Minimum alveolar concentrations (MAC) value is 0.2%-0.3%.

Regulatory Information

No withdrawal times are established for animals intended for food. Clearance is rapid and short withdrawal times are suggested. For extralabel use withdrawal interval estimates, contact FARAD at 1-888-USFARAD (1-888-873-2723) or send e-mail to FARAD@ncsu.edu.

Methylene Blue 0.1%

meth'ih-leen bloo

Trade and Other Names: New Methylene Blue and generic brands

Functional Classification: Antidote

Pharmacology and Mechanism of Action

Methylene blue acts as reducing agent to reduce methemoglobin to hemoglobin. It is an antidote for intoxication.

Indications and Clinical Uses

Methylene blue is used to treat for methemoglobinemia caused by chlorate and nitrate toxicosis. It also has been used to treat cyanide toxicosis.

Precautionary Information

Adverse Reactions and Side Effects

Methylene blue can cause Heinz body anemia in cats, but it is safe when used at therapeutic doses listed here.

Contraindications and Precautions

Use cautiously in cats.

Drug Interactions

No drug interactions reported for animals.

Instructions for Use

Comparison of effects for intoxication has only been performed in experimental effects. One study demonstrated that acetylcysteine produced the best response, but methylene blue also was helpful in some cats (*Am J Vet Res,* 56: 1529, 1995).

Patient Monitoring and Laboratory Tests

Monitor CBC in patients treated with methylene blue.

Formulations

Methylene blue is available in 1% solution (10 mg/mL).

M

Stability and Storage

Store in tightly sealed container, protected from light, and at room temperature.

Small Animal Dosage

Dogs and Cats

- 1.5 mg/kg IV once slowly.

Large Animal Dosage

Horses and Cattle

- 1.5 mg/kg IV slowly.

Regulatory Information

Cattle withdrawal time (meat): 14 days.
Cattle withdrawal time (milk): 4 days.

Methylprednisolone

meth-il-pred-niss'oh-lone

Trade and Other Names: Methylprednisolone: Medrol; Methylprednisolone acetate: Depo-Medrol; and Methylprednisolone sodium succinate: Solu-Medrol

Functional Classification: Corticosteroid

Pharmacology and Mechanism of Action

Methylprednisolone is a glucocorticoid antiinflammatory drug. Antiinflammatory effects are complex, but they operate primarily via inhibition of inflammatory cells and suppression of expression of inflammatory mediators. Compared to prednisolone, methylprednisolone is 1.25 times more potent.

Indications and Clinical Uses

Methylprednisolone acetate is a long-acting depot formulation of methylprednisolone. It is slowly absorbed from intramuscular injection site producing glucocorticoid effects for 3-4 weeks in some animals. Methylprednisolone acetate is used for intralesional therapy, intraarticular therapy, and inflammatory conditions. Methylprednisolone sodium succinate is a water-soluble formulation intended for acute therapy when high intravenous doses are needed for rapid effect. It is used for treatment of shock and CNS trauma. Methylprednisolone oral tablets are used for treatment of conditions in animals that require short-term to long-term therapy with an intermediate-acting corticosteroid. Conditions treated include dermatitis, immune-mediated diseases, intestinal diseases, and neurological and musculoskeletal diseases. In large animals, methylprednisolone acetate is used for treatment of inflammatory conditions of the musculoskeletal system (intraarticular).

Precautionary Information

Adverse Reactions and Side Effects

Side effects from corticosteroids are many, and include polyphagia, polydipsia/polyuria, and hypothalamic-pituitary-adrenal (HPA) axis suppression. However, manufacturer suggests that methylprednisolone causes less polyuria/polydipsia (PU/PD) than prednisolone. Adverse effects include GI ulceration, hepatopathy, diabetes, hyperlipidemia, decreased thyroid hormone, decreased protein synthesis, delayed wound healing, and immunosuppression. Dogs that receive high doses of methylprednisolone succinate (e.g., 30 mg/kg) have a high risk of GI bleeding. Secondary infections can occur as a result of immunosuppression and include demodicosis, toxoplasmosis, fungal infections, and UTIs. In cats, methylprednisolone acetate injections have caused injection site alopecia. In horses, additional adverse effects include risk of laminitis. In cats, methylprednisolone acetate administration causes volume expansion as a result of fluid shift secondary to hyperglycemia. This effect appears to increase risk of cats developing congestive heart failure (CHF) following methylprednisolone acetate administration.

Contraindications and Precautions

Use cautiously in patients prone to ulcers and infection or in animals in which wound healing is necessary. Use cautiously in diabetic animals, animals with renal failure, or pregnant animals. Use cautiously in cats because of volume expansion, especially cats at risk of CHF.

Drug Interactions

Like other corticosteroids, if methylprednisolone is administered with nonsteroidal antiinflammatory drugs (NSAIDs), there is increased risk of GI ulcers.

Instructions for Use

Use of methylprednisolone is similar to other corticosteroids. Dose adjustment should be made to account for difference in potency. Use of methylprednisolone acetate should be evaluated carefully because one injection will cause glucocorticoid effects that persist for several days to weeks. Results of clinical studies in animals have not been reported for use of methylprednisolone sodium succinate.

Patient Monitoring and Laboratory Tests

Monitor liver enzymes, blood glucose, and renal function during therapy. Monitor patients for signs of secondary infections. Perform adrenocorticotropic hormone stimulation test to monitor adrenal function. Monitor cats for diabetes and heart disease when treated with methylprednisolone acetate.

Formulations

Methylprednisolone is available in 1, 2, 4, 8, 18, and 32 mg tablets.

Methylprednisolone acetate is available in 20 and 40 mg/mL suspension for injection.

Methylprednisolone sodium succinate is available in 1 and 2 g and 125 and 500 mg vials for injection.

Stability and Storage

Store in tightly sealed container, protected from light, and at room temperature. Methylprednisolone is insoluble in water and slightly soluble in ethanol. Methylprednisolone acetate is slightly soluble in water. Methylprednisolone sodium succinate is highly soluble in water. When methylprednisolone sodium succinate is reconstituted it should be used within 48 hours at room temperature. Decomposition occurs with longer storage. It may be frozen at –20° C, for 4 weeks with no loss of potency.

Small Animal Dosage

Dogs

- Methylprednisolone: 0.22-0.44 mg/kg q12-24h PO.
- Methylprednisolone acetate: 1 mg/kg (or 20-40 mg/dog) IM q1-3wk.
- Methylprednisolone sodium succinate (for emergency use): 30 mg/kg IV and repeat at 15 mg/kg in 2-6 hours IV. Replacement or antiinflammatory therapy: use 0.25-0.5 mg/kg/day.

Cats

- Methylprednisolone: 0.22-0.44 mg/kg q12-24h PO.
- Methylprednisolone acetate: 10-20 mg/cat IM q1-3wk.
- Methylprednisolone sodium succinate (for emergency use): 30 mg/kg IV and repeat at 15 mg/kg in 2-6 hours IV. Replacement or antiinflammatory therapy: use 0.25-0.5 mg/kg/day.

Large Animal Dosage

Horses

- 200 mg as a single total dose injected IM.
- Intraarticular dose: 40 to 240 mg total dose, with the average dose of 120 mg is injected in the joint space using sterile technique.

Regulatory Information

Withdrawal times are not established. For extralabel use withdrawal interval estimates, contact FARAD at 1-888-USFARAD (1-888-873-2723) or send e-mail to FARAD@ncsu.edu.

RCI Classification: 4

Methyltestosterone

meth-ill-tess-toss'teh-rone

Trade and Other Names: Android and generic brands

Functional Classification: Hormone, Anabolic agent

Pharmacology and Mechanism of Action

Anabolic androgenic agent. Injections of methyltestosterone will mimic effects of testosterone.

Indications and Clinical Uses

Methyltestosterone is used for anabolic actions or testosterone hormone replacement therapy (androgenic deficiency). Testosterone has been used to stimulate erythropoiesis. Other similar agents used include testosterone cypionate and testosterone propionate.

Precautionary Information

Adverse Reactions and Side Effects

Adverse effects caused by excessive androgenic action of testosterone. Prostatic hyperplasia is possible in male dogs. Masculinization can occur in female dogs. Hepatopathy is more common with oral methylated testosterone formulations.

Contraindications and Precautions

Do not administer to pregnant animals.

Drug Interactions

No drug interactions reported for animals.

Instructions for Use

Use of testosterone androgens has not been evaluated in clinical studies in veterinary medicine. The clinical use is based primarily on experimental evidence or experiences in people.

Patient Monitoring and Laboratory Tests

Monitor hepatic enzymes and clinical signs for evidence of cholestasis and hepatotoxicity during treatment.

Formulations

Methyltestosterone is available in 10 and 25 mg tablets.

Stability and Storage

Store in tightly sealed container, protected from light, and at room temperature. Stability of compounded formulations has not been evaluated.

M

Small Animal Dosage

Dogs

- 5-25 mg/dog q24-48h PO.

Cats

- 2.5-5 mg/cat q24-48h PO.

Large Animal Dosage

No large animal doses have been reported.

Regulatory Information

Do not use in animals intended for food.
Methyltestosterone is a schedule III controlled drug.
RCI Classification: 4

Metoclopramide Hydrochloride

met-oh-kloe-prah′mide hye-droe-klor′ide

Trade and Other Names: Reglan and Maxolon

Functional Classification: Antiemetic

Pharmacology and Mechanism of Action

Prokinetic drug. Antiemetic. Metoclopramide stimulates motility of upper GI tract and is a centrally acting antiemetic. The mechanism of action of metoclopramide is not completely understood. Among the proposed mechanisms is stimulation of 5-HT_4 (serotonin) receptors or an increase in the release of acetylcholine in the

GI tract, possibly through a prejunctional mechanism. It also has anti-dopamine (D_2) action. It inhibits gastric relaxation induced by dopamine, thus enhancing the cholinergic responses of gastric smooth muscle to increase motility. It also increases the tone of the esophageal sphincter. Metoclopramide acts centrally to inhibit dopamine in the chemoreceptor trigger zone (CRTZ), which is responsible for antiemetic effects. The half-life in dogs is only 36 minutes; effects on esophageal sphincter persisted for only 30-60 minutes.

Indications and Clinical Uses

Metoclopramide is used primarily for gastroparesis and treatment of vomiting. It is not effective for dogs with gastric dilation. Because this drug transiently increases prolactin secretion, there has been interest in using this drug for treating agalactia in animals, but efficacy has not been determined. In people, metoclopramide has been also used to treat hiccups and lactation deficiency.

Precautionary Information

Adverse Reactions and Side Effects

Adverse effects are primarily related to blockade of central dopaminergic receptors. Adverse effects similar to what is reported for phenothiazines (e.g., acepromazine) have been reported in addition to behavioral changes. In horses, undesirable side effects have been common and limit the therapeutic use. Adverse effects in horses include behavioral changes, excitement, and abdominal discomfort. Excitement from intravenous infusions can be severe. In calves at doses >0.1 mg/kg, it produced neurologic effects.

Contraindications and Precautions

Do not use in epileptic patients, or with diseases caused by GI obstruction. Use cautiously in horses as dangerous behavior changes may occur.

Drug Interactions

Efficacy is diminished when administered with parasympatholytic (atropine-like) drugs.

Instructions for Use

Results of clinical studies in animals have not been reported. Use in animals (and doses) is based on experience in people or anecdotal experience in animals. Most use is for general antiemetic purposes, but doses as high as 2 mg/kg have been used to prevent vomiting during cancer chemotherapy. In horses, there is some increase in intestinal motility at recommended doses, but little effect on large bowel. In calves metoclopramide had little effect on rumen motility.

Patient Monitoring and Laboratory Tests

Monitor GI motility during treatment.

Formulations Available

Metoclopramide is available in 5 and 10 mg tablets, 1 mg/mL oral solution, and 5 mg/mL injection.

Stability and Storage

Store in tightly sealed container, protected from light, and at room temperature. Stability of compounded formulations has not been evaluated. It is incompatible with other drugs when mixed in solution. Stability is less than 24 hr if not protected from light.

Small Animal Dosage

Dogs and Cats

- 0.2-0.5 mg/kg q6-8h IV, IM, or PO. Higher doses have been used for antiemetic treatment with cancer chemotherapy, up to 2 mg/kg.
- Constant Rate Infusion (CRI): Administer a loading dose of 0.4 mg/kg IV, followed by a CRI of 0.3 mg/kg/hr IV. In refractory patients, this dose may be increased to a loading dose of 1.0 mg/kg, followed by a CRI or 1.0 mg/kg/hr IV.

Large Animal Dosage

Horses

- Infusion of metoclopramide (0.125-0.25 mg/kg/hr) added to IV fluids to reduce postoperative ileus in horses.

Calves and Cattle

Not recommended.

Regulatory Information

Withdrawal times are not established for animals that produce food. For extralabel use withdrawal interval estimates, contact FARAD at 1-888-USFARAD (1-888-873-2723) or send e-mail to FARAD@ncsu.edu.

RCI Classification: 4

Metoprolol Tartrate

meh-toe′proe-lole tar′trate

Trade and Other Names: Lopressor

Functional Classification: Beta-blocker

M

Pharmacology and Mechanism of Action

$Beta_1$ adrenergic blocker. Metoprolol has similar properties to propranolol, except that metoprolol is specific for $beta_1$ receptor. Metoprolol is a lipophilic beta-blocker and relies on the liver for clearance. Lipophilic beta-blockers, such as metoprolol, undergo high first-pass clearance, which reduces oral bioavailability and causes high interpatient variability in plasma concentrations and effects.

Indications and Clinical Uses

Metoprolol is used to control tachyarrhythmias and to control the response from adrenergic stimulation. Beta-blockers effectively slow heart rate.

Precautionary Information

Adverse Reactions and Side Effects

Adverse effects are primarily caused by excessive cardiovascular depression (decreased inotropic effects). Metoprolol may cause AV block.

Contraindications and Precautions

Use cautiously in animals prone to bronchoconstriction.

Drug Interactions

Lipophilic beta-blockers, such as metoprolol, are subject to hepatic metabolism and may be prone to drug interactions that affect hepatic metabolizing enzymes. If administered with digoxin, it may potentiate an AV-nodal conduction block.

Instructions for Use

Results of clinical studies in animals have not been reported. Use in animals (and doses) is based on experience in people or anecdotal experience in animals.

Patient Monitoring and Laboratory Tests

Monitor heart rate and rhythm during treatment.

Formulations

Metoprolol is available in 50 and 100 mg tablets and 1 mg/mL injection.

Stability and Storage

Store in tightly sealed container, protected from light, and at room temperature. Metoprolol tartrate is soluble in water and ethanol. Protect tablets from moisture and freezing. Suspensions have been prepared in syrups and other flavorings with no loss of stability after 60 days of storage.

Small Animal Dosage

Dogs

- 5-50 mg/dog (0.5-1.0 mg/kg) q8h PO.

Cats

- 2-15 mg/cat q8h PO.

Large Animal Dosage

No large animal doses have been reported.

Regulatory Information

Withdrawal times are not established for animals that produce food. For extralabel use withdrawal interval estimates, contact FARAD at 1-888-USFARAD (1-888-873-2723) or send e-mail to FARAD@ncsu.edu.
RCI Classification: 3

Metronidazole, Metronidazole Benzoate

meh-troe-nye'dah-zole

Trade and Other Names: Flagyl and generic brands

Functional Classification: Antibacterial, Antiparasitic

Pharmacology and Mechanism of Action

Antibacterial and antiprotozoal drug. It is a second-generation nitroimidazole in which the activity involves generation of free nitrordicals via metabolism of within protozoa and bacteria. Metronidazole disrupts DNA in organism via reaction with intracellular metabolite. Its action is specific for anaerobic bacteria and protozoa. Resistance is rare. It is active against some protozoa, including *Trichomonas, Giardia,* and intestinal protozoal parasites. It also has in vitro activity against anaerobic bacteria and *Helicobacter*. Metronidazole oral absorption is nearly complete in animals (75%-85% in horses and 60%-100% in dogs). Rectal absorption in horses is 30%. The half-life is 3-4 hours in horses and 4-5 hours in dogs. Metronidazole benzoate is formulated for cats to improve palatability. In this form, the oral absorption (12.4 mg/kg of the base) is 64%, with a half-life of 5 hr.

Indications and Clinical Uses

Metronidazole is indicated to treat diarrhea and other intestinal problems caused by intestinal protozoa such as *Giardia, Trichomonas,* and *Entamoeba*. Metronidazole may be used in small animals and horses for treatment of a variety of anaerobic infections. Metronidazole may have some immune-modulating activity in the intestine of animals and has been used to treat inflammatory bowel disease in animals. Metronidazole benzoate has been used in cats, because it is more palatable.

Precautionary Information

Adverse Reactions and Side Effects

Most severe adverse effect is caused by toxicity to CNS. High doses have caused lethargy, CNS depression, ataxia, tremors, seizures, vomiting, and weakness. Most CNS toxicity caused from metronidazole in animals occurs at high doses (>60 mg/kg/day). The CNS signs are related to inhibition of action of GABA and are responsive to benzodiazepines (diazepam 0.4 mg/kg q8h for 3 days). Like other nitroimidazoles, it has the potential to produce mutagenic changes in cells, but this has not been demonstrated in vivo. Like other nitroimidazoles, it has a bitter taste, and can cause vomiting and anorexia. Metronidazole benzoate has been used in some cats safely at 25 mg/kg q12h for 7 days. However, there is a caution about the effect of benzoate salts in cats, because it is a benzoic acid derivative. Benzoic acid can be toxic to cats and causes ataxia, blindness, respiratory problems, and other CNS disorders. However, it is estimated that 500 mg/kg/day of metronidazole benzoate would be needed to provide a toxic dose of benzoic acid to cats. Nevertheless, any cat showing CNS or other signs of toxicity should have the metronidazole benzoate discontinued immediately.

Contraindications and Precautions

Fetal abnormalities have not been demonstrated in animals with recommended doses, but use cautiously during pregnancy.

Drug Interactions

Like other nitroimidazoles, it can potentiate the effects of warfarin and cyclosporine via inhibition of drug metabolism.

Instructions for Use

Metronidazole is one of the most commonly used drugs for anaerobic infections. Although it is effective for giardiasis, other drugs used for *Giardia* include albendazole, fenbendazole, and quinacrine. CNS toxicity is dose related. Maximum dose that should be administered is 50-65 mg/kg per day in any species. Metronidazole is unpalatable and can produce a metallic taste. In cats, when the tablet is crushed or broken, the unpalatability is particularly a problem. Metronidazole benzoate has a bland taste and is better tolerated. It is a formulation not commercially available in the U.S. However, it may be available from compounding pharmacies. Metronidazole benzoate of 25 mg/mL contains 40 mg of benzoate. Because of the weight of metronidazole benzoate versus metronidazole hydrochloride, a factor of 1.6 times is used to convert a metronidazole hydrochloride dose to a metronidazole benzoate dose. Metronidazole benzoate is 62% metronidazole, therefore 20 mg/kg of metronidazole benzoate delivers 12.4 mg/kg metronidazole.

Metronidazole should not be injected directly; it is too acidic. See Stability and Storage section for mixing instructions.

Patient Monitoring and Laboratory Tests

Monitor for neurological adverse effects.

Formulations

Metronidazole is available in 250 and 500 mg tablets, 50 mg/mL suspension, and 5 mg/mL injection.

Metronidazole benzoate is a formulation not available in the U.S. but has been compounded for veterinary use. Metronidazole benzoate is 62% metronidazole.

Stability and Storage

It is slightly soluble in water. The benzoate form is practically insoluble; the hydrochloride form is soluble in water. Metronidazole has been crushed and mixed with some flavorings to mask the taste. When mixed with some syrups or water decomposition occurs within 28 days. Metronidazole benzoate prepared in vehicles such as Ora-Plus or Ora-Sweet was stable for 90 days. Metronidazole base (from tablets) also was mixed with these vehicles and found to be stable for 90 days. Reconstituted injectable forms are stable for 96 hours, but after dilution should be discarded after 24 hours.

Metronidazole hydrochloride when reconstituted is too acidic (pH 0.5-2) for direct injection. It should be further diluted with 100 mL (0.9% saline, 5% dextrose, or Ringer's solution) and neutralized with 5 mEq sodium bicarbonate per 500 mg for a pH of 6-7. Reconstituted injectable forms are stable for 96 hours, but after dilution should be discarded after 24 hours.

Small Animal Dosage

Dogs

- Anaerobes: 15 mg/kg q12h or 12 mg/kg q8h PO.
- *Giardia:* 12-15 mg/kg q12h for 8 days PO.

Cats

- Anaerobes: 10-25 mg/kg q24h PO.
- *Giardia:* 17 mg/kg (1/3 tablet per cat) q24h for 8 days.
- Metronidazole benzoate (for treatment of *Giardia*): 25 mg/kg PO 12h for 7 days. Metronidazole benzoate is 62% metronidazole, therefore 20 mg/kg of metronidazole benzoate delivers 12.4 mg/kg metronidazole.

Large Animal Dosage

Horses

- Treatment of anaerobic and protozoal infections: 10 mg/kg q12h PO. Note: some clinicians have used higher doses (up to 15-20 mg/kg q6h) but, at these doses, side effects are more likely.

Cattle

- Treatment of trichomoniasis (bulls): 75 mg/kg q12h IV for 3 doses.

Regulatory Information

Do not administer to animals that produce food. Administration of nitroimidazoles to animals intended for food is prohibited. Treated cattle must *not* be slaughtered for food.

Mexiletine

meks-il'eh-teen

Trade and Other Names: Mexitil

Functional Classification: Antiarrhythmic

Pharmacology and Mechanism of Action

Antiarrhythmic drug. Mexiletine is a Class IB antiarrhythmic agent. Mechanism of action is to block fast sodium channel and depress Phase 0 of depolarization.

Indications and Clinical Uses

Mexiletine has been used to treat ventricular arrhythmias. However, its use is not common in veterinary medicine. The first choice for acute treatment of ventricular arrhythmias is usually lidocaine.

Precautionary Information

Adverse Reactions and Side Effects

High doses may cause excitement and tremors. Mexiletine can be arrhythmogenic in some animals. In people, related drugs (flecainide and encainide) can be proarrhythmogenic and associated with excessive mortality.

Contraindications and Precautions

Use cautiously in animals with liver disease.

Drug Interactions

No drug interactions reported.

Instructions for Use

Results of clinical studies in animals have not been reported. Use in animals (and doses) is based on experience in people or anecdotal experience in animals.

Patient Monitoring and Laboratory Tests

Monitor ECG during use.

Formulations

Mexiletine is available in 150, 200, and 250 mg capsules.

Stability and Storage

Store in tightly sealed container, protected from light, and at room temperature. It is freely soluble in water and ethanol.

Small Animal Dosage

Dogs

- 5-8 mg/kg q8-12h PO (use cautiously).

Cats

Contraindicated.

Large Animal Dosage

No large animal doses have been reported.

Regulatory Information

Withdrawal times are not established for animals that produce food. For extralabel use withdrawal interval estimates, contact FARAD at 1-888-USFARAD (1-888-873-2723) or send e-mail to FARAD@ncsu.edu.
RCI Classification: 4

Mibolerone

mih-bole′er-one

Trade and Other Names: Cheque-drops

Functional Classification: Hormone

Pharmacology and Mechanism of Action
Androgenic steroid. Mibolerone will mimic androgens in the body.

Indications and Clinical Uses
Mibolerone is used to suppress estrus in animals.

Precautionary Information

Adverse Reactions and Side Effects
Many bitches show clitoral enlargement or discharge from treatment.

Contraindications and Precautions
Do not use in Bedlington terriers. Do not administer to pregnant animals. Do not use with perianal adenoma or carcinoma. Do not use in cats.

Drug Interactions
No drug interactions reported.

Instructions for Use
Treatment ordinarily is initiated 30 days prior to onset of estrus. It is not recommended to be used for more than 2 years.

Patient Monitoring and Laboratory Tests
Monitor hepatic enzymes periodically if used chronically.

Formulations
Mibolerone is available in 55 mcg/mL oral solution.

Stability and Storage
Store in tightly sealed container, protected from light, and at room temperature. Stability of compounded formulations has not been evaluated.

Small Animal Dosage

Dogs
- 2.6-5 mcg/kg/day PO.
- Bitches weighing 0.45-11.3 kg: 30 mcg/day PO.
- Bitches weighing 11.8-22.7 kg: 60 mcg/day PO.
- Bitches weighing 23-45.3 kg: 120 mcg/day PO.
- Bitches weighing more than 45.8 kg: 180 mcg/day PO.

Cats
Safe dose not established.

Large Animal Dosage
No large animal doses have been reported.

Regulatory Information
Do not administer to animals that produce food.

Midazolam Hydrochloride
mid'az'oe-lam hye-droe-klor'ide

Trade and Other Names: Versed

Functional Classification: Anticonvulsant

Pharmacology and Mechanism of Action

Benzodiazepine. Central acting CNS depressant. Mechanism of action appears to be via potentiation of GABA-receptor mediated effects in CNS, because it binds to the GABA binding site.

Indications and Clinical Uses

Midazolam is used as anesthetic adjunct. It is used for similar indications as diazepam, but because it is water soluble, midazolam can be administered in aqueous vehicle and administered IM compared to other drugs of this class (drugs such as diazepam are not water soluble).

It has been used as an anticonvulsant, muscle relaxant, sedative, and as an adjunct with anesthetic agents. In foals, it has been used to treat neonatal seizures (see following dose protocol).

Precautionary Information

Adverse Reactions and Side Effects

Midazolam given IV can cause serious cardiorespiratory depression. Some animals may experience paradoxical excitement. Chronic administration may lead to dependence and a withdrawal syndrome if discontinued.

Contraindications and Precautions

Use cautiously IV, especially with opiates.

Drug Interactions

No drug interactions reported.

Instructions for Use

Clinical trials have not been reported, although use of midazolam is reported in some anesthetic protocols for animals. Unlike other benzodiazepines, midazolam can be administered IM.

Patient Monitoring and Laboratory Tests

Samples of plasma or serum may be analyzed for concentrations of benzodiazepines. Plasma concentrations in the range of 100-250 ng/mL have been cited as the therapeutic range for people. Other references have cited this range as 150-300 ng/mL. However, there are no readily available tests for monitoring in many veterinary laboratories. Laboratories that analyze human samples may have nonspecific tests for benzodiazepines. With these assays, there may be cross-reactivity among benzodiazepine metabolites.

Formulations

Midazolam is available in 5 mg/mL injection.

Stability and Storage

Store in tightly sealed container, protected from light, and at room temperature. Solubility of midazolam in water is pH-dependent. At lower pH values (pH <4), it becomes more soluble. Mixed with syrups for flavoring, it was stable for 56 days.

Small Animal Dosage

Dogs

- 0.1-0.25 mg/kg IV or IM.
- 0.1-0.3 mg/kg/hr IV infusion.

Cats

- Sedation: 0.05 mg/kg IV.
- Induction of anesthesia: 0.3-0.6 mg/kg IV, combined with 3 mg/kg ketamine.

Large Animal Dosage

Pigs

- Up to 0.5 mg/kg IM, usually in combination with ketamine.

Horses

- Neonatal seizures in foals: 2-5 mg/kg IV, over 15-20 min or IM, followed by 1-3 mg/hr IV (2-6 mL/hr) to control seizures. Infusion dose is prepared by adding 10 mL (5 mg/mL) to 100 mL saline to make a solution of 0.5 mg/mL.

Regulatory Information

Withdrawal times are not established for animals that produce food. For extralabel use withdrawal interval estimates, contact FARAD at 1-888-USFARAD (1-888-873-2723) or send e-mail to FARAD@ncsu.edu.
Schedule IV controlled drug
RCI Classification: 2

Milbemycin Oxime

mil-beh-mye'sin ahk'seem

Trade and Other Names: Interceptor, Interceptor Flavor Tabs, and SafeHeart

Milbemycin also is an ingredient in Sentinel.

Functional Classification: Antiparasitic

Pharmacology and Mechanism of Action

Antiparasitic drug. Avermectins (ivermectin-like drugs) and milbemycins (milbemycin and moxidectin) are macrocyclic lactones and share similarities, including mechanism of action. These drugs are neurotoxic to parasites by potentiating glutamate-gated chloride ion channels in parasites. Paralysis and death of the parasite is caused by increased permeability to chloride ions and hyperpolarization of nerve cells. These drugs also potentiate other chloride channels, including ones gated by GABA. Mammals ordinarily are not affected, because they lack glutamate-gated chloride channels, and there is a lower affinity for other mammalian chloride channels. Because these drugs ordinarily do not penetrate the blood-brain barrier, GABA-gated channels in the CNS of mammals are not affected. Milbemycin is active against intestinal parasites, mites, bots, heartworm microfilaria, and developing larvae. Milbemycin has no effect on trematode or cestode parasites.

Indications and Clinical Uses

Milbemycin is used as heartworm preventative, miticide, and microfilaricide. It is also used to control infections of hookworm, roundworms, and whipworms. It also has been used in combination with flea control drugs (See Sentinel, which contains milbemycin oxime and lufenuron.) At high doses it has been used to treat *Demodex* infections in dogs.

Precautionary Information

Adverse Reactions and Side Effects

At doses of 5 mg/kg, it was well tolerated in most dogs (10 times the heartworm dose). At 10 mg/kg (20 times the heartworm dose), it caused depression, ataxia, and salivation in some dogs. Toxicity may occur at high doses and in breeds in which milbemycin crosses the blood-brain barrier. Sensitive breeds include Collies, Australian shepherds, Old English sheepdogs, Longhaired Whippets, and Shetland sheepdogs. Toxicity is neurotoxic and signs include depression, ataxia, difficulty with vision, coma, and death. Sensitivity to milbemycin occurs in certain breeds because of a mutation in the multidrug resistance gene (MDR1) that codes for the membrane pump p-glycoprotein. This mutation affects the efflux pump in blood-brain barrier. Therefore, milbemycin can accumulate in the brain of susceptible animals. High doses in normal animals may also produce similar toxicosis. However, at doses used for heartworm prevention, this effect is unlikely. At high doses used for treating *Demodex* infections, diarrhea may occur in some dogs.

Contraindications and Precautions

Do not use in dogs that have shown sensitivity to ivermectin or other drugs in this class (see previous breed list). Treatment using three times the daily doses, from mating to 1 week before weaning did not produce any adverse effects in the pregnant bitch, the fetus, or puppies. One-time doses of three times the monthly rate before or shortly after whelping caused no adverse effects on the puppies. Milbemycin is excreted in milk. Puppies given milbemycin at 19 times the regular dose showed adverse effects, but signs were transient for only 24-48 hours.

Drug Interactions

Do not use with drugs that may increase penetration across the blood-brain barrier. Such drugs include p-glycoprotein inhibitors such as ketoconazole, cyclosporine, quinidine, and some macrolide antibiotics (see Appendix for list of p-glycoprotein inhibitors).

Instructions for Use

Doses vary depending on parasite treated. Treatment of demodicosis requires high dose administered daily (*J Am Vet Med Assoc*, 207:1581, 1995; *Vet Dermatol*, 14:189-195, 2003). Using a protocol of 1 mg/kg/day until clinical cure, followed by 3 mg/kg/wk for a parasitological cure may require 4 months for a clinical cure and 8 months for a parasitological cure.

Patient Monitoring and Laboratory Tests

Monitor for heartworm status in dogs before initiating treatment with milbemycin.

Formulations Available

Milbemycin is available in 2.3, 5.75, 11.5, and 23 mg tablets.

Stability and Storage

Store in tightly sealed container, protected from light, and at room temperature. Stability of compounded formulations has not been evaluated.

Small Animal Dosage

Dogs

- Heartworm prevention and control of endoparasites: 0.5 mg/kg q30days PO.
- Demodicosis: 2 mg/kg q24h PO for 60-120 days or 1 mg/kg daily until a clinical cure is observed, followed by 3 mg/kg once per week until a parasitological cure (negative scraping) is observed.
- Sarcoptic mange: 2 mg/kg q7days for 3-5 weeks PO.
- Cheyletiellosis: 2 mg/kg/wk PO.

Cats

- Heartworm and endoparasite control: 2.0 mg/kg q30days PO.

Large Animal Dosage

No large animal doses have been reported.

Regulatory Information

Withdrawal times are not established for animals that produce food. For extralabel use withdrawal interval estimates, contact FARAD at 1-888-USFARAD (1-888-873-2723) or send e-mail to FARAD@ncsu.edu.

Mineral Oil

Trade and Other Names: Generic brands

Functional Classification: Laxative

Pharmacology and Mechanism of Action

Lubricant laxative. Mineral oil increases water content of stool and acts as a lubricant for intestinal contents.

Indications and Clinical Uses

Mineral oil is administered orally (via stomach tube in horses) to increase passage of feces for treatment of impaction and constipation.

Precautionary Information

Adverse Reactions and Side Effects

Adverse effects have not been reported. Chronic use may decrease absorption of fat-soluble vitamins.

Contraindications and Precautions

Use caution when administering via stomach tube. Accidental administration into the lungs has produced fatal reactions.

Drug Interactions

No drug interactions reported. Chronic use may inhibit absorption of fat-soluble vitamins.

Instructions for Use

Use is empirical. No clinical results reported.

Patient Monitoring and Laboratory Tests

No specific monitoring is necessary.

Formulations

Mineral oil is available in an oral liquid.

Stability and Storage

Store in tightly sealed container, protected from light, and at room temperature.

Small Animal Dosage

Dogs

- 10-50 mL/dog q12h PO.

Cats

- 10-25 mL/cat q12h PO.

Large Animal Dosage

Horses and Cattle

- 500-1000 mL (1 pint to 1 quart) per horse or cow PO, as needed. Up to 2-4 L per adult horse or cow PO.

Sheep and Pigs

- 500-1000 mL PO, as needed.

Regulatory Information

No regulatory information is available. Because of low risk of residues, no withdrawal times are suggested.

Minocycline Hydrochloride

min-oh-sye'kleen hye-droe-klor'ide

Trade and Other Names: Minocin

Functional Classification: Antibacterial

Pharmacology and Mechanism of Action

Tetracycline antibiotic. Like other tetracyclines, the mechanism of action of minocycline is to bind to 30S ribosomal subunit and inhibit protein synthesis. It is usually bacteriostatic. It has a broad spectrum of activity including gram-positive and gram-negative bacteria, some protozoa, *Rickettsiae,* and *Ehrlichiae.* Resistance among *Staphylococcus* species and gram-negative bacilli is common. Minocycline has a similar pharmacokinetic profile as doxycycline.

Indications and Clinical Uses

Minocycline is used when tetracyclines are indicated for treating bacterial infections in animals. It may be effective for *Rickettsiae* and *Ehrlichiae* infections. However, other tetracyclines such as doxycycline are used more frequently in animals.

Precautionary Information

Adverse Reactions and Side Effects

Adverse effects have not been reported for minocycline.

Contraindications and Precautions

Oral absorption is not affected by calcium products as much as with other tetracyclines.

Drug Interactions

No drug interactions are reported for animals.

Instructions for Use

Minocycline has received little attention for clinical veterinary use in North America. Clinical use has not been reported, but properties are similar to doxycycline. Doxycycline is more commonly used as the tetracycline of choice in small animals.

Patient Monitoring and Laboratory Tests

Susceptibility testing: CLSI (NCCLS) break points for sensitive organisms are less than or equal to 2 mcg/mL for streptococci and less than or equal to 4 for other organisms. Tetracycline is used as a marker to test susceptibility for other drugs in this class such as doxycycline, minocycline, and oxytetracycline.

Formulations

Minocycline is available in 50 and 100 mg tablets and 10 mg/mL oral suspension.

Stability and Storage

Store in tightly sealed container, protected from light, and at room temperature. Do not mix with other drugs.

Small Animal Dosage

Dogs and Cats

- 5-12.5 mg/kg q12h PO.

Large Animal Dosage

No large animal doses have been reported.
Oral absorption has not been established for large animals.

Regulatory Information

Withdrawal times are not established for animals that produce food. For extralabel use withdrawal interval estimates, contact FARAD at 1-888-USFARAD (1-888-873-2723) or send e-mail to FARAD@ncsu.edu.

Misoprostol

mee-soe-pross'tole

Trade and Other Names: Cytotec

Functional Classification: Antiulcer agent

Pharmacology and Mechanism of Action

Misoprostol is a synthetic prostaglandin. It is a synthetic analogue of PGE_1 and produces a cytoprotective effect on the GI mucosa. It has been shown in dogs and people to decrease the injury to GI mucosa caused by nonsteroidal antiinflammatory drugs (NSAIDs), such as aspirin. In studies in dogs, misoprostol was **not** effective for decreasing adverse effects caused by corticosteroids. Misoprostol also has antiinflammatory effects and has been used to treat pruritus in dogs.

Indications and Clinical Uses

Misoprostol is used to decrease the risk of GI ulceration when administered concurrently with NSAIDs. Efficacy has been established for this indication in trials with aspirin but not with other NSAIDs in animals. There is no evidence to show that it decreases GI bleeding caused from other drugs (e.g., corticosteroids). Clinical trials also are available to show that misoprostol is effective for treating pruritus in patients with atopic dermatitis, although it is less effective than other drugs.

Precautionary Information

Adverse Reactions and Side Effects

Adverse effects are caused by effects of prostaglandins. Most common side effect is GI discomfort, vomiting, and diarrhea.

Contraindications and Precautions

Do **not** administer to pregnant animals; it may cause abortion.

Drug Interactions

No drug interactions reported for animals.

Instructions for Use

Doses and recommendations are based on clinical trials in which misoprostol was administered to prevent GI mucosal injury caused by aspirin.

Patient Monitoring and Laboratory Tests

No specific monitoring is necessary.

Formulations

Misoprostol is available in 0.1 mg (100 mcg) and 0.2 mg (200 mcg) tablets.

Stability and Storage

Store in tightly sealed container, protected from light, and at room temperature. Stability of compounded formulations has not been evaluated.

Small Animal Dosage

Dogs

- 2-5 mcg/kg q8-12h PO.
- Treating atopic dermatitis 5 mcg/kg q8h PO.

Cats

Dose not established.

Large Animal Dosage

Horses

- 5 mcg/kg q8h PO. However, there may be unacceptable GI adverse effects in large animals.

Regulatory Information

Do not use in animals that produce food.
RCI Classification: 4

Mitotane

mye'toe-tane

Trade and Other Names: Lysodren and op-DDD

Functional Classification: Adrenolytic agent

Pharmacology and Mechanism of Action

Mitotane is a cytotoxic agent. Mitotane binds to adrenal proteins and is then converted to a reactive metabolite which then destroys cells of the adrenal cortex. Destruction of the adrenal cells is relatively specific and can be complete or partial, depending on the dose used. If only partial destruction of adrenal cortical cells occurs, repeated administration or maintenance doses are needed to suppress hypercortisolemia.

Mitotane is a highly lipophilic drug. It is poorly absorbed without food, but oral absorption is enhanced when administered with food or oil.

Indications and Clinical Uses

Mitotane is used primarily to treat pituitary-dependent hyperadrenocorticism (PDH) (Cushing's disease). It also has been used to treat adrenal tumors. Treatment is initiated with a loading dose, followed by weekly maintenance doses. Other drugs used to suppress cortisol in dogs include ketoconazole, selegiline, and trilostane. Treatment with mitotane has been compared with trilostane and shown that each drug, although acting through different mechanisms, produce similar survival times in dogs with PDH (*JVIM* 19: 810-815, 2005).

Precautionary Information

Adverse Reactions and Side Effects

Adverse effects, especially during induction period, include lethargy, anorexia, ataxia, depression, and vomiting. Corticosteroid supplementation (e.g., hydrocortisone or prednisolone) may be administered to minimize side effects. Hypertrophy may occur in dogs. Discontinue if signs of liver disease are observed.

Contraindications and Precautions

Do not administer to animals unless there is an ability to monitor response with cortisol serum measurements, preferably after adrenocorticotropic hormone (ACTH) stimulation.

Drug Interactions

No drug interactions are reported for animals.

Instructions for Use

Dose and frequency often is based on patient response. Adverse effects are common during initial therapy. Administration with food increases oral absorption. Maintenance dose should be adjusted on the basis of periodic cortisol measurements and ACTH stimulation tests (see also *Vet Rec,* 122:486, 1988). Prednisolone at 0.25 mg/kg is sometimes administered as a replacement in patients with PDH during the induction treatment. In some dogs, trilostane has been used when animal do not tolerate or respond to mitotane. Cats usually have not responded to mitotane treatment.

Patient Monitoring and Laboratory Tests

Monitor water consumption and appetite during the induction phase. Monitor ACTH response test to adjust dose. Monitor electrolytes periodically to screen for hyperkalemia that could result from adrenal destruction (iatrogenic hypoadrenocorticism)

Formulations

Mitotane is available in 500 mg tablets.

Stability and Storage

Store in tightly sealed container, protected from light, and at room temperature. Mitotane is not stable in aqueous solutions and may lose potency in some compounded formulations.

Small Animal Dosage

Dogs

- Pituitary-dependent hyperadrenocorticism (PDH): 50 mg/kg/day (in divided doses) PO for 5-10 days, then 50-70 mg/kg/week PO.
- Adrenal tumor: 50-75 mg/kg/day for 10 days, then 75-100 mg/kg/week PO.

Large Animal Dosage

No large animal doses have been reported.

Regulatory Information

Do not use in animals that produce food.

Mitoxantrone Hydrochloride

mye-toe-zan'trone hye-droe-klor'ide

Trade and Other Names: Novantrone

Functional Classification: Anticancer agent

Pharmacology and Mechanism of Action

Anticancer antibiotic. Mitoxantrone is an anticancer agent that is similar to doxorubicin in action. Like doxorubicin, it acts to intercalate between bases on DNA, disrupting DNA and RNA synthesis in tumor cell. Mitoxantrone may affect tumor cell membranes.

Indications and Clinical Uses

Mitoxantrone is used in anticancer drug protocols in animals for treatment of leukemia, lymphoma, and carcinomas.

Precautionary Information

Adverse Reactions and Side Effects

As with all anticancer agents, certain adverse effects are predictable and unavoidable and related to drug's action. Mitoxantrone produces myelosuppression, vomiting, anorexia, and GI upset, but it may be less cardiotoxic than doxorubicin.

Contraindications and Precautions

Do not administer to animals with bone marrow suppression.

Drug Interactions

No drug interactions are reported for animals.

Instructions for Use

Proper use of mitoxantrone usually follows a specific anticancer protocol. Consult specific protocol for dosing regimen.

Patient Monitoring and Laboratory Tests

Monitor CBC to look for evidence of bone marrow toxicity.

Formulations

Mitoxantrone is available in 2 mg/mL injection.

Stability and Storage

Store in tightly sealed container, protected from light, and at room temperature.

Small Animal Dosage

Dogs

- 6 mg/m^2 IV every 21 days.

Cats

- 6.5 mg/m^2 IV every 21 days.

Large Animal Dosage

No large animal doses have been reported.

Regulatory Information

Withdrawal times are not established for animals that produce food.

This drug should not be used in animals intended for food, because it is an anticancer agent.

Morphine Sulfate

mor′feen sul′fate

Trade and Other Names: Generic brands, MS Contin extended release tablets, Oramorph SR extended release tablets, and generic brand extended release tablets

Functional Classification: Analgesic, Opioid

Pharmacology and Mechanism of Action

Opioid agonist, analgesic. Prototype for other opioid agonists. Action of morphine is to bind to mu-opiate and kappa-opiate receptors on nerves and inhibit release of neurotransmitters involved with transmission of pain stimuli (such as Substance P). Morphine also may inhibit release of some inflammatory mediators. Central sedative and euphoric effects related to mu-receptor effects in brain. Other opiates used in animals include hydromorphone, codeine, oxymorphone, meperidine, and fentanyl.

Indications and Clinical Uses

Morphine is indicated for short-term analgesia, sedation, and as an adjunct to anesthesia. It is compatible with most anesthetics and can be used as part of a multimodal approach to analgesia/anesthesia. Administration of morphine may lower dose requirements for other anesthetics and analgesics used. Duration of morphine in dogs is short (2-4 hours). Morphine has been used in animals for treatment of pulmonary edema. Presumably, this effect is attributed to vasodilation and reduction of preload in animals. Although oral morphine (regular and sustained release) has been used in dogs, its absorption is poor and inconsistent. The oral dose formulations should not be relied on for treating severe pain in dogs. In horses, undesirable behavior and cardiovascular effects may occur at doses that are needed for analgesia, which diminishes its routine use.

Precautionary Information

Adverse Reactions and Side Effects

Like all opiates, side effects from morphine are predictable and unavoidable. Side effects from morphine administration include sedation, vomiting, constipation, urinary retention, and bradycardia. Panting may occur in dogs as a result of changes in thermoregulation. Histamine release occurs from administration of morphine, but it may be less likely with other opioids. Excitement can occur in some animals, but it is more common in cats and horses. Respiratory depression occurs with high doses. As with other opiates, a slight decrease in heart rate is expected. In most cases this decrease does not have to be treated with anticholinergic drugs (e.g., atropine), but it should be monitored. Tolerance and dependence occurs with chronic administration. In horses, there was ileus, constipation, and CNS stimulation (pawing and pacing) following 0.5 mg/kg. In horses, undesirable and even dangerous behavior actions can follow rapid intravenous opioid administration. If used in horses, they should receive a pre-anesthetic of acepromazine or an $alpha_2$ agonist.

Contraindications and Precautions

Morphine is a schedule II controlled substance. Cats and horses are more sensitive to excitement than other species.

Drug Interactions

Like other opiates, it will potentiate other drugs that cause CNS depression.

Instructions for Use

Effects from morphine administration are dose dependent. Low doses (0.1-0.25 mg/kg) produce mild analgesia. Higher doses (up to 1 mg/kg) produce greater analgesic effects and sedation. Usually morphine is administered IM, IV, or SQ. Constant Rate Infusions (CRI) also have been used, and doses cited have been shown to produce morphine concentrations in a therapeutic range. Oral morphine is available in sustained-release forms, but oral dosing can be highly variable and inconsistent. Epidural administration has been used for surgical procedures.

Patient Monitoring and Laboratory Tests

Monitor patient's heart rate and respiration. Although bradycardia rarely needs to be treated when it is caused by an opioid, if necessary atropine can be administered. If serious respiratory depression occurs, the opioid can be reversed with naloxone.

Formulations

Morphine is available in 1, 2, 4, 5, 8, 10, 15, 25, and 50 mg/mL injection (most common is 15 mg/mL), 15, 30 mg tablets, and extended release tablets in 15, 30, 60, 100, and 200 mg (MS Contin, Oramorph SR, or generic brands).

Stability and Storage

Store in tightly sealed container, protected from light, and at room temperature. Morphine sulfate is slightly water soluble and soluble in ethanol. It is more stable at pH <4. If mixed with high pH vehicles, oxidation occurs which may darken the formulation (brownish yellow). Solutions may be repackaged in plastic syringes and kept stable for 70 days. If mixed with sodium chloride (0.9%) for epidural injection, it is stable for 14 weeks. Protect from freezing.

Small Animal Dosage

Dogs

- Analgesia: 0.5 mg/kg q2h IV or IM. However, a dose range of 0.1-1 mg/kg IV, IM, or SQ q4h has also been used (dose is escalated as needed).
- CRI: Loading dose of 0.2 mg/kg IV, followed by 0.1 mg/kg/hr. This may be increased to a loading dose of 0.3 mg/kg, followed by 0.17 mg/kg/hr for more severe pain. Doses as high as a loading dose of 0.6 mg/kg, followed by 0.34 mg/kg IV have been used in experimental dogs.
- Oral dosing: Regular tablets should not be used. Sustained-release tablets have been used at a dose of 15 or 30 mg per dog, q8-12h PO, but studies have shown these tablets to be inconsistently and poorly absorbed in dogs.
- Epidural: 0.1 mg/kg.

Cats

- Analgesia: 0.1 mg/kg IM or SQ q3-6h (or as needed).

Large Animal Dosage

Horses

- 0.5-1 mg/kg IV or IM. Give IV dose slowly. Morphine may cause excitement in horses.

Regulatory Information

Morphine is a Schedule II controlled drug
Avoid use in animals intended for food.
RCI Classification: 1

Moxidectin

moks-ih-dek'tin

Trade and Other Names: ProHeart (canine), Quest (equine), and Cydectin (bovine)

Functional Classification: Antiparasitic

Pharmacology and Mechanism of Action

Antiparasitic drug in the milbemycin class. Avermectins (ivermectin-like drugs) and milbemycins (milbemycin and moxidectin) are macrocyclic lactones and share similarities, including mechanism of action. These drugs are neurotoxic to parasites by potentiating glutamate-gated chloride ion channels in parasites. Paralysis and death of the parasite is caused by increased permeability to chloride ions and hyperpolarization of nerve cells. These drugs also potentiate other chloride channels, including ones gated by GABA. Mammals ordinarily are not affected because they lack glutamate-gated chloride channels, and there is a lower affinity for other mammalian chloride channels. Because these drugs ordinarily do not penetrate the blood-brain barrier, GABA-gated channels in the CNS of mammals are not affected. Moxidectin is active against intestinal parasites, mites, bots, heartworm microfilaria, and developing larvae. Moxidectin has no effect on trematode or cestode parasites.

Indications and Clinical Uses

Moxidectin is used in dogs to prevent infection of heartworm *(Dirofilaria immitis)*. In horses, moxidectin is used for treatment of a variety of parasites, including large strongyles (*Strongylus vulgaris* [adults and L4/L5 arterial stages], *S. edentatus* [adult and tissue stages], *Triodontophorus brevicauda* [adults], and *T. serratus* [adults]); small strongyles ([adults] *Cyathostomum* species, *Cylicocyclus* species, *Cyliocostephanus* species, *Coronocyclus* species, and *Gyalocephalus capitatus*). It is also used to treat small strongyles, including larvae. It is used to treat ascarids, including *Parascaris equorum* (adults and L4 larval stages), pinworms (*Oxyuris equi* [adults and L4 larval stages]), hairworms (*Trichostrongylus axei* [adults]), large-mouth stomach worms (*Habronema muscae* [adults]), and horse stomach bots (*Gasterophilus intestinalis* [2nd and 3rd instars] and *G. nasalis* [3rd instars]). One dose also suppresses strongyle egg production for 84 days. Some formulations for horses also contain praziquantel for horses. This increases the spectrum to include other intestinal parasites such as tapeworms.

In cattle, moxidectin injectable is used to treat GI roundworms (*Ostertagia ostertagi* [adults and inhibited fourth-stage larvae], *Haemonchus placei* [adults], *Trichostrongylus axei* [adults], *T. colubriformis* [fourth-stage larvae], *Cooperia oncophora* [adults], *C. punctata* [adults and fourth-stage larvae], *C. surnabada* [adults and fourth-stage larvae], *Oesophagostomum radiatum* [adults and fourth-stage larvae], *Trichuris* spp. [adults]), lungworms (*Dictyocaulus viviparus* [adults and fourth-stage larvae]), grubs (*Hypoderma bovis* and *H. lineatum*), mites (*Psoroptes ovis [P. communis* var. *bovis]*, lice (*Linognathus vituli* and *Solenopotes capillatus*). One injection will protect cattle from reinfection with *D. viviparous* and *O. radiatum* for 42 days, *H. placei* for 35 days, and *O. ostertagi* and *T. axei* for 14 days after treatment.

M

Precautionary Information

Adverse Reactions and Side Effects

Toxicity may occur at high doses and in breeds in which moxidectin crosses the blood-brain barrier. Sensitive breeds may include Collies, Australian shepherds, Old English sheepdogs, Longhaired Whippets, and Shetland sheepdogs. Toxicity is neurotoxic and signs include depression, ataxia, difficulty with vision, coma, and death. Sensitivity to moxidectin occurs in certain breeds because of a mutation in the multidrug resistance gene (MDR1) that codes for the membrane pump p-glycoprotein. This mutation that affects the efflux pump in blood-brain barrier. Adverse effects may occur when high doses of moxidectin are used to treat dogs for demodicosis. These effects include lethargy, depressed appetite, vomiting, and lesions at the site of a SQ injection. Toxicity is more likely at high doses in dogs. At five times the label dose rate (15 mcg/kg) once every month, moxidectin was administered safely to Collies that were ivermectin-sensitive. However, at a single dose of 90 mcg/kg (30 times the label dose) administered to sensitive Collies, ataxia, lethargy, and salivation occurred in one sixth of dogs. At 30, 60, and 90 mcg/kg to ivermectin-sensitive Collies, (10 times, 20 times, and 30 times the label dose) there were no adverse effects observed (*Am J Vet Res*, 61:482-483, 2000). Nevertheless, caution is advised when administering moxidectin to sensitive breeds listed previously. Because of concern about adverse reactions and deaths in dogs from the 6-month injectable formulation (Pro-Heart 6), this product was discontinued. In horses, adverse effects (ataxia, depression, and lethargy) have been reported if young horses (younger than 6 months) or debilitated animals after treatment.

Contraindications and Precautions

Do not use in dogs younger than 6 months of age. The canine long-acting formulation ProHeart 6 has been removed from the market and is no longer available. Despite safety margin listed in the adverse effects section, caution is advised when administering moxidectin at high doses to ivermectin-sensitive breeds. Affected breeds may include Collies, Australian shepherds, Old English sheepdogs, Longhaired Whippets, and Shetland sheepdogs. Susceptible breeds may also be sensitive to other drugs such as loperamide, cardiovascular, and anticancer drugs. Administration to foals younger than 6 months of age is not recommended. Do not apply the pour-on formulation to small animals.

Drug Interactions

Do not administer with drugs that could potentially increase the penetration of ivermectin across the blood-brain barrier. Such drugs include ketoconazole, itraconazole, cyclosporine, and calcium-channel blockers.

Instructions for Use

Caution is recommended if bovine or equine formulation is considered for use in small animals. Toxic overdoses are likely because theses formulations are highly concentrated.

Patient Monitoring and Laboratory Tests

Animals should be checked for heartworm status prior to initiating treatment.

Formulations

Moxidectin is available in 30, 68, and 136 mcg tablets for dogs, 20 mg/mL equine oral gel, 5 mg/mL cattle pour-on, 10 mg/mL injectable solution for cattle, and Quest 2% gel for Horses (20 mg/mL). Quest Plus gel for horses contains 20 mg/mL (2%) plus 125 mg praziquantel (12.5%).

The 6-month injectable (Pro-Heart 6) has been suspended from the market in the U.S.

Stability and Storage

Store in tightly sealed container, protected from light, and at room temperature. Stability of compounded formulations has not been evaluated.

Small Animal Dosage

Dogs

- Heartworm prevention: 3 mcg/kg every 30 days PO.
- Endoparasite control: 25-300 mcg/kg.
- Sarcoptic mange: 200-250 mcg/kg (0.2-0.25 mg/kg) PO or SQ, once per week, for 3-6 weeks.
- Demodicosis: 200 mcg/kg SQ, weekly or every other week for 1-4 doses; alternatively, 400 mcg/kg/day PO.
- Higher doses are used for refractory cases: 500 mcg/kg (0.5 mg/kg)/day PO for 21-23 weeks or 0.5-1.0 mg/kg SQ, q72h, for 21-22 weeks. Duration of treatment for demodicosis is variable. Treat until two negative *Demodex* skin scrapings are achieved.

Large Animal Dosage

Horses

- GI parasites: 0.4 mg/kg PO. Avoid use in young horses, small ponies, or debilitated animals.

Cattle

- 0.2 mg/kg SQ, once.
- GI parasites, lungworms, mites, grubs, and lice: Topical treatment (pour-on): 0.5 mg/kg (0.23 mg/pound or 45 mL per 1000 pounds). Apply topically along the midline from the withers to the tail head. Avoid exposure to human skin and to other animals.

Regulatory Information

Do not use in horses intended for food.
Cattle withdrawal time (meat): 21 days.
No milk withholding time has been established. Do not use in female dairy cattle of breeding age. Do not use in veal calves.

Moxifloxacin

moks-ih-floks′ah-sin

Trade and Other Names: Avelox

Functional Classification: Antibacterial

Pharmacology and Mechanism of Action

Fluoroquinolone antibacterial. Moxifloxacin, like other quinolones, inhibits DNA gyrase and prevents bacterial cell DNA and RNA synthesis. Moxifloxacin is bactericidal with broad antimicrobial activity. It has a chemical structure slightly different from older veterinary fluoroquinolones. As a result of this modification, this newer generation of drugs, such as moxifloxacin, has greater activity against gram-positive bacteria and anaerobes than the veterinary fluoroquinolones (enrofloxacin, orbifloxacin, danofloxacin, and marbofloxacin).

Indications and Clinical Uses

Moxifloxacin, although a human drug, has been used in small animals for treatment of infections refractory to other drugs, including skin infections, pneumonia, and soft tissue infections. The spectrum of activity includes gram-positive cocci and anaerobic bacteria that may be resistant to other quinolones. Because other veterinary fluoroquinolones are preferred for initial use (enrofloxacin, orbifloxacin, danofloxacin, and marbofloxacin), moxifloxacin use is not common. Data for use in small animals is sparse and regimens are primarily extrapolated from the human label. In horses it has been administered at 5.8 mg/kg/day for 3 days. Although pharmacokinetics were favorable in horses, it caused diarrhea that may present a risk.

Precautionary Information

Adverse Reactions and Side Effects

High concentrations may cause CNS toxicity, especially in animals with renal failure. Moxifloxacin causes occasional vomiting. All of the fluoroquinolones may cause arthropathy in young animals. Dogs are most sensitive at 4 to 28 weeks of age. Large, rapidly growing dogs are the most susceptible. In horses, moxifloxacin caused diarrhea and is not recommended for routine use. Moxifloxacin at high doses has caused a dose-related prolongation of the Q-T interval. The clinical consequences of this observation for animals are not known.

Contraindications and Precautions

Avoid use in young animals due to risk of cartilage injury. Use cautiously in animals that may be prone to seizures, such as epileptics. Avoid use in horses, rodents, and rabbits because of risk of diarrhea.

Drug Interactions

Fluoroquinolones may increase concentrations of theophylline if used concurrently. Coadministration with divalent and trivalent cations, such as products containing aluminum (e.g., sucralfate), iron, and calcium may decrease absorption. Do not mix in solutions or in vials with aluminum, calcium, iron, or zinc, because chelation may occur.

Instructions for Use

Doses are based on plasma concentrations needed to achieve sufficient plasma concentration above minimum inhibitory concentrations (MIC) value. Efficacy studies have not been performed in dogs or cats.

Patient Monitoring and Laboratory Tests

Susceptibility testing: CLSI (NCCLS) break points for sensitive organisms are less than or equal to 1.0 mcg/mL. Most sensitive gram-negative bacteria of the *Enterobacteriaceae* have MIC values less than or equal to 0.1 mcg/mL. If ciprofloxacin is used to treat *Pseudomonas,* it may be several times more active than other fluoroquinolones. Otherwise, one should assume that if the organism is susceptible to ciprofloxacin, it is likely susceptible to others.

Formulations

Moxifloxacin is available in 400 mg tablets.

Stability and Storage

Store in tightly sealed container, protected from light, and at room temperature. Do not mix with products that contain ions (iron, aluminum, magnesium, and calcium).

Small Animal Dosage

Dogs and Cats

- 10 mg/kg q24h PO.

Large Animal Dosage

Horses

- 5.8 mg/kg q24h for 3 days, but it caused diarrhea. Therefore, there may be risks with long-term use.

Regulatory Information

There are no withdrawal times established because this drug should not be administered to animals that produce food.

Mycophenolate

mye-koe-fen′oh-late

Trade and Other Names: CellCept

Functional Classification: Immunosuppressant

Pharmacology and Mechanism of Action

Mycophenolate is metabolized to mycophenolic acid. It is used to suppress immunity for transplantation and for treatment of immune-mediated diseases. Mycophenolate, when metabolized to mycophenolic acid (MPA) inhibits inosine monophosphate dehydrogenase (IMPDH), which is an important enzyme for the de novo synthesis of purines in immune cells, especially stimulated lymphocytes. T and B-lymphocytes are critically dependent on de novo synthesis of purine nucleotides. Therefore it effectively suppresses lymphocyte proliferation and decreases antibody synthesis by B-cells. In people it is used as a replacement for azathioprine and has been primarily used for immune suppression in liver and kidney transplant patients, but other uses are being explored. It is usually used in combination with glucocorticoids and/or cyclosporine.

Indications and Clinical Uses

Mycophenolate is used to treat immune-mediated diseases in animals. In dogs, mycophenolate has been used on a limited basis to treat some immune-mediated diseases. According to pharmacokinetic studies with mycophenolate in dogs, the elimination rate was rapid (half-life less than 1 hour), which may require frequent dosing in dogs for successful therapy. For treatment of pemphigus foliaceous, it was given at a dose of 22-39 mg/kg/day divided into three treatments. It was well-tolerated, but only 3 out of 8 dogs completed the study and were improved. Azathioprine is more commonly used as an immunosuppressive agent.

Precautionary Information

Adverse Reactions and Side Effects

In dogs, GI problems (diarrhea and vomiting) have been the most common effects reported. Use in veterinary medicine has been rare, however.

Contraindications and Precautions

Mycophenolate is a potent immunosuppressive drug. Patients will be more prone to infection when receiving mycophenolate.

Drug Interactions

No drug interactions are reported. It is frequently administered with corticosteroids.

Instructions for Use

Mycophenolate is used in some patients that cannot tolerate other immunosuppressive drugs, such as azathioprine or cyclophosphamide. Mycophenolate has been used in combination with corticosteroids and cyclosporine.

Patient Monitoring and Laboratory Tests

Monitor for signs of infection in patients.

Formulations

Mycophenolate is available in 250 mg capsules.

Stability and Storage

Store in tightly sealed container, protected from light, and at room temperature. It is slightly soluble in water. It is more stable at low pH values (<4). It may be prepared in a syrup suspension for flavoring and stable for 121 days.

Small Animal Dosage

Dogs

- 10 mg/kg q8, PO.

Large Animal Dosage

No large animal dose has been reported.

Regulatory Information

There are no withdrawal times established because this drug should not be administered to animals that produce food.

Naloxone Hydrochloride

nal-oks'one hye-droe-klor'ide

Trade and Other Names: Narcan and Trexonil

Functional Classification: Opioid antagonist

Pharmacology and Mechanism of Action

Opiate antagonist. Naloxone competes for opiate receptors and displaces opioid drugs from these receptors, thus reversing their effects. It appears to antagonize all opiate receptors.

Indications and Clinical Uses

Naloxone is used to reverse the effects of opiate agonists on receptors. Naloxone should be used to reverse overdoses or toxicity. It will reverse effects of morphine, oxymorphone, butorphanol, hydromorphone, and other opioids. It is less effective for reversing buprenorphine and may be titrated in gradually to achieve the optimum amount of reversal. A formulation for wildlife use (Trexonil) is more concentrated and used to reverse tranquilization in wild animals. In horses, it will temporarily decrease crib biting, but the duration of action is short.

Precautionary Information

Adverse Reactions and Side Effects

Tachycardia and hypertension have been reported in people. In animals, reversal of opioid may precipitate a severe reaction that includes high blood pressure, excitement, pain, tachycardia, and cardiac arrhythmias.

Contraindications and Precautions

Administration to an animal that is experiencing pain will precipitate extreme reactions because of blockade of endogenous opioids.

Drug Interactions

Naloxone will reverse the action of other opioid drugs.

Instructions for Use

Administration may have to be individualized based on response in each patient. Naloxone's duration of action is short in animals (60 minutes) and it may have to be readministered. Start at the low end of the dosage rate and increase the dose to effect. Higher doses may be needed to reverse drugs that are mixed agonists/antagonists such as butorphanol or buprenorphine, compared to reversing drugs that are pure agonists.

A dose of 1 mL (0.4 mg) will reverse 1.5 mg oxymorphone, 15 mg morphine, 100 mg meperidine, and 0.4 mg fentanyl.

Patient Monitoring and Laboratory Tests

Naloxone is used to reverse opioid analgesic drugs. When opioids are reversed in some animals, serious reactions may occur. In some patients, changes in blood pressure, tachycardia, and discomfort may result.

Formulations Available

Naloxone is available in injectable vials with preservatives in 0.4 or 1 mg/mL, without preservatives in 0.02 mg (20 mcg), 0.4 mg or 1 mg per mL, and as Trexonil in 50 mg/mL.

Stability and Storage

When used IV, it may be diluted in other fluids. For intravenous infusion, it may be added to sodium chloride or 5% dextrose. After dilution it should be used within 24 hours. Do not mix with other drugs or solutions that are alkaline. Store in tightly sealed container, protected from light, and at room temperature.

Small Animal Dosage

Dogs and Cats

- 0.01-0.04 mg/kg IV, IM, or SQ, as needed to reverse opiate.

Large Animal Dosage

Horses

- 0.02-0.04 mg/kg IV (duration of effect is only 20 minutes).

Regulatory Information

No withdrawal times are established. It is anticipated that naloxone is cleared rapidly after administration. Because of low risk of residues, short (24-48 hour) withdrawal times are suggested.
RCI Classification: 3

Naltrexone

nal-treks'one

Trade and Other Names: Trexan

Functional Classification: Opioid antagonist

Pharmacology and Mechanism of Action

Opiate antagonist. Naltrexone competes for opiate receptors and displaces opioid drugs from these receptors, thus reversing their effects. It appears to antagonize all opiate receptors. Its action is similar to naloxone except that it is longer-acting and administered orally.

Indications and Clinical Uses

Naltrexone is used in people for treatment of opiate dependence. In animals some obsessive-compulsive disorders are believed to be mediated by endogenous opioids. It has been used successfully for treatment of some obsessive-compulsive behavioral disorders, such as tail chasing in dogs, acral lick granuloma in dogs, and crib biting in horses. The effect for each of these disorders is short-lived.

Precautionary Information

Adverse Reactions and Side Effects

Adverse effects have not been reported in animals.

Contraindications and Precautions

Do not administer to animals in pain, or it may elicit a severe reaction.

Drug Interactions

Naltrexone will reverse the action of other opioid drugs.

Instructions for Use

Treatment for obsessive-compulsive-disorders (canine compulsive disorder) in animals has been reported with naltrexone. Relapse rates may be high.

Patient Monitoring and Laboratory Tests

Monitor heart rate in treated animals.

Formulations

Naltrexone is available in 50 mg tablets.

Stability and Storage

Store in tightly sealed container, protected from light, and at room temperature. Naltrexone is soluble in water. It has been mixed with juices and syrups to mask the bitter taste and was stable for 60-90 days.

Small Animal Dosage

Dogs

- For behavior problems: 2.2 mg/kg q12h PO.

Large Animal Dosage

Horses

- Crib biting: 0.04 mg/kg IV or SQ. (Because injectable formulations are not available, it must be compounded for this indication.) Duration of effect 1-7 hours.

Regulatory Information

Withdrawal times are not established for animals that produce food. For extralabel use withdrawal interval estimates, contact FARAD at 1-888-USFARAD (1-888-873-2723) or send e-mail to FARAD@ncsu.edu.
RCI Classification: 3

Nandrolone Decanoate

nan'droe-lone dek-ah-noe'ate

Trade and Other Names: Deca-Durabolin

Functional Classification: Hormone, Anabolic agent

Pharmacology and Mechanism of Action

Anabolic steroid. Nandrolone is a derivative of testosterone used as an anabolic agent. Anabolic agents are designed to maximize anabolic effects, while minimizing androgenic action.

Indications and Clinical Uses

Anabolic agents have been used for reversing catabolic conditions, promoting weight gain, increasing muscling in animals, and stimulating erythropoiesis. There are no differences in efficacy among the anabolic steroids reported in animals.

Precautionary Information

Adverse Reactions and Side Effects

Adverse effects from anabolic steroids can be attributed to the pharmacologic action of these steroids. Increased masculine effects are common. There has been an increased incidence of some tumors in people. Some of the oral anabolic steroids that are 17 alpha-methylated (oxymetholone, stanozolol, and oxandrolone) are associated with hepatic toxicity.

Contraindications and Precautions

Use cautiously in patients with hepatic disease. Do not use in pregnant animals.

Drug Interactions

No drug interactions have been reported.

Instructions for Use

Results of clinical studies in animals have not been reported. Nandrolone use in animals (and doses) is based on experience in people or anecdotal experience in animals.

Patient Monitoring and Laboratory Tests

Monitor liver enzymes in treated patients.

Formulations

Nandrolone decanoate is available in 50, 100, and 200 mg/mL injection.

Stability and Storage

Store in tightly sealed container, protected from light, and at room temperature. Stability of compounded formulations has not been evaluated.

Small Animal Dosage

Dogs

- 1-1.5 mg/kg/wk IM.

Cats

- 1 mg/kg/wk IM.

Large Animal Dosage

Horses

- 1 mg/kg q4wk IM.

Regulatory Information

Nandrolone is a schedule III controlled drug.
Do not administer to animals intended for food.
RCI Classification: 4

Naproxen

nah-proks'en

Trade and Other Names: Naprosyn, Naxen, and Aleve (naproxen sodium)

Functional Classification: Nonsteroidal antiinflammatory drug (NSAID)

Pharmacology and Mechanism of Action

Naproxen and other NSAIDs have produced analgesic and antiinflammatory effects by inhibiting the synthesis of prostaglandins. The enzyme inhibited by NSAIDs is the cyclo-oxygenase enzyme (COX). The COX enzyme exists in two isoforms, called COX-1 and COX-2. COX-1 is primarily responsible for synthesis of prostaglandins important for maintaining a healthy GI tract, renal function, platelet function, and other normal functions. COX-2 is induced and responsible for synthesizing prostaglandins that are important mediators of pain, inflammation, and fever. Naproxen is a nonselective (COX-1 and COX-2) NSAID.

Indications and Clinical Uses

Naproxen has been used for treatment of musculoskeletal problems, such as myositis and osteoarthritis in dogs and horses. There are no veterinary formulations marketed. Its use has diminished, because there are registered drugs approved for these indications for horses and dogs.

Precautionary Information

Adverse Reactions and Side Effects

Naproxen is a potent NSAID. Adverse effects attributed to GI toxicity are common to all NSAIDs. Naproxen has produced serious ulceration in dogs because elimination in dogs is many times slower than in people or horses. Renal injury caused by renal ischemia also is possible with repeated doses.

Contraindications and Precautions

Caution is advised when using the OTC formulation designed for people, because the tablet size is much larger than safe dose for dogs. Therefore, warn pet owners about administration to dogs without consulting a veterinarian first. Do not administer to animals prone to GI ulcers. Do not administer with other ulcerogenic drugs, such as corticosteroids.

Drug Interactions

Do not administer with other NSAIDs or with corticosteroids. Corticosteroids have been shown to exacerbate the GI adverse effects. Some NSAIDs may interfere with the action of diuretic drugs and angiotensin-converting enzyme (ACE) inhibitors.

Instructions for Use

Results of clinical studies in animals have not been reported. Use in animals (and doses) is based on pharmacokinetic studies in experimental animals.

Patient Monitoring and Laboratory Tests

Monitor for signs of GI ulceration.

Formulations

Naproxen is available in 220 mg tablets (OTC). (A 220-mg dose of naproxen sodium is equivalent to 200 mg naproxen.) It is also available in 25 mg/mL oral suspension and 250, 375, and 500 mg tablets (prescription).

Stability and Storage

Store in tightly sealed container, protected from light, and at room temperature. Naproxen is practically insoluble in water at low pH, but it increases at high pH. It is soluble in ethanol.

Small Animal Dosage

Dogs

- 5 mg/kg initially, then 2 mg/kg q48h PO.

Large Animal Dosage

Horses

- 10 mg/kg q12h PO.

Regulatory Information

Withdrawal times are not established for animals that produce food. For extralabel use withdrawal interval estimates, contact FARAD at 1-888-USFARAD (1-888-873-2723) or send e-mail to FARAD@ncsu.edu.

RCI Classification: 4

N-Butylscopolammonium Bromide (Butylscopolamine Bromide)

en-byoo-til-skoe-pahl′ah-moe-nee-um broe′mide

Trade and Other Names: Buscopan

Functional Classification: Antispasmodic

Pharmacology and Mechanism of Action

Antispasmotic, Antimuscarinic, anticholinergic drug. Butylscopolamine, like other antimuscarinic drugs, blocks cholinergic receptors and produces a parasympatholytic effect. It affects receptors throughout the body, but it is used more commonly for its GI effects. It effectively inhibits secretions and motility of GI tract by blocking parasympathetic receptors.

Indications and Clinical Uses

Butylscopolamine bromide is indicated for treating pain associated with spasmodic colic, flatulent colic, and intestinal impactions in horses.

Precautionary Information

Adverse Reactions and Side Effects

Adverse reactions from anticholinergic drugs are related to their blocking of acetylcholine receptors and producing a systemic parasympatholytic response. As expected with this class of drugs, animals will have increased heart rate, decreased secretions, dry mucous membranes, decreased GI tract motility, and dilated pupils. In target animal safety studies in which doses of one times, three times, five times, and up to 10 times the doses were administered to horses, the above clinical signs were observed. However, at high doses there were no CBC or biochemical abnormalities or lesions identified at necropsy.

Contraindications and Precautions

N-butylscopolammonium bromide will decrease intestinal motility. Use cautiously in conditions where decreased motility will be a concern.

Drug Interactions

N-butylscopolammonium bromide is an anticholinergic drug, and therefore will antagonize any other medications that are intended to produce a cholinergic response (e.g., metoclopramide).

Instructions for Use

Experience is limited to treating spasmodic colic, flatulent colic, and intestinal impactions in horses. There is no experience in other animals.

Patient Monitoring and Laboratory Tests

Monitor equine intestinal motility (gut sounds and fecal output) during treatment. Monitor heart rate in treated animals.

Formulations

N-butylscopolammonium is available in a 20 mg/mL solution.

Stability and Storage

Store in tightly sealed container, protected from light, and at room temperature.

Small Animal Dosage

No dose is reported for small animals.

Large Animal Dosage

Horses

- 0.3 mg/kg, slowly IV as a single dose (1.5 mL per 100 kg).

Regulatory Information

Do not administer to animals intended for food.

Neomycin

nee-oh-mye'sin

Trade and Other Names: Biosol

Functional Classification: Antibacterial

Pharmacology and Mechanism of Action

Aminoglycoside antibiotic. The action of neomycin is to inhibit bacteria protein synthesis via binding to 30S ribosome. It is bactericidal with a broad spectrum of activity except against streptococci and anaerobic bacteria. Neomycin differs from other aminoglycosides, because it is only administered topically or orally. Systemic absorption is minimal from oral absorption.

Indications and Clinical Uses

Neomycin is only available in topical formulations. It is often combined with other antibiotics (Triple Antibiotics) in ointments for topical treatment of superficial infections. It is also used locally (oral local) for treatment of intestinal infections (colibacillosis). It is given orally, and because it is not absorbed systemically, it produces a local effect.

Precautionary Information

Adverse Reactions and Side Effects

Although oral absorption is so small that systemic adverse effects are unlikely, some oral absorption has been demonstrated in young animals (calves). Alterations in intestinal bacterial flora from therapy may cause diarrhea.

Contraindications and Precautions

Use cautiously in animals with renal disease. If oral absorption occurs because of compromised mucosal integrity, oral absorption may occur. Do not use longer than 14 days. Neomycin has been mixed with water and injected, but this practice is strongly discouraged.

Drug Interactions

Neomycin should not be mixed with other drugs before administration. Other drugs may bind and become inactivated.

Instructions for Use

Efficacy for treatment of diarrhea, especially for nonspecific diarrhea is questionable.

Patient Monitoring and Laboratory Tests

Monitor for signs of diarrhea. If sufficiently absorbed systemically, it could cause renal injury, therefore monitor BUN and creatinine with chronic use.

Formulations

Neomycin is available in 500 mg bolus, 50 mg/mL (equivalent to 35 mg/mL neomycin base), 200 mg/mL oral liquid (equivalent to 140 mg/mL of neomycin base), 325 mg soluble powder (equivalent to 20.3 grams per ounce of neomycin base).

Stability and Storage

It may be added to drinking water or milk. Do not add to other liquid supplements. Prepare a fresh solution daily. It is freely soluble in water and slightly soluble in ethanol. Aqueous solutions are stable over a wide pH range with optimum stability at pH 7. Store in tightly sealed container, protected from light, and at room temperature.

Small Animal Dosage

Dogs and Cats

- 10-20 mg/kg q6-12h PO.

Large Animal Dosage

Calves, Sheep, and Goats

- 22 mg/kg/day PO.

Regulatory Information

Slaughter withdrawal times: cattle 1 day; goats and sheep 2 days; swine and goats 3 days. Oral administration may cause residues in animals intended for food; therefore, do not administer to veal calves.

Neostigmine

nee-oh-stig′meen

Trade and Other Names: Prostigmin, Stiglyn, Neostigmine bromide, and Neostigmine methylsulfate

Functional Classification: Anticholinesterase

Pharmacology and Mechanism of Action

Cholinesterase inhibitor. Anticholinesterase drug and antimyasthenic drug. This drug inhibits the enzyme that breaks down acetylcholine. Therefore it prolongs the action of acetylcholine at the synapse. The major difference between physostigmine and neostigmine or pyridostigmine is that physostigmine crosses the blood-brain barrier, and the others do not.

Indications and Clinical Uses

Neostigmine is used as an antidote for anticholinergic intoxication. It is also used as a treatment of myasthenia gravis, treatment (antidote) for neuromuscular blockade, and treatment of ileus. It also has been used as a treatment of urinary retention (such as postoperative) retention by increasing tone of bladder smooth muscle.

Precautionary Information

Adverse Reactions and Side Effects

Adverse effects are caused by the cholinergic action resulting from inhibition of cholinesterase. These effects can be seen in the GI tract as diarrhea and increased secretions. Other adverse effects can include miosis, bradycardia, muscle twitching or weakness, constriction of bronchi and ureters. Adverse effects can be treated with anticholinergic drugs such as atropine. Pyridostigmine may be associated with fewer adverse effects than neostigmine.

Contraindications and Precautions

Do not use in urinary obstruction, intestinal obstruction, asthma or bronchoconstriction, pneumonia, and cardiac arrhythmias. Do not use in patients sensitive to bromide. Consider the amount of bromide in dose in any patient also receiving bromide (KBr) for treatment of seizures.

Drug Interactions

Do not use with other cholinergic drugs. Anticholinergic drugs (atropine and glycopyrrolate) will block the effects.

Instructions for Use

Neostigmine is indicated primarily only for treatment of intoxication. For routine systemic use of anticholinesterase drug, pyridostigmine may have fewer side effects. When used, frequency of dose may be increased based on observation of effects.

Patient Monitoring and Laboratory Tests

Monitor GI signs, heart rate, and rhythm.

Formulations

Neostigmine bromide is available in 15 mg tablets and neostigmine methylsulfate is available in 0.25, 0.5, and 1 mg/mL injections.

Stability and Storage

Store in tightly sealed container, protected from light, and at room temperature.

Small Animal Dosage

Dogs and Cats

- 2 mg/kg per day PO in divided doses.
- Antimyasthenic treatment: 10 mcg/kg IM or SQ, as needed.
- Antidote for neuromuscular blockade: 40 mcg/kg IM or SQ.
- Diagnostic aid for myasthenia: 40 mcg/kg IM or 20 mcg/kg IV.

Large Animal Dosage

When used as a treatment for neuromuscular blocking agents (cholinesterase inhibitor), the frequency of administration is determined by clinical response.

Cattle and Horses

- 22 mcg/kg (0.022 mg/kg) SQ.

Sheep

- 22-33 mcg/kg (0.022-0.033 mg/kg) SQ.

Swine

- 44-66 mcg/kg (0.044-0.066 mg/kg) IM.

Regulatory Information

Withdrawal times are not established for animals that produce food. For extralabel use withdrawal interval estimates, contact FARAD at 1-888-USFARAD (1-888-873-2723) or send e-mail to FARAD@ncsu.edu.
RCI Classification: 3

Niacinamide

nye'ah-sin'ah-mide

Trade and Other Names: Nicotinamide and Vitamin B_3

Functional Classification: Antiinflammatory

Pharmacology and Mechanism of Action

Immunosuppressant. Use primarily to treat skin diseases, such as discoid lupus erythematosus and pemphigus erythematosus in dogs. Mechanism of action is not entirely known. Niacinamide may have some antiinflammatory action such as suppression of inflammatory cells. Niacin and niacinamide are used to treat Vitamin B_3 deficiency. Do not confuse niacin with niacinamide. Niacin is converted to the active form niacinamide by intestinal bacteria.

Indications and Clinical Uses

Niacinamide has been used to treat immune-mediated skin disease in small animals. For skin disorders, it is usually administered with tetracycline. It also has been used to treat vitamin B_3 deficiency.

Precautionary Information

Adverse Reactions and Side Effects

Side effects are not common but have included vomiting, anorexia, lethargy, and diarrhea.

Contraindications and Precautions

No contraindications are reported for animals.

Drug Interactions

No drug interactions are reported.

Instructions for Use

For treatment of pemphigus skin disease, it is usually administered with a tetracycline.

Patient Monitoring and Laboratory Tests

Monitor blood CBC periodically during treatment.

Formulations

Niacinamide is available in 50, 100, 125, 250, and 500 mg tablets (OTC) and 100 mg/mL injection.

Stability and Storage

Store in tightly sealed container, protected from light, and at room temperature.

Small Animal Dosage

Dogs

- For a 10 kg dog, administer 500 mg niacinamide q8h PO, plus 500 mg tetracycline (dose is approximate). Eventually taper dose to q12h, then to q24h. For dogs <10 kg, start with 250 mg of each drug.

Large Animal Dosage

No large animal doses are reported.

Regulatory Information

No regulatory information is available. Because of low risk of residues, no withdrawal times are suggested.

Nifedipine

nye-fed'ih-peen

Trade and Other Names: Adalat and Procardia

Functional Classification: Calcium-channel blocker, vasodilator

Pharmacology and Mechanism of Action

Calcium-channel blocking drug of the dihydropyridine class. Vasodilator. The action of nifedipine is similar to other calcium-channel blocking drugs, such as amlodipine. They block voltage-dependent calcium entry into smooth muscle cells. Drugs of the dihydropyridine class are more specific for vascular smooth muscle than the cardiac tissue. Therefore, they have less effect on cardiac conduction than diltiazem.

Indications and Clinical Uses

Nifedipine is used for smooth muscle relaxation and to induce vasodilation. It is indicated for treatment of systemic hypertension.

Precautionary Information

Adverse Reactions and Side Effects

Adverse effects have not been reported in veterinary medicine. Most common side effect is hypotension.

Contraindications and Precautions

Do not administer to hypotensive patient. Nifedipine may be teratogenic in pregnant laboratory animals and/or embryotoxic. Avoid use in pregnant animals.

Drug Interactions

Do not administer with drugs known to inhibit drug metabolizing enzymes (e.g., ketoconazole). Nifedipine may be subject to interactions from drugs that inhibit the membrane multi-drug resistance (MDR1) pump (p-glycoprotein), which may lead to toxicity. See Appendix for drugs that may affect p-glycoprotein.

Instructions for Use

Use of nifedipine is limited in veterinary medicine. Other calcium-channel blockers, such as diltiazem, are used to control heart rhythm. Amlodipine is more commonly used for control of systemic hypertension.

Patient Monitoring and Laboratory Tests

Monitor blood pressure during therapy.

Formulations

Nifedipine is available in 10 and 20 mg capsules and 30, 60, and 90 mg extended release capsules.

Stability and Storage

Store in tightly sealed container, protected from light, and at room temperature. It is decomposed more rapidly if exposed to light. In extemporaneous solutions, nifedipine is unstable. If mixed with solutions, it should be used immediately.

Small Animal Dosage

Animal dose not established. In people, the dose is 10 mg/per person three times a day and increased in 10 mg increments to effect.

Large Animal Dosage

No large animal doses are reported.

Regulatory Information

Withdrawal times are not established for animals that produce food. For extralabel use withdrawal interval estimates, contact FARAD at 1-888-USFARAD (1-888-873-2723) or send e-mail to FARAD@ncsu.edu.
RCI Classification: 4

Nitazoxanide

nye-taz-oks'ah-nide

Trade and Other Names: Navigator (horse preparation) and Alinia (human preparation)

Functional Classification: Antiprotozoal

Pharmacology and Mechanism of Action

Antiprotozoal drug. Nitazoxanide (NTZ) is a nitrothiazolyl-salicylamide derivative. Its action against protozoa is unknown, but it may be related to the inhibition of the pyruvate-ferredoxin oxidoreductase (PFOR) enzyme-dependent electron transfer reaction essential to anaerobic and protozoal energy metabolism. Activity has been demonstrated against a variety of protozoa, including *Cryptosporidium parvum*, *Giardia*, *Isospora*, and *Entamoeba*. It also has activity against intestinal helminths, such as *Ascaris*, *Ancylostoma*, *Trichuris*, and *Taenia*. It also may be active against some anaerobic bacteria, including *Helicobacter*. One of the active metabolites is tizoxanide.

Indications and Clinical Uses

Nitazoxanide (NTZ) is used to treat equine protozoal myeloencephalitis (EPM). It has had only limited use in other veterinary species, but there is a form approved for use in people for treatment of protozoal infections, such as *C. parvum* and *Giardia*.

Precautionary Information

Adverse Reactions and Side Effects

Administration to some animals has produced diarrhea.

Contraindications and Precautions

No known contraindications.

Drug Interactions

No known drug interactions.

Instructions for Use

NTZ is administered for horses to treat EPM. Use in small animals has been extrapolated from the use in humans.

Patient Monitoring and Laboratory Tests

When treating patients for diarrhea, monitor electrolytes and fecal samples.

Formulations

Nitazoxanide is available in a 0.32 mg/mL oral paste. Human formulation is a powder for oral dosing, 100 mg of powder is mixed with 48 mL of water.

Stability and Storage

Stable if stored in manufacturer's original formulation. The oral solution for people can be mixed and remain stable for 7 days.

Small Animal Dosage

There is no small animal dosing instructions available. However, one dose that has been used is 100 mg per animal q12h PO for 3 days.

Large Animal Dosage

Horses

- 25 mg/kg q24h PO on days 1 through 5, followed by 50 mg/kg q24h PO on days 6 through 28.

Regulatory Information

Do not use in animals intended for food.

Nitenpyram

nye-ten-pye'ram

Trade and Other Names: Capstar

Functional Classification: Antiparasitic

Pharmacology and Mechanism of Action

Nitenpyram is an antiparasitic drug used for treatment of fleas. It will rapidly kill adult fleas.

Indications and Clinical Uses

Nitenpyram is used to kill fleas on dogs and cats. It is often used with other drugs that act to prevent flea infestations as part of a comprehensive flea-control program.

Precautionary Information

Adverse Reactions and Side Effects

No adverse reactions are reported. It was safe in studies in dogs and cats in which up to 10 times the dose was administered.

Contraindications and Precautions

Do not use in dogs or cats <1 kg (2 pounds) in weight. Do not use in cats or dogs younger than 4 weeks of age.

Drug Interactions

No drug interactions reported. It is safe to use with lufenuron and milbemycin.

Instructions for Use

Nitenpyram is often used with lufenuron to kill adult fleas and prevent flea eggs from hatching.

Patient Monitoring and Laboratory Tests

No specific monitoring is necessary.

Formulations

Nitenpyram is available in 11.4 or 57 mg tablets.

Stability and Storage

Store in tightly sealed container, protected from light, and at room temperature.

Small Animal Dosage

- 1 mg/kg daily PO, as needed to kill fleas.

Large Animal Dosage

No large animal dose is reported.

Regulatory Information

Withdrawal times are not established for animals that produce food. For extralabel use withdrawal interval estimates, contact FARAD at 1-888-USFARAD (1-888-873-2723) or send e-mail to FARAD@ncsu.edu.

Nitrofurantoin

nye-troe-fyoo′ran-toyn

Trade and Other Names: Macrodantin, Furalan, Furatoin, Furadantin, and generic brands

Functional Classification: Antibacterial

Pharmacology and Mechanism of Action

Antibacterial drug. Urinary antiseptic. Therapeutic concentrations are reached only in the urine. In the urine it is reduced by bacterial flavoproteins, and the reactive metabolites inhibit bacterial macromolecules (DNA and RNA). Resistance among bacteria is unusual, although *Proteus* and *Pseudomonas aeruginosa* are inherently resistant. Macrocrystalline form is slowly absorbed and less likely to cause gastric upset. Microcrystalline form is rapidly absorbed in intestine.

Indications and Clinical Uses

Nitrofurantoin is administered orally for treatment or prevention of UTIs. It does not attain high enough concentrations for systemic infections or kidney infections.

Precautionary Information

Adverse Reactions and Side Effects

Adverse effects include nausea, vomiting, and diarrhea. Turns urine color rust-yellow brown. In people, respiratory problems (pneumonitis) and peripheral neuropathy have been reported. These effects have not been reported in animals.

Contraindications and Precautions

Do not administer during pregnancy, especially at term because it may cause hemolytic anemia of newborn. Do not administer to neonates.

Drug Interactions

No drug interactions are reported for animals.

Instructions for Use
Two dosing forms exist. Microcrystalline is rapidly and completely absorbed. Macrocrystalline (Macrodantin) is more slowly absorbed and causes less GI irritation. Urine should be at acidic pH for maximum effect. Administer with food to increase absorption.

Patient Monitoring and Laboratory Tests
Monitor urine cultures and/or urinalysis. A microbiologic susceptibility test may overestimate the true activity against some bacteria.

Formulations
Macrodantin and generic brands are available in 25, 50, and 100 mg capsules (macrocrystalline) and Furalan, Furatoin, and generic brands are available in 50 and 100 mg tablets (microcrystalline). Furadantin is available in 5 mg/mL oral suspension.

Stability and Storage
Store in tightly sealed container, protected from light, and at room temperature. It is slightly soluble in water and ethanol but <1 mg/mL. It decomposes if exposed to metals other than stainless steel or aluminum.

Small Animal Dosage
Dogs and Cats
- 10 mg/kg/day divided into four daily treatments. Then 1 mg/kg at night PO.
- Macrocrystalline formulation: 2-3 mg/kg q8h PO, followed by 1-2 mg/kg once at nighttime.

Large Animal Dosage
Horses
- 2 mg/kg q8h PO.

Regulatory Information
It is prohibited from use in animals intended for food.

Nitroglycerin
nye-troe-glih'ser-in

Trade and Other Names: Nitrol, Nitro-bid, and Nitrostat

Functional Classification: Vasodilator

Pharmacology and Mechanism of Action
Nitrate. Nitrovasodilator. Like other nitrovasodilators, it relaxes vascular smooth muscle (especially venous) via generation of nitric oxide. Nitric oxide stimulates guanylate cyclase to produce cyclic guanosine monophosphate (GMP) in vascular smooth muscle and relax smooth muscle. Nitric oxide generating compounds may also help decrease gastric adverse effects associated with nonsteroidal antiinflammatory drugs (NSAIDs).

Indications and Clinical Uses
Nitroglycerin, like other nitrovasodilators, is used primarily in heart failure or pulmonary edema to reduce pre-load, or decrease pulmonary hypertension. In people, they are used to treat angina pectoris. In horses, nitroglycerin has been used to improve

N

blood flow to the feet in the management of laminitis. Efficacy is uncertain in horses.

Precautionary Information

Adverse Reactions and Side Effects

Most significant adverse effect is hypotension. Methemoglobinemia can occur with accumulation of nitrites, but it is a rare problem. Tolerance can develop with repeated use.

Contraindications and Precautions

Do not administer to hypotensive patients. Warn pet owners not to apply ointment without wearing gloves.

Drug Interactions

No drug interactions are reported for animals.

Instructions for Use

Tolerance can develop with repeated, chronic use. Use should be intermittent for optimum effect. Nitroglycerin has high presystemic metabolism, and oral availability is poor. When using ointment, 1 inch of ointment is approximately 15 mg.

Patient Monitoring and Laboratory Tests

Monitor patient's blood pressure during therapy.

Formulations

Nitroglycerin is available in 0.5, 0.8, 1, 5, and 10 mg/mL injection, 2% ointment, and transdermal systems (0.2 mg/hr patch).

Stability and Storage

Store in tightly sealed container, protected from light, and at room temperature.

Small Animal Dosage

Dogs

- 4-12 mg (up to 15 mg) topically q12h, ½ to 1.0 inch of 2% ointment on skin q8h.

Cats

- 2-4 mg topically q12h (or ¼ inch of ointment per cat).

Large Animal Dosage

Horses

- Treatment of laminitis: Apply 2% ointment to skin above hoof.

Regulatory Information

Do not administer to animals intended for food.

RCI Classification: 3

Nitroprusside (Sodium Nitroprusside)

nye-troe-pruss′ide

Trade and Other Names: Nitropress

Functional Classification: Vasodilator

Pharmacology and Mechanism of Action

Nitrate vasodilator. Like other nitrovasodilators, it relaxes vascular smooth muscle (especially venous) via generation of nitric oxide. Nitric oxide stimulates guanylate cyclase to produce cyclic guanosine monophosphate (GMP) in vascular smooth muscle and relax smooth muscle. Nitroprusside is used only as an intravenous infusion, and patients should be monitored carefully during administration. Nitroprusside has a rapid onset of effect (almost immediately) and a duration that lasts only minutes after discontinuation of intravenous administration.

Indications and Clinical Uses

Nitroprusside is used for acute management of pulmonary edema and other hypertensive conditions. It is administered only by intravenous infusion, and the dose is titrated carefully by monitoring systemic blood pressure. Titrate to maintain the arterial blood pressure to 70 mm Hg.

Precautionary Information

Adverse Reactions and Side Effects

Severe hypotension is possible during therapy. Reflex tachycardia can occur during treatment. Cyanide is generated via metabolism during nitroprusside treatment, especially at high infusion rates (>5 mcg/kg/min). Cyanide toxicity is possible with nitroprusside therapy. Sodium thiosulfate has been used in people to prevent cyanide toxicity. Methemoglobinemia is possible, and if necessary treated with methylene blue.

Contraindications and Precautions

Do not administer to hypotensive or dehydrated patients.

Drug Interactions

No drug interactions are reported for animals.

Instructions for Use

Nitroprusside is administered via intravenous infusion. Intravenous solution should be delivered in 5% dextrose solution. (For example, add 20-50 mg to 250 mL of 5% dextrose to a concentration of 50 to 200 mcg/mL.) Protect from light with opaque wrapping. Discard solutions if color change is observed. Titrate dose carefully in each patient.

Patient Monitoring and Laboratory Tests

Monitor blood pressure carefully during administration. Do not allow blood pressure to fall below 70 mm Hg during treatment. Monitor heart rate because reflex tachycardia is possible during infusion.

Formulations Available

Nitroprusside is available in 50 mg vial for injection at 10 and 25 mg/mL.

Stability and Storage

Not compatible in some fluids. For IV use, dilute with 5% dextrose. Protect from light and cover infusion solution during administration. Nitroprusside decomposes quickly in alkaline solutions or with exposure to light.

Small Animal Dosage

Dogs and Cats

- 1-5 mcg/kg/min IV, up to a maximum of 10 mcg/kg/min. Generally, start with 2 mcg/kg/min and increase gradually by 1 mcg/kg/min until desired blood pressure is achieved.

Large Animal Dosage

No large animal doses are reported.

Regulatory Information

Withdrawal times are not established for animals that produce food. For extralabel use withdrawal interval estimates, contact FARAD at 1-888-USFARAD (1-888-873-2723) or send e-mail to FARAD@ncsu.edu.

Nizatidine

nih-zah′tih-deen

Trade and Other Names: Axid

Functional Classification: Antiulcer agent

Pharmacology and Mechanism of Action

Histamine H_2-blocking drug. Nizatidine blocks histamine stimulation of gastric parietal cell to decrease gastric acid secretion. It is 4 to 10 times more potent than cimetidine. Nizatidine and ranitidine also have been shown to stimulate gastric emptying and colonic motility via anticholinesterase activity. It is also used to treat gastric ulcers and gastritis.

Indications and Clinical Uses

Nizatidine, like other H_2 receptor blockers, is used to treat ulcers and gastritis. These drugs inhibit secretion of stomach acid and have also been used to prevent ulcers caused from nonsteroidal antiinflammatory drugs (NSAIDs), but the efficacy for this use has not been demonstrated.

Precautionary Information

Adverse Reactions and Side Effects

Side effects from nizatidine have not been reported for animals.

Contraindications and Precautions

No contraindications have been reported for animals.

Drug Interactions

No drug interactions are reported for animals.

Instructions for Use

Results of clinical studies in animals have not been reported. Use in animals (and doses) is based on experience in people or anecdotal experience in animals. Nizatidine use in animals has not been as common as the use of other related drugs such as ranitidine or famotidine.

Patient Monitoring and Laboratory Tests

No specific monitoring is necessary.

Formulations

Nizatidine is available in 150 and 300 mg capsules.

Stability and Storage

Store in tightly sealed container, protected from light, and at room temperature. Nizatidine is slightly soluble in water. Nizatidine has been mixed with juices and syrups for oral administration and was stable for 48 hours. Avoid mixing with Maalox liquid.

Small Animal Dosage

Dogs

- 2.5-5 mg/kg q24h PO.

Large Animal Dosage

No large animal doses are reported.

Regulatory Information

Withdrawal times are not established for animals that produce food. For extralabel use withdrawal interval estimates, contact FARAD at 1-888-USFARAD (1-888-873-2723) or send e-mail to FARAD@ncsu.edu.

RCI Classification: 5

Norfloxacin

nor-floks′ah-sin

Trade and Other Names: Noroxin

Functional Classification: Antibacterial

Pharmacology and Mechanism of Action

Fluoroquinolone antibacterial drug. Norfloxacin acts via inhibition of DNA gyrase in bacteria to inhibit DNA and RNA synthesis. It is a bactericidal with a broad spectrum of activity. Sensitive bacteria include *Staphylococcus, Escherichia coli, Proteus, Klebsiella,* and *Pasteurella. Pseudomonas aeruginosa* is moderately sensitive. However norfloxacin is not as active as other drugs in the fluoroquinolone group.

Indications and Clinical Uses

Norfloxacin has been replaced by other veterinary fluoroquinolones because they have more favorable pharmacokinetics and improved spectrum of activity. However, it has been used to treat a variety of infections, including respiratory, urinary tract, skin, and soft tissue infections.

Precautionary Information

Adverse Reactions and Side Effects

High concentrations may cause CNS toxicity, especially in animals with renal failure. Norfloxacin may cause some nausea, vomiting, and diarrhea at high doses. All of the fluoroquinolones may cause arthropathy in young animals. Dogs are most sensitive at 4 to 28 weeks of age. Large, rapidly growing dogs are the most susceptible.

Contraindications and Precautions

Avoid use in young animals because of risk of cartilage injury. Use cautiously in animals that may be prone to seizures, such as epileptics. Norfloxacin may increase concentrations of theophylline if used concurrently. Coadministration with divalent and trivalent cations, such as products containing aluminum (e.g., sucralfate) may decrease absorption.

Drug Interactions

No drug interactions are reported for animals. However, like other quinolones, coadministration with divalent and trivalent cations, such as products containing aluminum (e.g., sucralfate), iron, and calcium may decrease absorption. Do not mix in solutions or in vials with aluminum, calcium, iron, or zinc, because chelation may occur.

Instructions for Use

Use in animals (and doses) is based on pharmacokinetic studies in experimental animals, experience in people, or anecdotal experience in animals.

Patient Monitoring and Laboratory Tests

Susceptibility testing: CLSI (NCCLS) break points for sensitive organisms are less than or equal to 4 mcg/mL.

Formulations

Norfloxacin is available in 400 mg tablets.

Stability and Storage

Store in tightly sealed container, protected from light, and at room temperature.

Small Animal Dosage

Dogs and Cats

- 22 mg/kg q12h PO.

Large Animal Dosage

No large animal doses have been reported.

Regulatory Information

It is prohibited from use in animals intended for food.

Olsalazine Sodium

ole-sal'ah-zeen soe'dee-um

Trade and Other Names: Dipentum

Functional Classification: Antidiarrheal

Pharmacology and Mechanism of Action

Antiinflammatory drug composed of two molecules of aminosalicylic acid joined by an azo bond. Each component is released in the colon by bacterial enzymes. The released drug is also known as mesalamine. Mesalamine is the active component of sulfasalazine, which is commonly administered for treatment of colitis. The action of mesalamine is not precisely known, but it appears to suppress the metabolism of arachidonic acid in the intestine. It inhibits both cyclo-oxygenase and lipoxygenase-mediated mucosal inflammation. Systemic absorption is small; most of the action is believed to be local. Other formulations of mesalamine include Asacol, Mesasal, and Pentasa. The others are coated tablets designed to release the active component in the intestine.

Indications and Clinical Uses

Olsalazine, like other forms of mesalamine, is used for treatment of inflammatory bowel disease, including colitis in animals. In small animals, most often sulfasalazine is used, however in some animals, olsalazine may be indicated.

Precautionary Information

Adverse Reactions and Side Effects

No adverse effects reported in animals.

Contraindications and Precautions

Do not administer to patients sensitive to salicylate compounds.

Drug Interactions

No drug interactions have been reported for animals.

Instructions for Use

Olsalazine is used in patients that cannot tolerate sulfasalazine.

Patient Monitoring and Laboratory Tests

No specific monitoring is necessary.

Formulations

Olsalazine is available in 500 mg tablets.

Stability and Storage

Store in tightly sealed container, protected from light, and at room temperature.

Small Animal Dosage

Dose not established, but 5-10 mg/kg q8h have been used. (The usual human dose is 500 mg twice daily.)

Large Animal Dosage

No doses are reported for large animals.

Regulatory Information

Withdrawal times are not established for animals that produce food. For extralabel use withdrawal interval estimates, contact FARAD at 1-888-USFARAD (1-888-873-2723) or send e-mail to FARAD@ncsu.edu.
RCI Classification: 4

Omeprazole

oh-mep′rah-zole

Trade and Other Names: Prilosec (formerly Losec; human preparation) GastroGard and UlcerGard (equine preparations)

Functional Classification: Antiulcer agent

Pharmacology and Mechanism of Action

Proton pump inhibitor (PPI). Omeprazole inhibits gastric acid secretion by inhibiting the K^+/H^+ pump (potassium pump). Omeprazole is more potent and longer acting than most available antisecretory drugs. Other proton pump inhibitors include pantoprazole (Protonix), lansoprazole (Prevacid), and rabeprazole (Aciphex). They all act via similar mechanism and are equally effective. PPIs also have some effect for inhibiting *Helicobacter* organisms in the stomach, when administered with antibiotics. Omeprazole is decomposed in the acid environment of the stomach. Therefore, formulations are designed to protect from acid to improve oral absorption. The formulation should not be modified (i.e., crushing of capsules) or the stability will be compromised.

Indications and Clinical Uses

Omeprazole, like other PPIs, is used for treatment and prevention of GI ulcers. It has been used in dogs, cats, and exotic species, but most efficacy data for animals has been produced in horses, in which it has been shown that omeprazole is effective for treating and preventing gastric ulcers. In foals, 4 mg/kg q24h, suppressed acid secretion for 22 hours (by comparison, ranitidine suppressed acid up to 8 hours at a dose of 6.6 mg/kg). In dogs, 1 mg/kg q24h PO is as effective as pantoprazole (1 mg/kg) and famotidine (0.5 mg/kg q12h) for maintaining stomach pH >3-4. Repeated doses may be necessary (2-5 doses) for complete inhibition of acid secretion. Because of their long duration of effect, PPIs may be more effective than other drugs (e.g., histamine H_2 blockers). In studies performed in horses, omeprazole was more effective than ranitidine for treating gastric ulcers. Effects were observed within 14 days, but recurrence was observed after treatment was discontinued. Omeprazole, like other PPIs, may be effective for preventing nonsteroidal antiinflammatory drug- (NSAID) induced ulcers. Omeprazole has been used in combination with other drugs (antibiotics) for treatment of *Helicobacter* infections in animals.

Precautionary Information

Adverse Reactions and Side Effects

Side effects have not been reported in animals. However, in people there is concern about hypergastrinemia with chronic use. Horses have tolerated 20 mg/kg q24h for 91 days and 40 mg/kg q24h PO for 21 days. Overgrowth of *Clostridium* bacteria has been a concern from chronic use because of chronic gastric acid suppression, but the clinical importance of this concern in animals has not been established.

Contraindications and Precautions

No contraindications reported for animals.

Drug Interactions

Although omeprazole has not been associated with drug interactions in animals, PPIs may inhibit some drug metabolizing enzymes (CYP-450 enzymes). Therefore, they may inhibit metabolism of other drugs. Do not administer with drugs that depend on acid stomach for absorption (e.g., ketoconazole and itraconazole).

Instructions for Use

Lansoprazole is a newer drug of this class, but it has not been used in animals. Other PPIs include pantoprazole (Protonix), lansoprazole (Prevacid), and abeprazole (Aciphex). No experience with these other products is reported for veterinary medicine. They are all considered equally efficacious. Pantoprazole and rabeprazole have the advantage in that they are available as tablets that can be crushed, and pantoprazole is less expensive than the other drugs in this class.

Patient Monitoring and Laboratory Tests

Omeprazole and PPIs are generally considered safe. No routine tests for monitoring adverse effects are recommended.

Formulations

Omeprazole is available in 20 mg capsules (human preparation) and in an equine paste, GastroGard. OTC Equine paste is UlcerGard. Paste for horses is 370 mg/g of paste.

Stability and Storage

Omeprazole should be maintained in manufacturer's original formulation (capsules or paste) for optimum stability and effectiveness. It is stable at pH 11, but rapidly decomposes at pH <7.8. Extemporaneously prepared mixtures may not be stable. Studies conducted on compounded formulations have shown that these formulations have low potency.

Small Animal Dosage

Dogs

- 20 mg/dog q24h PO or 0.7 mg/kg q24h PO.

Cats

Dose has not been established, but it has been assumed that the canine dose can be used in cats.

Large Animal Dosage

Horses

- Gastrogard to treat ulcers: 4 mg/kg once daily for 4 weeks PO.
- Gastrogard to prevent ulcers: 1-2 mg/kg q24h PO. (1 mg/kg was effective for prevention in studies performed in horses.)

Ruminants

Oral absorption may not be high enough for effective therapy.

Regulatory Information

Not intended for administration to animals that produce food. Oral absorption in ruminants is not established. Withdrawal times are not established for animals that produce food. For extralabel use withdrawal interval estimates, contact FARAD at 1-888-USFARAD (1-888-873-2723) or send e-mail to FARAD@ncsu.edu.
RCI Classification: 5

Ondansetron Hydrochloride

on-dan'sih-tron hye-droe-klor'ide

Trade and Other Names: Zofran

Functional Classification: Antiemetic

Pharmacology and Mechanism of Action

Antiemetic drug from the class of drugs called serotonin antagonists. Like other drugs of this class, ondansetron acts by inhibiting serotonin (5-HT, type 3) receptors. It is used primarily as an antiemetic during chemotherapy, for which they generally have been superior to other drugs in efficacy. During chemotherapy, there may be 5-HT released from injury to the GI tract that stimulates vomiting centrally, which is blocked by this class of drugs. These drugs also have been used to treat vomiting from other forms of gastroenteritis. Serotonin antagonists used for antiemetic therapy include granisetron, ondansetron, dolasetron, azasetron, and tropisetron.

Indications and Clinical Uses

Ondansetron, like other serotonin antagonists, is used to prevent vomiting. Although it may be effective for treating nausea and vomiting from other sources, the most common use is for preventing vomiting from chemotherapy.

Precautionary Information

Adverse Reactions and Side Effects

Ondansetron adverse effects have not been reported in animals. These drugs have little affinity for other 5-HT receptors. Some effects may be indistinguishable from concurrent cancer drugs.

Contraindications and Precautions

There are no important contraindications identified in animals.

Drug Interactions

No drug interactions reported for animals.

Instructions for Use

Ondansetron has been used in dogs and cats, despite its high expense. Granisetron is a similar drug that has been substituted for a similar purpose.

Patient Monitoring and Laboratory Tests

Monitor GI signs in vomiting patient.

Formulations

Ondansetron is available in 4 and 8 mg tablets, 4 mg/5 mL flavored syrup, and 2 mg/mL injection.

Stability and Storage

Store in tightly sealed container, protected from light, and at room temperature. Ondansetron is soluble in water. Solutions are stable, but pH should be <6 to prevent precipitation. Oral preparations have been mixed with syrups, juices, and other oral vehicles (e.g., Ora Sweet). It was stable for 42 days as long as pH remained low.

Small Animal Dosage

Dogs and Cats

- 0.5 to 1.0 mg/kg 30 min prior to administration of cancer drugs IV or PO.
- Vomiting from other causes: 0.1-0.2 mg/kg slow IV injection and repeated q6-12h.

Large Animal Dosage

None available.

Regulatory Information

No regulatory information is available. Because of low risk of residues, no withdrawal times are suggested.

O

Orbifloxacin

or-bih-floks'ah sin

Trade and Other Names: Orbax

Functional Classification: Antibacterial

Pharmacology and Mechanism of Action

Fluoroquinolone antimicrobial. Orbifloxacin acts via inhibition of DNA gyrase in bacteria to inhibit DNA and RNA synthesis. It is a bactericidal with a broad spectrum of activity. Spectrum includes staphylococci, gram-negative bacilli, and some *Pseudomonas* species. In dogs the half-life is 5.6 hours; in cats the half-life is 5.5 hours. In both species the oral absorption is nearly 100%. In horses, it has a half-life of 5 hours and oral absorption of 68%.

Indications and Clinical Uses

Orbifloxacin is registered for use in dogs and cats. Like other fluoroquinolones, it is used to treat susceptible bacteria in a variety of species. Treatment of infections has included skin, soft tissue, and UTIs in dogs and cats and soft tissue infections in horses.

Precautionary Information

Adverse Reactions and Side Effects

High concentrations may cause CNS toxicity, especially in animals with renal failure. It may cause some nausea, vomiting, and diarrhea at high doses. All of the fluoroquinolones may cause arthropathy in young animals. Dogs are most sensitive at 4 to 28 weeks of age. Large, rapidly growing dogs are the most susceptible. Blindness in cats have been reported from administration of some quinolones (nalidixic acid and enrofloxacin), but at doses up to 15 mg/kg, orbifloxacin has not produced this effect.

Contraindications and Precautions

Avoid use in young animals because of risk of cartilage injury. Use cautiously in animals that may be prone to seizures, such as epileptics.

Drug Interactions

Fluoroquinolones may increase concentrations of theophylline if used concurrently. Coadministration with divalent and trivalent cations, such as products containing aluminum, (e.g., sucralfate), iron, and calcium, may decrease absorption. Do not mix in solutions or in vials with aluminum, calcium, iron, or zinc, because chelation may occur.

Instructions for Use

At the registered label dose, orbifloxacin is active against most susceptible bacteria. Within the approved dose range, higher doses are needed for organisms with higher minimum inhibitory concentration (MIC) values.

Patient Monitoring and Laboratory Tests

Susceptibility testing: CLSI (NCCLS) break point for sensitive organisms is less than or equal to 1 mcg/mL. Other fluoroquinolones may be used in some cases to estimate susceptibility to this fluoroquinolone. However, other drugs may have lower MIC values for *Pseudomonas aeruginosa*. Against *P. aeruginosa,* ciprofloxacin has greater *in vitro* activity.

Formulations

Orbifloxacin is available in 5.7, 22.7, and 68 mg tablets.

Stability and Storage

Store in tightly sealed container, protected from light, and at room temperature. Orbifloxacin is slightly water soluble. It has been mixed with various syrups, flavorings, and vehicles and was stable at room temperature for 7 days. Do not mix with vehicles that contain aluminum, calcium, or iron as this may decrease oral absorption via chelation.

Small Animal Dosage

Dogs and Cats

- 2.5-7.5 mg/kg q24h PO.

Large Animal Dosage

Horses

- 5 mg/kg q24h PO.

Regulatory Information

Do not use fluoroquinolones off-label to animals that produce food. Orbifloxacin is prohibited from use in animals intended for food.

Ormetoprim + Sulfadimethoxine

or-met′oe-prim + sul-fa-dye-meth-oks′een

Trade and Other Names: Primor

Functional Classification: Antibacterial

Pharmacology and Mechanism of Action

Antibacterial drug. Ormetoprim sulfadimethoxine is a synergistic combination similar to trimethoprim sulfonamide combinations. Ormetoprim inhibits bacterial dihydrofolate reductase, and sulfonamide competes with para-aminobenzoic acid (PABA) for synthesis of nucleic acids. Bactericidal/bacteriostatic. It has a broad antibacterial spectrum that includes common gram-positive and gram-negative bacteria. It also is active against some coccidia.

Indications and Clinical Uses

Ormetoprim + sulfadimethoxine is used in small animals to treat a variety of bacterial infections caused by susceptible organisms, including pneumonia, skin, soft tissue, and UTIs in dogs and cats. In horses, it may be administered orally (see dosing section) for infections caused by susceptible gram-positive bacteria (*Actinomyces, Streptococcus* spp., and *Staphylococcus* spp.), but higher doses may be needed for gram-negative infections.

Precautionary Information

Adverse Reactions and Side Effects

Adverse effects associated with sulfonamides include allergic reactions, Type II and III hypersensitivity, arthropathy, anemia, thrombocytopenia, hepatopathy, hypothyroidism (with prolonged therapy), keratoconjunctivitis sicca, and skin reactions. Dogs may be more sensitive to sulfonamides than other animals because dogs lack the ability to acetylate sulfonamides to metabolites. Other, more toxic metabolites may persist. Ormetoprim has been associated with some CNS effects in dogs, which include behavioral changes, anxiety, muscle tremors, and seizures. In horses when IV doses were administered to experimental horses (IV formulation not commercially available), nervous system reactions such as tremors and muscle fasciculations were observed.

Contraindications and Precautions

Do not administer to animals sensitive to sulfonamides.

Drug Interactions

Sulfonamides may interact with other drugs, including warfarin, methenamine, and etodolac. They may potentiate adverse effects caused by methotrexate and pyrimethamine.

Instructions for Use

Doses listed are based on manufacturer's recommendations. Controlled trials have demonstrated efficacy for treatment of pyoderma on once daily schedule.

Patient Monitoring and Laboratory Tests

Monitor tear production with long-term use. For susceptibility testing, break point ranges have not been determined for ormetoprim + sulfadimethoxine. Use a test for trimethoprim-sulfonamide as a guide for susceptibility to ormetoprim + sulfadimethoxine. CLSI (NCCLS) break point for susceptible organisms is ≤2/38 mcg/mL (trimethoprim/sulfonamide).

Formulations

Ormetoprim + sulfadimethoxine is available in 120, 240, 600, and 1200 mg tablets in 5:1 ratio of sulfadimethoxine:ormetoprim.

Stability and Storage

Store in tightly sealed container, protected from light, and at room temperature.

Small Animal Dosage

Dogs

- 27 mg/kg on first day, followed by 13.5 mg/kg q24h PO. (All doses are based on the combined mg of both ormetoprim and sulfadimethoxine.)

Cats

Although doses are not reported by manufacturer, doses similar to those for dogs have been administered.

Large Animal Dosage

Horses

- Loading dose of 55 mg/kg (of the combined drugs) followed by 27.5 mg/kg (of the combined drugs) q24h PO.

Regulatory Information

Withdrawal times are not established for animals that produce food. Oral absorption has not been established for ruminants. For extralabel use withdrawal interval estimates, contact FARAD at 1-888-USFARAD (1-888-873-2723) or send e-mail to FARAD@ncsu.edu.

Oxacillin Sodium

oks-ah-sill'in soe'dee-um

Trade and Other Names: Pro-staphlin and generic brands

Functional Classification: Antibacterial

Pharmacology and Mechanism of Action

Beta-lactam antibiotic. Oxacillin, like other beta-lactam antibiotics, binds penicillin-binding proteins (PBP) that weaken or interfere with cell wall formation. After binding to PBP, the cell wall weakens or undergoes lysis. Like other beta-lactams, this drug acts in a time-dependent manner (i.e., it is more effective when drug concentrations are maintained above the minimum inhibitory concentrations [MIC] during the dose interval). Oxacillin has a limited spectrum of activity that includes primarily gram-positive bacteria. Resistance is common, especially among enteric gram-negative bacilli. Staphylococci are susceptible because oxacillin is resistant to the bacterial beta-lactamase produced by *Staphylococcus* spp.

Indications and Clinical Uses

Oxacillin has been used in small animals for treating soft tissue infections caused by gram-positive bacteria. Most common use has been for pyoderma in dogs. Use has diminished because of increased availability of other drugs, such as oral cephalosporins and amoxicillin-clavulanate.

Precautionary Information

Adverse Reactions and Side Effects

Adverse effects of penicillin-like drugs are most commonly caused by drug allergy. This can range from acute anaphylaxis when administered or other signs of allergic reaction when other routes are used. When administered orally, diarrhea is possible, especially with high doses.

Contraindications and Precautions

Use cautiously in animals allergic to penicillin-like drugs.

Drug Interactions

No drug interactions are reported. Food may inhibit oral absorption.

Instructions for Use

Doses based on empiricism or extrapolation from human studies. No clinical efficacy studies available for dogs or cats. Administer, if possible, on empty stomach.

Patient Monitoring and Laboratory Tests

Culture and sensitivity testing: CLSI (NCCLS) break points for sensitive organisms is less than or equal to 2 mcg/mL for *Staphylococcus.* If staphylococci are resistant to oxacillin, they should be interpreted as being resistant to all cephalosporins and penicillins regardless of sensitivity result. Oxacillin resistance is usually interpreted as equivalent to methicillin resistance, therefore oxacillin-resistant staphylococci are also referred to as methicillin-resistant *Staphylococcus aureus* (MRSA).

Formulations

Oxacillin is available in 250 and 500 mg capsules and 50 mg/mL oral solution.

Stability and Storage

Store in tightly sealed container, protected from light, and at room temperature. Oxacillin is soluble in water and alcohol. Reconstituted oral solution is stable for 3 days at room temperature and 14 days in the refrigerator.

Small Animal Dosage

Dogs and Cats

- 22-40 mg/kg q8h PO.

Large Animal Dosage

No doses are reported. Oral absorption has not been established for large animals.

Regulatory Information

Withdrawal times are not established for animals that produce food. Oral absorption has not been established for ruminants. For extralabel use withdrawal interval estimates, contact FARAD at 1-888-USFARAD (1-888-873-2723) or send e-mail to FARAD@ncsu.edu.

Oxazepam

oks-ay′zeh-pam

Trade and Other Names: Serax

Functional Classification: Anticonvulsant

Pharmacology and Mechanism of Action

Benzodiazepine. Oxazepam is a central acting CNS depressant with action similar to diazepam. Mechanism of action appears to be via potentiation of GABA-receptor mediated effects in CNS. Oxazepam is one of the active products of metabolism from diazepam. In contrast to diazepam, oxazepam does not undergo extensive hepatic metabolism in animals, but it is glucuronidated before excretion.

Indications and Clinical Uses

Oxazepam is used for sedation and to stimulate appetite. As a benzodiazepine it also may be considered for behavior problems and anxiety disorders in animals, but it has not been used as commonly as other drugs.

Precautionary Information

Adverse Reactions and Side Effects

Sedation is the most common side effect. It may also produce polyphagia. Some animals may experience paradoxical excitement. Chronic administration may lead to dependence and a withdrawal syndrome if discontinued.

Contraindications and Precautions

Oral administration of another benzodiazepine—diazepam—has caused idiosyncratic liver injury in cats. It is not known if the same concern applies to oxazepam—which is a metabolite of diazepam—although no cases of liver injury from oxazepam have been reported.

Drug Interactions

Use cautiously with other drugs that may cause sedation.

Instructions for Use

Doses based on empiricism. There have been no clinical trials in veterinary medicine, although it is widely believed to increase the appetite in cats.

Patient Monitoring and Laboratory Tests

Samples of plasma or serum may be analyzed for concentrations of benzodiazepines. Plasma concentrations in the range of 100-250 ng/mL have been cited as the therapeutic range for people. Other references have cited this range as 150-300 ng/mL. However, there are no readily available tests for monitoring in many veterinary laboratories. Laboratories that analyze human samples may have nonspecific tests for benzodiazepines. With these assays, there may be cross-reactivity among benzodiazepine metabolites.

Formulations

Oxazepam is available in 15 mg tablets.

Stability and Storage

Stable if stored in manufacturer's original formulation. Although oxazepam has been compounded for veterinary use, the potency and stability has not been evaluated for compounded products.

Small Animal Dosage

Cats

- Behavior disorders: 0.2-0.5 mg/kg q12-24h PO or 1-2 mg/cat q12h PO.
- Appetite stimulant: 2.5 mg/cat PO.

Dogs

- Behavior disorders or sedation: 0.2-1.0 mg/kg q12-24h PO.

Large Animal Dosage
No doses reported for large animals.

Regulatory Information
Do not administer to animals intended for food.
Schedule IV controlled drug
RCI Classification: 2

Oxfendazole
oks-fen′dah-zole

Trade and Other Names: Benzelmin and Synanthic

Functional Classification: Antiparasitic

Pharmacology and Mechanism of Action
Antiparasitic drug. Oxfendazole belongs to the benzimidazole class of antiparasitic drugs. Like other benzimidazole drugs it produces a degeneration of the parasite microtubule and irreversibly blocks glucose uptake in parasites. Inhibition of glucose uptake causes depletion of energy stores in parasites, eventually resulting in death. However, there is no effect on glucose metabolism in mammals. It is used to treat intestinal parasites in animals.

Indications and Clinical Uses
Oxfendazole is used in horses for treatment of large roundworms (*Parascaris equorum*), mature and immature pinworms (*Oxyuris equi*), large strongyles (*Strongylus edentatus, Strongylus vulgaris,* and *Strongylus equinus*), and small strongyles. In cattle, fendazole is used for treatment of lungworms (*Dictyocaulus viviparus*), stomach worms (barberpole worms [*Haemonchus contortus* and *H. placei,* adult]), small stomach worms (*Trichostrongylus axei,* adult), brown stomach worms (*Ostertagia ostertagi*), intestinal worms, nodular worms (*Oesophagostomum radiatum,* adult), hookworms (*Bunostomum phlebotomum,* adult), small intestinal worms (*Cooperia punctata, C. oncophora,* and *C. momasteri*), and tapeworms (*Moniezia benedeni,* adult).

O

Precautionary Information
Adverse Reactions and Side Effects

Adverse reactions are rare.

Contraindications and Precautions

Do not administer to sick or debilitated horses. Do not administer to female dairy cattle of breeding age.

Drug Interactions

No drug interactions are reported.

Instructions for Use
Administer to horses by mixing in a suspension and administer orally (e.g., via stomach tube) or mixing pellets with food. Administer to cattle orally with a dose syringe or intraruminally with a rumen injector. Treatment may be repeated in 6-8 weeks in horses or in 4-6 weeks in cattle.

Patient Monitoring and Laboratory Tests
No specific monitoring is necessary.

Formulations

Oxfendazole is available in 90.6 or 225 mg/mL suspension (cattle), 185 mg/gram paste (cattle), 0.375 grams per gram of paste (equine), 90.6 mg/mL suspension (equine), and 6.49 % pellets (equine).

Stability and Storage

Store in tightly sealed container, protected from light, and at room temperature. After mixing for oral administration, discard unused portion after 24 hours. Mix well before using, do not freeze suspension and avoid excessive heat.

Small Animal Dosage

Dogs and Cats

Dose not established.

Large Animal Dosage

Horses

- 10 mg/kg PO.

Cattle

- 4.5 mg/kg PO.

Regulatory Information

Do not use in dairy cattle.
Cattle withdrawal time: 7 days for suspension; 11 days for paste.

Oxibendazole

oks-ih-ben′dah-zole

Trade and Other Names: Anthelcide EQ

Functional Classification: Antiparasitic

Pharmacology and Mechanism of Action

Antiparasitic drug. Oxibendazole belongs to the benzimidazole class of antiparasitic drugs. Like other benzimidazole drugs, it produces a degeneration of the parasite microtubule and irreversibly blocks glucose uptake in parasites. Inhibition of glucose uptake causes depletion of energy stores in parasites, eventually resulting in death. However, there is no effect on glucose metabolism in mammals. It is used to treat intestinal parasites in animals.

Indications and Clinical Uses

Oxibendazole is used in horses for treatment of large strongyles (*Strongylus edentatus, S. equinus,* and *S. vulgaris*), small strongyles (species of the genera *Cylicostephanus, Cylicocyclus, Cyathostomum, Triodontophorus Cylicodontophorus,* and *Gyalocephalus*), large roundworms (*Parascaris equorum*), pinworms (*Oxyuris equi*) including various larval stages, and threadworms, (*Strongyloides westeri*).

Formulations for dogs may contain both diethylcarbamazine citrate and oxibendazole, for prevention of *Dirofilaria immitis* (heartworm disease), *Ancylostoma caninum* (hookworm infection), for treatment of *Trichuris vulpis* (whipworm infection), and intestinal *Toxocara canis* (ascarid infection).

Precautionary Information

Adverse Reactions and Side Effects

Adverse reactions are rare. Occasional vomiting and nausea may occur in dogs.

Contraindications and Precautions

Do not administer to dogs that may have heartworms.

Drug Interactions

No drug interactions are reported.

Instructions for Use

Administer suspension to horses by mixing with 1-2 liters of water (3-4 pints) and administer orally (e.g., via stomach tube). Alternatively mix powder with grain ration or use the paste. Horses should be retreated in 6 to 8 weeks if they are re-exposed. For dogs, medication may be mixed with food daily.

Patient Monitoring and Laboratory Tests

No specific monitoring is necessary.

Formulations

Oxibendazole is available in 10% suspension, 22.7% paste, 60, 120, and 180 mg diethylcarbamazine citrate + 45, 91, and 136 mg oxibendazole tablets.

Stability and Storage

Store in tightly sealed container, protected from light, and at room temperature. Mix well before using, do not freeze suspension and avoid excessive heat.

Small Animal Dosage

Dogs

- 5 mg/kg oxibendazole (combined with 6.6 mg/kg diethylcarbamazine) q24h PO.

Cats

No dose established.

Large Animal Dosage

Horses

- 10 mg/kg PO.
- Threadworms: 15 mg/kg PO once. Re-treat in 6 to 8 weeks if necessary.

Regulatory Information

No withdrawal times are established.

Withdrawal times are not established for animals that produce animals. For extralabel use withdrawal interval estimates, contact FARAD at 1-888-USFARAD (1-888-873-2723) or send e-mail to FARAD@ncsu.edu.

Oxtriphylline

oks-trih'fih-lin

Trade and Other Names: Choledyl-SA

Functional Classification: Bronchodilator

Pharmacology and Mechanism of Action

Choline theophyllinate. Methylxanthine bronchodilator. Free theophylline is released after absorption. Mechanism of action is unknown but may be related to increased cyclic adenosine monophosphate (AMP) levels or antagonism of adenosine. There appears to be antiinflammatory action as well as bronchodilating action.

Indications and Clinical Uses

Oxtriphylline is used for similar respiratory conditions as for theophylline. It is indicated in patients with reversible bronchoconstriction, such as cats with bronchial asthma or dogs with airway disease. Large animal uses have not been reported.

Precautionary Information

Adverse Reactions and Side Effects

Adverse effects include nausea, vomiting, and diarrhea. With high doses, tachycardia, excitement, tremors, and seizures are possible. Cardiovascular and CNS adverse effects appear to be less frequent in dogs than people.

Contraindications and Precautions

Some patients may be at a higher risk for adverse effects. Such patients may include animals with cardiac disease, animals prone to arrhythmias, and animals at risk for seizures.

Drug Interactions

Drugs that inhibit cytochrome P450 enzymes may increase drug concentrations and cause toxicity. See Appendix for list of drugs that may be P450 inhibitors.

Instructions for Use

Some formulations (Theocon) contain oxtriphylline and guaifenesin. When administering slow release tablet, do not crush tablet.

Patient Monitoring and Laboratory Tests

Therapeutic drug monitoring is recommended for chronic therapy. Interpretation of theophylline concentrations should be used to guide therapy. Generally, 10-20 mcg/mL is considered therapeutic.

Formulations

Oxtriphylline is available in 400 and 600 mg tablets. (Oral solutions and syrup are available in Canada but not in the U.S.)

Stability and Storage

Store in tightly sealed container, protected from light, and at room temperature.

Small Animal Dosage

Dogs

- 47 mg/kg (equivalent to 30 mg/kg theophylline) q12h PO.

Large Animal Dosage

No doses have been reported for large animals. Oral absorption has not been established for ruminants.

Regulatory Information

Withdrawal times are not established for animals that produce food. For extralabel use withdrawal interval estimates, contact FARAD at 1-888-USFARAD (1-888-873-2723) or send e-mail to FARAD@ncsu.edu.

Oxybutynin Chloride

oks-ih-byoo′tih-nin klor′ide

Trade and Other Names: Ditropan

Functional Classification: Anticholinergic

Pharmacology and Mechanism of Action

Anticholinergic agent. Oxybutynin produces an anticholinergic effect via blockade of muscarinic receptors. It will produce a general anticholinergic effect, but the predominant effect is on the urinary bladder. It inhibits smooth muscle spasms via blocking action of acetylcholine. It does not block skeletal muscle, autonomic ganglia, or receptors on blood vessels. A related drug used in people is tolterodine (Detrol).

Indications and Clinical Uses

Oxybutynin chloride has been used primarily to increase bladder capacity and to decrease spasms of urinary tract. In people it is used to treat urinary incontinence, but the use in animals is not common.

Precautionary Information

Adverse Reactions and Side Effects

Adverse effects are related to anticholinergic effects (atropine-like effects), but they are less frequent compared to other anticholinergic drugs. Constipation, dry mouth, and dry mucous membranes are possible from routine use. Administer physostigmine for treatment of overdose.

Contraindications and Precautions

Use cautiously in animals with heart disease or decreased intestinal motility. Use cautiously in animals with glaucoma.

Drug Interactions

Oxybutynin will potentiate other antimuscarinic drugs.

Instructions for Use

Results of clinical studies in animals have not been reported. Use in animals (and doses) is based on experience in people or anecdotal experience in animals. Although it increases urine retention, it may not be effective to treat incontinence in animals with decreased sphincter tone.

Patient Monitoring and Laboratory Tests

No specific monitoring is necessary.

Formulations

Oxybutynin is available in 5 mg tablets and 1 mg/mL oral syrup.

Stability and Storage

Store in tightly sealed container, protected from light, and at room temperature. Oxybutynin is soluble in water and ethanol.

Small Animal Dosage

Dogs

- 5 mg/dog q6-8h PO.

Large Animal Dosage

No doses have been reported for large animals.

Regulatory Information

Withdrawal times are not established for animals that produce food. Oral absorption has not been established for ruminants. For extralabel use withdrawal interval estimates, contact FARAD at 1-888-USFARAD (1-888-873-2723) or send e-mail to FARAD@ncsu.edu.

Oxymetholone

oks-ih-meth′oh-lone

Trade and Other Names: Anadrol

Functional Classification: Hormone, Anabolic agent

Pharmacology and Mechanism of Action

Anabolic steroid. Oxymetholone is a derivative of testosterone. Anabolic agents are designed to maximize anabolic effects, while minimizing androgenic action. Anabolic agents have been used for reversing catabolic conditions, increase weight gain, increasing muscling in animals, and stimulating erythropoiesis. Other anabolic agents include boldenone, nandrolone, stanozolol, and methyltestosterone.

Indications and Clinical Uses

Anabolic agents have been used for reversing catabolic conditions, increase weight gain, increasing muscling in animals, and stimulating erythropoiesis. Although other anabolic agents have been used in animals (methyltestosterone and stanozolol) there are no differences in efficacy among the anabolic steroids demonstrated in animals.

Precautionary Information

Adverse Reactions and Side Effects

Adverse effects from anabolic steroids can be attributed to the pharmacologic action of these steroids. Increased masculine effects are common. Increased incidence of some tumors have been reported in people. The 17a-methylated oral anabolic steroids (oxymetholone, stanozolol, and oxandrolone) have been associated with hepatic toxicity.

Contraindications and Precautions

Do not use in pregnant animals.

Drug Interactions

No drug interactions are reported.

Instructions for Use

Results of clinical studies in animals have not been reported. Use in animals (and doses) is based on experience in people or anecdotal experience in animals.

Patient Monitoring and Laboratory Tests

Monitor hepatic enzymes for evidence of cholestasis and hepatotoxicity.

Formulations

Oxymetholone is available in 50 mg tablets.

Stability and Storage

Store in tightly sealed container, protected from light, and at room temperature.

Small Animal Dosage

Dogs and Cats

- 1-5 mg/kg/day PO.

Large Animal Dosage

No doses reported for large animals.

Regulatory Information

Oxymetholone is a schedule III controlled drug.
Do not administer to animals intended for food.
RCI Classification: 4

Oxymorphone Hydrochloride

oks-ih-mor'fone hye-droe-klor'ide

Trade and Other Names: Numorphan

Functional Classification: Analgesic, Opioid

Pharmacology and Mechanism of Action

Opioid agonist, analgesic. Action is similar to morphine, except that oxymorphone is more lipophilic than morphine and 10 to 15 times more potent than morphine. Action is to bind to mu-opiate and kappa-opiate receptors on nerves and inhibit release of neurotransmitters involved with transmission of pain stimuli (such as Substance P). Central sedative and euphoric effects related to mu-receptor effects in brain. Other opiates used in animals include hydromorphone, codeine, morphine, meperidine, and fentanyl.

Indications and Clinical Uses

Oxymorphone is indicated for short-term analgesia, sedation, and as an adjunct to anesthesia. It is compatible with most anesthetics and can be used as part of a multimodal approach to analgesia/anesthesia. Although oxymorphone is registered for dogs, other opiates are used more commonly such as hydromorphone and morphine. Administration of oxymorphone may lower dose requirements for other anesthetics and analgesics used. Duration of action in dogs is short (2-4 hours). The oral dose formulations should not be relied upon for treating severe pain in dogs.

Precautionary Information

Adverse Reactions and Side Effects

Like all opiates, side effects from oxymorphone are predictable and unavoidable. Side effects from opiate administration include sedation, vomiting, constipation, urinary retention, and bradycardia. Panting may occur in dogs as a result of changes in thermoregulation. Histamine release, known to occur from administration of morphine, may be less likely with oxymorphone. Excitement can occur in some animals, but it is more common in cats and horses. Respiratory depression occurs with high doses. As with other opiates, a slight decrease in heart rate is expected. In most cases this decrease does not have to be treated with anticholinergic drugs (e.g., atropine), but should be monitored. Tolerance and dependence occurs with chronic administration. In horses, undesirable and even dangerous behavior actions can follow rapid intravenous opioid administration. Horses should receive a pre-anesthetic of acepromazine or an $alpha_2$ agonist.

Contraindications and Precautions

Oxymorphone is a schedule II controlled substance. Cats and horses may be more sensitive to opiates.

Drug Interactions

Like other opiates, it will potentiate other drugs that cause CNS depression.

Instructions for Use

There is some evidence that oxymorphone may have fewer cardiovascular effects compared to morphine. Because oxymorphone is more lipophilic than morphine, it is readily absorbed from epidural injection. Oxymorphone may be used with acepromazine, and together they have synergistic effects.

Patient Monitoring and Laboratory Tests

Monitor patient's heart rate and respiration. Although bradycardia rarely needs to be treated when it is caused by an opioid, atropine can be administered if necessary. If serious respiratory depression occurs, the opioid can be reversed with naloxone.

Formulations

Oxymorphone is available in 1.5 and 1 mg/mL injection.

Stability and Storage

pH of solution is 2.7-4.5. Oxymorphone is compatible with most fluid solutions. Store in tightly sealed container, protected from light, and at room temperature.

Small Animal Dosage

Dogs and Cats

- Analgesia: 0.1-0.2 mg/kg IV SQ or IM (as needed), re-dose with 0.05-0.1 mg/kg q1-2h.
- Preanesthetic: 0.025-0.05 mg/kg IM or SQ.
- Sedation: 0.05-0.2 mg/kg (with or without acepromazine) IM or SQ.

Large Animal Dosage

No doses have been reported for large animals.

Regulatory Information

Schedule II controlled drug
RCI Classification: 1

Oxytetracycline

oks'ih-tet-rah-sye'kleen

Trade and Other Names: Terramycin, Terramycin soluble powder, Terramycin scours tablets, Biomycin, Oxy-Tet, Oxybiotic Oxy 500, and Oxy 1000. Long-acting formulations include Liquamycin-LA 200 and Biomycin 200.

Functional Classification: Antibacterial

Pharmacology and Mechanism of Action

Tetracycline antibiotic. Mechanism of action of tetracyclines is to bind to 30S ribosomal subunit and inhibit protein synthesis. Oxytetracycline is usually bacteriostatic. It has a broad spectrum of activity including gram-positive and gram-negative bacteria, some protozoa, *Rickettsiae,* and *Ehrlichiae.* The spectrum also includes *Chlamydia,* spirochetes, *Mycoplasma,* L-form bacteria, and some protozoa (*Plasmodium* and *Entameba*). Resistance is common among gram-negative bacteria of the *Enterobacteriaceae* (e.g., *Escherichia coli*). Oxytetracycline has been available in a variety of formulations to control the release rate from an injection. Vehicles include polyethylene glycol, propylene glycol, povidone, or pyrrolidine. Oxytetracycline may be better absorbed orally than tetracycline.

Indications and Clinical Uses

Oxytetracycline is used to treat infections of the respiratory tract (pneumonia), urinary tract, soft tissues, and dermis. It is used for infections caused by a wide spectrum of bacteria, except that resistance is common among gram-negative bacilli of enteric origin and staphylococci. One of the most common uses is in cattle for treatment of bovine respiratory disease (BRD) caused by *Pasteurella multocida, Mannheimia haemolytica,* and *Histophilus somni* (formerly *Haemophilus somnus*). In pigs, tetracyclines have been used to treat atrophic rhinitis, pneumonic pasteurellosis, and *Mycoplasma* infections. In small animals, doxycycline, rather than oxytetracycline, is used as a treatment for *Rickettsiae* and *Ehrlichiae.* In newborn horses, oxytetracycline has been administered at high doses for the purpose of correcting angular limb deformities. The doses have been as high as 50-70 mg/kg IV q48h. There is no known explanation for the effect of oxytetracycline on tendon or ligament laxity in horses.

Precautionary Information

Adverse Reactions and Side Effects

Tetracyclines may cause renal tubular necrosis at high doses. Tetracyclines can affect bone and teeth formation in young animals. Tetracyclines have been implicated in drug fever in cats. Hepatotoxicity may occur at high doses in susceptible individuals. Oxytetracycline administration to horses has been associated with colic and diarrhea.

Contraindications and Precautions

Use cautiously in young animals as teeth discoloration is possible. Avoid injection volumes for IM >10 mL per site in cattle and >5 mL in pigs.

Drug Interactions

Tetracyclines bind to compounds containing calcium, which decreases oral absorption. Do not mix with solutions that contain iron, calcium, aluminum, or magnesium.

Instructions for Use

Oral dose forms are from large animal use. Use of injectable long-acting forms have not been studied in small animals. Use of tetracyclines in small animals has primarily relied on doxycycline. When using long-acting formulations in cattle, the long-acting properties only apply to intramuscular use, not intravenous administration. When products that are long-acting are compared to conventional injectable products, the long-acting products usually allow for longer dose intervals. However, in pigs, there were no differences in duration of plasma concentrations when equivalent doses were administered.

Patient Monitoring and Laboratory Tests

Susceptibility testing: CLSI (NCCLS) break points for sensitive organisms are less than or equal to 2 mcg/mL for streptococci and less than or equal to 4 for other organism. However, based on plasma concentrations achieved, a break point of less than or equal to 1 mcg/mL for all organisms is more realistic. Tetracycline is used as a marker to test susceptibility for other drugs in this class, such as doxycycline and minocycline.

Formulations

Oxytetracycline is available in 250 mg tablets, 500 mg bolus, 100 and 200 mg/mL injection, and 25, 166, and 450 g/lb of powder. Long-acting formulations are available in 200 mg/mL injection.

Stability and Storage

Store in tightly sealed container, protected from light, and at room temperature. If solutions are diluted prior to injection, they should be discarded if not used immediately. Solution may darken slightly without losing potency.

Small Animal Dosage

Dogs and Cats

- 7.5-10 mg/kg q12h IV or 20 mg/kg q12h PO.

Large Animal Dosage

Horses

- Treatment of Ehrlichiosis: 10 mg/kg q24h IM or IV (slowly).

Foals

- Treatment of flexural limb deformities: 44 mg/kg, up to 70 mg/kg (2-3 grams per foal), two doses, 24 hours apart.

Calves

- 11 mg/kg/day PO.
- Treatment of pneumonia: 11 mg/kg q12h PO.

Cattle

- Injection for treatment of anaplasmosis, enteritis, pneumonia, and other infections: 11 mg/kg q12h IV.
- Long-acting formulations: 20 mg/kg as a single dose.

Pigs

- 6.6-11 mg/kg, up to 10-20 mg/kg q24h IM or 20 mg/kg q48h IM.

Regulatory Information

Cattle and pig withdrawal times (meat): 7 days (oral tablets). For oral soluble powder, the withdrawal times vary greatly from one product to another for cattle and pigs. Generally, they are at least 5 days for meat, but consult specific product label for withdrawal times.

Cattle withdrawal times for injection: 18-22 days, depending on the product.

Cattle withdrawal times for long-acting formulations: 28 days.

Cattle withdrawal times (milk): 96 hours at a dose of 20 mg/kg.

Cattle withdrawal times (intrauterine administration): 168 hour (milk) and 28 days (meat).

Pig withdrawal times: 28 days and up to 42 days, depending on product.

Oxytocin

oks-ih-toe'sin

Trade and Other Names: Pitocin, Syntocinon (nasal solution), and generic brands

Functional Classification: Labor induction

Pharmacology and Mechanism of Action

Oxytocin stimulates uterine muscle contraction via action on specific oxytocin receptors.

Indications and Clinical Uses

Oxytocin is used to induce or maintain normal labor and delivery in pregnant animals. In surgery it may be used postoperatively following cesarean section to facilitate involution and resistance to the large inflow of blood. In large animals, oxytocin is used to augment uterine contractions and stimulate lactation. It will contract smooth muscle cells of the mammary gland for milk letdown if the udder is in proper physiological state. It is also used to expel placenta after delivery. However, efficacy for retained placenta is questionable, and some experts believe that estrogen should be administered in addition to oxytocin. Oxytocin does not increase milk production, but it will stimulate contraction leading to milk ejection.

Precautionary Information

Adverse Reactions and Side Effects

Adverse effects are uncommon if used carefully. However, careful monitoring of labor is necessary during its use.

Contraindications and Precautions

Do not administer to pregnant animals unless for induction of parturition. Do not administer unless cervix is fully relaxed. Do not use if there is abnormal presentation of fetus.

Drug Interactions

Beta-adrenergic agonists will inhibit induction of labor.

Instructions for Use

Oxytocin is used to induce labor. In people, oxytocin is administered via injection, constant intravenous infusion, and intranasal solution.

Patient Monitoring and Laboratory Tests

Fetal stress and progression of normal labor should be monitored closely.

Formulations

Oxytocin is available in 10 and 20 units/mL injection and 40 units/mL nasal solution.

Stability and Storage

Store in tightly sealed container, protected from light, and at room temperature.

Small Animal Dosage

Dogs

- 5-20 units per dog IM or SQ, (repeat every 30 min for primary inertia). **Note:** manufacturer's label lists higher doses of 5-30 units per dog.

Cats

- 2.5-3 units per cat IM or IV. Repeat up to 3 times every 30-60 minutes. (Maximum dose is 3 units/cat).

Large Animal Dosage

The following doses are all on a *per animal* basis rather than a *per kilogram* basis.

Cattle

- To stimulate uterine contractions: 30 units IM and repeat in 30 minutes if necessary. (Manufacturer lists 100 units per cow.)
- For retained placenta: 20 units IM given immediately after calving and repeated in 2-4 hours.
- For milk letdown: 10-20 units per cow, IV or IM.

Mares

- To stimulate uterine contractions: 20 units IM. (Manufacturer lists 100 units per mare.)
- For retained placenta: 30-40 units IM at 60-90 minute intervals or add 80-100 units to 500 mL saline solution and give IV.

Small Ruminants and Sows

- 5-10 Units IM. (Manufacturer lists 30-50 units per animal.)

Regulatory Information

No withdrawal times have been reported. Because of low risk of residues and rapid clearance after administration, a 24-hour withdrawal time is suggested.

Pamidronate Disodium

pam-ih-droe'nate dye-soe'dee-um

Trade and Other Names: Aredia

Functional Classification: Antihypercalcemic

Pharmacology and Mechanism of Action

Bisphosphonate drug. Drugs in this class include pamidronate, etidronate, and pyrophosphate. These drugs are a group of drugs characterized by a germinal bisphosphonate bond. They slow the formation and dissolution of hydroxyapatite crystals. Their clinical use resides in their ability to inhibit bone resorption. These drugs decrease bone turnover by inhibiting osteoclast activity, inducing osteoclast apoptosis, retard bone resorption, and decrease rate of osteoporosis. Inhibition of bone resorption is via inhibition of the mevalonate pathway. Pamidronate is eliminated by the kidneys in animals.

Indications and Clinical Uses

Pamidronate, like other bisphosphonate drugs, is used in people to treat osteoporosis and treatment of hypercalcemia of malignancy. In animals, pamidronate is used to decrease calcium in conditions that cause hypercalcemia, such as cancer and vitamin D toxicosis. It is helpful for managing neoplastic complications associated with pathologic bone resorption. It also may provide pain relief in patients with pathologic bone disease. It also may reduce glucocorticoid induced osteoporosis. Experimental work performed in dogs has shown it to be effective for treating cholecalciferol toxicosis, but it did not prevent decreases in renal function. After treating for hypercalcemia in dogs the duration of effect was 11 days to 9 weeks (median 8.5 weeks). Some bisphosphonates, such as pamidronate, have been used to treat navicular disease in horses, but this work is only preliminary.

Precautionary Information

Adverse Reactions and Side Effects

No serious adverse effects identified, however use in animals has been uncommon. One study in dogs reported slight decrease in food intake. In humans, acute renal necrosis after intravenous administration has been reported. Because pamidronate is eliminated by the kidneys in dogs, a dose-dependent nephropathy is possible. Risk of renal injury is more likely with doses exceeding 3 mg/kg IV. In people, there is some concern that it may result in excessive mineralization and hardening of the bone, which may result in a greater risk of fractures. However, this effect has not been reported for animals.

Contraindications and Precautions

No contraindications have been identified in animals.

Drug Interactions

Do not mix with solutions containing calcium (e.g., Lactated Ringer's solution).

Instructions for Use

For intravenous infusion, dilute in fluid solution (0.9% saline) and administer over 2 hours. (Dilute 30 mg pamidronate in 250 mL fluids.) Infusion can be repeated every 7 days. Although SQ route is listed for some veterinary applications, IV infusion is preferred route.

Patient Monitoring and Laboratory Tests

Monitor serum calcium and phosphorus. Treatment of vitamin D toxicosis with pamidronate may result in decreased renal function. Monitor urea nitrogen, creatinine, urine specific gravity, and food intake in treated animals.

Formulations

Pamidronate is available in 30, 60, and 90 mg vials for injection.

Stability and Storage

Store in tightly sealed container, protected from light, and at room temperature. Vials may be diluted in fluid solutions and infused over 2 hours or as long as 24 hours. Diluted solutions are stable for 24 hours at room temperature.

Small Animal Dosage

Dogs

- 2 mg/kg IV or SQ.
- Treatment for hypercalcemia: 1-2 mg/kg, IV, SQ.
- Treating malignant osteolytic disease: 1 mg/kg IV every 28 days as a 2 hour IV infusion.
- Treatment of cholecalciferol toxicosis: 1.3-2.0 mg/kg, IV, SQ for two treatments after toxin exposure.

Cats

- Treatment of hypercalcemia: 1.5-2.0 mg/kg, IV, SQ.

Large Animal Dosage

No doses have been reported for large animals.

Regulatory Information

Withdrawal times are not established for animals that produce food. For extralabel use withdrawal interval estimates, contact FARAD at 1-888-USFARAD (1-888-873-2723) or send e-mail to FARAD@ncsu.edu.

Pancrelipase

pan-kreh-lye′pase

Trade and Other Names: Viokase, Pancrezyme, Cotazym, Creon, Pancoate, Pancrease, and Ultrase

Functional Classification: Pancreatic enzyme

Pharmacology and Mechanism of Action

Pancreatic enzyme. Pancrelipase provides lipase, amylase, and protease. Pancrelipase is a mixture of enzymes (lipase, amylase, and protease) obtained from the pancreas of pigs. These enzymes enhance digestion of fats, proteins, and starches in the upper duodenum and jejunum. They are more active in alkaline environment. There are coated and uncoated tablets. The uncoated tablets are not as bioavailable, because degradation may occur in the acid of the stomach. Each milligram contains 24 units lipase, 100 units amylase, and 100 units of protease activity.

Indications and Clinical Uses

Pancrelipase is used to treat pancreatic exocrine insufficiency. It provides enzymes lacking for digestion. It should be administered before meals. It is inactivated in gastric acid and administration with a drug to suppress stomach acid (e.g., H_2 receptor blocker or proton pump inhibitor [PPI]) may improve activity.

Precautionary Information

Adverse Reactions and Side Effects

Oral bleeding has been reported from administration of tablets. The tablets contain potent enzymes and contact with mucosal membranes may cause lesions and mucosal ulcers. Ensure that tablets are not trapped in the esophagus or esophageal erosions may occur. *Warn owners that if they handle tablets, avoid hand-to-mucosa contact (e.g., contact with eyes).*

Contraindications and Precautions

Enteric-coated tablets may not be as effective as mixing powder with food.

Drug Interactions

If antacids are used concurrently, magnesium hydroxide and calcium carbonate may reduce effectiveness.

Instructions for Use

Mix pancrelipase with food when administering approximately 20 minutes prior to feeding. After successful results are obtained, the dose may be reduced gradually to identify the minimum effective dose. Pancreatic enzymes are more effective if administered with acid-suppressing drugs (H_2 blockers, PPIs, bicarbonate, or some antacids). If delayed-release capsules are used (granules), do not crush. Different brands have varying activity. If switching from one brand to another, not all products will result in the same therapeutic results.

Patient Monitoring and Laboratory Tests

No specific monitoring is necessary.

Formulations

Pancrelipase is available in a composition of 16,800 units of lipase, 70,000 units of protease, and 70,000 units of amylase per 0.7 gram. It is also available in capsules and tablets. Various formulations contain a variety of activity. For example, Viokase powder contains 16,000 units/70,000 units/70,000 units (lipase/protease/amylase) per 0.7 grams of powder. Tablets range from 8000/30,000/30,000 units (lipase/protease/amylase) to 11,000/30,000/30,000 units (lipase/protease/amylase) per tablet.

Stability and Storage

Store in tightly sealed container, protected from light, and at room temperature. It is inactivated in acid environment.

Small Animal Dosage

Dogs

- Mix 2 tsp powder with food per 20 kg body weight or 1-3 tsp/0.45 kg of food 20 minutes prior to feeding. Formulations with granules in capsules may be opened and sprinkled on food (approximately 1 capsule with meals for a dog).

Cats

- ½ teaspoon per cat with food.

Large Animal Dosage

No doses have been reported for large animals.

Regulatory Information

Because of low risk of residues and rapid clearance after administration, no withdrawal time is suggested.

Pancuronium Bromide

pan-kyoo-roe′nee-um bro′mide

Trade and Other Names: Pavulon

Functional Classification: Muscle relaxant

Pharmacology and Mechanism of Action

Neuromuscular blocking agent (nondepolarizing). Pancuronium, like other drugs in this class, competes with acetylcholine at neuromuscular end plate to produce paralysis. Sensory nerves are intact.

Indications and Clinical Uses

Pancuronium is a paralytic agent used during anesthesia or for mechanical ventilation. It is used primarily during anesthesia or other conditions in which it is necessary to inhibit muscle contractions. It is sometimes used as an alternative to atracurium, because it is longer acting.

Precautionary Information

Adverse Reactions and Side Effects

Pancuronium produces respiratory depression and paralysis. Neuromuscular blocking drugs have no effect on analgesia.

Contraindications and Precautions

Do not use in patients unless mechanical ventilation support can be provided.

Drug Interactions

Some drugs may potentiate the action (e.g., aminoglycosides) and should not be used concurrently.

Instructions for Use

Administer only in situations in which careful control of respiration is possible. Doses may need to be individualized for optimum effect. Do not mix with alkalinizing solutions or Lactated Ringer's solution.

Patient Monitoring and Laboratory Tests

Monitor patient's respiration rate, heart rate, and rhythm during use. If possible, monitor the oxygenation status during anesthesia.

Formulations

Pancuronium is available in 1 and 2 mg/mL injection.

Stability and Storage

Store in tightly sealed container, protected from light, and at room temperature.

Small Animal Dosage

Dogs and Cats

- 0.1 mg/kg IV, or start with 0.01 mg/kg and additional 0.01 mg/kg doses q30min.
- Constant rate infusion (CRI): 0.1 mg/kg IV, followed by 2 mcg/kg/min infusion.

Large Animal Dosage

No doses have been reported for large animals.

Regulatory Information

Withdrawal times are not established for animals that produce food. For extralabel use withdrawal interval estimates, contact FARAD at 1-888-USFARAD (1-888-873-2723) or send e-mail to FARAD@ncsu.edu.
RCI Classification: 2

Pantoprazole

pan-toe-pray'zole

Trade and Other Names: Protonix

Functional Classification: Antiulcer agent

Pharmacology and Mechanism of Action

Proton pump inhibitor (PPI). Pantoprazole inhibits gastric acid secretion by inhibiting the K^+/H^+ pump. Pantoprazole, like other PPIs, have potent and long-acting effects. Acid suppression may have a duration >24 hours in animals. Pantoprazole is the first PPI that can be administered IV. After a dose, it inhibits acid secretion for >24 hours.

Indications and Clinical Uses

Pantoprazole is used for treatment and prevention of GI ulcers. Other PPIs include omeprazole, lansoprazole (Prevacid), and rabeprazole (AcipHex). All PPIs act via similar mechanism and are equally effective. However, there has been more experience with omeprazole in animals than the other drugs of this group. In dogs, pantoprazole (1 mg/kg) maintained stomach pH >3-4 when administered IV. Pantoprazole, being the only one in an IV formulation, is often used when an intravenous drug is preferred for treatment.

P

Precautionary Information

Adverse Reactions and Side Effects

Side effects have not been reported in animals. However, in people there is concern about hypergastrinemia with chronic use. Overgrowth of *Clostridium* bacteria has been a concern from chronic use because of chronic gastric acid suppression, but the clinical importance of this concern in animals has not been established.

Contraindications and Precautions

No known contraindications.

Drug Interactions

Do not mix intravenous solution with other drugs. Do not administer with drugs that depend on acid stomach for absorption (e.g., ketoconazole, itraconazole, iron supplements). PPIs may inhibit some drug metabolizing enzymes (CYP 450 enzymes), although in people there was low risk of drug interactions caused by enzyme inhibition.

Instructions for Use

For treating GI ulcers, administer once per day for 7-10 days. For gastrin-secreting tumors use higher dose (1 mg/kg) twice daily. Other PPIs include omeprazole (Prilosec), lansoprazole (Prevacid), and rabeprazole (AcipHex). They all act via similar mechanism and are equally effective. The primary difference with pantoprazole is that it is available in an intravenous dosage formulation and can be mixed with fluid solutions. For intravenous use, mix 40 mg vial with 10 mL saline and further dilute with saline, Lactated Ringer's solution, or 5% dextrose to 0.4 mg/mL for intravenous infusion. Administer intravenous infusion over at least 15 minutes.

Patient Monitoring and Laboratory Tests

No specific monitoring is necessary. When treating ulcers, monitor hematocrit or CBC to detect bleeding. Monitor for signs of vomiting and diarrhea.

Formulations

Pantoprazole is available in 0.4 mg/mL in a 40 mg vial for intravenous use and 40 mg tablets.

Stability and Storage

Store in tightly sealed container, protected from light, and at room temperature. Do not freeze reconstituted solutions. Once diluted for intravenous use, it is stable for 12 hours.

Small Animal Dosage

Dogs and Cats

- 0.5-0.6 mg/kg once daily PO.
- Intravenous use: 0.5-1 mg/kg IV infusion over 24 hours. For intravenous administration, the entire dose also can be administered within 15 minutes and repeated once every 24 hours.

Large Animal Dosage

No dose is reported for large animals. Doses have been extrapolated from human use (0.5 mg/kg q24h IV).

Regulatory Information

Withdrawal times are not established for animals that produce food. For extralabel use withdrawal interval estimates, contact FARAD at 1-888-USFARAD (1-888-873-2723) or send e-mail to FARAD@ncsu.edu.

RCI Classification: 5

Paregoric

pare-eh-gore'ik

Trade and Other Names: Corrective mixture

Functional Classification: Antidiarrheal

Pharmacology and Mechanism of Action

Paregoric (opium tincture) is an outdated product used to treat diarrhea. Paregoric contains 2 mg of morphine in every 5 mL of paregoric. The action is via stimulation of intestinal mu-opiate receptors to cause a decrease in intestinal peristalsis.

Indications and Clinical Uses

Paregoric will decrease signs of diarrhea via opiate effects, but its use is somewhat outdated.

Precautionary Information

Adverse Reactions and Side Effects

Like all opiates, side effects are predictable and unavoidable. Side effects may include sedation, constipation, and bradycardia. Respiratory depression occurs with high doses. Tolerance and dependence occurs with chronic administration.

Contraindications and Precautions

Contains opium and may be abused by humans. Use cautiously in horses and ruminants because intestinal motility may be decreased.

Drug Interactions

No drug interactions have been reported in animals.

Instructions for Use

Use of paregoric has been replaced by more specific products such as loperamide or diphenoxylate.

Patient Monitoring and Laboratory Tests

No specific monitoring is necessary.

Formulations

For every 5 mL of paregoric, there is 2 mg morphine.

Stability and Storage

Store in tightly sealed container, protected from light, and at room temperature.

Small Animal Dosage

Dogs and Cats

- 0.05-0.06 mg/kg q12h PO.

Large Animal Dosage

No doses have been reported for large animals.

Regulatory Information

Withdrawal times are not established for animals that produce food. For extralabel use withdrawal interval estimates, contact FARAD at 1-888-USFARAD (1-888-873-2723) or send e-mail to FARAD@ncsu.edu.

Paromomycin Sulfate

pare-oe-moe-mye'sin sul'fate

Trade and Other Names: Humatin

Functional Classification: Antiparasitic

Pharmacology and Mechanism of Action

Antibiotic drug of the aminoglycoside class. The mechanism of action of paromomycin is similar to other aminoglycosides; it inhibits the ribosomal 30S subunit with subsequent inhibition of bacterial protein synthesis.

Indications and Clinical Uses

Paromomycin has been used to treat intestinal infections, such as cryptosporidiosis. The use is based on limited accounts, and efficacy has not been tested in controlled studies.

Precautionary Information

Adverse Reactions and Side Effects

Paromomycin has been associated with renal failure and blindness when used in cats. Although systemic absorption is not expected to be high, cats treated with high doses for intestinal organisms developed problems.

Contraindications and Precautions

Extreme caution is recommended when administering this drug to animals that may have compromised bowel due to intestinal disease, because increased systemic absorption may occur.

Drug Interactions

No drug interactions have been reported in animals.

Instructions for Use

In cats, doses of 125-165 mg/kg every 12 hours have been administered for 5 to 7 days, PO. However, there are reports in the veterinary literature that these doses have produced toxicity in cats, including renal injury. It is suggested to use lower doses to avoid toxicity, monitor the patient's renal parameters carefully, and when there is a compromised integrity of the intestinal mucosa as may occur with diarrhea, use of paromomycin is discouraged.

Patient Monitoring and Laboratory Tests

Monitor patient's renal function during treatment, such as urine specific gravity, serum creatinine, and BUN.

Formulations

Paromomycin is available in 250 mg capsules.

Stability and Storage

Store in tightly sealed container, protected from light, and at room temperature.

Small Animal Dosage

Cats

- Doses of 125-165 mg/kg q12h PO for 7 days have been recommended. However, caution is recommended when using doses this high.

Large Animal Dosage

No doses have been reported for large animals.

Regulatory Information

Withdrawal times are not established for animals that produce food. Although not absorbed systemically to a large extent, it is expected that concentrations may persist in the kidneys, producing long extended withdrawal times for slaughter.

Paroxetine

par-oks'eh-teen

Trade and Other Names: Paxil

Functional Classification: Behavior modification

Pharmacology and Mechanism of Action

Antidepressant drug. Paroxetine, like other drugs in this class is classified as a selective serotonin reuptake inhibitor (SSRI). It resembles fluoxetine (Prozac) in action. Mechanism of action appears to be via selective inhibition of serotonin reuptake and down regulation of 5-HT_1 receptors. SSRI drugs are more selective for inhibiting serotonin reuptake than the tricyclic antidepressant drugs (TCAs).

Indications and Clinical Uses

Paroxetine, like other SSRI drugs, is used to treat behavioral disorders such as obsessive-compulsive disorders (canine compulsive disorder) and dominance aggression. In cats, it has been effective for decreasing urine spraying.

Precautionary Information

Adverse Reactions and Side Effects

Some effects similar to fluoxetine, but in some animals paroxetine is better tolerated.

Contraindications and Precautions

Use cautiously in patients with heart disease. Do not use in pregnant animals. There is a risk of fetal malformations if used early in pregnancy.

Drug Interactions

Do not use with monoamine oxidase inhibitors (MAOIs), such as selegiline. Do not use with other behavior-modifying drugs, such as other SSRIs or TCAs.

Instructions for Use

Dosing recommendations are empirical. Paroxetine has been used for conditions similar to what has been treated with fluoxetine (Prozac). Since paroxetine is available in small tablets, it can be easier to administer convenient doses to smaller animals, rather than drugs available in capsules. Paroxetine has caused constipation in some animals, and veterinarians may administer a feline laxative for the first week of therapy to avoid problems.

Patient Monitoring and Laboratory Tests

Use in animals has been relatively safe, and one should only monitor behavior changes.

Formulations

Paroxetine is available in 10, 20, 30, and 40 mg tablets and 2 mg/mL oral suspension.

Stability and Storage

Stable if stored in manufacturer's original formulation. Although paroxetine has been compounded for veterinary use, the potency and stability has not been evaluated for compounded products.

Small Animal Dosage

Dogs
- 0.5 mg/kg/day PO.

Cats
- 1/8 to 1/4 of a 10 mg tablet daily PO.

Large Animal Dosage

No doses have been reported for large animals.

Regulatory Information

Do not administer to animals intended for food.
RCI Classification: 2

Penicillamine

pen-ih-sill'ah-meen

Trade and Other Names: Cuprimine and Depen

Functional Classification: Antidote

Pharmacology and Mechanism of Action

Penicillamine is also called 3 mercaptovaline. It is a chelating agent for lead copper, iron, and mercury. When used to treat copper toxicity, it helps to solubilize copper in the cells to allow for more rapid urinary excretion. Treated animals should have increased copper urinary excretion. Other drugs that have been used as chelating agents include tetrathiomolybdate, trientine, and zinc. Penicillamine also has antiinflammatory properties which may contribute to its positive effect for treating animals with hepatitis.

Indications and Clinical Uses

Penicillamine has been used in people to treat rheumatoid arthritis. In animals it is used primarily for treatment of copper toxicity and hepatitis associated with accumulation of copper. Treatment duration for animals with copper-storage hepatic disease may require 2-4 months. It also has been used to treat cystine calculi.

Precautionary Information

Adverse Reactions and Side Effects

In people, allergic reactions have been reported as well as agranulocytosis and anemia. In animals, there have been no adverse reactions associated with its used for treating copper-storage liver disease. In treated dogs, corticosteroid hepatopathy has been observed. Therefore it may produce steroid-like effects in the liver.

Contraindications and Precautions

Do not use in pregnant animals. There appears to be little cross-reaction between penicillin and penicillamine in allergic animals.

Drug Interactions

No drug interactions have been reported in animals.

Instructions for Use

Administer on an empty stomach (2 hours before meals).

Patient Monitoring and Laboratory Tests

Monitor liver biochemistry tests during treatment. Monitor metal concentrations if used to treat intoxication.

Formulations

Penicillamine is available in 125 and 250 mg capsules and 250 mg tablets.

Stability and Storage

Store in tightly sealed container, protected from light, and at room temperature. Penicillamine is soluble in water. Preparations of penicillamine in a suspension for oral use have been combined with syrups and flavorings and were stable for 5 weeks.

Small Animal Dosage

Dogs and Cats

- 10-15 mg/kg q12h PO.
- Doberman pinschers: use 200 mg q12h PO.

Large Animal Dosage

Horses and Cattle

- 10-15 mg/kg q12h PO.

Regulatory Information

Cattle withdrawal time (meat): 21 days.
Cattle withdrawal time (milk): 3 days.

Penicillin G

Trade and Other Names: Penicillin G potassium or sodium, Penicillin G benzathine (Benza-Pen), Penicillin G, Procaine, and generic Penicillin V (Pen-Vee)

Functional Classification: Antibacterial

Pharmacology and Mechanism of Action

Beta-lactam antibiotic. Penicillin G is also called benzyl penicillin. Its action is similar to other penicillins. It binds penicillin binding proteins (PBP) to weaken or cause lysis of cell wall. Penicillin G is bactericidal with a time-dependent action. Increased bactericidal effect is observed when drug concentrations are maintained above minimum inhibitory concentration (MIC) values. Spectrum of penicillin G is limited to gram-positive bacteria and anaerobes. Penicillin sodium or penicillin potassium when injected IV has a half-life of one hour or less in most animals. However, the same dose of procaine penicillin given IM may produce more prolonged concentrations and a half-life of 20-24 hours because of slow absorption from the injection site.

There are several formulations of penicillin G:

- Sodium or potassium penicillin G [crystallin penicillin]), which is water soluble and can be administered IV or IM. It may also be mixed with fluids for IV administration.
- Penicillin G benzathine, which is insoluble and available as a suspension. It is slowly absorbed from an injection site to produce low, but prolonged (several days of) penicillin concentrations. All benzathine penicillin G forms are combined with procaine penicillin G in commercial formulation (1:1 ratio).

- Penicillin G procaine is a poorly soluble suspension for intramuscular or subcutaneous administration. It is absorbed slowly producing concentrations for 12-24 hours after injections.
- Penicillin V, oral penicillin is not highly absorbed and narrow spectrum in comparison with other penicillin derivatives.

Indications and Clinical Uses

Penicillin G is administered by injection either IV (potassium or sodium penicillin) or IM (procaine or procaine/benzathine penicillin G). Penicillin G is indicated for treatment of gram-positive cocci. Many staphylococci are resistant because of beta-lactamase synthesis. Streptococci are usually susceptible. Other susceptible organisms include gram-positive bacilli and anaerobic bacteria. Most gram-negative bacilli, especially those of enteric origin, are resistant. Some gram-negative respiratory pathogens such as *Pasteurella multocida, Mannheimia haemolytica* are susceptible.

Penicillin concentrations in the urine are at least 100-fold higher than plasma concentrations in treated animals, therefore some urinary pathogens may be more susceptible.

Precautionary Information

Adverse Reactions and Side Effects

Penicillin G is usually well tolerated. Allergic reactions are possible. Diarrhea is common with oral doses. Pain and tissue reactions may occur with IM or SQ injections.

Contraindications and Precautions

Use cautiously in animals allergic to penicillin-like drugs. Avoid injection volumes >30 mL per site.

Drug Interactions

No drug interactions have been reported in animals.

Instructions for Use

Penicillin G benzathine is not recommended for most infections because concentrations are too low to provide therapeutic drug concentrations. A possible exception is for treatment of streptococcal infections. Avoid SQ injection with procaine penicillin G because of tissue injury and residue problems. Penicillin V should be administered on an empty stomach for maximum absorption.

Patient Monitoring and Laboratory Tests

Susceptibility testing: CLSI (NCCLS) break points for sensitive organisms are less than or equal to 8 mcg/mL for enterococci and less than or equal to 0.12 mcg/mL for staphylococci and streptococci.

Formulations

Penicillin G potassium is available in 5-20 million unit vials. Penicillin G benzathine is available in 150,000 units/mL and can be combined with 150,000 units/mL of Procaine Penicillin G suspension. Penicillin G, Procaine is available in 300,000 units/mL suspension. Penicillin is one of the few antibiotics that is still measured in terms of units rather than weight in mg or mcg. One unit of penicillin represents the specific activity in 0.6 mcg of sodium penicillin. Thus, 1 mg of penicillin sodium represents 1667 units of penicillin.

Penicillin V is available in 250 and 500 mg tablets (250 mg is equal to 400,000 units).

Stability and Storage

Sodium and potassium forms of penicillin G retain their potency for 24 hours at room temperature and 7 days if refrigerated. Penicillin potassium or penicillin sodium are freely soluble in water. Degradation may occur at high pH (>8).

Small Animal Dosage

- Penicillin G potassium or sodium: 20,000-40,000 units/kg q6-8h IV or IM.
- Penicillin G benzathine: 24,000 units/kg q48h IM.
- Procaine Penicillin G: 20,000-40,000 units/kg q12-24h IM.
- Penicillin V: 10 mg/kg q8h PO.

Large Animal Dosage

Cattle and Sheep

- Procaine Penicillin G: 24,000-66,000 units/kg q24h IM. Subcutaneous use is discouraged.
- Sodium or potassium penicillin G: 20,000 units/kg IM or IV, q6h.

Pigs

- Procaine penicillin G: 15,000-25,000 units/kg q24h IM.

Horses

- Penicillin sodium or penicillin potassium: 20,000-24,000 units/kg q6-8h IV. (Doses up to 44,000 units/kg q6h have been used for refractory cases.)
- Procaine penicillin G: 20,000-24,000 units/kg q24h IM.
- Potassium penicillin G: 20,000-24,000 units/kg q12h IM.

Regulatory Information

Horses: Injections of procaine penicillin may cause a positive test for procaine prior to racing.

Horses may be tested positive with a procaine urine test for as long as 30 days after an injection.

Withdrawal times for benzathine penicillin at label dose of 6000-7000 units/kg in cattle: 30 days meat (14 days Canada).

Withdrawal times for procaine penicillin at label dose of 6000-7000 units/kg in cattle: 10 days meat, 4 days milk; sheep 9 days; swine 7 days.

Withdrawal times for procaine penicillin G at a dose of 15,000 units/kg in pigs: 8 days.

Withdrawal times for procaine penicillin G at a dose of 21,000 units/kg in cattle: 10 days meat, 96 hours milk.

Procaine Penicillin G at a dose of 60,000 units/kg: 21 days cattle, 15 days pigs.

RCI Classification: penicillin is not classified; procaine 3

Pentastarch

Trade and Other Names: Pentaspan

Functional Classification: Fluid replacement

Pharmacology and Mechanism of Action

Pentastarch is a synthetic colloid volume expander that is used to maintain vascular volume in animals with circulatory shock. It is prepared from hydroxyethyl starch and is derived from amylopectin. Because pentastarch is a large molecular weight compound (280 kd), it tends to remain in the vasculature and prevent loss of intravascular volume and prevent tissue edema. There are two hydroxyethyl starch preparations: hetastarch and pentastarch. Other colloids used are dextrans (Dextran 40 and Dextran 70).

Indications and Clinical Uses

Pentastarch is used primarily to treat acute hypovolemia and shock. It is administered IV in acute situations. Pentastarch has a duration of effective volume expansion of 12-48 hours. Pentastarch is used in similar situations as hetastarch, but it is used less frequently.

Precautionary Information

Adverse Reactions and Side Effects

There has only been limited use in veterinary medicine, therefore adverse effects have not been reported. However, it may cause allergic reactions and hyperosmotic renal dysfunction. Coagulopathies are possible, but rare and less likely than with hetastarch.

Contraindications and Precautions

No contraindications are reported for animals.

Drug Interactions

Pentastarch is compatible with most fluid solutions.

Instructions for Use

Pentastarch is used in critical care situations and is infused via constant rate infusion (CRI). Pentastarch may be more effective and produce fewer side effects than Dextran. Because of lower molecular weight, it can be infused more quickly than hetastarch.

Patient Monitoring and Laboratory Tests

Monitor patient's hydration status and blood pressure during administration.

Formulations

Pentastarch is available in 10% injectable solution.

Stability and Storage

Pentastarch is stable in original packaging. Compatible with most fluid administration sets.

Small Animal Dosage

Dogs

- CRI: 10-25 mL/kg/day IV.

Cats

- CRI: 5-10 mL/kg/day IV.

Large Animal Dosage

No doses have been reported for large animals.

Regulatory Information

No regulatory requirements.

Pentazocine

pen-taz'oh-seen

Trade and Other Names: Talwin-V

Functional Classification: Analgesic, Opioid

Pharmacology and Mechanism of Action

Synthetic opiate analgesic. The action of pentazocine results from its effect as a mu-opiate receptor partial agonist and a kappa-receptor agonist. Most of the sedative and analgesic effects are believed to be caused by the kappa-receptor effects. Pentazocine may partially reverse some mu-receptor agonist effects. Its effects are believed to be similar to buprenorphine or butorphanol, but efficacy is less.

Indications and Clinical Uses

Pentazocine has been used for sedation and analgesia, primarily in horses. However, its efficacy is not as good as other drugs and the use of pentazocine has declined.

Precautionary Information

Adverse Reactions and Side Effects

Adverse effects are similar to other opioid analgesic drugs and include constipation, ileus, vomiting, and bradycardia. Sedation is common at analgesic doses. Respiratory depression can occur with high doses. Dysphoric effects have been observed with these agonist/antagonist drugs.

Contraindications and Precautions

Pentazocine is a schedule IV controlled substance.

Drug Interactions

Pentazocine may potentiate other sedative drugs such as $alpha_2$ agonists. Pentazocine may interfere with mu-opiate effects of other drugs, such as morphine or fentanyl.

Instructions for Use

Pentazocine is a mixed agonist/antagonist. It is relatively modest to weak in efficacy for pain control.

Patient Monitoring and Laboratory Tests

Monitor patient's heart rate and respiration. Although bradycardia rarely needs to be treated when it is caused by an opioid, atropine can be administered if necessary. If serious respiratory depression occurs, the opioid can be reversed with naloxone.

Formulations

Pentazocine is available in 30 mg/mL injection (availability has been limited).

Stability and Storage

Store in tightly sealed container, protected from light, and at room temperature.

Small Animal Dosage

Dogs

- 1.65-3.3 mg/kg q4h IM, or as needed.

Cats

- 2.2-3.3 mg/kg q4h IM, IV, or SQ, or as needed.

Large Animal Dosage

Horses

- 200-400 mg per horse, IV.

Regulatory Information

Pentazocine is a Schedule IV controlled drug. Withdrawal times are not established for animals that produce food. For extralabel use withdrawal interval estimates, contact FARAD at 1-888-USFARAD (1-888-873 -2723) or send e-mail to FARAD@ncsu.edu.

RCI Classification: 3

Pentobarbital Sodium

pen-toe-bar′bih-tahl soe′dee-um

Trade and Other Names: Nembutal and generic brands

Functional Classification: Anesthetic, Barbiturate

Pharmacology and Mechanism of Action

Short-acting barbiturate anesthetic. The action of pentobarbital is via nonselective depression of CNS. Duration of action may be 3-4 hours.

Indications and Clinical Uses

Pentobarbital usually is used as intravenous anesthetic. It also is used to control severe seizures in animals for treatment during status epilepticus. In some instances, pentobarbital is included in mixtures used to induce euthanasia in animals.

Precautionary Information

Adverse Reactions and Side Effects

Adverse effects are related to anesthetic action. Cardiac depression and respiratory depression are common.

Contraindications and Precautions

Rapid intravenous doses can be lethal. Monitor respiration rate carefully after injection because respiratory depression may occur.

Drug Interactions

Pentobarbital will potentiate sedative and cardiorespiratory depressing effects of other anesthetics. Pentobarbital is subject to effects from other drugs that may either induce or inhibit cytochrome P450 metabolizing enzymes (see Appendix).

Instructions for Use

Pentobarbital has narrow therapeutic index. When administering IV, inject first half of dose initially, then remainder of calculated dose gradually until anesthetic effect is achieved.

Most euthanasia solutions contain pentobarbital as their active ingredient. Often other ingredients to facilitate euthanasia are included such as muscle relaxants and drugs with lethal cardiac effects (e.g., edetate disodium 0.05%). The concentration of pentobarbital in most euthanasia solutions is 390 mg/mL with a dose of 1 mL per 10 pounds, which is equivalent to 1 mL per 4.5 kg or 87 mg/kg IV.

Patient Monitoring and Laboratory Tests

Monitor vital signs, especially heart rate and rhythm and respiration during anesthesia.

Formulations

Pentobarbital is available in 50 and 65 mg/mL solution for injection (contains propylene glycol).

Stability and Storage

Store in tightly sealed container, protected from light, and at room temperature. pH of solution is 9-10.5 and may affect stability of other coadministered drugs. It will precipitate if combined with most hydrochloride-based drugs or drugs with low pH.

Small Animal Dosage

Dogs and Cats

- General Anesthesia: 25-30 mg/kg IV, to effect.
- Constant rate infusion (CRI): 2-15 mg/kg IV to effect, followed by 0.2-1.0 mg/kg/hr.
- Euthanasia: see Instructions for Use section.

Large Animal Dosage

Cattle

- To produce standing sedation: 1-2 mg/kg IV.

Cattle, Sheep, and Goats

- General anesthesia: 20-30 mg/kg IV given to effect.

Regulatory Information

Withdrawal times are not established for animals that produce food. For extralabel use withdrawal interval estimates, contact FARAD at 1-888-USFARAD (1-888-873-2723) or send e-mail to FARAD@ncsu.edu.
Schedule II controlled drug
RCI Classification: 2

P

Pentoxifylline

pen-toks'ih-fill-in

Trade and Other Names: Trental, Oxpentifylline, and generic brands

Functional Classification: Antiinflammatory agent

Pharmacology and Mechanism of Action

Methylxanthine. Pentoxifylline is used primarily as a rheological agent in people (increases blood flow through narrow vessels). An improved rheological effect has also been demonstrated with equine blood cells. As a phosphodiesterase inhibitor (PDE 4 inhibitor) it produces antiinflammatory effects. It may have antiinflammatory action via inhibition of cytokine synthesis. Pentoxifylline suppresses synthesis of inflammatory cytokines, such as interleukin-1 (IL-1), interleukin-6 (IL-6), and tumor necrosis factor (TNF) alpha and may inhibit lymphocyte activation.

There are 7 metabolites produced in animals, with some being biologically active.

Indications and Clinical Uses

Pentoxifylline is used in dogs for some dermatoses, vasculitis, contact allergy, atopy, familial canine dermatomyositis, and erythema multiforme. In horses, pentoxifylline is used for a variety of conditions in which suppression of inflammatory cytokines or increased blood perfusion is desired. Such conditions have included intestinal ischemia, colic, sepsis, laminitis, and navicular disease. However, the efficacy for treating these diseases has not been shown. It may have improved efficacy for sepsis if combined with a nonsteroidal antiinflammatory drug (NSAID; e.g., flunixin).

Precautionary Information

Adverse Reactions and Side Effects

Pentoxifylline may cause effects similar to other methylxanthines, such as nausea, vomiting, and diarrhea. Nausea, vomiting, dizziness, and headache have been reported in people. Vomiting is reported in dogs. If crushed tablets are used, plasma concentration will increase more rapidly than with intact tablets, leading to headaches, nausea, and possible vomiting.

Contraindications and Precautions

None reported. When broken tablet is administered to cats, the taste is unpleasant.

Drug Interactions

No drug interactions are reported. However, as a methylxanthine, adverse reactions are possible from coadministration with a cytochrome P450 inhibitor (see Appendix).

Instructions for Use

Although pharmacokinetic studies in dogs and horses have been reported, results of clinical studies in animals have been limited. Pentoxifylline undergoes extensive hepatic metabolism and systemic availability after oral administration is only 20%-30%, and it has a rapid elimination half-life (less than 1 hour). Because of rapid half-life, frequent administration is necessary, at least three times daily; however some regimens used for dermatology have used every 12 hour frequency. Most of use in animals (and doses) is based on anecdotal experience in animals. When a broken tablet is administered to cats, the taste is unpleasant.

Patient Monitoring and Laboratory Tests

No specific monitoring is necessary.

Formulations

Pentoxifylline is available in 400 mg tablets.

Stability and Storage

Store in tightly sealed container, protected from light, and at room temperature. Aqueous solubility is only 77 mg/mL. Oral suspensions may be stable for up to 90 days, but it will settle requiring resuspension (shaking) before oral administration.

Small Animal Dosage

Dogs

- Dermatologic use: 10 mg/kg q12h PO, and up to 15 mg/kg q8h PO.
- Familial canine dermatomyositis: 25 mg/kg q12h PO.
- Other uses: 10-15 mg/kg q8 PO or 400 mg/dog for most animals.

Cats

- 1/4 of a 400 mg tablet (100 mg) q8-12h PO.

Large Animal Dosage

Horses

- 8.5 mg/kg q8h PO, (oral absorption is unpredictable).
- Respiratory disease (airway obstruction): 36 mg/kg q12h PO.

Regulatory Information

Withdrawal times are not established for animals that produce food. For extralabel use withdrawal interval estimates, contact FARAD at 1-888-USFARAD (1-888-873-2723) or send e-mail to FARAD@ncsu.edu.
RCI Classification: 4

Pergolide, Pergolide Mesylate

per'goe-lide

Trade and Other Names: Permax

Functional Classification: Dopamine agonist

Pharmacology and Mechanism of Action

Dopaminergic agonist. Pergolide is a potent dopamine agonist that stimulates postsynaptic dopamine receptors (D_1 and D_2 receptors). It is used to stimulate dopamine receptors in conditions that dopamine is deficient, regardless of the state of the presynaptic dopamine stores. Other drugs that may share similar effects are selegiline, apomorphine, and lisuride (previously called lysuride).

Indications and Clinical Uses

In people, pergolide is used for neurodegenerative disease in which dopamine is deficient, such as Parkinson's disease, in which pergolide is used with levodopa or carbidopa. In animals it also has been used for dopamine-deficient states. It is believed that horses and some dogs develop hyperadrenocorticism (Cushing's Disease)—pituitary-dependent hyperadrenocorticism (PDH)— because of a loss of dopamine antagonism of adrenocorticotropic hormone (ACTH) release. Most horses with Cushing's disease have hyperplasia or adenoma of the pars intermedia of the pituitary. This adenoma is deficient in dopamine and produces excess ACTH. Administration of dopamine agonists acts to suppress ACTH release from the pituitary and subsequently restore cortisol levels to normal states. This effect is better established in horses than in dogs, and there are no reports of efficacy for treating PDH in dogs. It has been used successfully to treat equine pituitary pars intermedia dysfunction (Cushing's Syndrome).

Precautionary Information

Adverse Reactions and Side Effects

Pergolide inhibits secretion of prolactin and will increase growth hormone. It may inhibit lactation. CNS effects may include ataxia and dyskinesia. In horses, adverse effects include anorexia, diarrhea, and colic. Worsening of laminitis from pergolide (it is theoretically a vasoconstrictive drug) has not been proven.

Contraindications and Precautions

Unlike bromocriptine, pergolide can be used in pregnant animals.

Drug Interactions

No drug interactions have been reported in animals. It may interact with droperidol and phenothiazines (e.g., acepromazine), and it will exacerbate the effects of selegiline. Do not administer with monoamine oxidase inhibitors (MAOIs).

Instructions for Use

Use in horses is often accomplished by compounding the preparation for horses and administered daily. Start with low dose listed for 4-6 weeks and gradually increase the dose until desired results are obtained. It may be possible to obtain better efficacy when pergolide is used concurrently with cyproheptadine. When treating horses, consider supplementing their diet with magnesium and chromium.

Patient Monitoring and Laboratory Tests

Monitor ACTH levels in animals to document pituitary function. In horses, endogenous ACTH concentrations that exceed 27-50 pcg/mL are considered abnormal. Dexamethasone suppression tests can also be performed to monitor treatment in horses. Consult Dexamethasone monograph for procedure to perform this test.

Formulations

Pergolide tablets are available in 50 mcg (0.05 mg), 250 mcg (0.25 mg), 1 mg (all strengths as the base)

Stability and Storage

Store in tightly sealed container, protected from light, and at room temperature. Stability of compounded formulations has not been evaluated.

Small Animal Dosage

- Small animal doses have not been established but have been extrapolated from human use, which is to start with 1 mcg/kg (0.001 mg/kg) daily PO, and increase the dose gradually by 2 mcg/kg at a time until desired effects are observed.

Large Animal Dosage

Horses

- Low dose: 0.002 mg/kg q24h PO (1 mg/day for 500 kg horse).
- High dose: 0.006-0.01 mg/kg q24h PO (3-5 mg/day for 500 kg horse). Start with low dose and increase to high dose gradually if needed.

Regulatory Information

Do not administer to animals intended for food.

Phenobarbital, Phenobarbital Sodium

fee-noe-bar′bih-tahl

Trade and Other Names: Luminal, Phenobarbitone, and generic brands

Functional Classification: Anticonvulsant

Pharmacology and Mechanism of Action

Long-acting barbiturate. Phenobarbital has actions similar to other barbiturates on the CNS. However, phenobarbital will produce anticonvulsant effects without significant other barbiturate effects. As an anticonvulsant it stabilizes neurons by increased chloride conductance via GABA-mediated channels.

Indications and Clinical Uses

Phenobarbital is widely used as a drug of choice for treating seizure disorders, such as idiopathic epilepsy, in dogs, cats, horses, and exotic animals. Phenobarbital also has been used as a sedative.

Precautionary Information

Adverse Reactions and Side Effects

Most adverse effects are dose related. Phenobarbital causes polyphagia, sedation, ataxia, and lethargy. Some tolerance develops to side effects after initial therapy. Liver enzyme elevations are common but may not always be associated with liver pathology. Elevations in alkaline phosphatase are usually higher than other enzymes. However, hepatotoxicity also has been reported in some dogs and is more likely with high doses. Neutropenia, anemia, and thrombocytopenia has been associated with phenobarbital therapy in dogs. It is likely an idiosyncratic reaction and recovery may occur if phenobarbital is discontinued. In dogs, superficial necrolytic dermatitis has been associated with phenobarbital administration, without concurrent liver pathology. Affected dogs may have high serum concentrations of phenobarbital.

Contraindications and Precautions

Administer with caution to animals with liver disease. Phenobarbital may induce its own metabolism. Therefore, chronic administration may lower plasma concentrations, resulting in increases in dose requirement. Pregnant animals may have increase in seizure frequency and an increase in dose may be necessary.

Drug Interactions

Phenobarbital is one of the most potent drugs for inducing hepatic microsomal metabolizing enzymes. Therefore, many drugs administered concurrently will have lower (and perhaps subtherapeutic) concentrations because of more rapid clearance. Drugs affected may include theophylline, digoxin, corticosteroids, anesthetics, and many others (see Appendix list for drugs that affect cytochrome P450 enzymes). Administration of phenobarbital may lower Total T-4 thyroid concentrations, but thyroid-stimulating hormone (TSH) and T-3 concentrations are unaffected. Solutions are alkaline (pH 9-11), therefore avoid mixing with acidic solutions or drugs that will become unstable at alkaline pH.

Instructions for Use

Adjust dose based on blood levels of phenobarbital. If bromide is used concurrently (sodium or potassium bromide) lower doses of phenobarbital may be used.

Patient Monitoring and Laboratory Tests

Phenobarbital doses should be carefully adjusted via monitoring serum/plasma concentrations. Collect a sample at any time during the dose interval as the timing of the sample is not critical. Avoid the use of plasma separation devices if the tube is to be stored (these devices will cause a false lowering of concentrations). The therapeutic range in dogs is considered 15-40 mcg/mL (65-180 mmol/L). If dogs are also receiving bromide, phenobarbital concentrations in the range of 10-36 mcg/mL have been considered therapeutic. To convert from mmol/L to mcg/mL use a multiplication factor of 0.232. To convert from mcg/mL to mmol/L multiply by 4.3. In cats the optimum range for therapeutic effect is 23-28 mcg/mL

(99-120 mmol/L). In horses the optimum range for therapeutic effect is 15-20 mcg/mL (65-86 mmol/L). Monitor liver enzymes periodically in animals receiving phenobarbital because of risk of hepatopathy. Monitor liver function with bile acid determinations. Monitor CBC periodically in animals treated with phenobarbital because of risk of neutropenia, anemia, and thrombocytopenia. Phenobarbital administration will lower other drug concentrations. It will lower thyroid T-4 and free T-4, but not T-3 and TSH concentrations in dogs.

Formulations

Phenobarbital is available in 15, 30, 60, and 100 mg tablets, 30, 60, 65, and 130, mg/mL injection, and 4 mg/mL oral elixir solution.

Stability and Storage

Store in tightly sealed container, protected from light, and at room temperature. Phenobarbital is slightly soluble in water (100 mg/mL), but phenobarbital sodium is more soluble (1 g/mL). Solutions prepared in water have an alkaline pH (9-11). Precipitation may occur at lower pH values (avoid mixing with acidic syrups or flavorings). It is subject to hydrolysis in aqueous solutions. However, if prepared in propylene glycol it is stable for 56 weeks.

Small Animal Dosage

Dogs

- 2-8 mg/kg q12h PO.
- Status epilepticus: administer in increments of 10-20 mg/kg IV (to effect).

Cats

- 2-4 mg/kg q12h PO.
- Status epilepticus: administer in increments of 10-20 mg/kg IV (to effect).

Large Animal Dosage

Horses

- 12 mg/kg q24h PO. Note that in some horses, after initial therapy, higher doses of 12 mg/kg q12h may be needed.
- 5-20 mg/kg IV over 30 minutes (may be diluted in sodium chloride).

Regulatory Information

Withdrawal times are not established for animals that produce food. For extralabel use withdrawal interval estimates, contact FARAD at 1-888-USFARAD (1-888-873-2723) or send e-mail to FARAD@ncsu.edu.
Schedule IV controlled drug
RCI Classification: 2

Phenoxybenzamine Hydrochloride

fen-oks-ih-ben′zah-meen hye-droe-klor′ide

Trade and Other Names: Dibenzyline

Functional Classification: Vasodilator

Pharmacology and Mechanism of Action

Alpha$_1$ adrenergic antagonist. Phenoxybenzamine binds to and antagonizes alpha$_1$ receptor on smooth muscle causing relaxation. It is a potent and long-acting vasodilator.

Indications and Clinical Uses

Phenoxybenzamine is used primarily to treat peripheral vasoconstriction. In some animals, it has been used to relax urethral smooth muscle, for example when treating urethral spasm in cats after urethral blockage. Experimentally, phenoxybenzamine has been used to relax vascular smooth muscle in horses for treating laminitis. However, this has not been a common clinical use.

Precautionary Information

Adverse Reactions and Side Effects

Phenoxybenzamine causes prolonged hypotension in animals. Signs of an excessive hypotension may include rapid heart rate, weakness, and syncope. In horses, phenoxybenzamine has caused diarrhea.

Contraindications and Precautions

Use carefully in animals with cardiovascular compromise. Do not use in dehydrated animals. Use carefully in animals with low cardiac output.

Drug Interactions

Phenoxybenzamine is a potent alpha-adrenergic agonist. It will compete with other drugs that act on the alpha-receptor. It will cause vasodilation and should be used cautiously with drugs that may cause vasodilation or depress the heart.

Instructions for Use

Results of clinical studies in animals have not been reported. Use in animals (and doses) is based on experience in people or limited experimental experience in animals.

Patient Monitoring and Laboratory Tests

Phenoxybenzamine can lower blood pressure significantly. Monitor patient's blood pressure and heart rate if possible during treatment.

Formulations

Phenoxybenzamine is available in 10 mg capsules.

Stability and Storage

Phenoxybenzamine is only slightly soluble in water, but soluble in propylene glycol and ethanol. It is not stable in aqueous solutions and undergoes rapid degradation; therefore, it may not be stable in some compounded formulations. Store in tightly sealed container, protected from light, and at room temperature.

Small Animal Dosage

Dogs

- 0.25 mg/kg q8-12h or 0.5 mg/kg q24h PO.

Cats

- 2.5 mg/cat q8-12h or 0.5 mg/kg q12h PO. (Doses as high as 0.5 mg/kg IV have been used to relax urethral smooth muscle.)

Large Animal Dosage

Horses

- 1 mg/kg q24h IV or 0.7 mg/kg q6h PO.

Regulatory Information

Withdrawal times are not established for animals that produce food. For extralabel use withdrawal interval estimates, contact FARAD at 1-888-USFARAD (1-888-873-2723) or send e-mail to FARAD@ncsu.edu.
RCI Classification: 3

Phentolamine Mesylate

fen-tole'ah-meen mess'ih-late

Trade and Other Names: Regitine and Rogitine (in Canada)

Functional Classification: Vasodilator

Pharmacology and Mechanism of Action

Nonselective alpha-adrenergic blocker. Vasodilator. Phentolamine blocks both $alpha_1$ and $alpha_2$ receptors on smooth muscle.

Indications and Clinical Uses

Phentolamine is a potent vasodilator and is used primarily to treat acute hypertension.

Precautionary Information

Adverse Reactions and Side Effects

Phentolamine may cause excess hypotension with high doses or in animals that are dehydrated and may cause tachycardia.

Contraindications and Precautions

Use carefully in animals with cardiovascular compromise. Do not use in dehydrated animals. Use carefully in animals with low cardiac output.

Drug Interactions

Phentolamine is an alpha-adrenergic agonist. It will compete with other drugs that act on the alpha-receptor. It will cause vasodilation and should be used cautiously with drugs that may cause vasodilation or depress the heart.

Instructions for Use

Results of clinical studies in animals have not been reported. Use in animals (and doses) is based on experience in people or anecdotal experience in animals. Titrate dose for each patient to produce desired vasodilation.

Patient Monitoring and Laboratory Tests

Phentolamine can lower blood pressure significantly. Monitor patient's blood pressure and heart rate if possible during treatment.

Formulations

Phentolamine is available in 5 mg vials for injection.

Stability and Storage

Store in tightly sealed container, protected from light, and at room temperature.

Small Animal Dosage

Dogs and Cats

- 0.02-0.1 mg/kg IV.

Large Animal Dosage

No doses have been reported for large animals.

Regulatory Information

Withdrawal times are not established for animals that produce food. For extralabel use withdrawal interval estimates, contact FARAD at 1-888-USFARAD (1-888-873-2723) or send e-mail to FARAD@ncsu.edu.

RCI Classification: 3

Phenylbutazone

fen-ill-byoo′tah-zone

Trade and Other Names: Butazolidin, PBZ, and generic brands

Functional Classification: Nonsteroidal Antiinflammatory Drug (NSAID)

Pharmacology and Mechanism of Action

Phenylbutazone and other NSAIDs produce analgesic and antiinflammatory effects by inhibiting the synthesis of prostaglandins. The enzyme inhibited by NSAIDs is the cyclo-oxygenase enzyme (COX). The COX enzyme exists in two isoforms, called COX-1 and COX-2. COX-1 is primarily responsible for synthesis of prostaglandins important for maintaining a healthy GI tract, renal function, platelet function, and other normal functions. COX-2 is induced and responsible for synthesizing prostaglandins that are important mediators of pain, inflammation, and fever. Phenylbutazone is a nonselective inhibitor of COX-1 and COX-2.

P

Indications and Clinical Uses

The major use of phenylbutazone is in horses for musculoskeletal pain and inflammation, arthritis, soft tissue injury, and racing injuries. The duration of action in horses after a single administration is approximately 24 hours. Phenylbutazone is registered for use in dogs (and cats in Europe), however the use in small animals is not common because of the availability of other drugs.

Precautionary Information

Adverse Reactions and Side Effects

In horses, GI ulcers are well-documented. Ulcers are more likely as the dose increases and in animals undergoing extensive training. Phenylbutazone is generally well tolerated in dogs, but there is no data for cats. Adverse effects possible are GI toxicity such as gastritis and gastric ulcers. Phenylbutazone also is associated with renal injury. In horses that are dehydrated or have renal compromise, phenylbutazone can cause ischemia and renal papillary necrosis. Phenylbutazone is rarely used in people because it has caused bone marrow depression. This effect also has been observed in dogs. In experimental horses, phenylbutazone (4.4 mg/kg q12h for 14 days) decreased proteoglycan synthesis in articular cartilage.

Contraindications and Precautions

Do not administer injectable formulation IM. Do not administer to animals prone to GI ulcers or with compromised renal function. Do not administer with other ulcerogenic drugs, such as corticosteroids.

Drug Interactions

Do not administer with other NSAIDs or with corticosteroids. Corticosteroids have been shown to exacerbate the GI adverse effects. Phenylbutazone will interfere with the action of furosemide in horses. Some NSAIDs also may interfere with the action of angiotensin-converting enzyme (ACE) inhibitors.

Instructions for Use

Doses are based primarily on manufacturer's recommendations and clinical experience. Although a range of 4.4-8.8 mg/kg per day has been administered to horses, studies have not shown an advantage for the higher dose, and the higher dose is more likely to cause GI injury.

Patient Monitoring and Laboratory Tests

Monitor CBC for signs of bone marrow toxicity with chronic use.

Formulations

Phenylbutazone is available in 100, 200, 400 mg and 1 g tablets and 200 mg/mL injection.

Stability and Storage

Store in tightly sealed container, protected from light, and at room temperature. Phenylbutazone is not water soluble. It should not be compounded in aqueous vehicles.

Small Animal Dosage

Dogs

- 15-22 mg/kg q8-12h (44 mg/kg/day; 800 mg/dog maximum) PO or IV.

Cats

- 6-8 mg/kg q12h IV or PO.

Large Animal Dosage

Horses

- 4.4-8.8 mg/kg/day (generally 2 grams to 4 grams per horse) PO. It is not recommended to use the highest dose for more than 48-96 hours.
- Injection: 2.2-4.4 mg/kg/day for 48-96 hours. Give injections IV only as intramuscular injections will cause tissue irritation.

Cattle

- 17-25 mg/kg loading dose, then 2.5-5 mg/kg q24h or 10-14 mg/kg q48h PO or IV. (See regulatory restrictions in cattle.)

Pigs

- 4 mg/kg q24h IV.

Regulatory Information

Phenylbutazone is prohibited from use in female dairy cattle younger than 20 months of age. Other withdrawal times have not been established for animals intended for food. However, FARAD recommends: Swine 15 days and cattle 12 days meat at 6 gram per dose and 21 days meat at repeated doses.

RCI Classification: not classified

Phenylephrine Hydrochloride

fen-ill-ef′rin hye-droe-klor′ide

Trade and Other Names: Neo-synephrine

Functional Classification: Vasopressor

Pharmacology and Mechanism of Action

Alpha$_1$-adreneric receptor agonist. Phenylephrine will stimulate alpha$_1$ receptors and cause smooth muscle contraction, primarily in vascular smooth muscle to cause vasoconstriction. It may be applied topically (e.g., mucous membranes) to constrict superficial blood vessels.

Indications and Clinical Uses

Phenylephrine is used primarily in critical care patients or during anesthesia to increase peripheral resistance and increase blood pressure. Phenylephrine also is used commonly as topical vasoconstrictor (as in nasal decongestants or for ophthalmic use).

Precautionary Information

Adverse Reactions and Side Effects

Adverse effects related to excessive stimulation of alpha$_1$ receptor (prolonged peripheral vasoconstriction). Reflex bradycardia may occur. Prolonged topical use may cause tissue inflammation.

Contraindications and Precautions

Do not use in animals with compromised cardiovascular status. It will cause vasoconstriction and can increase blood pressure.

Drug Interactions

Phenylephrine will potentiate other alpha$_1$ agonists.

P

Instructions for Use

Phenylephrine has a rapid onset and short duration of action.

Patient Monitoring and Laboratory Tests

When administered IV, monitor blood pressure and heart rate.

Formulations

Phenylephrine is available in 10 mg/mL injection, 1% nasal solution, and 2.5 and 10% ophthalmic solutions.

Stability and Storage

Phenylephrine is soluble in water and may be mixed in intravenous solutions. It is also soluble in ethanol. It is subject to oxidation and will turn a darker color in some solutions, especially alkaline solutions. Discard formulations that turn a dark color. Store in tightly sealed container, protected from light, and at room temperature.

Small Animal Dosage

Dogs and Cats

- 10 mcg/kg (0.01 mg/kg) q15min IV, as needed or 0.1 mg/kg q15min IM or SQ.
- Constant rate infusion (CRI): 10 mcg/kg IV, followed by 3 mcg/kg/min IV.

Large Animal Dosage

No large animal dose is available.

Regulatory Information

Withdrawal times are not established for animals that produce food. For extralabel use withdrawal interval estimates, contact FARAD at 1-888-USFARAD (1-888-873-2723) or send e-mail to FARAD@ncsu.edu.

RCI Classification: 3

Phenylpropanolamine Hydrochloride

fen-ill-proe-pah-nole'ah-meen hye-droe-klor'ide

Trade and Other Names: Dexatrim, Propagest, and PPA (human preparations) Proin-ppa, UriCon, and Propalin (veterinary preparations)

Functional Classification: Adrenergic agonist

Pharmacology and Mechanism of Action

Adrenergic agonist. Sympathomimetic. It nonselectively acts as an agonist for the alpha-adrenergic and beta-adrenergic receptor. These receptors are found throughout the body, such as on sphincters, blood vessels, smooth muscle, and heart.

Indications and Clinical Uses

Phenylpropanolamine (PPA) has been used as a decongestant, mild bronchodilator, and to increase tone of urinary sphincter. Pseudoephedrine and ephedrine are related drugs that produce similar alpha-receptor and beta-receptor effects. The most common use in animals is for treating urinary incontinence. The mechanism for this action appears to be via stimulating receptors on sphincter. Abuse potential and adverse effects in people have limited its use in human medicine.

Precautionary Information

Adverse Reactions and Side Effects

Adverse effects are attributed to excess stimulation of adrenergic (alpha and beta) receptors. Side effects include tachycardia, cardiac effects, CNS excitement, restlessness, and appetite suppression. There are recent reports of adverse effects caused by PPA in people. In particular, it has caused problems with blood pressure in some people and also caused strokes. Such a concern should also apply to animals, but there have been no specific reports of these problems in animals.

Contraindications and Precautions

Use cautiously in any animal with cardiovascular disease. PPA has been abused by people and used as a recreational drug.

Drug Interactions
PPA and other sympathomimetic drugs can cause increased vasoconstriction and changes in heart rate. Use cautiously with other vasoactive drugs. Use cautiously with other drugs that may lower seizure threshold. Use of inhalant anesthetics with PPA may increase cardiovascular risk. Do not use with tricyclic antidepressants (TCAs) or monoamine oxidase inhibitors (MAOIs; e.g., selegiline or amitraz).

Instructions for Use

In some animals, pseudoephedrine has been substituted for PPA with good success.

Patient Monitoring and Laboratory Tests

Monitor heart rate and blood pressure in animals receiving treatment. Animals with urinary incontinence should be checked periodically for presence of UTIs.

Formulations

Phenylpropanolamine is available 25, 50, and 75 flavored tablets, 25 mg vanilla flavored liquid, 50 mg scored tablets (veterinary preparations). 15, 25, 30, and 50 mg tablets (human preparations) are no longer available, but compounded veterinary formulations have been distributed.

Stability and Storage

Since the availability of human preparations have been taken off the market, the only formulations currently available are nonapproved compounded preparations. The stability and potency of these preparations has not been evaluated by the FDA.

Small Animal Dosage

Dogs

- 1 mg/kg q8h PO. Increase dose to 1.5-2 mg/kg q8h PO, if necessary. In some animals it may be possible to decrease frequency to q12h PO.

Large Animal Dosage

No large animal dose is available.

Regulatory Information

There are no formulations currently marketed in the U.S. for human use because of abuse potential and adverse cardiovascular events. Veterinary formulations currently are not regulated.
RCI Classification: 3

Phenytoin, Phenytoin Sodium

fen-ih-toe-in

Trade and Other Names: Dilantin

Functional Classification: Anticonvulsant, antiarrhythmic

Pharmacology and Mechanism of Action

Anticonvulsant. Depresses nerve conduction via blockade of sodium channels. Phenytoin is also classified as Class-I cardiac antiarrhythmic. In cardiac tissue, phenytoin increases threshold for triggering ventricular arrhythmias. It also decreases conduction velocity and does not shorten the refractory period as much as lidocaine.

Indications and Clinical Uses

Phenytoin is commonly used as an anticonvulsant in people, but it is not effective in dogs and not used in cats. In dogs, elimination is so rapid that dosing is impractical. Phenytoin is used in horses for treating ventricular arrhythmias, controlling myotonia, rhabdomyolysis, hyperkalemic periodic paresis, and stringhalt.

Precautionary Information

Adverse Reactions and Side Effects

Adverse effects include sedation, gingival hyperplasia, skin reactions, and CNS toxicity. In horses, at high doses recumbency and excitement have been observed. Sedation in horses may be an initial sign of high plasma concentrations. Monitoring plasma concentrations in horses can prevent adverse effects.

Contraindications and Precautions

Do not administer to pregnant animals.

Drug Interactions

Phenytoin will interact with drugs undergoing hepatic metabolism. Phenytoin is a potent cytochrome P450 enzyme inducer. When used with cytochrome P450 inhibitors, increased levels of phenytoin may occur.

Instructions for Use

Because of short half-life and poor efficacy in dogs and questionable safety in cats, other anticonvulsants are used as first choice before phenytoin.

Patient Monitoring and Laboratory Tests

Therapeutic drug monitoring can be performed, however therapeutic concentrations have not been established for dogs and cats. In horses, effective plasma concentrations are 5-20 mcg/mL (average 8.8 mcg/mL +/− 2 mcg/mL). Therapy should be aimed at producing concentrations above 5 mcg/mL in horses.

Formulations

Phenytoin is available in 25 mg/mL oral suspension, 30, 100 mg capsules (sodium salt), and 50 mg/mL injection (sodium salt).

Stability and Storage

Store protected from light at room temperature. Phenytoin sodium will absorb carbon dioxide and must be kept in a tight container. Phenytoin is practically insoluble in water, but phenytoin sodium has a solubility of 15 mg/mL. It is soluble in ethanol and propylene glycol. pH of phenytoin is 10-12, and it may not be compatible with acidic solutions. It may precipitate from solution if mixed with solutions at a lower pH. Protect from freezing.

Small Animal Dosage

Dogs

- Anticonvulsant: 20-35 mg/kg q8h.
- Antiarrhythmic: 30 mg/kg q8h PO or 10 mg/kg IV over 5 min.

Cats

Do not use.

Large Animal Dosage

Horses

- Initial bolus of 20 mg/kg q12h PO, for 4 doses, followed by 10-15 mg/kg q12h PO. A single IV dose in horses of 7.5-8.8 mg/kg can be used followed by oral maintenance doses.

Regulatory Information

Withdrawal times are not established for animals that produce food. For extralabel use withdrawal interval estimates, contact FARAD at 1-888-USFARAD (1-888-873-2723) or send e-mail to FARAD@ncsu.edu.

RCI Classification: 4

Physostigmine

fye-zoe-stig′meen

Trade and Other Names: Antilirium

Functional Classification: Anticholinesterase

Pharmacology and Mechanism of Action

Cholinesterase inhibitor. Anticholinesterase drug. This drug inhibits the enzyme that breaks down acetylcholine. Therefore it prolongs the action of acetylcholine at the synapse. The major difference between physostigmine and neostigmine or pyridostigmine is that physostigmine crosses the blood-brain barrier, and the others do not.

Indications and Clinical Uses

Physostigmine is used as an antidote for anticholinergic intoxication and as a treatment (antidote) for neuromuscular blockade. It also has been used as a treatment of ileus and urinary retention (such as postoperative urine retention) by increasing tone of bladder smooth muscle.

Precautionary Information

Adverse Reactions and Side Effects

Adverse effects caused by the cholinergic action result from inhibition of cholinesterase. These effects can be seen in the GI tract as diarrhea and increased secretions. Other adverse effects can include miosis, bradycardia, muscle twitching or weakness, and constriction of bronchi and ureters. Adverse effects can be treated with anticholinergic drugs such as atropine.

Contraindications and Precautions

Do not administer with choline esters such as bethanechol.

Drug Interactions

No drug interactions have been reported in animals.

Instructions for Use

Physostigmine is indicated primarily only for treatment of intoxication. For routine systemic use of anticholinesterase drug, neostigmine and pyridostigmine have fewer side effects. When used, frequency of dose may be increased based on observation of effects.

Patient Monitoring and Laboratory Tests

Monitor heart rate and rhythm and GI signs.

Formulations

Physostigmine is available in 1 mg/mL injection.

Stability and Storage

Store in tightly sealed container, protected from light, and at room temperature.

Small Animal Dosage

Dogs and Cats

- 0.02 mg/kg q12h IV.

Large Animal Dosage

No doses have been reported for large animals.

Regulatory Information

Withdrawal times are not established for animals that produce food. For extralabel use withdrawal interval estimates, contact FARAD at 1-888-USFARAD (1-888-873-2723) or send e-mail to FARAD@ncsu.edu.

RCI Classification: 3

Phytonadione

fye-toe-nah-dye′one

Trade and Other Names: AquaMEPHYTON, Mephyton. Veta-K1, Vitamin K1, Phylloquinone, and Phytomenadione

Functional Classification: Vitamin

Pharmacology and Mechanism of Action

Vitamin K supplement. Phytonadione and phytomenadione are synthetic lipid-soluble forms of vitamin K_1. (Phytomenadione is the British spelling of Phytonadione.) Menadiol is vitamin K_4, which is a water-soluble derivative converted in the body to vitamin K_3 (menadione).

Vitamin K_1 is a fat-soluble vitamin used to treat coagulopathies caused by anticoagulant toxicosis (warfarin or other rodenticides). These anticoagulants deplete vitamin K in the body, which is essential for synthesis of clotting factors. Administration of vitamin K, in its various formulations, can be used to reverse the effect of anticoagulant toxicity.

Indications and Clinical Uses

Phytonadione is used to treat coagulopathies caused by anticoagulant toxicosis (warfarin or other rodenticides). In large animals, it is used to treat sweet clover poisoning.

Precautionary Information

Adverse Reactions and Side Effects

In people, a rare hypersensitivity-like reaction has been observed after rapid intravenous injection. Signs resemble anaphylactic shock. These signs also have been observed in animals. To avoid anaphylactic reactions, do not administer IV.

Contraindications and Precautions

Accurate diagnosis to rule-out other causes of bleeding is suggested. Other forms of vitamin K may not be as rapidly acting as vitamin K_1, therefore consider using a specific preparation. To avoid anaphylactic reactions, do not administer IV.

Drug Interactions

No drug interactions are reported.

Instructions for Use

Consult poison control center for specific protocol if specific rodenticide is identified. Use vitamin K_1 for acute therapy of toxicity because it is more highly bioavailable. Administer with food to enhance oral absorption. The injection can be diluted in 5% dextrose or 0.9% saline but not other solutions. Although vitamin K_1 veterinary labels have listed the intravenous route for administration, these labels have not been approved by the FDA. Therefore, avoid intravenous administration of vitamin K_1. The preferred route is SQ, but IM can also be used.

Patient Monitoring and Laboratory Tests

Monitoring bleeding times in patients is essential for accurate dosing of vitamin K_1 preparations. When treating long-acting rodenticide poisoning, periodic monitoring of the bleeding times is suggested.

Formulations

Phytonadione is available in 5 mg tablets (Mephyton) and 25 mg capsules (Veta-K1).

Phytonadione (AquaMEPHYTON) is available in 2 or 10 mg/mL injection.

Stability and Storage

Store in tightly sealed container at room temperature. It is light sensitive and should be protected from light. Phytonadione is practically insoluble in water. However it is soluble in oils and slightly soluble in ethanol. Do not mix with aqueous solutions. If mixed as a suspension for oral use, administer soon after preparation. Do not freeze.

Small Animal Dosage

Dogs and Cats

- Treatment of short-acting rodenticides: 1 mg/kg/day for 10-14 days IV, SQ, or PO.
- Treatment of long-acting rodenticides: 2.5-5 mg/kg/day for 3-4 weeks IM, SQ, or PO.

Birds

- 2.5-5 mg/kg q24h.

Large Animal Dosage

Cattle, Calves, Horses, Sheep, and Goats

- 0.5-2.5 mg/kg SQ or IM.

Regulatory Information

Withdrawal times are not established for animals that produce food. It is anticipated that milk and meat withdrawal times will be short. For extralabel use withdrawal interval estimates, contact FARAD at 1-888-USFARAD (1-888-873-2723) or send e-mail to FARAD@ncsu.edu.

P

Pimobendan

pim-oh-ben'dan

Trade and Other Names: Vetmedin

Functional Classification: Cardiac inotropic agent

Pharmacology and Mechanism of Action

Pimobendan is a positive inotrope by acting as a phosphodiesterase III inhibitor. Therefore, its action is to increase intracellular concentrations of cyclic adrenomonophosphate (AMP). Phosphodiesterase III is the enzyme that degrades cyclic AMP. Most of the therapeutic effect of pimobendan may reside in its action as a *calcium* sensitizer rather than the phosphodiesterase inhibition. By acting as a calcium sensitizer, it increases the interaction of troponin C with contractile proteins and acts as a inotropic agent. It also has vasodilating properties. The benefits in heart failure are caused by both positive inotropic effects and vasodilating properties. Effects occur after 1 hour and persist for 8-12 hours after administration.

Indications and Clinical Uses

Pimobendan is indicated for use in dogs for treatment of CHF. It has been used in dogs with either valvular insufficiency or cardiomyopathy. When used in dogs, it has improved signs of heart failure and increased survival. When used in dogs, it may be administered with diuretics and angiotensin-converting enzyme (ACE) inhibitors. In trials in North America, pimobendan showed significant improvement compared to placebo in dogs treated with an ACE inhibitor and a diuretic. It has been used with furosemide, ACE inhibitors, and spironolactone. There has been anecdotal experience in cats. When administered at 1.25 mg/cat q12h, it has been well tolerated and has improved some cats.

Precautionary Information

Adverse Reactions and Side Effects

Pimobendan is potentially arrhythmogenic. There is some concern as to whether or not pimobendan will increase the risk of atrial fibrillation arrhythmia in dogs.

Contraindications and Precautions

Use cautiously in animals prone to cardiac arrhythmias.

Drug Interactions

Use cautiously with other phosphodiesterase inhibitors such as theophylline, pentoxifylline, and sildenafil (Viagra) and related drugs. Sildenafil is a phosphodiesterase V inhibitor; theophylline is a phosphodiesterase IV inhibitor.

Instructions for Use

Follow label instruction for use. Evaluate stage of heart failure in animals before use. Formulations have been imported from Europe, where it has been approved previously.

Patient Monitoring and Laboratory Tests

Monitor patient's heart rate and rhythm during use.

Formulations

Pimobendan is available in 2.5 and 5 mg capsules. Until it is registered by FDA in the U.S., permission from FDA is needed to import from Europe.

Stability and Storage

Store in tightly sealed container, protected from light, and at room temperature.

Small Animal Dosage

Dogs

- 0.15-0.25 mg/kg q24h PO, and up to 0.25-0.3 mg/kg q12h PO.
- Dogs 4-8 kg: 1.25 mg.
- Dogs 8-20 kg: 2.5 mg.
- Dogs 20-40 kg: 5 mg.
- Dogs 40-60 kg: 10 mg.
- Dogs >60 kg: 15 mg.

Cats

- 1.25 mg/cat q12h PO (experience is limited).

Large Animal Dosage

No doses have been reported for large animals.

Regulatory Information

Do not administer to animals intended for food.

Piperacillin Sodium

pih'per-ah-sill'in soe'dee-um

Trade and Other Names: Pipracil and Zosyn

Functional Classification: Antibacterial, Beta-lactam

Pharmacology and Mechanism of Action

Beta-lactam antibiotic of the acylureidopenicillin class. Like other beta-lactams, piperacillin binds penicillin-binding proteins (PBP) that weaken or interfere with cell wall formation. After binding to PBP, the cell wall weakens or undergoes lysis. Like other beta-lactams, this drug acts in a time-dependent manner (i.e., it is more effective when drug concentrations are maintained above the minimum inhibitory concentration [MIC] values during the dose interval). Similar to other penicillins, piperacillin has a high activity against *Pseudomonas aeruginosa*. It also has good activity against streptococci. Piperacillin has a short half-life in animals and must be given by injection (usually IV) which limits its usefulness. Some formulations of piperacillin also contain tazobactam (Zosyn), which is a beta-lactamase inhibitor and increases the spectrum to include beta-lactamase strains of gram-negative and gram-positive bacteria.

P

Indications and Clinical Uses

Piperacillin has similar activity as ampicillin, but it is extended to include many organisms that otherwise are resistant to ampicillin, such as *Pseudomonas aeruginosa*, and other gram-negative bacilli. Its activity is enhanced when administered with an aminoglycoside (e.g., gentamicin or amikacin).

Precautionary Information

Adverse Reactions and Side Effects

Allergy to penicillin is most common adverse effect. High doses may inhibit platelet function.

Contraindications and Precautions

Do not use in patients allergic to penicillin drugs. High doses contribute to the sodium load in a patient.

Drug Interactions

Do not mix in vials or syringes with other drugs.

Instructions for Use

Piperacillin is combined with tazobactam (beta-lactamase inhibitor) in Zosyn, which increases the spectrum to include beta-lactamase producing strains of *Staphylococcus* and gram-negative bacteria. Ticarcillin has a similar spectrum of activity and may be used as a substitute for piperacillin.

Patient Monitoring and Laboratory Tests

Susceptibility testing: CLSI (NCCLS) break points for sensitive organisms are less than or equal to 64 mcg/mL for *Pseudomonas aeruginosa* and less than or equal to 16 mcg/mL for all other gram-negative organisms.

Formulations

Piperacillin is available in 2, 3, 4, and 40 g vials for injection.

Stability and Storage

Reconstituted solution should be used within 24 hours or 7 days if refrigerated.

Small Animal Dosage

Dogs and Cats

- 40 mg/kg q6h IV or IM.

Large Animal Dosage

No doses have been reported for large animals.

Regulatory Information

Withdrawal times are not established for animals that produce food. However, because of rapid elimination, it is anticipated that withdrawal times will be similar as for other beta-lactams such as ampicillin.

For extralabel use withdrawal interval estimates, contact FARAD at 1-888-USFARAD (1-888-873-2723) or send e-mail to FARAD@ncsu.edu.

Piperazine

pih-peer′e-zeen

Trade and Other Names: Pipa-Tabs and generic brands

Functional Classification: Antiparasitic

Pharmacology and Mechanism of Action

Antiparasitic compound. Piperazine produces neuromuscular blockade in parasite through selective antagonism of GABA receptors, resulting in opening of chloride channels, hyperpolarization of parasite membrane, and paralysis of worms. Efficacy is limited primarily to roundworms. In horses it is active against small strongyles and roundworms.

Indications and Clinical Uses

Piperazine is a common antiparasitic drug and is widely available, even OTC. It is used primarily for treatment of roundworm (ascarid) infections in animals.

Precautionary Information

Adverse Reactions and Side Effects

Piperazine is remarkably safe in all species, but can cause ataxia, muscle tremors, and changes in behavior.

Contraindications and Precautions

No contraindications in animals. It may be used in all ages.

Drug Interactions

No drug interactions have been reported in animals.

Instructions for Use

Piperazine is a widely used antiparasitic drug with a wide margin of safety. It may be used in combination with other antiparasitic drugs.

Patient Monitoring and Laboratory Tests

No specific monitoring is necessary.

Formulations

Piperazine is available in 860 mg powder, 140 mg capsules, 50 and 250 mg tablets, and 128, 160, 170, 340, 510, and 800 mg/mL oral solution.

Stability and Storage

Store in tightly sealed container, protected from light, and at room temperature.

Small Animal Dosage

Dogs and Cats

- 44-66 mg/kg administered once PO.

Large Animal Dosage

Horses and Pigs

- 110 mg/kg PO in the drinking water as the sole water source.
- Oral solution (horses): 30 mL (one ounce) of 17% piperazine solution administered PO for each 45 kg body weight.

Regulatory Information

Withdrawal times are not established for animals that produce food. For extralabel use withdrawal interval estimates, contact FARAD at 1-888-USFARAD (1-888-873-2723) or send e-mail to FARAD@ncsu.edu.

Piroxicam

peer-oks′ih-kam

Trade and Other Names: Feldene and generic brands

Functional Classification: Nonsteroidal antiinflammatory drug (NSAID)

Pharmacology and Mechanism of Action

Piroxicam is an NSAID of the oxicam class. Clinical effects are similar to other NSAIDs (see aspirin and flunixin). These drugs appear to have analgesic and antiinflammatory effects by inhibiting the synthesis of prostaglandins. The enzyme inhibited by NSAIDs is the cyclo-oxygenase enzyme (COX). The COX enzyme exists in two isoforms, called COX-1 and COX-2. COX-1 is primarily responsible for synthesis of prostaglandins important for maintaining a healthy GI tract, renal function, platelet function, and other normal functions. COX-2 is induced and responsible for synthesizing prostaglandins that are important mediators of pain, inflammation, and fever. (There may be some crossover of COX-1 and COX-2 effects in some situations.) Piroxicam may be more COX-2 selective in dogs than in people. Piroxicam also may have some antitumor or tumor-preventative effects and is used in some anticancer protocols.

Indications and Clinical Uses

Piroxicam is primarily used to treat arthritis and other musculoskeletal conditions. However, a common use in dogs and cats has been as an adjunct for treating cancer. This use is based on reports of its activity for treating or suppressing some tumors, including transitional cell carcinoma of bladder, squamous cell carcinoma, and mammary adenocarcinoma. Piroxicam has been used in combination with cisplatin to treat oral malignant melanoma and oral squamous cell carcinoma in dogs (0.3 mg/kg).

Precautionary Information

Adverse Reactions and Side Effects

Elimination of piroxicam is slow. Adverse effects are primarily GI toxicity (e.g., gastric ulcers). Renal toxicity also is a risk, especially in animals prone to dehydration or that have compromised renal function. Piroxicam has been administered to dogs and cats as a treatment for cancer with few adverse effects, but GI erosions and ulcers are possible.

Contraindications and Precautions

Use cautiously in dogs. The human formulation is too large a dose for most dogs. Warn pet owners about overdoses that could produce GI ulceration. Do not administer to animals prone to GI ulcers. Do not administer to pregnant animals. Use cautiously in any animal with renal disease.

Drug Interactions

Do not administer with other NSAIDs or with corticosteroids. Corticosteroids have been shown to exacerbate the gastrointestinal adverse effects. Some NSAIDs may interfere with the action of diuretic drugs and angiotensin-converting enzyme (ACE) inhibitors.

Instructions for Use

Most experience with dosing has been accumulated from studies in which dogs were treated with piroxicam for transitional cell carcinoma of the bladder. Some of these dogs tolerated piroxicam better, with respect to GI toxicity, if the drug was administered with misoprostol. Piroxicam has been used in dogs for treatment of squamous cell carcinoma.

Patient Monitoring and Laboratory Tests

Piroxicam has the potential of inducing GI ulceration. Monitor for signs of vomiting, bleeding, and lethargy. If bleeding is suspected, monitor patient's hematocrit or CBC. Monitor renal function in treated animals.

Formulations

Piroxicam is available in 10 mg capsules.

Stability and Storage

Piroxicam is only slightly soluble in water. It is soluble in acidic solutions and some organic solvents. Compounded formulations made for small animals may be stable for only 48 hours.

Small Animal Dosage

Dogs

- 0.3 mg/kg q48h PO.
- Cancer treatment: Dogs also have tolerated 0.3 mg/kg q24h PO.

Cats

- 0.3 mg/kg q24h PO.

Large Animal Dosage

No doses have been reported for large animals.

Regulatory Information

Withdrawal times are not established for animals that produce food. For extralabel use withdrawal interval estimates, contact FARAD at 1-888-USFARAD (1-888-873-2723) or send e-mail to FARAD@ncsu.edu.
RCI Classification: 4

Plicamycin

plye-kah-mye'sin

Trade and Other Names: Mithracin and Mithramycin

Functional Classification: Anticancer agent

Pharmacology and Mechanism of Action

Anticancer agent. The action of plicamycin is to complex with DNA in presence of divalent cations and inhibit DNA and RNA synthesis. It lowers serum calcium and may have direct action on osteoclasts to decrease serum calcium.

Indications and Clinical Uses

Plicamycin is used in cancer protocols for carcinomas and treatment of hypercalcemia.

Precautionary Information

Adverse Reactions and Side Effects

Adverse effects have not been reported in animals. In people, hypocalcemia and GI toxicity have been reported. Plicamycin may cause bleeding problems.

Contraindications and Precautions

Do not use with drugs that may increase the risk of bleeding (e.g., nonsteroidal antiinflammatory drugs [NSAIDs], heparin, or anticoagulants).

Drug Interactions

No drug interactions have been reported.

Instructions for Use

Results of clinical studies in animals have not been reported. Use in animals (and doses) is based on experience in people or anecdotal experience in animals.

Patient Monitoring and Laboratory Tests

Monitor serum calcium concentrations.

Formulations

Plicamycin is available in 2.5 mg vial for injection and 0.5 mg/mL when diluted.

Stability and Storage

Store in tightly sealed container, protected from light, and at room temperature.

Small Animal Dosage

Dogs and Cats

- Antihypercalcemic: 25 mcg/kg/day IV (slow infusion) over 4 hours.
- Antineoplastic (dogs): 25-30 mcg/kg/day IV (slow infusion) for 8-10 days

Large Animal Dosage

No doses have been reported for large animals.

Regulatory Information

Withdrawal times are not established for animals that produce food. This drug should not be used in animals intended for food, because it is an anticancer agent.

Polyethylene Glycol Electrolyte Solution

pahl-ee-eth′ill-een glye′kole

Trade and Other Names: GoLytely, PEG, Colyte, and Co-Lav

Functional Classification: Laxative

Pharmacology and Mechanism of Action

Saline cathartic. Polyethylene glycol electrolyte solution is a nonabsorbable compound that increases water secretion into bowel via osmotic effect. These isosmotic liquids pass through the bowel without absorption.

Indications and Clinical Uses

Polyethylene glycol electrolyte solution is a cathartic that is used primarily for evacuating the bowel and cleansing of the intestine prior to endoscopy and surgical procedures. It is administered PO and will induce a rapid osmotic cathartic effect. It is effective for bowel cleansing, but it requires high volumes to be effective. In some human patients, smaller volumes can be used if it is combined with another laxative, such as bisacodyl.

Precautionary Information

Adverse Reactions and Side Effects

Water and electrolyte loss with high doses or prolonged use are common. Large volumes required may cause nausea.

Contraindications and Precautions

Do not administer to animals that are dehydrated, because it may cause fluid and electrolyte loss. It is not indicated for chronic use.

Drug Interactions

No specific drug interactions.

Instructions for Use

Used for bowel evacuation prior to surgical or diagnostic procedures. Large volumes are required. In human patients, administration of only half the volume can be used if taken with bisacodyl (1-4 tablets) 2 hours prior to procedure. This combination is called HalfLytely.

Patient Monitoring and Laboratory Tests

Monitor electrolytes if it is administered repeatedly.

Formulations

Polyethylene glycol electrolyte is an oral solution. Preparations contain polyethylene glycol (PEG) 3350, sodium chloride, potassium chloride, sodium bicarbonate, and sodium sulfate.

Stability and Storage

Store in tightly sealed container, protected from light, and at room temperature.

Small Animal Dosage

Dogs and Cats

- 25 mL/kg, repeat in 2-4 hours PO.

Large Animal Dosage

Horses and Cattle

- Via stomach tube: 500 mL to 4 L once PO.

Regulatory Information

No withdrawal times necessary.

Polysulfated Glycosaminoglycan

pahl-ee-sul′fate-ed glye-koe-sah-mee-noe-glye-kan

Trade and Other Names: Adequan Canine, Adequan IA, and Adequan IM

Functional Classification: Antiarthritic agent

Pharmacology and Mechanism of Action

Polysulfated glycosaminoglycan (PSGAG) provides large molecular weight compounds similar to normal constituents of healthy joints. It is chondroprotective and inhibits enzymes that may degrade articular cartilage, such as metalloproteinase.

Indications and Clinical Uses

PSGAG is used in dogs and horses to treat or prevent degenerative joint disease. Intraarticular injections have been effective, but intramuscular doses may be too low to be effective in some animals.

Precautionary Information

Adverse Reactions and Side Effects

Adverse effects are rare. Allergic reactions are possible. PSGAG has heparin-like effects and may elicit bleeding problems in some animals, but this has not been observed clinically.

Contraindications and Precautions

Intraarticular injections should be done using aseptic technique. Use cautiously in animals receiving heparin therapy.

Drug Interactions

No drug interactions are reported in animals.

Instructions for Use

Doses are derived from empirical evidence, experimental studies, and clinical studies in dogs. Although effective for acute arthritis, it may not be as effective for chronic arthropathy. In horses, it is sometimes combined with amikacin (125 mg) for intraarticular use to prevent infection.

Patient Monitoring and Laboratory Tests

Observe injected joints for signs of infection after treatment.

Formulations

Polysulfated glycosaminoglycan is available in 100 mg/mL injection in 5 mL vial, 100 mg/mL for IM use, and 250 mg/mL for intraarticular use in horses.

Stability and Storage

Store in tightly sealed container, protected from light, and at room temperature.

Small Animal Dosage

Dogs

- 4.4 mg/kg IM, twice weekly for up to 4 weeks.

Large Animal Dosage

Horses

- 500 mg every 4 days IM for 28 days or 250 mg once weekly for 5 weeks intraarticular.

Regulatory Information

No withdrawal times necessary.

Ponazuril

poe-naz'yoo-ril

Trade and Other Names: Marquis

Functional Classification: Antiprotozoal

Pharmacology and Mechanism of Action

Antiprotozoal drug. Coccidiostat. Ponazuril (also known as toltrazuril sulfone) is a metabolite of the antiprotozoal drug, toltrazuril. Ponazuril is a triazine-based drug that acts to inhibit enzyme systems in protozoa and/or decreasing pyrimidine synthesis. It is specific in action to protozoa.

Indications and Clinical Uses

Toltrazuril, the parent drug, has been used for protozoa such as *Isospora, Coccidia* spp., *Toxoplasma gondii,* and *Eimeria* spp. Ponazuril has a long half-life in horses (>4 days) and concentrations in cerebrospinal fluid (CSF) are 3.5%-4% of serum concentrations but high enough to inhibit protozoa. Ponazuril is specifically registered for use as a treatment of equine protozoal myeloencephalitis (EPM), caused by *Sarcocystis neurona*. In clinical studies in horses with EPM, 62% of 101 horses were treated successfully with doses of 5 or 10 mg/kg for 28 days.

Precautionary Information

Adverse Reactions and Side Effects

Administration of 50 mg/kg to horses (10 times the recommended dose) produced minor adverse effects. There were minimal changes in the serum analysis. Soft feces may occur at high doses.

Contraindications and Precautions

Avoid use in pregnant or breeding mares until more information becomes available on safety.

Drug Interactions

No drug interactions have been reported.

Instructions for Use

Use in horses is based on careful clinical trials and pharmacokinetic studies in horses. Field trials were conducted by manufacturer. In a trial with either 5 or 10 mg/kg per day in horses, 62% were improved by 28 days. Although successful treatment was reported after 28 days, longer treatment duration may be needed in some animals to resolve the infection and prevent relapse. Ponazuril has not been used clinically in other animals.

Patient Monitoring and Laboratory Tests

In horses treated for EPM, monitor neurological status during treatment. IgG and albumin quotient has been measured in CSF of treated horses to monitor treatment, but this may not indicate clinical cure.

Formulations

Ponazuril is available in 15% (150 mg/mL) oral paste for horses.

Stability and Storage

Store in tightly sealed container, protected from light, and at room temperature.

Small Animal Dosage

No small animal dose has been reported.

Large Animal Dosage

Horses

- Treatment of EPM: 5 mg/kg q24h PO for 28 days.

Regulatory Information

No regulatory information is available. For extralabel use withdrawal interval estimates, contact FARAD at 1-888-USFARAD (1-888-873-2723) or send e-mail to FARAD@ncsu.edu.

Potassium Chloride

Trade and Other Names: Generic brands

Functional Classification: Potassium supplement

Pharmacology and Mechanism of Action

Potassium supplement. Potassium is used for treatment of hypokalemia. A dose 1.9 g of potassium chloride is equivalent to 1 g of potassium. One gram of potassium chloride is equal to 14 mEq of potassium. Other potassium supplements include potassium gluconate, potassium acetate, potassium bicarbonate, and potassium citrate.

Indications and Clinical Uses

Potassium supplements are indicated for treating hypokalemia. Hypokalemia may occur with some diseases or as a consequence of diuretic use. In most patients, potassium chloride is the supplement of choice for hypokalemia. It is better absorbed than other supplements, and the chloride ion may be helpful because hypochloremia may also occur in some patients.

Precautionary Information

Adverse Reactions and Side Effects

Toxicity from high potassium concentrations can be dangerous. Hyperkalemia can lead to cardiovascular toxicity (bradycardia and arrest) and muscular weakness. Oral potassium supplements can cause nausea and stomach irritation.

Contraindications and Precautions

Use cautiously in animals with renal disease. Do not use potassium chloride if metabolic acidosis and hyperchloremia is present. Use another potassium supplement instead. Intravenous use should be done cautiously because of risk of hyperkalemia. Use potassium cautiously in digitalized patients. Do not use with potassium penicillin or potassium bromide.

Drug Interactions

Interactions between potassium supplements and the following drugs may occur: digoxin, thiazide diuretics, spironolactone, amphotericin B, corticosteroids, penicillins, angiotensin-converting enzyme (ACE) inhibitors, and laxatives.

Instructions for Use

One gram of potassium chloride provides 13.41 mEq of potassium. It is usually added to fluid solutions. When potassium is supplemented in fluids, do not administer at a rate faster than 0.5 mEq/kg/hr.

Patient Monitoring and Laboratory Tests

Monitor serum potassium levels. Monitor ECG in patients that may be prone to arrhythmias. Normal potassium is 4-5.5 mEq/L (dogs) and 4.3-6.0 mEq/L (cats).

Formulations

Potassium chloride is available in various concentrations for injection (usually 2 mEq/mL). It is available in an oral suspension and oral solution as 10-20 mEq of potassium per packet. 1 gram potassium chloride contains 14 mEq potassium ion.

Stability and Storage

Store in tightly sealed container, protected from light, and at room temperature. Potassium chloride is freely soluble in water.

Small Animal Dosage

Dogs and Cats

- 0.5 mEq potassium/kg/day or supplement 10-40 mEq/500 mL of fluids, depending on serum potassium.

Large Animal Dosage

Cattle and Horses

- Supplement in intravenous fluids to 20-40 mEq potassium per liter of fluids. Do not exceed a rate of 0.5 mEq/kg/hr IV.

Regulatory Information

No withdrawal times necessary.

Potassium Citrate

Trade and Other Names: Generic and Urocit-K

Functional Classification: Alkalinizing agent

Pharmacology and Mechanism of Action

Potassium citrate ($K_3C_6H_5O_7$) alkalinizes urine and may increase urine citric acid. Increase in urine excretion of citrate and alkaline urine may decrease urinary calcium oxalate crystallization. Urinary excretion of calcium also is decreased. Other potassium supplements include: potassium gluconate, potassium acetate, potassium bicarbonate, and potassium chloride.

Indications and Clinical Uses

Potassium citrate is used for prevention of calcium oxalate urolithiasis. It is also used for renal tubular acidosis. In dogs, after administration of 150 mg/kg (of potassium citrate) q12h PO, the urine pH was not significantly increased, but urine concentration of calcium oxalate was decreased.

Precautionary Information

Adverse Reactions and Side Effects

Toxicity from high potassium concentrations can be dangerous. Hyperkalemia can lead to cardiovascular toxicity (bradycardia and arrest) and muscular weakness. Oral potassium supplements can cause nausea and stomach irritation.

Contraindications and Precautions

Use cautiously in animals with renal disease. Do not use with potassium penicillin or potassium bromide.

Drug Interactions

No drug interactions are reported in animals.

Instructions for Use

One gram of potassium citrate provides 9.26 mEq of potassium. Administer with meals.

Patient Monitoring and Laboratory Tests

Monitor serum potassium levels. Normal potassium is 4-5.5 mEq/L (dogs) and 4.3-6.0 mEq/L (cats). Monitor ECG in patients that may be prone to arrhythmias.

Formulations

Potassium citrate is available in 5 mEq and 10 mEq tablets. Some formulations are in combination with potassium chloride. Potassium citrate tablets in a in a delayed-released tablet also is available.

Stability and Storage

Store in tightly sealed container, protected from light, and at room temperature.

Small Animal Dosage

Dogs and Cats

- 2.2 mEq/100 kCal of energy/day PO or 0.5 mEq/kg per day, PO. Higher doses have been used safely in some animals. (1000 mg potassium citrate = 9.26 mEq potassium.)

Large Animal Dosage

No doses have been reported for large animals.

Regulatory Information

No withdrawal times necessary.

Potassium Gluconate

Trade and Other Names: Kaon, Tumil-K, and generic brands

Functional Classification: Potassium supplement

Pharmacology and Mechanism of Action

Potassium supplement. Used for treatment of hypokalemia. Potassium gluconate exists in an anhydrous form and a monohydrate form. Six grams of potassium gluconate anhydrous is equivalent to 1 g potassium; 6.45 g potassium gluconate monohydrate is equivalent to 1 g potassium. One gram potassium gluconate is equal to 4.27 mEq of potassium. Other potassium supplements include: potassium chloride, potassium acetate, potassium bicarbonate, and potassium citrate.

Indications and Clinical Uses

Potassium gluconate is used for treatment of hypokalemia and renal tubular acidosis. Potassium supplements are indicated for treating hypokalemia. Hypokalemia may occur with some diseases or as a consequence of diuretic use. In most patients, potassium chloride is the supplement of choice for hypokalemia.

Precautionary Information

Adverse Reactions and Side Effects

Toxicity from high potassium concentrations can be dangerous. Hyperkalemia can lead to cardiovascular toxicity (bradycardia and arrest) and muscular weakness. Oral potassium supplements can cause nausea and stomach irritation.

Contraindications and Precautions

Use cautiously in animals with renal disease.

Drug Interactions

No drug interactions are reported in animals.

Instructions for Use

One gram of potassium gluconate provides 4.27 mEq of potassium.

Patient Monitoring and Laboratory Tests

Monitor serum potassium levels. Normal potassium is 4-5.5 mEq/L (dogs) and 4.3-6.0 mEq/L (cats). Monitor ECG in patients that may be prone to arrhythmias.

Formulations

Potassium gluconate is available in 2 mEq tablet (equivalent to 500 mg potassium gluconate).

Kaon elixir is 20 mEq potassium/15 mL elixir (containing 4.68 grams potassium gluconate).

Stability and Storage

Store in tightly sealed container, protected from light, and at room temperature. Potassium gluconate is soluble in water.

Small Animal Dosage

Dogs

- 0.5 mEq/kg q12-24h PO.

Cats

- 2-8 mEq/day divided twice daily, PO.

Large Animal Dosage

No doses have been reported for large animals.

Regulatory Information

No withdrawal times necessary.

Potassium Iodide

Trade and Other Names: Quadrinal

Functional Classification: Antifungal, Expectorant

P

Pharmacology and Mechanism of Action

Potassium iodide is used as an iodine supplement. It also has some antimicrobial properties, although the exact mechanism is uncertain. Potassium iodide also may irritate the respiratory tract and has been used as an expectorant.

Indications and Clinical Uses

Potassium iodide is used to treat fungal infections, although sodium iodide is often preferred. It has been used for bacterial, actinomycete, and fungal infections, primarily in horses and cattle. In small animals it has been used for sporotrichosis. Proof of efficacy for these indications has not been established. Iodine supplements are also administered PO to protect the thyroid gland from radioactive iodine fallout in case of a nuclear disaster. For this purpose, iodine is administered 30-100 mg/day PO.

Precautionary Information

Adverse Reactions and Side Effects

High doses can produce signs of iodism, which include lacrimation, irritation of mucous membranes, cough, dry scruffy coat, and hair loss. Potassium iodide has a bitter taste and can cause nausea and salivation. Potassium iodide administration has been associated with cardiomyopathy in cats.

Contraindications and Precautions

Do not administer to foals or pregnant animals (abortion is possible). Do not administer IV.

Drug Interactions

No known drug interactions.

Instructions for Use

Clinical use in animals is primarily empirical. The doses and indications listed have not been tested in clinical trials. Other, more proven drugs for these indications should be considered as alternatives.

Patient Monitoring and Laboratory Tests

No specific monitoring is necessary.

Formulations

Potassium iodide is available in 1 g/mL saturated solutions. Saturated solution (1 g/mL) yields 38 mg per drop. In tablets, there is 145 mg iodine and potassium iodide (10%) yields 6.3 mg of iodine per drop.

Stability and Storage

Store in tightly sealed container, protected from light, and at room temperature.

Small Animal Dosage

Dogs and Cats

- Antifungal: 25-40 drops per animal q8h PO of the saturated solution.
- Expectorant: 50 mg/kg/day.

Large Animal Dosage

Cattle and Horses

- 10-15 g/day (adult) PO, for 30-60 days.
- 5-10 g/day (calves or pony) PO, for 30-60 days.

Regulatory Information

No regulatory information is available. Because of low risk of residues, no withdrawal times are suggested.

Potassium Phosphate

Trade and Other Names: K-Phos, Neutra-Phos-K, and generic brands

Functional Classification: Phosphate supplement

Pharmacology and Mechanism of Action

Phosphorous supplement. Potassium phosphate if used for severe hypophosphatemia associated with diabetic ketoacidosis. It also acidifies the urine.

Indications and Clinical Uses

Potassium phosphate has been used to reduce calcium urinary secretion in patients prone to calcium urinary calculi and to promote a more acid urine. This drug should not be used to supplement potassium. In most patients, potassium chloride is the supplement of choice for hypokalemia.

Precautionary Information

Adverse Reactions and Side Effects

Intravenous administration can cause hypocalcemia.

Contraindications and Precautions

Use cautiously in animals with renal disease.

Drug Interactions

No drug interactions are reported in animals.

Instructions for Use

Potassium phosphate use in animals is primarily as a urinary acidifier or treatment of hypophosphatemia.

Patient Monitoring and Laboratory Tests

Monitor calcium, potassium, and phosphorus levels in treated animals.

Formulations

Potassium phosphate is available in 500 mg tablets (contains 114 mg [3.7 mmol] phosphorus) and 1.45 g (containing 250 mg or 8 mmol phosphorus) oral solution. Oral solutions can be made from concentrates and mixed with water for oral administration.

It is also available in 224 mg monobasic potassium phosphate and 236 mg of dibasic potassium phosphate (3 mmol [93 mg] of phosphorus) per mL injection.

Stability and Storage

Store in tightly sealed container, protected from light, and at room temperature.

Small Animal Dosage

Dogs and Cats

- 0.1 mmol/kg/day IV supplementation.
- 4 mg/kg phosphorus (approximately 0.1 mmol/kg) PO, up to 4 times daily.
- 0.03-0.12 mmol/kg/hr IV.

Large Animal Dosage

No doses have been reported for large animals.

Regulatory Information

No withdrawal times necessary.

P

Pralidoxime Chloride

prah-lih-doks'eem klor'ide

Trade and Other Names: 2-PAM and Protopam chloride

Functional Classification: Antidote

Pharmacology and Mechanism of Action

Pralidoxime chloride is an oxime that is used as an adjunct to atropine for treatment of intoxication. Organophosphate (OP) intoxication results in inactivation of cholinesterase enzymes and excess accumulation of acetylcholine. Pralidoxime (also known as 2-PAM) is used to reactivate acetylcholinesterase by promoting dephosphorylation. Pralidoxime is well absorbed from intramuscular administration, but it does not cross the blood-brain barrier. After absorption, the half-life is short necessitating repeated administrations.

Indications and Clinical Uses

Pralidoxime chloride is used for treatment of organophosphate toxicosis. Administer promptly after organophosphate intoxication is identified. It also has been used to treat overdoses of neostigmine, pyridostigmine, and edrophonium, which are anticholinesterase drugs.

Precautionary Information

Adverse Reactions and Side Effects

Intramuscular injections cause pain. Rapid intravenous injections may cause heart and respiratory problems.

Contraindications and Precautions

Pralidoxime treatment should not be used for carbamate intoxication. Do not administer rapidly IV or it may cause respiratory depression.

Drug Interactions

No drug interactions. However, other drugs should be avoided when treating organophosphate poisoning. These drugs include aminoglycosides, barbiturates, phenothiazine tranquilizers (acepromazine), and neuromuscular blocking agents.

Instructions for Use

Dilute formulation in glucose solution before intravenous administration. Give slowly IV. Administer atropine (0.1 mg/kg) when using pralidoxime. Recovery from organophosphate poisoning may take 48 hours. When treating intoxication, consult poison control center for precise guidelines.

Patient Monitoring and Laboratory Tests

Monitor for signs of organophosphate poisoning to determine if repeated doses are necessary. Monitor heart rate and rhythm and respiratory rate. It may be possible to monitor cholinesterase activity from a blood sample to confirm organophosphate poisoning (consult local diagnostic laboratory for details).

Formulations

Pralidoxime chloride is available in 1 g vial to be reconstituted in 20 mL water (50 mg/mL injection).

Stability and Storage

Store powder at room temperature and protect from light. Discard reconstituted solution after 3 hours.

Small Animal Dosage

- 20 mg/kg, up to 50 mg/kg q8-12h IM or IV (initial dose slow).

Large Animal Dosage

Cattle, Sheep, and Pigs

- 20-50 mg/kg q8h (administered as a 10% solution) IM or via slow IV infusion, or as needed. Frequency can be assessed by monitoring clinical signs.

Regulatory Information

Cattle and pig withdrawal times (extralabel): 6 days for milk and 28 days for meat.

Praziquantel

pray-zih-kwon'tel

Trade and Other Names: Droncit and Drontal (combination with febantel)

Functional Classification: Antiparasitic

Pharmacology and Mechanism of Action

Antiparasitic drug. Action on parasites related to neuromuscular toxicity and paralysis via altered permeability to calcium.

Indications and Clinical Uses

Praziquantel is widely used to treat intestinal infections caused by cestodes (*Dipylidium caninum, Taenia pisiformis,* and *Echinococcus granulosus*) and removal and control of canine cestode *Echinococcus multilocularis.* In cats it is used for removal of feline cestodes *Dipylidium caninum* and *Taenia taeniaeformis.* In horses it is used to treat tapeworms *(Anoplocephala perfoliata).*

Precautionary Information

Adverse Reactions and Side Effects

Vomiting occurs at high doses. Anorexia and transient diarrhea have been reported. It is safe in pregnant animals.

Contraindications and Precautions

Avoid use in cats younger than 6 weeks and dogs younger than 4 weeks.

Drug Interactions

No drug interactions have been reported in animals.

Instructions for Use

Praziquantel is one of the most common drugs used for tapeworm treatment. It has a wide margin of safety. Some formulations of praziquantel are available in combination, e.g., combination of praziquantel and febantel, combination of ivermectin and praziquantel, moxidectin, and praziquantel.

P

Patient Monitoring and Laboratory Tests

No specific monitoring is necessary.

Formulations

Praziquantel is available in 23 and 34 mg tablets and 56.8 mg/mL injection. It is also available in pastes and gels, and they are available in pastes and gels for horses in combination with other drugs (ivermectin, moxidectin, febantel, etc.).

Stability and Storage

Store in tightly sealed container, protected from light, and at room temperature.

Small Animal Dosage

Dogs

- Dogs <6.8 kg: 7.5 mg/kg once PO.
- Dogs >6.8 kg: 5 mg/kg once PO.
- Dogs <2.3 kg, 7.5 mg/kg, once IM or SQ.
- Dogs 2.7-4.5 kg: 6.3 mg/kg once IM or SQ.
- Dogs >5 kg: 5 mg/kg once IM or SQ.

Cats (all doses given once)

- Cats 2.2 kg: 11.4 mg/cat, SC or IM
- Cats 2.2 kg to 4.5 kg: 22.7 mg/cat, SC or IM
- > 5 kg: 34.1 mg/cat, SC or IM
- <1.8 kg: 11.4 mg/cat PO.
- 2.3 kg to 5 kg: 23 mg/cat, PO
- > 5 kg: 34.5 mg/cat, PO

Large Animal Dosage

Horses

- 1 mg/kg (454 mg/pound) PO.

Regulatory Information

Withdrawal times are not established for animals that produce food. For extralabel use withdrawal interval estimates, contact FARAD at 1-888-USFARAD (1-888-873-2723) or send e-mail to FARAD@ncsu.edu.

Prazosin

pray'zoe-sin

Trade and Other Names: Minipress

Functional Classification: Vasodilator

Pharmacology and Mechanism of Action

Alpha$_1$ adrenergic blocker. Prazosin is a vasodilator that is a selective blocker for the alpha$_1$ adrenergic receptor. Its action is similar to phenoxybenzamine, but it produces less tachycardia than nonselective alpha-antagonist drugs. Prazosin decreases tension in both arterial and venous vascular smooth muscle. Prazosin relaxes smooth muscle, especially of vasculature. Prazosin is used as vasodilator and to relax smooth muscle (occasionally urethral muscle).

Indications and Clinical Uses

Prazosin has been used in people for vasodilation, and the management of hypertension that is not responsive to other drugs. Prazosin has been used to a limited extent in veterinary medicine to produce balanced vasodilation. It has also been used experimentally in horses in improve digital perfusion in the treatment of laminitis. Long-term administration is not common because tolerance may develop with chronic use.

Precautionary Information

Adverse Reactions and Side Effects

High doses cause vasodilation and hypotension.

Contraindications and Precautions

Use cautiously in animals with compromised cardiac function. It may lower blood pressure and decrease cardiac output.

Drug Interactions

No drug interactions have been reported in animals.

Instructions for Use

Titrate dose to needs of individual patient. Results of clinical studies in animals have not been reported; therefore, use in animals (and doses) is based on experience in people or anecdotal experience in animals.

Patient Monitoring and Laboratory Tests

Monitor for hypotension and reflex tachycardia.

Formulations

Prazosin is available in 1, 2, and 5 mg capsules.

Stability and Storage

Store in tightly sealed container, protected from light, and at room temperature.

Small Animal Dosage

Dogs and Cats

- 0.5-2 mg/animal (1 mg/15 kg) q8-12h PO.

Large Animal Dosage

No doses have been reported for large animals.

Regulatory Information

Withdrawal times are not established for animals that produce food. For extralabel use withdrawal interval estimates, contact FARAD at 1-888-USFARAD (1-888-873-2723) or send e-mail to FARAD@ncsu.edu.

RCI Classification: 3

Prednisolone Sodium Succinate

pred-niss-oh'lone soe'dee-um suk'sih-nate

Trade and Other Names: Solu-Delta-Cortef

Functional Classification: Corticosteroid

Pharmacology and Mechanism of Action

Prednisolone sodium succinate is the same as prednisolone, except that this is a water-soluble formulation intended for acute therapy when high intravenous doses are needed for rapid effect.

Indications and Clinical Uses

Prednisolone sodium succinate has similar uses as prednisolone in other forms, except this is used when prompt response is needed from injection (especially at high doses). Uses include treatment of immune-mediated diseases (e.g., pemphigus and hemolytic anemia), spinal cord trauma, and adrenocortical insufficiency. Large animal uses include treatment of inflammatory conditions and treatment of recurrent airway obstruction (RAO) in horses. In cattle, corticosteroids have been used in the treatment of ketosis. The use of prednisolone for treatment of shock, snakebites, and head trauma is discouraged because of lack of proven efficacy, or high risk of adverse effects.

Precautionary Information

Adverse Reactions and Side Effects

Adverse effects are not expected from single administration. However, with repeated use, other side effects are possible. Side effects from corticosteroids are many, and include polyphagia, polydipsia/polyuria, and hypothalamic-pituitary-adrenal (HPA) axis suppression. Adverse effects include GI ulceration, diarrhea, hepatopathy, diabetes mellitus, hyperlipidemia, decreased thyroid hormone, decreased protein synthesis, impaired wound healing, and immunosuppression. With high doses of prednisolone sodium succinate, there is a high risk of GI bleeding. In horses, in addition to adverse effects listed above, may be an increased risk of laminitis, although this documentation of this effect has been controversial.

Contraindications and Precautions

Use cautiously in patients with a risk of GI ulcers and bleeding, infection, or in animals that growing or healing is necessary. Use prednisolone sodium succinate cautiously in patients with renal disease, because it may cause azotemia. Use cautiously in pregnant animals, because fetal abnormalities have been reported in laboratory rodents.

Drug Interactions

Administration of corticosteroids with nonsteroidal antiinflammatory drugs (NSAIDs) will increase the risk of GI injury. Do not mix prednisolone sodium succinate with solutions containing calcium.

Instructions for Use

Doses for prednisolone are based on severity of underlying condition. Use of prednisolone sodium succinate is often at high doses for acute treatment.

Patient Monitoring and Laboratory Tests

Monitor liver enzymes, blood glucose, and renal function during therapy. Monitor patients for signs of secondary infections. Perform adrenocorticotropic hormone (ACTH) stimulation test to monitor adrenal function. Corticosteroids can increase liver enzymes—especially alkaline phosphatase—without inducing liver pathology. Corticosteroid administration may decrease conversion of thyroid hormones to active form.

Formulations

Prednisolone sodium succinate is available in 100 and 500 mg vials for injection (10, 20, and 50 mg/mL).

Stability and Storage

Store in tightly sealed container, protected from light, and at room temperature. Prednisolone sodium succinate should be used immediately after reconstitution. Do not freeze. If solution becomes cloudy, do not administer IV.

Small Animal Dosage

Dogs and Cats

- Shock: (although this use is controversial) 15-30 mg/kg IV (repeat in 4-6 hours)
- CNS trauma: 15-30 mg/kg IV, taper to 1-2 mg/kg q12h.
- Antiinflammatory: 1 mg/kg/day IV.
- Replacement therapy: 0.25-0.5 mg/kg/day IV.
- For intermittent treatment (pulse therapy) of pemphigus foliaceus, it has been administered at 10 mg/kg IV.

Large Animal Dosage

Horses

- 0.5-1.0 mg/kg q12-24h IM or IV. Intravenous dose should be given slowly over 30-60 seconds.
- Treatment of shock: Although efficacy for treating shock has not been established, recommended doses are 15-30 mg/kg IV, repeat dose in 4-6 hours.

Regulatory Information

Withdrawal times are not established for animals that produce food. For extralabel use withdrawal interval estimates, contact FARAD at 1-888-USFARAD (1-888-873-2723) or send e-mail to FARAD@ncsu.edu.
RCI Classification: 4

Prednisolone, Prednisolone Acetate

Trade and Other Names: Delta-cortef, PrednisTab, and generic brands

Functional Classification: Corticosteroid

Pharmacology and Mechanism of Action

Glucocorticoid antiinflammatory drug. Antiinflammatory effects are complex, but via binding to cellular glucocorticoid receptors, prednisolone acts to inhibit inflammatory cells and suppresses expression of inflammatory mediators. Prednisolone is approximately four times more potent than cortisol, but only one seventh as potent as dexamethasone. Prednisolone is available as the base (usually as a tablet) or as an injectable acetate form, which can be administered IM or intraarticularly.

Indications and Clinical Uses

Prednisolone, like other corticosteroids, is used to treat a variety of inflammatory and immune-mediated disease. Dosing section contains range of doses for replacement therapy, antiinflammatory therapy, and immunosuppressive therapy. Large animal uses include treatment of inflammatory conditions, especially musculoskeletal disorders. In horses prednisolone has been used for treatment of recurrent airway obstruction (RAO), formerly called chronic obstructive pulmonary disease (COPD). In cattle, corticosteroids have been used in the treatment of ketosis.

Precautionary Information

Adverse Reactions and Side Effects

Side effects from corticosteroids are many and include polyphagia, polydipsia/polyuria, behavior changes, and hypothalamic-pituitary-adrenal (HPA) axis suppression. Adverse effects include GI ulceration, hepatopathy, diabetes, hyperlipidemia, decreased thyroid hormone, decreased protein synthesis, delayed wound healing, increased risk of diabetes, and immunosuppression. Secondary infections can occur as a result of immunosuppression and include demodicosis, toxoplasmosis, fungal infections, and UTIs.

Contraindications and Precautions

Use cautiously in patients with a risk of GI ulcers and bleeding, infection, or in animals that growing or healing is necessary. Use prednisolone cautiously in patients with renal disease, because it may cause azotemia. Use prednisolone cautiously in pregnant animals, because fetal abnormalities have been reported in laboratory rodents. Do not administer prednisolone acetate intravenously.

Drug Interactions

Administration of corticosteroids with nonsteroidal antiinflammatory drugs (NSAIDs) will increase the risk of GI injury.

Instructions for Use

Doses for prednisolone are of a broad range and based on severity of underlying condition. Doses for long-term treatment may eventually be tapered to 0.5 mg/kg q48h, PO.

Patient Monitoring and Laboratory Tests

Monitor liver enzymes, blood glucose, and renal function during therapy. Monitor patients for signs of secondary infections. Perform adrenocorticotropic hormone (ACTH) stimulation test to monitor adrenal function. Corticosteroids can increase liver enzymes—especially alkaline phosphatase—without inducing liver pathology. Corticosteroid administration may decrease conversion of thyroid hormones to active form.

Formulations

Prednisolone is available in 5 and 20 mg tablets, 3 mg/mL syrup, and 25 mg/mL acetate suspension injection (10 and 50 mg/mL in Canada).

Stability and Storage

Store in tightly sealed container, protected from light, and at room temperature. Prednisolone is slightly soluble in water, but it is more soluble in ethanol. If diluted first in ethanol, it may be compounded into oral liquid formulations with good stability for 90 days. Prednisolone acetate is insoluble in water. Do not freeze.

Small Animal Dosage

Dogs

- Antiinflammatory: 0.5-1 mg/kg q12-24h IV, IM, or PO initially, then taper to q48h.
- Immunosuppressive: 2.2-6.6 mg/kg/day IV, IM, or PO initially, then taper to 2-4 mg/kg q48h.
- Replacement therapy: 0.2-0.3 mg/kg/day PO.

Cats

Same as for dogs, except that for many conditions they require twice the dog dose.

Large Animal Dosage

Horses

- Prednisolone acetate suspension: 100-200 total dosage IM.
- Prednisolone tablets: 0.5-1.0 mg/kg q12-24h PO. Taper to lower dose for long-term treatment.

Cattle

- Treatment of ketosis: 100-200 mg total dosage IM.

Regulatory Information

Cattle withdrawal times for prednisolone acetate: 5 days for meat, 72 hours for milk (in Canada).

Withdrawal times are not established for animals that produce food in the U.S.

For extralabel use withdrawal interval estimates, contact FARAD at 1-888-USFARAD (1-888-873-2723) or send e-mail to FARAD@ncsu.edu.
RCI Classification: 4

Prednisone

pred'nih-sone

Trade and Other Names: Deltasone, Meticorten, and generic brands

Functional Classification: Corticosteroid

Pharmacology and Mechanism of Action

Glucocorticoid antiinflammatory drug. The effect of prednisone is attributed to prednisolone. After administration, prednisone is converted to prednisolone. Antiinflammatory effects are complex, but via binding to cellular glucocorticoid receptors, prednisolone acts to inhibit inflammatory cells and suppresses expression of inflammatory mediators. Prednisolone is approximately four times more potent than cortisol, but only one seventh as potent as dexamethasone. Prednisone appears to be well absorbed and converted to active drug in dogs. However, in horses and cats, administration of prednisone results in low systemic levels of the active drug prednisolone, either because of poor absorption of prednisone or because of a deficiency in converting prednisone into prednisolone.

Indications and Clinical Uses

Prednisone, like other corticosteroids, is used to treat a variety of inflammatory and immune-mediated diseases. In cats, prednisone may produce therapeutic failures, and prednisolone (active drug) is preferred. There are several large animal doses cited (similar to prednisolone), however because of poor activity in horses, the use is discouraged.

P

Precautionary Information

Adverse Reactions and Side Effects

Side effects from corticosteroids are many and include polyphagia, polydipsia/polyuria, behavior changes, and hypothalamic-pituitary-adrenal (HPA) axis suppression. Adverse effects include GI ulceration, diarrhea hepatopathy, diabetes, hyperlipidemia, decreased thyroid hormone, decreased protein synthesis, delayed wound healing, and immunosuppression. Secondary infections can occur as a result of immunosuppression and include demodicosis, toxoplasmosis, fungal infections, and UTIs.

Contraindications and Precautions

Use cautiously in patients with a risk of GI ulcers and bleeding, infection, or in animals in which growing or healing is necessary. Use prednisone cautiously in patients with renal disease, because it may cause azotemia. Use prednisone cautiously in pregnant animals, because fetal abnormalities have been reported in laboratory rodents.

Drug Interactions

Administration of corticosteroids with nonsteroidal antiinflammatory drugs (NSAIDs) will increase the risk of GI injury.

Instructions for Use

As for prednisolone, the doses vary across a broad range, based on severity of underlying condition. For long-term treatment, doses can be tapered to 0.5 mg/kg q48h, PO.

Patient Monitoring and Laboratory Tests

Monitor liver enzymes, blood glucose, and renal function during therapy. Monitor patients for signs of secondary infections. Perform adrenocorticotrophic hormone (ACTH) stimulation test to monitor adrenal function. Corticosteroids can increase liver enzymes—especially alkaline phosphatase—without inducing liver pathology. Corticosteroid administration may decrease conversion of thyroid hormones to active form.

Formulations

Prednisone is available in 1, 2.5, 5, 10, 20, 25, and 50 mg tablets, 1 mg/mL syrup (Liquid Pred in 5% alcohol), 1 mg/mL oral solution (in 5% alcohol), and 10 and 40 mg/mL prednisone suspension for injection (Meticorten; availability has been limited).

Stability and Storage

Store in tightly sealed container, protected from light, and at room temperature. Prednisone is slightly soluble in water, and it is soluble in ethanol. Prednisone has been prepared by first dissolving in ethanol, then mixing with syrups and flavorings. No loss occurred, but crystallization is common in aqueous vehicles. Prednisone tablets have been crushed and mixed with syrups and other flavorings, stored for 60 days and found to produce equal bioavailability as tablets in people.

Small Animal Dosage

Dogs

- Antiinflammatory: 0.5-1 mg/kg q12-24h IV, IM, or PO initially, then taper to q48h.
- Immunosuppressive: 2.2-6.6 mg/kg/day IV, IM, or PO initially, then taper to 2-4 mg/kg q48h.
- Replacement therapy: 0.2-0.3 mg/kg/day PO.

Cats

Not recommended for cats, because of inability to form active metabolite. However, if use is attempted, higher doses than used in dogs will be needed.

Large Animal Dosage

Horses

- Prednisone suspension (Meticorten) (label dose): 100-400 mg per horse (0.22-0.88 mg/kg) as a single dose, IM, to be repeated every 3-4 days. No oral doses are listed for horses, because inability of oral treatment to produce active prednisolone concentrations.

Regulatory Information

Withdrawal times are not established for animals that produce food. For extralabel use withdrawal interval estimates, contact FARAD at 1-888-USFARAD (1-888-873-2723) or send e-mail to FARAD@ncsu.edu.

RCI Classification: 4

Primidone

prih'mih-done

Trade and Other Names: Mylepsin, Neurosyn, and Mysoline (in Canada)

Functional Classification: Anticonvulsant

Pharmacology and Mechanism of Action

Anticonvulsant. Primidone is converted to phenylethylmalonamide (PEMA) and phenobarbital both of which have anticonvulsant activity, but most of activity (85%) is probably because of the phenobarbital. Phenobarbital acts to potentiate the inhibitory effects of GABA-mediated chloride channels.

Indications and Clinical Uses

Primidone is used for treating seizure disorders in animals, including epilepsy. The effects of primidone are primarily produced by the presence of the active metabolite, phenobarbital. Although it is possible that some epileptic patients refractory to phenobarbital alone will respond better to primidone, the number of such cases is low.

Precautionary Information

Adverse Reactions and Side Effects

Adverse effects are same as for phenobarbital. Primidone has been associated with idiosyncratic hepatotoxicity in dogs. Although some labels caution its use in cats, one study in experimental cats determined that it is safe if used at recommended doses.

Contraindications and Precautions

There may be a higher risk of hepatic toxicity with primidone as compared to other anticonvulsants. Primidone should be avoided in animals with liver disease.

Drug Interactions

Primidone is converted to phenobarbital, which is one of the most potent drugs for inducing hepatic microsomal metabolizing enzymes. Therefore, many drugs administered concurrently will have lower (and perhaps subtherapeutic) concentrations because of more rapid clearance. Drugs affected may include theophylline, digoxin, corticosteroids, anesthetics, and many others (see Appendix list for drugs that affect cytochrome P450 enzymes).

Instructions for Use

Recommendations are similar as for phenobarbital. When monitoring therapy with primidone, phenobarbital plasma concentrations should be measured to estimate anticonvulsant effect. When converting a patient from primidone therapy to phenobarbital the conversion is as follows: 60 mg phenobarbital is approximately 250 mg primidone.

Patient Monitoring and Laboratory Tests

Doses should be carefully adjusted via monitoring serum/plasma phenobarbital concentrations. Collect a sample at any time during the dose interval as the timing of the sample is not critical. Avoid the use of plasma separation devices if the tube is to be stored. The therapeutic range in dogs is considered 15-40 mcg/mL (65-180 mmol/L). However, in cats the optimum range for therapeutic effect is 23-28 mcg/mL. Monitor liver function with bile acid determinations.

Formulations

Primidone is available in 50 and 250 mg tablets.

Stability and Storage

Store in tightly sealed container, protected from light, and at room temperature. Stability of compounded formulations has not been evaluated.

Small Animal Dosage

Dogs and Cats

- 8-10 mg/kg q8-12h as initial dose PO, then is adjusted via monitoring to 10-15 mg/kg q8h.

Large Animal Dosage

No doses have been reported for large animals.

Regulatory Information

Withdrawal times are not established for animals that produce food. For extralabel use withdrawal interval estimates, contact FARAD at 1-888-USFARAD (1-888-873-2723) or send e-mail to FARAD@ncsu.edu.

RCI Classification: 3

Procainamide Hydrochloride

proe-kane-ah′mide hye-droe-klor′ide

Trade and Other Names: Pronestyl and generic brands

Functional Classification: Antiarrhythmic

Pharmacology and Mechanism of Action

Class-I antiarrhythmic drug. Like other Class I antiarrhythmic drugs (similar to quinidine), procainamide will inhibit sodium influx into cardiac cell via sodium channel blockade. It will suppress cardiac automaticity and reentrant arrhythmias, primarily in the ventricle. Procainamide is metabolized in people to n-acetyl procainamide (NAPA), which produces other antiarrhythmic actions (Class III drug: potassium channel blocking effects). However, dogs do not form this metabolite because of inability to acetylate some drugs.

Indications and Clinical Uses

Procainamide is used in small animals to suppress ventricular ectopic beats and treat ventricular arrhythmias. It is used primarily during acute treatment by injection or tablet. Rarely is long-term treatment used. Procainamide has occasionally been used in horses to suppress ventricular arrhythmias.

Precautionary Information

Adverse Reactions and Side Effects

Adverse effects include cardiac arrhythmias, cardiac depression, tachycardia, and hypotension. In people, procainamide produces hypersensitivity effects (Lupus-like reactions), but these have not been reported in animals.

Contraindications and Precautions

Procainamide can suppress the heart and produce proarrhythmic effects. Use cautiously in animals receiving digoxin because it may potentiate arrhythmias.

Drug Interactions
Drugs that inhibit cytochrome P450 enzymes (e.g., cimetidine) can potentially increase procainamide concentrations.

Instructions for Use

Because dogs do not produce active metabolite N-acetyl procainamide (NAPA), dose may be higher to control some arrhythmias compared to people. In animals, there is no evidence that slow-release oral formulations produce longer duration of sustained blood concentrations.

Patient Monitoring and Laboratory Tests

Monitor plasma concentrations during chronic therapy. Effective plasma concentrations in experimental dogs are 20 mcg/mL. However, in some references, concentrations as low as 8-10 mcg/mL are cited to be effective. The metabolite, NAPA, is monitored in people, but dogs do not produce this metabolite. ECG should be monitored in treated animals.

Formulations

Procainamide is available in 250, 375, and 500 mg tablets or capsules, and 100 and 500 mg/mL injection.

Stability and Storage

Store in tightly sealed container, protected from light, and at room temperature. Procainamide is soluble in water. When stored, solutions may turn yellow in color without losing potency. Darker coloration indicates oxidation. Storage of injectable vials in refrigerator will prevent oxidation. pH of oral compounded products should be 4-6 for maximum stability. Compounded oral products in syrups and flavorings may be stable for 60 days or more, but they should be kept in refrigerator.

Small Animal Dosage

Dogs

- 10-30 mg/kg q6h PO, to a maximum dose of 40 mg/kg.
- 8-20 mg/kg IV or IM.
- Constant Rate Infusion (CRI): 25-50 mcg/kg/min IV.

Cats

- 3-8 mg/kg q6-8h IM or PO.
- CRI: 1-2 mg/kg IV slowly, then 10-20 mcg/kg/min IV.

Large Animal Dosage

Horses

- 25-35 mg/kg q8h PO.
- Up to 20 mcg/kg IV.

Regulatory Information

Withdrawal times are not established for animals that produce food. For extralabel use withdrawal interval estimates, contact FARAD at 1-888-USFARAD (1-888-873-2723) or send e-mail to FARAD@ncsu.edu.

Prochlorperazine Edisylate, Prochlorperazine Maleate

proe-klor-pare'ah-zeen ed-iss'ih-late, proe-klor-pare'ah-zeen mal'ee-ate

Trade and Other Names: Compazine

Functional Classification: Antiemetic, Phenothiazine

Pharmacology and Mechanism of Action

Phenothiazine. Central acting dopamine (D_2) antagonist. Prochlorperazine suppresses dopamine activity in the CNS to produce sedation and prevent vomiting. Antiemetic action also may be related to $alpha_2$ and muscarinic blocking effects. There are two salt formulations of prochlorperazine: prochlorperazine edisylate and prochlorperazine maleate. They are therapeutically equivalent. Other phenothiazines include chlorpromazine, perphenazine, promazine, trifluoperazine, and triflupromazine.

Indications and Clinical Uses

Prochlorperazine is used for sedation, tranquilization, and as antiemetic. In people it is used to treat psychotic disorders.

Precautionary Information

Adverse Reactions and Side Effects

Prochlorperazine causes sedation and other side effects attributed to other phenothiazines. It also produces extrapyramidal side effects (involuntary muscle movements) in some individuals.

Contraindications and Precautions

Like other phenothiazines it may be contraindicated in some CNS disorders. It may lower seizure threshold in susceptible animals.

Drug Interactions

Prochlorperazine may potentiate other sedatives.

Instructions for Use

Prochlorperazine is used primarily as antiemetic in animals. Clinical trials are not available; doses are based primarily on extrapolation and anecdotal experience.

Patient Monitoring and Laboratory Tests

No specific monitoring is necessary.

Formulations

Prochlorperazine is available in 5, 10, and 25 mg tablets (prochlorperazine maleate), 1 mg/mL oral solution, and 5 mg/mL injection (prochlorperazine edisylate).

Stability and Storage

Store in tightly sealed container, protected from light, and at room temperature. Prochlorperazine is slightly soluble in water and soluble in ethanol. However the maleate form is more insoluble in water. Prochlorperazine edisylate may be mixed with fluids such as water for injection. Some yellow discoloration may not affect potency. However, if milky white precipitate forms in vial, do not use.

Small Animal Dosage

Dogs and Cats

- 0.1-0.5 mg/kg q6-8h IM, IV, or SQ.
- 0.15-2.5 mg/kg q6-8h PO.

Large Animal Dosage

No doses have been reported for large animals.

Regulatory Information

Withdrawal times are not established for animals that produce food. For extralabel use withdrawal interval estimates, contact FARAD at 1-888-USFARAD (1-888-873-2723) or send e-mail to FARAD@ncsu.edu.

Prochlorperazine Edisylate + Isopropamide Iodide, Prochlorperazine Maleate + Isopropamide Iodide

Trade and Other Names: Darbazine

Functional Classification: Antiemetic, Antidiarrheal

Pharmacology and Mechanism of Action

Combination product. This combination combines either prochlorperazine edisylate (injectable form) or prochlorperazine maleate (oral form) with isopropamide (isopropamide iodide). Chlorpromazine is a central acting dopamine antagonist (antiemetic); isopropamide is an anticholinergic drug (atropine-like effects).

Indications and Clinical Uses

Prochlorperazine is a phenothiazine used to control vomiting; isopropamide is an anticholinergic used to decrease intestinal motility and GI secretions. Its use is not common because of decreased availability of formulations and lack of proven efficacy.

P

Precautionary Information

Adverse Reactions and Side Effects

Side effects are attributed to each component. Prochlorperazine produces phenothiazine-like effects. Isopropamide produces antimuscarinic effects (see Atropine monograph).

Contraindications and Precautions

Use of antimuscarinic drugs is contraindicated in animals with gastroparesis and should be used cautiously in animals with diarrhea.

Drug Interactions

Isopropamide will interfere with cholinergic drug or drugs that promote motility (e.g., metoclopramide). Prochlorperazine will potentiate other sedatives.

Instructions for Use

This combination should be used with caution, especially if considered for repeated doses, in animals with intestinal disease. It can produce ileus.

Patient Monitoring and Laboratory Tests

No specific monitoring is necessary.

Formulations

Prochlorperazine edisylate + isopropamide iodide is available in 3.33 mg prochlorperazine and 1.67 mg isopropamide capsules and prochlorperazine maleate + isopropamide iodide is available in 4 mg prochlorperazine and 0.28 mg isopropamide per mL injection.

Stability and Storage

Store in tightly sealed container, protected from light, and at room temperature. Stability of compounded formulations has not been evaluated.

Small Animal Dosage

Cats

- 0.14-0.2 mL/kg q12h SQ.

Dogs

- 0.14-0.2 mL/kg q12h SQ.
- Dogs 2-7 kg: 1 capsule q12h PO.
- Dogs 7-13 kg: 1-2 capsules q12h PO.

Large Animal Dosage

No doses have been reported for large animals. The use is discouraged because isopropamide may decrease GI motility.

Regulatory Information

Withdrawal times are not established for animals that produce food. For extralabel use withdrawal interval estimates, contact FARAD at 1-888-USFARAD (1-888-873-2723) or send e-mail to FARAD@ncsu.edu.

RCI Classification: 2

Promethazine Hydrochloride

proe-meth'ah-zeen hye-droe-klor-ide

Trade and Other Names: Phenergan

Functional Classification: Antiemetic, Phenothiazine

Pharmacology and Mechanism of Action

Phenothiazine with strong antihistamine effects. Promethazine is used mostly for its antiemetic effects, for which it acts either via the antihistamine receptors or by blocking dopamine receptors associated with vomiting.

Indications and Clinical Uses

Promethazine is used for treatment of allergy (antihistamine effect) and as antiemetic (motion sickness). The efficacy for treating allergies in animals has not been established.

Precautionary Information

Adverse Reactions and Side Effects

Adverse effects include sedation and antimuscarinic (atropine-like) effects. Both phenothiazine effects (see acepromazine) and anticholinergic (see Atropine monograph) effects are possible in some patients.

Contraindications and Precautions
Promethazine may produce antimuscarinic side effects.

Drug Interactions
No drug interactions have been reported in animals.

Instructions for Use
Results of clinical studies in animals have not been reported. Therefore, the use in animals (and doses) is based on experience in people or anecdotal experience in animals.

Patient Monitoring and Laboratory Tests
No specific monitoring is necessary.

Formulations
Promethazine is available in 6.25 and 25 mg/5 mL syrup, 12.5, 25, and 50 mg tablets, and 25, 50 mg/mL injection.

Stability and Storage
Promethazine hydrochloride is soluble in water. If oxidized it will turn a blue color and should be discarded. It is sensitive to light and should be protected from light.

Small Animal Dosage
Dogs and Cats
- 0.2-0.4 mg/kg q6-8h IV, IM, PO, up to a maximum dose of 1 mg/kg.

Large Animal Dosage
No doses have been reported for large animals.

Regulatory Information
Withdrawal times are not established for animals that produce food. For extralabel use withdrawal interval estimates, contact FARAD at 1-888-USFARAD (1-888-873-2723) or send e-mail to FARAD@ncsu.edu.
RCI Classification: 3

P

Propantheline Bromide
proe-pan′theh-leen broe′mide

Trade and Other Names: Pro-Banthine

Functional Classification: Antidiarrheal

Pharmacology and Mechanism of Action
Anticholinergic (antimuscarinic) drug. Propantheline blocks acetylcholine receptor to produce parasympatholytic effects (atropine-like effects). Propantheline will produce systemic parasympatholytic effects that include decreased GI secretions and motility.

Indications and Clinical Uses
Propantheline is used to decrease smooth muscle contraction and secretion of GI tract. Via the anticholinergic effects, it also has been used to treat vagal-mediated cardiovascular effects, such as bradycardia and heart block. Because it will produce a profound decrease in gastrointestinal tract motility, its use should be carefully weighed against the potential for adverse effects.

Precautionary Information

Adverse Reactions and Side Effects

Side effects are attributed to excess anticholinergic (antimuscarinic) effects and include ileus, urine retention, tachycardia, xerostomia (dry mouth), and behavior changes. Treat overdoses with physostigmine.

Contraindications and Precautions

Do not use in animals with decreased intestinal motility. Use cautiously in animals with heart disease, because it may increase heart rate. Do not use in animals with glaucoma.

Drug Interactions

Propantheline will interfere with cholinergic drugs or drugs that promote motility (e.g., metoclopramide).

Instructions for Use

Propantheline has not been evaluated in clinical trials in animals, but propantheline is often the drug of choice for oral therapy in cases where an anticholinergic effect is desired.

Patient Monitoring and Laboratory Tests

No specific monitoring is necessary.

Formulations

Propantheline is available in 7.5 and 15 mg tablets.

Stability and Storage

Store in tightly sealed container, protected from light, and at room temperature.

Small Animal Dosage

Dogs and Cats

- 0.25-0.5 mg/kg q8-12h PO.

Large Animal Dosage

No doses have been reported for large animals. The use is discouraged because of adverse effect on GI motility.

Regulatory Information

Withdrawal times are not established for animals that produce food. For extralabel use withdrawal interval estimates, contact FARAD at 1-888-USFARAD (1-888-873-2723) or send e-mail to FARAD@ncsu.edu.

RCI Classification: 4

Propiopromazine Hydrochloride

proe-pee-oh-prom′ah-zeen hye-droe-klor′ide

Trade and Other Names: Tranvet

Functional Classification: Antiemetic, Phenothiazine

Pharmacology and Mechanism of Action

Propiopromazine is a phenothiazine with antihistamine effects. It has actions similar to other systemic phenothiazine drugs. Propiopromazine is used mostly for its antiemetic and sedative effects, for which it acts either via the antihistamine receptors or by blocking dopamine receptors. A similar human drug, propiopromazine, has been discontinued.

Indications and Clinical Uses

Propiopromazine has been used for its antiemetic and sedative effects, for which it acts either via the antihistamine receptors or by blocking dopamine receptors.
It also has sedative and tranquilizing effects, and has been used in cats and dogs to facilitate handling difficult, excited, or unruly animals. It is used as a preanesthetic.

Precautionary Information

Adverse Reactions and Side Effects

Phenothiazines can cause sedation as a common side effect. Propiopromazine produces extrapyramidal side effects in some individuals.

Contraindications and Precautions

It may lower blood pressure via alpha-adrenergic blockade.

Drug Interactions

Do not use with other phenothiazines, organophosphates, or procaine.

Instructions for Use

Results of clinical studies in animals have not been reported. Use in animals (and doses) is based on anecdotal experience in animals and product label.

Patient Monitoring and Laboratory Tests

No specific monitoring is necessary.

Formulations

Propiopromazine is available as 20 mg chewable tablet and 5 or 10 mg/mL injection. Similar human drugs (e.g., propiopromazine) have been discontinued.

Stability and Storage

Store in tightly sealed container, protected from light, and at room temperature.

P

Small Animal Dosage

Dogs and Cats

- 1.1-4.4 mg/kg q12-24h, PO.
- 0.1-1.1 mg/kg IV, IM (range of injectable doses depends on level of sedation needed).

Large Animal Dosage

No doses have been reported for large animals.

Regulatory Information

Withdrawal times are not established for animals that produce food. For extralabel use withdrawal interval estimates, contact FARAD at 1-888-USFARAD (1-888-873-2723) or send e-mail to FARAD@ncsu.edu.

Propofol

proe′poe-fole

Trade and Other Names: Rapinovet, Propoflo (veterinary preparation), and Diprivan (human preparation)

Functional Classification: Anesthetic

Pharmacology and Mechanism of Action

Anesthetic. Mechanism of action is not well-defined but may be barbiturate-like. Propofol produces a short acting (10 minutes) anesthesia, followed by a rapid and smooth recovery.

Indications and Clinical Uses

Propofol is used as a short-term injectable anesthetic. It may be used as induction agent followed by inhalation with halothane or isoflurane. The advantage of propofol over other agents is smooth, rapid recovery. It can be used with acepromazine, diazepam, butorphanol, and inhalant anesthetics.

Precautionary Information

Adverse Reactions and Side Effects

Apnea and respiratory depression is most common adverse effect. Cardiovascular effects are similar to those of thiopental, but the incidence of cardiac adverse events is generally low. However, propofol can induce vasodilation, which can be minimized by supplementing with intravenous fluids. Less frequent adverse reactions include vomiting during recovery and pain.

Contraindications and Precautions

Propofol can induce apnea and hypoxia upon induction. Supplemental oxygen should be available to prevent adverse effects. Do not administer to hypotensive animals. When propofol has been used to sedate animals for intradermal skin testing, it may produce a greater number of positive reactions.

Drug Interactions

Propofol can be used with several other anesthetics and adjuncts safely. Propofol has been mixed with thiopental sodium (2.5%) in a 1:1 mixture without loss of effectiveness. However, it should not be mixed in a syringe with other anesthetics unless compatibility is known.

Instructions for Use

Shake well before using. Use strict aseptic technique for administration. Propofol may be diluted in 5% dextrose, lactated Ringer's solution, and 0.9% saline but not to less than 2 mg/mL concentration. Delay in penetration to brain is approximately 3 minutes; therefore there is a delayed CNS effect during injection. When using with other drugs, (acepromazine, opiates, etc.) lower doses should be administered. A mixture of 1:1 thiopental (2.5%) and propofol can be used in dogs and results in a smooth induction.

Patient Monitoring and Laboratory Tests

Monitor respiration rate and character during anesthesia with propofol.

Formulations

Propofol is available in 1% (10 mg/mL) injection in 20 mL ampules.

Stability and Storage

Shake well before use. Once an ampule has been opened, discard within 6 hours. Use careful technique to prevent microbial contamination of vial. Propofol has been mixed with thiopental sodium in a 1:1 mixture, and they are physically and chemically compatible. However, do not mix with other drugs unless compatibility is known. Propofol has a pH of 7-8.5. Protect from light. Store at 40° F to 72° F (4° C-22° C). Do not freeze.

Small Animal Dosage

Dogs and Cats

- 6.6 mg/kg IV slowly over 60 seconds. If necessary, an additional dose can be given at 0.5-1.0 mg/kg for intubation.
- Constant Rate Infusion (CRI): 5 mg/kg slowly IV, followed by 100-400 mcg/kg/min (or 6-24 mg/kg/hour).
- CRI infusion with ketamine in cats: 0.025 mg/min/kg + ketamine 23-46 mcg/kg/min.

Large Animal Dosage

Small Ruminants

- 4 mg/kg IV.

Pigs

- 2-5 mg/kg IV.

Regulatory Information

Withdrawal times are not established for animals that produce food. For extralabel use withdrawal interval estimates, contact FARAD at 1-888-USFARAD (1-888-873-2723) or send e-mail to FARAD@ncsu.edu.

RCI Classification: 2

Propranolol Hydrochloride

proe-pran'oh-lole hye-droe-klor'ide

Trade and Other Names: Inderal and generic brands

Functional Classification: Beta blocker

P

Pharmacology and Mechanism of Action

Beta-adrenergic blocker. Nonselective for $beta_1$ and $beta_2$ adrenergic receptors. Class-II antiarrhythmic. Propranolol is a lipophilic beta blocker and relies on the liver for clearance. Lipophilic beta blockers such as propranolol undergo high first-pass clearance, which reduces oral bioavailability, and causes high interpatient variability in plasma concentrations and effects. Drug concentrations may be higher when there is impaired liver blood flow.

Indications and Clinical Uses

Propranolol is used primarily to decrease heart rate, decrease cardiac conduction, control tachyarrhythmias, and decrease blood pressure. Propranolol is effective to control the response from adrenergic stimulation. Beta blockers such as propranolol are among the most effective drugs for slowing heart rate.

Precautionary Information

Adverse Reactions and Side Effects

Adverse effects related to $beta_1$-blocking effects on heart. Propranolol causes cardiac depression and decreases cardiac output. $Beta_2$-blocking effects can cause bronchoconstriction and decrease insulin secretion. Beta blockers can cause weakness and fatigue.

Contraindications and Precautions

Do not administer to animals with low cardiac reserve, animals with bradycardia, or animals with poor systolic function. Use cautiously in animals with respiratory problems; bronchoconstriction can occur from $beta_2$ effects. Hyperthyroid cats may have reduced clearance and increased risk of toxicity.

Drug Interactions

Lipophilic beta blockers, such as propranolol, rely on the liver for clearance. These drugs are subject to interactions from drugs that affect liver blood flow and interact with hepatic enzymes. Decrease liver blood flow will reduce propranolol clearance.

Instructions for Use

Usually dose is titrated according to patient's response. Start with low dose and increase gradually to desired effect. Clearance relies on hepatic blood flow; use cautiously in animals with impaired hepatic perfusion. In cats with hyperthyroidism, consider reducing the dose to prevent adverse effects. Cats with hyperthyroidism may have decreased clearance or increased oral absorption compared to other cats.

Patient Monitoring and Laboratory Tests

Monitor heart rate during treatment. Monitor respiratory function in patients prone to bronchoconstriction.

Formulations

Propranolol is available in 10, 20, 40, 60 , 80, and 90 mg tablets, 1 mg/mL injection, and 4 and 8 mg/mL oral solution.

Stability and Storage

Store in tightly sealed container, protected from light, and at room temperature. Propranolol is soluble in water and ethanol. Suspensions prepared in various syrups and flavorings were stable for 4 months, but some settling may occur. pH of formulations should be kept at 2.8-4 for maximum stability. In alkaline solutions it will decompose.

Small Animal Dosage

Dogs

- 20-60 mcg/kg over 5-10 min IV (titrate dose to effect).
- 0.2-1 mg/kg q8h PO (titrate dose to effect).

Cats

- 0.4-1.2 mg/kg (2.5-5 mg/cat) q8h PO.

Large Animal Dosage

Horses

- Up to 0.1 mg/kg IV, slowly. Repeat in 6-8 hours if necessary.

Regulatory Information

Withdrawal times are not established for animals that produce food. For extralabel use withdrawal interval estimates, contact FARAD at 1-888-USFARAD (1-888-873-2723) or send e-mail to FARAD@ncsu.edu.

RCI Classification: 3

Propylthiouracil

pro-pil-thye-oh-yoo'rah-sil

Trade and Other Names: Propyl-Thyracil, PTU, and generic brands

Functional Classification: Antithyroid

Pharmacology and Mechanism of Action

Antithyroid drug. Propylthiouracil inhibits synthesis of thyroid hormones; specifically, it interferes with conversion of T-4 to T-3.

Indications and Clinical Uses

Propylthiouracil has been used for the treatment of feline hyperthyroidism. Because of adverse effects, use of propylthiouracil in most cats has been replaced with methimazole.

Precautionary Information

Adverse Reactions and Side Effects

Adverse effects in cats include hepatopathy, hemolytic anemia, thrombocytopenia, and other signs of immune-mediated disease (*J Am Vet Med Assoc*, 184:806, 1984).

Contraindications and Precautions

Do not use in cats with low platelet counts or bleeding problems.

Drug Interactions

No drug interactions have been reported in animals.

Instructions for Use

Propylthiouracil has been largely replaced in therapy with methimazole.

Patient Monitoring and Laboratory Tests

Monitor CBC to look for evidence of hematologic abnormalities. Monitor T4 levels to assess therapy.

Formulations

Propylthiouracil is available in 50 and 100 mg tablets.

Stability and Storage

Store in tightly sealed container, protected from light, and at room temperature. Propylthiouracil is slightly soluble in water and soluble in ethanol.

Small Animal Dosage

Cats

- 11 mg/kg q12h PO.

Large Animal Dosage

No doses have been reported for large animals.

Regulatory Information

Withdrawal times are not established for animals that produce food. For extralabel use withdrawal interval estimates, contact FARAD at 1-888-USFARAD (1-888-873-2723) or send e-mail to FARAD@ncsu.edu.

Prostaglandin F_2 Alpha

pross-teh-glan'din

Trade and Other Names: Lutalyse, Dinoprost, and PGF_2 alpha

Functional Classification: Prostaglandin

Pharmacology and Mechanism of Action

Prostaglandin F_2 (PGF_2) alpha simulates the action of endogenous PGF_2 alpha in animals. It induces luteolysis and will terminate pregnancy. It is also called Dinoprost.

Indications and Clinical Uses

PGF_2 alpha has been used to treat open pyometra in animals. In cattle, Dinoprost has been used for treatment of chronic endometritis. Use for inducing abortion in small animals has been questioned. However, in large animals, Dinoprost is used to induce abortion in first 100 days of gestation. Dinoprost is used for estrous synchronization in cattle and horses by causing luteolysis. In pigs, Dinoprost is used to induce parturition when given within 3 days of farrowing.

Precautionary Information

Adverse Reactions and Side Effects

PGF_2 alpha causes increased smooth muscle tone, resulting in diarrhea, abdominal discomfort, bronchoconstriction, and increase in blood pressure. In small animals, other side effects include vomiting. Induction of abortion may cause retained placenta.

Contraindications and Precautions

Do not administer IV. PGF_2 alpha induces abortion in pregnant animals. Use caution when handling this drug. It should not be handled by pregnant women. Absorption through the skin is possible. People with respiratory problems also should not handle Dinoprost.

Drug Interactions

According to the label, dinoprost should not be used with nonsteroidal antiinflammatory drugs (NSAIDs), because these drugs inhibit synthesis of prostaglandins. However, NSAIDs should not affect concentrations of PGF_2 alpha after administration with this product. When using oxytocin concurrently, it should be used cautiously, because there is a risk of uterine rupture.

Instructions for Use

Use in treating pyometra should be monitored carefully.

Patient Monitoring and Laboratory Tests

Monitor for signs of estrus after treatment.

Formulations

PGF_2 is available in 5 mg/mL solution for injection.

Stability and Storage

Store in tightly sealed container, protected from light, and at room temperature. It should be stored in a manner to avoid skin contact with humans.

Small Animal Dosage

Dogs

- Pyometra: 0.1-0.2 mg/kg once daily for 5 days SQ.
- Abortion: 0.025-0.05 mg (25-50 mcg)/kg q12h IM.

Cats

- Pyometra: 0.1-0.25 mg/kg once daily for 5 days SQ.
- Abortion: 0.5-1 mg/kg IM for 2 injections.

Large Animal Dosage

Cattle

- Abortion: 25 mg total dosage, administered once IM.
- Estrus synchronization: 25 mg once IM or twice at 10-12 day intervals.
- Pyometra: 25 mg IM administered once.

Horses

- Estrus synchronization: 1 mg/100 pounds (1 mg/45 kg) IM or 1-2 mL administered once IM. Mares should return to estrus within 2-4 days and ovulate 8-12 days after treatment.

Pigs

- Induction of parturition: 10 mg administered once IM. Parturition occurs within 30 hours.

Regulatory Information

No withdrawal time required for meat or milk.

Pseudoephedrine Hydrochloride

soo-doh-eh-fed'rin hye-droe-klor'ide

Trade and Other Names: Sudafed and generic brands

Functional Classification: Adrenergic agonist

Pharmacology and Mechanism of Action

Adrenergic agonist. Pseudoephedrine is a sympathomimetic. It nonselectively acts as an agonist for the alpha-adrenergic and beta-adrenergic receptors. These receptors are found throughout the body, such as on sphincters, blood vessels, smooth muscle, and heart.

Pseudoephedrine produces a similar effect as ephedrine and phenylpropanolamine. However, compared to ephedrine it may have fewer CNS effects.

Indications and Clinical Uses

Pseudoephedrine has been used as decongestant, mild bronchodilator, and to increase tone of urinary sphincter. Pseudoephedrine, phenylpropanolamine, and ephedrine have similar alpha receptor and beta receptor effects. The most common use in animals is for treating urinary incontinence. The mechanism for this action appears to be via stimulating receptors on sphincter. In people, it is still used as a decongestant, whereas products such as phenylpropanolamine (PPA) have been removed from the human market.

Precautionary Information

Adverse Reactions and Side Effects

Side effects attributed to adrenergic effects (excitement, rapid heart rate, and arrhythmias).

Contraindications and Precautions

Pseudoephedrine may cause some effects that are similar to phenylpropanolamine. Use cautiously in patients with cardiovascular disease. Use cautiously, or not at all, with monoamine oxidase inhibitors (MAOIs; e.g., selegiline). Beta agonists may increase blood glucose. Pseudoephedrine has been used in clandestine laboratories to illegally manufacture methamphetamine. Therefore, some states may regulate the sales of this drug and restrict some distribution.

Drug Interactions

Pseudoephedrine, like other sympathomimetic agents, is expected to potentiate other alpha- and beta-receptor agonists. It may cause increased vasoconstriction and changes in heart rate. Use cautiously with other vasoactive drugs. Use cautiously with other drugs that may lower seizure threshold. Use with inhalant anesthetics may increase cardiovascular risk. Do not use with tricyclic antidepressants (TCAs) or monoamine oxidase inhibitors (MAOIs; e.g., selegiline or amitraz).

Instructions for Use

Although clinical trials have not been conducted for comparison, it is believed that the action and efficacy of pseudoephedrine is similar to ephedrine and phenylpropanolamine.

Patient Monitoring and Laboratory Tests

Monitor heart rate in patients. If possible, monitor blood pressure and ECG in patients that may be susceptible to cardiovascular problems.

Formulations Available

Pseudoephedrine is available in 30 and 60 mg tablets, 120 mg capsules, and 6 mg/mL syrup. (Some combination formulations have other ingredients such as antitussives or antihistamines.)

Stability and Storage

Store in tightly sealed container, protected from light, and at room temperature. Pseudoephedrine is soluble in water and ethanol. Keep compounded formulations at a low pH for maximum stability. Protect from freezing.

Small Animal Dosage

Dogs

- 0.2-0.4 mg/kg (or 15-60 mg/dog) q8-12h PO.

Large Animal Dosage

No doses have been reported for large animals.

Regulatory Information

Withdrawal times are not established for animals that produce food. For extralabel use withdrawal interval estimates, contact FARAD at 1-888-USFARAD (1-888-873-2723) or send e-mail to FARAD@ncsu.edu.

RCI Classification: 3

Psyllium

sill'ee-um

Trade and Other Names: Metamucil and generic brands

Functional Classification: Laxative

Pharmacology and Mechanism of Action

Bulk-forming laxative. The action of psyllium is to absorb water and expand to provide increased bulk and moisture content to the stool, which encourages normal peristalsis and bowel motility. Psyllium also may have antilipidemia effects.

Indications and Clinical Uses

Psyllium is administered orally for treatment of constipation and bowel evacuation. In horses, it has been used for treating sand colic, but the effectiveness for this indication has not been shown.

Precautionary Information

Adverse Reactions and Side Effects

Adverse effects have not been reported in animals. Intestinal impaction can occur with overuse or in patients with inadequate fluid intake. In horses, it may be difficult to administer via stomach tube because it is prone to forming a gel when mixing with water.

Contraindications and Precautions

No contraindications are reported for animals.

Drug Interactions

No drug interactions have been reported in animals.

Instructions for Use

Results of clinical studies in animals have not been reported. Use in animals (and doses) is based on experience in people or anecdotal experience in animals.

Patient Monitoring and Laboratory Tests

Psyllium may lower serum cholesterol measurements.

Formulations

Psyllium is available as powder, usually 3.4 g/tsp.

Stability and Storage

Store in tightly sealed container, protected from light, and at room temperature.

Small Animal Dosage

Dogs and Cats

- 1 teaspoon/5-10 kg (added to each meal).

Large Animal Dosage

Horses

- Up to 1000 mg/kg per day PO, via stomach tube or added to feed.

Regulatory Information

No withdrawal times are necessary.

Pyrantel Pamoate, Pyrantel Tartrate

pye-ran'tel

Trade and Other Names: Nemex, Strongid, Priex, Pyran, and Pyr-A-Pam

Functional Classification: Antiparasitic

Pharmacology and Mechanism of Action

Antiparasitic drug. Pyrantel is in the class of tetrahydropyrimidines. Others in this class include morantel. Pyrantel acts to interfere with ganglionic neurotransmission via blocking with acetylcholine receptors and other sites. This causes paralysis of the parasites. Paralyzed worms are expelled from the intestinal lumen by peristalsis. Pyrantel is poorly water soluble and not absorbed systemically in ruminants, although some absorption occurs in monogastric animals. Most of the activity is confined to the intestinal lumen.

Indications and Clinical Uses

Pyrantel is indicated for treatment of intestinal nematodes. In horses, pyrantel is used for treatment and prevention of nematodes, including pinworms *(Oxyuris equi)*, large roundworms *(Parascaris equorum)*, large strongyles *(Strongylus edentatus, S. equinus,* and *S. vulgaris)*, and small strongyles. When added to medicated feed it is used to control nematodes, including pinworms *(O. equi)*, large roundworms *(P. equorum)*, large strongyles *(S. edentatus, S. vulgaris,* and *Triodontophorus* species*)*, and small strongyles. In pigs it is used for prevention of large roundworm *(Ascaris suum)* and prevention of the nodular worm, *Oesophagostomum* species. In dogs and cats, it is used for treatment nematodes, including hookworms *(Ancylostoma* species*)*, and roundworms *(Toxocara cati, T. canis* and *Toxascaris leonina)*. There is some evidence that it is effective for control of some tapeworms, but ordinarily other drugs should be used for tapeworms.

Precautionary Information

Adverse Reactions and Side Effects

No adverse effects reported.

Contraindications and Precautions

No contraindications in animals. It may be used in all ages, in lactating and pregnant animals.

Drug Interactions

CNS toxicity may be more likely when coadministered with levamisole, but this is not reported from clinical use in animals.

Instructions for Use

Shake suspension prior to use. Doses listed are for single dose, but they may be repeated as part of a parasite management program. Lower doses may be added to daily feed for prevention of parasites.

Patient Monitoring and Laboratory Tests

Monitor fecal samples for presence of intestinal parasites.

Formulations

Pyrantel is available in 171, 180, and 226 mg (base) per mL paste, 22.7 and 113.5 mg (base) tablets, and 2.27, 4.54, and 50 mg (base) per mL suspension. It is also available in 12.6, 10.6, and 21.1 g/kg of pellets for medicated feed.

Pyrantel pamoate is a salt and contains 34.7% pyrantel base. Doses are based on the amount of pyrantel base. Pyrantel tartrate contains 57.9% pyrantel base. Many of the formulations contain other antiparasitic drugs (e.g., praziquantel).

Stability and Storage

Store in tightly sealed container, protected from light, and at room temperature. Protect from freezing.

Small Animal Dosage

Dogs

- 5 mg/kg once PO, repeat in 7-10 days.

Cats

- 20 mg/kg once PO.

Doses may be mixed with food.

Large Animal Dosage

Horses

- Nematodes: 6.6 mg/kg PO.
- Cestodes: 13.2 mg/kg.
- Medicated feed: 12.5 mg/kg as a single dose or 2.6 mg/kg/day for prevention.

Pigs

- 22 mg/kg administered in feed, as a single treatment.

Regulatory Information

Pigs: 1 day withdrawal (U.S.); 7 days (Canada).

Withdrawal times for other species are not established. For extralabel use withdrawal interval estimates, contact FARAD at 1-888-USFARAD (1-888-873-2723) or send e-mail to FARAD@ncsu.edu.

P

Pyridostigmine Bromide

peer-id-oh-stig′meen broe′mide

Trade and Other Names: Mestinon and Regonol

Functional Classification: Anticholinesterase, Antimyasthenic

Pharmacology and Mechanism of Action

Cholinesterase inhibitor and antimyasthenic drug. This drug inhibits the enzyme that breaks down acetylcholine. Therefore it prolongs the action of acetylcholine at the synapse. The major difference between physostigmine and neostigmine or pyridostigmine is that physostigmine crosses the blood-brain barrier, and the others do not. Compared to neostigmine, pyridostigmine has longer duration of action.

Indications and Clinical Uses

Pyridostigmine is used as an antidote for anticholinergic intoxication and treatment (antidote) for neuromuscular blockade. It is also used as a treatment of myasthenia gravis, ileus, and urinary retention (such as postoperative) retention by increasing tone of bladder smooth muscle. Most often, pyridostigmine is the first drug of choice for myasthenia gravis and is preferred over neostigmine.

Precautionary Information

Adverse Reactions and Side Effects

Adverse effects are caused by the cholinergic action resulting from inhibition of cholinesterase. These effects can be seen in the GI tract as diarrhea and increased secretions. Other adverse effects can include miosis, bradycardia, muscle twitching or weakness, and constriction of bronchi and ureters. Adverse effects can be treated with anticholinergic drugs, such as atropine. Pyridostigmine may be associated with fewer adverse effects than neostigmine, but the effects of pyridostigmine may persist longer. If adverse effects are observed, treat with 0.125 mg of hyoscyamine sulfate. Atropine also may be used.

Contraindications and Precautions

Do not use in these conditions: urinary obstruction, intestinal obstruction, asthma or bronchoconstriction, pneumonia, and cardiac arrhythmias. Do not use in patients sensitive to bromide. Consider the amount of bromide in dose in any patient also receiving bromide (KBr) for treatment of seizures.

Drug Interactions

Use cautiously in patients receiving potassium bromide.

Instructions for Use

Pyridostigmine is used for treatment of myasthenia gravis. Neostigmine and pyridostigmine have fewer side effects than physostigmine. When used, frequency of dose may be increased based on observation of effects. After administration, pyridostigmine benefits should be observed in approximately 15-30 minutes. The duration of action may be 3-4 hours.

Patient Monitoring and Laboratory Tests

Monitor GI effects. Monitor cardiac rate and rhythm.

Formulations

Pyridostigmine is available in 12 mg/mL oral syrup, 60 mg tablets (scored), and 5 mg/mL injection.

Stability and Storage

Store in tightly sealed container, protected from light, and at room temperature. Pyridostigmine is soluble in water. Store in acid solutions; it may decompose in alkaline vehicles.

Small Animal Dosage

Dogs and Cats

- Antimyasthenic: 0.02-0.04 mg/kg q2h IV or 0.5-3 mg/kg q8-12h PO.
- Antidote for muscle blockade: 0.15-0.3 mg/kg IM or IV, as needed.

Large Animal Dosage

No doses have been reported for large animals.

Regulatory Information

Withdrawal times are not established for animals that produce food. For extralabel use withdrawal interval estimates, contact FARAD at 1-888-USFARAD (1-888-873-2723) or send e-mail to FARAD@ncsu.edu.

RCI Classification: 3

Pyrimethamine

peer-ih-meth'ah-meen

Trade and Other Names: Daraprim

Functional Classification: Antibacterial

Pharmacology and Mechanism of Action

Antibacterial and antiprotozoal drug. Pyrimethamine blocks dihydrofolate reductase enzyme which inhibits synthesis of reduced folate and nucleic acids. Activity of pyrimethamine is more specific against protozoa than bacteria. Pyrimethamine is often combined with a sulfonamide to produce a synergistic effect.

Indications and Clinical Uses

Pyrimethamine is used to treat protozoal infections in animals. It is most often combined with a sulfonamide, either separately, or in a combined formulation. See Pyrimethamine + Sulfadiazine monograph for additional information.

Precautionary Information

Adverse Reactions and Side Effects

When administered with trimethoprim sulfonamide combinations, anemia has been observed. Folic or folinic acid has been supplemented to prevent anemia, but benefit of this treatment is unclear.

Contraindications and Precautions

Do not administer to animals that may be prone to anemia or in which a CBC cannot be monitored.

Drug Interactions

Drug interactions are not reported for animals. However, combination of pyrimethamine with trimethoprim/sulfonamides will enhance the bone marrow toxicity.

Instructions for Use

Pyrimethamine is used either alone or in combination with sulfonamides. (See pyrimethamine + sulfadiazine combination for further details.)

Patient Monitoring and Laboratory Tests

Monitor CBC periodically in animals receiving treatment.

Formulations

Pyrimethamine is available in 25 mg tablets.

Stability and Storage

Store in tightly sealed container, protected from light, and at room temperature. Pyrimethamine is poorly soluble in water, but it is more soluble in ethanol. Tablets have been crushed to make extemporaneous suspensions in syrups and other flavorings. These formulations have been stable for 7 days and up to 90 days, depending on the formulation.

Small Animal Dosage

Dogs

- 1 mg/kg q24h PO for 14-21 days (5 days for *Neospora caninum*).

Cats

- 0.5-1 mg/kg q24h PO for 14-28 days.

Large Animal Dosage

- Horses, equine protozoal myeloencephalitis (EPM), caused by *Sarcocystis neurona:* 1 mg/kg q24h PO in combination with a sulfonamide (see details on pyrimethamine + sulfadiazine.)

Regulatory Information

Withdrawal times are not established for animals that produce food. For extralabel use withdrawal interval estimates, contact FARAD at 1-888-USFARAD (1-888-873-2723) or send e-mail to FARAD@ncsu.edu.

Pyrimethamine + Sulfadiazine

peer-ih-meth'ah-meen + sul-fa-dye'ah-zeen

Trade and Other Names: ReBalance

Functional Classification: Antiprotozoal

Pharmacology and Mechanism of Action

Antibacterial, antiprotozoal drug, and sulfonamide combination. Pyrimethamine blocks dihydrofolate reductase enzyme, which inhibits synthesis of reduced folate and nucleic acids. Activity of pyrimethamine is more specific against protozoa than bacteria. Sulfadiazine provides a false PABA substrate for synthesis of dihydrofolic acid by bacteria and protozoa. Together the combination is synergistic against protozoa.

Indications and Clinical Uses

Pyrimethamine + sulfadiazine is used to treat horses with Equine Protozoal Myeloencephalitis (EPM). Although not registered for use to treat other animals, the equine formulation has been administered to small animals to treat protozoal infections caused by *Toxoplasma*, *Neospora*, and *Sarcocystis* species.

Precautionary Information

Adverse Reactions and Side Effects

There is a risk of folic acid anemia when pyrimethamine and sulfonamide combinations are administered. This has been observed in 12% of treated horses in a field trial. Folic or folinic acid (preferably folinic acid) has been supplemented to prevent anemia, but benefit of this treatment is unclear. Bone marrow suppression usually resolves after discontinuation of treatment. Diarrhea may occur after oral administration. Multiple adverse effects have been documented from administration of sulfonamides. These include allergic reactions, Type II and III hypersensitivity, arthropathy, anemia, thrombocytopenia, hepatopathy, hypothyroidism (with prolonged therapy), keratoconjunctivitis sicca, and skin reactions. Dogs may be more sensitive to sulfonamides than other animals because dogs lack the ability to acetylate sulfonamides to metabolites.

Contraindications and Precautions

Do not administer to animals sensitive to sulfonamides.

Drug Interactions

Drug interactions are not reported for animals. However, combination of pyrimethamine with trimethoprim/sulfonamides will enhance the bone marrow toxicity.

Instructions for Use

Use of pyrimethamine sulfadiazine has been primarily for treatment of protozoal infections in horses. However, there is anecdotal evidence that pyrimethamine + sulfadiazine may be indicated for treatment of some protozoa (e.g., *Toxoplasma, Neospora, or Sarcocystis)* in small animals.

Patient Monitoring and Laboratory Tests

Monitor CBC periodically in animals receiving treatment. A CBC should be performed at least monthly in treated animals.

Formulations

Pyrimethamine + sulfadiazine is available in an oral suspension that is 250 mg sulfadiazine and 12.5 mg pyrimethamine per mL.

Stability and Storage

Store in tightly sealed container, protected from light, and at room temperature. Do not freeze.

Small Animal Dosage

Dogs and Cats

- 1 mg/kg pyrimethamine and 20 mg/kg sulfadiazine once daily PO. (Equivalent to one third mL, 0.33 mL, per 4 kg of body weight.)

Large Animal Dosage

- EPM caused by *S. neurona:* 1 mg/kg pyrimethamine, 20 mg/kg sulfadiazine q24h PO (4 mL per 110 pounds). Treatment duration in horses varies from 90-270 days.

Regulatory Information

Do not administer to animals intended for food.

Quinacrine Hydrochloride

kwin'eh-krin hye-droe-klor'ide

Trade and Other Names: Atabrine (No longer available in U.S.)

Functional Classification: Antiparasitic

Pharmacology and Mechanism of Action

Antimalarial drug. Quinacrine is an outdated antimalarial drug. It inhibits nucleic acid synthesis in parasite.

Indications and Clinical Uses

Quinacrine is used occasionally for treatment of protozoa *(Giardia)*. But other drugs (e.g., metronidazole and tinidazole) are used more often.

Precautionary Information

Adverse Reactions and Side Effects

Side effects are common. Vomiting occurs after oral administration.

Contraindications and Precautions

No contraindications are reported for animals.

Drug Interactions

No drug interactions have been reported in animals.

Instructions for Use

Doses listed are for treatment of giardiasis. Effects for other organisms are not reported.

Patient Monitoring and Laboratory Tests

No specific monitoring is necessary.

Formulations

Quinacrine is available in 100 mg tablets. Quinacrine may no longer be marketed in the U.S., but it may be available from some pharmacies in a compounded formulation.

Stability and Storage

Store in tightly closed container, protected from light, and at room temperature. Stability of compounded formulations has not been evaluated.

Small Animal Dosage

Dogs

- 6.6 mg/kg q12h PO for 5 days.

Cats

- 11 mg/kg q24h PO for 5 days.

Large Animal Dosage

No doses have been reported for large animals.

Regulatory Information

Withdrawal times are not established for animals that produce food. For extralabel use withdrawal interval estimates, contact FARAD at 1-888-USFARAD (1-888-873-2723) or send e-mail to FARAD@ncsu.edu.

Quinidine, Quinidine Sulfate

kwin-ih-deen

Trade and Other Names: Quinidine gluconate: Quiniglute, Duraquin and Quinidine polygalacturonate: Cardioquin, and Quinidine sulfate: Cin-Quin, and Quinora

Functional Classification: Antiarrhythmic

Pharmacology and Mechanism of Action

Antiarrhythmic drug. Class-I antiarrhythmic. Like other Class I antiarrhythmic drugs, its action is to inhibit sodium influx via blockade of sodium channels. Therefore it suppresses cardiac Phase 0 action potential and decreases ectopic arrhythmic foci.

Indications and Clinical Uses

Quinidine is used to treat ventricular arrhythmias and occasionally to convert atrial fibrillation to sinus rhythm. In small animals it is rarely used, because there are other more effective and safer alternatives available. In horses and cattle, quinidine has been the drug of choice to treat atrial fibrillation. However, other alternatives are considered because of frequency of adverse effects in horses. Alternatives include diltiazem and electrical cardioversion. Rapid clearance in cattle (half-life is 2.25 hour) results in the need for frequent administration. Equine doses are usually administered orally via stomach tube.

Precautionary Information

Adverse Reactions and Side Effects

Side effects with quinidine are more common than procainamide and include nausea and vomiting. Adverse effects include hypotension and tachycardia (because of vagolytic effect). With intravenous dosing, adverse effects such as hypotension and tachyarrhythmias are common in cattle. Note that in horses, adverse effects are common, which include hypotension, gastrointestinal problems, and supraventricular tachycardia. Sudden cardiac death is possible but uncommon in horses.

Contraindications and Precautions

Quinidine may increase heart rate. Use cautiously in animals with heart disease.

Drug Interactions

Quinidine is a well-known multi-drug resistance (MDR1) membrane pump (p-glycoprotein) inhibitor. It will interfere with membrane channels and increase concentrations of some coadministered drugs. Coadministration with digoxin may increase digoxin concentrations. See Appendix for list of potential p-glycoprotein substrates.

Instructions for Use

Quinidine is not used as commonly as other Class I antiarrhythmic drugs. Doses calculated according to amount of quinidine base in each product. Preparation of 324 mg quinidine gluconate has a 202 mg quinidine base. Preparation of 275 mg quinidine polygalacturonate has a 167 mg quinidine base. Preparation of 300 mg quinidine sulfate has a 250 mg quinidine base.

Patient Monitoring and Laboratory Tests

Quinidine can be hypotensive and vagolytic. Monitor patient's ECG for arrhythmias and monitor blood pressure.

Formulations

In some countries, quinidine is being discontinued and may be difficult to obtain.

Quinidine gluconate is available in 324 mg tablets and 80 mg/mL injection.

Quinidine polygalacturonate is available in 275 mg tablets.

Quinidine sulfate is available in 100, 200, and 300 mg tablets, 200 and 300 mg capsules, and 200 mg/mL injection.

Stability and Storage

Store in tightly sealed container, protected from light, and at room temperature. Quinidine is slightly soluble in water. Quinidine salts may form a dark color when exposed to light and should not be used. Quinidine has been compounded for oral use in syrups (e.g., Ora-Sweet) and stable for 60 days.

Small Animal Dose

Dogs

- Quinidine gluconate: 6-20 mg/kg q6h IM or 6-20 mg/kg q6-8h PO (of base).
- Quinidine polygalacturonate: 6-20 mg/kg q6h PO (of base).
- Quinidine sulfate: 6-20 mg/kg q6-8h PO (of base) or 5-10 mg/kg q6h IV.

Large Animal Dosage

Cattle

- Treatment of atrial fibrillation: Quinidine is poorly absorbed orally in cattle and must be given IV. A loading dose of 49 mg/kg (given over 4 hours), followed by 42 mg/kg IV maintenance dose. Or give 40 mg/kg diluted in 4 L of fluid slowly at a rate of 1 L/hr until fibrillation is converted.

Horses

- Atrial fibrillation treatment: 5 grams per 450 kg BW (per 1000 pounds) for the first treatment; thereafter give 10 grams per 450 kg every 2 hours until sinus rate is achieved. IV dose is 1-1.5 mg/kg every 10-15 min to a total dose of 10 mg/kg or until sinus rate conversion.

Regulatory Information

Withdrawal times are not established for animals that produce food. Because of rapid elimination, short withdrawal times can be used. For extralabel use withdrawal interval estimates, contact FARAD at 1-888-USFARAD (1-888-873-2723) or send e-mail to FARAD@ncsu.edu.

RCI Classification: 4

Racemethionine

rah-see′meth-eye′oh-neen

Trade and Other Names: Uroeze, Methio-Form, and generic brands and Pedameth, Uracid, and generic brands (human preparations)

Functional Classification: Acidifier

Pharmacology and Mechanism of Action

Urinary acidifier. Methionine lowers urinary pH. Racemethionine also has been used to protect against acetaminophen overdose in people, by restoring hepatic concentrations of glutathione.

Indications and Clinical Uses

It is used as a urinary acidifier. In people it also is used to treat dermatitis caused by urinary incontinence (reduces urine ammonia).

Precautionary Information

Adverse Reactions and Side Effects

Adverse effects have not been reported.

Contraindications and Precautions

Do not use in animals with metabolic acidosis. Do not use in young cats. Do not use in animals with hepatic disease.

Drug Interactions

No drug interactions have been reported in animals.

Instructions for Use

Use for acetaminophen toxicity has been replaced by acetylcysteine.

Patient Monitoring and Laboratory Tests

Monitor CBC and hepatic enzymes if used to treat toxicity.

Formulations

Racemethionine is available in 500 mg tablets, 75 mg/5 mL pediatric oral solution, 200 mg capsules, and powders to add to an animal's food.

Stability and Storage

Store in tightly sealed container, protected from light, and at room temperature.

Small Animal Dosage

Dogs

- 150-300 mg/kg/day PO.

Cats

- 1-1.5 gm/cat PO (added to food each day).

Large Animal Dosage

No doses have been reported for large animals.

Regulatory Information

Withdrawal times are not established for animals that produce food. For extralabel use withdrawal interval estimates, contact FARAD at 1-888-USFARAD (1-888-873-2723) or send e-mail to FARAD@ncsu.edu.

R

Ramipril

ram'ih-pril

Trade and Other Names: Vasotop

Functional Classification: Vasodilator, Angiotensin-converting enzyme (ACE) inhibitor

Pharmacology and Mechanism of Action

Like other ACE inhibitors, ramipril inhibits conversion of angiotensin I to angiotensin II. Angiotensin II is a potent vasoconstrictor, and will stimulate sympathetic stimulation, renal hypertension, and synthesis of aldosterone. The ability of aldosterone to cause sodium and water retention contributes to congestion. Ramipril, like other ACE inhibitors will cause vasodilation, and decrease aldosterone-induced congestion. But ACE inhibitors also contribute to vasodilation by increasing concentrations of some vasodilating kinins and prostaglandins. Ramipril appeared to have a cardio-protective effect when used to treat dogs with heart disease caused by cardiomyopathy or valvular disease.

Indications and Clinical Uses

Ramipril is used to treat hypertension and CHF. It is primarily used in dogs, but its benefit in cats with heart failure or with systemic hypertension has not been reported.

Precautionary Information

Adverse Reactions and Side Effects

Ramipril was well tolerated in clinical studies in dogs.

Contraindications and Precautions

Studies performed in experimental dogs indicated that dose adjustments are not necessary when administering ramipril in dogs with impaired renal function. Discontinue ACE inhibitors in pregnant animals; they cross the placenta and have caused fetal malformations and death of the fetus.

Drug Interactions

Use cautiously with other hypotensive drugs and diuretics. Nonsteroidal antiinflammatory drugs (NSAIDs) may decrease vasodilating effects.

Instructions for Use

Clinical efficacy has been demonstrated in dogs with dilated cardiomyopathy. Other drugs used for treatment of heart failure may be used concurrently. Dogs also may receive digoxin and/or furosemide with ramipril.

Patient Monitoring and Laboratory Tests

Monitor patients carefully to avoid hypotension. With all ACE inhibitors, monitor electrolytes and renal function 3-7 days after initiating therapy and periodically thereafter.

Formulations

Ramipril is available in 1.25, 2.5, 5, and 10 mg capsules.

Stability and Storage

Store in tightly sealed container, protected from light, and at room temperature.

Small Animal Dosage

Dogs

- 0.125-0.25 mg/kg daily PO.

Large Animal Dosage

No doses have been reported for large animals.

Regulatory Information

Withdrawal times are not established for animals that produce food. For extralabel use withdrawal interval estimates, contact FARAD at 1-888-USFARAD (1-888-873-2723) or send e-mail to FARAD@ncsu.edu.

Ranitidine Hydrochloride

rah-nit′ih-deen hye-droe-klor′ide

Trade and Other Names: Zantac

Functional Classification: Antiulcer agent

Pharmacology and Mechanism of Action

Histamine$_2$ antagonist (H_2 blocker). Ranitidine, like other H_2 blockers, suppresses histamine stimulation of gastric parietal cell to decrease gastric acid secretion. Ranitidine will increase stomach pH. Ranitidine is longer-acting and 4 to 10 times more potent than cimetidine. Ranitidine hydrochloride is 89% ranitidine.

Indications and Clinical Uses

Ranitidine is used to treat ulcers and gastritis. It is used to prevent nonsteroidal antiinflammatory drug (NSAID) induced ulcers in animals, although efficacy has not been demonstrated for this effect. It does not produce a sustained increase in stomach pH as much as proton pump inhibitors (omeprazole). Ranitidine (6.6 mg/kg PO) in foals suppressed acid for 6 hours, but omeprazole suppressed acid for 22 hours at 4 mg/kg. In horses, ranitidine did not improve healing of ulcers induced by NSAIDs, and it was not as effective as omeprazole for treating ulcers. Ranitidine may stimulate stomach emptying and colon motility via anticholinesterase action.

Precautionary Information

Adverse Reactions and Side Effects

Adverse effects are usually seen only with decreased renal clearance. In people, CNS signs may occur with high doses. Ranitidine may have fewer effects on endocrine function and drug interactions compared to cimetidine.

Contraindications and Precautions

Fewer drug interactions are possible with ranitidine compared to cimetidine, because ranitidine does not inhibit cytochrome P450 enzymes.

Drug Interactions

Ranitidine and other H_2 receptor blockers block secretion of stomach acid. Therefore, they will interfere with oral absorption of drugs dependent on acidity, such as ketoconazole, itraconazole, and iron supplements. Unlike cimetidine, ranitidine is not known to inhibit microsomal P450 enzymes.

Instructions for Use

Pharmacokinetic information in dogs suggests that ranitidine may be administered less often than cimetidine to achieve continuous suppression of stomach acid secretion.

Patient Monitoring and Laboratory Tests

No specific monitoring is necessary.

Formulations

Ranitidine is available in 75, 150, and 300 mg tablets, 50 and 300 mg capsules, and 25 mg/mL injection. Some forms are available over-the-counter (OTC).

Stability and Storage

Store in tightly sealed container, protected from light, and at room temperature. Ranitidine hydrochloride is soluble in water. Tablets have been crushed and mixed with water and syrup and was stable for 7 days. Protect from freezing.

Small Animal Dosage

Dogs

- 2 mg/kg q8h IV or PO.

Cats

- 2.5 mg/kg q12h IV.
- 3.5 mg/kg q12h PO.

Large Animal Dosage

Horses

- 2.2-6.6 mg/kg q6-8h PO. The higher dose (6.6 mg/kg) is more effective at suppressing stomach acid.
- 2 mg/kg q6-8h IV.

Calves

- 50 mg/kg q8h PO in milk-fed calves.

Regulatory Information

Withdrawal times are not established for animals that produce food. For extralabel use withdrawal interval estimates, contact FARAD at 1-888-USFARAD (1-888-873-2723) or send e-mail to FARAD@ncsu.edu.

RCI Classification: 5

Riboflavin (Vitamin B_2)

rye'boe-flay-vin

Trade and Other Names: Vitamin B_2

Functional Classification: Vitamin

Pharmacology and Mechanism of Action

Vitamin B_2 supplement. Thiamine is commonly an ingredient in Vitamin B complex aqueous solutions for injection. In these formulations it is available as 5′ phosphate sodium riboflavin. Vitamin B-Complex often contains thiamine (B_1), riboflavin, niacinamide, and cyanocobalamin B_{12}.

Indications and Clinical Uses

Riboflavin is used as a Vitamin B_2 supplement. It is usually administered for maintenance in deficient patients.

Precautionary Information

Adverse Reactions and Side Effects

Adverse effects are rare because water soluble vitamins are easily excreted. Riboflavin may discolor the urine.

Contraindications and Precautions

Do not administer injectable solution IV rapidly if it contains thiamine (vitamin B_{12}), because this may cause an anaphylactic reaction.

Drug Interactions

No drug interactions have been reported in animals.

Instructions for Use

It is not necessary to supplement in animals with well-balanced diets.

Patient Monitoring and Laboratory Tests

No specific monitoring is necessary.

Formulations

Riboflavin is available in various sized tablets in increments from 10 to 250 mg. Riboflavin is most commonly formulated with other vitamins in a "vitamin B complex" aqueous solution for injection (2 and 5 mg/mL of riboflavin).

Stability and Storage

Store in tightly sealed container, protected from light, and at room temperature.

Small Animal Dosage

Dogs

- 10-20 mg/day PO.
- 1-4 mg/dog q24h SQ.

Cats

- 5-10 mg/day PO.
- 1-2 mg/cat q24h SQ.

Large Animal Dosage

Lambs

- 2-4 mg q24h IM, or SQ.

Calves and Foals

- 6-10 mg q24h IM or SQ.

Cattle and Horses

- 20-40 mg q24h IM or SQ.

Sheep and Pigs

- 10-20 mg q24h IM or SQ.

Regulatory Information

Because of low risk of harmful residues in animals intended for food, no withdrawal time is necessary.

Rifampin

rih-fam'pin

Trade and Other Names: Rifadin and Rifampicin

Functional Classification: Antibacterial

Pharmacology and Mechanism of Action

Antibacterial. Action of rifampin is to inhibit bacterial RNA synthesis. Rifampin has a spectrum of activity that includes primarily gram-positive bacteria. Rifampin is lipophilic and shows good intracellular penetration compared with many other antibiotics. Subsequently, it may be effective against some intracellular pathogens.

Indications and Clinical Uses

Rifampin is highly lipid-soluble and has been used to treat intracellular infections. Rifampin is used in people primarily for treatment of tuberculosis. Spectrum of action includes staphylococci, streptococci, and mycobacteria. However, resistance develops quickly. One of the most common uses of rifampin is for treating infections caused by *Rhodococcus equi* in horses. For this treatment, it is frequently combined with erythromycin, azithromycin, or clarithromycin. In small animals, it is occasionally used to treat staphylococcal infections.

Precautionary Information

Adverse Reactions and Side Effects

In people, hypersensitivity and flu-like symptoms are reported. Hepatotoxicity is seen more commonly in dogs when high doses are administered, for example 10 mg/kg. Urine will be colored orange to reddish-orange in treated patients. It will also discolor saliva, tears, feces, sclera, and mucous membranes to a reddish-orange color. Pancreatitis has been associated with rifampin administration.

Contraindications and Precautions

When administered with other drugs, consideration for more rapid elimination of other drugs should be considered. Use cautiously in animals that are at a risk for pancreatitis. Because of risk of hepatitis, use cautiously with any other drug that may be potentially hepatotoxic (e.g., sulfonamides, anticonvulsants, acetaminophen).

Drug Interactions

Multiple drug interactions are possible. Rifampin is a potent inducer of cytochrome P450 hepatic enzymes. Drugs affected include barbiturates, chloramphenicol, and corticosteroids.

Instructions for Use

Most of the documented clinical experience has been in horses when rifampin was combined with a macrolide antibiotic for use in foals. Use in small animals (and doses) is based on experience in people or anecdotal experience in animals. Use in combination with other drugs to decrease emergence of resistance. Administer on an empty stomach.

Patient Monitoring and Laboratory Tests

Susceptibility testing: CLSI (NCCLS) break point for sensitive organisms is less than or equal to 1.0 mcg/mL for streptococci and less than or equal to 1.0 mcg/mL for other organisms.

Formulations

Rifampin is available in 150 mg and 300 mg capsules and 600 mg Rifadin IV injectable solution.

Stability and Storage

Store in tightly sealed container, protected from light, and at room temperature. Rifampin is slightly soluble in water and ethanol. It is more soluble at acidic pH. Acid should be added to solutions (e.g., ascorbic acid) to prevent oxidation and improve solubility. Rifampin has been mixed with syrups and flavorings for oral administration and was stable for 4-6 weeks. Injectable solution is prepared by adding 10 mL saline to 600 mg vial and mix (60 mg/mL). It may be infused with 0.9% saline or 5% dextrose solution. Reconstituted injectable solution is stable for 24 hours.

Small Animal Dosage

Dogs and Cats

- 5 mg/kg q12-24h PO.

Large Animal Dosage

Horses

- 10 mg/kg q24h PO.
- Foals for treatment of *R. equi:* 5 mg/kg q12h PO, combined with erythromycin (25 mg/kg q8h PO).

Cattle

- 20 mg/kg q24h PO.

Regulatory Information

No regulatory information is available. Withdrawal times have not been established for animals that produce food. For extra label use withdrawal interval estimates, contact FARAD at 1-888-USFARAD (1-888-873-2723) or send e-mail to FARAD@ncsu.edu.

Ringer's Solution

Trade and Other Names: Generic brands

Functional Classification: Fluid replacement

Pharmacology and Mechanism of Action

Intravenous solution for fluid replacement. Ringer's solution contains (in mEq/L) 147 sodium, 4 mEq/L potassium, 155 mEq/L chloride, and 4 mEq/L calcium.

Indications and Clinical Uses

Ringer's solution is used as fluid replacement and for maintenance. It has a balanced electrolyte concentration, but it does not contain any bases (see Lactated Ringer's for solutions that contain bases).

Precautionary Information

Adverse Reactions and Side Effects

Ringer's solution is considered an acidifying solution, because with prolonged administration the chloride will increase renal excretion of bicarbonate. Fluid overload occurs at high infusion rates.

Contraindications and Precautions

Do not exceed fluid rates of 80 mL/kg/hr. Consider supplementing with potassium, because this fluid will not meet maintenance potassium needs.

Drug Interactions

Ringer's solution contains calcium; do not mix with drugs that may bind to calcium.

Instructions for Use

When administering intravenous fluid solution, monitor rate carefully and electrolyte concentrations. Add bicarbonate to fluids if necessary based on calculation of base deficit.

Fluid administration rates are as follows: normal maintenance rates: 40-65 mL/kg/24hour (approximately 2-2.5 mL/kg/hr). For replacement fluid use the following calculation:

Liters needed = % dehydration × Body Weight (kg)

or

mL needed = % dehydration × Body Weight (kg) × 1000

Patient Monitoring and Laboratory Tests

Monitor pulmonary pressure when infusing high doses. Monitor electrolyte balance, especially potassium during treatment.

Formulations

Ringer's solution is available in 250, 500, and 1000 mL bags for infusion.

Stability and Storage

Store in tightly sealed container, protected from light, and at room temperature.

Small Animal Dosage

Dogs and Cats

- 55-65 mL/kg day (2.5 mL/kg/hr) IV, SQ, or IP (intraperitoneal), maintenance.
- 15-30 mL/kg/hr IV for moderate dehydration.
- 50 mL/kg/hr IV for severe dehydration.

Large Animal Dosage

Large Animals

- 40-50 mL/kg day IV, SQ, or IP (itraperitoneal) for maintenance
- 15-30 mL/kg/hr IV for moderate dehydration.
- 50 mL/kg/hr IV for severe dehydration.

Calves

- Moderate dehydration: 45 mL/kg given at a rate of 30-40 ml/kg/hr.
- Severe dehydration: 80-90 mL/kg given at a rate of 30-40 mL/kg/hr, or as fast as 80 mL/kg/hr, if necessary.

Regulatory Information

Because of low risk of harmful residues in animals intended for food, no withdrawal time is suggested.

Romifidine Hydrochloride

roe-mif'ih-deen hye-droe-klor'ide

Trade and Other Names: Sedivet

Functional Classification: Analgesic, Alpha$_2$ agonist

Pharmacology and Mechanism of Action

Alpha$_2$ adrenergic agonist. Alpha$_2$ agonists decrease release of neurotransmitters from the neuron. The proposed mechanism whereby they decrease transmission is via binding to presynaptic $alpha_2$ receptors (negative feedback receptors). The result is decreased sympathetic outflow, analgesia, sedation, and anesthesia. Romifidine is structurally similar to clonidine. Other drugs in this class include xylazine, detomidine, medetomidine, and clonidine. Romifidine has an onset of effect of 2 minutes and a duration of 1-1.5 hours.

Indications and Clinical Uses

Romifidine, like other $alpha_2$ agonists, is used as a sedative, anesthetic adjunct, and analgesia. Romifidine produces the longest duration of sedative effects, followed by detomidine, medetomidine, and xylazine. Its use is primarily limited to horses in which it is used as a sedative and analgesic to facilitate handling, clinical examinations, clinical procedures, and minor surgical procedures and for use as a preanesthetic prior to the induction of general anesthesia.

Precautionary Information

Adverse Reactions and Side Effects

Romifidine, like other $alpha_2$ agonists, decreases sympathetic output. Bradycardia is common and cardiovascular depression may occur. Cardiac effects can include sinoatrial block, first-degree and second-degree AV block, bradycardia, and sinus arrhythmia. In horses it causes effects similar to other $alpha_2$ agonists, including ataxia, head drooping, sweating, and bradycardia. Facial edema is common, especially with higher doses. At high doses (up to 600 mcg/kg) to horses, there were no deaths.

Contraindications and Precautions

Romifidine, like other $alpha_2$ agonists should be used cautiously in animals with heart disease. Use may be contraindicated in older animals with preexisting cardiac disease. Xylazine causes problems in pregnant animals, and this should be considered for other $alpha_2$ agonists as well. Use cautiously in animals that are pregnant; it may induce labor. In addition, it may decrease oxygen delivery to fetus in late gestation. In case of overdose, reverse with atipamezole or yohimbine.

Drug Interactions

Do not use with other drugs that may cause cardiac depression. It may be used in horses with diazepam or ketamine. Do not mix in vial or syringe with other anesthetics. Use with opioid analgesic drugs will greatly enhance the CNS depression. Consider lowering doses if administered with opioids.

R

Instructions for Use

Romifidine is an $alpha_2$ agonist. Medetomidine, romifidine, and detomidine are more specific for the $alpha_2$ receptor than xylazine. Romifidine, like other $alpha_2$ agonists, can be administered with ketamine or benzodiazepines. It can be reversed with $alpha_2$ antagonists such as atipamezole or yohimbine. A range of doses is used in horses for romifidine; 40 and 120 mcg/kg IV have been compared, which showed that sedation, cardiac effects, analgesia are all dose-dependent effects. Deeper sedation occurs with higher doses. Each dose produced effects for at least 60 minutes, and some were observed for 180 minutes. Duration of 180 minutes is more likely with higher doses.

Patient Monitoring and Laboratory Tests

Monitor vital signs during anesthesia. Monitor heart rate, blood pressure, and ECG if possible during anesthesia.

Formulations

Romifidine is available in a 1% injection (10 mg/mL).

Stability and Storage

Store in tightly sealed container, protected from light, and at room temperature.

Small Animal Dosage

Dogs and Cats

Doses not established for small animals.

Large Animal Dosage

Horses

- Sedation and analgesia: 40 to 120 mcg/kg IV.
- Preanesthetic: 100 mcg/kg IV.

Regulatory Information

Do not administer in animals intended for food.

Ronidazole

roe'nid'ah-zole

Trade and Other Names: Generic

Functional Classification: Antibacterial, Antiparasitic

Pharmacology and Mechanism of Action

Antibacterial and antiprotozoal drug. It is a nitroimidazole in which the activity involves generation of free nitroradicals via metabolism within protozoa and bacteria. Ronidazole disrupts DNA in organism via reaction with intracellular metabolite. Its action is specific for anaerobic bacteria and protozoa. Like other nitroimidazoles, it is active against some protozoa, including *Trichomonas, Giardia,* and intestinal protozoal parasites.

Indications and Clinical Uses

Ronidazole is currently not a registered drug, but it has been used in cats to treat intestinal protozoal parasites. Studies for treatment of other organisms are not available. For treatment of feline *Tritrichomonas foetus* intestinal infections it has been administered orally at a dose of 30 mg/kg twice daily for 2 weeks. Efficacy for long-term remission has not been established, but temporary resolution of feline *Tritrichomonas foetus* intestinal infections has been observed.

Precautionary Information

Adverse Reactions and Side Effects

Like other nitroimidazoles, the most severe adverse effect is caused by toxicity to CNS. High doses may cause lethargy, CNS depression, ataxia, vomiting, and weakness. The CNS signs are related to inhibition of action of GABA and are responsive to benzodiazepines (diazepam). Like other nitroimidazoles, it has the potential to produce mutagenic changes in cells, but this has not been demonstrated in vivo. Like other nitroimidazoles, it has bitter taste and can cause vomiting and anorexia.

Contraindications and Precautions

Fetal abnormalities have not been demonstrated in animals with recommended doses, but use cautiously during pregnancy.

Drug Interactions

Like other nitroimidazoles, it may potentiate the effects of warfarin and cyclosporine via inhibition of drug metabolism.

Instructions for Use

Ronidazole is currently not a marketed drug but has been prepared from bulk powder in compounding pharmacies. There is currently little information about systemic absorption and toxicity from ronidazole in cats.

Patient Monitoring and Laboratory Tests

Monitor for neurologic adverse effects.

Formulations

No available formulation exists; it is compounded from bulk chemical.

Stability and Storage

Store in tightly sealed container, protected from light, and at room temperature. Stability of compounded formulations has not been evaluated.

Small Animal Dosage

Dogs

No dose has been reported.

Cats

- 30 mg/kg q12h PO for 2 weeks.

Large Animal Dose

No doses have been reported for large animals.

Regulatory Information

Do not administer to animals that produce food. Administration of nitroimidazoles to animals intended for food is prohibited. Treated cattle must not be slaughtered for food.

S-Adenosylmethionine (SAMe)

ess'ah-den'oh-sill-meh-thye'oh-neen

Trade and Other Names: Denosyl and SAMe

Functional Classification: Nutritional supplement

Pharmacology and Mechanism of Action

Nutritional supplement. SAMe has been associated with improvement in acetaminophen-induced hepatotoxicity in humans and one report in veterinary medicine. It serves as a methyl donor in metabolic reactions and generates glutathione (GSH), which may conjugate certain drug metabolites to enhance excretion. Cats and dogs have low levels of GSH, and SAMe may help restore GSH in animals that have been intoxicated and perhaps in animals that have liver disease.

Indications and Clinical Uses

SAMe has been used as a dietary supplement to support patients with hepatic disease. It may help restore hepatic GSH concentrations in deficient animals. It also has been administered to treat liver injury caused by intoxication of acetaminophen and other drugs that produce hepatotoxic drug injury.

Precautionary Information

Adverse Reactions and Side Effects

No adverse effects are reported.

Contraindications and Precautions

No contraindications are reported for animals.

Drug Interactions

Reactions of SAMe with tricyclic antidepressants (TCAs) have been reported, although the mechanism is not known. In laboratory animals, administration with clomipramine has caused serotonin syndrome.

Instructions for Use

SAMe is a dietary supplement widely available OTC. Potency of formulations may vary. Absorption is decreased when given with a meal. Administer 30 minutes to 1 hour before feeding. To ensure passage into the stomach of cats administer with water. Coated tablets (such as Denosyl) protect the active ingredient from destruction by stomach acid. Do not break tablets or disrupt coating.

Patient Monitoring and Laboratory Tests

Monitor liver enzymes in animals being treated for toxicity.

Formulations

SAMe is widely available OTC in tablets and powder. The brand Denosyl is available in 90, 225, and 425 mg tablets.

Stability and Storage

Store in tightly sealed container, protected from light, and at room temperature. Do not disrupt coating on tablet.

Small Animal Dosage

Dogs

- 90 mg (small dogs); 225 mg (medium dogs); and 425 mg (large dogs).

Cats

• 90 mg/cat/day PO, for cats up to 5 kg body weight.

Large Animal Dosage

No dose has been reported for large animals.

Regulatory Information

Because of low risk of harmful residues in food animals, no withdrawal time is suggested.

Selamectin

sel-ah-mek'tin

Trade and Other Names: Revolution

Functional Classification: Antiparasitic

Pharmacology and Mechanism of Action

Antiparasitic. Microfilaricide for heartworm prevention in dogs and cats. Selamectin is a semisynthetic avermectin. Avermectins (ivermectin-like drugs) and milbemycins (milbemycin, doramectin, and moxidectin) are macrocyclic lactones and share similarities, including mechanism of action. Avermectins are neurotoxic to parasites by potentiating effects of inhibitory neurotransmitter, GABA. Therefore, these drugs paralyze and kill susceptible parasites. Ordinarily, mammals are resistant because sufficient concentrations for toxicity are not achieved in the CNS. After topical application selamectin has high affinity for sebaceous glands and skin. Terminal half-life of selamectin is 11 days in dogs and 8 days in cats.

Indications and Clinical Uses

Selamectin is approved for prevention of heartworms, control of fleas, mites, and ticks in dogs and prevention of heartworms, control of fleas, mites, hookworms, and roundworms in cats.

Precautionary Information

Adverse Reactions and Side Effects

Transient, localized alopecia with or without inflammation at or near the site of application was observed in approximately 1% of treated cats. Other adverse effects included nausea, lethargy, salivation, tachypnea, and muscle tremors.

Contraindications and Precautions

Do not use in dogs younger than 6 weeks of age. Do not use in cats younger than 8 weeks of age.

Drug Interactions

No drug interactions have been reported in animals.

Instructions for Use

Apply as indicated on product label to skin of dogs and cats.

Patient Monitoring and Laboratory Tests

Monitor heartworm status in animals.

Formulations

Selamectin is available in 60 and 120 mg/mL topical solution.

Stability and Storage

Store in tightly sealed container, protected from light, and at room temperature.

Small Animal Dosage

Dogs and Cats

- Heartworm prevention: 6-12 mg/kg applied topically, every 30 days. (This dose also may be applied for treatment and prevention of ear mites and fleas.)
- Sarcoptic mange treatment: 6-12 mg/kg twice 30 days apart. (However, many dermatologists administer it at 2-3 week intervals.)

Large Animal Dosage

No dose has been reported for large animals.

Regulatory Information

Withdrawal times are not established for animals that produce food. For extralabel use withdrawal interval estimates, contact FARAD at 1-888-USFARAD (1-888-873-2723) or send e-mail to FARAD@ncsu.edu.

Selegiline Hydrochloride

se-leh′jeh-leen hye-droe-klor′ide

Trade and Other Names: Anipryl (also known as deprenyl and l-deprenyl), Eldepryl (human preparation), and Emsam transdermal patch

Functional Classification: Dopamine agonist

Pharmacology and Mechanism of Action

Dopamine agonist. Selegiline has been known by many names. Selegiline hydrochloride is the official USP drug name, but most clinicians know it by the older name l-deprenyl. (l-deprenyl is distinguished from its steroisomer d-deprenyl.) It was used in humans for treatment of Parkinson's disease and occasionally for Alzheimer's disease with the trade name *Eldepryl.* (Efficacy for Alzheimer's disease has not been established.) The veterinary formulation is registered for treatment of Cushing's disease in dogs and canine cognitive dysfunction.

The action of selegiline is to inhibit MAO type B (and other MAOs at higher doses). The proposed mechanism of action is to inhibit the metabolism of dopamine in the central nervous system and secondarily inhibits the metabolism of phenylethylamine. (Phenylethylamine in laboratory animals produces amphetamine-like effects.) There are two active metabolites, which are l-amphetamine and l-methamphetamine, but it is not known to what extent these contribute to pharmacologic effects.

The action for pituitary-dependent hyperadrenocorticism may be through increased dopamine levels in the brain, which decreases ACTH release, resulting in lower cortisol levels.

Indications and Clinical Uses

In dogs, selegiline is registered to control clinical signs of pituitary-dependent hyperadrenocorticism (PDH; Cushing's Disease) and to treat cognitive dysfunction in older dogs. However, the efficacy for Cushing's Disease may not be as high as for other drugs such as mitotane or trilostane. Selegiline may not be effective for some forms of PDH but may improve some clinical signs without lowering cortisol levels in dogs with PDH administered 1.0 mg/kg once daily. For canine cognitive dysfunction (dementia) in old dogs, treatment with selegiline inhibits MAO type B and increases dopamine concentrations in the brain, which restores dopamine and balance and may improve cognitive ability. It has been administered to some older cats with age-related behavior problems, but clinical results in cats have not been reported. It does not appear to produce any clinical effects in horses from oral administration.

In people it is primarily used to treat Parkinson's disease and other neurodegenerative diseases (in combination with levodopa). However, other drugs are used more often.

Precautionary Information

Adverse Reactions and Side Effects

Adverse effects are rare in dogs but have included vomiting, diarrhea, and hyperactive/restlessness. Amphetamine-like signs can be produced in experimental animals. At high doses in dogs, hyperactivity has been observed (doses >3 mg/kg) that included salivation, panting repetitive movements, decreased weight, and changes in activity level.

There are two active metabolites, which are l-amphetamine and l-methamphetamine. Even though there were increases in amphetamine concentrations in dogs, they were not high enough to produce adverse effects. However, at high doses (>3 mg/kg) it may produce behavioral changes. The l-isomer metabolites are not as active as their d-forms, and studies have not supported a potential for amphetamine-like abuse or dependency from selegiline compared with other amphetamine-like drugs.

Contraindications and Precautions

Not indicated for adrenal tumors. Use cautiously with other drugs. (See the following list of interactions.)

Drug Interactions

Do not use with other monoamine oxidase inhibitors (MAOIs). Do not use with tricyclic antidepressants (TCAs), such as clomipramine and amitriptyline or with selective serotonin-reuptake inhibitors (SSRIs), such as fluoxetine. Do not administer with meperidine, dobutamine, or amitraz. Use cautiously with sympathetic amines such as phenylpropanolamine.

Instructions for Use

Dose titration to effect. Start with low dose and increase gradually until clinical effect is observed. Transdermal patch for humans has not been evaluated for animals.

Patient Monitoring and Laboratory Tests

No specific monitoring is required. Serum cortisol testing is not valuable for evaluating efficacy.

Formulations

Selegiline is available in 2, 5, 10, 15, and 30 mg tablets for animals, and 20, 30, 40 cm^2 transdermal patch for humans.

Stability and Storage

Stable if stored in manufacturer's original formulation.

Small Animal Dosage

Dogs

- Begin with 1 mg/kg q24h PO. If there is no response within 2 months increase dose to maximum of 2 mg/kg q24h PO.

Cats

- 0.25-0.5 mg/kg q12-24h PO.

Large Animal Dosage

No dose has been reported for large animals. In preliminary studies in which selegiline was administered at a dose of 30 mg/horse PO or IV, there were no observed effects on behavior or locomotor activity.

Regulatory Information

Do not administer to animals intended for food.
RCI Classification: 2

Senna

sen'na

Trade and Other Names: Senokot

Functional Classification: Laxative

Pharmacology and Mechanism of Action

Laxative. Senna acts via local stimulation or via contact with intestinal mucosa.

Indications and Clinical Uses

Senna is indicated for treatment of constipation.

Precautionary Information

Adverse Reactions and Side Effects

Adverse effects not reported for animals. However, excessive doses are expected to cause fluid and electrolyte loss.

Contraindications and Precautions

Do not administer to animals with GI obstruction. Do not administer to dehydrated animals.

Drug Interactions

No drug interactions have been reported in animals.

Instructions for Use

Doses and indications are not well established for veterinary medicine. Use is strictly based on anecdotal experience.

Patient Monitoring and Laboratory Tests

No specific monitoring is necessary.

Formulations

Senna is available in granules in concentrate or syrup.

Stability and Storage

Store in tightly sealed container, protected from light, and at room temperature.

Small Animal Dosage

Dogs

- Syrup: 5-10 mL/dog/day PO.
- Granules: 1/2 to 1 tsp/dog/day PO.

Cats

- Syrup: 5 mL/cat q24h.
- Granules: 1/2 tsp/cat q24h (with food).

Large Animal Dosage

No doses have been reported for large animals.

Regulatory Information

Because of low risk of harmful residues in animals intended for food, no withdrawal time is suggested.

Sevoflurane

see-voe-floo'rane

Trade and Other Names: Aerrane

Functional Classification: Anesthetic

Pharmacology and Mechanism of Action

Inhalant anesthetic. Like other inhalant anesthetics, the mechanism of action is uncertain. Sevoflurane produces a generalized, reversible, depression of the CNS. The inhalant anesthetics vary in their solubility in blood, their potency, and the rate of induction and recovery. Those with low blood/gas partition coefficients are associated with the most rapid rates of induction and recovery. Sevoflurane has a vapor pressure of 160 mm Hg (at 20° C), a blood/gas partition coefficient of 0.65, and a fat/blood coefficient of 48. Sevoflurane is similar to isoflurane in many respects, except that it has lower solubility, resulting in faster induction and recovery times.

Indications and Clinical Uses

Sevoflurane is used as an inhalant anesthetic. There are not any significant advantages over the use of isoflurane and it is approximately five times more expensive than isoflurane. It has a minimum alveolar concentration (MAC) value of 2.58%, 2.36%, and 2.31% in cats, dogs, and horses, respectively.

Precautionary Information

Adverse Reactions and Side Effects

Adverse effects related to anesthetic effects (e.g., cardiovascular and respiratory depression). Sevoflurane can produce byproducts of fluoride ions and Compound A, which can be toxic to the kidneys.

Contraindications and Precautions

Do not use unless there is adequate facilities to monitor patients.

Drug Interactions

No drug interactions reported for animals.

Instructions for Use
Use of inhalant anesthetics require careful monitoring. Dose is determined by depth of anesthesia.

Patient Monitoring and Laboratory Tests
Carefully monitor patient's heart rate and rhythm and respiratory rate during use.

Formulations
Sevoflurane is available in a 100 mL bottle.

Stability and Storage
Sevoflurane is highly volatile, and should only be stored in approved containers.

Small Animal Dosage
- Induction: 8%, Maintenance: 3%-6%

Large Animal Dosage
Horses
- MAC value: 2.31.

Regulatory Information
No withdrawal times are established for animals intended for food. Clearance is rapid and short withdrawal times are suggested. For extralabel use withdrawal interval estimates, contact FARAD at 1-888-USFARAD (1-888-873-2723) or send e-mail to FARAD@ncsu.edu.

Silymarin
sill-ih-mare'in

Trade and Other Names: Silybin, Marin, Milk Thistle, and generic brands

Functional Classification: Hepatic protectant

Pharmacology and Mechanism of Action
Silymarin contains silybin as the most active ingredient. It is also known as Milk Thistle, from which it is derived. Silymarin is a mixture of antihepatotoxic flavonolignans (derived from the plant Silybum). Silymarin has three components that are considered flavonolignans: silidianin, silcristin, and the major component, which is silybin (also called silymarin and silibinin). Silymarin has been used for the treatment of a variety of liver disorders in humans. The mechanism of silymarin's action is thought to be as an antioxidant inhibiting both peroxidation of lipid membranes and glutathione oxidation. Experimental data has supported the hepatoprotective properties of silymarin as an antioxidant and a free radical scavenger.

Indications and Clinical Uses
Silymarin has been used to treat hepatic disease, including hepatotoxic reactions in people and animals. In cats it may provide antioxidant activity. Silymarin is used as a complementary treatment in canine and feline liver disease. However, there is no scientific information on the oral absorption, correct dose, or evidence of efficacy of silymarin treatment.

Precautionary Information

Adverse Reactions and Side Effects

No adverse reactions have been reported.

Contraindications and Precautions

No contraindications are reported for animals.

Drug Interactions

No drug interactions have been reported.

Instructions for Use

Silymarin is a dietary supplement, and forms available may vary in potency and stability.

Patient Monitoring and Laboratory Tests

Monitor liver enzymes in animals being treated for toxicity.

Formulations

Silymarin tablets are widely available OTC. Commercial veterinary formulations (Marin) also contain zinc and vitamin E in a phosphatidylcholine complex in tablets for dogs and cats.

Stability and Storage

Store in tightly sealed container, protected from light, and at room temperature.

Small Animal Dosage

Dogs and Cats

Effective dose has not been established. It is recommended to start with a minimum of 30 mg/kg PO/day.

Large Animal Dosage

No dose has been reported for large animals.

Regulatory Information

Because of low risk of harmful residues in animals intended for food, no withdrawal time is suggested.

S

Sodium Bicarbonate

Trade and Other Names: Baking soda, Soda mint, Citrocarbonate, and Arm and Hammer pure baking soda

Functional Classification: Alkalinizing agent

Pharmacology and Mechanism of Action

Alkalizing agent. Antacid. It increases plasma and urinary concentrations of bicarbonate. One gram sodium bicarbonate is equal to 12 mEq sodium and bicarbonate ions; 3.65 g sodium bicarbonate is equal to 1 g sodium.

Indications and Clinical Uses

Sodium bicarbonate is a typical alkalinizing solution. It is the most frequent alkalinizing solution used for intravenous therapy of systemic acidosis and to treat severe hyperkalemia. When adding to fluid therapy, the goal is to maintain $PaCO_2$ within 37-43 mm Hg. It also has been administered to alkalize urine.

Precautionary Information

Adverse Reactions and Side Effects

Adverse effects attributed to alkalizing activity. Hypokalemia may occur with excessive administration. Hyperosmolality, hypernatremia, paradoxical CNS, and intracellular acidosis may occur.

Contraindications and Precautions

Do not administer to animals with hypocalcemia (may exacerbate tetany). Do not administer to animals with excessive chloride loss because of vomiting. Do not administer to animals with alkalosis. Administration of sodium bicarbonate may increase risk of hypernatremia, paradoxical CNS acidosis, and hyperosmolality.

Drug Interactions

Sodium bicarbonate should not be mixed with drugs that require an acidic medium for stability and solubility. Such drugs may include solutions containing hydrochloride (HCl) salts. When mixing intravenous solutions, do not mix bicarbonate with solutions containing calcium (chelation may result) or with drugs given as the hydrochloride salt (instability may result). When administered orally, interaction may occur to decrease absorption of other drugs (partial list includes anticholinergic drugs, ketoconazole, fluoroquinolones, and tetracyclines).

Instructions for Use

When used for systemic acidosis, doses should be adjusted on basis of blood gas measurements or assessment of acidosis. The following equation may be used to estimate requirement:

mEq Bicarbonate = Body Weight (kg) × Base Deficit (mEq/L) × 0.3.

Initially, administer 25%-50% of this dose in intravenous fluids over 20-30 minutes. In calves or neonates, use a factor of 0.5 instead of 0.3. 12 mEq of bicarbonate = 1 g of sodium bicarbonate. Note: 1.4% solution = 0.17 mEq/mL and provides 13 g of bicarbonate per L. 8.5 % solution = 1 mEq/mL of $NaHCO_3$. One 1 teaspoon of baking soda is approximately 2 g of $NaHCO_3$. When used during cardiac resuscitation, caution is advised because of risk of hyperosmolality, hypernatremia, and paradoxical CNS acidosis.

Patient Monitoring and Laboratory Tests

Monitor acid-base status.

Formulations

Sodium bicarbonate is available in 325, 520, and 650 mg tablets. Per teaspoonful (3.9 g) of Citrocarbonate, there is 780 mg sodium bicarbonate and 1.82 grams sodium citrate. It is also available in injections of various strengths: 4.2% is 0.5 mEq/mL (11.5 mg/mL sodium) and 8.4% is 1 mEq/mL (23 mg/mL sodium).

Stability and Storage

Store in tightly sealed container at room temperature. Alkaline solution with pH of 7-8.5. Do not mix with acid solutions. Sodium bicarbonate is soluble in water. If exposed to air, it may decompose to sodium carbonate, which is more alkaline.

Small Animal Dosage

Dogs and Cats

- Metabolic acidosis: 0.5-1 mEq/kg IV.

- Renal failure: 10 mg/kg q8-12h PO.
- Alkalization of urine: 50 mg/kg q8-12h PO.
- Antacid: 2-5 g mixed with water PO.
- CPR: 1 mEq/kg with additional doses of 0.5 mEq/kg at 10 minute intervals.

Large Animal Dosage

- Metabolic acidosis: 0.5-1 mEq/kg IV slowly. Other doses should be calculated based on base deficits. Oral doses vary. 10-12 grams of sodium bicarbonate may be given orally to adult large animals (horses and cattle) and 2-5 grams to calves, foals, and pigs.

Regulatory Information

Because of low risk of harmful residues in animals intended for food, no withdrawal time is suggested.

Sodium Chloride 0.9%

Trade and Other Names: Normal saline and generic brands

Functional Classification: Fluid replacement

Pharmacology and Mechanism of Action

Sodium chloride is used for intravenous infusion as replacement fluid. It is not a suitable maintenance solution. Sodium chloride (0.9%) contains 154 mEq/L sodium and 154 mEq/L chloride. See Appendix for comparison to other fluid solutions.

Indications and Clinical Uses

Sodium chloride is used for intravenous fluid supplementation. However, it is not a balanced electrolyte solution and should not be used for maintenance. It also is frequently used as a vehicle to deliver intravenous medications via constant rate infusion (CRI).

Precautionary Information

Adverse Reactions and Side Effects

It is not a balanced electrolyte solution. Long-term infusion may cause electrolyte imbalance. Saline solution is not balanced and it may cause acidemia, because it will increase renal elimination of bicarbonate. Prolonged use may cause hypokalemia.

Contraindications and Precautions

Do not exceed maximum dose rate of 80 mL/kg/hr. This solution does not contain electrolyte balance for maintenance.

Drug Interactions

No drug interactions have been reported in animals.

Instructions for Use

When administering intravenous fluid solution, monitor rate carefully and electrolyte concentrations.

Fluid administration rates are as follows:

Replacement fluid: calculate as Liters needed = % dehydration × Body Weight (kg) or mL needed = % dehydration × Body Weight (kg) × 1000.

Add bicarbonate to fluids if necessary based on calculation of base deficit.

Patient Monitoring and Laboratory Tests

Monitor hydration status and serum electrolytes, particularly potassium.

Formulations

Sodium chloride 0.9% is available in 500 and 1000 mL infusion.

Stability and Storage

Store in tightly sealed container at room temperature.

Small Animal Dosage

Dogs and Cats

- Moderate dehydration: 15-30 mL/kg/hr IV.
- Severe dehydration: 50 mL/kg/hr IV.

Large Animal Dosage

- 40-50 mL/kg day IV, IP, or SQ maintenance.
- Moderate dehydration: 15-30 mL/kg/hr IV.
- Severe dehydration: 50 mL/kg/hr IV.

Calves

- Moderate dehydration: 45 mL/kg given at a rate of 30-40 mL/kg/hr.
- Severe dehydration: 80-90 mL/kg given at a rate of 30-40 mL/kg/hr or as fast as 80 mL/kg/hr if necessary.

Regulatory Information

Because of low risk of harmful residues in animals intended for food, no withdrawal time is suggested.

Sodium Chloride 7.2%

Trade and Other Names: Hypertonic saline and HSS

Functional Classification: Fluid replacement

Pharmacology and Mechanism of Action

Concentrated sodium chloride used for acute treatment of hypovolemia. Hypertonic saline solution causes rapid expansion of plasma volume and may improve microvascular blood flow. Hypertonic saline solution contains 2566 mOsm/L, 1232 mEq/L sodium, and 1232 mEq/L chloride.

Indications and Clinical Uses

Hypertonic saline is used to treat hypovolemic shock in animals. The duration of its benefit is short lived. There may be benefits for combination with colloids such as Dextran 70. It has been used at doses of 4 mL/kg IV to dogs during a 5-minute infusion to be effective for treatment of septic shock.

Precautionary Information

Adverse Reactions and Side Effects

Not a balanced electrolyte solution. Long-term infusion may cause electrolyte imbalance.

Contraindications and Precautions

Do not administer to hypernatremic animals. Do not administer solutions high in sodium to animals with renal insufficiency.

Drug Interactions

No drug interactions have been reported in animals.

Instructions for Use

Hypertonic saline is used for short-term infusion for rapid replacement of vascular volume.

Patient Monitoring and Laboratory Tests

Monitor hematocrit and blood pressure in treated animals.

Formulations

Sodium chloride 7.2% is available as an infusion.

Stability and Storage

Store in tightly sealed container at room temperature.

Small Animal Dosage

Dogs and Cats

- 2-8 mL/kg IV of 7.5% solution.

Large Animal Dosage

- 4-8 mL/kg of 7.2% solution IV at a rate of 1 mL/kg/min.

Regulatory Information

Because of low risk of harmful residues in animals intended for food, no withdrawal time is suggested.

Sodium Iodide (20%)

Trade and Other Names: Iodopen and generic brands

Functional Classification: Iodine replacement

Pharmacology and Mechanism of Action

Sodium iodide is used to treat iodine deficiency.

Indications and Clinical Uses

Sodium iodide is used to treat fungal infections and is preferred over potassium iodide. It has been used for bacterial, actinomycete, and fungal infections, primarily in horses and cattle. In cattle it has been used for actinomycosis (lumpy jaw) and actinobacillosis (wooden tongue and necrotic stomatitis). In small animals it has been used for sporotrichosis. Proof of efficacy for these indications has not been established.

Precautionary Information

Adverse Reactions and Side Effects

Overuse causes iodism (burning of mouth, gastric irritation, and skin lesions).

Contraindications and Precautions

Do not use in pregnant animals; it may cause abortion.

Drug Interactions

No drug interactions are reported.

Instructions for Use

For treatment in cattle, administer slowly IV. Be careful not to inject outside the vein or tissue necrosis may occur.

Patient Monitoring and Laboratory Tests

No specific monitoring is necessary.

Formulations

Sodium iodide is available in 20 g/100 mL (20%) injection, and there is 100 mcg elemental iodide (118 mcg sodium iodide) per mL injection.

Stability and Storage

Store in tightly sealed container, protected from light, and at room temperature.

Small Animal Dosage

Dogs and Cats

- 20-40 mg/kg q8-12h PO.

Large Animal Dosage

Horses

- 125 mL of a 20% solution IV daily for 3 days, then 30 g/horse daily for 30 days.

Cattle

- 67 mg/kg IV (15 mL per 100 pounds) slowly, repeat weekly.

Regulatory Information

Because of low risk of harmful residues in animals intended for food, no withdrawal time is suggested.

Sotalol Hydrochloride

soe′tah-lole hye-droe-klor′ide

Trade and Other Names: Betapace

Functional Classification: Beta blocker, antiarrhythmic

Pharmacology and Mechanism of Action

Nonspecific Beta-receptor ($Beta_1$ and $Beta_2$) adrenergic blocker (Class II antiarrhythmic). Action is similar to propranolol (1/3 potency), however its beneficial effect may be caused more by the other antiarrhythmic effects. In addition to being a Class II antiarrhythmic drug, sotalol may have some Class III (potassium-channel-blocking) activity. The Class III activity prolongs the refractory period by decreasing potassium conduction in delayed rectifier currents. Sotalol is a water-soluble beta blocker and relies less on the liver for clearance than other beta blockers. Plasma levels and interindividual differences in clearance are expected to be less than other beta blockers.

Indications and Clinical Uses

Sotalol is indicated for control of refractory ventricular arrhythmias. It has also been used for refractory atrial fibrillation.

Precautionary Information

Adverse Reactions and Side Effects

Adverse effects have not been reported for animals but are expected to be similar to propranolol. Like many antiarrhythmics, sotalol may have some proarrhythmic activity. Negative inotropic effects may cause concern in some animals with poor cardiac contractility.

Contraindications and Precautions

Administer cautiously to patients with heart failure or AV block. Use cautiously in patients with poor cardiac reserve.

Drug Interactions

Use cautiously with other drugs that may decrease cardiac contractility or lower heart rate.

Instructions for Use

The beta-blocking effects occur at low doses; Class III antiarrhythmic effects at higher doses. In people, it may be a more effective maintenance agent for controlling arrhythmias than other drugs.

Patient Monitoring and Laboratory Tests

Monitor heart rate during treatment.

Formulations

Sotalol is available in 80, 120, 160, and 240 mg tablets.

Stability and Storage

Store in tightly sealed container, protected from light, and at room temperature. Sotalol is water-soluble and ethanol. It has been mixed with syrups and flavorings and stable for 12 weeks, but it should be stored in the refrigerator.

Small Animal Dosage

Dogs

- 1-2 mg/kg q12h PO. (For medium to large breed dogs, begin with 40 mg/dog q12h, then increase to 80 mg, if no response)

Cats

- 1-2 mg/kg q12h PO.

Large Animal Dosage

No dose has been reported for large animals.

Regulatory Information

Withdrawal times are not established for animals that produce food. For extralabel use withdrawal interval estimates, contact FARAD at 1-888-USFARAD (1-888-873-2723) or send e-mail to FARAD@ncsu.edu.

RCI Classification: 3

Spectinomycin, Spectinomycin Dihydrochloride Pentahydrate

spek-tih-noe-mye'sin

Trade and Other Names: Spectam, Spectogard, Prospec, and Adspec

Functional Classification: Antibiotic, Aminocyclitol

Pharmacology and Mechanism of Action

Spectinomycin is an aminocyclitol antibiotic, which shares similar features as an aminoglycoside. However it does not contain amino sugars or glycosidic bonds. It has a broad spectrum of activity.

Indications and Clinical Uses

Spectinomycin has been used in cattle to treat respiratory infections caused by *Pasteurella, Mannheimia*, and *Histophilus somni* (formerly *Haemophilus somnus)*. It also has activity against *Mycoplasma*. It has been used in dogs but not commonly.

Precautionary Information

Adverse Reactions and Side Effects

Injection site lesions may occur from administration to cattle.

Contraindications and Precautions

The powder intended to be used in drinking water should not be formulated with water or saline for intravenous injection. This solution has produced severe pulmonary edema and death.

Drug Interactions

No drug interactions are reported.

Instructions for Use

Injections in cattle should be made in the neck muscle.

Patient Monitoring and Laboratory Tests

No specific monitoring is necessary.

Formulations

Spectinomycin is available in an oral solution, powder for drinking water, and injection for cattle. Spectinomycin is available in a 100 mg spectinomycin sulfate/mL solution.

Stability and Storage

Store in tightly sealed container, protected from light, and at room temperature. Stability of compounded formulations has not been evaluated.

Small Animal Dosage

Dogs

- 22 mg/kg q12h PO for 4 days.
- 5.5-11 mg/kg q12h IM for 4 days.

Large Animal Dosage

Pigs

- 50-100 mg/pig PO.

Cattle

- 10-15 mg/kg q24h SQ (in neck) for 3-5 days.

Regulatory Information

Cattle withdrawal time (meat): 11 days.
Pig withdrawal time (meat): 21 days.
Do not administer to calves to be slaughtered for veal. A milk discard time has not been established. Do not administer to dairy cattle 20 months of age or older.

Spironolactone

speer-one-oh-lak'tone

Trade and Other Names: Aldactone

Functional Classification: Diuretic

Pharmacology and Mechanism of Action

Potassium-sparing diuretic. Action of spironolactone is to interfere with sodium reabsorption in distal renal tubule by competitively inhibiting the action of aldosterone. It binds directly to the aldosterone receptor, but at usual doses it does not block the action of other steroid receptors.

Indications and Clinical Uses

Spironolactone is used for treating high blood pressure and congestion caused by heart failure. Spironolactone may be used with angiotensin-converting enzyme (ACE) inhibitors to achieve a synergistic effect for treatment of heart failure in animals. The proposed benefit is via aldosterone antagonism. Spironolactone is a common drug in humans for managing hepatic cirrhosis, because it will inhibit ascites formation caused by excess aldosterone.

Precautionary Information

Adverse Reactions and Side Effects

Spironolactone can produce hyperkalemia in some patients. High doses and long-term use may produce some steroid-like side effects.

Contraindications and Precautions

Do not use in dehydrated patients. Nonsteroidal antiinflammatory drugs (NSAIDs) may interfere with action. Avoid concurrent use of supplements that are high in potassium. Do not administer to patients with gastric ulcers or who may be prone to GI disease such as gastritis or diarrhea.

Drug Interactions

Spironolactone is often used together with ACE inhibitors, such as enalapril. It acts synergistically with those drugs. Risk of hyperkalemia may increase when used with an ACE inhibitor, but this has not been a clinical problem in dogs. Use cautiously with other drugs that can increase potassium concentrations such as trimethoprim and NSAIDs.

Instructions for Use

Spironolactone usually is administered with other drugs (e.g., ACE-inhibitors, inotropic agents, vasodilators) for treating congestive heart failure.

Patient Monitoring and Laboratory Tests

Monitor serum potassium concentration when administering with an ACE inhibitor (e.g., enalapril maleate). Administration of spironolactone may cause a slightly false-positive result for digoxin assay.

Formulations

Spironolactone is available in 25, 50, and 100 mg tablets. Tablets can be split easily.

Stability and Storage

Store in tightly sealed container, protected from light, and at room temperature. Spironolactone is insoluble in water, but it is slightly more soluble in ethanol. It has been mixed with syrups for an oral suspension (after first mixing with ethanol) and found to be stable for 90-160 days.

Small Animal Dosage

Dogs and Cats

- 2-4 mg/kg/day (or 1-2 mg/kg q12h) PO. In dogs, start with 2 mg/kg/day and increase gradually, not to exceed 4 mg/kg/day.

Large Animal Dosage

No dose has been reported for large animals.

Regulatory Information

Withdrawal times are not established for animals that produce food. For extralabel use withdrawal interval estimates, contact FARAD at 1-888-USFARAD (1-888-873-2723) or send e-mail to FARAD@ncsu.edu.

RCI Classification: 4

Stanozolol

stan-oh'zoe-lole

Trade and Other Names: Winstrol-V

Functional Classification: Hormone, Anabolic agent

Pharmacology and Mechanism of Action

Anabolic steroid. Stanozolol is a derivative of testosterone. Anabolic agents are designed to maximize anabolic effects, while minimizing androgenic action. Other anabolic agents include boldenone, nandrolone, oxymetholone, and methyltestosterone.

Indications and Clinical Uses

Anabolic agents, such as stanozolol, have been used for reversing catabolic conditions, increasing weight gain, increasing muscling in animals, and stimulating erythropoiesis. It has been used in horses during training. Stanozolol has been used in animals with chronic renal failure and there is some evidence of an improvement in the nitrogen balance in dogs with renal disease treated with stanozolol. Use in cats is associated with toxicity.

Precautionary Information

Adverse Reactions and Side Effects

Adverse effects from anabolic steroids can be attributed to the pharmacologic action of these steroids. Increased masculine effects are common. Increased incidence of some tumors have been reported in people. Some 17-alpha-methylated oral anabolic steroids (oxymetholone, stanozolol, and oxandrolone) are associated with hepatic toxicity. Stanozolol administration in cats with renal disease has been shown to consistently produce increased hepatic enzymes and hepatic toxicosis.

Contraindications and Precautions

Do not administer to cats with renal disease. Use cautiously in dogs. This drug is abused by humans to enhance athletic performance.

Drug Interactions

No drug interactions have been reported in animals.

Instructions for Use

However, for many indications, use in animals (and doses) is based on experience in people or anecdotal experience in animals.

Patient Monitoring and Laboratory Tests

Monitor liver enzymes for signs of hepatic injury (cholestatic) during treatment.

Formulations

Stanozolol is available in 50 mg/mL injection as a sterile suspension and 2 mg tablets.

Stability and Storage

Store in tightly sealed container, protected from light, and at room temperature. Stability of compounded formulations has not been evaluated.

Small Animal Dosage

Dogs

- 2 mg/dog (or range of 1-4 mg/dog) q12h PO.
- 25-50 mg/dog/week IM.

Cats

- 1 mg/cat q12h PO.
- 25 mg/cat/week IM (use cautiously in cats).

Large Animal Dosage

Horses

- 0.55 mg/kg (5 mL per 1000 pounds) IM, once a week for up to 4 weeks.

Regulatory Information

Stanozolol is a schedule III controlled drug and should not be administered to animals that produce food.

RCI Classification: 4

Streptozocin

strep-toe-zoe′sin

Trade and Other Names: Streptozotocin and Zanosar

Functional Classification: Antihyperglycemic agent

Pharmacology and Mechanism of Action

Streptozocin (also known as streptozotocin) is an agent with specific effects on pancreatic beta cells. It is a nitrosourea alkylating agent with a specific cytotoxic effect on the pancreatic cells. There is selective uptake into pancreatic beta cells. It can produce diabetes mellitus in normal animals, but it is used primarily for treating insuloma tumors in animals. Occasionally it has been used as a cytotoxic agent for treating other tumors in humans (e.g., lymphoma, sarcomas), but these uses are not reported for animals. Streptozocin has a rapid half-life in animals but metabolites may be active. Metabolites rapidly cross the blood-brain barrier.

Indications and Clinical Uses

In animals, streptozocin is used primarily for treating insulin-secreting tumors (insulinoma).

Precautionary Information

Adverse Reactions and Side Effects

Diabetes mellitus is anticipated in treated animals. In humans the major adverse effect is renal injury caused by tubular necrosis. Renal injury has been reported in dogs at doses of >700 mg/m^2. Other adverse effects include vomiting, nausea, and diarrhea. Increases in hepatic enzymes and hepatic injury have been reported in dogs, however hepatotoxicity appears to be reversible. Bone marrow suppression is rare in animals. Local phlebitis may occur from intravenous administration.

Contraindications and Precautions

Streptozocin may produce diabetes mellitus in treated animals. In addition, there may be a sudden release of insulin after intravenous administration and intravenous dextrose should be available to treat acute hypoglycemia. Monitor animals for evidence of renal and hepatic injury. Do not administer to pregnant animals.

Drug Interactions

No specific drug interactions are reported for animals, however, use with any other nephrotoxic, hepatotoxic, or myelotoxic drug will exacerbate toxicity.

Instructions for Use

Risk of renal toxicosis caused by streptozocin may be decreased with administration of fluid diuresis. The diuresis should consist of administration of fluids (e.g., 0.9% saline) IV prior to drug administration. Antiemetics should be administered with each infusion, because vomiting is common. Treatment is continued every 3 weeks until signs of tumor recurrence occurs or until toxicosis limits the continuation of treatments. Reconstitute vial prior to use by adding 9.5 mL of 5% dextrose or 0.9% saline to vial. Resulting solution is 100 mg per mL. Further dilute this vial with 5% dextrose or 0.9% saline for intravenous infusion.

Patient Monitoring and Laboratory Tests

Monitor serum glucose in treated animals. Monitor serum creatinine, urea nitrogen, and hepatic enzymes for evidence of hepatotoxcity and renal injury. Although myelotoxicity is unusual, monitor CBC before each treatment.

Formulations

Streptozocin is available in 1 g vials for injection.

Stability and Storage

Store vial between 2-8° C. Use vial within 12 hours after reconstitution at room temperature. Formulation also contains citric acid. Do not use if color changes from pale yellow to a darker brown color.

Small Animal Dosage

Dogs

- 500 mg/m^2 IV, infused over 2 hours, every 3 weeks.

Large Animal Dosage

No dose has been reported for large animals.

Regulatory Information

Do not administer to animals that produce food.

Succimer

suks′ih-mer

Trade and Other Names: Chemet

Functional Classification: Antidote

Pharmacology and Mechanism of Action

Chelating agent. Succimer chelates lead and other heavy metals such as mercury and arsenic and increases their elimination from the body.

Indications and Clinical Uses

Succimer is used for treatment of metal toxicosis, primarily toxicosis caused by lead.

Precautionary Information

Adverse Reactions and Side Effects

No adverse effects reported in dogs. However, renal injury has been associated with succimer treatment in cats.

Contraindications and Precautions

No contraindications are reported for animals.

Drug Interactions

No drug interactions have been reported in animals.

Instructions for Use

Doses cited are based on studies in dogs (*J Am Vet Med Assoc,* 208:371, 1996). In cats, succimer has been used at 10 mg/kg q8h PO for 2 weeks.

Patient Monitoring and Laboratory Tests

Monitor patient's blood lead levels during treatment. Monitor renal function during treatment, because renal failure has been associated with succimer administration in cats.

Formulations

Succimer is available in 100 mg capsules.

Stability and Storage

Store in tightly sealed container, protected from light, and at room temperature. Stability of compounded formulations has not been evaluated.

Small Animal Dosage

Dogs and Cats

- 10 mg/kg q8h PO for 5 days, then 10 mg/kg q12h PO for 2 more weeks.

Large Animal Dosage

No dose has been reported for large animals.

Regulatory Information

Withdrawal times are not established for animals that produce food. For extralabel use withdrawal interval estimates, contact FARAD at 1-888-USFARAD (1-888-873-2723) or send e-mail to FARAD@ncsu.edu.

Sucralfate

soo-krahl'fate

Trade and Other Names: Carafate and Sulcrate (in Canada)

Functional Classification: Antiulcer agent

Pharmacology and Mechanism of Action

Gastric mucosa protectant. Antiulcer agent. Action of sucralfate is to bind to ulcerated tissue in GI tract to aid healing of ulcers. It has an affinity for negatively charged injured tissue. There is some evidence that sucralfate may act as a cytoprotectant (via increasing prostaglandin synthesis).

Indications and Clinical Uses

Sucralfate is used to prevent and treat gastric ulcers. However, in clinical use, there is little evidence that it will prevent ulcers from nonsteroidal antiinflammatory drugs (NSAIDs), although experimental evidence is available for horses. Sucralfate is administered orally and may protect ulcerated tissue and promote healing.

Precautionary Information

Adverse Reactions and Side Effects

Adverse effects have not been reported. It is not absorbed systemically.

Contraindications and Precautions

No contraindications listed for animals.

Drug Interactions

Sucralfate may decrease absorption of other drugs administered orally via chelation with aluminum (such as fluoroquinolones and tetracyclines). If mixed with other drugs (antimicrobials), inactivation may occur.

Instructions for Use

Dosing recommendations are based largely on empiricism. There are no clinical studies to demonstrate efficacy in animals with sucralfate. Sucralfate may be administered concurrently with histamine type 2 inhibitors, (H_2-blockers) (e.g., cimetidine) without causing an interaction.

Patient Monitoring and Laboratory Tests

No specific monitoring is necessary.

Formulations

Sucralfate is available in 1 g tablets and 200 mg/mL oral suspension.

Stability and Storage

Store in tightly sealed container, protected from light, and at room temperature. Sucralfate is insoluble in water, unless exposed to strong acid or alkaline conditions.

Small Animal Dosage

Dogs

- 0.5-1 g q8-12h PO.

Cats

- 0.25 g q8-12h PO.

Large Animal Dosage

Foals

- 1 g q8h PO.

Regulatory Information

Because of low risk of harmful residues in animals intended for food, no withdrawal time is suggested.

Sufentanil Citrate

soo-fen'tah-nil sih'trate

Trade and Other Names: Sufenta

Functional Classification: Analgesic, Opioid

Pharmacology and Mechanism of Action

Opioid agonist. Action of fentanyl derivatives is via mu-opiate receptor. Sufentanil is five to seven times more potent than fentanyl. Doses of 13 to 20 mcg of sufentanil produce analgesia equal to 10 mg of morphine.

S

Indications and Clinical Uses

Sufentanil, like other opiate derivatives, is used for sedation, general anesthesia, and analgesia. The use of sufentanil, compared to other opiates, has been limited in animals.

Precautionary Information

Adverse Reactions and Side Effects

Adverse effects similar to morphine. Like all opiates, side effects are predictable and unavoidable. Side effects include sedation, constipation, and bradycardia. Respiratory depression occurs with high doses.

Contraindications and Precautions

Use cautiously in animals with respiratory disease. Because of its high potency compared with morphine and other opiates, calculate dose carefully.

Drug Interactions

Like other opiates, sufentanil may potentiate other sedatives and anesthetics.

Instructions for Use

When used for anesthesia, animals are often premedicated with acepromazine or a benzodiazepine.

Patient Monitoring and Laboratory Tests

Monitor patient's heart rate and respiration. Although bradycardia rarely needs to be treated when it is caused by an opioid, atropine can be administered if necessary. If serious respiratory depression occurs, the opioid can be reversed with naloxone.

Formulations

Sufentanil is available in 50 mcg/mL injection.

Stability and Storage

Store in tightly sealed container, protected from light, and at room temperature. Stability of compounded formulations has not been evaluated. Sufentanil is a schedule II drug and should be stored in locked compartment.

Small Animal Dosage

Dogs and Cats

- 2 mcg/kg IV (0.002 mg/kg), up to a maximum dose of 5 mcg/kg (0.005 mg/kg).

Large Animal Dosage

No doses have been reported for large animals.

Regulatory Information

Schedule II controlled drug

Avoid use in animals intended for food. Withdrawal times are not established. However, for extralabel use withdrawal interval estimates, contact FARAD at 1-888-USFARAD (1-888-873-2723) or send e-mail to FARAD@ncsu.edu.

RCI Classification: 1

Sulfachlorpyridazine

sul-fah-klor-peer-id'ah-zeen

Trade and Other Names: Vetisulid

Functional Classification: Antibacterial

Pharmacology and Mechanism of Action

Sulfonamide antibacterial. Sulfonamides compete with para-aminobenzoic acid (PABA) for enzyme that synthesizes dihydrofolic acid in bacteria. It is synergistic with trimethoprim. Bacteriostatic. Like other sulfonamides, it has a broad spectrum of activity, including gram-positive bacteria, gram-negative bacteria, and some protozoa. However, when used alone, resistance is common.

Indications and Clinical Uses

Sulfachlorpyridazine is used as a broad-spectrum antimicrobial to treat or prevent infections caused by susceptible organisms. Infections treated may include pneumonia, intestinal infections (especially coccidia), soft tissue infections, and UTIs. However, resistance is common. The use of sulfachlorpyridazine has not been reported for small animals. It is used primarily for pigs and cattle. However, other drugs may be equally effective.

Precautionary Information

Adverse Reactions and Side Effects

Adverse effects associated with sulfonamides (primarily in dogs) include allergic reactions, Type II and Type III hypersensitivity, hepatotoxicity, hypothyroidism (with prolonged therapy), keratoconjunctivitis sicca, and skin reactions.

Contraindications and Precautions

Do not administer in animals with sensitivity to sulfonamides.

Drug Interactions

There are several interactions reported for sulfonamide administration in small animals. (See sulfonamide manuscripts.) However, these interactions have not been relevant for its use in cattle and pigs.

Instructions for Use

The most common use of sulfachlorpyridazine is for treatment of enteritis in pigs and calves.

Patient Monitoring and Laboratory Tests

Sulfonamides are known to decrease thyroxine (T4) concentrations in dogs after 6 weeks of treatment. Susceptibility testing: CLSI (NCCLS) break point for sensitive organisms is less than or equal to 256 mcg/mL. One sulfonamide can be used as a marker for susceptibility to other sulfonamides. According to NCCLS, susceptibility tests for sulfonamides can be used to interpret urinary bacteria isolates only.

Formulations

Sulfachlorpyridazine is available in 2 g bolus and 200 mg/mL injection.

Stability and Storage

Store in tightly sealed container, protected from light, and at room temperature. Stability of compounded formulations has not been evaluated.

S

Small Animal Dosage

No doses reported for dogs and cats.

Large Animal Dosage

Cattle

- 33-50 mg/kg q12h PO or IV.

Pigs

- 22-39 mg/kg q12h PO or 44-77 mg/kg/day PO in the drinking water.

Regulatory Information

Extralabel use of sulfonamides is prohibited from use in lactating dairy cattle.
Cattle withdrawal time (meat): 7 days.
Pig withdrawal time (meat): 4 days.

Sulfadiazine

sul-fa-dye'a-zeen

Trade and Other Names: Generic brands and combined with trimethoprim as Tribrissen

Functional Classification: Antibacterial

Pharmacology and Mechanism of Action

Sulfonamide antibacterial. Sulfonamides compete with para-aminobenzoic acid (PABA) for enzyme that synthesizes dihydrofolic acid in bacteria. It is synergistic with trimethoprim. Bacteriostatic. Like other sulfonamides, it has a broad spectrum of activity, including gram-positive bacteria, gram-negative bacteria, and some protozoa. However, when used alone, resistance is common.

Indications and Clinical Uses

Sulfadiazine is used occasionally alone; however efficacy is not established for many infections. Most often, it is used with trimethoprim to treat a variety of infections, including UTIs and skin infections. (See section on Trimethoprim-Sulfonamides for a more complete description.)

Precautionary Information

Adverse Reactions and Side Effects

Adverse effects associated with sulfonamides include allergic reactions, Type II and Type III hypersensitivity, arthropathy, anemia, thrombocytopenia, hepatopathy, hypothyroidism (with prolonged therapy), keratoconjunctivitis sicca, and skin reactions. Dogs may be more sensitive to sulfonamides than other animals because dogs lack the ability to acetylate sulfonamides to metabolites. Other, more toxic metabolites may persist.

Contraindications and Precautions

Do not administer to animals with sensitivity to sulfonamides. Doberman pinschers may be more sensitive than other species to reactions to sulfonamides. Use cautiously in this species.

Drug Interactions

Sulfonamides may interact with other drugs, including warfarin, methenamine, dapsone, and etodolac. They may potentiate adverse effects caused by methotrexate and pyrimethamine. Sulfonamides will increase metabolism of cyclosporine resulting in decreased plasma concentrations. Methenamine is metabolized to formaldehyde that may form a complex and precipitate with sulfonamides. Sulfonamides administered to horses that are receiving detomidine may develop cardiac arrhythmias. This precaution is only listed for intravenous forms of trimethoprim-sulfonamides.

Instructions for Use

Usually, sulfonamides are combined with trimethoprim or ormetoprim in 5:1 ratio and in small animals and horses, sulfonamides are rarely used alone. There is no clinical evidence that one sulfonamide is more or less toxic or efficacious than another sulfonamide.

Patient Monitoring and Laboratory Tests
Sulfonamides are known to decrease thyroxine (T4) concentrations in dogs after 6 weeks of treatment. Susceptibility testing: CLSI (NCCLS) break point for sensitive organisms is less than or equal to 256 mcg/mL. One sulfonamide can be used as a marker for susceptibility to other sulfonamides. According to NCCLS, susceptibility tests for sulfonamides can be used to interpret urinary bacteria isolates only.

Formulations
Sulfadiazine is available in 500 mg tablets.

Stability and Storage
Store in tightly sealed container, protected from light, and at room temperature. Stability of compounded formulations has not been evaluated.

Small Animal Dosage
Dogs and Cats
- 100 mg/kg IV PO (loading dose), followed by 50 mg/kg q12h IV or PO (see also Trimethoprim).

Large Animal Dosage
For horses, see dosing for Trimethoprim combinations.

Regulatory Information
Extralabel use of sulfonamides is prohibited from use in lactating dairy cattle. No withdrawal times are established. However, for extralabel use withdrawal interval estimates, contact FARAD at 1-888-USFARAD (1-888-873-2723) or send e-mail to FARAD@ncsu.edu.

Sulfadimethoxine
sul-fah-dye-meth-oks′een

Trade and Other Names: Albon, Bactrovet, and generic brands

Functional Classification: Antibacterial

Pharmacology and Mechanism of Action
Sulfonamide antibacterial. Sulfonamides compete with para-aminobenzoic acid (PABA) for enzyme that synthesizes dihydrofolic acid in bacteria. It is synergistic with trimethoprim. Bacteriostatic. Like other sulfonamides, it has a broad spectrum of activity, including gram-positive bacteria, gram-negative bacteria, and some protozoa. However, when used alone, resistance is common.

Indications and Clinical Uses
Sulfadimethoxine is used as a broad-spectrum antimicrobial to treat or prevent infections caused by susceptible organisms. Infections treated may include pneumonia, intestinal infections (especially coccidia), soft tissue infections, and UTIs. However resistance is common, unless combined with ormetoprim (see Primor).

Precautionary Information

Adverse Reactions and Side Effects

Adverse effects associated with sulfonamides include allergic reactions, Type II and Type III hypersensitivity, arthropathy, anemia, thrombocytopenia, hepatopathy, hypothyroidism (with prolonged therapy), keratoconjunctivitis sicca, and skin reactions. Dogs may be more sensitive to sulfonamides than other animals because dogs lack the ability to acetylate sulfonamides to metabolites. Other, more toxic metabolites may persist.

Contraindications and Precautions

Do not administer in animals with sensitivity to sulfonamides. Doberman pinschers may be more sensitive than other species to reactions to sulfonamides. Use cautiously in this species.

Drug Interactions

Sulfonamides may interact with other drugs, including warfarin, methenamine, dapsone, and etodolac. They may potentiate adverse effects caused by methotrexate and pyrimethamine. Sulfonamides will increase metabolism of cyclosporine resulting in decreased plasma concentrations. Methenamine is metabolized to formaldehyde that may form a complex and precipitate with sulfonamides. Sulfonamides administered to horses that are receiving detomidine may develop cardiac arrhythmias. This precaution is only listed for intravenous forms of trimethoprim-sulfonamides.

Instructions for Use

Usually, sulfonamides are combined with trimethoprim or ormetoprim in 5:1 ratio and in small animals and horses, sulfonamides are rarely used alone. There is no clinical evidence that one sulfonamide is more or less toxic or efficacious than another sulfonamide. Sulfadimethoxine has been combined with ormetoprim in Primor.

Patient Monitoring and Laboratory Tests

Sulfonamides are known to decrease thyroxine (T4) concentrations in dogs after 6 weeks of treatment. Susceptibility testing: CLSI (NCCLS) break point for sensitive organisms is less than or equal to 256 mcg/mL. One sulfonamide can be used as a marker for susceptibility to other sulfonamides. According to NCCLS, susceptibility tests for sulfonamides can be used to interpret urinary bacteria isolates only.

Formulations

Sulfadimethoxine is available in 125, 250, and 500 mg tablets, 400 mg/mL injection, and 50 mg/mL suspension.

Stability and Storage

Store in tightly sealed container, protected from light, and at room temperature. Stability of compounded formulations has not been evaluated.

Small Animal Dosage

Dogs and Cats

- 55 mg/kg PO (loading dose), followed by 27.5 mg/kg q12h PO. (For doses of combination with ormetoprim, see Primor.)

Large Animal Dosage

Cattle

- Treatment of pneumonia and other infections: 55 mg/kg as initial dose, followed by 27 mg/kg q24h PO for 5 days.
- Sustained release bolus (Albon-SR): 137.5 mg/kg PO, as a single dose.

Regulatory Information

Cattle withdrawal time (meat): 7 days.

Cattle withdrawal time (milk): 60 hours.

Withdrawal time for sustained-released bolus 21 days.

Extralabel use of sulfonamides is prohibited from use in lactating dairy cattle. Currently, sulfadimethoxine is the only sulfonamide with approved indications in dairy cattle.

Sulfamethazine

sul-fah-meth'ah-zeen

Trade and Other Names: Sulmet and generic brands

Functional Classification: Antibacterial

Pharmacology and Mechanism of Action

Sulfonamide antibacterial. Sulfonamides compete with para-aminobenzoic acid (PABA) for enzyme that synthesizes dihydrofolic acid in bacteria. It is synergistic with trimethoprim. Bacteriostatic. Like other sulfonamides, it has a broad spectrum of activity, including gram-positive bacteria, gram-negative bacteria, and some protozoa. However, when used alone, resistance is common.

Indications and Clinical Uses

Sulfamethazine is used as a broad-spectrum antimicrobial to treat or prevent infections caused by susceptible organisms. Infections treated may include pneumonia, intestinal infections (especially coccidia), soft tissue infections and UTIs. However, resistance is common.

Precautionary Information

Adverse Reactions and Side Effects

Adverse effects associated with sulfonamides include allergic reactions, Type II and Type III hypersensitivity, arthropathy, anemia, thrombocytopenia, hepatopathy, hypothyroidism (with prolonged therapy), keratoconjunctivitis sicca, and skin reactions. Dogs may be more sensitive to sulfonamides than other animals because dogs lack the ability to acetylate sulfonamides to metabolites. Other, more toxic metabolites may persist.

Contraindications and Precautions

Do not administer in animals with sensitivity to sulfonamides. Doberman pinschers may be more sensitive than other species to reactions to sulfonamides. Use cautiously in this species.

S

Drug Interactions

Sulfonamides may interact with other drugs, including warfarin, methenamine, dapsone, and etodolac. They may potentiate adverse effects caused by methotrexate and pyrimethamine. Sulfonamides will increase metabolism of cyclosporine resulting in decreased plasma concentrations. Methenamine is metabolized to formaldehyde that may form a complex and precipitate with sulfonamides. Sulfonamides administered to horses that are receiving detomidine may develop cardiac arrhythmias. This precaution is only listed for intravenous forms of trimethoprim-sulfonamides.

Instructions for Use

Usually, sulfonamides are combined with trimethoprim or ormetoprim in 5:1 ratio and in small animals and horses, sulfonamides are rarely used alone. There is no clinical evidence that one sulfonamide is more or less toxic or efficacious than another sulfonamide.

Patient Monitoring and Laboratory Tests

Sulfonamides are known to decrease thyroxine (T4) concentrations in dogs after 6 weeks of treatment. Susceptibility testing: CLSI (NCCLS) break point for sensitive organisms is less than or equal to 256 mcg/mL. One sulfonamide can be used as a marker for susceptibility to other sulfonamides. According to NCCLS, susceptibility tests for sulfonamides can be used to interpret urinary bacteria isolates only.

Formulations

Sulfamethazine is available in a 30 g bolus.

Stability and Storage

Store in tightly sealed container, protected from light, and at room temperature. Stability of compounded formulations has not been evaluated.

Small Animal Dosage

Dogs and Cats

- 100 mg/kg PO (loading dose), followed by 50 mg/kg q12h PO.

Large Animal Dosage

Cattle

- Treatment of pneumonia and other infections: 220 mg/kg as initial dose, followed by 110 mg/kg q24h PO.
- Use of soluble powder as a drench or in drinking water: 237 mg/kg as initial dose, followed by 119 mg/kg q24h PO.
- Sustained-release bolus: 350-400 mg/kg PO as a single dose.

Pigs

- Use of soluble powder as a drench or in drinking water: 237 mg/kg as initial dose, followed by 119 mg/kg q24h PO.

Regulatory Information

Extralabel use of sulfonamides is prohibited from use in lactating dairy cattle.
Cattle withdrawal time (meat): 10 or 11 days.
Cattle withdrawal time (meat; soluble powder): 10 days,
Pig withdrawal time (meat; soluble powder): 15 days.
Cattle withdrawal time (meat; sustained-release bolus): 8-18 days, depending on the product.

Sulfamethoxazole

sul-fah-meth-oks'ah-zole

Trade and Other Names: Gantanol

Functional Classification: Antibacterial

Pharmacology and Mechanism of Action

Sulfonamide antibacterial. Sulfonamides compete with para-aminobenzoic acid (PABA) for enzyme that synthesizes dihydrofolic acid in bacteria. It is synergistic with trimethoprim. Bacteriostatic. Like other sulfonamides, it has a broad spectrum of activity, including gram-positive bacteria, gram-negative bacteria, and some protozoa. However, when used alone, resistance is common.

Indications and Clinical Uses

Sulfamethoxazole is used as a broad-spectrum antimicrobial to treat or prevent infections caused by susceptible organisms. Infections treated may include pneumonia, intestinal infections (especially coccidia), soft tissue infections, and UTIs. However, resistance is common, unless combined with trimethoprim.

Precautionary Information

Adverse Reactions and Side Effects

Adverse effects associated with sulfonamides include allergic reactions, Type II and Type III hypersensitivity, arthropathy, anemia, thrombocytopenia, hepatopathy, hypothyroidism (with prolonged therapy), keratoconjunctivitis sicca, and skin reactions. Dogs may be more sensitive to sulfonamides than other animals because dogs lack the ability to acetylate sulfonamides to metabolites. Other, more toxic metabolites may persist.

Contraindications and Precautions

Do not administer in animals with sensitivity to sulfonamides. Doberman pinschers may be more sensitive than other species to reactions to sulfonamides. Use cautiously in this species.

Drug Interactions

Sulfonamides may interact with other drugs, including warfarin, methenamine, dapsone, and etodolac. They may potentiate adverse effects caused by methotrexate and pyrimethamine. Sulfonamides will increase metabolism of cyclosporine resulting in decreased plasma concentrations. Methenamine is metabolized to formaldehyde that may form a complex and precipitate with sulfonamides. Sulfonamides administered to horses that are receiving detomidine may develop cardiac arrhythmias. This precaution is only listed for intravenous forms of trimethoprim-sulfonamides.

Instructions for Use

Usually, sulfonamides are combined with trimethoprim or ormetoprim in 5:1 ratio and in small animals and horses, sulfonamides are rarely used alone. There is no clinical evidence that one sulfonamide is more or less toxic or efficacious than another sulfonamide.

Patient Monitoring and Laboratory Tests

Sulfonamides are known to decrease thyroxine (T4) concentrations in dogs after 6 weeks of treatment. Susceptibility testing: CLSI (NCCLS) break point for sensitive organisms is less than or equal to 256 mcg/mL. One sulfonamide can be used as a marker for susceptibility to other sulfonamides. According to NCCLS, susceptibility tests for sulfonamides can be used to interpret urinary bacteria isolates only.

Formulations

Sulfamethoxazole is available in 500 mg tablets and is combined with trimethoprim in Bactrim, Septra, and generic products (see Trimethoprim).

Stability and Storage

Store in tightly sealed container, protected from light, and at room temperature. Stability of compounded formulations has not been evaluated.

Small Animal Dosage

Dogs and Cats

- 100 mg/kg PO (loading dose), followed by 50 mg/kg q12h PO.

Large Animal Dosage

No doses have been reported for large animals.

Regulatory Information

Extralabel use of sulfonamides is prohibited from use in lactating dairy cattle. Withdrawal times are not established. However, for extralabel use withdrawal interval estimates, contact FARAD at 1-888-USFARAD (1-888-873-2723) or send e-mail to FARAD@ncsu.edu.

Sulfaquinoxaline

sul-fah-kwin-oks'ah-leen

Trade and Other Names: Sulfa-Nox

Functional Classification: Antibacterial

Pharmacology and Mechanism of Action

Sulfonamide antibacterial. Sulfonamides compete with para-aminobenzoic acid (PABA) for enzyme that synthesizes dihydrofolic acid in bacteria. It is synergistic with trimethoprim. Bacteriostatic. Like other sulfonamides, it has a broad spectrum of activity, including gram-positive bacteria, gram-negative bacteria, and some protozoa. However, when used alone, resistance is common.

Indications and Clinical Uses

Sulfaquinoxaline is used as a broad-spectrum antimicrobial to treat or prevent infections caused by susceptible organisms. Infections treated may include pneumonia, intestinal infections (especially coccidia), soft tissue infections and UTIs. However, resistance is common.

Precautionary Information

Adverse Reactions and Side Effects

Adverse effects associated with sulfonamides include allergic reactions, Type II and Type III hypersensitivity, arthropathy, anemia, thrombocytopenia, hepatopathy, hypothyroidism (with prolonged therapy), keratoconjunctivitis sicca, and skin reactions. Dogs may be more sensitive to sulfonamides than other animals because dogs lack the ability to acetylate sulfonamides to metabolites. Other, more toxic metabolites may persist.

Contraindications and Precautions

Do not administer in animals with sensitivity to sulfonamides. Avoid contact with skin or mucous membranes when mixing in water.

Drug Interactions

Sulfonamides may interact with other drugs, including warfarin, methenamine, dapsone, and etodolac. They may potentiate adverse effects caused by methotrexate and pyrimethamine. Sulfonamides will increase metabolism of cyclosporine resulting in decreased plasma concentrations. Methenamine is metabolized to formaldehyde that may form a complex and precipitate with sulfonamides. Sulfonamides administered to horses that are receiving detomidine may develop cardiac arrhythmias. This precaution is only listed for intravenous forms of trimethoprim-sulfonamides.

Instructions for Use

Mix in the drinking water. Make fresh solutions daily. The most common use of sulfaquinoxaline is for treatment of enteritis caused by coccidia in calves, sheep, and poultry.

Patient Monitoring and Laboratory Tests

Sulfonamides are known to decrease thyroxine (T4) concentrations in dogs after 6 weeks of treatment. Susceptibility testing: CLSI (NCCLS) break point for sensitive organisms is less than or equal to 256 mcg/mL. One sulfonamide can be used as a marker for susceptibility to other sulfonamides. According to NCCLS, susceptibility tests for sulfonamides can be used to interpret urinary bacteria isolates only.

Formulations

Sulfaquinoxaline is available in 34.4, 128.5, 192, 200, 286.2, and 340 mg/mL solution.

S

Stability and Storage

Store in tightly sealed container, protected from light, and at room temperature. Stability of compounded formulations has not been evaluated.

Small Animal Dosage

No doses reported for dogs and cats.

Large Animal Dosage

Calves

- 13.2 mg/kg/day PO (usually administered in the drinking water as a 0.015% solution for 5 days).

Regulatory Information

Extralabel use of sulfonamides is prohibited from use in lactating dairy cattle. Cattle withdrawal time: 10 days.

Sheep withdrawal time: 10 days.
Poultry withdrawal time: 10 days.
Rabbit withdrawal time: 10 days.

Sulfasalazine

sul-fah-sal'ah-zeen

Trade and Other Names: Azulfidine and Salazopyrin (in Canada)

Functional Classification: Antibacterial

Pharmacology and Mechanism of Action

Sulfonamide combined with an antiinflammatory drug. Sulfasalazine has little effect and salicylic acid (mesalamine) has antiinflammatory effects. (See manuscript for mesalamine for more details on mesalamine use.) When administered as the combination of salicylic acid and the sulfonamide, sulfapyridine, the salicylic acid is released by colonic bacteria to produce an antiinflammatory effect. The antiinflammatory effect is believed to be either through antiprostaglandin action, antileukotriene activity, or both.

Indications and Clinical Uses

Sulfasalazine is used in small animals for the treatment of idiopathic colitis and other inflammatory intestinal diseases. It is often the first drug of choice for treatment when dietary therapy has been unsuccessful.

Precautionary Information

Adverse Reactions and Side Effects

Adverse effects are all attributed to sulfonamide component. Adverse effects associated with sulfonamides and include allergic reactions, Type II and Type III hypersensitivity, hypothyroidism (with prolonged therapy), keratoconjunctivitis sicca, and skin reactions. Keratoconjunctivitis sicca has been reported in dogs that received sulfasalazine for chronic treatment. The amount of salicylate absorbed appears to be small in cats, therefore adverse effects from salicylate in cats is unlikely.

Contraindications and Precautions

Do not administer to animals that are sensitive to sulfonamides. Drug interactions are possible, but have not been reported in animals, probably because low systemic drug levels are achieved. Mesalamine from any source can potentially interfere with thiopurine methyltransferase and, therefore, increase the risk of toxicity from azathioprine.

Drug Interactions

Sulfonamides may interact with other drugs, including warfarin, methenamine, dapsone, and etodolac. They may potentiate adverse effects caused by methotrexate and pyrimethamine. Sulfonamides will increase metabolism of cyclosporine resulting in decreased plasma concentrations. Methenamine is metabolized to formaldehyde which may form a complex and precipitate with sulfonamides.

Instructions for Use

Usually used for treatment of idiopathic colitis, often in combination with dietary therapy. For animals sensitive to sulfonamides, consider other forms of mesalamine (see Mesalamine section for more details).

Patient Monitoring and Laboratory Tests

Monitor tear production in dogs that receive chronic therapy.

Formulations

Sulfasalazine is available in 500 mg tablets and as a pediatric suspension.

Stability and Storage

Store in tightly sealed container, protected from light, and at room temperature. Stability of compounded formulations has not been evaluated.

Small Animal Dosage

Dogs

- 10-30 mg/kg q8-12h PO.

Cats

- 20 mg/kg q12 PO.

Large Animal Dosage

No doses have been reported for large animals.

Regulatory Information

Extralabel use of sulfonamides is prohibited from use in lactating dairy cattle.
RCI Classification: 4

Tacrolimus

tak-roe-lih'mus

Trade and Other Names: Protopic, FK506

Functional Classification: Immuno-suppressant

Pharmacology and Mechanism of Action

Tacrolimus is a microbial product isolated from the organism *Streptomyces tsukubaensis.* Tacrolimus binds to a receptor and subsequently binds to calcineurin and inhibits the calcineurin pathway that stimulates nuclear factor, NFAT. The action resembles that of cyclosporine, although the cellular receptors differ. By inhibiting the action of NFAT, tacrolimus decreases synthesis of inflammatory cytokines. In particular, synthesis of IL-2 is inhibited, which results in decreased activation of T-lymphocytes. It is 10-100 times more potent than cyclosporine. Tacrolimus inhibits release of mast cell and basophil mediators and decreases inflammatory mediator expression.

Indications and Clinical Uses

Tacrolimus is used as an immunosuppressive drug to treat autoimmune disease, prevent organ transplant rejection, and to treat atopic dermatitis. Most use in animals is with a topical formulation. It has been applied topically (ointment) for localized areas of atopic dermatitis. There has been limited use for preventing renal transplant rejection in cats, because the pharmacokinetics have been highly variable. A related drug, pimecrolimus, also has been used topically.

Precautionary Information

Adverse Reactions and Side Effects

There may be a slight burning or pruritic sensation with initial topical application. These reactions are mild and decrease as the skin heals. With systemic administration, dogs may show GI signs, which include diarrhea, intestinal discomfort, vomiting, intestinal intussusception, and intestinal injury. Tacrolimus is minimally absorbed systemically from topical application.

Contraindications and Precautions

Tacrolimus is a potent immunosuppressant. Use cautiously in animals prone to infection.

Drug Interactions

No drug interactions identified from topical administration.

Instructions for Use

There are no reports of safe systemic doses used in dogs.

Patient Monitoring and Laboratory Tests

No specific monitoring is necessary with topical use.

Formulations Available

Tacrolimus is available in 0.1% topical ointment.

Stability and Storage

Ointment is stable if stored in manufacturer's original formulation. Compounded formulations of tacrolimus have been available from pharmacists, but the stability and potency of these formulations has not been evaluated. It is practically insoluble in water. When prepared in a suspension, it was stable for several weeks.

Small Animal Dosage

Dogs and Cats

Apply topical ointment (0.1%) to localized lesions on affected areas of skin. It has been used in dogs twice daily.

Large Animal Dosage

No doses have been reported for large animals.

Regulatory Information

Do not administer to animals intended for food.

Tamoxifen Citrate

tah-moks'ih-fen sih'trate

Trade and Other Names: Nolvadex

Functional Classification: Antiestrogen

Pharmacology and Mechanism of Action

Nonsteroidal estrogen receptor blocker. Tamoxifen also has weak estrogenic effects. Tamoxifen also may increase release of gonadotropin-releasing hormone (Gn-RH).

Indications and Clinical Uses

Tamoxifen is used as adjunctive treatment for certain tumors, especially estrogen-responsive tumors. The most common use in animals is adjunctive treatment for mammary neoplasia. In women it has been used to induce ovulation by stimulating release of Gn-RH from the hypothalamus.

Precautionary Information

Adverse Reactions and Side Effects

Adverse effects have not been thoroughly documented in animals. However, in people, tamoxifen has been reported to cause increased tumor pain.

Contraindications and Precautions

Do not use in pregnant animals.

Drug Interactions

Tamoxifen is a potent cytochrome P450 enzyme inhibitor.

Instructions for Use

Tamoxifen is often used with other anticancer drug protocols.

Patient Monitoring and Laboratory Tests

No specific monitoring is necessary.

Formulations Available

Tamoxifen is available in 10 and 20 mg tablets.

Stability and Storage

Store in tightly sealed container, protected from light, and at room temperature.

Small Animal Dosage

Veterinary dose not established. Human dose is 10 mg q12h PO (approximately 0.14 mg/kg q12h).

Large Animal Dosage

No doses have been reported for large animals.

Regulatory Information

Do not administer to animals intended for food.

Taurine

tore'een

Trade and Other Names: Generic brands

Functional Classification: Nutritional supplement

Pharmacology and Mechanism of Action

Nutritional supplement. Taurine is a naturally occurring amino acid considered essential for cats. Deficiencies in animals may lead to blindness and heart disease. Taurine may have some cardiac inotropic effects.

Indications and Clinical Uses

Taurine is used in prevention and treatment of ocular and cardiac disease (dilated cardiomyopathy) caused by taurine deficiency. Taurine may be supplemented in dogs and cats with heart disease.

Precautionary Information

Adverse Reactions and Side Effects

Adverse effects have not been reported.

Contraindications and Precautions

No contraindications are reported for animals.

Drug Interactions

No drug interactions have been reported in animals.

Instructions for Use

Routine supplementation with taurine may not be necessary in animals that are receiving a balanced diet. However, supplementation may be necessary in animals with diseases associated with taurine deficiency.

Patient Monitoring and Laboratory Tests

Taurine concentrations can be measured in some laboratories to detect deficiencies.

Formulations Available

Taurine is available in powder or supplemented in some diets. Consult a compounding pharmacy for availability.

Stability and Storage

Store in tightly sealed container, protected from light, and at room temperature.

Small Animal Dosage

Dogs
- 500 mg/dog q12h PO.

Cats
- 250 mg/cat q12h PO.

Large Animal Dosage

No doses have been reported for large animals.

Regulatory Information

Because of low risk of harmful residues in animals intended for food, no withdrawal time is suggested.

Tepoxalin

tep-oks'ah-lin

Trade and Other Names: Zubrin

Functional Classification: Antiinflammatory

Pharmacology and Mechanism of Action

Tepoxalin is a nonsteroidal antiinflammatory drug (NSAID). Like other drugs in this class, tepoxalin produces analgesic and antiinflammatory effects by inhibiting the synthesis of prostaglandins. However, tepoxalin also inhibits the action of lipoxygenase (LOX) to decrease synthesis of inflammatory leukotrienes in dogs. This produces a "dual action" in dogs by inhibiting both prostaglandins and leukotrienes. Tepoxalin, using in vitro assays, is more cyclo-oxygenase (COX) 1 selective than COX-2 selective. It has not been established if the specificity for COX-1 or COX-2 is related to efficacy or safety. Tepoxalin forms an active metabolite after administration to dogs, cats, and horses. In dogs, tepoxalin has a half-life of 2 hours and the acid-metabolite has a half-life of 13 hours. It is highly protein bound. Feeding increases oral absorption in dogs.

Indications and Clinical Uses

Tepoxalin is used to decrease pain and inflammation. It has been used for the acute and chronic treatment of pain and inflammation in dogs. One of the most common uses is osteoarthritis, but it also has been used for pain associated with surgery. Because of the dual action of tepoxalin, it has been investigated for treating other inflammatory conditions in dogs and cats. Use in large animals has not been reported.

T

Precautionary Information

Adverse Reactions and Side Effects

GI problems are the most often adverse effects associated with tepoxalin and can include vomiting, diarrhea, nausea, ulcers, and erosions of the GI tract. Both acute and long-term safety and efficacy have been established for dogs. In field trials, vomiting was the most often reported adverse effect. In studies performed in dogs, dogs have tolerated 10 times and 30 times the labeled dose. Renal effects and bleeding studies have been performed on healthy dogs. Tepoxalin in these studies was not shown to adversely affect bleeding times or renal function. Nevertheless, renal toxicity, especially in dehydrated animals or animals with preexisting renal disease has been shown for some NSAIDs.

Contraindications and Precautions

Dogs and cats with preexisting GI problems or renal problems may be at a greater risk of adverse effects from NSAIDs. Safety in pregnancy is not known, but adverse effects have not been reported.

Drug Interactions

Do not administer with other NSAIDs or with corticosteroids. Corticosteroids have been shown to exacerbate the GI adverse effects. Some NSAIDs may interfere with the action of diuretic drugs and angiotensin-converting enzyme (ACE) inhibitors. However, in experimental studies in dogs, tepoxalin combined with an ACE inhibitor did not produce adverse renal effects.

Instructions for Use

Rapidly dissolving tablets can be administered with or without food. In some animals, it is helpful to wet tablet before placing on animal's tongue. Long-term studies have not been completed in cats; only single-dose studies have been reported in which a dose of 10 mg/kg did not produce adverse effects.

Patient Monitoring and Laboratory Tests

Monitor GI signs for evidence of diarrhea, GI bleeding, or ulcers. Because of risk of renal injury, monitor renal parameters (water consumption, BUN, creatinine, and urine specific gravity) periodically during treatment.

Formulations

Tepoxalin is available in 30, 50, 100, and 200 mg tablets (rapidly dissolving).

Stability and Storage

Store in tightly sealed container, protected from light, and at room temperature. Shelf life is 2 years if maintained in manufacturer's original packaging.

Small Animal Dosage

Dogs

- 10 mg/kg q24h PO. It is safe to start with 20 mg/kg initially and use a dose of 10-20 mg/kg because of wide safety margin.

Cats

- Cats have tolerated 10 mg/kg as a single dose, but long-term safety has not been evaluated.

Large Animal Dosage

No doses have been reported for large animals.

Regulatory Information

Do not administer to animals that produce food.

Terbinafine Hydrochloride

ter-bin'ah-feen hye-droe-klor'ide

Trade and Other Names: Lamisil

Functional Classification: Antifungal

Pharmacology and Mechanism of Action

Antifungal drug. Terbinafine belongs to the allylamine group of antifungal drugs. It acts on ergosterol biosynthesis by targeting fungal squalene epoxidase (SE). SE is a membrane-bound enzyme and is involved in the conversion of squalene into squalene 2,3-epoxide, which is subsequently converted into lanosterol and ergosterol. Terbinafine is selective for fungal SE. Terbinafine is active against dermatophytes.

Indications and Clinical Uses

Terbinafine is indicated for treatment of dermatophyte infections in dogs, cats, birds, and some exotic animals. For dermatophytes in animals, the doses necessary for efficacy are much higher than those used in people. There is no evidence that terbinafine is more effective than other antifungal agents, such as itraconazole. In dogs it has been used for *Malassezia* yeast infections. Treatment of infections in horses with terbinafine has not been successful probably because of poor absorption.

Precautionary Information

Adverse Reactions and Side Effects

Vomiting has been the most common adverse effect. Nausea and anorexia also are possible. Hepatotoxicity is possible, but it has not been reported from use in animals.

Contraindications and Precautions

No contraindications reported for animals.

Drug Interactions

No drug interactions have been reported in animals.

Instructions for Use

Treatment of dogs and cats requires much higher doses compared to doses used in people.

Patient Monitoring and Laboratory Tests

No specific monitoring is necessary.

Formulations

Terbinafine is available in 250 mg tablets, 1% topical solution, and 1% topical cream.

Stability and Storage

Store in tightly sealed container, protected from light, and at room temperature. Terbinafine is slightly soluble in water and alcohol. When suspensions have been prepared from crushed tablets in a vehicle (Ora-Sweet) it was stable for 42 days.

Small Animal Dosage

Dogs

- 30 mg/kg q24h PO (with food) for 3 weeks.

Cats

- 30-40 mg/kg/day PO for at least 2 weeks.

Large Animal Dosage

There are no effective doses reported for large animals. It is not effective for horses.

Regulatory Information

Withdrawal times are not established for animals that produce food. For extralabel use withdrawal interval estimates, contact FARAD at 1-888-USFARAD (1-888-873-2723) or send e-mail to FARAD@ncsu.edu.

Terbutaline Sulfate

ter-byoo'tah-leen sul'fate

Trade and Other Names: Brethine and Bricanyl

Functional Classification: Bronchodilator, Beta agonist

Pharmacology and Mechanism of Action

$Beta_2$ adrenergic agonist. Bronchodilator. Stimulates $beta_2$ receptors to relax bronchial smooth muscle. Terbutaline is more $beta_2$ specific than drugs such as isoproterenol. Other $beta_2$ specific drugs include albuterol and metaproterenol. In addition to the $beta_2$ effects to relax bronchial smooth muscle and relieve bronchospasm, the $beta_2$ agonists also may inhibit release of inflammatory mediators, especially from mast cells.

Indications and Clinical Uses

Terbutaline, like other $beta_2$ agonists, is indicated in animals with reversible bronchoconstriction, such as cats with bronchial asthma. It also has been used in dogs to relieve bronchoconstriction and in animals with bronchitis and other airway diseases. Albuterol injection may be used as an alternative for terbutaline injection (4 mcg/kg bolus, up to 8 mcg/kg as needed). Oral absorption in horses is nil, therefore it is not effective in horses for oral administration. Clenbuterol usually is the drug of choice for horses.

Precautionary Information

Adverse Reactions and Side Effects

Terbutaline is a potent beta agonist and causes dose-related beta-adrenergic stimulation that can result in tachycardia, tachyarrhythmias, and tremors. Arrhythmias are more likely with high doses or overdoses.

Contraindications and Precautions

Administer cautiously to animals with cardiac disease, particularly animals that may be susceptible to tachyarrhythmias.

Drug Interactions

Use cautiously with other drugs that may stimulate the heart and cause tachycardia.

Instructions for Use

May be administered PO, IM, or SQ. Terbutaline (and other $beta_2$ agonists) have also been used in people to delay labor (dose in people is 2.5 mg q6h PO). Other $beta_2$ agonists used in animals for relief of bronchoconstriction include albuterol and salmeterol. Animals with acute bronchoconstriction also may benefit from corticosteroid treatment and oxygen therapy. Caution should be used when administering repeated subcutaneous doses. The maximum subcutaneous dose in people is 500 mcg/person (0.5 mg) within a 4-hour period.

Patient Monitoring and Laboratory Tests

Monitor heart rate in animals during treatment.

Formulations

Terbutaline is available in 2.5 and 5 mg tablets and 1 mg/mL (equivalent to 0.82 mg/mL) injections.

Stability and Storage

Store in tightly sealed container, protected from light, and at room temperature. Terbutaline sulfate is soluble in water. Solutions may be subject to degradation. Observe for color change, and discard if solution turns a dark color. Suspensions have been prepared from tablets in syrup and stable for 55 days.

Small Animal Dosage

Dogs

- 1.25-5 mg/dog q8h PO.
- 3-5 mcg/kg (0.003-0.005 mg/kg) SQ.

Cats

- 0.1 mg/kg q8h PO.
- 0.625 mg/cat (1/4 of 2.5 mg tablet) q12h PO.
- 5-10 mcg/kg (0.005-0.01 mg/kg) q4h SQ or IM.

Large Animal Dosage

Horses

- Not absorbed orally. Use IV for treatment of chronic recurrent airway obstruction (RAO): 2-5 mcg/kg q6-8h IV, or as needed.

Regulatory Information

Terbutaline has similar properties as clenbuterol and should not be administered to animals intended for food.

RCI Classification: 3

Testosterone

tess-toss'ter-one

Trade and Other Names: Testosterone cypionate ester: Andro-Cyp, Andronate, Depo-Testosterone, and generic brands and testosterone propionate ester: Testex and Malogen (in Canada)

Functional Classification: Hormone

Pharmacology and Mechanism of Action

Testosterone ester for injection, available in two forms: testosterone cypionate and testosterone propionate. It is used to supplement testosterone in deficient animals. It will produce anabolic effects. Testosterone esters are administered IM to avoid first-pass effects that occur from oral administration. Esters in oil are absorbed more slowly from intramuscular injections. Esters are then hydrolyzed to free testosterone. Other agents with more specific anabolic activity include boldenone, oxymetholone, nandrolone, stanozolol, and methyltestosterone.

Indications and Clinical Uses

Anabolic agents have been used for reversing catabolic conditions, increasing weight gain, increasing muscling in animals, and stimulating erythropoiesis.

Precautionary Information

Adverse Reactions and Side Effects

Adverse effects caused by excessive androgenic action of testosterone. Prostatic hyperplasia is possible in male dogs. Masculinization can occur in female dogs. Hepatopathy is more common with oral methylated testosterone formulations than with injected formulations.

Contraindications and Precautions

Use cautiously in patients with hepatic disease. Do not administer to pregnant animals. This drug has potential for abuse in humans for anabolic uses.

Drug Interactions

No drug interactions have been reported in animals.

Instructions for Use

Use of testosterone androgens has not been evaluated in clinical studies in veterinary medicine. Use is based primarily on experimental evidence or experiences in people.

Patient Monitoring and Laboratory Tests

Monitor hepatic enzymes in treated patients periodically.

Formulations

Testosterone cypionate ester is available in 100 and 200 mg/mL injections.
Testosterone propionate ester is available in 100 mg/mL injections.

Stability and Storage

Testosterone is insoluble in water but soluble in oils and ethanol. Protect from light, heat, and freezing. When mixed with oil, it has been stable for 60 days.

Small Animal Dosage

Dogs and Cats

- Testosterone cypionate ester: 1-2 mg/kg q2-4weeks IM.
- Testosterone propionate ester: 0.5-1 mg/kg 2-3 times/week IM.

Large Animal Dosage

There are no large animal formulations available, except for implants for calves. Do not administer injections to animals intended for food.

Regulatory Information

Testosterone is a schedule III controlled drug.
RCI Classification: 4

Tetracycline, Tetracycline Hydrochloride

tet-rah-sye'kleen

Trade and Other Names: Panmycin, Duramycin powder, and Achromycin V

Functional Classification: Antibacterial

Pharmacology and Mechanism of Action

Tetracycline antibiotic. Mechanism of action of tetracyclines is to bind to 30S ribosomal subunit and inhibit protein synthesis. The action is time-dependent and against some bacteria is bacteriostatic. Tetracycline, like other tetracyclines, has a broad spectrum of activity including bacteria, some protozoa, *Rickettsiae,* and *Ehrlichiae*. Resistance is common.

Indications and Clinical Uses

Tetracyclines are used to treat a variety of infections, including soft tissue infections, pneumonia, and UTIs. Other drugs in this group that are used more frequently in animals for treatment include oxytetracycline and doxycycline.

Precautionary Information

Adverse Reactions and Side Effects

Tetracyclines in general may cause renal tubular necrosis at high doses. Tetracyclines can affect bone and teeth formation in young animals. Tetracyclines have been implicated in drug fever in cats. Hepatotoxicity may occur at high doses in susceptible individuals.

Contraindications and Precautions

Do not use in young animals as can affect bone and teeth formation.

Drug Interactions

Tetracyclines bind to compounds that contain calcium, which decreases oral absorption. Do not mix with solutions that contain iron, calcium, aluminum, or magnesium.

Instructions for Use

Pharmacokinetic and experimental studies have been conducted in small animals, but not in clinical studies. Use of tetracyclines in small animals has primarily been replaced by doxycycline.

Patient Monitoring and Laboratory Tests

Susceptibility testing: CLSI (NCCLS) break point for sensitive organisms is less than or equal to 2 mcg/mL for streptococci and less than or equal to 4 mcg/mL for other organisms. However, on the basis of plasma concentrations achieved, 1 mcg/mL or less should be used for animals. Tetracycline is used as a marker to test susceptibility for other drugs in this class such as doxycycline, minocycline, and oxytetracycline.

Formulations

Tetracycline is available in 250 and 500 mg capsules, 500 mg calf bolus, 100 mg/mL oral suspension, and 25 and 324 g/lb of powder.

Stability and Storage

Store in tightly sealed container, protected from light, and at room temperature. Tetracycline has poor aqueous solubility. However, tetracycline hydrochloride is more soluble (100 mg/mL). The pH of tetracycline hydrochloride solution is approximately 2.0. It will decompose if kept at alkaline pH. Tetracycline hydrochloride is unstable, and compounded preparations are better prepared from tetracycline base as a suspension. Tetracycline will darken with exposure to light. Protect from freezing.

Small Animal Dosage

Dogs and Cats

- 15-20 mg/kg q8h PO.
- 4.4-11 mg/kg q8h IV or IM.
- Rickettsial infection (dogs): 22 mg/kg q8h for 14 days PO.

Large Animal Dosage

Calves and Pigs

- For treatment of enteritis and pneumonia: 11 mg/kg q12h administered in the water or as a bolus. When administered in the water, the dose may actually vary among animals, depending on their water intake.

Regulatory Information

Cattle and pig withdrawal times: 5 days meat for oral powder; 18 days meat; and 72 hours milk when used as intrauterine bolus in cattle; 12, 14, 24 days when oral tablets are used, depending on product (check label).

Thenium Closylate

thee'nee-um kloe'sill-ate

Trade and Other Names: Canopar

Functional Classification: Antiparasitic

Pharmacology and Mechanism of Action

Antiparasitic drug. Thenium is antiparasitic drug with action specific for hookworms.

Indications and Clinical Uses

Thenium closylate is used to treat adult forms of the species *Ancylostoma caninum* and *Uncinaria stenocephala* (hookworms).

Precautionary Information

Adverse Reactions and Side Effects

Thenium may cause occasional vomiting after oral administration.

Contraindications and Precautions

No contraindications are reported for animals.

Drug Interactions

No drug interactions have been reported in animals.

Instructions for Use

Tablet is bitter if coating is broken.

Patient Monitoring and Laboratory Tests

Monitor fecal samples for evidence of parasites.

Formulations

Thenium closylate is available in 500 mg tablets (veterinary preparation).

Stability and Storage

Store in tightly sealed container, protected from light, and at room temperature.

Small Animal Dosage

- Dogs weighing greater than 4.5 kg: 500 mg PO once repeat in 2-3 weeks.
- Dogs weighing 2.5-4.5 kg: 250 mg (half-tablet) twice a day PO for 1 day, repeat in 2-3 weeks.

Large Animal Dosage

No doses have been reported for large animals.

Regulatory Information

Do not administer to animals intended for food.

Theophylline

thee-off′ih-lin

Trade and Other Names: Many generic brands and theophylline sustained-release. Theo Dur, Slo-bid, and Gyrocaps

Functional Classification: Bronchodilator

Pharmacology and Mechanism of Action

Methylxanthine bronchodilator. Nonselective phosphodiesterase (PDE) inhibitor. Phosphodiesterase is the enzyme that converts cyclic adenosine monophosphate (cyclic-AMP) to inactive forms. Therapeutic effects may be caused by cyclic-AMP, or antagonism of adenosine. There appears to be antiinflammatory action as well as bronchodilating action. Sustained-release preparations are used to decrease frequency of administration. Theophylline is the active component of aminophylline.

Indications and Clinical Uses

Theophylline is indicated for control of reversible airway constriction, such as seen with feline asthma. Used for inflammatory airway disease in cats, dogs, and horses. In dogs, the uses include collapsing trachea, bronchitis, and other airway diseases. It has not been effective for respiratory diseases in cattle. In dogs and cats, human-labeled extended release tablets and capsules may be used twice daily in dogs and once daily in cats to achieve effective blood concentrations.

Precautionary Information

Adverse Reactions and Side Effects

Adverse effects include nausea, vomiting, and diarrhea. With high doses, tachycardia, excitement, tremors, and seizures are possible. Cardiovascular and CNS adverse effects appear to be less frequent in dogs than people.

Contraindications and Precautions

Administer with caution to patients with cardiovascular disease or patients with seizure disorders.

Drug Interactions

Use cautiously with other phosphodiesterase inhibitors such as pentoxifylline, sildenafil (Viagra), and pimobendan. Many drugs will inhibit the metabolism of theophylline and potentially increase concentrations. Drugs responsible include cimetidine, erythromycin, fluoroquinolones, and propranolol. Some drugs will decrease concentrations by increasing metabolism. Such drugs include phenobarbital and rifampin.

Instructions for Use

Adjust dose to maintain therapeutic blood levels. Older slow-release and extended-release formulations are no longer available. Pharmacokinetic studies have established doses for human-labeled Inwood Laboratories tablets and capsules in dogs and cats. These formulations have produced the most consistent plasma concentrations from oral dosing.

Patient Monitoring and Laboratory Tests

Plasma concentrations of theophylline should be monitored in patients receiving chronic therapy to maintain plasma concentrations between 10 and 20 mcg/mL. Regularly monitor plasma concentrations in patients receiving chronic treatment. Peak-trough concentration measurements are encouraged.

Formulations

Theophylline is available in 100, 125, 200, 250, and 300 mg tablets, 27 mg/5 mL (5.3 mg/mL) oral solution or elixir, and injection in 5% dextrose. Theophylline extended-release is available in 200 and 300 mg tablets and 125 and 200 mg capsules (Theochron, TheoCap, or Inwood formulation). However, availability of various sizes of extended-release formulations may vary. The manufacturers have discontinued other extended-release formulations such as Slo-Bid and Theo-Dur.

Stability and Storage

Store in tightly sealed container, protected from light, and at room temperature. Theophylline is slightly soluble in water (8 mg/mL). Theophylline has been mixed with some oral liquids and found to be stable if administered shortly after mixing. When using the slow-release tablets or capsules in dogs and cats, do not disrupt coating on formulation.

Small Animal Dosage

Dogs

- Theophylline: 9 mg/kg q6-8h PO (immediate-release formulations)
- Theophylline sustained-release: 10 mg/kg q12h (Inwood laboratories formulation) PO.

Cats

- 4 mg/kg q8-12h PO (immediate release formulations)
- Theophylline sustained-release: 20 mg/kg for tablets (100 mg per cat) q24h PO or 25 mg/kg for capsule (125 mg per cat) q24h PO (Inwood laboratories formulation). With long-term use in cats, this interval may be increased to q48h.

Large Animal Dose

- Horses, treatment of recurrent airway obstruction (RAO): 5 mg/kg q12h PO.
- Although theophylline has been administered to horses IV, this administration has caused transient excitement and restlessness. Give IV administration slowly.
- Cattle use as a bronchodilator: 20 mg/kg q12h PO. When treating diseases secondary to virus infections, decrease frequency to once every 24 hours.

Regulatory Information

Withdrawal times are not established. However, for extralabel use withdrawal interval estimates, contact FARAD at 1-888-USFARAD (1-888-873-2723) or send e-mail to FARAD@ncsu.edu.

RCI Classification: 3

Thiabendazole

thye-ah-ben′dah-zole

Trade and Other Names: Omnizole, Equizole, TBZ, and Thibenzole

Functional Classification: Antiparasitic

Pharmacology and Mechanism of Action

Benzimidazole antiparasitic drug. Like other benzimidazoles, it produces a degeneration of the parasite microtubule and irreversibly blocks glucose uptake in parasites. Inhibition of glucose uptake causes depletion of energy stores in parasite, eventually resulting in death. However, there is no effect on glucose metabolism in mammals.

Indications and Clinical Uses

Availability of commercial forms of thiabendazole has been limited. In horses, thiabendazole has been used for control of large and small strongyles, *Strongyloides,* and pinworms of the genera *Strongylus, Cyathostomum, Cylicobrachytus* and related genera, *Craterostomum, Oesophagodontus, Poteriostomum, Oxyuris,* and *Strongyloides.* In ruminants it has been used for infections of GI roundworms in sheep and goats (*Trichostrongylus* spp. *Haemonchus* spp., *Ostertagia* spp., *Cooperia* spp., *Nematodirus* spp., *Bunostomom* spp., *Strongyloides* spp., *Chabertia* spp., *Oesophagostomum* spp., *Trichostrongylus colubriformis* and *T. axei*, and *Ostertagia* spp.).

Precautionary Information

Adverse Reactions and Side Effects

Adverse effects are uncommon.

Contraindications and Precautions

No contraindications are reported for animals.

Drug Interactions

No drug interactions have been reported in animals.

Instructions for Use

Thiabendazole is ordinarily administered to horses and cattle. Experience in small animals is limited.

Patient Monitoring and Laboratory Tests

Monitor fecal samples for evidence of intestinal parasites.

Formulations Available

Thiabendazole is available in paste, pellets, and solution for oral administration and pre-mix for feeds. Some formulations are no longer commercially available.

Stability and Storage

Store in tightly sealed container, protected from light, and at room temperature.

Small Animal Dosage

Dogs

- 50 mg/kg q24h for 3 days, repeat in 1 month.
- Treating respiratory parasites: 30-70 mg/kg q12h PO.

Cats

- *Strongyloides* spp: 125 mg/kg q24h for 3 days.

Large Animal Dosage

Horses

- 44 mg/kg PO (single dose).

Sheep and Goats

- 44 mg/kg PO (single dose); up to 67 mg/kg PO for some infections.

Cattle

- 67 mg/kg PO (single dose), up to 111 mg/kg PO for more severe infections.

Pigs (baby pigs)

- 67-90 mg/kg PO.

Regulatory Information

Withdrawal time for milk 96 hours.
Sheep and goats withdrawal time (meat): 30 days.
Cattle withdrawal time (meat): 3 days.
Pig withdrawal time (meat): 30 days.

Thiacetarsemide Sodium

thye-ass-et-ars'ah-mide soe-dee-um

Trade and Other Names: Caparsolate

Functional Classification: Antiparasitic

Pharmacology and Mechanism of Action

Organic arsenical

Indications and Clinical Uses

Thiacetarsemide is used for treatment of adult heartworm infections. Melarsomine is considered by many experts safer and has replaced thiacetarsemide for routine treatment.

Precautionary Information

Adverse Reactions and Side Effects

Adverse effects are common, especially anorexia, vomiting, and hepatic injury. Pulmonary thromboembolism may occur as consequence of heartworm kill.

Contraindications and Precautions

Not recommended in cats unless they can be carefully monitored. Cats are less susceptible to arsenical toxicity than dogs, but they are more prone to pulmonary thromboembolism. If cats are treated, they should be confined under close observation for 3-4 weeks.

Drug Interactions

No drug interactions have been reported in animals.

Instructions for Use

Thiacetarsemide is administered via 4 injections over 2 days, however, if severe adverse effects are observed, discontinue regimen. Extravasation can result in skin slough.

It is recommended to substitute melarsomine for thiacetarsemide, if possible, for treating heartworm disease.

Patient Monitoring and Laboratory Tests

Monitor renal and hepatic function.

Formulations

Thiacetarsemide is available in 10 mg/mL injections. There are no longer commercial supplies of thiacetarsemide, and its availability is uncertain.

Stability and Storage

Store in tightly sealed container, protected from light, and at room temperature.

Small Animal Dosage

Dogs

- 2.2 mg/kg IV twice daily for 2 days.

Cats

- Not recommended, unless the cat can be closely supervised. Dose is 2.2 mg/kg twice daily IV for 2 consecutive days.

Large Animal Dosage

No doses have been reported for large animals.

Regulatory Information

Do not administer to animals intended for food.

Thiamine Hydrochloride

thye'ah-min hye-droe-klor'ide

Trade and Other Names: Vitamin B_1, Bewon, and generic brands

Functional Classification: Vitamin

Pharmacology and Mechanism of Action

Vitamin B_1 used for treatment of vitamin deficiency. Vitamin B complex often contains thiamine (B_1), riboflavin, niacinamide, and cyanocobalamin B_{12}.

Indications and Clinical Uses

Thiamine is used to provide Vitamin B_1 supplementation or to treat vitamin B_1 deficiency.

T

Precautionary Information

Adverse Reactions and Side Effects

Adverse effects are rare, because water soluble vitamins are easily excreted.

Contraindications and Precautions

Administer solutions of Vitamin B_1 very slowly IV, if at all. Rapid intravenous administration has caused anaphylactic reactions.

Drug Interactions

Thiamine hydrochloride may be susceptible in incompatibility when this hydrochloride is mixed with alkalinizing solutions.

Instructions for Use

Vitamin B supplements are administered often in combination with other B vitamins as vitamin B complex solutions.

Patient Monitoring and Laboratory Tests

No specific monitoring is necessary.

Formulations

Thiamine is available in 250 mcg/5 mL elixir, 5 mg to 500 mg tablets and 100 and 500 mg/mL injections.

Vitamin B complex aqueous solutions for injection usually contain 12.5 mg/mL of vitamin B_1.

Stability and Storage

Store in tightly sealed container, at room temperature, protected from light. When mixed with other solutions (e.g., fluid solutions), incompatibility may result.

Small Animal Dosage

Dogs

- 10-100 mg/dog/day PO.
- 12.5-50 mg/dog/day IM or SQ.

Cats

- 5-30 mg/cat/day PO, up to a maximum dose of 50 mg/cat/day.
- 12.5-25 mg/cat/day IM or SQ.

Large Animal Dosage

All doses listed on a per animal basis.

Lambs

- 12.5-25 mg/day IM.

Sheep and Pigs

- 65-125 mg/day IM.

Calves and Foals

- 37.5-65 mg/day IM.

Cattle and Horses

- 125-250 mg/day IM.

Regulatory Information

Withdrawal time for animals intended for food: 0 days.

Thioguanine

thye-oh-gwah'neen

Trade and Other Names: Generic brands

Functional Classification: Anticancer agent

Pharmacology and Mechanism of Action

Anticancer agent. Antimetabolite of purine analog type. Thioguanine inhibits DNA synthesis in cancer cells.

Indications and Clinical Uses

Thioguanine is used in some anticancer protocols. It is not commonly used in animals.

Precautionary Information

Adverse Reactions and Side Effects

Adverse effects, as with any anticancer drug, are expected. Adverse effects from thioguanine may be similar to those observed from mercaptopurine. Immunosuppression and leukopenia are common.

Contraindications and Precautions

Do not administer to patients with depressed bone marrow.

Drug Interactions

No drug interactions have been reported in animals.

Instructions for Use

Thioguanine is combined with other agents for treatment of cancer.

Patient Monitoring and Laboratory Tests

Monitor CBC to screen for evidence of bone marrow toxicity.

Formulations

Thioguanine is available in 40 mg tablets.

Stability and Storage

Store in tightly sealed container, protected from light, and at room temperature.

Small Animal Dosage

Dogs

- 40 mg/m^2 q24h PO.

Cats

- 25 mg/m^2 q24h PO for 1-5 days, then repeat every 30 days.

Large Animal Dosage

No dose has been reported for large animals.

Regulatory Information

Withdrawal times are not established for animals that produce food. This drug should not be used in animals intended for food, because it is an anticancer agent.

T

Thiopental Sodium

thye-oh-pen'tahl soe'dee-um

Trade and Other Names: Pentothal

Functional Classification: Anesthetic, Barbiturate

Pharmacology and Mechanism of Action

Ultrashort-acting barbiturate. Anesthesia is produced by CNS depression, without analgesia. Anesthesia is terminated by redistribution in the body.

Indications and Clinical Uses

Thiopental is used primarily for induction of anesthesia or for short duration of anesthesia (10-15 minute procedures). It induces a rapid, smooth, and generally excitement-free induction.

Precautionary Information

Adverse Reactions and Side Effects

Most common effect is transient apnea and respiratory depression. Other adverse effects are related to the anesthetic effects of the drug. Thiopental may cause cardiovascular depression with a slight decrease in stroke volume and little change in cardiac output or blood pressure. Premedication will reduce the risk of cardiovascular events. Supplementation with oxygen during induction also will decrease cardiovascular events. Overdoses are caused by rapid or repeated injections. Avoid extravasation outside of vein.

Contraindications and Precautions

Use carefully in patients with respiratory or cardiac disease. Do not use unless there is an ability to monitor and maintain respiration.

Drug Interactions

Thiopental is compatible with other anesthetics. However, use of other sedatives and anesthetics will lower dose of thiopental. Thiopental has been combined with propofol in a 1:1 mixture without loss of effectiveness. This mixture of 1:1 2.5% thiopental and propofol has been used to induce anesthesia in dogs.

Instructions for Use

Therapeutic index is low. Use only in patients in which it is possible to monitor cardiovascular and respiratory functions. Thiopental is often administered with other anesthetic adjuncts.

Patient Monitoring and Laboratory Tests

Monitor cardiovascular and respiratory function during anesthesia with thiopental.

Formulations

Thiopental is available in 250 mg to 10 g vials (mix to desired concentration).

Stability and Storage

Thiopental, when prepared properly, is chemically stable and resists bacterial growth for up to 4 weeks when refrigerated. Thiopental has a pH of 10-11 and should not be mixed with acidifying solutions. If mixed with other drugs the alkalinity may affect their stability. Propofol has been mixed with thiopental sodium in a 1:1 mixture and they are physically and chemically compatible if used promptly.

Small Animal Dosage

Dogs

- 10-25 mg/kg IV (to effect).

Cats

- 5-10 mg/kg IV (to effect).

Large Animal Dosage

Cattle

- Induction: 6-12 mg/kg IV (to effect).

Pigs

- 10-20 mg/kg IV (to effect).

Regulatory Information

Extralabel use: establish a withdrawal time of at least 1 day for meat and 24 hours for milk.
Pig withdrawal time (meat): 0 days.
Schedule II controlled drug
RCI Classification: 2

Thiotepa

thye-oh-tep'ah

Trade and Other Names: Thioplex and generic brands

Functional Classification: Anticancer agent

Pharmacology and Mechanism of Action

Anticancer agent. Thiotepa is an alkylating agent of the nitrogen mustard type (similar to cyclophosphamide).

Indications and Clinical Uses

Thiotepa is used for various tumors, especially malignant effusions. The most common mode of administration is in a lesion or locally (e.g., in a bladder). For cancer of the bladder, 30 mg is diluted in 30 mL of distilled water and instilled directly in the bladder once per week.

Precautionary Information

Adverse Reactions and Side Effects

Adverse effects are similar to other anticancer agents and alkylating drugs (many of which are unavoidable). Bone marrow suppression is the most common effect.

Contraindications and Precautions

Avoid use in animals with depressed bone marrow.

Drug Interactions

No drug interactions have been reported in animals.

Instructions for Use

One should consult specific cancer chemotherapy protocol for guidance on administration. Thiotepa usually is administered directly in body cavities.

Patient Monitoring and Laboratory Tests

Monitor CBC for evidence of bone marrow suppression.

Formulations

Thiotepa is available in 15 mg injections (usually in solution of 10 mg/mL).

Stability and Storage

Store in tightly sealed container, protected from light, and at room temperature. When mixing solution, add 1.5 mL of sterile water to each vial. This solution is stable for 5 days if refrigerated. Solutions may be clear to slightly opaque, but if cloudiness or precipitate appears, discard vial.

Small Animal Dosage

Dogs and Cats

- 0.2-0.5 mg/m^2 weekly or daily for 5-10 days IM, intracavitary, or intratumor.

Large Animal Dosage

No dose has been reported for large animals.

Regulatory Information

Withdrawal times are not established for animals that produce food. This drug should not be used in animals intended for food, because it is an anticancer agent.

Thyroid Releasing Hormone

Trade and Other Names: TRH

Functional Classification: Hormone, Thyroid

Pharmacology and Mechanism of Action

Thyroid releasing hormone (TRH) is used to detect hyperthyroidism when T-4 is not elevated, yet hyperthyroidism is suspected.

Indications and Clinical Uses

TRH has been used for diagnostic testing, but the value has been questioned. See thyrotropin (TSH) for diagnostic testing for hypothyroidism.

Precautionary Information

Adverse Reactions and Side Effects

No significant adverse effects. Allergic reactions are possible.

Contraindications and Precautions

No contraindications are reported for animals.

Drug Interactions

No drug interactions have been reported in animals.

Instructions for Use

Used for diagnostic purposes.

Patient Monitoring and Laboratory Tests

Monitor thyroid concentrations. Collect post TRH T4 sample at 4 hours after test dose.

Formulations

TRH is available in injections.

Stability and Storage

Store in tightly sealed container, protected from light, and at room temperature.

Small Animal Dosage

- Collect baseline T4, followed by 0.1 mg/kg IV. Collect post-TRH T4 sample at 4 hours.

Large Animal Dosage

No dose has been reported for large animals.

Regulatory Information

Because of low risk of harmful residues in animals intended for food, no withdrawal time is suggested.

Thyrotropin

thye-roe-troe′pin

Trade and Other Names: Thytropar, Thyrogen, and TSH

Functional Classification: Hormone, Thyroid

Pharmacology and Mechanism of Action

Thyroid stimulating hormone (TSH) is used for diagnostic testing; it stimulates normal secretion of thyroid hormone.

Indications and Clinical Uses

TSH is used to stimulate secretion of thyroid hormone for diagnostic testing. Because of the limited availability of TSH for diagnostic testing and the high cost of the human form, this test is rarely performed.

Precautionary Information

Adverse Reactions and Side Effects

Adverse reactions are rare. In people, allergic reactions have occurred.

Contraindications and Precautions

No contraindications are reported for animals.

Drug Interactions

No drug interactions have been reported in animals.

Instructions for Use

To prepare solution, add 2 mL sodium chloride to 10 unit vial. Consult testing laboratory for specific guidelines for thyroid testing.

Patient Monitoring and Laboratory Tests

After 0.1 units/kg IV, collect post TSH sample at 6 hours.

Formulations

Recombinant human TSH, also known as Thyrogen, is available in a 1.1 mg vial. Other forms (Thytropar) are difficult to obtain.

Stability and Storage

Store in tightly sealed container, protected from light, and at room temperature. Reconstituted solutions retain potency for 2 weeks at 2-8° C.

Small Animal Dosage

Dogs

- Collect baseline sample, followed by 0.1 units/kg IV (maximum dose is 5 units); collect post-TSH sample at 6 hours.

Large Animal Dosage

No dose has been reported for large animals.

Regulatory Information

Because of low risk of harmful residues in animals intended for food, no withdrawal time is suggested.

Ticarcillin + Clavulanate Potassium

tye-kar-sill'in + klav'yoo-lan'ate

Trade and Other Names: Timentin

Functional Classification: Antibacterial

Pharmacology and Mechanism of Action

Action and spectrum are the same as ticarcillin, except clavulanic acid has been added to inhibit bacterial beta-lactamase and increase spectrum of activity. Clavulanate does not increase activity against *Pseudomonas* compared to ticarcillin alone, however.

Indications and Clinical Uses

Ticarcillin + clavulanate has been used in animals for treatment of various infections, including pneumonia, soft tissue infections, and bone infections. Ticarcillin has similar activity as ampicillin, but is extended to include many organisms that otherwise are resistant to ampicillin, such as *Pseudomonas aeruginosa* and other gram-negative bacilli. When combined with clavulanate, the activity against some strains of gram-negative bacteria and *Staphylococcus* is improved. Its activity is enhanced when administered with an aminoglycoside. It is administered IV in most animals; intramuscular administration can be painful.

Precautionary Information

Adverse Reactions and Side Effects

Adverse effects are uncommon. However, allergic reactions are possible. High doses can produce seizures and decreased platelet function.

Contraindications and Precautions

Administer cautiously, if at all, to animals with penicillin allergies.

Drug Interactions

Do not combine in same syringe or in vial with aminoglycosides.

Instructions for Use

Ticarcillin is synergistic with, and often combined with, aminoglycosides (e.g., amikacin and gentamicin). Lidocaine (1%) may be used for reconstitution to decrease pain from intramuscular injection.

Patient Monitoring and Laboratory Tests

Susceptibility testing: CLSI (NCCLS) break point for sensitive organisms is less than or equal to 64/2 mcg/mL for *Pseudomonas* and less than or equal to 16/2 mcg/mL for gram-negative bacilli. (The "/" distinguishes the ticarcillin from the clavulanate concentrations.)

Formulations Available

Ticarcillin + clavulanate is available in 3 g/vial injections.

Stability and Storage

Store in tightly sealed container, protected from light, and at room temperature.

Small Animal Dosage

Dogs and Cats

- Dose according to rate for ticarcillin: 33-50 mg/kg q4-6h IV or IM.

Large Animal Dosage

Horses

- 44 mg/kg q6-8h IV or IM (of the ticarcillin component).
- Ticarcillin-clavulanate also has been used in horses as an intrauterine infusion at a dose of 12.4 mg/kg ticarcillin and 0.4 mg/kg clavulanate diluted in 60-100 mL saline.

Regulatory Information

Withdrawal times are not established. However, excretion is similar to other beta-lactam antibiotics, such as ampicillin. Follow ampicillin guidelines for withdrawal times.

Ticarcillin Disodium

tye-kar-sill'in dye-soe-dee-um

Trade and Other Names: Ticar and Ticillin

Functional Classification: Antibacterial

Pharmacology and Mechanism of Action

Beta-lactam antibiotic. Like other beta-lactams, ticarcillin binds penicillin-binding proteins (PBP) that weaken or interfere with cell wall formation. After binding to PBP, the cell wall weakens or undergoes lysis. Like other beta-lactams, this drug acts in a time-dependent manner (i.e., it is more effective when drug concentrations are maintained above the minimum inhibitory concentration [MIC] values during the dose interval. Ticarcillin has action similar to ampicillin/amoxicillin and a spectrum similar to carbenicillin. Ticarcillin is primarily used for gram-negative infections, especially those caused by *Pseudomonas* species.

Indications and Clinical Uses

Ticarcillin has been used in animals for treatment of various infections, including pneumonia, soft tissue infections, and bone infections. Ticarcillin has similar activity as ampicillin, but it is extended to include many organisms that otherwise are resistant to ampicillin, such as *Pseudomonas aeruginosa* and other gram-negative bacilli. Its activity is enhanced when administered with an aminoglycoside. It is administered IV in most animals; intramuscular administration can be painful. Ticarcillin also has been infused in the uterus of horses to treat metritis.

Precautionary Information

Adverse Reactions and Side Effects

Adverse effects are uncommon. However, allergic reactions are possible. High doses can produce seizures and decreased platelet function.

Contraindications and Precautions

Administer cautiously, if at all, to animals with penicillin allergies.

Drug Interactions

Do not combine in same syringe or in vial with aminoglycosides.

Instructions for Use

Ticarcillin is synergistic with, and often combined with, aminoglycosides (e.g., amikacin and gentamicin). Lidocaine (1%) may be used for reconstitution to decrease pain from intramuscular injection.

Patient Monitoring and Laboratory Tests

Susceptibility testing: CLSI (NCCLS) break point for sensitive organisms is less than or equal to 64 mcg/mL for *Pseudomonas* and less than or equal to 16 mcg/mL for gram-negative enteric organisms.

Formulations

Ticarcillin is available in 6 gram/50 mL vial. The vials contain 1, 3, 6, 20, and 30 g. The equine formulation has become difficult to obtain.

Stability and Storage

Store in tightly sealed container, protected from light, and at room temperature.

Small Animal Dosage

Dogs and Cats

- 33-50 mg/kg q4-6h IV or IM.

Large Animal Dosage

Horses

- 44 mg/kg q6-8h IV or IM.
- Ticarcillin also has been used in horses as an intrauterine infusion at a dose of 12.4 mg/kg diluted in 60-100 mL saline.

Regulatory Information

Withdrawal times are not established. However, excretion is similar to other beta-lactam antibiotics, such as ampicillin. Follow ampicillin guidelines for withdrawal times.

Tiletamine + Zolazepam

till-eh'tah-meen + zole-az'eh-pam

Trade and Other Names: Telezol and Zoletil

Functional Classification: Anesthetic

Pharmacology and Mechanism of Action

Anesthetic. It is a combination of tiletamine (dissociative anesthetic agent similar in action to ketamine) and zolazepam (benzodiazepine similar in action as diazepam). Tiletamine + zolazepam produces a short duration (30 minutes) of anesthesia. In cats, the effect of the zolazepam will have a longer duration than tiletamine. In dogs, the tiletamine will have a longer duration than the zolazepam. Therefore, anesthesia appears to be smoother in cats than in dogs.

Indications and Clinical Uses

Tiletamine + zolazepam is used for short-term anesthesia in animals. For longer procedures, other drugs should be used.

Precautionary Information

Adverse Reactions and Side Effects

Tiletamine + zolazepam has a wide margin of safety, which is greater in cats than dogs. Side effects include excessive salivation (may be antagonized with atropine), erratic recovery, and muscle twitching. Drying of the cornea may occur unless ophthalmic ointment is applied to the eyes. Adverse reactions have been observed when administered to ferrets.

Contraindications and Precautions

Low doses do not provide sufficient anesthesia for surgery. Do not use in patients with pancreatic disease.

Drug Interactions

No drug interactions have been reported in animals.

Instructions for Use

Administer by deep intramuscular injection.

Patient Monitoring and Laboratory Tests

Monitor heart rate and rhythm during anesthesia. Monitor body temperature because of risk of hypothermia.

Formulations

Tiletamine + zolazepam is available in 50 mg of each component per mL (100 mg total).

Stability and Storage

Store in tightly sealed container, protected from light, and at room temperature.

Small Animal Dosage

Dogs

- Initial IM dose is 6.6-10 mg/kg for minor procedures.
- Short-term anesthesia: 10-13 mg/kg.

Cats

- 10-12 mg/kg IM for minor procedures and higher doses of 14-16 mg/kg IM for surgery.

Doses are based on combined mg of each component.

Large Animal Dosage

No dose has been reported for large animals.

Regulatory Information

No regulatory information is available. For extralabel use withdrawal interval estimates, contact FARAD at 1-888-USFARAD (1-888-873-2723) or send e-mail to FARAD@ncsu.edu.
Schedule III controlled drug

Tilmicosin Phosphate

til-mye'koe-sin foss'fate

Trade and Other Names: Micotil and Pulmotil tilmicosin premix

Functional Classification: Antibacterial

Pharmacology and Mechanism of Action

Macrolide antibiotic. It inhibits bacteria by binding to 50S ribosome and inhibiting protein synthesis. Spectrum of activity limited primarily to gram-positive aerobic bacteria, *Mycoplasma,* and respiratory pathogens such as *Pasteurella multocida, Mannheimia haemolytica*, and *Histophilus somni* (formerly *Haemophilus somnus*). Tilmicosin administered to calves (15 mg/kg SQ) reduced expression of prostaglandin (PGE_2) stimulated by bacteria. There also may be some antiinflammatory effects such as reduced leukocyte release of inflammatory mediators in the lungs associated with tilmicosin treatment. There also may be reduced prostaglandin synthesis with tilmicosin administration in alveolar macrophages.

Indications and Clinical Uses

Tilmicosin activity against respiratory pathogens is sufficient for efficacy for treating bovine respiratory disease (BRD). In cattle, one injection has duration of at least 72 hours, based on high concentrations achieved in lung. Tilmicosin also has been used as a prophylactic treatment for calves that are entering feedlots. The use of tilmicosin at the time of feedlot arrival has reduced incidence of respiratory disease in cattle. Tilmicosin (Pulmotil) is used in medicated feed for swine for control of swine respiratory disease (SRD).

Precautionary Information

Adverse Reactions and Side Effects

Tilmicosin may be cardiotoxic in some animals. Injections to pigs have been fatal because of cardiotoxicity. The cardiac effects are increased heart rate and decreased contractility. However, administration of tilmicosin premix in feed of pigs has been safe. In dogs, tilmicosin injections have caused cardiac toxicosis and may be caused by calcium-channel blockade; it was reversed by administration of calcium. In goats, injections >10 mg/kg IM or SQ can cause toxicity. In horses, injections of tilmicosin IM or SQ >10 mg/kg can lead to toxicity. Do not administer IV to any species.

Contraindications and Precautions

Tilmicosin reaches high concentrations in milk for up to 42 days. Do not administer to lactating dairy cattle. Do not administer to goats. Do not administer to any animals IV or death can result. *People handling tilmicosin should take precautions to prevent accidental injection. Fatal injections have been reported in people.*

Drug Interactions

The cardiac adverse effects are exacerbated by administration of beta-blockers such as propranolol. Dobutamine and administration of calcium may offset cardiac effects.

Instructions for Use

Administer SQ. *If a person handling the drug is accidentally injected, consult physician immediately.* Severe cardiac toxicity has occurred in some species of animals.

Patient Monitoring and Laboratory Tests

Susceptibility information: Use of break points for other macrolides may identify organisms sensitive or resistant to tilmicosin.

Formulations

Tilmicosin is available in 300 mg/mL injection (Micotil) and 200 g/kg (90.7 g/lb) of premix (Pulmotil).

Stability and Storage

Store in tightly sealed container, protected from light, and at room temperature.

Small Animal Dosage

Not recommended for small animals.

Large Animal Dosage

Cattle

- 10 mg/kg SQ single dose. Avoid intravenous or intramuscular administration.

Sheep

- 10 mg/kg SQ.

Goats

Do not use.

Horses

Do not use. Safety not established.

Pigs

- Pneumonia: 181-383 g/ton of feed. Feed only this ration for 21 days, beginning at the time of disease outbreak.

Regulatory Information

Cattle withdrawal time (meat): 28 days. No withdrawal time established for milk.
Pig withdrawal time (meat): 7 days.
Sheep withdrawal time (meat): 28 days.

Tinidazole

tih-nih'dah-zole

Trade and Other Names: Tindamax

Functional Classification: Antiprotozoal

Pharmacology and Mechanism of Action

Antiprotozoal with action similar to metronidazole. It is a second-generation nitroimidazole in which the activity involves generation of free nitroradicals via metabolism of within protozoa. It has action against *Trichomonas*, *Giardia*, and intestinal protozoal parasites. It also has in vitro activity against anaerobic bacteria and *Helicobacter*. Half-life is approximately 5.5 hours in horses, 8.5 hours in cats, and 4.5 hours in dogs. Oral absorption in dogs, cats, and horses is approximately 100%.

Indications and Clinical Uses

Tinidazole is indicated to treat diarrhea and other intestinal problems caused by intestinal protozoa such as *Giardia*, *Trichomonas*, and *Entamoeba*. Tinidazole also is active against many anaerobic bacteria and may be used as a substitute for metronidazole in small animals and horses for treatment of a variety of anaerobic infections.

Precautionary Information

Adverse Reactions and Side Effects

Tinidazole has similar action as metronidazole. With high doses it can cause neurological problems, including ataxia, tremors, nystagmus, and seizures. The CNS signs are related to inhibition of action of GABA and are responsive to benzodiazepines (diazepam). Like other nitroimidazoles, it has the potential to produce mutagenic changes in cells, but this has not been demonstrated in vivo. Like other nitroimidazoles, it has bitter taste and can cause vomiting and anorexia. However, the bitter taste is not as bad as metronidazole.

Contraindications and Precautions

Do not administer to animals that may be prone to seizures. Do not administer to animals already known to be sensitive to metronidazole. Do not administer to pregnant animals.

Drug Interactions

Like other nitroimidazoles, it can potentiate the effects of warfarin and cyclosporine via inhibition of drug metabolism.

Instructions for Use

Give oral dose with food to minimize the unpleasant taste and decrease nausea.

Patient Monitoring and Laboratory Tests

No specific monitoring is necessary. Most anaerobic bacteria have minimum inhibitory concentration (MIC) values below 2 mcg/mL.

Formulations

Tinidazole is available in 250 and 500 mg tablets.

Stability and Storage

Tablets have been crushed and mixed with flavorings to improve palatability. These suspensions are stable for 7 days.

Small Animal Dosage

Dogs

- 15 mg/kg q12h PO.

Cats

- 15 mg/kg q24h PO. Duration of therapy will depend on whether one is treating *Giardia* (5 days) or other anaerobic infections (longer than 5 days).

Large Animal Dosage

Horses

- 10-15 mg/kg q12h PO.

Regulatory Information

Do not administer to animals that produce food. Administration of nitroimidazoles to animals intended for food is prohibited.

Tobramycin Sulfate

toe-brah-mye'sin sul'fate

Trade and Other Names: Nebcin

Functional Classification: Antibacterial

Pharmacology and Mechanism of Action

Aminoglycoside antibacterial drug. Like other aminoglycosides, tobramycin is bactericidal. It binds to the 30S ribosomal subunit in bacteria to inhibit protein synthesis and lead to cell death. It is concentration-dependent in its antibacterial action. It has a similar spectrum to amikacin and gentamicin, although it is more active than gentamicin against gram-negative bacteria. Generally, if an organism is sensitive to tobramycin it will also be sensitive to amikacin.

Indications and Clinical Uses

Tobramycin, like other aminoglycosides, is used to treat serious systemic infections caused by gram-negative bacteria. It is often administered simultaneously with beta-lactam antibiotics to produce a synergistic effect. The infections treated include pneumonia, soft tissue infections, and sepsis. Tobramycin has also been used topically. Tobramycin has been used in nebulizing solutions for respiratory infections.

Precautionary Information

Adverse Reactions and Side Effects

Nephrotoxicity is the most dose-limiting toxicity. Ensure that patients have adequate fluid and electrolyte balance during therapy. Ototoxicity and vestibulotoxicity also are possible.

Contraindications and Precautions

When used with anesthetic agents, neuromuscular blockade is possible. Do not mix in vial or syringe with other antibiotics.

Drug Interactions

Avoid mixing in vials with other drugs. It is incompatible with other antibiotics and inactivation occurs rapidly.

Instructions for Use

Inject IV or IM. Administer with a beta-lactam antibiotic for a synergistic effect. For nebulization treatment of respiratory infections, administer 160 mg of tobramycin (total dose) twice daily for 28 days. The solution used for nebulization (in individual packets with no preservatives) is called TOBI, but it is expensive. Tobramycin injectable is used instead, but contains preservatives that could induce bronchospasm. Use diluted tobramycin with 3 mL of saline and administer albuterol before nebulization to decrease bronchospasm.

Patient Monitoring and Laboratory Tests

Susceptibility testing: The CLSI (NCCLS) minimum inhibitory concentration (MIC) value break point for susceptibility is less than or equal to 4 mcg/mL. Monitor BUN, creatinine, and urine for evidence of renal toxicity. Blood levels can be monitored to detect problems with systemic clearance. When monitoring trough levels in patient dosed once daily, the trough levels should be below the limit of detection. Alternatively measure half-life from samples taken at 1 hour and

2 to 4 hours post-dosing. Clearance should be above 1.0 mL/kg/min and half-life should be less than 2 hours.

Formulations

Tobramycin is available in 40 mg/mL injections.

Stability and Storage

Store in tightly sealed container, protected from light, and at room temperature. Store powder at room temperature. Reconstituted solutions are stable for 24 hours at room temperature and 96 hours refrigerated. Do not use discolored solutions. Tobramycin sulfate diluted in fluids can be frozen and stable for 30 days. Ophthalmic solutions have been compounded and shown to be stable for 90 days. Do not mix with other antibiotics, especially beta-lactam agents (penicillins and cephalosporins), because inactivation may occur.

Small Animal Dosage

Dogs

- 2-4 mg/kg q8h or 9-14 mg/kg q24h SQ, IM, or IV.

Cats

- 3 mg/kg q8h or 5-8 mg/kg q24h SQ, IM, or IV.

Nebulization therapy is sometimes used in small animals. (See Instructions for Use section for details on nebulization therapy.)

Large Animal Dosage

Horses

- 6.6 mg/kg q24h IV or IM.

Regulatory Information

Do not administer to animals intended for food or animals that produce food. Other drugs in this class require extra-label withdrawal times of 18 months.

Tocainide Hydrochloride

toe-kay'nide hye-droe-klor'ide

Trade and Other Names: Tonocard

Functional Classification: Antiarrhythmic

Pharmacology and Mechanism of Action

Antiarrhythmic drug. Tocainide is a Class-Ib antiarrhythmic. Like other Class I drugs, such as lidocaine, it blocks sodium channels in cardiac tissues and inhibits Phase 0 depolarization to suppress spontaneous depolarization.

Indications and Clinical Uses

Tocainide is an oral substitute used for treatment and control of ventricular arrhythmias. The use in veterinary medicine has been uncommon.

Precautionary Information

Adverse Reactions and Side Effects

In dogs, anorexia and GI toxicity have been reported. Arrhythmias, vomiting, and ataxia also are possible. (In one study, 35% of dogs showed GI effects.)

Contraindications and Precautions

Use cautiously in animals that are also receiving beta blockers. Do not use in patients with heart block.

Drug Interactions

No drug interactions have been reported for animals.

Instructions for Use

Tocainide has limited experience in animals. However, clinical studies demonstrate efficacy.

Patient Monitoring and Laboratory Tests

Therapeutic concentrations are 6-10 mcg/mL.

Formulations

Tocainide is available in 400 and 600 mg tablets.

Stability and Storage

Store in tightly sealed container, protected from light, and at room temperature.

Small Animal Dosage

Dogs

- 15-20 mg/kg q8h PO.

Cats

No dose established.

Large Animal Dosage

No dose has been reported for large animals.

Regulatory Information

No regulatory information is available. For extralabel use withdrawal interval estimates, contact FARAD at 1-888-USFARAD (1-888-873-2723) or send e-mail to FARAD@ncsu.edu.

RCI Classification: 4

Toltrazuril

tole-traz'yoo'ril

Trade and Other Names: Baycox

Functional Classification: Antiprotozoal

T

Pharmacology and Mechanism of Action

Antiprotozoal drug. Coccidiostat. Toltrazuril is a triazinone effective for *Isospora* and coccidiosis, *Toxoplasma gondii*, and *Eimeria* spp. Toltrazuril is a derivative of another drug, ponazuril, that is also used for the same conditions. Toltrazuril sulfone (ponazuril) is found in serum and cerebral spinal fluid (CSF) of treated horses. See section on ponazuril for more details.

Indications and Clinical Uses

Toltrazuril has been used as a treatment of equine protozoal myeloencephalitis (EPM) caused by *Sarcocystis neurona*. However, it is recommended to use an approved drug, ponazuril (Marquis), for treatment of horses.

Precautionary Information

Adverse Reactions and Side Effects

Administration of 50 mg/kg to horses (five times and 10 times the recommended dose) produced minor adverse effects according to manufacturer. There were minimal changes in the serum analysis.

Contraindications and Precautions

No contraindications are reported for animals.

Drug Interactions

No drug interactions have been reported in animals.

Instructions for Use

Although toltrazuril has been used in horses, the registered drug ponazuril is preferred for use.

Patient Monitoring and Laboratory Tests

No specific monitoring is necessary.

Formulations

Toltrazuril is not currently available in commercial formulations in the U.S. for horses. It is available in suspension for poultry in other countries and has been imported to the U.S. after permission from the FDA.

Stability and Storage

Store in tightly sealed container, protected from light, and at room temperature. Stability of compounded formulations has not been evaluated.

Small Animal Dosage

None reported for small animals.

Large Animal Dosage

Horses

- EPM caused by *S. neurona:* 5-10 mg/kg (7.5 for most horses) q24h PO, for minimum of 30 days.

Regulatory Information

No regulatory information is available. For extralabel use withdrawal interval estimates, contact FARAD at 1-888-USFARAD (1-888-873-2723) or send e-mail to FARAD@ncsu.edu.

Tramadol Hydrochloride

tram'ah-dole

Trade and Other Names: Ultram and generic brands

Functional Classification: Analgesic

Pharmacology and Mechanism of Action

Analgesic. Tramadol has some mu-opioid receptor action, and it may also inhibit the reuptake of norepinephrine (NE) and serotonin (5 HT). One of the isomers has greater effect on 5 HT reuptake and greater affinity for mu-opiate receptors.

The other isomer is more potent for NE reuptake and less active for inhibiting 5 HT reuptake. Taken together, the effects of tramadol may be explained through inhibition of 5 HT reuptake (similar to fluoxetine and other antidepressant drugs), action on alpha$_2$ receptors (similar to medetomidine and xylazine), and also activity for opiate mu receptors (similar to morphine). The metabolite (desmethyltramadol, also called M1) may have greater opiate effects than the parent drug (for example, 200 times in opiate receptor binding and six times more potent for analgesia than tramadol). Therefore, analgesic action may be attributed to opiate mediated effects from the active metabolite. Oral administration of tramadol in dogs, horses, and cats indicate that the M1 metabolite is produced by all species, with the highest levels appearing in cats.

Indications and Clinical Uses

Tramadol is used to treat pain. It is an alternative to pure opiate analgesics and nonsteroidal antiinflammatory drugs (NSAIDs) in patients that require treatment for mild to moderate pain. It is considered a mild analgesic, but it can safely be used with other analgesic drugs (including NSAIDs) for multimodal therapy. Tramadol has been used in dogs, cats, and horses. Tramadol, through its serotonin effects may be active as a behavior-modifying drug (similar to other antidepressants), however, this action has not been investigated for animals.

Precautionary Information

Adverse Reactions and Side Effects

Sedation may occur in some animals, especially at high doses. In cats, some vomiting, behavior changes, and mydriasis may be observed at high doses. At very high doses in dogs, seizures may occur. It is only partially antagonized by naloxone.

Contraindications and Precautions

Use cautiously with other drugs that have CNS depressing effects, such as opiates, alpha$_2$ agonists, or serotonin uptake inhibitors (for example, antidepressant and behavior-modifying drugs). Tramadol may potentiate their actions. Metabolites may be eliminated via the urine. Use with caution in animals with renal disease, or seizure disorders.

Drug Interactions

No drug interactions have been reported in animals. However, because of multiple effects from tramadol (serotonin reuptake inhibition, adrenergic effects, and opiate effects) interactions are possible with other drugs that act via similar mechanisms.

Instructions for Use

Dosing information is based on experimental studies in dogs, cats, and horses and experimental efficacy studies. Dosing information is also derived from clinical experience in dogs.

Tramadol extended-release (ER) tablets have been used in people but in dogs these tablets show delayed absorption and plasma levels 5 times less than people at equivalent (mg/kg) doses. Therefore, ER tablets for people may be inequitable in dogs and cats.

Patient Monitoring and Laboratory Tests

No specific monitoring is necessary. However, owners should watch for signs of pain and side effects caused from opiate and other sedative drugs.

Formulations

Tramadol immediate release tablets are available in 50 mg tablets.
Tramadol extended-release (ER) is available in 100, 200, or 300 mg tablets.

Stability and Storage

Store in tightly sealed container, protected from light, and at room temperature. Tramadol is water soluble. When mixed with aqueous vehicles has maintained potency and been stable for weeks. However, stability of compounded formulations that may contain flavorings and other excipients has not been evaluated.

Small Animal Dosage

Dogs

- 5 mg/kg q6h to q8h PO.

Cats

- 2 mg/kg q12h PO.

Large Animal Dosage

Horses

- 10 to 24 mg/kg q12h PO.

Regulatory Information

No regulatory information is available. For extralabel use withdrawal interval estimates, contact FARAD at 1-888-USFARAD (1-888-873-2723) or send e-mail to FARAD@ncsu.edu.

RCI Classification: 2

Trandolapril

tran-doe'lah-pril

Trade and Other Names: Mavik

Functional Classification: Vasodilator, angiotensin-converting enzyme (ACE) inhibitor

Pharmacology and Mechanism of Action

Like other ACE inhibitors, it inhibits conversion of angiotensin I to angiotensin II. Angiotensin II is a potent vasoconstrictor and will stimulate sympathetic stimulation, renal hypertension, and synthesis of aldosterone. The ability of aldosterone to cause sodium and water retention contributes to congestion. Trandolapril, like other ACE inhibitors, will cause vasodilation and decrease aldosterone-induced congestion; but ACE inhibitors also contribute to vasodilation by increasing concentrations of some vasodilating kinins and prostaglandins. Trandolapril is converted to active trandolaprilat after administration.

Indications and Clinical Uses

Trandolapril, like other ACE inhibitors, is used for treatment of hypertension and for management of CHF. Compared to other ACE inhibitors, such as enalapril, it is not used commonly in veterinary medicine.

Precautionary Information

Adverse Reactions and Side Effects

Trandolapril may cause azotemia in some patients; carefully monitor patients receiving high doses of diuretics.

Contraindications and Precautions

Use cautiously with other hypotensive drugs and diuretics. Nonsteroidal antiinflammatory drugs (NSAIDs) may decrease vasodilating effects. Discontinue ACE inhibitors in pregnant animal; they cross the placenta and have caused fetal malformations and death of the fetus.

Drug Interactions

Use cautiously with other hypotensive drugs and diuretics. NSAIDs may decrease vasodilating effects.

Instructions for Use

Not used extensively in veterinary patients. Most of the experience has been extrapolated from uses in people.

Patient Monitoring and Laboratory Tests

Monitor patients carefully to avoid hypotension. With all ACE inhibitors, monitor electrolytes and renal function 3-7 days after initiating therapy and periodically thereafter.

Formulations Available

Trandolapril is available in 1, 2, and 4 mg tablets.

Stability and Storage

Store in tightly sealed container, protected from light, and at room temperature. Stabilty of compounded formulations has not been evaluated.

Small Animal Dosage

The dose has not been established for dogs. Dose in people is 1 mg/person/day to start, then increase to 2-4 mg/day.

Large Animal Dosage

No dose has been reported for large animals.

Regulatory Information

No regulatory information is available. For extralabel use withdrawal interval estimates, contact FARAD at 1-888-USFARAD (1-888-873-2723) or send e-mail to FARAD@ncsu.edu.

Triamcinolone Acetonide, Triamcinolone Hexacetonide, Triamcinolone Diacetate

trye-am-sin'oh-lone

Trade and Other Names: Vetalog, Triamtabs, Aristocort, and generic brands

Functional Classification: Corticosteroid

Pharmacology and Mechanism of Action

Glucocorticoid antiinflammatory drug. Antiinflammatory effects are complex, but they are primarily via inhibition of inflammatory cells and suppression of expression of inflammatory mediators. There is disagreement on the potency of triamcinolone. Most human references indicate that triamcinolone has potency that is approximately equal to methylprednisolone (about five times cortisol and 1.25 times prednisolone).

However, many veterinary dermatologists suggest that potency is higher—six to 10 times more potent than prednisolone or approximately equal to dexamethasone. Triamcinolone acetonide is an injectable suspension that is slowly absorbed from intramuscular or intralesional injection site.

Indications and Clinical Uses

Triamcinolone, like other corticosteroids, is used to treat inflammatory and immune-mediated diseases in animals. It is used for similar purposes as prednisolone. The long-acting injectable formulation (triamcinolone acetonide) is used for intralesional therapy of tumors and similar purposes as methylprednisolone acetate. Large animal uses include treatment of inflammatory conditions and of recurrent airway obstruction (RAO), formerly called chronic obstructive pulmonary disease (COPD) in horses. Triamcinolone acetonide is also given intra-articularly to horses for treatment of arthritis.

Precautionary Information

Adverse Reactions and Side Effects

Side effects from corticosteroids are many and include polyphagia, polydipsia/polyuria, and hypothalamic-pituitary adrenal (HPA) axis suppression. Adverse effects include GI ulceration, hepatopathy, diabetes, hyperlipidemia, decreased thyroid hormone, decreased protein synthesis, impaired wound healing, and immunosuppression. When triamcinolone acetonide is used for ocular injections, there is some concern that granulomas may occur at injection site. In horses, adverse effects include increased risk of laminitis in horses.

Contraindications and Precautions

Use cautiously in patients prone to ulcers, infection, or in animals in which wound healing is necessary. Use cautiously, in diabetic animals, animals with renal failure, or pregnant animals.

Drug Interactions

Use cautiously, if at all, with nonsteroidal antiinflammatory drugs (NSAIDs), because it may potentiate the GI toxicity.

Instructions for Use

Triamcinolone, like other corticosteroids such as prednisolone, is administered in a variety of doses, depending on the severity of the condition being treated. Note that cats may require higher doses than dogs (sometimes twice as high).

Patient Monitoring and Laboratory Tests

Monitor liver enzymes, blood glucose, and renal function during therapy. Monitor patients for signs of secondary infections. Perform adrenocorticotropic hormone (ACTH) stimulation test to monitor adrenal function.

Formulations

Vetalog (veterinary preparation) is available in 0.5 and 1.5 mg tablets. Human preparation of triamcinolone is available in 1, 2, 4, 8, and 16 mg tablets and 10 mg/mL injection.

Triamcinolone acetonide is available in 2 and 6 mg/mL suspension injections.

Triamcinolone hexacetonide is available in 20 mg/mL suspension.

Triamcinolone diacetate is available in 25 mg/mL suspension.

Stability and Storage

Store in tightly sealed container, protected from light, and at room temperature. Stability of compounded formulations has not been evaluated.

Small Animal Dosage

- Antiinflammatory: 0.5-1 mg/kg q12-24h PO, then taper dose to 0.5-1 mg/kg q48h PO. (However, manufacturer recommends doses of 0.11 to 0.22 mg/kg/day.)
- Dermatologists have used triamcinolone tablets at doses of 0.2-0.6 mg/kg/day for treatment of immune-mediated diseases, with maintenance doses of 0.1-0.2 mg/kg q48h, PO.
- Triamcinolone acetonide: 0.1-0.2 mg/kg IM or SQ, repeat in 7-10 days.
- Intralesional: 1.2-1.8 mg or 1 mg for every cm diameter of tumor q2wks.

Large Animal Dosage

Horses

- 0.5-1.0 mg/kg q12-24h PO.
- Triamcinolone acetonide suspension: 0.022-0.044 mg/kg as a single dose IM.
- Recurrent airway obstruction (RAO): 0.09 mg/kg IM as a single dose.
- Intra-articular: 6-18 mg as a total dose (usually 12 mg). Repeat in 4-13 days if necessary.

Cattle

- Induction of parturition: 0.016 mg/kg IM, 1 week before induction of parturition with dexamethasone.

Regulatory Information

No regulatory information is available. For extralabel use withdrawal interval estimates, contact FARAD at 1-888-USFARAD (1-888-873-2723) or send e-mail to FARAD@ncsu.edu.

RCI Classification: 4

Triamterene

trye-am′ter-een

Trade and Other Names: Dyrenium

Functional Classification: Diuretic

T

Pharmacology and Mechanism of Action

Potassium-sparing diuretic. Triamterene has similar action to spironolactone, except that spironolactone has competitive inhibiting effect on aldosterone, triamterene does not.

Indications and Clinical Uses

Triamterene has been used infrequently in veterinary medicine. For treating congestive diseases, spironolactone is used more frequently.

Precautionary Information

Adverse Reactions and Side Effects

Triamterene can produce hyperkalemia in some patients.

Contraindications and Precautions

Do not use in dehydrated patients. Nonsteroidal antiinflammatory drugs (NSAIDs) may interfere with action. Avoid supplements that are high in potassium.

Drug Interactions

No specific drug interactions are reported for animals. However, use cautiously with other drugs that may contain potassium or cause potassium retention. Such drugs include trimethoprim.

Instructions for Use

There is little clinical experience available for triamterene. There is no convincing evidence that triamterene is more effective than spironolactone.

Patient Monitoring and Laboratory Tests

Monitor hydration status, serum potassium levels, and renal function.

Formulations

Triamterene is available in 50 and 100 mg capsules.

Stability and Storage

Store in tightly sealed container, protected from light, and at room temperature. Stability of compounded formulations has not been evaluated.

Small Animal Dosage

Dogs and Cats

- 1-2 mg/kg q12h PO.

Large Animal Dosage

No dose has been reported for large animals.

Regulatory Information

No regulatory information is available. For extralabel use withdrawal interval estimates, contact FARAD at 1-888-USFARAD (1-888-873-2723) or send e-mail to FARAD@ncsu.edu.

RCI Classification: 4

Trientine Hydrochloride

trye-en′teen hye-droe-klor′ide

Trade and Other Names: Syprine

Functional Classification: Antidote

Pharmacology and Mechanism of Action

Chelating agent. Trientine chelates copper to enhance its clearance.

Indications and Clinical Uses

Trientine is used to chelate copper when penicillamine cannot be tolerated in a patient.

Precautionary Information

Adverse Reactions and Side Effects

Adverse effects have not been reported in animals.

Contraindications and Precautions

No contraindications are reported for animals.

Drug Interactions

No drug interactions have been reported in animals.

Instructions for Use

Trientine is used only in patients that cannot tolerate penicillamine. It usually induces less cupruresis than penicillamine.

Patient Monitoring and Laboratory Tests

Monitor copper levels in treated patients.

Formulations

Trientine is available in 250 mg capsules.

Stability and Storage

Store in tightly sealed container, protected from light, and at room temperature. Stability of compounded formulations has not been evaluated.

Small Animal Dosage

Dogs

- 10-15 mg/kg q12h PO.

Large Animal Dosage

No dose has been reported for large animals.

Regulatory Information

No regulatory information is available. For extralabel use withdrawal interval estimates, contact FARAD at 1-888-USFARAD (1-888-873-2723) or send e-mail to FARAD@ncsu.edu.

Trifluoperazine Hydrochloride

trye-floo-oh-pare'ah-zeen hye-droe-klor'ide

Trade and Other Names: Stelazine

Functional Classification: Antiemetic, Phenothiazine

T

Pharmacology and Mechanism of Action

Phenothiazine. Like other phenothiazines, it is a central acting dopamine (D_2) antagonist and suppresses dopamine activity in the CNS to produce sedation and prevent vomiting. Other phenothiazines include acepromazine, chlorpromazine, perphenazine, prochlorperazine, promazine, propiopromazine and triflupromazine.

Indications and Clinical Uses

Trifluoperazine is used for treatment of anxiety, to produce sedation, and as an antiemetic. It is a weaker sedative than some of the other phenothiazines. In people it is used to treat psychotic disorders.

Precautionary Information

Adverse Reactions and Side Effects

Adverse effects not reported in animals but are expected to be similar to other phenothiazines. Phenothiazines can lower the seizure threshold in susceptible animals. They can also cause sedation as a common side effect and extrapyramidal side effects (involuntary muscle movements) in some individuals.

Contraindications and Precautions

Use cautiously in patients that are hypotensive.

Drug Interactions

No drug interactions have been reported in animals. However, these drugs may be subject to cytochrome P450 drug interactions.

Instructions for Use

Results of clinical studies in animals have not been reported. Use in animals (and doses) is based on experience in people or anecdotal experience in animals.

Patient Monitoring and Laboratory Tests

No specific monitoring is necessary.

Formulations

Trifluoperazine is available in 10 mg/mL oral solution, 1, 2, 5, and 10 mg tablets, and 2 mg/mL injections.

Stability and Storage

Store in tightly sealed container, protected from light, and at room temperature. Trifluoperazine is soluble in water and slightly soluble in ethanol. It is oxidized rapidly if exposed to air or light.

Small Animal Dosage

Dogs and Cats

- 0.03 mg/kg q12h IM.

Large Animal Dosage

No dose has been reported for large animals.

Regulatory Information

No regulatory information is available. For extralabel use withdrawal interval estimates, contact FARAD at 1-888-USFARAD (1-888-873-2723) or send e-mail to FARAD@ncsu.edu.

RCI Classification: 2

Triflupromazine Hydrochloride

trye-floo-proe'mah-zeen hye-droe-klor'ide

Trade and Other Names: Vesprin and Fluopromazine (former name)

Functional Classification: Antiemetic, Phenothiazine

Pharmacology and Mechanism of Action

Phenothiazine. Central acting dopamine (D_2) antagonist. Triflupromazine suppresses dopamine activity in the CNS to produce sedation and prevent vomiting.

Monitor sodium and potassium concentrations in treated dogs. If necessary, supplement with potassium because of aldosterone inhibition.

Formulations

There are no formulations available in the U.S. Trilostane has been imported from Europe in 60 mg capsules with permission from FDA. European brand is Vetoryl (Arnold Veterinary Products, UK).

Stability and Storage

Store in tightly sealed container, protected from light, and at room temperature. Stability of compounded formulations has not been evaluated.

Small Animal Dosage

Dogs

- 6 mg/kg/day PO, (range of 4-9 mg/kg/day). Adjust dose based on cortisol measurements.
- Dogs <5kg: 30 mg q24h PO.
- Dogs 5-20 kg: 60 mg q24h PO.
- Dogs >20 kg: 120 mg, q24h PO.
- Dose interval: twice daily treatment has been considered in some dogs with an average dose of 3 mg/kg q12h PO.
- Treatment of Alopecia-X: 9-12 mg/kg/day PO.

Cats

- 6 mg/kg q24h PO, and gradually increase (as needed) to 10 mg/kg q24h.

Large Animal Dosage

Horses

- 0.4-1.0 mg/kg/day PO (added to feed).

Regulatory Information

Trilostane is not approved for use in the U.S. It should not be used in animals that produce food.

Trimeprazine Tartrate

trye-mep′rah-zeen tar′trate

Trade and Other Names: Temaril, Panectyl (in Canada), and Temaril-P (with prednisolone)

Functional Classification: Antiemetic, Phenothiazine

T

Pharmacology and Mechanism of Action

Phenothiazine with antihistamine activity. It has actions similar to other antihistamines, but it also produces sedation similar to other phenothiazines.

Indications and Clinical Uses

Trimeprazine is used alone, or in combination with corticosteroids, for inflammatory and allergic problems. The most common use is for pruritus in dogs. It also has been used for treating motion sickness. The combination product, Temaril-P with prednisolone, is used to treat pruritus in animals. Therapeutic effect is attributed to combined antihistamine and sedative effect of trimeprazine and the antiinflammatory effect of prednisolone. This combination may be more effective for pruritus than prednisolone alone.

Precautionary Information

Adverse Reactions and Side Effects

Adverse effects are attributed to the antihistamine and phenothiazine effects. The most common is sedation, but ataxia and behavior changes also can occur.

Contraindications and Precautions

Phenothiazines can potentially lower seizure threshold in sensitive animals, although this effect has not been reported for trimeprazine.

Drug Interactions

No drug interactions are reported for animals.

Instructions for Use

There is evidence that trimeprazine is more effective when combined with prednisolone for treatment of pruritus. Combination product is Temaril-P, which contains trimeprazine and prednisolone.

Patient Monitoring and Laboratory Tests

No specific monitoring is necessary.

Formulations

Trimeprazine is available in 2.5 mg/5 mL syrup and 2.5 mg tablets.
Temaril-P is available in tablets that contain 5 mg trimeprazine + 2 mg prednisolone.

Stability and Storage

Store in tightly sealed container, protected from light, and at room temperature.

Small Animal Dosage

Dogs and Cats

- 0.5 mg/kg q12h PO.

Large Animal Dosage

No dose has been reported for large animals.

Regulatory Information

No regulatory information is available. For extralabel use withdrawal interval estimates, contact FARAD at 1-888-USFARAD (1-888-873-2723) or send e-mail to FARAD@ncsu.edu.

RCI Classification: 4

Trimethobenzamide

trye-meth-oh-ben′zah-mide

Trade and Other Names: Tigan

Functional Classification: Antiemetic

Pharmacology and Mechanism of Action

Antiemetic. Trimethobenzamide inhibits vomiting at the chemoreceptor trigger zone (CRTZ).

Indications and Clinical Uses

Trimethobenzamide is used for antiemetic treatment, especially when vomiting is induced from the CRTZ (e.g., from chemotherapeutic drugs).

Precautionary Information

Adverse Reactions and Side Effects

Adverse effects not reported in animals.

Contraindications and Precautions

Not recommended for use in cats.

Drug Interactions

No drug interactions have been reported in animals.

Instructions for Use

Efficacy as antiemetic not reported in animals.

Patient Monitoring and Laboratory Tests

No specific monitoring is necessary.

Formulations

Trimethobenzamide is available in 100 mg/mL injections and 100 and 250 mg capsules.

Stability and Storage

Store in tightly sealed container, protected from light, and at room temperature.

Small Animal Dosage

Dogs

- 3 mg/kg q8h IM or PO.

Cats

Not recommended.

Large Animal Dosage

No dose has been reported for large animals.

Regulatory Information

Because of low risk of harmful residues in animals intended for food, no withdrawal time is suggested.

Trimethoprim + Sulfadiazine

trye-meth′oh-prim + sul-fah-dye′ah-zeen

Trade and Other Names: Tribrissen, Uniprim, Tucoprim, and Di-Trim

Functional Classification: Antibacterial

Pharmacology and Mechanism of Action

Trimethoprim sulfonamides combine the antibacterial drug action of trimethoprim and a sulfonamide. The combination is synergistic with a broad spectrum of activity. Used for treatment of UTIs, wound infections, protozoal infections (e.g., toxoplasmosis), skin infections, prostate infections, and infections of the CNS.

Trimethoprim has been combined with both sulfadiazine and sulfamethoxazole. Trimethoprim + sulfadiazine is only available as a veterinary preparation; trimethoprim + sulfamethoxazole is a human preparation. There are no published reports of differences in efficacy between trimethoprim + sulfadiazine versus trimethoprim + sulfamethoxazole. The primary difference between sulfamethoxazole and sulfadiazine is that sulfamethoxazole is metabolized more extensively and sulfadiazine may attain higher active urine concentrations in some patients.

Indications and Clinical Uses

Trimethoprim + sulfadiazine is used to treat a variety of infections in dogs, cats, horses, and some exotic animals. The combination has efficacy for susceptible bacterial infections (gram-negative and gram-positive), including pneumonia, soft tissue and skin infections, and UTIs. In horses, they have been used for respiratory infections, joint infections, abdominal infections, and soft tissue infections. The combination has not been successful for treating infections in abscesses or infections caused by anaerobic bacteria. The combination also is used occasionally for infections caused by protozoa (e.g., coccidial and *Toxoplasma* infections).

Precautionary Information

Adverse Reactions and Side Effects

Adverse effects associated with sulfonamides include allergic reactions, Type II and Type III hypersensitivity, arthropathy, anemia, thrombocytopenia, hepatopathy, keratoconjunctivitis sicca, and skin reactions. Dogs may be more sensitive to sulfonamides than other animals because dogs lack the ability to acetylate sulfonamides to metabolites. Other, more toxic metabolites may persist. Trimethoprim sulfonamides may decrease thyroid hormone after treatment in dogs. Effects on thyroid function are most apparent after 2 weeks of treatment, but they are reversible.

Contraindications and Precautions

Do not administer in animals with sensitivity to sulfonamides. Doberman pinschers may be more sensitive than other species to reactions to sulfonamides. Use cautiously in this species.

Drug Interactions

Sulfonamides may interact with other drugs, including warfarin, methenamine, dapsone and etodolac. They may potentiate adverse effects caused by methotrexate and pyrimethamine. Sulfonamides will increase metabolism of cyclosporine resulting in decreased plasma concentrations. Methenamine is metabolized to formaldehyde that may form a complex and precipitate with sulfonamides. Sulfonamides administered to horses that are receiving detomidine may develop cardiac arrhythmias. This precaution is only listed for intravenous forms of trimethoprim-sulfonamides.

Instructions for Use

Dose listed is of the combined components; 30 mg/kg = 5 mg/kg trimethoprim and 25 mg sulfonamide. There is evidence that 30 mg/kg/day is efficacious for pyoderma; for other infections, 30 mg/kg twice daily has been recommended. Oral trimethoprim is not absorbed in ruminants.

Patient Monitoring and Laboratory Tests

Culture and sensitivity testing: CLSI (NCCLS) break point for sensitive organisms is less than or equal to 2/38 mcg/mL. For streptococci, this break point is less than or equal to 2/38 mcg/mL. Values listed are the concentration of trimethoprim/ sulfonamide ratio. Trimethoprim sulfonamides may affect the monitoring of thyroid hormones. In dogs, trimethoprim + sulfadiazine may cause a functional hypothyroidism and lower total T-4 concentrations. Trimethoprim + sulfamethoxazole decreased thyroid function at 30 mg/kg q12h and also at 15 mg/kg q12h. Trimethoprim + sulfadiazine at 15 mg/kg q12h for 4 weeks did not affect thyroid function in one study. Effects of trimethoprim sulfonamides on thyroid function in dogs are reversible. In horses, trimethoprim + sulfadiazine did not affect assays of thyroid function.

Formulations

Trimethoprim + sulfadiazine is available in 30, 120, 240, 480, and 960 mg tablets. (All formulations have ratio of 5 to 1, sulfadiazine to trimethoprim.) It is also available as an oral paste for horses. As a powder for horses, each gram contains 67 mg trimethoprim and 333 mg of sulfadiazine.

Stability and Storage

Store in tightly sealed container, protected from light, and at room temperature. Stability of compounded formulations has not been evaluated.

Small Animal Dosage

Dogs and Cats

(doses listed as the combined sulfonamide + trimethoprim)

- 15 mg/kg q12h PO or 30 mg/kg q12-24h PO.
- *Toxoplasma:* 30 mg/kg q12h PO.

Large Animal Dosage

Horses

- 30 mg/kg (25 mg sulfonamide + 5 mg trimethoprim) q12h PO for acute treatment. For some infections, treatment once a day at 30 mg/kg may be sufficient.

Cattle

No dose established. Trimethoprim is not absorbed orally in ruminants, but it is absorbed in calves. Trimethoprim + sulfadoxine has been used in cattle (16 mg/kg combined drug every 24 hours IV or IM), but this drug is not available in the U.S.

Regulatory Information

Withdrawal times are not available. Extralabel use of sulfonamides is prohibited from use in lactating dairy cattle.

Trimethoprim + Sulfamethoxazole

trye-meth'oh-prim + sul-fah-meth-oks'ah-zole

Trade and Other Names: Bactrim, Septra, and generic brands

Functional Classification: Antibacterial

Pharmacology and Mechanism of Action

Trimethoprim sulfonamides combine the antibacterial drug action of trimethoprim and a sulfonamide. The combination is synergistic with a broad spectrum of activity. Trimethoprim + sulfamethoxazole is used for treatment of UTIs, wound infections, protozoal infections (e.g., toxoplasmosis), skin infections, prostate infections, and infections of the CNS. Trimethoprim has been combined with both sulfadiazine and sulfamethoxazole. Trimethoprim + sulfadiazine is only available as a veterinary preparation; trimethoprim + sulfamethoxazole is a human preparation. There are no published reports of differences in efficacy between trimethoprim + sulfadiazine versus trimethoprim + sulfamethoxazole. The primary difference between sulfamethoxazole and sulfadiazine is that sulfamethoxazole is metabolized more extensively. Sulfadiazine may attain higher active urine concentrations in some patients.

Indications and Clinical Uses

Trimethoprim + sulfamethoxazole is used to treat a variety of infections in dogs, cats, horses, and some exotic animals. The combination has efficacy for susceptible bacterial infections (gram-negative and gram-positive), including pneumonia, soft tissue and skin infections, and UTIs. In horses, they have been used for respiratory infections, joint infections, abdominal infections, and soft tissue infections. The combination has not been successful for treating infections in abscesses or infections caused by anaerobic bacteria. The combination also is used occasionally for infections caused by protozoa (e.g., coccidial and *Toxoplasma* infections).

Precautionary Information

Adverse Reactions and Side Effects

Adverse effects associated with sulfonamides include allergic reactions, Type II and Type III hypersensitivity, arthropathy, anemia, thrombocytopenia, hepatopathy, keratoconjunctivitis sicca, and skin reactions. Dogs may be more sensitive to sulfonamides than other animals because dogs lack the ability to acetylate sulfonamides to metabolites. Other, more toxic metabolites may persist. Trimethoprim sulfonamides may decrease thyroid hormone after treatment in dogs. Effects on thyroid function are most apparent after 2 weeks of treatment, but they are reversible.

Contraindications and Precautions

Do not administer in animals with sensitivity to sulfonamides. Doberman pinschers may be more sensitive than other species to reactions to sulfonamides. Use cautiously in this species. The injectable preparation contains benzyl alcohol which may cause reactions in small patients. The injectable preparation should be diluted and injected slowly IV.

Drug Interactions

Sulfonamides may interact with other drugs, including warfarin, methenamine, dapsone, and etodolac. They may potentiate adverse effects caused by methotrexate and pyrimethamine. Sulfonamides will increase metabolism of cyclosporine resulting in decreased plasma concentrations. Methenamine is metabolized to formaldehyde that may form a complex and precipitate with sulfonamides. Sulfonamides administered to horses that are receiving detomidine may develop cardiac arrhythmias. This precaution is only listed for intravenous forms of trimethoprim-sulfonamides.

Instructions for Use

Dose listed is of the combined components; 30 mg/kg = 5 mg/kg trimethoprim and 25 mg sulfonamide. There is evidence that 30 mg/kg/day is efficacious for pyoderma; for other infections, 30 mg/kg twice daily has been recommended. When using the injectable formulation, each 5 mL vial should be diluted in 75-125 mL of 5% dextrose. The diluted formulation should then be administered by intravenous infusion over 60 minutes.

Patient Monitoring and Laboratory Tests

Culture and sensitivity testing: CLSI (NCCLS) break point for sensitive organisms is less than or equal to 2/38 mcg/mL. For streptococci, this break point is less than or equal to 2/38 mcg/mL. Values listed are the concentration of trimethoprim/sulfonamide ratio. In dogs, trimethoprim + sulfadiazine may cause a functional hypothyroidism and lower total T-4 concentrations. Trimethoprim + sulfamethoxazole decreased thyroid function at 30 mg/kg q12h and also at 15 mg/kg q12h. Trimethoprim + sulfadiazine at 15 mg/kg q12h for 4 weeks did not affect thyroid function in one study. Effects of trimethoprim sulfonamides on thyroid function in dogs are reversible. In horses, trimethoprim + sulfadiazine did not affect assays of thyroid function.

Formulations

Trimethoprim + sulfamethoxazole is available in 480 and 960 mg tablets and 240 mg/5 mL oral suspension (all formulations have ratio of 5:1 sulfamethoxazole to trimethoprim).

As an injection, it is available as 80 mg sulfamethoxazole and 16 mg trimethoprim per mL in 5 mL vials.

Stability and Storage

Store in tightly sealed container, protected from light, and at room temperature. Injectable formulations should be stored at room temperature and not refrigerated. Injectable formulation contains 0.3% sodium hydroxide.

Small Animal Dosage

Dogs and Cats

(doses listed as the combined sulfonamide + trimethoprim)

- 15 mg/kg q12h PO or 30 mg/kg q12-24h PO.
- 30 mg/kg q12h IV (see Instructions for Dosing section for preparation of intravenous formulation).

Large Animal Dosage

Horses

- 30 mg/kg (25 mg sulfonamide + 5 mg trimethoprim) q12h PO for acute treatment. For some infections, treatment once a day at 30 mg/kg may be sufficient.

Cattle

No dose is established. Trimethoprim is not absorbed orally in ruminants, but it is absorbed in calves. Trimethoprim + sulfadoxine has been used in cattle (16 mg/kg combined drug every 24 hours IV or IM), but this drug is not available in the U.S.

Regulatory Information

Extralabel use of sulfonamides is prohibited from use in lactating dairy cattle. However, trimethoprim + sulfadoxine has a withdrawal time in Canada for cattle of 10 days (meat) and 96 hours (milk).

Tripelennamine Citrate

tri-peh-len'eh-meen sih'trate

Trade and Other Names: Pelamine and PBZ

Functional Classification: Antihistamine

Pharmacology and Mechanism of Action

Antihistamine (H_1 blocker). Similar to other antihistamines, tripelennamine acts by blocking the histamine type 1 receptor (H_1) and suppresses inflammatory reactions caused by histamine. The H_1 blockers have been used to control pruritus and skin inflammation in dogs and cats; however, success rates in dogs have not been high. More commonly used antihistamines include clemastine, chlorpheniramine, diphenhydramine, and hydroxyzine.

Indications and Clinical Uses

Tripelennamine is used to prevent allergic reactions and for pruritus therapy in dogs and cats. However, success rates for treatment of pruritus have not been high. In addition to the antihistamine effect for treating allergies, these drugs block the effect of histamine in the vomiting center, vestibular center, and other centers that control vomiting in animals.

Precautionary Information

Adverse Reactions and Side Effects

Sedation is most common side effect. Antimuscarinic effects (atropine-like effects) also are common. Members of this class (ethanolamines) have greater antimuscarinic effects than other antihistamines. GI adverse effects may occur, such as ileus and decreased stomach emptying.

Contraindications and Precautions

No contraindications are reported for animals.

Drug Interactions

No drug interactions are reported for animals.

Instructions for Use

There are no clinical reports of use in veterinary medicine. No evidence that it is more efficacious than other drugs in this class.

Patient Monitoring and Laboratory Tests

No specific monitoring is necessary.

Formulations

Tripelennamine is available in 25 and 50 mg tablets, 20 mg/mL injections (generic), and 5 mg/mL elixir oral liquid.

Stability and Storage

Store in tightly sealed container, protected from light, and at room temperature.

Small Animal Dosage

Dogs and Cats

The dose is not clearly established. It has been listed as 1 mg/kg q12h PO. In humans, the dose is 1.25 mg/kg q4-6h PO.

Large Animal Dosage

No dose has been reported for large animals.

Regulatory Information

No regulatory information is available. For extralabel use withdrawal interval estimates, contact FARAD at 1-888-USFARAD (1-888-873-2723) or send e-mail to FARAD@ncsu.edu.

RCI Classification: 3

Tulathromycin

too-lath-roe-mye'sin

Trade and Other Names: Antibacterial and Macrolide

Functional Classification: Draxxin

Pharmacology and Mechanism of Action

Antibacterial related to the macrolide class of drugs. It is considered a triamilide macrolide, which is derived from azalide macrolides, such as azithromycin. Like other macrolides it inhibits bacterial protein synthesis by binding to the ribosomal 50S subunit. It is considered bacteriostatic, but it may have bactericidal properties in vitro. Because of a positively charged molecule, it may penetrate gram-negative bacteria more easily than other macrolide antibiotics. Tulathromycin has a spectrum of activity that is limited to gram-positive bacteria and some gram-negative bacteria that cause respiratory diseases in cattle and pigs (e.g., *Mannheimia haemolytica* and *Pasteurella multocida*). It also is active against *Mycoplasma bovis.* The half-life is long (e.g., 92 hour plasma half-life and 8 day tissue half-life in cattle), which prolongs the drug concentration at the site of infection. Other antiinflammatory effects may explain the clinical effects for respiratory infections, such as reduced inflammatory effects from leukocytes.

Indications and Clinical Uses

In cattle, tulathromycin is used for treatment of bovine respiratory disease (BRD) caused by *Mannheimia haemolytica, Pasteurella multocida,* and *Histophilus somni* (formerly *Haemophilus somnus).* It also has been used to prevent infections caused by these pathogens when used prophylactically. Tulathromycin is also effective for treatment of *Mycoplasma bovis* infections in cattle. In pigs, it has been used for treatment of swine respiratory disease (SRD) associated with *Actinobacillus pleuropneumoniae, P. multocida, Bordetella bronchiseptica,* and *H. parasuis.*

Precautionary Information

Adverse Reactions and Side Effects

Serious adverse reactions have not been observed. Injection site reactions are possible in some animals with swelling or irritation at the injection site. High doses (five times the dose) produced myocardial lesions in some animals. However, most animals have tolerated up to 10 times the labeled dose without toxicity.

Contraindications and Precautions

No specific contraindications.

Drug Interactions

No drug interactions are reported.

Instructions for Use

In cattle, administer as a single subcutaneous injection in the neck. In pigs, administer as a single intramuscular injection in the neck.

Patient Monitoring and Laboratory Tests

CLSI (NCCLS) break point for susceptibility is less than or equal to 16.0 mcg/mL been established. For susceptibility testing, also use erythromycin as a guide.

Formulations

Tulathromycin is available in 100 mg/mL solution for injection.

Stability and Storage

Store in tightly sealed container, protected from light, and at room temperature.

Small Animal Dosage

No small animal doses have been established.

Large Animal Dosage

Cattle

- 2.5 mg/kg SQ (neck) as a single injection.

Pigs

- 2.5 mg/kg IM (neck) as a single injection.

Regulatory Information

No milk withdrawal times are established.

Do not use in female dairy cattle 20 months of age or older. Do not use in veal calves.

Cattle withdrawal time (meat): 18 days.

Pig withdrawal time (meat): 5 days.

Tylosin

tye'loe-sin

Trade and Other Names: Tylocine, Tylan, and Tylosin tartrate

Functional Classification: Antibacterial

Pharmacology and Mechanism of Action

Macrolide antibiotic. Like other macrolide antibiotics, tylosin inhibits bacteria by binding to 50S ribosome and inhibiting protein synthesis. Spectrum of activity limited primarily to gram-positive aerobic bacteria. *Clostridium* and *Campylobacter* are usually sensitive. *Escherichia coli* and *Salmonella* are resistant. In pigs, *Lawsonia intracellularis* is sensitive.

Indications and Clinical Uses

In cattle, tylosin is used for treatment of bovine respiratory disease (BRD) caused by *Mannheimia*, *Pasteurella Multocida*, and *Histophilus somni* (formerly *Haemophilus somnus*). It is used for interdigital necrobacillosis (foot rot) in cattle caused by *Fusobacterium necrophorum* or *Bacteroides melaninogenicus*. In pigs it is used for treatment of swine arthritis caused by *Mycoplasma hyosynoviae*, swine pneumonia caused by *Pasteurella* spp., swine erysipelas caused by *Erysipelothrix rhusiopathiae*, swine dysentery associated with *Serpulina (Treponema) hyodysenteriae* and proliferative enteropathy caused by *Lawsonia intracellularis*. Often in pigs it is added to feed or drinking water. In small animals, it is used for gram-positive soft tissue and skin infections. However, the most common use in dogs is for treatment of diarrhea, referred to as "antibiotic-responsive diarrhea" that has not responded to other antibiotics. The etiology of the diarrhea is not known but may be caused by *Clostridium* or *Camphylobacter*. For this use, the powdered formulation (swine formulation) is most often added to food daily for maintenance.

Precautionary Information

Adverse Reactions and Side Effects

Tylosin may cause diarrhea in some animals. However, oral treatment for colitis in dogs has been administered for several months with safety. Skin reactions have been observed in pigs. Administration to horses has been fatal.

Contraindications and Precautions

Do not administer orally to rodents or rabbits. Do not administer to horses. Avoid intravenous administration. Do not inject more than 10 mL in one intramuscular site.

Drug Interactions

No drug interactions are reported for animals.

Instructions for Use

Tylosin is used in pigs for managing respiratory tract infections. It is rarely used in small animals for uses other than intestinal disease. Powdered formulation (tylosin tartrate) has been administered on food for control of signs of colitis in dogs. Tablets are approved for treatment of colitis in Canada.

Patient Monitoring and Laboratory Tests

No specific monitoring is necessary.

Formulations

Tylosin is available in a soluble powder with 3 g/teaspoon (Tylosin-100). Tylosin tartrate is equal to 1.1g/1g of tylosin base. Also available as 50 and 200 mg/mL injection (with propylene glycol).

Stability and Storage

Store in tightly sealed container, protected from light, and at room temperature.

Small Animal Dosage

Dogs

- 7-15 mg/kg q12-24h PO.
- 8-11 mg/kg q12h IM.
- Colitis: 12-20 mg/kg q8h with food, then if there is a response increase the interval to q12h and eventually to q24h. (20 mg/kg is approximately 1/8 teaspoon of Tylan for a 20 kg dog.)

Cats

- 7-15 mg/kg q12-24h PO.
- 8-11 mg/kg q12h IM.

Large Animal Dosage

Swine

- Treatment of arthritis, erysipelas, and swine dysentery: 8.8 mg/kg q12h IM.

Cattle

- Pododermatitis and pneumonia: 17.6 mg/kg q24h IM.
- Swine: medicated feed dose is administered at a dose of 22-220 g/kg (of the premix), with dose depending on specific product. Consult package information.

Regulatory Information

Pig withdrawal time (meat): 14 days.
Cattle withdrawal time (meat): 21 days.
Not to be used in lactating cattle.

Urofollitropin

yoo-roe-fah'lih-troe-pin

Trade and Other Names: Metrodin, FSH, and Fertinex

Functional Classification: Hormone

Pharmacology and Mechanism of Action

Urofollitropin contains follicle stimulating hormone (FSH) and stimulates ovulation. In people it is used in combination with human chorionic gonadotropin (hCG) to stimulate ovulation.

Indications and Clinical Uses

Although urofollitropin is used in people in combination with hCG to stimulate ovulation, the use in animals is not common.

Precautionary Information

Adverse Reactions and Side Effects

Side effects have not been reported in animals. In people, thromboembolism or severe ovarian hyperstimulation syndrome has been reported. In humans, ovarian enlargement and ovarian cysts have been reported.

Contraindications and Precautions

Do **not** use in pregnant animals.

Drug Interactions

No drug interactions are reported for animals.

Instructions for Use

Results of clinical studies in animals have not been reported. Use in animals is extrapolated from the experience in people. Use in humans is followed by administration of hCG.

Patient Monitoring and Laboratory Tests

Monitor estrogen and/or progesterone with treatment.

Formulations

Urofollitropin is available in 75 units per vial for injection.

Stability and Storage

Store in tightly sealed container, protected from light, and at room temperature.

Small Animal Dosage

Doses not established. However, the usual human dose is 75 units/day IM for 7 days. This may be increased to 150 units/day IM for an additional 7 days.

Large Animal Dosage

Doses not established. However, the usual human dose is 75 units/day IM for 7 days. This may be increased to 150 units/day IM for an additional 7 days.

Regulatory Information

It is expected to pose little risk from residues in animals intended for food, and no withdrawal times are recommended.

Ursodiol, Ursodeoxycholic Acid

er-soe-dye'ole, er-soe-dee-oks-ih-koe-lik ass'id

Trade & Other Names: Actigall and Ursodeoxycholic acid

Functional Classification: Laxative, Choleretic

Pharmacology and Mechanism of Action

Hydrophilic bile acid. Anticholelithic and choleretic. Ursodiol is the short name for ursodeoxycholic acid. This is a naturally occurring, water-soluble bile acid. Ursodiol, like other bile acids, can act as a choleretic and increase bile flow. In dogs, it may alter pool of circulating bile acids, displacing the more hydrophobic bile acids or enhance their secretion in liver and bile. By modulating the composition of biliary bile salts in favor of more hydrophilic bile salts, injury to the biliary epithelium is less likely than with hydrophobic bile salts.

Indications and Clinical Uses

Ursodiol is used for treatment of liver diseases. It is used to treat primary biliary cirrhosis, cholestatic liver disorders, and chronic liver disease. Although experimental evidence exists for its benefit in dogs, there are no well-controlled clinical trials that demonstrate efficacy. In people it has been used as a laxative and to prevent or treat gallstones.

Precautionary Information

Adverse Reactions and Side Effects

Adverse effects not reported in animals. Ursodiol may cause diarrhea.

Contraindications and Precautions

No contraindications are reported for animals.

Drug Interactions

No drug interactions identified for animals.

Instructions for Use

Results of clinical studies in animals have not been reported. Use in animals (and doses) is based on experience in people or anecdotal experience in animals. Administer with meals.

Patient Monitoring and Laboratory Tests

Monitor bile acids and hepatic enzymes during treatment to monitor effects.

Formulations

Ursodiol is available in 300 mg capsules and 250 mg tablets.

Stability and Storage

Store in tightly sealed container, protected from light, and at room temperature. Suspensions have been prepared in vehicles for oral use and found to be stable for 35-60 days.

Small Animal Dosage

Dogs and Cats

- 10-15 mg/kg q24h PO.

Large Animal Dosage

No large animal doses are available.

Regulatory Information

It is expected to pose little risk from residues in animals intended for food, and no withdrawal times are recommended.

Valproic Acid, Valproate Sodium

val-proe'ik ass'id, val'proe-ate soe'dee-um

Trade and Other Names: Depakene (Valproic acid), Depakote (Divalproex), and Epival (in Canada)

Functional Classification: Anticonvulsant

Pharmacology and Mechanism of Action

Anticonvulsant. Action is not known, but valproate may increase GABA concentrations in the CNS. Both valproic acid and valproate sodium are used. Divalproex is composed of both valproic acid and sodium valproate. Equivalent oral doses of divalproex sodium and valproic acid deliver equivalent quantities of valproate ion.

Indications and Clinical Uses

Valproate is used, usually in combination with phenobarbital, to treat refractory epilepsy in animals. Most use has been in dogs, but limited efficacy studies have been reported.

Precautionary Information

Adverse Reactions and Side Effects

Adverse effects have not been reported in animals, but hepatic failure has been reported in people. Sedation may be seen in some animals.

Contraindications and Precautions

Do not use in pregnant animals.

Drug Interactions

Valproate may cause bleeding if used with drugs that inhibit platelets.

Instructions for Use

This drug is usually used as an add-on with phenobarbital.

Patient Monitoring and Laboratory Tests

Therapeutic drug monitoring can be performed, however therapeutic concentrations have not been established for dogs and cats, and ranges cited for people, 50-100 mcg/mL (desired trough concentration), should be used. Concentrations greater than 100 mcg/mL are associated with adverse effects.

Formulations

Depakote is available in 125, 250, and 500 mg tablets. Depakene is available in 250 mg capsules and 50 mg/mL syrup. Valproate sodium (Depacon) is available in 100 mg/mL injections.

Stability and Storage

Store in tightly sealed container, protected from light, and at room temperature. Valproic acid is slightly soluble in water, but valproate sodium is soluble in water. Extemporaneous emulsions have been prepared and were comparable to absorption of syrup.

Small Animal Dosage

Dogs

- 60-200 mg/kg q8h PO.
- 25-105 mg/kg/day PO when administered with phenobarbital.

Cats

Dose not established.

Large Animal Dosage

No dose has been reported for large animals.

Regulatory Information

No regulatory information is available. For extralabel use withdrawal interval estimates, contact FARAD at 1-888-USFARAD (1-888-873-2723) or send e-mail to FARAD@ncsu.edu.

Vancomycin

van-koe-mye'sin

Trade and Other Names: Vancocin and Vancoled

Functional Classification: Antibacterial

Pharmacology and Mechanism of Action

Antibacterial drug. Mechanism of action is to inhibit cell wall and cause bacterial cell lysis (via different mechanism as beta-lactams). Spectrum includes *Streptococcus, Enterococcus*, and *Staphylococcus.* Strains of *Staphylococcus* treated are often called *methicillin-resistant Staphylococcus* (e.g. methicillin-resistant *Staphylococcus aureus* [MRSA]).

Indications and Clinical Uses

Vancomycin is used for resistant strains of *Staphylococcus* or *Enterococcus* in animals. It is not effective against gram-negative bacteria. Vancomycin use is not common in animals, because it is inconvenient to administer. However, it is valuable for treatment of enterococci or staphylococci that are resistant to other antibiotics.

Precautionary Information

Adverse Reactions and Side Effects

Adverse effects have not been reported in animals. Adverse effects in people include renal injury (more common with older products that contained impurities) and histamine release.

Contraindications and Precautions

Do not administer rapidly IV. Administer by slow infusion.

Drug Interactions

Do not mix with other drugs in infusion solution; there are incompatibilities identified for many drugs. It is incompatible with alkaline solutions.

Instructions for Use

Doses are derived from pharmacokinetic studies in dogs. Infusion solution can be prepared in 0.9% saline or 5% dextrose, but not in alkalinizing solutions. Administer IV;

it causes severe pain and tissue injury if administered IM or SQ. Do not administer rapidly. Use slow infusion if possible (e.g., over 30 minutes).

Patient Monitoring and Laboratory Tests

Monitoring of trough plasma concentrations is recommended to ensure proper dose. Maintain trough concentration above 5 mcg/mL. CLSI (NCCLS) guidelines for susceptibility testing list a break point of less than or equal to mcg/mL for *Enterococcus*, less than or equal to 1 mcg/mL for *Streptococcus*, and less than or equal to 4 mcg/mL for *Staphylococcus*.

Formulations

Vancomycin is available in 500 mg, 1, 5, and 10 g vials for injection.

Stability and Storage

Stability may be compromised if mixed with other drugs in infusion solutions. Store in tightly sealed container, protected from light, and at room temperature. It is soluble in water and ethanol. After reconstitution with sterile water, it may be further diluted in 5% dextrose or saline. Solutions may have a dark color. After reconstitution it is stable for 14 days either at room temperature or in refrigerator. Some ophthalmic compounded formulations are not stable and have a low pH that can be irritating to the eyes.

Small Animal Dosage

Dogs

- 15 mg/kg q6-8h IV infusion.

Cats

- 12-15 mg/kg q8h IV infusion.

Large Animal Dosage

Horses

- 4.3-7.5 mg/kg q8h IV given as an infusion over 1 hour.
- Regional limb perfusion: infuse 300 mg diluted to make a 0.5% solution.

Regulatory Information

Do not administer to animals intended for food.

Vasopressin

vay-zoe-press'in

Trade and Other Names: Pitressin

Functional Classification: Hormone

Pharmacology and Mechanism of Action

Antidiuretic hormone. Vasopressin mimics the effect of antidiuretic hormone (ADH) on the tubule of the renal tubule. ADH permits reabsorption of water in renal tubule. Without ADH, more diluted urine is excreted. (See Desmopressin manuscript for additional formulations and use.)

Indications and Clinical Uses

Vasopressin is used for treatment of polyuria caused by central diabetes insipidus. Not effective for polyuria caused by renal disease. Desmopressin is a preferred formulation and used more frequently in animals.

Precautionary Information

Adverse Reactions and Side Effects

Adverse effects have not been reported. Allergic reactions and increase in blood pressure have been reported in people.

Contraindications and Precautions

No contraindications are reported for animals.

Drug Interactions

No drug interactions have been reported in animals.

Instructions for Use

Doses are adjusted on the basis of monitoring of water intake and urine output.

Patient Monitoring and Laboratory Tests

Monitor water intake, urine output, and urine specific gravity.

Formulations

Vasopressin is available in 20 units/mL (aqueous) solution.

Stability and Storage

Store in tightly sealed container, protected from light, and at room temperature.

Small Animal Dosage

Dogs and Cats

- 10 units IV or IM.

Large Animal Dosage

No dose has been reported for large animals.

Regulatory Information

Because of low risk of harmful residues in animals intended for food, no withdrawal time is suggested.

Verapamil Hydrochloride

ver-ap'ah-mill hye-droe-klor'ide

Trade and Other Names: Calan and Isoptin

Functional Classification: Calcium antagonist

Pharmacology and Mechanism of Action

Calcium-channel blocking drug of the nondihydropyridine group. Verapamil blocks calcium entry into cells via blockade of voltage-dependent slow channel. Verapamil produces vasodilation, negative chronotropic, and negative inotropic effects.

Indications and Clinical Uses

Verapamil is indicated for control of supraventricular arrhythmias. The use of verapamil has diminished because of adverse effects. The preferred drug from this class to use in animals is usually diltiazem.

Precautionary Information

Adverse Reactions and Side Effects

Adverse effects include hypotension, cardiac depression, bradycardia, and AV block. It may cause anorexia in some patients. Verapamil has caused sudden cardiac arrest in some patients with intravenous administration.

Contraindications and Precautions

Do not use in patients with decompensated CHF or advanced heart block. Not well tolerated in cats.

Drug Interactions

Verapamil, like other calcium-channel-blocking drugs, is subject to interaction with drugs that interfere with the multi-drug resistance (MDR) membrane pump (p-glycoprotein) and the cytochrome P450 enzymes. (See Appendix for list of drugs that may cause interference.)

Instructions for Use

Diltiazem is preferred over verapamil in patients with heart failure because of less myocardial depression. Oral formulation not absorbed sufficiently (of the active stereoisomer) for adequate effects.

Patient Monitoring and Laboratory Tests

Monitor heart rate and rhythm during treatment.

Formulations

Verapamil is available in 40, 80, and 120 mg tablets and 2.5 mg/mL injection.

Stability and Storage

Store in tightly sealed container, protected from light, and at room temperature. Verapamil is soluble in water. Aqueous solutions are stable for 3 months. Maximum stability is at pH 3-6. It can be mixed with infusion solutions and is compatible. Suspensions have been prepared for oral administration and found to be stable for 60 days.

Small Animal Dosage

Dogs

- 0.05 mg/kg q10-30min IV (maximum cumulative dose is 0.15 mg/kg). Oral dose is not established.

Cats

Not recommended.

Large Animal Dosage

No dose has been reported for large animals.

Regulatory Information

Do not administer to animals intended for food.

RCI Classification: 4

Vinblastine Sulfate

vin-blast'een sul'fate

Trade and Other Names: Velban

Functional Classification: Anticancer agent

Pharmacology and Mechanism of Action

Anticancer agent. Vinblastine causes arrest of cancer cell division by binding to microtubules and inhibiting mitosis. Vinblastine is related to vincristine. It is used in anticancer drug protocols.

Indications and Clinical Uses

Vinblastine is used in cancer chemotherapy protocols for various tumors. It is sometimes used as an alternative to vincristine. Vinblastine has been used in protocols to treat mast cell tumors. Do not use vinblastine to increase platelet numbers as is done occasionally with vincristine. (Vinblastine may actually cause thrombocytopenia.)

Precautionary Information

Adverse Reactions and Side Effects

Vinblastine does not produce neuropathy as does vincristine, but there may be a higher incidence of myelosuppression. It causes tissue necrosis if injected outside vein.

Contraindications and Precautions

If perivascular injection occurs, immediate flushing of area with fluids is recommended.

Drug Interactions

No drug interactions have been reported in animals.

Instructions for Use

Consult specific chemotherapy protocol for regimens.

Patient Monitoring and Laboratory Tests

Monitor CBC during treatment.

Formulations

Vinblastine is available in 1 mg/mL injection.

Stability and Storage

Store in tightly sealed container, protected from light, and at room temperature.

Small Animal Dosage

Dogs and Cats

- 2 mg/m^2 IV (slow infusion) once/week.

Large Animal Dosage

No dose has been reported for large animals.

Regulatory Information

Withdrawal times are not established for animals that produce food. This drug should not be used in animals intended for food, because it is an anticancer agent.

Vincristine Sulfate

vin-kriss'teen sul'fate

Trade and Other Names: Oncovin, Vincasar, and generic brands

Functional Classification: Anticancer agent

Pharmacology and Mechanism of Action

Anticancer agent. Vincristine causes arrest of cancer cell division by binding to microtubules and inhibiting mitosis. For thrombocytopenia, vincristine increases thrombopoiesis, increases fragmentation of megakaryocytes, and decreases platelet destruction. It may also decrease destruction of platelets by macrophages.

Indications and Clinical Uses

Vincristine is used in combination chemotherapy protocols. It is included in several anticancer chemotherapy protocols, usually with corticosteroids, alkylating agents, and other drugs. Vincristine also increases numbers of functional circulating platelets and is used for thrombocytopenia. When used to treat immune-mediated thrombocytopenia, it may be administered with a corticosteroid (e.g., prednisone at 2 mg/kg) to produce a rapid increase in functional platelets. This regimen (compared to prednisone alone) has shortened the duration of hospitalization for dogs with immune-mediated thrombocytopenia.

Precautionary Information

Adverse Reactions and Side Effects

Vincristine is generally well-tolerated. It is less myelosuppressive than other anticancer drugs. Neuropathy has been reported, but it is rare. Constipation can occur. Vincristine is irritating to tissues. Avoid extravasation outside vein during administration. If accidental injection is made outside the vein, prompt action is needed to avoid severe tissue injury.

Contraindications and Precautions

If perivascular injection occurs, immediate flushing of area with fluids is recommended to decrease tissue injury. When handling vincristine, pharmacy and hospital staff should take appropriate precautions to prevent exposure to people.

Drug Interactions

There are no significant drug interactions.

Instructions for Use

Vincristine is used in cancer chemotherapy protocols for various tumors. For example in the COAP protocol, which is an acronym for cyclophosphamide, Oncovin, asparaginase, and Prednisolone; the Oncovin component is vincristine. For use in treating thrombocytopenia, it is advised to administer vincristine with a corticosteroid (prednisolone or prednisone).

Patient Monitoring and Laboratory Tests

Monitor platelets during therapy if used to increase platelet numbers.

Formulations

Vincristine is available in 1 mg/mL injection.

Stability and Storage

Maintain in the injectable vial. Do not mix with other drugs in vial.

Small Animal Dosage

Dogs and Cats

- Antitumor: 0.5-0.7 mg/m^2 IV (or 0.025-0.05 mg/kg) once/week.
- Thrombocytopenia: 0.02 mg/kg IV once/week.

Large Animal Dosage

No dose has been reported for large animals.

Regulatory Information

Withdrawal times are not established for animals that produce food. This drug should not be used in animals intended for food, because it is an anticancer agent.

Vitamin A

Trade and Other Names: Retinol, Aquasol-A, Vitamin AD, and Vitamins A and D

Functional Classification: Vitamin

Pharmacology and Mechanism of Action

Vitamin A supplement. See also Isotretinoin (Accutane) for analogues used for other conditions.

Indications and Clinical Uses

Vitamin A is used as a supplement for animals with deficiency.

Precautionary Information

Adverse Reactions and Side Effects

Excessive doses can cause bone or joint pain and dermatitis. Other signs of hypervitaminosis A can be excessive bleeding, confusion, diarrhea, and peeling of skin.

Contraindications and Precautions

Hypervitaminosis can occur from high doses of vitamin A administered chronically. Doses needed to cause toxicity can be as high as 10,000 units/kg/day.

Drug Interactions

No drug interactions have been reported in animals.

Instructions for Use

Dosing of vitamin A may be expressed as units or retinol equivalents (RE) or mcg of retinol. One RE equals 1 mcg of retinol. One RE of vitamin A is equal to 3.33 units of retinol.

Patient Monitoring and Laboratory Tests

Monitor for signs of toxicity if high doses are used.

Formulations

Vitamin A is available in 5000 units (1500 RE) per 0.1 mL oral solution and in 10,000, 25,000, and 50,000 unit tablets. These tablets are listed as 3000, 7500, and 15,000 REs, respectively. Injectable formulations used in veterinary medicine usually are included with vitamin D. These combinations contain 100,000 units/mL, 200,000 units/mL, or 500,000 units/mL.

Stability and Storage

Store protected from light at room temperature. Vitamin A, like other fat-soluble vitamins, is insoluble in water but soluble in oils. It is subject to oxidation and should be kept in a tightly sealed container.

Small Animal Dosage

Dogs and Cats

- 625-800 units/kg q24h PO.

Large Animal Dosage

All doses are listed as per animal and may be repeated in 2-3 months.

Calves

- 500,000-1 million units IM.

Sheep and Swine

- 500,000-1 million units IM.

Cattle

- 1-2 million units IM.

Regulatory Information

Because of low risk of harmful residues in animals intended for food, no withdrawal time is suggested.

Vitamin E

Trade and Other Names: Tocopherol, Alpha-tocopherol, Aquasol E, and generic brands

Functional Classification: Vitamin

Pharmacology and Mechanism of Action

Vitamin E also is known as Alpha-tocopherol. It is a fat-soluble vitamin that is considered an antioxidant. Vitamin E also is found in solutions as d-alpha-tocopherol (natural source of vitamin E).

Indications and Clinical Uses

Vitamin E is used as supplement and as treatment of some immune-mediated dermatoses and hepatobiliary disorders. Vitamin E has been used as an oral treatment for discoid lupus in dogs, however, efficacy for many skin diseases has been questioned.

Precautionary Information

Adverse Reactions and Side Effects

Vitamin E at high doses can cause coagulopathies. Doses known to cause coagulopathy are 1000 units/day (15 units/kg/day) in humans. Coagulopathies are caused by a decrease in vitamin-K-dependent coagulation factors.

Contraindications and Precautions

Use carefully in animals with coagulopathies.

Drug Interactions

Vitamin E may interact with anticoagulants. Vitamin E may exacerbate the anticoagulant effect of warfarin.

Instructions for Use

Vitamin E has been proposed as treatment for a wide range of human illnesses, but evidence for efficacy in animals is lacking. In animals it is used as adjunctive antioxidant therapy for a variety of diseases.

Patient Monitoring and Laboratory Tests

Monitor for bleeding in animals treated with high doses.

Formulations

Vitamin E is available in capsules, tablets, and an oral solution (e.g., 1000 units/capsule). Injectable formulations for veterinary medicine may also contain vitamins A and D. Usually injectable combinations contain 300 units/mL. Vitamin E also is found in solutions as d-alpha-tocopherol (natural source of vitamin E).

Stability and Storage

Vitamin E, like other fat-soluble vitamins, is insoluble in water but soluble in oils. Store in tightly sealed container, protected from light, and at room temperature.

Small Animal Dosage

Dogs and Cats

- 100-400 units q12h PO (as alpha-tocopherol)
- Immune-mediated skin disease: 400-600 units q12h PO.
- Discoid lupus erythematosus (dogs): 200-400 units q12h PO.

Large Animal Dosage

All doses are listed as per animal and may be repeated in 2-3 months.

Calves

- 1200-1800 units IM.

Cattle

- 2400-3000 units IM.

Sheep and Swine

- 1200-1800 units IM.

Regulatory Information

Because of low risk of harmful residues in animals intended for food, no withdrawal time is suggested.

Vitamin K

Trade and Other Names: AquaMEPHYTON (injection), Mephyton (tablets), Veta-K1 (capsules), Veda-K1 (oral and injectable), Vitamin K, Phylloquinone, and Phytomenadione

Functional Classification: Vitamin

Pharmacology and Mechanism of Action

See also Phytonadione for additional information. Vitamin K is a cofactor used to synthesize coagulation factors in the liver (factors II, VII, IX, and X). Vitamin K-1 also is known as phytonadione and phylloquinone (Phytomenadione is the British spelling of Phytonadione). Vitamin K-2 is also known as menaquinone. Vitamin K-3 is known as menadione. Vitamin K-3 is a synthetic analogue and is not equivalent to Vitamin K-1. Vitamin K-3 is not recommended for clinical use. Vitamin K-1 is absorbed better with meals that contain fat.

Indications and Clinical Uses

Vitamin K-1 is a fat-soluble vitamin used to treat coagulopathies caused by anticoagulant toxicosis (warfarin or other rodenticides). Anticoagulants deplete Vitamin K in the body, which is essential for synthesis of clotting factors. In large animals, it is used to treat sweet clover poisoning.

Precautionary Information

Adverse Reactions and Side Effects

In people, a rare hypersensitivity-like reaction has been observed after rapid intravenous injection. This reaction may be caused by histamine release from a reaction from the drug vehicle, Polysorbate 80. Signs resemble anaphylactic shock. These signs also have been observed in animals. To avoid anaphylactic reactions, do not administer IV. Reactions from intramuscular injection, such as hematoma, may occur in animals with coagulopathies.

Contraindications and Precautions

Accurate diagnosis to rule out other causes of bleeding is suggested. Other forms of vitamin K may not be as rapidly acting as vitamin K-1, therefore consider using a specific preparation. To avoid anaphylactic reactions, do not administer IV.

Drug Interactions

Some drugs, such as cephalosporins, may decrease vitamin K-dependent clotting factors.

Instructions for Use

Consult poison control center for specific protocol if specific rodenticide is identified. Use vitamin K-1 for acute therapy, because it is more highly bioavailable. Administer with food to enhance absorption. Phytonadione and Phytomenadione are synthetic lipid-soluble forms of vitamin K-1. Menadiol is vitamin K-4, which is a water-soluble derivative, converted in the body to vitamin K-3 (menadione).

Injection can be diluted in 5% dextrose or 0.9% saline but not other solutions. Although Vitamin K-1 veterinary labels have listed intravenous route for administration, these labels have not been approved by the FDA. Therefore, avoid intravenous administration of Vitamin K-1. The preferred route is subcutaneous, but intramuscular can also be used. When treating for poisoning by second-generation rodenticides, which have long half-lives, 6 weeks of therapy may be necessary.

Patient Monitoring and Laboratory Tests

Monitoring bleeding times in patients is essential for accurate dosing of vitamin K-1 preparations. When treating long-acting rodenticide poisoning, periodic monitoring of the bleeding times is suggested.

Formulations

Vitamin K is available in 2 or 10 mg/mL injection. Mephyton is 5 mg tablet. Veta-K1 is 25 mg capsule. Phytonadione (AquaMEPHYTON) is a 2-mg/mL or 10-mg/mL injection.

Stability and Storage

Vitamin K, like other fat-soluble vitamins, is insoluble in water but soluble in oils. Store in tightly sealed container, protected from light, and at room temperature.

Small Animal Dosage

Dogs and Cats

- Short-acting rodenticides: 1 mg/kg/day IM, SQ, or PO for 10-14 days.
- Long-acting rodenticides: 2.5-5 mg/kg/day IM, SQ, or PO for 3-4 weeks, and up to 6 weeks.

Birds

- 2.5-5 mg/kg q24h.

Large Animal Dosage

Cattle, Calves, Horses, Sheep, and Goats

- 0.5-2.5 mg/kg SQ or IM.

Regulatory Information

There is no meat or milk withdrawal time necessary.

Voriconazole

vor-ih-kahn'ah-zole

Trade and Other Names: Vfend

Functional Classification: Antifungal

Pharmacology and Mechanism of Action

Azole (triazole) antifungal drug. Voriconazole is a second-generation triazole antifungal drug. Similar to the other currently available azole and triazole antifungals, voriconazole inhibits the fungal cytochrome P450-dependent 14 alpha-sterol demethylase which is essential for formation of ergosterol in the fungal cell wall. Voriconazole is similar in structure to fluconazole; however it is more active and potent. Voriconazole is active against dermatophytes and systemic fungi, such as *Blastomyces, Histoplasma*, and *Coccidioides.* It also has activity against yeast, such as *Candida* and *Malassezia*. Voriconazole has greater activity against *Aspergillus* than other drugs of this class and is indicated for systemic treatment. Oral absorption is higher than in most other drugs in this class. In horses, voriconazole was absorbed 92% and had a half-life of 13 hours.

Indications and Clinical Uses

Voriconazole has been used to treat dermatophytes and systemic fungi, such as *Blastomyces, Histoplasma,* and *Coccidioides.* It has been used to treat infections caused by *Aspergillus* and *Fusarium.* The efficacy in humans for treating *Aspergillus* is better than with other oral antifungal drugs and comparable to amphotericin B. Penetration into the CNS and eye is high enough to treat infections in these areas.

Precautionary Information

Adverse Reactions and Side Effects

Voriconazole is better tolerated than ketoconazole. However, vomiting and hepatotoxicity are possible, especially at high doses.

Contraindications and Precautions

Use cautiously in any animal with signs of liver disease. Use cautiously in pregnant animals. At high doses in laboratory animals, drugs in this class have caused fetal abnormalities.

Drug Interactions

Voriconazole is a cytochrome P450 enzyme inhibitor. It may cause drug interactions because of inhibition of P450 enzymes. However, this inhibition is not expected to be as prominent as with ketoconazole.

Instructions for Use

Doses are based on experimental studies in animals with voriconazole. Some uses in animals are based on empiricism or extrapolation from human literature. When used IV, 10 mg/mL solution should be further diluted with fluids to a concentration <5 mg/mL and infused slowly.

Patient Monitoring and Laboratory Tests

Monitor liver enzyme concentrations.

Formulations

Voriconazole is available in 50 and 200 mg tablets and 200 mg (10 mg/mL) injection.

Stability and Storage

Store in a tightly sealed container, protected from light, at room temperature. Compounded formulations may be stable and potent if used immediately after mixing. Use intravenous formulation immediately after mixing.

Small Animal Dosage

Dogs and Cats

- 4-5 mg/kg q12h PO.

Large Animal Dosage

Horses

- 2 mg/kg q24h PO.
- 1.5 mg/kg q24h IV.

Regulatory Information

No regulatory information is available. For extralabel use withdrawal interval estimates, contact FARAD at 1-888-USFARAD (1-888-873-2723) or send e-mail to FARAD@ncsu.edu.

Warfarin sodium

war′far-in soe′dee-um

Trade and Other Names: Coumadin and generic brands

Functional Classification: Anticoagulant

Pharmacology and Mechanism of Action

Anticoagulant. Warfarin sodium depletes vitamin K, which is responsible for generation of clotting factors. Half-life of warfarin in animals is 36-42 hours (20-30 hours in cats).

Indications and Clinical Uses

In small animals, it has been used to treat hypercoagulation disease and prevent thromboembolism. In horses, warfarin has been used to treat navicular disease, although it is not popular for this use.

Precautionary Information

Adverse Reactions and Side Effects

Adverse effects are attributable to decreased blood clotting. Spontaneous bleeding can result in blood loss, hemoperitoneum, hemarthrosis, gastrointestinal bleeding, epistaxis, and excessive bleeding from trauma or surgery.

Contraindications and Precautions

Do not administer to animals that may be prone to bleeding. Administer carefully with other drugs that are known to interfere with coagulation.

Drug Interactions

There are multiple drugs and some foods that may affect warfarin's action. Some of these that may potentiate warfarin's action include aspirin, chloramphenicol, phenylbutazone, ketoconazole, and cimetidine. Drug interactions are possible with administration with other highly protein-bound drugs, but such reactions are poorly documented in animals. Drug interactions are also possible with trimethoprim sulfonamides and metronidazole. Do not administer with some cephalosporin drugs (particularly those with N-methylthiotetrazole [NMTT]), because cephalosporins may induce bleeding through anti-vitamin-K-dependent mechanisms.

Instructions for Use

Warfarin response can be highly variable among animals. Pharmacokinetic studies have attempted to correlate plasma pharmacokinetics with clinical response (prothrombin time [PT]). However, such a correlation has been difficult to obtain. A particular dose and plasma concentration that produces an effective prolongation of prothrombin time in one patient may not be effective in another individual. Because of the variation in response, adjust doses by monitoring bleeding times in treated animals. For a rapid effect, consider a loading dose of 6 mg/kg once daily for 2 treatments in dogs. In one study (*J Vet Pharmacol Ther*, 23:339, 2000), a starting dose in cats was calculated to be 0.06-0.09 mg/kg (0.25-0.5 mg/cat/day). When dividing tablets for treatment, it is best to crush up a whole tablet into a powder and divide the doses equally from the powder. When tablets are cut into halves or quarters, there is uneven distribution of warfarin within the tablet. Some fractions of the tablet may contain a higher amount than others (*J Vet Pharmacol Ther*, 23:329-337, 2000).

Patient Monitoring and Laboratory Tests

Adjust dose by monitoring clotting time. Optimum dose is highly individualistic. The best method to monitor warfarin therapy is with the one stage prothrombin time. Prothrombin times are reported in seconds and recorded as a ratio of the prothrombin time of the patient to the mean normal prothrombin time of the laboratory and as the international normalized ratio (INR). The INR is the most reliable way to monitor the prothrombin time. In animals the dose is adjusted to maintain PT at 1.5 to 2 times normal (or INR of 2-3). Consult specific reference for guidance (Harpster and Batey, *Current Veterinary Therapy XII*. Philadelphia, PA: WB Saunders, 1995: 868).

Formulations

Warfarin sodium is available in 1, 2, 2.5, 4, 5, 7.5, and 10 mg tablets.

Stability and Storage

Warfarin sodium is soluble in water. It is light sensitive and should be packaged in tight containers. Solutions should have pH >8 to maintain solubility. Some tablets do not have drug distributed evenly, therefore uneven doses can result from splitting tablets.

Small Animal Dosage

Dogs

- 0.1-0.2 mg/kg q24h PO with loading doses of 6 mg/kg PO, once daily for 2 days.

Cats

- Start with 0.5 mg/cat/day and adjust dose based on clotting time assessment.

Large Animal Dosage

Horses

- 0.02 mg/kg q24h PO (9 mg per 450 kg of body weight [1000 pounds]). Increase this dose gradually until bleeding time is sufficiently prolonged. Allow 7 days between changes in dose.

Regulatory Information

Do not administer to animals intended for food.
RCI Classification: 5

Xylazine hydrochloride

zye'lah-zeen hye-droe-klor'ide

Trade and Other Names: Rompun and generic brands

Functional Classification: $Alpha_2$ adrenergic agonist, Analgesic, Sedative

Pharmacology and Mechanism of Action

$Alpha_2$ adrenergic agonist. $Alpha_2$ agonists decrease release of neurotransmitters from the neuron. They decrease transmission via binding to presynaptic $alpha_2$ receptors (negative feedback receptors). The result is decreased sympathetic outflow, analgesia, sedation, and anesthesia. Other drugs in this class include medetomidine, romifidine, detomidine, and clonidine. Receptor binding studies indicate that $alpha_2/alpha_1$ adrenergic receptor selectivity was 1620 for medetomidine and 160 for xylazine.

Indications and Clinical Uses

Xylazine is used for short-term sedation, anesthesia, and analgesia in horses, dogs, cats, cattle, and exotic animals. Like other $alpha_2$ agonists, it is used as an anesthetic adjunct and analgesic. Duration of effect is approximately 30 minutes. Compared to xylazine, medetomidine has produced better sedation and analgesia than xylazine in dogs. Romifidine produces the longest duration of sedative effects, followed by detomidine, medetomidine, and xylazine.

Precautionary Information

Adverse Reactions and Side Effects

In small animals, vomiting is the most common acute effect. Xylazine produces sedation and ataxia. Xylazine, like other $alpha_2$ agonists, decreases sympathetic output. Cardiovascular depression may occur. Cardiac effects can include sinoatrial block, first- and second-degree AV block, bradycardia, and sinus arrhythmia. Xylazine produces emesis after intravenous injection, especially in cats. In ruminants, use of xylazine may decrease GI motility and cause bloating, salivation, and regurgitation. Note that cattle, sheep, and goats are much more sensitive to xylazine than other animals, which requires lowering the dose. Like other $alpha_2$ agonists it produces transient hyperglycemia, which may increase urine flow.

Contraindications and Precautions

Ruminants are much more sensitive to xylazine than other species. Lower doses must be used compared with other animals. Use cautiously in animals that are pregnant; it may induce labor. In addition, it may decrease oxygen delivery to fetus in late gestation. Use cautiously, if at all, in patients with cardiac disease. Because of cardiac depression, it should not ordinarily be used with tranquilizers such as phenothiazines. Reverse effects of xylazine with an $alpha_2$ antagonist (e.g., yohimbine or atipamezole) if there are dangerous adverse effects.

Drug Interactions

Use with opioid analgesic drugs will greatly enhance the CNS depression. Consider lowering doses if administered with opioids. Do not administer with other drugs that cause significant cardiac depression.

Instructions for Use

Xylazine is often used in combination with other drugs, e.g., ketamine. It is not necessary to premedicate animals with atropine. For large animals, if sedation is needed without recumbency, use the lower end of the dose range.

Patient Monitoring and Laboratory Tests

Monitor heart rate and rhythm during anesthesia with xylazine. It may cause increased plasma glucose in animals.

Formulations Available

Xylazine is available in 20 and 100 mg/mL injection.

Stability and Storage

Store in tightly sealed container, protected from light, and at room temperature.

Small Animal Dosage

Dogs

- 1.1 mg/kg IV.
- 2.2 mg/kg IM.
- Short-term treatment of pain: 0.1-0.5 mg/kg IM, IV, or SQ.

Cats

- 1.1 mg/kg IM.
- Emetic dose: 0.4-0.5 mg/kg IV.
- Short-term treatment of pain: 0.1-0.5 mg/kg IM, IV, or SQ.

Large Animal Dosage

Horses

- 1-2 mg/kg IM.
- 0.5-1.1 mg/kg IV.

Pigs

- 0.5-3 mg/kg IM. (Use in combination with other drugs in swine. It is unreliable alone.)

Cattle

- 0.1-0.2 mg/kg IM.
- 0.03-0.1 mg/kg IV.

Sheep

- 0.1-0.3 mg/kg IM.
- 0.05-0.1 mg/kg IV.

Goats

- 0.05-0.5 mg/kg IM.
- 0.01-0.5 mg/kg IV.

Regulatory Information

Withdrawal time for cattle: In the U.S., 4 days meat; 24 hours milk after IM administration at doses of 0.05-0.3 mg/kg. In Canada it is listed as 3 days for meat and 48 hours for milk, whereas in the U.K. it is listed as 14 days for meat and 48 hours for milk.

RCI Classification: 3

Yohimbine

yoe-him' been

Trade and Other Names: Yobine

Functional Classification: $Alpha_2$ receptor antagonist

Pharmacology and Mechanism of Action

$Alpha_2$ adrenergic antagonist. It antagonizes the action of other drugs that stimulate the $alpha_2$ receptor.

Indications and Clinical Uses

Yohimbine is used primarily to reverse actions of xylazine or detomidine. Atipamezole is another $alpha_2$ antagonist that may be used to reverse xylazine or medetomidine.

Precautionary Information

Adverse Reactions and Side Effects

High doses can cause tremors and seizures.

Contraindications and Precautions

When administering to reverse an $alpha_2$ agonist, monitor heart rate and rhythm carefully during treatment.

Drug Interactions

No drug interactions are reported, except the antagonism of $alpha_2$ agonists.

Instructions for Use

Reverses signs of sedation and anesthesia caused by $alpha_2$ agonists.

Patient Monitoring and Laboratory Tests

Monitor heart rate and rhythm during use of yohimbine.

Formulations

Yohimbine is available in a 2 mg/mL injection.

Stability and Storage

Store in tightly sealed container, protected from light, and at room temperature.

Small Animal Dosage

Dogs and Cats

- 0.11 mg/kg IV.
- 0.25-0.5 mg/kg SQ or IM.

Large Animal Dosage

Cattle and Sheep

- To reverse xylazine or medetomidine: 0.125-0.2 mg/kg IV.

Regulatory Information

Extralabel use: establish a withdrawal time of at least 7 days for meat and 72 hours for milk.

RCI Classification: 2

Zidovudine

zye-doe'vyoo-deen

Trade and Other Names: Retrovir

Functional Classification: Antiviral

Pharmacology and Mechanism of Action

Antiviral drug. Zidovudine (AZT) acts to inhibit the viral enzyme reverse transcriptase that prevents conversion of viral RNA into DNA. Other drugs in this class include lamivudine, didanosine, and zalcitabine.

Indications and Clinical Uses

In people, AZT is used to treat HIV (AIDS). In animals has been experimentally used for treatment of feline leukemia virus (FeLV) and feline immunodeficiency virus (FIV) infection in cats. In cats, doses of 25 mg/kg q12h IV or PO produced drug concentrations in effective range. However, efficacy in cats has been controversial (less effective than expected).

Precautionary Information

Adverse Reactions and Side Effects

Anemia and leucopenia have been observed in treated animals.

Contraindications and Precautions

No contraindications are reported for animals.

Drug Interactions

No drug interactions have been reported in animals.

Instructions for Use

At this time, experience with using AZT for treating viral disease in animals is largely experimental or anecdotal. This drug may help some cats with FIV and may prevent persistent FeLV, but documentation of efficacy is lacking.

Patient Monitoring and Laboratory Tests

Monitor the packed-cell volume (PCV) in treated cats and perform a CBC periodically.

Formulations

AZT is available in a 10 mg/mL syrup and a 10 mg/mL injection.

Stability and Storage

Store in tightly sealed container, protected from light, and at room temperature.

Small Animal Dosage

Cats

- 15 mg/kg q12h PO, up to 20 mg/kg q8h PO. (Doses as high as 30 mg/kg/day also have been used.)

Large Animal Dosage

No dose has been reported for large animals.

Regulatory Information

Do not administer to animals intended for food.

Zinc

Trade and Other Names: Zinc

Functional Classification: Nutritional supplement

Pharmacology and Mechanism of Action

Zinc is an essential element important in over 200 metalloenzymes. It also is important for nucleic acid, cell membrane, and protein synthesis. It is also important for growth, tissue repair, and cell division. Zinc acts as a chelating agent, and it competes with iron to inhibit fibrosis and collagen formation. The benefits have been seen in experimental animals and in humans with liver disease. One of the uses has been to manage hepatic cirrhosis. Zinc also may act as an antioxidant and prevent membrane damage. Zinc binds to intestinal copper to decrease oral absorption.

Indications and Clinical Uses

Zinc is used as a chelating agent in animals. It has been used to treat zinc-deficient diseases such as those that cause dermatologic problems. It is also used as an antifibrotic agent in liver disease. Zinc has been used as a cupruretic to decrease copper concentrations in animals with liver disease.

Precautionary Information

Adverse Reactions and Side Effects

Most common effect is GI problems, including nausea and vomiting. Hemolysis can be observed with high doses.

Contraindications and Precautions

No contraindications are reported for animals.

Drug Interactions

Oral absorption is impaired from tetracyclines, iron, copper, phytates (found in bran and grains), and penicillamine.

Instructions for Use

Administer without food to improve oral absorption.

Patient Monitoring and Laboratory Tests

Monitor blood zinc concentrations to prevent high levels which cause hemolysis. Blood zinc concentrations should ideally be 200-500 mcg/dL. A concentration above 800 mcg/dL is considered toxic.

Formulations

Zinc is available in several forms, including zinc sulfate (23% zinc), zinc gluconate (14% zinc), and zinc acetate (35% zinc). Zinc gluconate is available in tablets ranging from 1.4-52 mg (10 mg zinc gluconate = 1.4 mg of elemental zinc).

Zinc sulfate is available in capsules 25 and 50 mg elemental zinc (110 mg zinc sulfate = 25 mg elemental zinc).

Zinc sulfate is available in tablets: 15, 25, 45, and 50 mg (elemental zinc, 66 mg zinc sulfate = 15 mg elemental zinc).

Stability and Storage

Store in tightly sealed container, protected from light, and at room temperature.

Small Animal Dosage

Dogs and Cats

Adjust dose based on measuring plasma zinc concentrations.

- Zinc gluconate: 1 mg/kg elemental zinc three times/day PO.
- Zinc sulfate: 1 mg/kg elemental zinc three times/day PO.
- Zinc acetate: 1.5-3 mg (of elemental zinc) daily per animal PO.
- Dermatologic use: 10 mg/kg daily (zinc sulfate or zinc gluconate).

Large Animal Dosage

No specific doses have been reported. Extrapolate dose needed from small animal use (approximately 1 mg/kg elemental zinc three times per day PO) and adjust dose by monitoring zinc concentrations.

Regulatory Information

Because of low risk of harmful residues in animals intended for food, no withdrawal time is suggested.

Zonisamide

zoe-nis′a-mide

Trade and Other Names: Zonegran

Functional Classification: Anticonvulsant

Pharmacology and Mechanism of Action

Anticonvulsant. Mechanism of action is uncertain, but it may potentiate the action of GABA, an inhibitory neurotransmitter, or it may stabilize membranes via changes in sodium and calcium conductance. Half-life in dogs has been reported to be approximately 15 hours in one study and 16 hours (plasma) to 57 hours (red blood cells [RBCs]) in another study.

Indications and Clinical Uses

Zonisamide is used to treat refractory seizures in dogs when other drugs have not been effective. It has been effective in approximately 50% of dogs with refractory epilepsy. It has been used as an add-on with other anticonvulsant drugs.

Precautionary Information

Adverse Reactions and Side Effects

At the suggested clinical doses, adverse effects have not been reported for dogs. Adverse reactions can include lethargy, ataxia, and vomiting. Like other anticonvulsants, ataxia, sedation, and CNS changes are possible. In safety studies, Beagles received 75 mg/kg/day for 1 year with minimal side effects.

Contraindications and Precautions

Because zonisamide resembles sulfonamides in structure, use cautiously in animals that are sensitive to these drugs. (See sulfonamide manuscripts for full details on sulfonamide adverse effects.)

Drug Interactions

When administered concurrently with phenobarbital, the half-life of elimination is more rapid for zonisamide, which may require higher doses. It is expected to potentiate other CNS depressants and anticonvulsants.

Instructions for Use

Most experience with zonisamide in animals has been preliminary work in dogs with refractory epilepsy. In one study 10 mg/kg twice daily PO produced plasma concentrations within the therapeutic range reported for people. When administered with phenobarbital, it was shown that drug metabolism is increased. Zonisamide half-life was shorter in dogs receiving phenobarbital concurrently, and therefore dose may have to be increased for combination therapy compared to monotherapy.

Patient Monitoring and Laboratory Tests

Effective plasma concentrations in animals have been suggested to be 10-40 mcg/mL, but in people the effective concentrations are 10-70 mcg/mL.

Formulations

Zonisamide is available in 100 mg capsules.

Stability and Storage

Store in tightly sealed container, protected from light, and at room temperature. Stability of compounded formulations has not been evaluated.

Small Animal Dosage

Dogs

- 5-10 mg/kg q12h PO.

Large Animal Dosage

No dose has been reported for large animals.

Regulatory Information

No regulatory information is available. For extralabel use withdrawal interval estimates, contact FARAD at 1-888-USFARAD (1-888-873-2723) or send e-mail to FARAD@ncsu.edu.

RCI Classification: 3

APPENDIX A
Calculation of Drug Doses

How to Calculate Milliliters (mL) Needed

$$\text{Dose (mg/kg)} \times \text{kilograms body weight} = \text{total dose needed (mg)}$$

$$\text{Strength of solution (mg/mL)} = (\text{\% strength}) \times 10$$

$$\frac{\text{Total dose needed}}{\text{Strength of solution (mg/mL)}} = \text{mL needed}$$

Example

20 kg dog needs 15 mg/kg of a 20% solution
20 kg × 15 mg/kg = 300 mg total dose needed
Strength of solution = 20% × 10 = 200 mg/mL
mL needed = 300 mg/200 mg/mL = 1.5 mL

How to Calculate Tablets Needed

$$\text{Dose (mg/kg)} \times \text{kilograms body weight} = \text{total dose needed (mg)}$$

$$\frac{\text{Total dose needed}}{\text{Strength of tablet}} = \text{Number of tablets needed}$$

Example

20 kg dog needs 12 mg/kg
Tablet size is 100 mg
20 kg × 12 mg/kg = 240 mg total dose needed
240 mg/100 mg tablets = 2.4 tablets

(In most instances, you would round up to 2½ tablets if the medication has sufficient safety.)

How to Calculate Infusion Rates

$$\text{Dose (mg/kg/min)} \times \text{kilograms body weight} = \text{total dose needed (mg) per minute}$$

If dose is listed in micrograms/kg/min, multiply by 1000 for mg/kg/min

$$\text{Strength of solution (mg/mL)} = (\text{\% strength}) \times 10$$

$$\frac{\text{Total dose needed per minute}}{\text{Strength of solution (mg/mL)}} = \text{mL needed per minute}$$

$$\text{mL needed per minute} \times 60 = \text{mL needed per hour}$$

Administer the total mL to fluid administered in each hour interval. If fluid is to be administered over 24 hours: mL needed per hour × 24 = mL needed per day.

Example:

20 kg dog needs 0.15 mg/kg/min (150 mcg/kg/min) of a 10% solution
Fluid rate (Lactated Ringers solution) is 60 mL/kg/day
20 kg × 0.15 mg/kg/min = 3.0 mg needed per minute
Strength of solution = 10% × 10 = 100 mg/mL
mL needed per min = (3.0 mg per min)/100 mg/mL = 0.03 mL per min
0.03 mL per minute × 60 min/hr = 1.8 mL added to each hour of fluids
Fluid rate is 60 mL/kg/day = 2.5 mL/kg/hr = 50 mL/hr for a 20 kg dog.

To each 50 mL/hr fluid volume to be infused, add 1.8 mL of medication. If drug is stable in solution for 24 hours, total amount can be added to a 24 hour volume of fluid:

Total fluid needed per 24 hours = 60 mL/kg/day × 20 kg = 1200 mL

1.8 mL per hour × 24 hr = 43.2 mL per day added to 1200 mL total fluid requirement.

APPENDIX B
Controlled Substance Charts: United States and Canada

Controlled Substance Charts

Drug Examples	United States*
Heroin, LSD, peyote, marijuana, mescaline	**Schedule I** • High abuse potential • No currently accepted medical use • No veterinary uses identified
Morphine and morphine derivatives and Synthetic opioids. Drugs used in veterinary medicine include: morphine, meperidine, etorphine, hydrocodone, hydromorphone, oxymorphone, codeine (in some forms), and pentobarbital.	**Schedule II** • High abuse potential; potentially severe psychologic or physical dependence • Currently accepted medical use but may be severely restricted • Telephone orders to a pharmacy are allowed only in emergencies if written Rx follows promptly • No refills allowed
Drugs used in veterinary medicine include: anabolic steroids (stanozolol, oxymethalone, testosterone, methyltestosterone, boldenone, trenbolone), barbiturates (thiamylal, thiopental), opioids (burpenorphine and codeine in some forms), and ketamine and derivatives (ketamine and tiletamine + zolazepam).	**Schedule III** • Abuse potential less than the drugs/ substances in Schedules I and II; potentially moderate or low physical dependence or high psychologic dependence • Currently accepted medical use • Telephone orders to pharmacy permitted • Veterinarian may authorize limited refills
Drugs used in veterinary medicine include opioids (butorphanol and pentazocine), benzodiazepines (diazepam, oxazepam, midazolam, clonazepam, clorazepate, and alprazolam), and phenobarbital	**Schedule IV** • Abuse potential relative to drugs/ substances in Schedule III; potentially limited to physical or psychologic dependence • Currently accepted medical use • Telephone orders to pharmacy permitted • Veterinarian may authorize limited refills
Codeine preparations used as antitussives and some opioids used as antidiarrheals (e.g., diphenoxylate).	**Schedule V** • Lowest abuse potential; potentially very limited physical or psychologic dependence • Currently accepted medical use • Veterinarian can determine refills • Some products containing limited amounts of Schedule V substances (e.g., cough suppressants) available OTC.
Drug Examples	**Canada**
LSD, mescaline (peyote), harmaline, psilocin and psilocybin (magic mushrooms)	**Part J of the Food and Drug Regulation (FDR)** • Considered "restricted drugs" • High misuse potential • No recognized medical use

*Complete list for the U.S. can be located at: http://www.usdoj.gov/dea/pubs/scheduling.html

Continued

Controlled Substance Charts—cont'd

Drug Examples	Canada
	• Marijuana exemption from FDR if produced for medical reasons
Sedatives such as barbiturates and derivatives (secobarbital), thiobarbiturates (pentothal sodium); anabolic steroids	**Part G of the FDR** • Controlled drugs • Misuse potential • Verbal and written prescriptions under certain conditions • Only prescribed if required for medical condition • Specified number of refills (conditions apply) • Records must be kept • May be administered under emergency situations (conditions apply)
Amphetamines	**Part G of the FDR** • Designated controlled drug • May be used for designated medical conditions outlined in FDR
Benzodiazepine tranquilizers such as diazepam, and lorazepam,	**Benzodiazepines and Other Targeted Substances Regulations** • Misuse potential • Verbal and written prescriptions under certain conditions • Only prescribed if required for medical condition • Specified number of refills (conditions apply) • Records must be kept • May be administered under emergency situations (conditions apply)
Opiates: heroin, morphine, codeine (in some forms), and analgesics such as pentazocine or fentanyl	**Narcotic Control Regulation** • High misuse potential • Written prescriptions for specific medical conditions† • Records of opiate prescription file must be kept • No refills (limited amounts in a prescription) • Heroin and methadone are subject to specific controls
LSD, mescaline (peyote), harmaline, psilocin and psilocybin (magic mushrooms)	**Part J of the Food and Drug Regulation (FDR)** • Considered "restricted drugs" • High misuse potential • No recognized medical use • Marijuana exemption from FDR if produced for medical reasons

†Verbal prescriptions are permitted for certain opioid preparations (such as Tylenol No. 2 and No. 3), but not for opiate alone, or opiates with 1 other active non-opioid ingredient.

APPENDIX C Drugs for Infections Commonly Seen in Veterinary Medicine

Infection Site	First-Choice Drugs	Alternate-Choice Drugs
Skin: pyoderma or other skin infection	Amoxicillin-clavulanate Cephalosporin	Trimethoprim-sulfonamides Fluoroquinolone* Clindamycin Oxacillin
Urinary tract	Cephalosporin Amoxicillin/ampicillin Amoxicillin-clavulanate	Trimethoprim-sulfonamides Fluoroquinolone* Tetracycline
Respiratory tract	Amoxicillin-clavulanate Fluoroquinolone Cephalosporin	Macrolide (erythromycin, azithromycin) Aminoglycosides (amikacin, gentamicin) Clindamycin Chloramphenicol Extended-spectrum cephalosporin†
Septicemia‡	Amoxicillin-clavulanate Cephalosporin Fluroroquinolone	Aminoglycoside Extended-spectrum cephalosporin
Bone and joint	Cephalosporin Amoxicillin-clavulanate	Trimethoprim-sulfonamides Clindamycin Extended-spectrum cephalosporins Fluoroquinolone
Intracellular pathogens	Doxycycline Fluoroquinolone*	Azithromycin Clindamycin

*Fluoroquinolone = enrofloxacin, difloxacin, marbofloxacin, or orbifloxacin (difloxacin not registered for cats).
†Extended-spectrum cephalosporin = second-generation or third-generation drugs (eg, cefotetan, cefotaxime, cefpodoxime).
‡Combinations of drugs are often used in acute febrile septicemia. Such combinations may include a beta-lactam plus an aminoglycoside or a fluoroquinolone plus amoxicillin-clavulanate.

APPENDIX D
Antibiotic Choices for Specific Organ System Infections

Antibiotics for Skin Infection

- Amoxicillin-clavulanate (Clavamox)
- Oxacillin (generic)
- Cefadroxil (Cefa-Tabs, Cefa-Drops)
- Cephalexin (generic, off-label)
- Cefpodoxime proxetil (Simplicef)
- Clindamycin (Antirobe)
- Trimethoprim-sulfadiazine (Tribrissen, Di-Trim)
- Ormetoprim-sulfadimethoxine (Primor)
- Enrofloxacin (Baytril)
- Marbofloxacin (Zeniquin)
- Orbifloxacin (Orbax)
- Difloxacin (Dicural)

Antibiotics for Uncomplicated Urinary Tract Infection (Oral Drugs)

- Amoxicillin/ampicillin
- Amoxicillin-clavulanate (Clavamox)
- Cefadroxil (Cefa-Tabs, Cefa-Drops)
- Cefpodoxime proxetil (Simplicef)
- Cephalexin (generic, off-label)
- Trimethoprim-sulfadiazine (Tribrissen, Di-Trim)
- Ormetoprim-sulfadimethoxine (Primor)
- Tetracycline (not doxycycline)

Antibiotics for Respiratory Infection

- Amoxicillin-clavulanate (Clavamox)
- Azithromycin (Zithromax)
- Cefadroxil (Cefa-Tabs, Cefa-Drops)
- Cephalexin (generic)
- Cefpodoxime proxetil (Simplicef)
- Clindamycin (Antirobe)
- Enrofloxacin (Baytril)
- Marbofloxacin (Zeniquin)
- Orbifloxacin (Orbax)
- Difloxacin (Dicural)
- Chloramphenicol

APPENDIX E
Drugs That May Induce Cytochrome P-450 Enzymes

- Alcohol
- Chlorinated hydrocarbons
- Diazepam (Valium)
- Diphenhydramine
- Estrogens
- Griseofulvin
- Hyperthyroidism
- Pentobarbital
- Phenobarbital
- Phenylbutazone
- Phenytoin (Dilantin)
- Progestogens
- Rifampin
- St. John's wort

APPENDIX F
Drugs That May Inhibit Cytochrome P-450 Enzymes

- Amiodarone
- Chloramphenicol
- Cimetidine
- Cisapride
- Clarithromycin
- Cyclophosphamide
- Diltiazem
- Erythromycin
- Felbamate
- Fluoroquinolones
- Interferon (vaccines)
- Itraconazole
- Ketoconazole
- Organophosphates
- Phenylbutazone
- Quinidine
- Tetracycline
- Verapamil
- Voriconazole

APPENDIX G
Drugs That May Inhibit MDR1 (P-Glycoprotein)

- Bromocriptine
- Carvedilol
- Chlorpromazine
- Cyclosporine
- Erythromycin
- Fluoxetine
- Grapefruit juice
- Itraconazole
- Ketaconazole
- Methadone
- Paroxetine
- Pentazocine
- Quinidine
- St. John's wort
- Tamoxifen
- Verapamil

APPENDIX H
Drugs That Are Substrates for MDR1 (P-Glycoprotein)

- Aldosterone
- Amitriptyline
- Cortisol
- Cyclosporine
- Dexamethasone
- Digoxin
- Diltiazem
- Doxorubicin
- Doxycycline
- Erythromycin
- Itraconazole
- Ivermectin
- Ketoconazole
- Levofloxacin
- Loperamide
- Methylprednisolone
- Morphine
- Ondansetron
- Phenothiazines
- Tacrolimus
- Terfenadine
- Tetracycline
- Verapamil
- Vinblastine
- Vincristine

APPENDIX I
Fluid Solutions for Intravenous Use

Solution Type	Na^+ (mEq/L)	K^+ (mEq/L)	Cl^- (mEq/L)	Ca^{++} (mEq/L)	Mg^{++} (mEq/L)	Buffer (mEq/L)	Osmolality (mOsm/L)	pH
Ringer's Solution	147	4	156	4	0	0	310	5-7.5
Lactated Ringer's solution	130	4	109	3	0	28 (lactate)	275	6-7.5
0.9 % NaCl	154	0	154	0	0	0	308	4.5
5% dextrose	0	0	0	0	0	0	252	4-6.5
2.5% dextrose/ 0.45% NaCL	77	0	77	0	0	0	280	4.5
Plasma-Lyte	140	5	98	0	3	27 (acetate) 23 (gluconate)	294	4-6.5
Dextran 6% and 0.9% NaCl	154	0	154	0	0	0	310	3.0-7.0
Hetastarch	154	0	154	0	0	0	309	5.5
Pentastarch	154	0	154	0	0	0	326	5.0
Hemoglobin glutamer (Oxyglobin)							300	7.8
Normosol-R	140	5	98	0	3	27 (acetate) 23 (gluconate)	294	6.6

APPENDIX J
Compounded Formulations: What to Look for to Detect Incompatibility or Instability

Liquid Dose Forms

Color change (pink or amber)
Signs of microbial growth
Cloudiness, haze, flocculent or film formation
Separation of phases (e.g., oil and water, emulsion)
Precipitation, clumping, crystal formation
Droplets for fog forming on inside of container
Gas or odor release
Swelling of container

Solid Dose Forms

Odor (sulfur or vinegar odor)
Excessive powder or crumbling
Cracks or chips in tablets
Swelling of tablets or capsules

"Rules of Thumb"

Do not mix drugs that require reconstitution in a vial with other drugs, and do not add other drugs to the vial.

Do not mix drugs that are not in aqueous vehicle (e.g., propylene glycol) with IV fluids

Do not mix hydrochloride salts (HCl) of drugs with buffers (citrates, bicarbonates, phosphates)

APPENDIX K Prescription Writing Reference . . . Do's & Don'ts

Veterinarian Information

Always Include

Prescribing veterinarian's name
Practice address
Practice telephone number
DEA # (if written for a controlled substance)
Current date
Rx

- **Drug Name:** (Print FULL brand name or generic name. . . NEVER abbreviate)
- **Dosage Form:** (Specify tablet, capsule, suspension, other)
- **Strength:** (mg, g, μg, etc.) or concentration (mg/ml). . . Use metric units and use mcg for μg whenever possible
- **Total Quantity:** (# 10 [for 10 tablets]; 60 ml)
- **Sig:** *Include the following:* Dose (individual); route; frequency; duration; indication or use
- **Number of Refills:** Define the number permitted
- **Designate:** Whether or not generic substitution is permissible
- **Signature**

Owner Information

Always Include

Patient's name (in "quotes")
Patient's age or date of birth
Owner's name (or that of an owner representative)
Owner's address
Owner's phone number

Common Prescription Writing Errors

- Always use metric units: e.g., **g** (gram) for solids; **ml** or **mL** (milliliter) for liquids.
- Use **per** instead of a slash (/), which can be interpreted as the number **1.**
- Use **units** instead of the abbreviation **u**, which can be interpreted as **0** or 4 or **μ.**
- Use **once daily** instead of **sid,** which has been interpreted as **5/d** or **5 per day!** (NOTE: "sid" is *not* a conventional prescription abbreviation.)
- Use **three times daily** instead of **tid,** and **four times daily** instead of **qid.**
- Use **every other day** instead of **qod.**
- REMEMBER—abbreviations like **qd, qid,** and **qod** are easily confused with each other
- When writing numbers:
  - Use a **leading zero** with decimals: e.g., use **0.5 ml** rather than **.5 ml.**
  - Avoid using a **trailing zero:** e.g., use **3** rather than **3.0.**
- And FINALLY—When in doubt...spell it out.

From Ford: *Kirk & Bistner's Handbook of Veterinary Procedures and Emergency Treatment*, 8th ed. Philadelphia, W.B. Saunders, 2006, p. 684.

APPENDIX L
How to Report an Adverse Drug Reaction

1. Phone the drug sponsor to report an Adverse Drug Experience (ADE) if it is an FDA-approved animal drug. Obtain drug sponsor phone numbers from the product label, or from the company's internet web site. When phoning the pharmaceutical company, inform them that you wish to speak with a veterinarian on their staff to report an adverse drug experience.
2. Contact the FDA and complete Form 1923a. This form may be completed regardless of whether or not the drug is an animal-approved drug or human-approved drug. The FDA can be contacted from their web site at:
   http://www.fda.gov/cvm/adetoc.htm
   The FDA also may be contacted at this address:
   Center for Veterinary Medicine
   Division of Surveillance, HFV-210
   7519 Standish Place
   Rockville, MD 20855
   Telephone: 1-888-FDA-VETS

When completing Form 1932a, supply as much history and clinical data as possible, including concurrent medications administered to the animal.

Animal Biologics: Vaccines, Bacterins

Contact the U.S. Department of Agriculture (USDA)
(800) 752-6255
http://www.aphis.usda.gov/

Pesticides: Topically Applied External Parasiticides

Contact the U.S. Environmental Protection Agency (EPA)
(800) 858-PEST
http://www.epa.gov/pesticides/

APPENDIX M
Drugs Prohibited from Use in Food-Producing Animals

Because they present a risk to public health, the following drugs are prohibited in food producing animals.

Chloramphenicol
Clenbuterol
Diethylstilbestrol
Dimetridazole
Furazolidone
Nitrofurazone (and other Nitrofurans)
Fluoroquinolones (extra-label use)
Glycopeptide antibiotics
Ipronidazole (and other Nitroimidazoles)
Phenylbutazone in female dairy cattle > 20 months of age
Sulfonamide drugs in Lactating Dairy Cattle*

*With the exception of sulfadimethoxine, sulfabromomethazine, and sulfaethoxypyradazine, approved for use in some feeds.

APPENDIX N
Association of Racing Commissioners International, Inc., Uniform Classification Guidelines for Foreign Substances (Revised April 2004)
http://www.arci.com/index.html

RCI Drug Classification Scheme is based on (1) pharmacology, (2) drug use patterns, and (3) the appropriateness of a drug for use in the racing horse.

Classification Definitions

Class 1

Stimulant and depressant drugs that have the highest potential to affect performance and that have no generally accepted medical use in the racing horse. Many of these agents are Drug Enforcement Agency (DEA) schedule II substances. These include the following drugs and their metabolites: Opiates, opium derivatives, synthetic opioids and psychoactive drugs, amphetamines and amphetamine-like drugs as well as related drugs, including but not limited to apomorphine, nikethamide, mazindol, pemoline, and pentylenetetrazol. Though not used as therapeutic agents, all DEA Schedule 1 agents are included in Class 1 because they are potent stimulant or depressant substances with psychotropic and often habituative actions.

Penalty Recommendations (in the absence of mitigating circumstances): 1-5 year suspension and $5,000 fine and loss of purse.

Class 2

Drugs that have a high potential to affect performance, but less of a potential than drugs in Class 1. These drugs are (1) not generally accepted as therapeutic agents in racing horses, or (2) they are therapeutic agents that have a high potential for abuse. Drugs in this class include: psychotropic drugs, certain nervous system and cardiovascular system stimulants, depressants, and neuromuscular blocking agents. Injectable local anesthetics are included in this class because of their high potential for abuse as nerve blocking agents. **Penalty Recommendations** (in the absence of mitigating circumstances): 6 months-1 year suspension and $1,500-$2,500 fine and loss of purse.

Class 3

Drugs that may or may not have generally accepted medical use in the racing horse, but the pharmacology of which suggests less potential to affect performance than drugs in Class 2. Drugs in this class include bronchodilators and other drugs with primary effects on the autonomic nervous system, procaine, antihistamines with sedative properties and the high-ceiling diuretics.

Penalty Recommendations (in the absence of mitigating circumstances): 60 days-6 months suspension and up to $1,500 fine and loss of purse.

Class 4

This class includes therapeutic medications that would be expected to have less potential to affect performance than those in Class 3. Drugs in this class includes less potent diuretics; anabolic steroids; corticosteroids; antihistamines and skeletal muscle relaxants without prominent central nervous system (CNS) effects;

expectorants and mucolytics; hemostatics; cardiac glycosides and anti-arrhythmics; topical anesthetics; antidiarrheals and mild analgesics. This class also includes the non-steroidal anti-inflammatory drugs (NSAIDs), at concentrations greater than established limits. **Penalty Recommendations** (in the absence of mitigating circumstances): 15-60 days suspension and up to $1,000 fine and loss of purse.

Class 5

This class includes those therapeutic medications for which concentration limits have been established by the racing jurisdictions as well as certain miscellaneous agents such as dimethylsulfoxide (DMSO) and other medications as determined by the regulatory bodies. Included specifically are agents that have very localized actions only, such as anti-ulcer drugs, and certain anti-allergic drugs. The anticoagulant drugs are also included. **Penalty Recommendations** (in the absence of mitigating circumstances): 0-15 days suspension with possible loss of purse and/or fine.

Non-Classified Substances

Substances that are considered to have no effect on the physiology of a racing animal except to improve nutrition or treat or prevent infections or parasite infestations are not classified. These Substances normally include antimicrobials, antiparasitic drugs, and nutrients such as vitamins.

APPENDIX O Important Internet Sites for Drug Information

Drug Compounding

http://www.fda.gov/ora/compliance_ref/cpg/default.htm
http://www.fda.gov/OHRMS/DOCKETS/98fr/03d-0290-gd10001.pdf

Drug Interactions

http://www.drug-interactions.com
http://www.druginteractioninfo.org/
http://medicine.iupui.edu/flockhart/index.htm

FDA Adverse Drug Reports: Cumulative Summary

http://www.fda.gov/cvm/ade_cum.htm

FDA Home Page

http://www.fda.gov/cvm/

FDA Approved Animal Drug Products

http://www.fda.gov/cvm/greenbook.html
http://dil.vetmed.vt.edu/

FDA Approved Human Drug Products

http://www.fda.gov/cder/orange/default.htm
http://www.accessdata.fda.gov/scripts/cder/drugsatfda/index.cfm

FDA Adverse Drug Reaction Reporting

http://www.fda.gov/cvm/adetoc.htm
http://www.fda.gov/cvm/ade_cum.htm

Horse Racing Drug Regulations

http://www.arci.com/index.html
http://www.arci.com/druglisting.pdf

USP Veterinary Drug Information

http://www.usp.org/audiences/veterinary/
http://www.usp.org/audiences/veterinary/monographs/main.html

AVMA Guidelines on Antimicrobial Use

http://avma.org/scienact/jtua/default.asp

Extra-Label (off label) Drug Use Information

http://www.avma.org/scienact/amduca/amduca1.asp
or e-mail questions to: FARAD@ncsu.edu

Euthanasia Formulations and References:

http://www.avma.org/issues/animal_welfare/euthanasia.pdf

APPENDIX P Important Contacts for Veterinary Drug Information

Animal Blood Banks

Animal Blood Bank phone: (800) 243-5759

A 24-hour hotline that focuses on transfusion medicine (particularly blood component therapy), recommending dosages and infusion rates.

Eastern Veterinary Blood Bank: (800) 949-EVBB [(800) 949-3822]

A 24-hour, commercial blood bank that focuses on transfusion medicine; gives recommendations and referrals to distribution centers when it cannot ship the requested product; for complicated cases, offers a paid consultation service.

HEMOPET: (949) 252-8455

A national, full-service, nonprofit blood bank and educational network for animals, in Irvine, Calif; accessible 24 hours.

Midwest Animal Blood Services: (517) 851-8244

A 24-hour, commercial all-species blood bank providing blood components, blood typing services, and transfusion medicine consultation (special emphasis on red blood cell typing and transplantation matching)

Poison Control Center

ASPCA National Animal Poison Control Center: (888) 4ANI-HELP [(888) 426-4435]

Fee $45 per case; credit cards only; no extra charge for follow-up calls. (900) 680-0000—$30 per case. The charge is billed directly to caller's phone. Follow-up calls can be made for no additional charge by dialing (888) 426-4435.

Drug Enforcement Agency (DEA)

Office of Diversion Control, Registration Section: (800) 882-9539

Food and Drug Administration Center for Veterinary Medicine (FDA/CVM):

(888) FDA-VETS [(888) 332-8387]

Food Animal Residue Avoidance Databank (FARAD)

(888) USFARAD [(888) 873-2723], send an e-mail to: FARAD@ncsu.edu, or visit web site at: www.farad.org

FARAD is sponsored by the USDA to prevent residues of drugs and other chemicals in food animals.

APPENDIX Q
Solution Compatibility Chart

Intravenous Medication	D2 1/2W	D5W	D10W	D5/ 1/4NS	D5/ 1/2NS	D5NS	NS	1/2NS	R	LR	D5R	D5LR	Dextran 6%/D5W/NS	Fruc 10%/W/NS	Invert sug 10%/W/NS	Na lactate 1/6 M
Acetazolamide	C	C	C	C	C	C	C	C	C	C	C	C	C	C	C	C
Acyclovir		C		C	C	C	C				C					
Aminophylline	C	C	C	C	C	C	C	C	C	C	C	C	C	C		
Ammonium Chloride							C									
Amikacin		C					C									
Amphotericin B		C														
Ampicillin		C					C									
Ascorbic acid	C	C	C	C	C	C	C	C	C	C	C	C	C	C	C	C
Calcium chloride		C	C	C	C	C	C		C	C	C					
Calcium Gluconate		C	C			C	C			C		C		W		C
Cefazolin Na		C	C	C	C	C	C		C	C		C			W	
Cefotaxime Na		C	C	C	C	C	C			C					W	C
Cefotetan		C					C									
Cefoxitin Na		C	C	C	C	C	C		C	C		C				C
Ceftazidime		C	C	C	C	C	C		C	C					W	C
Cimetidine		C	C	C	C	C	C		C	C		C			W	
Ciprofloxacin		C					C									
Clindamycin		C	C		C	C	C			C	C					
Cyclosporine		C					C									
Dexamethasone		C					C									
Dobutamine HCl		C	C		C	C	C	C		C		C				C
Dopamine HCl		C	C		C	C	C			C		C				C
Doxycycline		C					C		C						W	

Epinephrine	C	C	C	C	C	C	C		C	C	C	C	C	C	C	C
Famotidine		C	C				C			C						
Fentanyl		C					C									
Furosemide		C	C			C	C			C		C				C
Gentamicin		C	C				C		C	C						
Heparin Na	C	C		C	C	C	C	C	C		C	C	C	C	C	
Hydrocortisone phosphate		C	C				C	C								
Hydrocortisone Na succinate	C	C	C	C	C	C	C	C	C	C	C	C	C	C	C	C
Hydromorphone HCl		C	C		C	C	C	C	C	C	C	C		W		C
Imipenem-Cilastatin		C^{4}	C^{4}	C^{4}	C^{4}	C^{4}	C^{10}									
Insulin (regular)		C^{P}	C		C		C^{P}			C	C					
Isoproterenol	C	C^{P}	C	C	C	C	C^{P}		C	C	C	C	C	C	C	
Kanamycin		C	C			C	C			C						
Lidocaine		C^{P}			C	C	C	C		C		C				
Magnesium sulfate		C					C			C						
Meperidine HCl	C	C	C	C	C	C	C	C	C	C	C	C	C	C	W	C
Meropenem		C^{1}	C^{1}	C^{1}		C^{1}	C^{4}		C^{4}	C^{4}		C^{1}				C^{2}
Metoclopramide HCl		C			C		C		C	C						
Morphine	C	C	C	C	C	C	C	C	C	C	C	C	C	C	C	C
Multivitamin		C	C			C	C			C		C		W		C
Nitroglycerin		C			C	C	C	C		C		C				C
Norepinephrine		C^{P}				C^{P}	C			C						
Ondansetron HCl		C			C	C	C									
Oxacillin Na		C	C			C	C			C		C				
Pancuronium		C			C	C	C			C						
Penicillin G, K	C	C	C	C	C	C	C	C	C	C	C	C	C	C	C	
Pentobarbital Na	C	C	C	C	C	C	C	C	C	C	C	C	C	C	C	C
Piperacillin/Tazobactam		C				C	C						NS			
Potassium chloride	C	C	C	C	C	C	C	C	C	C	C	C	C	C	C	C
Potassium phosphate	C	C	C	C	C	C	C	C					C	C	C	C
Prochlorperazine	C	C	C	C	C	C	C	C	C	C	C	C	C	C	C	C
Propranolol		C^{P}			C	C	C	C		C						

Continued

APPENDIX Q
Solution Compatibility Chart—cont'd

Intravenous Medication	D2 1/2W	D5W	D10W	D5/ 1/4NS	D5/ 1/2NS	D5NS	NS	1/2NS	R	LR	D5R	D5LR	Dextran 6%/D5W/NS	Fruc 10%/W/NS	Invert sug 10%/W/NS	Na lactate 1/6 M
Ranitidine		C	C		C		C			C						
Sodium bicarbonate	C	C	C	C	C	C	C	C			C		C	C	C	
Sodium chloride	C	C	C	C	C	C	C	C	C	C	C	C	C	C	C	C
Thiamine	C	C	C	C	C	C	C	C	C	C	C	C	C	C	C	C
Thiopental	C	C		C	C	C^6	C	C					C			C
Ticaracillin		C					C			C						
Tobramycin		C					C									
Warfarin		C	C		C	C	C					C				
Zidovudine		C^P					C									

C, compatible; W, compatible in water only; NS, compatible in normal saline only; C with a superscript number indicates the number of hours for which a solution is compatible and stable; C^P indicates the preferred diluent; no entry, no documented information.

Index

Entries can be identified as follows: generic name, Trade name.

N

O

P

U

V

Mini CD to Accompany Saunders Handbook of Veterinary Drugs

Minimum System Requirements

Microsoft Windows

- Windows 98 SE, ME, 2000, or XP
- 800 × 600 pixels screen resolution
- 16.7 million colors
- 256 MB RAM
- Pentium III, 1 GHz (Pentium IV recommended)
- CD-ROM drive

Notes

1. If the application is used on a system with a processor with lower speed than recommended, the application may run slowly or become unresponsive.
2. The Macromedia Flash Player Settings for Local Storage must be set to maximum. If the Flash Player Settings are not enabled, on launching the application, a web page will open. Use the slide bar displayed on the web page to set the local storage limit to "unlimited," and then relaunch the Papich application.

Installation Instructions

1. Insert the CD into the CD-ROM drive.
2. The application will auto-start on your system.

Notes

If the application does not start automatically, then:

a. Right click on the "My Computer" icon on the Desktop and choose "Explore."
b. Click once on the CD-ROM drive icon that appears on the screen.
c. Double-click on "Papich.exe," available on the right side of the screen, to launch the application.

Technical Support

Technical support for this product is available between 7:30 a.m. and 7 p.m. CST, Monday through Friday. Before calling, be sure that your computer meets the minimum system requirements to run this software.

Inside the United States and Canada, call 1-800-692-9010. Outside North America, call 314-872-8370. You may also fax your questions to 314-523-4932, or contact Technical Support through e-mail: technical.support@elsevier.com.

Part Number: 9996011089